NATIONAL AUDUBON SO

A Chanticleer Press Edition

WETLANDS

By William A. Niering

Birds
John Bull, Field Associate, The American Museum of Natural History; John Farrand, Jr., Editor, *American Birds,* National Audubon Society; and Miklos D. F. Udvardy, Professor of Biological Sciences, California State University, Sacramento

Butterflies
Robert Michael Pyle, Consulting Lepidopterist, International Union for Conservation of Nature and Natural Resources

Fishes
James D. Williams, Research Associate, National Museum of Natural History

Insects and Spiders
Lorus Milne and Margery Milne, Lecturers, University of New Hampshire

Mammals
John O. Whitaker, Jr., Professor of Life Sciences, Indiana State University

Mushrooms
Peter Katsaros, Mycologist

Reptiles and Amphibians
John L. Behler, Curator of Herpetology, New York Zoological Society; and F. Wayne King, Director, Florida State Museum

Trees
Elbert L. Little, Jr., U.S. Forest Service

Wildflowers
William A. Niering, Professor of Botany, Connecticut College, New London; Nancy C. Olmstead, former Research Associate, Connecticut Arboretum; and Richard Spellenberg, Professor of Biology, New Mexico State University

Alfred A. Knopf, New York

This is a Borzoi Book.
Published by Alfred A. Knopf, Inc.

 Published in the United States by Alfred A. Knopf, Inc., New York, and simultaneously in Canada by Random House of Canada Limited, Toronto. Distributed by Random House, Inc., New York.

Prepared and produced by Chanticleer Press, Inc., New York.

Printed and bound by Toppan Printing Co., Ltd., Tokyo, Japan.
Typeset in Garamond by Dix Type, Inc., Syracuse, New York.

Published March 1985
Seventh Printing, March 1997

Library of Congress Cataloging-in-Publication Data
Niering, William A., 1924–
The National Audubon Society nature guides. Wetlands.
Includes index.
1. Natural history–North America–Handbooks, manuals, etc. 2. Wetland ecology–North America–Handbooks, manuals, etc. 3. Zoology–North America–Handbooks, manuals, etc. 4. Botany–North America–Handbooks, manuals, etc. 5. Wetland flora–North America–Identification. 6. Animals–Identification.
I. National Audubon Society. II. Title. III. Title: Wetlands.
QH102.N54 1985 574.5'26325'097 84-48672
ISBN 0-394-73147-6 (pbk.)

Cover photograph: A Fragrant Water Lily shimmers in the sunlight in Georgia's Okefenokee Swamp.

CONTENTS

NATIONAL AUDUBON SOCIETY

The mission of the NATIONAL AUDUBON SOCIETY *is to conserve and restore natural ecosystems, focusing on birds and other wildlife, for the benefit of humanity and the earth's biological diversity.*

With more than 560,000 members and an extensive chapter network, our staff of scientists, educators, lobbyists, lawyers, and policy analysts works to save threatened ecosystems and restore the natural balance of life on our planet. Through our sanctuary system we manage 150,000 acres of critical habitat. *Audubon* magazine, sent to all members, carries outstanding articles and color photography on wildlife, nature, and the environment. We also publish *Field Notes,* a journal reporting bird sightings, and *Audubon Adventures,* a bimonthly children's newsletter reaching 600,000 students.

NATIONAL AUDUBON SOCIETY produces television documentaries and sponsors books, electronic programs, and nature travel to exotic places.

For membership information:

NATIONAL AUDUBON SOCIETY
700 Broadway
New York, NY 10003-9562
(212) 979-3000

THE AUTHOR

William A. Niering
The author is Katherine Blunt Professor of Botany at Connecticut College in New London and also director of the Connecticut Arboretum. A member of the National Wetlands Technical Council, he has written numerous articles on wetlands and ecological subjects. He is the author of *The Life of the Marsh* and *National Audubon Society Field Guide to North American Wildflowers (Eastern Region)*.

HOW TO USE THIS GUIDE

This guide is designed for use both at home and in the field. Its clear arrangement in four parts—habitat essays, color plates, species descriptions, and appendices—puts information at your fingertips that would otherwise only be accessible through a small library of field guides.
The habitat essays enable you to discover the many kinds of wetlands, the relationships among the plants and animals found there, and highlights not to be missed. The color plates feature wetland scenes and over 600 photographs of different plant and animal species. The species descriptions cover the most important information about a plant or animal, including a description, the range, specific habitat, and comments. Finally, the appendices include a bibliography, a glossary, and a comprehensive index.

Using This Guide at Home
Before planning an outing, you will want to know what you can expect to see.
1. Begin by leafing through the color plates for a preview of wetlands.
2. Read the habitat section. For quick reference, at the end of each chapter you will find a list of some of the most common plants and animals found in that habitat.
3. Look at the color plates of some of the animals and plants so that you will be able to recognize them later in the field. The table called How to Use the Color Plates provides a visual table of contents to the color section, explains the arrangement of the plates, and tells the caption information provided. The habitats where you are likely to encounter the species are listed in blue type so that you can easily refer to the correct habitat chapter. The page number for the full species description is also included in the caption.
4. Turn to the species descriptions to learn more about the plants and animals that interest you. A range map or drawing appears in the margin for birds, fishes, mammals, reptiles, and amphibians, and for many of the trees, wildflowers, ferns, and grasses. Poisonous mushrooms and reptiles are indicated by the danger symbol ⊗ next to the species name.
5. Consult the appendices for definitions of technical terms and suggestions for further reading.

Using This Guide in the Field
When you are out in the field, you will want to find information quickly and easily.
1. Turn to the color plates to locate the plant or animal you have seen. At a glance the captions will help you narrow down the possibilities. First, verify the habitat by checking the blue type information to the left of the color plate. Next, look for important field marks, which are also indicated in blue type—for example, how and where a mushroom grows, an insect's food, or a caterpillar's host plants. To find out whether a bird, fish, mammal, reptile, or amphibian is in your area, check the range map next to the color plate.
2. Now turn to the species description to confirm your identification and to learn more about the species.

First frontispiece: A Brown Bear holds his catch of Sockeye Salmon, just taken from the Brooks River in Alaska.

Second frontispiece: A colony of Wood Storks nests along the Lane River in Florida's Everglades National Park.

Third frontispiece: Fragrant Water Lilies illuminate the dark waters of a beaver pond in Acadia National Park, Mount Desert Island, Maine.

Fourth frontispiece: A White-tailed Deer, with its tail up to signal danger, dashes through a marsh in Everglades National Park, Florida.

Fifth frontispiece: A Great Blue Heron pauses along a wooded stream, waiting for prey in Aransas National Wildlife Refuge, in Texas.

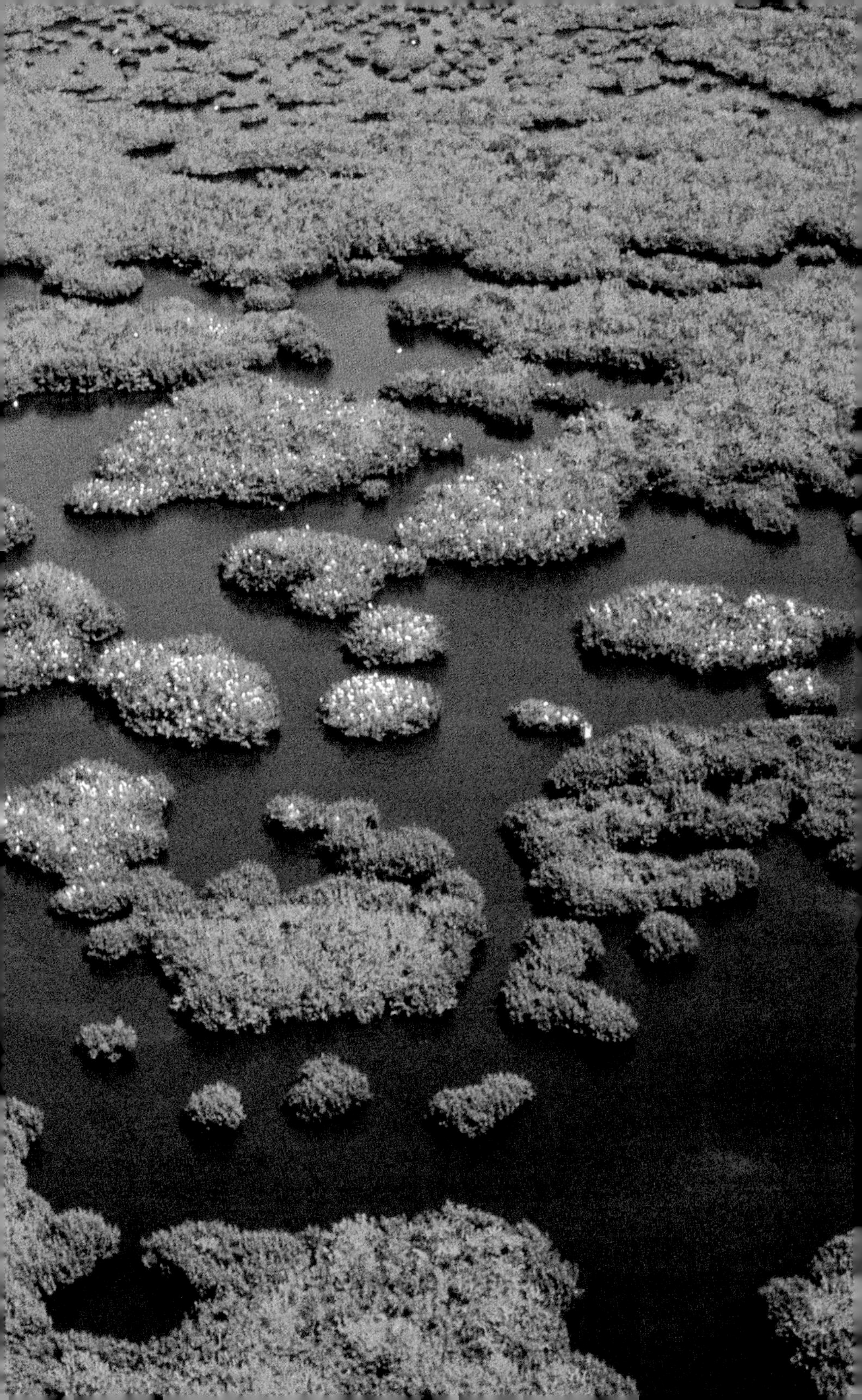

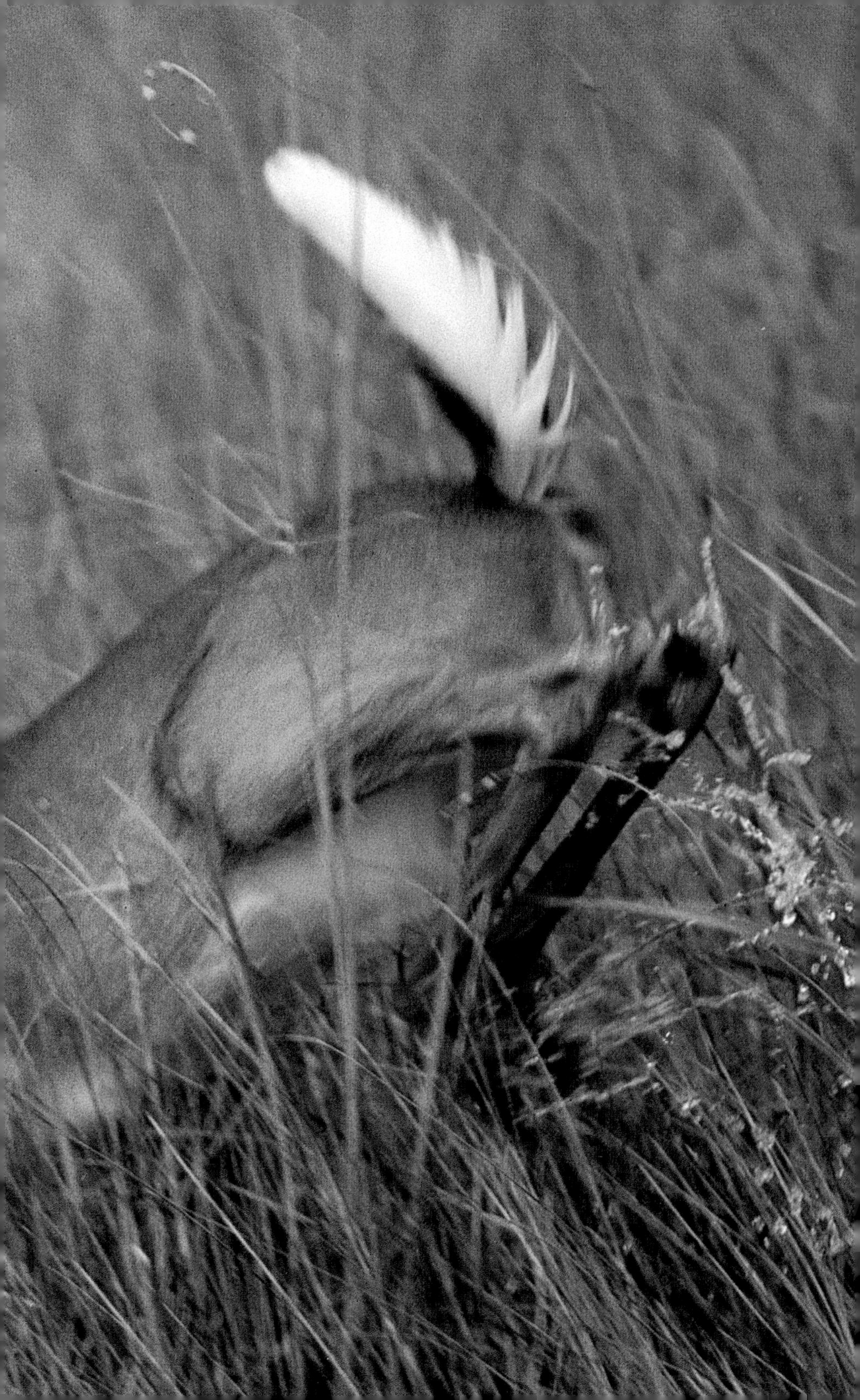

PART I WETLANDS

PREFACE

Wetlands—long considered insect-ridden, unattractive, and dangerous areas—have in this century begun to be recognized as beautiful places with a rich and exciting variety of plant and animal life just waiting to be explored by the curious and the adventuresome. Historically, the importance of wetlands has been overlooked, but recently this outlook has changed dramatically because the vital ecological roles that wetlands serve have been documented. Conservation organizations, like the National Audubon Society or The Nature Conservancy, have been and are actively preserving wetlands. The Everglades National Park and the nation's system of Wildlife Refuges with wetlands areas are heavily visited.

With the habitat approach taken in this volume it is hoped that the reader can gain a better ecological understanding of the complex wetlands found in the United States. The more important types you are liable to encounter are included, with special emphasis on those that are most accessible.

Practically speaking, when visiting wetlands without a boardwalk, it is best to wear boots or old sneakers. A good, effective mosquito repellent will be handy. In general, wetlands are perfectly safe places to visit. Nonetheless, it is best not to visit a bog alone—you may need an extra hand if you get "bogged down." Except in the South, poisonous snakes are usually not common in wetlands. In bogs, Poison Sumac is one plant to avoid, because it can give you a rash like that of Poison Ivy.

If you explore a large wetland area, it is advisable to take a compass along and to note the direction of the upland as you enter the wetland. It is easy to lose your bearings—I was once temporarily bewildered in a cranberry bog after the sun disappeared. Because open bogs with floating mats are rather fragile habitats, it is best to visit them by canoe, if open water permits.

To record your visit and check your observations, carry a camera, notebook, and a field guide; using a small snapsack will keep your hands free. There will be ample opportunities to photograph both plant and animal life. In addition to recording your photos, you may wish to list the plants and wildlife observed on the trip as well as the nature of the habitat and its associated life—just as I have attempted to do here for the various wetland habitats. Reading this volume will help you learn about some of the ecological interactions that you may be lucky enough to see going on: What ecological factors are influencing the community of plants and animals? What kinds of changes are occurring? Are the high or low water levels affecting the biota?

Wetlands are fragile places. Plant collecting is not recommended; for the health of the environment, identify specimens in their natural habitats and leave the area as you found it.

With these few precautions in mind, and with fresh curiosity and awareness, you will be assured of adventure in the wetlands. Many surprises and thrills await you as you discover the diversity of freshwater wetlands found in our country.

INTRODUCTION

Wetlands evoke powerful emotions. To some they are dark, mysterious, forbidding places, to be avoided at all costs. To many novelists, poets, and artists, however, they have been a source of inspiration. Who can forget the marsh in Dickens's *Great Expectations* or these lines from Sidney Lanier's "The Marshes of Glynn"?

The creeks overflow: a thousand rivulets run
'Twixt the roots of the sod, the blades of the marshgrass stir;
Passeth a hurrying sound of wings that westward whirr;
Passeth, and all is still; and the currents cease to run;
And the sea and the marsh are one.

Perhaps one of the most memorable descriptions of a wetland occurs in Sir Arthur Conan Doyle's "The Hound of the Baskervilles," in which he describes the Great Grimpen Mire, where the villain meets his horrible fate:

Rank weeds and lush, slimy water plants send an odour of decay and a heavy miasmatic vapor into our faces, while a false step plunged us more than once thigh-deep into the dark, quivering mire, which shook for yards in soft undulations around our feet.

This is surely a masterful description of a bog, one of North America's most fascinating wetlands.

Water and wetlands have been immortalized by artists of both the European and American schools. The water lilies of Monet and the many renderings of wetlands by painters of the Hudson River School are only a few of the many masterpieces dealing with this subject. Yet despite this kind of appreciation, wetlands have often been considered wastelands. This was the image conveyed in the mid-1800s by the Swamp Wetland Acts; enacted by the U.S. Congress, these laws gave fifteen states sixty-five million acres of federal land for "reclamation." This obviously meant draining the wetlands so that they could be used for more "constructive" purposes. Today, less than half, only forty-six percent, of the wetlands that existed at the time of the Europeans' arrival remains. At the time of the nation's settlement there were 215 million acres; in the mid-1970s only 99 million acres remained. Nonetheless, a new image of these habitats has emerged. These areas have finally been recognized as a vital part of our landscape. Many are directly related to one of our most basic needs—water. However, their other functions are equally important. Wetlands mitigate flooding, provide habitats for waterfowl, filter pollutants, and stabilize the biosphere, upon which all life is dependent. A new wetland ethic now advocates the protection and preservation of these areas.

What Are Wetlands?

Wetlands are areas where water is the primary factor controlling the environment and the associated plant and animal life. These transitional habitats occur between upland and aquatic environments where the water table is at or near the surface of the land, or where the land is covered by shallow

Wetland Ecoregions of the United States

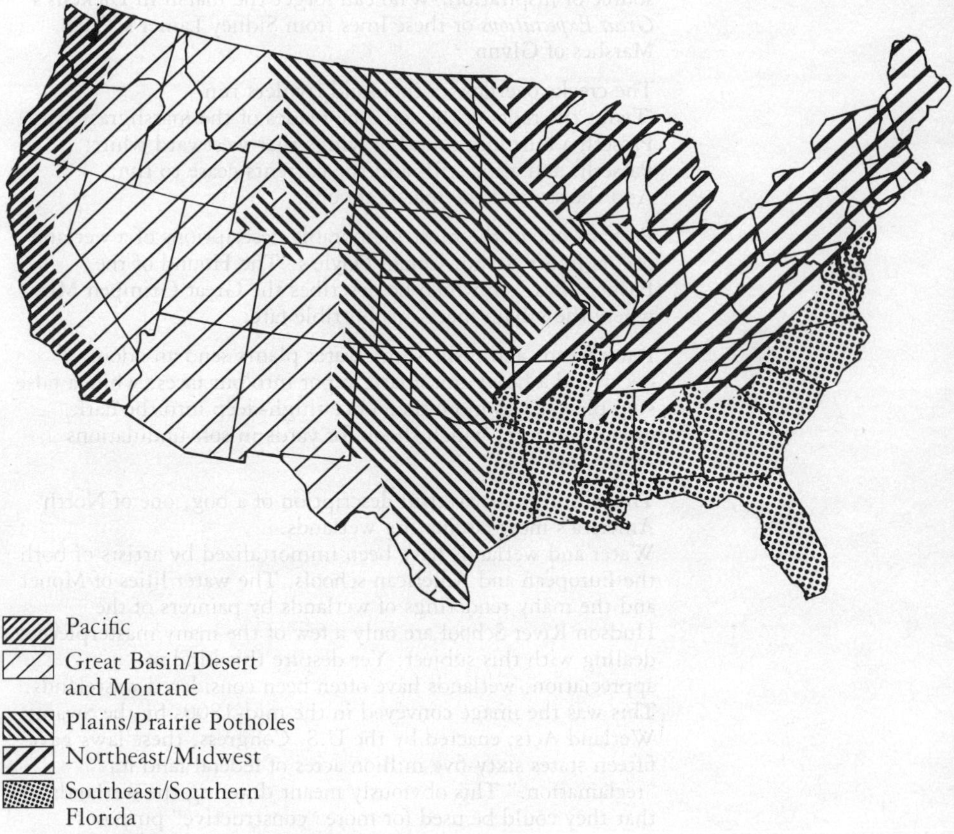

Source: National Wetlands Technical Council

water that may be up to six feet deep. This definition was developed by the U.S. Fish and Wildlife Service, which is currently undertaking a nationwide inventory of these areas. Most wetlands are dominated by hydrophytes, or wetland plants; these can tolerate various degrees of flooding or live in frequently saturated areas. Most wetlands are characterized by fluctuating water levels and by soils that are distinctly different from those of dry, upland areas.

Habitats with flowing or deep water, such as rivers, streams, lakes, and ponds, are closely associated with many wetlands and are therefore also discussed in this volume.

Kinds of Wetlands

Scientists recognize five major wetland systems: marine, estuarine, lacustrine, riverine, and palustrine. (Marine and estuarine habitats include coastal wetlands, such as tidal marshes and mangrove swamps; these are discussed in the coastal volumes of this series.) The other three categories represent freshwater systems, which account for ninety percent of the nation's wetlands. Lacustrine wetlands are associated with lakes; riverine wetlands are found along rivers and streams. The word palustrine means marshy; wetland areas within this category include marshes, swamps, and bogs—terms commonly used to designate distinct wetland types. We shall use these terms since they are familiar to most people. However, it should be noted that the U.S. Fish and Wildlife Service has developed a more precise hierarchical system, by means of which each wetland can be mapped or described with reference to its general structure or vegetation, flooding pattern, water chemistry, and soils.

Marshes

Marshes are characterized by soft-stemmed herbaceous plants, such as cattails and pickerelweed. These plants, called emergents, grow with their stems partly in and partly out of the water. Shallow marshes are those with up to six inches of water; deep marshes have as much as two to three feet of water. In the deeper marshes, floating and submerged aquatics —such as water lilies, pondweeds, and the carnivorous bladderworts—may be closely associated with cattails, arrowheads, and other emergents common in shallow areas. Seasonal fluctuations in the water level may occur: The water may rise in spring after being fed by freshets and recede somewhat during drier periods. Certain marshes dry out completely; this is sometimes the case in the prairie pothole country dotting the grasslands of Minnesota and North and South Dakota.

Some marshes begin as shallow lakes and depressions that gradually fill in with decomposed vegetation. Others occur in the shallow water along the edges of lakes and rivers. River floodplains, oxbow lakes, and sloughs are especially favorable sites for the establishment of emergent and floating marsh plants. The Everglades is a vast expanse of marshland where such exotic creatures as Alligators, Anhingas, and the rare Snail Kite are permanent residents. The prairie pothole marshes of the upper Midwest are important duck-breeding areas, and in Minnesota and Wisconsin, Wild Rice, a culinary delicacy, is harvested from the wetlands.

Wet meadows are closely associated with marshes. They are covered by moisture-loving grasses, sedges, and such showy broadleaved flowering plants as Turk's–cap Lily and ironweeds. These areas are usually not as wet or as frequently flooded as marshes and indeed often resemble grasslands; for this reason, they are not emphasized in this book.

Swamps and Floodplain Forests

Unlike marshes, swamps are dominated by woody plants—namely, trees and shrubs. Some are forested with hardwood trees, such as Red Maple, gums, and ashes; others by evergreens, such as cedars, firs, and spruces. In the Northeast, swamps dominated by Red Maple are most common. Beneath the Maple, a variety of wetland shrubs—including Highbush Blueberry, Spicebush, and Sweet Pepperbush—may be present. On the forest floor, which is periodically flooded, Skunk Cabbage is the first plant to appear in the spring; it is followed by the yellow Marsh Marigold, showy orchids, and the brilliant red Cardinal Flower. Willows, alders, shrubby dogwoods, and Buttonbush form shrub swamps. Some of these shrub wetlands are relatively permanent; others are transitional and will eventually be replaced by forested wetlands. Some wooded swamps develop from marshes, while others do not result from a transition of this sort, but originate directly in poorly drained depressions.

Swamp soils are saturated during the growing season, and standing water—from a few inches to a foot or more deep—is not uncommon at certain times of the year. In both marshes and swamps, highly organic soils commonly form a black muck. The underlying mineral soils are usually fairly close to the surface.

Along the larger rivers, distinctive wetland forests develop on the floodplains. In the North, Silver Maple, cottonwoods, and willows are among the common trees that occur on the silty or sandy alluvial soils laid down by rivers. Marshy areas may also develop on these floodplains. In the Southeast and along the Gulf of Mexico, extensive bottomland hardwood swamp forests occur alongside sluggish rivers. Here tupelos, Baldcypress, Overcup Oak, Sweetgum, Red Maple, and ashes are exposed to varying degrees of flooding. Some of these forest trees are highly valued for their wood.

On the coastal plain from Virginia southward through the Carolinas, one encounters unusual boggy shrub wetlands known as pocosins. These areas are covered with beautiful evergreen hollies and bays, as well as scattered stands of stunted Pond Pine. Although pocosins are often underlain by peaty deposits and thus are akin to bogs, we shall consider them as shrub swamps, with which they share many features.

Bogs

Some of the most interesting wetlands in North America are bogs. They occur primarily in formerly glaciated areas of the

Northeast, the north-central states, and Canada. Bogs are peatlands, usually lacking an overlying layer of mineral soils. The substrate—peat—is formed by the building up and gradual decomposition of plant material; this accumulation is especially favored in highly acidic, poorly drained areas where bacteria and other decomposers cannot thrive. Peat forms a floating mat of vegetation over water, and may accumulate in deposits of twenty to forty feet. Bogs often develop in deep glacial lakes. They are characterized by evergreen trees and shrubs, and are often blanketed with a carpet of sphagnum moss.

Typical bog shrubs include Leatherleaf, Bog Rosemary, Labrador-tea, Sheep Laurel, and Bog Laurel (which is related to cultivated rhododendrons). Sunny openings are filled with unusual insectivorous plants such as Sundews and Pitcher Plants. Showy orchids are also common. In northern bogs, Black Spruce and the light green, feathery-leaved Larch, or Tamarack, occur frequently. Farther south, in coastal bogs from Cape Cod southward, Atlantic White-cedar is the conspicuous evergreen tree.

Bogs offer an unusual source of information for biologists and others interested in the ecological history of the continent. The underlying peat preserves a record—in the form of fossil pollens—of the kinds of plants that have grown in the area over the last 10,000 to 15,000 years.

Rivers and Streams

Flowing water and currents characterize rivers and streams. The nature of individual streams may vary greatly and depends largely upon the speed at which the water flows. Fast-moving streams are usually associated with hilly or mountainous areas, while slower-moving or sluggish water courses exist where the gradient is very slight, for example, along the coastal plain from the Carolinas south to Georgia.

Fast- and slow-moving aquatic systems harbor very different flora and fauna. In rapidly moving streams, the plants and animals must in some way anchor themselves or they will be flushed downstream. Threadlike, filamentous algae and boxlike algae called diatoms, the primary captors of energy, are attached to rocks by special holdfast cells or slimy secretions. If you have ever tried to wade across a rapidly flowing stream, you know how slippery the rocks can be. This slipperiness is usually caused by a coating of diatoms.

These slippery rocks are places where one type of stream food chain—the grazing chain—begins. Snails, glued to the rocks by a single foot, slide along, eating algae. Some of the aquatic insects are also attached to the stream bottom, where they strain out their food as it passes by. These food particles are mostly decomposed bits of leaves that have washed into the stream from the surrounding trees. Such material, called detritus, forms part of a second important type of aquatic food chain.

In contrast to such fast systems, the slow-moving rivers of the Southeast accumulate large amounts of energy-rich organic sediments and therefore support a great number of aquatic organisms. On the floodplains of these rivers, extensive bottomland hardwood forests develop, composed of trees that can withstand varying degrees of flooding. Along other rivers, sizable marshes occur in the shallower waters of the shore.

Lakes and Ponds

Ranging in size from less than one acre to several thousands of acres, lakes and ponds—standing bodies of water—offer yet another level of diversity in wetlands habitats. The primary difference between a lake and a pond is size—lakes are usually deep, large bodies of water, and ponds are smaller and shallower. In addition, ponds usually have water of uniform temperature, whereas that of a lake changes with depth. These lacustrine environments often include areas of shallow water along their margins, where marshes and swamp forests may develop. Beyond the shoreline, one encounters deep-water habitats, where rooted aquatic plants may be absent because of a lack of light. Lakes and ponds may be of natural glacial origin, but many have been built by people. Farmers build ponds as a source of water for livestock, and sometimes ponds are constructed for the purposes of growing fish, which can be a profitable enterprise.

Large, deep lakes in northern climates are usually not highly productive environments, since the water is cold and its nutrient level is rather low. Limnologists—the scientists who specialize in the study of lakes and ponds—refer to these kinds of lakes as oligotrophic, meaning low in nutrients. Lake Tahoe is a good example of an oligotrophic lake.

Shallower, warmer lakes are much more favorable for life, and as algae or phytoplankton increase, the food chain builds rapidly. Soon a diverse population of aquatic organisms fills the lake waters. Along lake shores in spots that are sufficiently shallow, bulrushes, cattails, and other emergents are quick to claim a foothold; water lilies appear; ducks arrive; and we have the beginnings of a marsh. When the nutrient level in a lake has built to a certain point, it is said to be mesotrophic (somewhat enriched). Most of the lakes in Connecticut, for example, are now in this middle-aged stage. This process has occurred both naturally and partly as a result of human activity.

With continued algal blooms, the nutrient or food level of a lake can build up until the lake becomes eutrophic, or very enriched. In late summer, I have seen lakes in Minnesota's Itasca State Park that looked green and soupy because the algal blooms had exploded. This explosion was due to the fact that temperature, nutrients, and other factors were at the most favorable levels for the growth of blue-green algae. Such lakes are moving into a mesotrophic or eutrophic state.

Lakes and ponds may eventually be transformed into wetlands. Silt-laden rivers and streams that feed into lakes can dramatically contribute to this filling process. In the West, some of the large, man-made lakes that were built for recreation and irrigation are silting in at an amazing rate.

The Formation of Wetlands

Wetlands vary greatly in age. Some—especially man-made ones—are of relatively recent origin, while others had their beginnings following the retreat of the glaciers that once covered much of North America. As the northern part of the United States emerged from the Ice Age some 10,000 to 12,000 years ago, thousands of glacial lakes were left on the newly exposed, barren landscape. Buried ice blocks melted to form kettle lakes, which were ideal sites for the development of bogs. Scoured-out basins or streams dammed by glacial debris also became bodies of water where wetlands formed.

Along major rivers, floodplains develop as a normal part of the rivers' evolution. These bottomlands, which fringe either side of a river's channel, are formed as the river periodically floods its banks and lays down alluvial deposits, or layers of silt and sand. The floodplain is a vital geomorphic feature. It is here that the river temporarily "stores" water during floods. Floodplains may also support a mosaic of wetland types: marshes, floodplain forests, or bottomland hardwood swamps. Some of the trees in these bottomland forests grow to be very large. In Congaree Swamp in South Carolina, which was recently established as a national monument, over half of the forty-five species of trees have attained record size.

Beavers also play a vital role in creating wetlands. In many northern states, thousands of wetlands can be traced to the activity of these animals. A Beaver builds its dam with trees felled near a stream course. Once the food supply near the dam is exhausted, the animal abandons the dam and moves on to a new location, where it repeats the operation. The old dam holds for a while, but eventually begins to leak. Some sort of wetland will eventually claim the former pond. Regardless of the water's depth, wetland species will persist as long as the dam site is saturated.

Near the coast, where upland groundwater or seepage provides an adequate water supply, freshwater wetlands commonly form among or on the inland side of dunes or barrier beaches. In the Sandhills of Nebraska, for example, wetlands have formed within the dunes.

In Florida, the Everglades represents a unique shallow basin that was formed on eroded limestone bedrock and is fed by underground and surface water flowing primarily from Lake Okeechobee. In northern Florida, Kentucky, Indiana, and other limestone areas, sinkholes develop as percolating water dissolves the underlying limestone. In Tennessee, Reelfoot Lake, a national wildlife refuge, was formed by earthquake activity.

Many wetlands have been created by human beings. Flood-control and hydroelectric dams, reservoirs, impoundments for irrigation, farm ponds, and the pits, ponds, and depressions associated with mining, quarrying, and road construction are among the more obvious examples.

The Dynamics of Wetland Ecosystems

Within a given area, the plants and animals interacting with one another and their environment constitute an ecological system, or ecosystem. Within this system, there are certain organisms that are more important than others. These are the dominant species.

In the northeastern hardwood swamps, Red Maple is often the dominant species and forms the main tree canopy. Beneath the maples, a shrubby layer may develop, and on the forest floor, wild flowers may make up a conspicuous ground cover or herbaceous layer. This layering of vegetation is referred to as stratification.

Various sets of species have different tolerances; some, for example, need more light than others to grow and reproduce. Competition among organisms is also an important aspect of an ecosystem, and one that can limit the presence or size of a given species population. For example, under a dense layer of maple foliage, the shrub layer may be sparsely developed because of inadequate light—the result of competition with the trees. In an open marsh, however, competition for light is not a consideration; most of the plants are present because they require a great deal of sunlight to live and because they can tolerate wet conditions. Green plants may also compete for mineral nutrients, which they require in addition to light, whereas bird and animal populations may compete for food or nesting sites. As the various wetland systems have evolved, natural selection has tended to weed out certain species, minimizing the competitive interaction among those remaining. After many years, a mature system will finally function in a relatively harmonious fashion.

Adapting to Water

Wetness—in the form of saturated soils or long periods of flooding—is another special condition to which wetland plants must be adapted. Saturation brings with it special problems, one of the most important being the low levels of oxygen that plants must tolerate. (Oxygen diffuses about four times more slowly in water than in air.) Upland plants, on the other hand, do not have this problem, since there is usually ample oxygen between the soil particles around their roots.

Aquatic plants respond to this oxygen problem in various ways. In some, extensive intercellular networks link the aerial leaves to the roots. Water lilies have small openings (stomata) on the upper surfaces of their leaves to facilitate the exchange of oxygen and carbon dioxide. These openings allow oxygen to enter and move down the long leaf stalks to the underwater stems and the roots, which are buried in the mucky marsh sediments. Submerged aquatic plants also have many air spaces in their stems and leaves.

Wetland trees and shrubs have several unusual adaptations for coping with low levels of oxygen. Some, such as willow and ash, are stimulated when flooded to produce new, air-filled roots to replace those that the flood has killed. Flooding can also promote the growth of tiny openings in the bark, called lenticels, which allow air to move more readily into the plant. And some species are capable of switching to oxygenless, or anaerobic, respiration. When this occurs, the plant begins to generate potentially poisonous products such as alcohols. However, the tree converts these substances to useful organic acids; it transports these to the leaves, where they are used for growth.

Animals have also evolved many adaptations that allow them to cope with life in water. Fish, of course, extract oxygen directly from the water by passing it over their gills. Other animals, including some aquatic insects and spiders, periodically rise to the surface and pick up a bubble of air, which they then use in the way that a diver uses an oxygen tank.

Still others live part of their lives in the water and part on land. Dragonflies and damselflies lay their eggs on the water's surface. The immature aquatic forms that develop from these eggs are underwater carnivores, but they eventually emerge as aerial predators that skim across the marsh and pond waters in search of insects. Some frogs and salamanders spend most of their lives in upland areas and only come to the wetlands to breed and to lay their eggs. Nevertheless, their aquatic origin is evident in the fact that these amphibians must maintain a moist skin—even when away from a watery environment—in order to absorb oxygen.

Energy Flow

A basic ecological process occurring in all natural ecosystems is energy flow, which is the movement of chemical energy within a particular food chain—from plants (the primary producers) to herbivores (plant eaters) and ultimately to one or more carnivores (meat eaters). The process may begin in a plant's leaves, where the energy of the sun's light combines with chlorophyll to produce sugars, or carbohydrates.

In many wetlands, there are two major energy-flow patterns. One—the grazing food chain—involves the direct consumption of green plants, while the second—the detrital food chain—involves those organisms that depend primarily on detritus, or organic debris, as their food source. Often the patterns intertwine.

In lake and pond ecosystems, submerged aquatic plants and tiny floating algae (phytoplankton) serve as the basis of the food chain. Tiny aquatic animals (zooplankton) feed on the algae, and small aquatic insects eat the zooplankton. These are eaten by small fish, which in turn are consumed by larger fish. A plug cast into a clump of water lilies in the shallow zone of a lake may raise a bass, and the food chain—in this case a grazing food chain—thus ends up on the supper table.

In streams, the main sources of organic input, or food for stream organisms, include partly decomposed leaves or other organic material flowing downstream. This debris, or detritus, may be caught in the nets set by the larvae of caddisflies, and stoneflies also glean the rocks for algae. These insects are in turn consumed—often by Brook Trout.

In the riverine bottomland hardwood swamps, the detrital food chain is particularly important, as the leaves of the swamp trees are broken down by bacteria and fungi. Detritus, which is energy-rich to begin with, is often further enriched by bacterial protein that is high in nitrogen. This mixture is a vital food source for many wetland organisms, such as worms and aquatic insects.

In the Florida Everglades, one food chain leads from plants to snails to the Snail Kite. Since most animals can feed on more than one kind of organism, a complex network of feeding interactions, or food web, usually develops. However, the Snail Kite is an ecological specialist, because in North America it feeds solely on the Apple Snail. This can be hazardous to survival, and indeed has been for the Snail Kite. Shell collectors have greatly depleted the snail populations, and the loss of suitable habitats to draining activities and periodic droughts has severely affected snail populations. As a result, the Snail Kite has been listed as an endangered species since 1966.

It should be pointed out that energy flow is a noncyclical ecological process: The chemical energy used at each trophic, or feeding, level is not recoverable. The plants, herbivores, and carnivores have transformed the energy, and some has been made into new cells and tissues. However, the cellular activity (involving cellular respiration) that has accomplished this has also resulted in the production of a considerable amount of heat, which represents energy that is lost to the atmosphere.

Therefore, as energy moves from one trophic level to the next, there is less available for each succeeding set of organisms. As a rule of thumb, ecologists calculate that, on average, ten percent of the useful energy at one level will actually be passed on to the next trophic level—for example, to the Mink that ate the Muskrat in the cattail marsh. (This is known as the ten-percent rule.) Since there is an inevitable loss of available energy at each trophic level, there is a limit to the number of top-level carnivores that can exist in any wetland ecosystem. Since the Mink is rather high on the food chain, there are only a limited number of predators above this level.

Depending on the availability of nutrients—from the most basic level on up—an ecosystem can support only a certain number of organisms and still function adequately. If this number is exceeded, the ecosystem will suffer and begin to degrade. The number of organisms that any given ecosystem can support without damage is known as the carrying capacity of that ecosystem.

Nutrient Cycling

Looking at the constant flow of energy through wetland ecosystems, one finds that not all green plants are consumed by grazers. In fact, few aquatic invertebrates feed on submerged aquatic plants, being primarily detritus feeders. All of the uneaten leaves, as well as twigs and dead branches, that accumulate in the wetland are taken over by the decomposers—bacteria, worms, and aquatic insects that produce detritus. These creatures use some of the energy that resides in dead plant and animal remains, but in the process, also release mineral nutrients and soluble organic compounds that enable the wetland ecosystems to be self-perpetuating. Thus marshes and swamps don't need the additional fertilizers that agricultural lands do. Wetlands are naturally productive. This process of nutrient release through decomposition varies from one kind of wetland to another. For example, the rate of decomposition in bogs is extremely slow. Therefore the dead plant remains—roots, stems, and leaves—tend to accumulate. Peat builds up, because the highly acidic conditions are unfavorable to the mircoorganisms in charge of recycling. In contrast, southern bottomland hardwood swamps are tremendous producers of detritus. The decomposers are superactive in breaking down the leaves that fall and in recharging the system with nutrients, which in turn support an abundance of life.

Wetland Productivity

Biological productivity is the "living output," in terms of organisms—plants, Muskrats, and ducks, to name a few—that occurs because of the efficient interaction of organisms within the ecosystem. Wetlands are among the most productive ecosystems in the world. They rival the best agricultural lands and appear to be exceeded only by the sugarcane fields of Hawaii. The high productivity of wetlands is due to their ability to capture large amounts of the sun's energy and store it as chemical energy, as well as to their efficient recycling of that which is produced.

The rate at which photosynthesis produces energy or stores sugars in plants is the rate of primary productivity. The total amount actually produced by an organism in a given time is referred to as its gross productivity. Some of this energy is used to maintain the organism's life processes (in cellular respiration); the stored energy that remains is net productivity.

The harvesting of plants and animals in a given area of the wetland also provides an indication of productivity. For example, harvested plants can be dried in an oven and weighed to yield the standing crop, or biomass. Cattail marshes are among the most productive wetlands, with yields as great as twelve tons of biomass per acre per year. A sedge marsh is about one–third as productive, yet its biomass exceeds that of grasslands and equals or exceeds the productivity of many forests. This high plant productivity is the basis for the high overall production of ducks, Muskrats, and other wildlife in marshes.

Wetland productivity is related to several factors. The efficient functioning of both the grazing and detritus food chains contributes significantly to the productivity of many wetlands. In addition, wetlands are what is known as "pulsed," or energy-subsidized, ecosystems. The periodic rise and fall of the water level creates a rhythm in wetlands; nutrients may be brought in by flooding, or made more accessible when the water level retreats. This pulsing also helps to keep the system oxygenated, a factor that is especially critical, since (as noted earlier) low levels of oxygen can limit growth, especially in wetlands. Studies have shown that the stagnant water of unpulsed wetlands is less productive than the refreshed water of areas with periodic flooding. In bogs, where there is little or no pulsing, organic matter tends to accumulate as peat rather than be broken down or recycled, and potential productivity is locked up in the sediments. In both saltwater and freshwater tidal wetlands, the tidal cycle provides the energy subsidy that accounts for the high productivity.

Biotic Change

"All lakes are doomed to die!"

I have never forgotten these words, spoken by my first limnology professor. This statement dramatically describes the fate of lakes, but the rate at which this process occurs is highly variable. For while the Great Lakes will persist for a very long time—even though Lake Erie was threatened some years ago by pollution—other, smaller bodies of water may be much shorter-lived.

The nutrient enrichment of lakes is a natural trend that increases over time. An abundance of phytoplankton feeds the zooplankton and a lake food chain is begun. As nutrient availability increases, productivity also increases.

Lakes have a unique mechanism for keeping nutrients in circulation. Twice a year, the lake water overturns. During the summer, there is a distinct stratification in the lake: The surface waters are warmed by the wind as it mixes the upper layers of the water. However—as you may well have experienced when swimming in a mountain lake—warm water near the surface gives way to colder water beneath. The abrupt temperature change between the two layers prevents further mixing of the surface water with the deeper water. With cooler weather in the fall, however, the temperature profile of the lake water becomes uniform. Mineral-rich waters from the bottom now rise to the surface to nourish algae and other plants that can live only in the upper waters, where there is ample light.

This biannual recirculation of nutrients in lakes not only increases productivity; it is also partly responsible for lake filling. Just as peat accumulation causes bogs to form in deep kettle lakes, the process of nutrient enrichment can cause shallower lakes to fill in and become marshes and swamps. As cattails appear, Muskrats and Red-winged Blackbirds arrive. In time a pond or lake is replaced by a marsh.

Lake filling can also be accelerated by silt and clay, which are carried into lakes and ponds by streams. These sediments mix with the detritus from aquatic plants and further help to fill lakes. We can conclude that there is a definite trend for lakes and ponds to fill in over a period of time.

The Value of Wetlands

Our attitude toward wetlands has changed dramatically since 1764, when the Virginia Assembly chartered the Dismal Swamp Company to drain 40,000 acres of the Great Dismal

Swamp so that the excellent timber could be cut. George Washington was a member of the company, and a canal that was dug across the swamp still bears his name—Washington Ditch. After the trees had been cut down, the plan for converting the swamp to agricultural land failed. In 1970, the Nature Conservancy, a national organization concerned with the preservation of natural areas, received a gift of 50,000 acres of the swamp from the Union Camp Corporation. Today a large portion of the swamp is a national wildlife refuge; one can hike along Washington Ditch to Lake Drummond, a mysterious lake in the middle of the swamp. The mystery is that no one really knows how the lake was formed, although it has been suggested that a catastrophic fire may have burned an enormous hole in the peat, thereby forming the lake basin.

Wetlands play many roles. They are invaluable in controlling floodwaters, recharging groundwater, and filtering pollutants; as a habitat for waterfowl and other wildlife, a support for fisheries, and sanctuaries for rare and endangered species; and for their educational, recreational, and aesthetic promise. In a recent study of the importance of wetlands by the U.S. Department of Transportation, ten major roles were recognized. An overview of some of these roles will help us to better appreciate the value of these liquid assets.

Flood Control and Groundwater Recharge

Wetlands are of major importance in the hydrologic cycle—the pattern of evaporation, precipitation, and flow to the seas. They can serve as temporary storage basins, lower flood crests, and contribute to groundwater recharge. They can also reduce erosion and the destructive potential of severe floods. With increased development and the paving over of large areas with asphalt and concrete, we greatly speed up the rate at which storm waters move off the land and thus increase the likelihood of flooding.

During the great flood in northeastern Pennsylvania in 1955, many highway bridges in the Pocono Mountains region were washed out; however, those in an area below a sizable bog remained intact. In Wisconsin it has been found that watersheds containing fifteen percent of their area as wetlands had flood peaks that were sixty percent lower than those with no wetlands. By slowing the velocity of flood waters, wetlands can also act as sediment or siltation traps, thereby slowing erosion. In addition, wetlands sometimes lessen erosion along shorelines, where marsh plants help to buffer wave action.

Some wetlands recharge groundwater, which is the source of drinking water in many communities. Groundwater recharge is the movement of surface water down through the soil to the underlying groundwater system or aquifer. In the glaciated lake country of Wisconsin, twenty-six percent of the wetlands are involved in recharging the groundwater reserves. In the prairie pothole region of the Midwest, wetlands are more important than uplands in groundwater recharge.

Not all wetlands contribute to the water table, but that does not mean they are not serving many other functions. Greater interest and new philosophies are developing concerning the part that wetlands play in human well-being.

Wildlife and Fisheries

Almost everyone associates such animals as ducks, Muskrats, Beavers, and Alligators with wetlands. These creatures, as well as many other kinds of wildlife, are absolutely dependent on these habitats. It has been estimated that 150 kinds of birds and some 200 kinds of fish are wetland-dependent. Other animals, including deer, bear, and Raccoon, also use wetlands. During the winter, White-tailed Deer often yard up and feed in evergreen swamps, especially those dominated by Northern White-cedar and Balsam Fir. In northern regions, Moose obtain sodium, a required dietary nutrient, from aquatic plants.

The term wetland wildlife also has powerful economic implications. Two million Americans hunt the waterfowl that breed, nest, and feed in wetlands. An estimated 600,000 ducks—mostly Mallards, Pintails, and Green-winged Teals—were harvested between 1967 and 1969. The prairie pothole marshes, which represent only ten percent of the wetlands in the United States, produce fifty percent of these ducks. Thousands of Muskrats are trapped annually in the wetlands; their pelts provide an additional source of income for many people.

Many freshwater fish are directly connected to the wetlands. Several species require areas of shallow water for breeding and feeding, or some other part of their life cycle. They retreat to these areas to avoid predators, which are generally less common in shallow water. In the deeper swamps of the southern bottomlands, fish are an integral part of the food web. In fact, it has recently come to light that the nutrient-rich waters from these riverine ecosystems strongly influence the fish catch in the brackish estuarine waters at the mouths of rivers. The latter circumstance dramatically illustrates the close interrelationship of freshwater and saltwater ecosystems. In the fertile prairie pothole wetlands, one acre yields up to 100 pounds of rough fish (species that are not commercially important) and 200 to 300 pounds of game fish. Most of the rough fish ends up as supplements in animal foods, some of which may be used in raising poultry. Thus, when we sit down to a chicken dinner, we partake—at a distance—of the energy of the wetlands.

Pollution Filtration

It has long been recognized that aquatic systems have a certain self-cleansing ability. If sewage is added upstream, the organic level will have been considerably reduced by the time the water has traveled several miles. Dilution is one reason for this, but another factor is the ability of aquatic organisms such as algae and bacteria to take up minerals and break down organic matter. This process will obviously not work if more sewage is added than the riverine system can process. This overloading has happened in many of our rivers and lakes in recent years, necessitating the construction of numerous sewage-treatment plants.

Runoff from agricultural land often puts excess nitrogen and phosphorous—the components of fertilizers—into rivers and lakes. Wetlands can absorb some of these nutrients and thus improve water quality, and some of the nitrogen is returned to the atmosphere in the form of gas. Most, however, is buried in sediments and used by wetland plants at a later date. The portion that is not used may be flushed from the marshes or swamps by spring freshets. Wetlands, it seems, possess an inherent ability to trap nutrients. They often hold them back when there is an abundance, frequently releasing them when they are most needed.

Within the last decade, this nutrient-trapping role has stimulated research into the possibility of using wetlands to filter our pollutants, especially sewage. In southern Florida, two cypress domes (small, doughnut-shaped cypress swamps nestled within the pinelands) have been receiving 15,000 gallons of effluent per day, which has caused the water level to rise an inch per week. In response to this nutrient enrichment, the surface water has quickly become covered with a green carpet of duckweed, a tiny, floating aquatic plant that is relished by ducks. As these plants die and fall to the bottom, they decay and release their nutrients to stimulate the growth of the cypress trees. The domes actually retained ninety-seven percent of the coliform bacteria, heavy metals, and nutrients from the sewage. As the swamp water percolated into underlying sediments, it was further filtered, and relatively little contamination of the groundwater occurred.

A sedge marsh near Clermont, Florida, has effectively taken care of the waste water from the local treatment plant. Near Philadelphia the level of nitrogen and phosphorous in the waste water was reduced by fifty to sixty percent after it flowed across a 500-acre freshwater tidal marsh. Some Florida wetlands have fortuitously taken care of such wastes for many years—presumably with no undesirable effects—and certain home septic systems are no doubt receiving unsuspected help from adjacent wetlands. Wetlands near large metropolitan or industrial areas probably play a significant part in lessening both air and water pollution. The Hackensack Meadows, which lie in the shadows of Manhattan and Newark, are much more important in their undeveloped state than most people realize.

These experimental studies—and others in Wisconsin, Michigan, New Jersey, and Massachusetts, as well as in Europe—appear promising; nonetheless, one must be extremely careful about overly enriching wetland systems. Changes usually occur, as they did in the cypress domes in Florida, where duckweed became much more abundant in the treated swamp. Some changes may be quite benign, but others may be undesirable or even harmful. It appears that certain wetlands have the potential of helping with our pollution problems, whereas others are not suitable for such purposes. There are many variables involved—including the flora, the water flow patterns, retention time, and soil type—that determine a particular wetland's ability to process pollutants.

One of the most exciting recent developments in pollution filtration is the proposal to use artificially created wetlands; research in this area is under way in both Europe and the United States. According to estimates, a man-made marsh-pond complex of one hundred acres could deal effectively with the domestic sewage from a community of 10,000 people. In fact, artificial marsh-pond systems can be three times more efficient in taking up wastes than natural wetlands.

It has even been proposed that bulrushes be used to absorb certain industrial pollutants, including phenols and cyanide. Another idea involves using catfish and small crustaceans to feed on the organic matter contained in sewage.

Whatever the results of these projects may be, one thing is clear: Wetlands and wetland plants are nutrient traps and in the future will probably help us with some of our air- and water-pollution problems.

Maintaining Biospheric Stability

The thin skin of air, water, and soil that encircles the globe and supports all life is the biosphere. The interaction of elements, including human beings, that keeps this gigantic system working in harmony is not well understood. However, wetlands may perform significant, essential functions. How might this be occurring? One example of their contribution involves the production of oxygen. In the process of photosynthesis, all green plants use carbon dioxide from the air and return oxygen to it. Although upland plants contribute a significant proportion of this oxygen, plants in the wetlands are especially efficient in the process.

Wetlands are also important in the nitrogen cycle, the natural process through which nitrogen in the atmosphere is converted into the compounds that are used by plants and animals to create protein—and later is eventually returned to its original state. All green plants require nitrogen, but they cannot use the gaseous form that makes up most of the air we breathe, and so must convert it to another form. Microorganisms in the soil are capable of converting nitrogen gas into a form plants can use. However, some of these microorganisms are also capable of working in the other direction—converting excess nitrate to nitrogen gas and putting it back into the atmosphere. On agricultural land, the nitrogen used as fertilizer is in the form of nitrate or ammonia compounds. There is some concern that, as a result of the use of fertilizers, the nitrogen cycle may be slipping out of balance.

Now how do the wetlands come into play? Most wetlands contain vast hordes of bacteria, which can take the excess nitrates or other nitrogenous pollutants that we generate in our industrial society, put them back into the atmosphere as harmless inert gas, and thus help to balance the nitrogen cycle.

Finally, the wetlands may be helping to prevent our being burned by the sun. In many wetland soils, oxygen levels are so low that organisms must employ anaerobic respiration, which is the type of respiration that takes place in the flooded roots of certain trees that cannot obtain enough oxygen. Recent studies suggest that an anaerobic world preceded our present oxygen-demanding way of life. The gas given off by respiration without oxygen is methane, or marsh gas. It is thought to function as a kind of regulator of the ozone layer, which provides protection from ultraviolet radiation. Scientists do not have all the answers, but the preservation of wetlands may be more important to us than we once realized.

Education, Recreation, and Aesthetics

Wetlands are living museums, where the dynamics of ecological systems can be taught. These outdoor laboratories can demonstrate such basic ecological principles as energy flow, recycling, and limited carrying capacity. The way in which wetlands serve people can also be highlighted, as it is in the Connecticut Arboretum guided tour. There the presentation makes the point that a one-acre swamp, when flooded to a depth of one foot, contains 330,000 gallons of water. Thus the swamp acts as a kind of natural reservoir, storing the excess and allowing it to filter slowly into the groundwater system. If the swamp were filled or drained, however, this huge quantity of water would be lost to the groundwater system—and in all likelihood would cause destructive flooding farther downstream.

Wetlands are exemplary teaching and research laboratories in a variety of scientific disciplines. Environmental education is a major theme in many national parks and public areas established around wetlands. In the Everglades National Park, visitors are introduced to the wetland food chain along the famous Anhinga Trail, where the energy flows from mosquitoes to small fishes to larger garfish to Alligators. Apart from the experience of seeing the actual participants, the process is portrayed artistically in a designed display. In the last few years, 600,000 visitors have enjoyed this recreational experience each year, which is testimony to the enduring attraction of wetlands.

Indeed, our ancestors were attracted to and highly dependent on wetlands. The Indians' settlements were often located near these areas; they harvested Wild Rice and cattails in marshes along rivers and lakes and depended heavily on shellfish, as evidenced by the many large shell middens along river estuaries. They exploited wetland resources in thoroughgoing and often ingenious ways, but were protective and appreciative of them at the same time.

Wetlands are beautiful. There is something ineffable about them—ducks rising off a marsh, a heron intent on its prey, a Moose lifting emergent-laden antlers, the night sounds of a swamp in spring—that evokes pleasure and awe. They are an integral part of our natural heritage.

BOGS

Bogs, one of North America's most distinctive kinds of wetlands, are characterized by a growth of evergreen trees and shrubs and a floor covered by a thick carpet of sphagnum moss. Bogs form in very wet places—often in old glacial lakes, which were created as ice blocks deposited by glaciers that melted or as valleys were dammed by glacial debris. Some have considerable amounts of open water surrounded by floating boggy vegetation; in others, vegetation may have completely filled a lake.

In a bog decomposition is hindered severely due to the highly acidic environment. Thus, peat accummulates, often to considerable depths, and gives bogs their distinctive nature. Because peat is not decomposed by the action of bacteria and other decay-producing organisms, it is deficient in many minerals needed for plant growth. Therefore the species that populate bogs are hardy evergreens and other plants—especially sphagnum mosses—that are adapted to extremely acidic, nutrient-poor soils.

Sphagnum Moss
Sphagnum spp.

Not all bogs are forested, nor have they all developed in glacial lakes. Shallow depressions with impervious subsoil will allow standing water to accumulate. This condition, in turn, slows decomposition, and eventually paves the way for the growth of a boggy flora.

Peat makes bogs spongy. Although you can get "bogged down" in any kind of wetland, the term is especially apt in these peatlands, and visitors must exercise care. For this reason, many bogs in nature preserves have boardwalks that protect the fragile surface of the bog while allowing the visitor to get close to some of the unique plants and animals found there.

Since bogs are typically underlaid by many feet of spongy peat, it is possible for the visitor to experience a "quaking bog" sensation when jumping up and down on the mossy bog surface. If there is still open water, a floating mat of sedges and sometimes sphagnum moss may develop out over the water. Such areas can be especially hazardous. There is always the chance of falling through—an unpleasant prospect even though you can rest assured that you would be permanently preserved, thanks to the same lack of bacterial activity that is responsible for the accumulation of peat. One amazingly preserved body, known as Tollund Man, was discovered in a Danish bog in 1950. He is thought to have been a sacrificial victim who was buried in the bog more than 2000 years ago. Tollund Man is so well preserved that his fingernails and facial features, including whiskers, are incredibly lifelike.

Distribution

Since lakes are especially common in the parts of North America that were once glaciated, bogs are also frequent there. Most occur in eastern Canada and New England and across the Great Lakes states. One of the largest peatland complexes in North America is in northern Minnesota.

Bogs are also scattered throughout the western mountains and the Pacific Northwest. In the east, boggy areas extend down

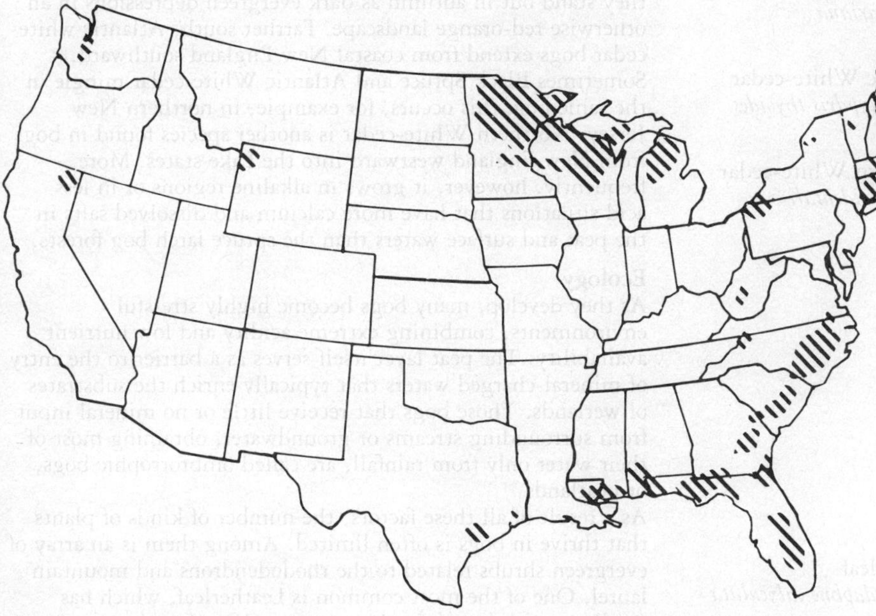

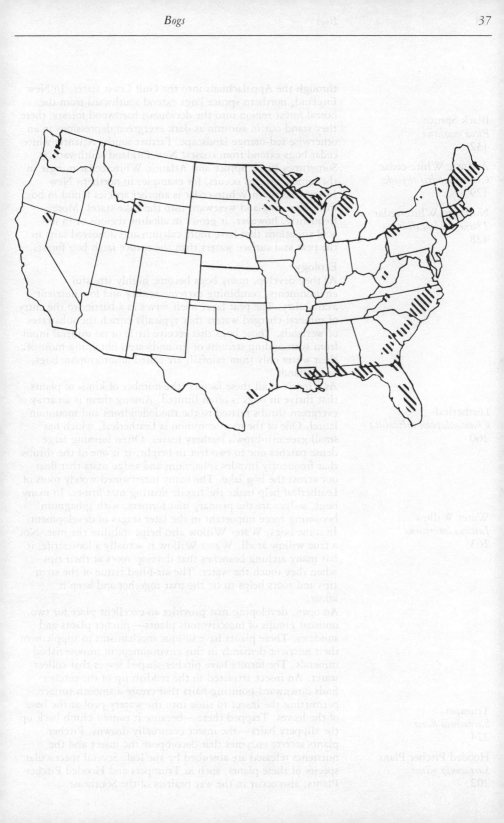

Black Spruce
Picea mariana
432

Atlantic White-cedar
Chamaecypdris thyoides
429

Northern White-cedar
Thuja occidentalis
428

through the Appalachians into the Gulf Coast states. In New England, northern spruce bogs extend southward from the boreal forest region into the deciduous hardwood forests; there they stand out in autumn as dark evergreen depressions in an otherwise red-orange landscape. Farther south, Atlantic white-cedar bogs extend from coastal New England southward. Sometimes Black Spruce and Atlantic White-cedar mingle in the same bog; this occurs, for example, in northern New Jersey. Northern White-cedar is another species found in bogs from New England westward into the Lake states. More frequently, however, it grows in alkaline regions or in less acid situations that have more calcium and dissolved salts in the peat and surface waters than the spruce larch bog forests.

Ecology

As they develop, many bogs become highly stressful environments, combining extreme acidity and low nutrient availability. The peat layer itself serves as a barrier to the entry of mineral-charged waters that typically enrich the substrates of wetlands. Those bogs that receive little or no mineral input from surrounding streams or groundwater, obtaining most of their water only from rainfall, are called ombrotrophic bogs, or peatlands.

Leatherleaf
Chamaedaphne calyculata
260

Water Willow
Justicia americana
263

As a result of all these factors, the number of kinds of plants that thrive in bogs is often limited. Among them is an array of evergreen shrubs related to the rhododendrons and mountain laurel. One of the most common is Leatherleaf, which has small greenish-brown leathery leaves. Often forming large dense patches one to two feet in height, it is one of the shrubs that frequently invades sphagnum and sedge mats that float out across the bog lake. The many intertwined woody roots of Leatherleaf help make the fragile floating mat firmer. In many bogs, sedges are the primary mat formers, with sphagnum becoming more important in the later stages of development. In some bogs, Water Willow also helps stabilize the mat. Not a true willow at all, Water Willow is actually a loosestrife; it has many arching branches that develop roots at their tips when they touch the water. The air-filled tissue of the stem tips and roots helps to tie the mat together and keep it afloat.

Trumpet
Sarracenia flava
224

Hooded Pitcher Plant
Sarracenia minor
202

An open, developing mat provides an excellent place for two unusual groups of insectivorous plants—pitcher plants and sundews. These plants have unique mechanisms to supplement their nutrient demands in this environment of impoverished minerals. The former have pitcher-shaped leaves that collect water. An insect attracted to the reddish lip of the pitcher finds downward-pointing hairs that create a smooth surface, permitting the insect to slide into the watery pool at the base of the leaves. Trapped there—because it cannot climb back up the slippery hairs—the insect eventually drowns. Pitcher plants secrete enzymes that decompose the insect and the nutrients released are absorbed by the leaf. Several spectacular species of these plants, such as Trumpets and Hooded Pitcher Plants, also occur in the wet prairies of the Southeast.

The smaller sundews, only a few inches high, have a rosette of reddish leaves with sticky glandular hairs. An insect that lands on a leaf becomes stuck. Then the plant secretes enzymes that kill the insect and break down its nutrients, which are eventually absorbed into the leaf.

Butterwort
Pinguicula spp.
208, 302

The butterwort, another insect catcher, is most common in the Southeast. At the base of the flower stalk there is a rosette of leaves; their upper surfaces are covered with a sticky substance that captures and digests insects in the same manner as the sundews.

Certain evergreen trees and shrubs are well suited to the bog's short growing season. Because evergreens do not shed their leaves as regularly as deciduous species do, they do not need to constantly make new leaves. This situation is advantageous where nutrients are scarce, allowing the plants to conserve energy.

Sheep Laurel
Kalmia angustifolia
288

Labrador Tea
Ledum groenlandicum
234

Cranberry
Vaccinium macrocarpon
266, 330

Some of the interesting evergreen shrubs that contribute to shrub mat formation are Sheep Laurel, which has pink laurel-like flowers; Labrador Tea, with its dense brownish fuzz on the leaf undersurface; and two native species of cranberry. In fact, bogs are so well suited to the growth of cranberries that they are used extensively in New Jersey, Cape Cod, and elsewhere for commercial cranberry culture.

Highbush Blueberry
Vaccinium corymbosum
259

Grass Pink
Calopogon pulchellus
269

Taller shrubs that flourish in bogs include Highbush Blueberry and Bog Holly; the latter has red velvety fruits. As these shrubs develop, they block the light that pitcher plants, sundews, and other light-demanding plants require, causing these to decrease or disappear. Yet in mossy openings among the shrubs one may encounter two beautiful pink bog orchids —the Grass Pink and the Pogonia during the summer.

Rose Pogonia
Pogonia ophioglossoides
268

Tamarack/Larch
Larix laricina
430

Red Maple
Acer rubrum
479

Black Ash
Fraxinus nigra
435

Poison-sumac
Toxicodendron vernix
441

The open developing bog mat provides ample light for the lovely, feathery, light-green deciduous conifer, Tamarack. Also called Larch, this tree has soft needlelike leaves that grow in little rosettes, readily distinguishing it. Other trees that may be present are Red Maple, Black Ash, Poison-sumac, and, in northern bogs, the distinctive Black Spruce.

Sometimes bogs exhibit very clear belts or zones of vegetation that range from the water's edge to the upland. As one might expect with the entry of all of these plants, there will be competitive interactions among the species. Some species will be lost and others will gain over the years.

One of the most extensive peatlands in North America occurs in northern Minnesota. The Upper Red Lake area is a 300-square-mile region of unbroken wetland north of the Red Lakes. An aerial view reveals teardrop-shaped forested bog "islands," several miles long and dominated by Black Spruce and Tamarack. These are surrounded by treeless, patterned fens looking much like waves in a lake when viewed from the air. Shrubs cover the ridges and sedges, and other bog species the wetter hollows. Such areas are referred to as string bogs.

Fens receive water that has percolated through mineral soil; they therefore have a richer array of plant species, especially sedges and grasses—and in some cases, shrubs—rather than the carpet of sphagnum typical of ombrotrophic bogs.

Wildlife of the Bog

White-tailed Deer
Odocoileus virginianus
617

Black Bear
Ursus americanus
615

Northern Leopard Frog
Rana pipiens
130, 143

Wood Frog
Rana sylvatica
149

Pine Barrens Treefrog
Hyla andersoni
138

Bog (Muhlenberg's) Turtle
Clemmys muhlenbergi
165

Golden-crowned Kinglet
Regulus satrapa

Red-breasted Nuthatch
Sitta canadensis

Connecticut Warbler
Oporornis agilis

Lincoln's Sparrow
Melospiza lincolnii
577

Northern Waterthrush
Seiurus noveboracensis

Palm Warbler
Dendroica palmarum
583

Snowshoe Hare
Lepus americanus

Bobcat
Felis rufus
616

Northern Bog Lemming
Synaptomys borealis

Beaver
Castor canadensis
611

Hessel's Hairstreak
Mitoura hesseli
387

Although bogs do have some characteristic species, some of the animals found here are visitors from the surrounding upland. Among the larger animals are the White-tailed deer and Black Bear. Bears are most common when berry-producing shrubs, such as Highbush Blueberry, are at their peak; broken branches and the absence of berries attest to the presence of these large animals.

A variety of amphibians depend on boggy wetlands, especially during the breeding season. In one bog study in Minnesota, ecologists reported that different frogs inhabited different vegetation belts from the open water to the upland forest. On the sedge mat near the open water, Leopard Frogs were most abundant, whereas Wood Frogs were more common farther from the water in the spruce bog forest belt. Leopard Frogs can tolerate full sunlight and apparently prefer being near open water, where they can readily escape their enemies. The Wood Frog prefers cooler, shadier areas, where it can hide under logs. If a bog forest eventually encroaches on a sedge mat, one might accurately predict an increase in the Wood Frog population, and a corresponding decrease in Leopard Frogs.

One of the most beautiful bog frogs, the rare Pine Barrens Treefrog, is now being threatened by the destruction of its habitat. The relatively rare Bog, or Muhlenberg's, Turtle also needs every bit of protection possible. Despite its secretive habits, this attractive species is still endangered by eager collectors.

Spruce bogs are shady and cool and reflect a somewhat northerly vegetation; where they occur southward into the deciduous forest region birds typical of coniferous forests are often found. Golden-crowned Kinglets, Red-breasted Nuthatches, and various wood warblers frequent bogs. The Connecticut Warbler and Lincoln's Sparrow are especially typical of Larch, or Tamarack, bogs. The sparrow-size Northern Waterthrush, an unusual wood warbler, searches the water's edge for insects; the drab, rufous-capped Palm Warbler, constantly wagging its tail, is another summer visitor to these wetlands.

Although the truly northern Snowshoe Hare is usually found on the upland, it also frequents bogs, especially when searching for evergreens in winter. The furry coats of these hares are white in winter and brownish in summer, thus serving as excellent camouflage from various predators: owls, foxes, and Bobcats. A small, mouselike herbivore, the Northern Bog Lemming, often feeds on sedges and grasses; its presence can be detected by the little piles of grassy cuttings that it leaves along its runways. Beavers too have a strong impact on the life of bogs, damming and manipulating the water flow in these areas.

Among the insects, there are several butterflies that are distinctly creatures of the bogs. Hessel's Hairstreak is closely associated with Atlantic white-cedar, and therefore is found almost exclusively in bogs or swamps. Other butterflies of the

Bog Elfin
Incisalia lanoraieensis
415

Bog fritillary
Proclossiana eunomia
396

Spruce Bog Alpine
Erebia disa
418

northern bogs include the Bog Elfin, Bog Fritillary, and Spruce Bog Alpine.

Pollen Records

Because bogs are subject to such little decomposition, they serve as a kind of time capsule, preserving microfossils of pollen from those plants that grew around the developing bog thousands of years ago.

The forest trees—such as oaks, birches, and pines—that may grow near bogs produce large quantities of wind-borne pollen. In this relatively inefficient mode of pollination, many of the grains fall on the surrounding landscape, never reaching a female flower. The pollen that falls on the surface of the bog lake sinks and becomes incorporated into the developing peat at the bottom of the lake, to be preserved for thousands of years.

By taking a continuous core sample from the peat and extracting and staining the pollen that has been preserved at different levels, it is possible to reconstruct the dominant upland vegetation types that once grew around the bog.

In the Northeast, pollen studies indicate that the initial growth that followed the retreat of the glaciers—10,000 to 12,000 years ago—was an open, tundralike, stunted spruce-fir vegetation. As climatic conditions altered and these areas grew warmer, forests of spruce and fir became dominant. Next there followed a period when pines were most common. Eventually deciduous trees, such as oaks, birches, hickories, and other hardwoods, became more important in the upper levels. Thus the record preserved in the bogs has provided scientists an opportunity to learn the paleoecology of these wetland regions.

The Fate of Bogs

As kettle-hole lakes continue to fill with peat, and as the bog forest grows larger and denser, one might suspect that these areas would eventually give way to incursions of the vegetation types that develop on the surrounding uplands. It is not the rule unless the water level or substrate in a bog is drastically modified. Many of these boggy areas have developed over the past 10,000 to 15,000 years—surely enough time for this transition to take place and the upland forests to dominate. Yet this has not happened.

Why?

One reason is that the highly acidic, wet, peaty substrate is not congenial to most upland trees. In fact, many plants found in bogs are unusual in their ability to tolerate such harsh conditions; many other species—including upland species—cannot. In addition, the cooler conditions that prevail in bogs probably favor the occurrence of northern species, such as Tamarack and Black Spruce, in areas somewhat south of their normal range. These hardy species are not likely to give way in the face of a challenge from less well-adapted upland trees that require warmer, as well as drier, conditions.

In bogs, as in many wetland areas, Beavers play a crucial role in development and maintenance of the system. In a bog that has an outlet, a Beaver dam can dramatically raise the water level. The floating mat of vegetation is usually not affected, because it simply floats higher as the water rises. However, because grounded portions of the mat cannot rise with the water, the vegetation in such areas often dies. In northern Connecticut, I have observed the death of a mature spruce forest, with very little effect on the floating mat nearby. Thus flooding in a bog can arrest development or return the bog to more open conditions.

A series of distinct vegetation belts may develop as a bog forms. A sedgy or mossy floating mat near open water may give way to an evergreen shrub mat or a larch zone, which in turn gives way to grounded bog forest near the upland. This belting gives the illusion that there is a clear succession of vegetation zones, with one grading into the next. Although this may sometime be the case, the development of these zones is usually much more complex, and is often the result of fluctuating water levels within a bog. Certain field studies have proved especially illuminating. For example, at Cedar Creek bog in Minnesota, it was found that over a period of thirty-five years the floating bog mat next to the water did not change its position; rather, the tree and shrub belts on it merely progressed outward. Apparently, droughts followed by times of high water levels had interacted to account for the pattern. During the extended dry periods, with low water levels, the typical growth of the mat out over the water was arrested.

In a Michigan bog, over a fifty-year dry period, tall shrubs and trees replaced the Leatherleaf mat; then, as water levels began to rise again, the tall woody growth was killed and the Leatherleaf became reestablished. And at Beckley Bog in northwestern Connecticut, it has been reported that the trees in the various zones, although of different heights, are approximately the same age, thus indicating that no real progression or succession is occurring.

In the Great Lakes states, bog fires can also undermine forest development, allowing the area to be reclaimed by Leatherleaf or other shrubs. Fire often also favors the development of Atlantic White-cedar, which grows best in open, sunny places.

Despite their apparently somewhat static nature, bogs are nonetheless dynamic ecosystems, constantly undergoing change. Although some lakes are completely filled in with bog vegetation, large amounts of open water persist in many bog lakes. Such areas may eventually be filled—slowly—by the inexorable process that has dominated bog development for century after century. Taking into account the thousands of years that have elapsed since the glaciers retreated, we can rest assured that these fascinating wetlands will be part of the North American landscape for some time to come.

BOGS: PLANTS AND ANIMALS

Fish
Central Mudminnow 102

Amphibians
Carpenter Frog 139
Four-toed Salamander 114
Pine Barrens Treefrog 138

Reptiles
Bog Turtle 165
Brown Snake 189
Eastern Ribbon Snake 187
Redbelly Snake 180
Striped Crayfish Snake 188

Wildflowers
Bog Rein Orchid 262
Bog Rosemary 261
Buck Bean 258
California Pitcher Plant 282
Cotton Grass 238
Cranberry 266, 330
Crimson Pitcher Plant 280
Goldthread 256
Grass Pink 269
Great Laurel 230
Hooded Pitcher Plant 202
Horned Bladderwort 218
Labrador Tea 234
Leatherleaf 260
Northern Pitcher Plant 281
Rose Pogonia 268
Round-leaved Sundew 251
Sheep Laurel 288
Swamp Loosestrife 286
Swamp Pink 270
Swamp Saxifrage 319
Trumpets 224
Water Arum 225
Yellow Butterwort 208

Mushrooms
Blueberry Cup 341
Blue-staining Cup 340
Chocolate Milky 336
Emetic Russula 335
Spotted Gomphidius 333
Swamp Beacon 339
Turpentine Waxy Cap 334
Yellow Unicorn
Entoloma 331

Butterflies and Moths
Appalachian Brown 400
Arctic Skipper 395
Baltimore 391
Black Dash 426
Bog Copper 399
Bog Elfin 415
Bog Fritillary 396
Common Alpine 417
Frigga's Fritillary 397
Hessel's Hairstreak 387
Jutta Arctic 412
Mitchell's Marsh Satyr 401
Mulberry Wing 423
Northern Blue 405
Pink Edged Sulfur 385
Scudder's Willow
Sulfur 386
Spruce Bog Alpine 418
Swamp Metalmark 398
Two-spotted Skipper 421

Trees
Atlantic White-cedar 429
Balsam Willow 459
Black Spruce 432
Northern White-cedar 428
Poison-sumac 441
Tamarack 430

Birds
Bufflehead 508
Lincoln's Sparrow 577
Palm Warbler 583

Mammals
Arctic Shrew 594
Black Bear 615
Masked Shrew 589
Southern Bog Lemming 600
Southern Red-backed
Vole 601, 602
White-tailed Deer 617

EMERGENT WETLANDS: MARSHES

Common Cattail
Typha latifolia
220

Red-winged Blackbird
Agelaius phoeniceus
580, 588

It is easy to recognize a freshwater marsh: Cattails, reeds, lily pads, feeding ducks, and singing Red-winged Blackbirds are some of the signs that call our attention to these wetlands. Unlike the wooded swamps discussed elsewhere in the book, marshes are dominated by soft-stemmed plants; you can test this by pressing a cattail or reed between your fingers. Marshes may be shallow or deep, with water levels ranging from a few inches to several feet. Some have soil that is always saturated, while others are only flooded periodically. Some marshes—known as prairie potholes—dry out completely during periods of prolonged drought, rejuvenating when the rain comes. Shallow or deep, marshes support a variety of amphibious plants, called emergents, that grow partly in and partly out of the water. Deeper marshes also often harbor beds of floating and submerged aquatics. Cattails, grasses, and sedges have narrow leaves that persist throughout the winter; other emergents have broad leaves that die at the end of the growing season. Various kinds of emergents, such as cattails, may dominate a marsh, and, depending on the water level, they can be arranged in belts from the shallow to the deeper water. Other marshes are dominated by wetland grasses, and although these places look like meadows, they are wet underfoot.

Distribution

Freshwater marshes are found throughout the United States. There is a large concentration of marshes in the north-central prairie pothole country, especially in the Dakotas and in the Canadian province of Saskatchewan. The famous Florida Everglades is covered with saw grass; in the West, along the Pacific Flyway—a major waterfowl migration route—the tule or bulrush marshes in California and southern Oregon attract millions of ducks and geese annually. Marshes frequently occur along streams in poorly drained depressions. They also develop in the shallow water along the borders of lakes, ponds, and rivers. Some inland marshes of the West are saline; this is especially true in closed basins where salts accumulate because evaporation rates exceed precipitation.

Ecology

Marshes are among North America's most fascinating and diverse wetlands. Often they are named for the most conspicuous vegetation: there are cattail, bulrush, sedge, and saw grass marshes, to name just a few. The Everglades saw grass marshes are such distinctive subtropical wetlands that they are considered in a separate chapter.

The kinds of marsh plants that will be found in a particular wetland are related to the water regime and, in some cases, to the mineral content of the water or soil. If the marsh is continuously flooded, emergents—such as cattails—floating water lilies, and submerged aquatics play a major role. If, on the other hand, the soils are merely saturated, few of the truly aquatic plants will be present.

The various marsh types include deep marshes and shallow marshes as well as wet meadows. Deep marshes are

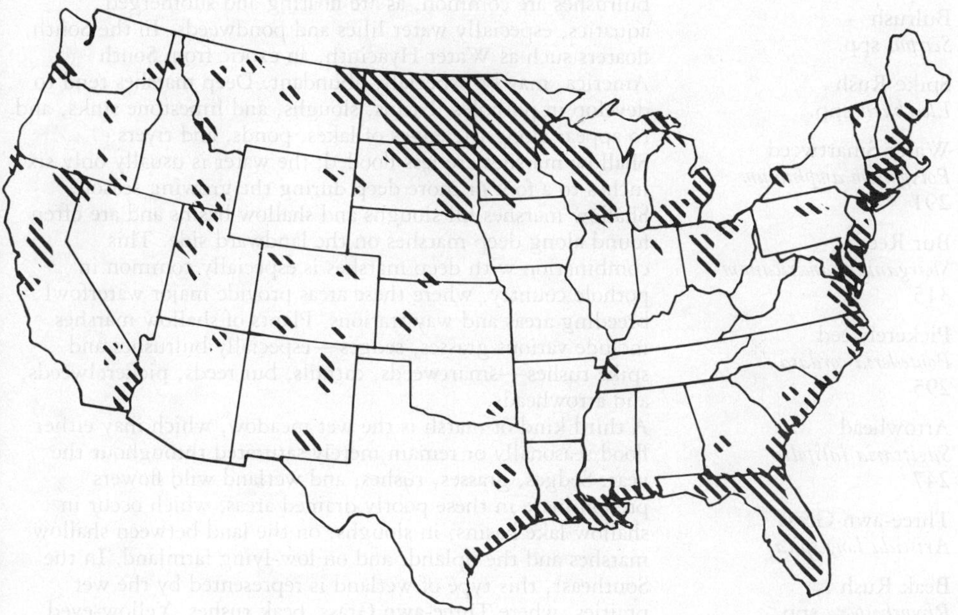

Water Hyacinth
Eichhornia crassipes
296

Bulrush
Scirpus spp.

Spike Rush
Eleocharis spp.

Water Smartweed
Polygonum amphibium
291

Bur Reed
Sparganium americanum
315

Pickerelweed
Pontederia cordata
295

Arrowhead
Sagittaria latifolia
247

Three-awn Grass
Aristida longespica

Beak Rush
Rhynchospora spp.

Yellow-eyed Grass
Xyris iridifolia
210

Grass Pink
Calopogon pulchellus
269

permanently flooded, except perhaps during the most severe droughts. Water levels may reach six feet, and there may be large areas of open water. Emergents such as cattails and bulrushes are common, as are floating and submerged aquatics, especially water lilies and pondweeds. In the South, floaters such as Water Hyacinth, an exotic from South America, may be especially abundant. Deep marshes tend to develop in potholes, basins, sloughs, and limestone sinks, and to appear along the edges of lakes, ponds, and rivers.

Shallow marshes are less flooded; the water is usually only six inches to a foot or more deep during the growing season. Shallow marshes fill sloughs and shallow basins and are often found along deep marshes on the landward side. This combination with deep marshes is especially common in pothole country, where these areas provide major waterfowl breeding areas and way stations. Plants of shallow marshes include various grasses, sedges—especially bulrushes and spike rushes—smartweeds, cattails, bur reeds, pickerelweeds, and arrowheads.

A third kind of marsh is the wet meadow, which may either flood seasonally or remain merely saturated throughout the year. Sedges, grasses, rushes, and wetland wild flowers predominate in these poorly drained areas, which occur in shallow lake basins, in sloughs, on the land between shallow marshes and the upland, and on low-lying farmland. In the Southeast, this type of wetland is represented by the wet prairies, where Three-awn Grass, beak rushes, Yellow-eyed Grass and Grass Pink orchid are found.

In the arid West, where there are high concentrations of dissolved sulfate or chloride salts in the soil, evaporation of moisture often leaves behind high concentrations of salts. In such places, alkali or saline marshes occur. These marshes are well represented in Utah, Nevada, Idaho,Oregon, and parts of California. Tule marshes are good examples; these are alkali-bulrush wetlands in California and Oregon, where millions of waterfowl congregate during annual migrations.

The Marsh Ecosystem

Muskrat
Ondatra zibethicus
609

Wild Rice
Zizania aquatica
321

A typical flooded marsh is often a mosaic of emergents, submergents, and floating plants, interspersed with areas of open water. These marsh plants, the primary producers, are at the base of the food chain. In some marshes, algae—including phytoplankton—also make a significant contribution to the base of the food chain. Among the primary consumers are Muskrats, ducks, and even people, when they harvest Wild Rice.

As a member of the subfamily of field mice, the Muskrat is in essence a large mouse; its diet includes cattails and other aquatic plants. It shreds great quantities of vegetation when building its lodge. The Muskrat's waterproof fur, flattened tail, and webbed feet are all features that aid it in its aquatic existence. Of course, ducks, with their webbed feet and well-insulated, waterproof plumage, are also well adapted to life in the water.

Algae are consumed by zooplankton, small crustaceans, various aquatic insects, and tadpoles. These in turn are eaten by small fishes, which provide sustenance for larger fish, herons, snakes, and turtles. Muskrats may be preyed upon by Mink, and ducks by snapping turtles and people.

Mink
Mustela vison
613

As in the other wetland systems, plant production in marshes exceeds direct consumption, and the resulting surplus becomes part of the marsh sediments. The rooted marsh plants take up some minerals; others may be lost to the area as streams sweep them away; and the remainder are stored in the marsh sediments. Bacteria, aquatic insects, worms, and other decomposers help to break down and recycle these nutrients, and the algae are also favored by this nutrient enrichment. This recycling is essential to keeping the system recharged and productive.

Let us examine the diverse plant and bird life typical of marshes, and focus on two important marsh mammals, the Muskrat and the Mink. Since the aquatic insects and other life in many marshes is similar to that found in lakes and ponds and even to that found along rivers and streams, the reader is referred to these chapters for details about marsh life.

The Plant Parade

Marsh plants are highly varied, yet some look very much alike —especially grasses, sedges, and rushes. Vegetation in a marsh can be divided into three categories: the emergents, the floaters, and the submergents. In many marshes there is a parade of plants, a belting or mosaic of these different growth forms. The progression is sometimes dramatic, with cattails in the shallower water, water lilies floating beyond, and the submerged forms in the deepest water. However, sometimes these vegetation types occur together with shrubs and trees. This condition, in which various wetland types intermingle, is called interspersion. It forms a favorite habitat for waterfowl.

Emergents

The emergents include narrow- and broad-leaved plants. Some have showy flowers, while some, namely the grasses and sedges, bear inconspicuous flowers. Although many of the sedges and some of the grasses are emergents, many species in these families also occur in less flooded parts of the marsh.

Narrowleaf Cattail
Typha angustifolia

Cattails are typical emergents; their lower stems are flooded and their upper leaves and flowering stalks stick out of the water. There are several species. The Narrowleaf Cattail, which can tolerate a degree of salinity, has very narrow leaves and forms extensive marshes along the mid-Atlantic coastal rivers and estuaries. Narrowleaf Cattail marshes are transitional areas found as one moves upstream from the cordgrass-dominated salt marshes to freshwater marshes that no longer feel the influence of the tides. The Common Cattail, which has a broader leaf, is more common in the freshwater marshes of the interior.

Although the differences in leaf width may help to distinguish the two species when they are side by side, the flowering stalks are often a better aid in identification of these cattails. In the narrow-leaved form there is usually a wide gap—lacking in the broad-leaved form—between the tightly packed green cluster of female flowers below and the yellowish-green, male flowers above, which fall away after producing pollen. However, there is also a hybrid with narrow leaves, which complicates the identification process. (This exchange of genetic material is a widespread phenomenon; it handily illustrates that species are evolving entities rather than precise ones, as implied in giving a name to a species.)

Cattails often occur in relatively pure stands, which sometimes cover many acres. Under the favorable conditions of flooding, they can spread via underground rootstocks, called rhizomes, in the same manner as grass in our lawns. When they spread like this, cattails form clones—large colonies of identical individuals. This procedure, known as vegetative reproduction, is advantageous; once a clone has become established, individuals can bypass the vulnerable seedling stage.

Because they are perennials, cattails store up large food reserves in their underground parts for the next growing season but this reserve is frequently tapped by Muskrats. Since cattails persist at the end of the growing season, their flowering stalks are especially conspicuous and are frequently collected for floral arrangements. The tip of the fruiting stalk is where the male flowers have fallen off; what remains are thousands of tiny, tightly packed brown fruits. The fact that cattails persist is very important to Red-winged Blackbirds, which, when they arrive in spring, fasten their nests to the old stalks.

Water Plantain
Alisma subcordatum
248

Arrow Arum
Peltandra virginica
310

Golden Club
Orontium aquaticum
222

The broad-leaved emergents—such as showy Pickerelweed, Arrowhead and Water Plantain, Arrow Arum, and the striking Golden Club—die down at the end of the growing season. Some of these also reproduce vegetatively and form large patches. When in flower, the many blue spikes of Pickerelweed make an especially beautiful display. Several of these emergents have arrow-shaped leaves; the Arrowhead, which has white flowers and various leaf forms, is striking in this regard. For the many dabbling ducks of these marshes, duck potatoes (which are little storage organs on the Arrowhead's roots) are of great interest. The widespread Arrow Arum may be confused with the Arrowhead, but the former has an elongated, tapering flower that is distinctive. Related to Skunk Cabbage and Jack-in-the-pulpit, Arrow Arum has an enclosing flower sheath, or spathe, which is wrapped around its flower cluster, or spadix.

Skunk Cabbage
Symplocarpus foetidus
312

Jack-in-the-pulpit
Arisaema triphyllum
309

Many marsh plants look so much like grasses that they have taken on the name. Jamaican Saw Grass, which occurs in the Everglades, is a good example: It is not a grass, but rather a sedge. What is the difference between the two? The stems of grasses are round, while the stems of sedges usually have edges and a triangular configuration. (This can be easily checked by twirling a stem between the fingers.)

Like cattails, bulrushes are emergent sedges. Many bulrushes

Leafy Three-square
Scirpus americanus

have angular stems, but in some species the stems are round—in nature there are usually exceptions to any rule. With long, spearlike stems and little clusters of scaly flowers breaking out near the tips of the stems, bulrushes form extensive colonies. Their underwater rootstocks are eaten by Muskrats. One species, Leafy Three-square, is also an especially important source of food for ducks and other marsh birds, which consume its seeds. The round stem of the Hardstem Bulrush or Tule, which is typical of western tule marshes, is difficult to crush between the fingers, whereas the soft-stemmed variety is easily crushed.

Tussock Sedge
Carex stricta

Sedges of the genus *Carex* number more than 500 species in the United States; of these, most are found in wetlands. One of the most easily recognized members of this genus is Tussock Sedge, which forms widespread marshes in the Northeast and westward into the Great Lakes states. Often found in low, poorly drained farm meadows, the scattered tufted clumps of this species can serve as stepping stones across a flooded marsh—if you are agile. The various sedges are easily identified by a three-sided stem, drooping or erect spikes, and little fruits, each of which is enclosed in a small sac.

Wool Grass
Scirpus cyperinus
322

Members of another group of sedges, the Spike Rushes, have slender stems capped by a scaly spike sticking out of the water. Muskrats and ducks feed heavily on these soft, succulent stems. Wool Grass, another sedge, has tiny brown heads with clusters of woolly flowers. Since many other sedges can be found in marshes throughout North America, your chances of recognizing a sedge are excellent.

Soft Rush
Juncus effusus
324

The rushes represent yet another kind of grasslike marsh plant. Some species—for example, the Soft Rush, which grows in big, waist-high clumps—have solid, spearlike leaves. Like bulrushes, they sprout their greenish-brown, scaly flowers near the stem tip. A close examination of a single, tiny flower will reveal six scaly petals and six stamens—the same arrangement as in a lily or a tulip. These plants were used as torches by our ancestors. When the plant is collected in the fall, most of the outer, green covering can be removed from the stem, exposing the beautiful white pith; the pith can be dipped in tallow and set alight, giving off a wonderful light. Rushes were used in both Europe and the United States for hundreds of years, and people still make rush lights from the Soft Rush growing in our marshes. In addition, Muskrats feed on these rootstalks, and the stems provide shelter for various birds.

The many wetland grasses are easily distinguished from the sedges and other plants by their stems, which—like bamboo—are round and hollow with solid joints. Grasses also have distinctive leaves, which come in two parts: the blade that sticks out from the stem, and the sheathing portion, which wraps around the stem and attaches at the joint. (You can observe these characteristics by examining a lawn grass before going to a marsh.)

Giant Reed
Phragmites australis
323

In the fall, the tan plumy heads of the Giant Reed cannot be missed. This species covers large areas of the Hackensack Meadows along the New Jersey Turnpike between Newark and

New York City, where it filters pollutants from the metropolitan area. In the salt marshes of southern New England, where adequate saltwater flushing has been reduced by flood-control gates, the aggressive Giant Reed has replaced vast areas of Salt-marsh Cordgrass in the tidal marshes. The underground rhizomes of Giant Reed can spread at a fantastic rate, and it quickly takes over disturbed brackish and freshwater wetlands. However, it is not of high value to wildlife—except as cover—and once established tends to crowd out other species.

Salt-marsh Cordgrass
Spartina patens

Reed Canary
Phalaris arundinacea

Rice Cut Grass
Leersia oryzoides

Manna Grass
Glyceria obtusa

Fox Tail Grass
Alopecurus spp.

Slough Grass
Spartina pectinata

Millet
Panicum miliaceum

Reed Canary, Rice Cut, Manna, Fox Tail, Slough, White Top, Millet, and Maiden Cane are some of the many marsh grasses that provide wildlife with food and cover. Like the sedges and rushes, grasses have inconspicuous flowers—a typical feature of plants that do not depend on insects for pollination—and are dependent instead on the wind for pollination.

Whether along an eastern riverine marsh or a wetland in Minnesota, the large flower stalks of Wild Rice in full bloom are a spectacular sight. The plant's many tiny yellow stamens dangle beneath the branches where the female flowers grow. Like corn, which is also a grass, rice bears its male and female flowers on different parts of the plant.

Bur Reeds may be mistaken for grasses, but they constitute their own family, which includes one species bearing the same name. Their burrlike fruit clusters are not like the open, highly branched flower clusters of most grasses. One northern species, Floating Bur Reed, has a floating stem.

Floating Bur Reed
Sparganium

Floaters

The floating plants include both those that float freely on the surface of the water and those that, like water lilies, are rooted in the bottom muck and extend their leaves to the surface on long leafstalks, or petioles. In the latter type, tiny openings, or stomates, on the dry upper surface of each leaf are part of a direct connection between the leaves and the rootstocks; they facilitate the exchange of gases, allowing the entire plant to breathe. This adaptation is quite striking, because most other plants have their openings on the underside of the leaves.

Growing in water that is several feet deep, floaters may cover marshy pools, and when hundreds flower, they put on a spectacular show. Muskrats prize their energy-rich stems (rhizomes), which are buried in the mud.

Duckweed
Lemna spp.
313

Water Meal
Wolffia spp.

Nearby, the surface of the water is carpeted with millions of green midgets, each a few millimeters in size. These amazing little plants are known as duckweed. Duckweed reproduces vegetatively (rather than sexually) by making plantlets from existing ones: If you pick up a handful of duckweed, you will see clusters of new individuals adhering to one another, each with its own miniature root dangling down. The most minute member of this unusual family is Water Meal, which is a millimeter in size, rootless, and barely visible to the naked eye. Smaller than a pinhead, it is the tiniest flowering plant known.

Water Lettuce
Pistia stratiotes
308

There are several southern floaters. Water Lettuce is easily recognized by its light green rosettes of hairy leaves, which superficially resemble those of Leafy Lettuce. It is most often found in quiet water. The most vigorous and conspicuous free-floater is Water Hyacinth, which has attractive blue flowers. An inflated leafstalk helps it to float; indeed all of its tissue is spongy and air-filled. Water Hyacinth reproduces at a prodigious rate, clogging open, watery areas. Like water lilies, Alligator Weed is rooted; it often forms huge floats along the edges of lakes or waterways. A number of interesting water ferns also can be found floating on the water in southern marshy areas.

Submergents

If you have a fish tank, it probably contains submerged plants. Some of these may have highly dissected leaves (leaves with many lobes or segments), while others are likely to have long, narrow leaves, like grass. The lobes found in some submerged aquatics provide maximum surface area and help to buoy the plants.

Bladderworts, milfoils, pondweeds, Water Celery, and Elodea are some of the many submerged aquatics that are typically found in deep marshes and ponds. The carnivorous bladderworts are an especially interesting group. Their highly forked leaves have tiny bladders, which are only visible if you pull up a handful. In flower, bladderworts are easy to recognize; the showy yellow or blue flowers stick up out of the water, looking like very small snapdragons. A close examination of the tiny bladders with a hand lens will reveal that each bladder forms a sac, which has a flap resembling a trapdoor and branched hairs at the mouth. When stimulated by aquatic organisms passing by, the indented sac inflates, sucking in the prey. After the prey has been digested, the trap is set again, ready for the next catch.

Like many terrestrial plants, bladderworts are pollinated through the action of insects. In contrast, the submerged Water Celery has evolved an unusual water-pollination technique. When the separate male and female flowers are produced, the female flower rises and opens on the water's surface. The underwater male flowers break off and also float to the surface, where they open and drift about until they meet a female flower. Once pollination has occurred, the female flower coils downward, and the fruit matures underwater.

The pondweeds, the largest group of submerged seed-bearing aquatics, have narrow, ribbonlike leaves. Sago Pondweed is a favorite of most ducks because of its large seeds.

Plant Productivity

Salt marshes are well known for their high productivity. This situation is partly owing to tidal action, which makes nutrients more available and also aerates these marshes, thus providing an energy subsidy.

Freshwater marshes, however, are even more productive, as the abundance of animal life within them indicates. The tide-influenced riverine marshes of the mid-Atlantic region can

Sweetflag
Acorus calamus
221

Mallard
Anas platyrhynchos
492

produce a biomass of twelve to fifteen tons per acre, an amount that includes only the stems and leaves growing above ground. To this figure must be added the underground production, which can be several times greater than the yield obtained above. Indeed, much of the food produced by aquatic plants is stored in their rootstocks, which are consumed by various animals. Aquatics that are often found in marshes along rivers include cattails, Pickerelweed, Arrow Arum, Arrowhead, Sweetflag, water smartweeds, and Wild Rice.

The prolific and fast-growing Water Hyacinth of the South may hold the world record for productivity, yielding thirty tons of biomass per acre in open, watery areas. With such a growth rate, it is easy to see that this plant could become a problem in certain wetlands.

Marshes, Ducks, and the Prairie Potholes

Northern Pintail
Anas acuta
498

Canvasback
Aythya valisineria
499

Gadwall
Anas strepera
496

In North America, the prairie pothole region extends from south-central Canada into the north-central United States, covering some 300,000 square miles. This formerly glaciated landscape is pockmarked with huge numbers of potholes, which fill with snowmelt and rain in the spring. Some prairie pothole marshes are temporary, while others may be virtually permanent. Here as in other marshes, submerged and floating aquatic plants take over the deeper water; bulrushes and cattails grow closer to shore, and wet, sedgy marshes lie next to the upland.

American Wigeon
Anas americana
494

Northern Shoveler
Anas clypeata
493

Green-winged Teal
Anas crecca
490

Lesser Scaup
Aythya affinis
503

Redhead
Aythya americana
500

The high productivity of freshwater marshes is reflected in the abundance of animal life they support—and the prairie potholes are no exception. Marshes and ducks go together: The area is home to fifty percent of North American waterfowl. The ducks arrive in late March or early April. Some fifteen species nest in the prairie pothole marshes. Mallards, Pintails, and Canvasbacks arrive first, followed by Gadwalls, American Wigeons, Northern Shovelers, Green-winged Teal, Lesser Scaup, and Redheads. Spring is a time of great activity on the marsh: Courtship antics, nuptial flights, and displays occur constantly in the air and on the water until mates and nest sites have been selected. Numerous nesting possibilities may be surveyed; the Redheads, Canvasbacks, Ruddies, and Ring-necked Ducks usually select cattails, bulrushes, and smartweeds, as cover. Sometimes even the Mallards nest in the emergents. Bulrushes and smartweeds provide food for nesting waterfowl, but the birds may also graze the surrounding stubble fields in search of weed seeds.

Ruddy Duck
Oxyura jamaicensis
510

Ring-necked Duck
Aythya collaris
501

Young ducklings begin to appear in June, and new broods are produced through August. For a month or more, the ducklings are kept under close supervision near the nest sites —at least until their downy coats are replaced by flight feathers. For the ducklings, the larvae of dragonflies, damselflies, mayflies, caddisflies, and midges provide a high-protein diet, which they supplement with freshwater shrimp, snails, tadpoles, and leeches.

Raccoon
Procyon lotor
614

Although the marsh is an ideal habitat for ducks, there are hazards. Minks, foxes, Raccoons, crows, magpies, gulls,

Coyote
Canis latrans

ground squirrels, bullsnakes, and Coyotes regularly take eggs; the ducklings that do hatch are challenged by snakes, snapping turtles, and hawks. Botulism, algal poisoning, and parasitic infections are also problems that ducks must face. And severe hailstorms can kill many young ducks.

In the pothole region, drought can also have a major impact on breeding populations; there are years when thousands fail to nest. But with the return of rain, the nesting readily resumes. Studies have shown that prairie pothole marshes can support 140 ducks per square mile.

Marsh ducks may be divided into those that dabble for their food in shallow water and those that dive for it in deeper water. The dabblers—which include American Wigeon (or "Baldpate"), Northern Shoveler, Pintail, Mallard, and Gadwall—tip up their tails as they feed on aquatic plants and animals on or near the bottom. The relatively tame ducks that are so commonly seen in ponds and pools around inhabited areas are Mallards. The males have a distinctive green head and a white neck ring. The Wigeon, which can be identified by its white crown, gets some of its food by waiting until diving ducks return to the surface and then snatching their catch away from them. Wigeons also graze like geese in the meadows and grain fields around marshes. Northern Shovelers have an unusually large, spoon-shaped bill that is equipped with comblike teeth to strain out aquatic organisms. The male Pintail, as the name implies, has a long, pointed tail, a feature the inconspicuous female lacks. The gray Gadwall, which bears a distinct white patch behind its wings, has a wide breeding range.

Diving ducks are typical of deeper marshes, lakes, and ponds. They maneuver with great facility underwater, aided by short legs that are placed farther back on their bodies than those of the dabbling ducks. Canvasbacks, Redheads, Ruddy Ducks, and Lesser Scaup are a few of the divers that frequent freshwater marshes. The Canvasback has an unusual, sloping forehead that distinguishes it from the Redhead. It dives for Water Celery and pondweeds, its favorite foods. The similar Redhead, which sometimes lays its eggs in the nests of other ducks, feeds mostly at night on submerged vegetation. The

Pied-billed Grebe
Podilymbus podiceps
483

Ruddy Duck, which is chestnut-brown with white cheeks, has an extraordinarily bright blue bill. Like the Pied-billed Grebe, Ruddies can sink slowly beneath the water to escape predators, instead of flying or diving. The Lesser Scaup has an iridescent purple head and white wing stripes, which are especially evident when it rises out of the water and flaps its wings. Often found in closely knit flocks, Lesser Scaup feed on aquatic plants and animals.

The northern marshes provide excellent summer nesting and feeding grounds for waterfowl, but as the days begin to shorten, the birds head south. North American waterfowl move along four major routes from east to west across the continent: the Atlantic, Mississippi, Central, and Pacific flyways. Each spring and fall, millions of birds funnel along these routes from Alaska and northern Canada to the southern

United States, Mexico, and Central America. Many of the national wildlife refuges established during these flyways provide areas where great numbers of waterfowl can nest and feed during their long migratory flights.

Canada Goose
Branta canadensis
512

Wood Duck
Aix sponsa
491

Snow Goose
Chen caerulescens
513, 514

Common Goldeneye
Bucephala clangula
506

Common Merganser
Mergus merganser
507

Blue-winged Teal
Anas discors
497

Eared Grebe
Podiceps nigricollis
486

Along the Atlantic Flyway, Canada Geese, Mallards, Wood Ducks, and teal nest in the 6000-acre Montezuma National Wildlife Refuge in the Finger Lakes region of New York. During peak migration periods, 140,000 Canada Geese and 150,000 ducks may stop by. This area was once highly productive, but suffered a decline after being drained at the turn of the century. The area was later restored; and today it is one of the most productive freshwater marshes in North America.

On the Central Flyway in the Nebraska Sandhills, Crescent Lake Wildlife Refuge is used by Snow Geese, Goldeneyes, Mergansers, Pintails, Redheads, and Lesser Scaup during migration, as well as during the nesting season. Mallards, Blue-winged Teal, Ruddy Ducks, and Eared Grebes raise their young in these wetlands. Teal, the bantams among the ducks, nest well back from the water in sedge or grass cover.

The Pied-bill Grebe is a small, chunky, solitary bird that rarely flies. It has the endearing habit, common to all grebes, of ferrying its young about on its back. The Eared Grebe is a similarly small diving bird that has a sharp bill, thin neck, and hardly any tail. Like other grebes, it builds a floating nest on a dense, matted raft that it constructs of rushes or other marsh plants. Even though the eggs may be partly flooded, they still manage to hatch.

On the Mississippi Flyway, the Agassiz National Wildlife Refuge in Minnesota has over 30,000 acres of open water and marshes that are used by thirteen species of breeding ducks. In the Klamath Basin of California and Oregon, a complex of national wildlife refuges covering more than one hundred million acres accommodates most of the birds using the Pacific Flyway. At Tule Lake in California, there are sometimes four million birds at one time. October is the best time to witness these enormous gatherings. The basin is also home to some 80,000 nesting ducks and geese each year.

The Elegant Waders and Other Water Birds

The waders are birds that stride into the water in pursuit of their prey or that stand poised, waiting until something edible moves or swims by. They have spearlike bills and long legs, which allow them to hunt among the emergent plants.

Great Blue Heron
Ardea herodias
528

Great Egret
Casmerodius albus
526

Snowy Egret
Egretta thula
527

Cattle Egret
Bubulcus ibis

Most waders belong to the heron family. The three-foot-tall Great Blue Heron is one of the largest and most spectacular. It feeds on fish, frogs, and snakes, which it catches by standing motionless until its prey appears. In winter it migrates to southern marshes, including the Everglades. Nearly as large, the Great Egret has a yellow bill and black legs and feet. The smaller Snowy Egret wears a striking pair of yellow "overshoes" at the end of its black legs. The Cattle Egret, which is white with a yellowish bill and legs, is more typical in wet meadows and pastures, where it feeds on the insects stirred up by the cattle. Originating in the Old World, this egret moved from South America northward into Florida and up the East Coast. This new species has become very abundant in the South and now breeds as far north as New England.

Green Heron
Butorides striatus

Great "White" Heron
Ardea herodias

Reddish Egret
Egretta rufescens

Louisiana Heron
Egretta tricolor

If you hear a peculiar cry—one that sounds like the sound you get when you blow on a blade of grass held tightly between your fingers—it is the little Green Heron. Greenish-blue with orange legs, it feeds along muddy borders, craning its neck forward as it takes the measure of its prey. Some very interesting feeding techniques have evolved among the various herons found in marshes and other wetlands. The "Great White," Great Blue, and Green herons stand and wait until their prey moves or swims by. The Reddish Egret, found in coastal wetlands, uses a canopy feeding method; this involves dashing around with wings outspread; the shadow cast by the wings eliminates reflection and offers a refuge to the fish unlucky enough to be caught. The Snowy Egret feeds itself by stirring up the water with one foot while in flight, thereby flushing out its meal. The most unusual method is the pirouetting technique employed by the slim Louisiana Heron: It steps forward with wings outspread, then raises one wing, and sticks its head underneath to look into the water. As it turns, it raises its other wing and takes another look. The shadows cast by the wings attract the prey.

American Bittern
Botaurus lentiginosus
532

Least Bittern
Ixobrychus exilis
533

The elusive bitterns are also long-legged waders. The American Bittern—sometimes called the "Stake-driver" because of its distinctive and oft-repeated "oong-KA-chunk!" call—is one of the truly remarkable marsh birds. When disturbed, it freezes with its neck erect and its bill pointing skyward, becoming practically indistinguishable from the surrounding vegetation. A cousin, the Least Bittern, is the smallest heron; it has a cuckoolike voice.

King Rail
Rallus elegans
541

Virginia Rail
Rallus limicola
540

Sora
Porzana carolina
538

Clapper Rail
Rallus longirostris

The rails are among the most secretive of marsh birds. The expression "as thin as a rail" derives from the narrow, compressed body of these birds, which are adapted to slipping through the marsh sedges and rushes. The King and Virginia rails and the Sora are the three most common members of this family in freshwater marshes, while the Clapper Rail is frequently found in salt marshes. Somewhat chickenlike, rails belong to an ancient family that dates back seventy million years. They haunt the twilight, when they are heard but seldom seen.

Common Moorhen
Gallinula chloropus
536

Purple Gallinule
Porphyrula martinica
537

American Coot
Fulica americana
535

Coots and gallinules, also members of the rail family, are ducklike birds frequently associated with marshes. The widely distributed Common Moorhen (formerly called the Common Gallinule) prefers the cover of emergent plants when swimming. The Purple Gallinule, which is found farther south, is characteristically seen walking on water-lily pads in open, marshy sloughs. The widespread American Coot is the only American gray, ducklike bird with a white bill. Coots often feed with ducks. Their feet are not webbed like ducks' feet; instead, each toe has a series of lobes along its length to assist in paddling. Coots appear to have difficulty getting airborne; when they take off, they patter across the water, flapping their wings furiously. They prefer a habitat that harbors reeds and rushes, as they weave platform nests with these aquatic plants, which are also a primary item in their diet.

American Avocet
Recurvirostra americana
547

Black-necked Stilt
Himantopus mexicanus

Willet
Catoptrophorus semipalmatus

Three western shorebirds also associated with marshes are American Avocet, Black-necked Stilt, and Willet. The long-legged, beautiful American Avocet has a long, upcurved bill, which it uses like a sickle, swinging it from side to side near the bottom in search of snails, diving beetles, and other aquatic life. The Black-necked Stilt, sometimes called "Daddy-long-legs," has long, pinkish legs and eats the same food as the Avocet. These two birds were once common along the East Coast, but overhunting in the nineteenth century depleted their populations. The Willet is a long-legged, sandy gray bird that lives on muddy shores and in meadows. It is unusually noisy; in fact, its whistle—"pill-will-willet"—gave it its name. All of these birds can be found in western alkali wetlands, such as the tule marshes in the Central Valley of California. The Willet also breeds in the Great Basin and the northern prairie states, as well as on the East Coast.

Redwings and Other Marsh Birds

"O-ka-LEEEE! O-ka-LEEEE!" This rich musical sound comes from the Red-winged Blackbird, which prefers to nest and feed in cattail marshes because of the abundance of stalks and aquatic insects. The male has showy red patches on its wings, while the female is a drab brown with streaked underparts. These gregarious birds often form huge flocks and can, on occasion, be highly destructive to grain fields. However, studies have shown that only about ten percent of their diet consists of grain; the major portion is made up of insect pests and weed seeds.

Yellow-headed Blackbird
Xanthocephalus xanthocephalus
586

Found throughout the United States, Redwings mingle with more western Yellow-headed Blackbirds in the pothole marshes of the western and central parts of their range. When both species nest in the same marsh, their behavioral patterns are especially interesting. The Redwings usually arrive first and tentatively stake out their territory, but as the more aggressive Yellow-heads appear and move into the best sites among the bulrushes and cattails, the Redwings are slowly pushed shoreward. Visiting a marsh at nesting time is an exciting experience. The males present conspicuous display flights, their wings beating and tails drooping.

Although both species are polygamous, the number of mates an individual takes is often determined by how much food is available. Studies have shown that, in productive marshes, both Red-winged and Yellow-headed blackbirds are very gregarious and have high nest densities. Their breeding periods are synchronized with the emergence of mayflies, dragonflies, and damselflies.

Common Yellowthroat
Geothlypis trichas
584

A piercing "witchity-witchity" announces the presence of a Common Yellowthroat. This small warbler lives in damp thickets at the edge of marshes. Feeding near the ground—where this species nests—the male is easily recognizable by the black Lone Ranger mask across the eyes (Sometimes you can get a better look at these beautiful, naturally curious songbirds by coaxing them closer to you with the classic birdwatcher's ploy: Expel your breath sharply through your mouth, making a "pssh-pssh" sound, or loudly kiss the back of your hand.)

Swamp Sparrow
Melospiza georgiana
576

Sharp-tailed Sparrow
Ammodramus candacutus
582

Two plump little sparrows also reside in the marsh. The Swamp Sparrow, which is wide-ranging throughout the eastern half of the United States, also extends into Canada. It has a rufous cap and a sweet musical trill. The Sharp-tailed Sparrow's insectlike song is often heard in coastal as well as freshwater marshes, especially in central and western Canada.

Marsh Wren
Cistothorus palustris
574

Sedge Wren
Cistothorus platensis
575

Among the smallest songbirds are the Marsh and Sedge wrens. The black-capped Marsh Wren, which prefers an environment of cattails and bulrushes, has a liquid, gurgling song that is sometimes accompanied by a chattering prelude or postlude. The female wren, on her own, builds a globular nest in bulrushes or cattails, while the male sometimes constructs several dummy nests as well, probably to confuse rivals or predators. Locating the real nest of a pair is often time-consuming. The much rarer Sedge Wren prefers the drier sedge or grass marshes nearer the upland. If flushed, it flies up and then drops back into the grassy cover. The Sedge Wren also builds dummy nests, hiding its real one close to the ground.

Black Tern
Chlidonias niger
549

Forster's Tern
Sterna forsteri
551

Caspian Tern
Sterna caspia
552

Franklin's Gull
Larus pipixcan
553

California Gull
Larus californicus
556

Several terns and two gulls are closely associated with freshwater marshes. Although the Black and Forster's Terns are found in the prairie pothole region—where they patrol adjacent grasslands for insects—they nest in marshes. When mayflies emerge, flocks of Black Terns fly above them and catch them as they rise. These terns also feed on damselflies. Caspian Terns, which nest in a variety of habitats, are sometimes resident in marshes. Franklin's Gull, which has a black head and white underparts, is also common in the prairie. It is considered a highly beneficial bird, since it eats dragonflies, grasshoppers, and other insects that damage crops. The California Gull, which nests on marsh islands within its range, is another important insect-eater.

Short-eared Owl
Asio flammeus
565

Northern Harrier
Circus cyaneus
561

Meadow Vole
Microtus pennsylvanicus
603

Two birds of prey—the Short-eared Owl and the Northern Harrier—are also marsh dwellers. This owl is sometimes seen in the late afternoon as it prepares for its evening hunt, which is primarily for mice. On foggy days, it may even hunt in the daytime. In the winter and during migrations, these birds are quite gregarious, often gathering in flocks of one hundred or more. The Northern Harrier's wings and tail are long and slim, and it has a distinctive white rump. Its sensitive ears enable it to pick up the squeaks of Meadow Voles. Harriers also surprise ducks and other birds that feed above and around the marsh. They often nest on the ground in dried sedges.

Muskrats and Mink

Two furbearers, namely, the Muskrat and the Mink, are characteristically associated with marshes. The Muskrat, which looks like an overgrown rat with partly webbed feet and a vertically flattened tail, prefers cattail or bulrush marshes, where it can feed and build its lodge. Muskrats are related to the Beaver and are good swimmers. Beginning in the spring, Muskrats make nightly rounds to their breeding platforms. As they travel, they leave behind a musky scent, which is produced by special glands and is probably intended to attract mates. Muskrats mate frequently and often have several litters per year.

Beaver
Castor canadensis
611

A Muskrat lodge may be up to ten feet in diameter and four feet high, but most are smaller. The dome-shaped house is made of cattails or other aquatic plants and has a channel, or plunge hole, that provides access to the water during the winter. The number of lodges in a marsh may reflect both the size of the Muskrat population and the health of the marsh. One lodge with five Muskrats can be sustained on an acre of marsh with little or no damage to the environment. However, if the population explodes, the emergent vegetation may be so heavily grazed that "eat-outs" occur. When this happens, all of the marsh plants are consumed and areas of open water begin to appear in the marsh. With overpopulation, the weak or sickly Muskrats fall prey to Mink or other predators; others may move to better marshes.

There are also hazards during the winter, especially if the ice is thick. Muskrats normally feed below the ice, exiting from inside the lodge through the plunge hole. If the exit is frozen shut, however, they may be forced to feed on the open marsh. This is a cold and perilous business, especially if Mink are present. Sometimes Muskrats, unable to feed, starve in their lodges. In such instances, the Mink's uncanny ability to search out dead flesh becomes evident, for it will dig through a lodge or through ice to get at the carcass.

During bad winters, Muskrats may trek long distances in search of other marshes. Therefore, "freeze-outs," like "eat-outs," can be fatal to Muskrats, and sharply reduce their population. Despite all these hazards, Muskrats are nonetheless a hardy lot and tend to rebound after most catastrophes.

The word "mink" usually brings to mind fur coats and other valuable items. Most of these coats are made from the fur of commercially grown Mink, which are bred to produce many different colors. This has removed some of the pressure from the wild Mink, a member of the weasel family that is found in association with wetlands. This dark brown creature is nocturnal and inclined to be solitary. Males grow to two feet in length and weigh about two pounds; females are smaller. The nest is constructed among rocks or in cavities, and the four to ten kits are born in the spring.

The Mink spends much of its time in water and feeds on small mammals, birds, frogs, and fish, storing some of this food in the den. The mink gives off a very strong, unpleasant odor, which is especially noticeable when the animal is angered. A ferocious fighter, its enemies include Bobcat, fox, Great Horned Owl, and man. On the marsh, this small creature

Bobcat
Felis rufus
616

Great Horned Owl
Bubo virginianus

performs the valuable service of keeping down the numbers of Muskrats, whose population, if unchecked, might prove harmful to the marsh ecosystem.

Other Animal Life

Although birds are the most conspicuous form of animal life in marshes, many other animals are present in and around these wetlands. We have looked at the association of Muskrats and Minks, both important marsh mammals. Two other important furbearers are the Beaver and the Nutria. (For a more comprehensive discussion of the Beaver, see the chapter on lakes and ponds.)

Nutria or Coypu
Myocastor coypus
610

The Nutria, or Coypu, is an exotic. Imported from South America at the turn of the century, it has become abundant in southern marshes. These animals feed only on the tops of marsh plants and thus unlike Muskrats do not cause "eat-outs." The reddish-brown fur of the Nutria is becoming increasingly popular as a substitute for Beaver.

Marsh Rabbit
Sylvilagus palustris
605

Cottontail
Sylvilagus spp.

The dark brown Marsh Rabbit of the southeastern wetlands looks somewhat like the Cottontail except that it has a less conspicuous tail. It makes trails through the marsh as it feeds on wetlands grasses and other plants. If pursued, it may take to the water, where it floats with only its eyes and nose exposed.

Eastern Harvest Mouse
Reithrodontomys humulis

Masked Shrew
Sorex cinereus
589

Least Shrew
Cryptotis parva

Common Garter Snake
Thamnophis sirtalis

Marsh Rice Rat
Oryzomys palustris
596

Other small mammals commonly found in wet meadows and marshes include the Meadow Vole, Eastern Harvest Mouse, and several species of shrew. The tiny Masked Shrew is a voracious carnivore that each day consumes more than its own weight in beetle larvae, slugs, snails, and spiders. The Least Shrew, which is active day and night, feeds almost constantly on earthworms, spiders, and insects. The Meadow Vole, or Field Mouse, which is typical of grassy fields, makes runways and spherical grass nests. Feeding primarily on plants, Meadow Voles are occasionally taken by Garter Snakes and Northern Harriers around the edges of the marsh. The Rice Rat, which lives in southeastern marshes, forages for aquatic plants, crabs, and snails. Sometimes this species' feeding platforms, which are made of plants, can be found over the water, with the remains of crabs lying atop them.

Mosquito Fish
Gambusia affinis
97

Pickerel
Esox spp.
75

Northern Pike
Esox lucius
76

Warmouth
Lepomis gulosus
47

Large-mouthed Bass
Micropterus salmoides
34

The fishes that are found in marshes are primarily warm-water species, and small foragers are the most common. Killifish and the Mosquito Fish are frequent in southern wetlands, although some killifish occur in northeastern freshwater tidal marshes. These forage fishes are joined by bottom feeders, including several species of bullhead catfish. The predaceous species in deep marshes include pickerel, Northern Pike, Warmouth, and Large-mouthed Bass. Although really a northern-lake species, the Northern Pike depends upon nearby marshes for its spawning grounds.

Northern Leopard Frog
Rana pipiens
130, 143

Frogs, toads, and salamanders return to the open water of marshes and ponds to lay their eggs. Some—for example, the Leopard, Chorus, and Cricket frogs—are often found in or near marshy areas. Various species and subspecies of the wide-ranging Chorus Frog, which has three dark stripes down its

Southern Chorus Frog
Pseudacris nigrita

Spring Peeper
Hyla crucifer
150

Cricket Frog
Acris spp.

Bullfrog
Rana catesbeiana
137

Green Frog
Rana clamitans
134

Mud Puppy or Waterdog
Necturus maculosus
104

Hellbender
Cryptobranchus alleganiensis
105

Spotted Salamander
Ambystoma maculatum
126, 127

Tiger Salamander
Ambystoma tigrinum
129

Spotted Turtle
Clemmys guttata
156

Painted Turtle
Chrysemys picta
159, 161, 162

Northern Water Snake
Nerodia sipedon
195

Cottonmouth
Agkistrodon piscivorus
175, 177, 194

American Alligator
Alligator mississippiensis
172

Spectacled Caiman
Caiman crocodilus
173

American Crocodile
Crocodylus acutus
174

back, ranges from Texas well up into Canada. The nocturnal Southern Chorus Frog can be recognized by the three rows of black spots on its back, and the rather warty Diurnal Cricket Frog has a dark triangle between its eyes. The Chorus Frog makes a rasping, rising trill that sounds like fingers running over a comb and—like the Spring Peeper, which it resembles—is heard in early spring. Cricket Frogs emerge later in the season. Their call is a kind of clicking sound, like pebbles striking together.

The Bullfrog, Pig Frog, and Green Frog are also associated with ponds, sloughs, and marshes. The Bullfrog, a widespread species, is the largest North American frog. The Green Frog, also widespread, has a twanging call, in contrast to the Bullfrog's rather impressive roar; the Pig Frog of the south is named for the guttural grunt that it utters. The Pig Frog is often found among the Water Hyacinth, where it feeds on crayfish. The sexes of all three species can be distinguished by their eardrums, which are larger than the eye in the males and eye-sized or smaller in the females.

Among the water-dependent salamanders, Mud Puppies (or Waterdogs), Hellbenders, sirens, and congo-eels can be found in deep, permanently flooded marshes. Others—such as the Spotted Salamander—come to marshes to lay their eggs. The widespread Tiger Salamander can be found in wet meadows, where it feeds on earthworms, insects, and even small mice.

Turtles, such as the Spotted and Painted turtles are frequently seen sunning themselves in marshes. In the Great Lakes states, Blanding's Turtle, which is marked by a bright yellow throat, is tolerant of cold water and is often seen basking in the sun on a Muskrat lodge. Box turtles, which are common throughout the eastern half of the country, thrive on the earthworms as well as on slugs in wet meadows and marshes.

Marshes are congenial habitats for a variety of snakes, including mud snakes, swamp snakes, brown snakes, and a variety of water snakes. One of the most common and widespread species is the Northern Water Snake, which feeds on minnows, tadpoles, and frogs. In the southern part of their range, several water snakes (the Northern in particular because of its variation in color and pattern) can be mistaken for the poisonous Water Moccasin, or Cottonmouth. When the Cottonmouth gapes, the white cottony lining of its mouth—which gives it its name—is very conspicuous.

In the marshes is also found the largest of our reptiles, the American Alligator. The Alligator suffered depredation in Florida, but has made a spectacular comeback since measures were undertaken to protect it from hunters. The Spectacled Caiman, an import from Central and South America, is more aggressive although smaller. Intended originally for the pet trade in this country, Spectacled Caimans have escaped or been released into the wild, where they are still occasionally sighted. Typical of brackish waters near the coast, the American Crocodile is the third gator found in the southern wetlands.

Swamp Milkweed
Asclepias incarnata
267

Swamp Milkweed Leaf Beetle
Labidomera clivicollis
351

Waterlily Leaf Beetle
Donacia spp.
355

Great Gray Copper
Gaeides xanthoides
403

Pink-edged Sulfur
Colias interior
385

Swamp Metalmark
Calephelis muticum
398

Mosquitoe
Culex spp.
376

Marsh Fly
Tetanocera spp.
380

Phantom Midge
Chaoborus spp.

Horse Fly
Tabanus spp.
378

Vinegar Fly
Drosophila melanogaster
381

Marsh Insects

In the wet meadows and marshes, where Swamp Milkweed is part of a rich cover of wild flowers, the Swamp Milkweed Leaf Beetle is frequently found. Its elongated yellow eggs are attached to the undersides of the leaves. Also look for the Waterlily Leaf Beetle among the lily pads; it is a bronzy insect that eats the foliage of water lilies and Skunk Cabbage. The butterflies that frequent marshes and meadows include the Great Gray Copper, Pink-edged Sulfur, Swamp Metalmark, and several skippers.

Mosquitoes breed in the shallow water of wetlands, and their larvae are eaten by frogs, fish, and aquatic insects. Marsh Flies and Phantom Midges are often mistaken for mosquitoes, but they do not bite. When the Midges hatch, they may come off the marsh in huge swarms. The Horse Fly, unlike the Phantom Midge, delivers a painful bite. It attaches its eggs to wetland plants overhanging the water. The female sucks blood, while the male feeds on pollen and nectar. The red-eyed Vinegar Fly feeds on fermenting fruits and decaying organic matter. This little fly, well known to generations of biology students, has been the subject of many studies into the principles of genetics.

Other marsh invertebrates include snails, crayfish, and worms, as well as many aquatic insects, such as dragonflies, damselflies, and mayflies. These organisms are especially important in the food chains of both birds and fishes. Many of the larval forms of these invertebrates serve as shredders in the initial breakdown of plant material; others rework the detritus. Worms and insect larvae in the bottom sediments further assist in the recycling process.

The Recyclers

The high productivity of marsh plants results in the addition each year of a considerable amount of plant material that must be processed by the decomposers. Muskrats are especially important as recyclers.

They shred enormous quantities of marsh vegetation in making their lodges, thereby increasing the surface area for bacteria and other decomposers to attack. In deep marsh sediments, the large invertebrate population is made up of tiny, swimming protozoans and crustaceans, snails, worms, and aquatic insects—including the nymphs of damselflies, dragonflies, caddisflies, and mayflies. Bacteria and water fungi also play a role.

As dead plants fall into the water, nutrients begin to leach from the plant parts. This dissolved organic matter can be used directly by certain aquatic organisms, including plankton. As the plant material is broken down—first by worms, insects, and other decomposers into coarse and then into progressively finer particulate matter—nutrients such as phosphorus, nitrogen, and calcium are released. Rooted aquatic plants have been described as nutrient pumps that mine these minerals, which are required in their photosynthesis and respiratory processes.

The nutrient flux in a marsh will vary according to the rates of water flow and decomposition. There is a considerable intake of nutrients during the growing season, and some loss from the system at other times of the year. Riverine marshes have a greater tendency to lose nutrients than do depression marshes that are drained by small, sluggish streams. Some of the nutrients stored in the sediments are periodically flushed from the system during severe storms. Nutrients can also be added, however, through sediments carried into the marsh by streams and groundwater leaching, and through precipitation.

Although there is still much to learn about nutrient cycling in wetlands, it is clear that the role of the silent decomposers is essential in maintaining the high productivity of marsh ecosystems.

Biotic Change

The fate of a marsh may be directly related to the activity of the recyclers. If the annual accumulation of dead plant material is not fully recycled or broken down, the marsh tends to fill in and the black muck soil increases in depth. This filling process can ultimately cause a shallow marsh to become a wet meadow, in which a smaller amount of standing water and more exposed soil inhibit the potential invasion of woody wetland plants such as willows, alders, maples, and cedars. In the Northeast, Tussock Sedge marshes are often invaded, and sometimes replaced, by Red Maples. Some of these sedge marshes were probably grazed in the past; however, the trend of agricultural abandonment in the Northeast, has led to an increase of forested wetlands. If the water levels remain high, this woody invasion will probably not occur, but with increased filling or silting, even a deep marsh may be affected, in time turning into a shallow marsh, with concomitant changes in the plant and animal life.

Tussock Sedge
Carex stricta

Red Maple
Acer rubrum
479

As a shallow marsh becomes a wet meadow and is gradually taken over by a shrub or forested swamp, light-demanding marsh plants will decline and eventually be replaced by a new wetland community. The replacement of one such community by another has been termed vegetation change, or succession. As the plant species change, the animal populations change as well. Where does the process end? Successional diagrams in some books give the impression that the wetland will eventually resemble the surrounding upland. However, this is an oversimplification and often misleading. The underlying soil of a marsh may not be favorable for upland plants; in addition, if periodic flooding continues, the wetland will persist. Some marshes have persisted for a long time.

An intriguing example of a long-lived marsh can be seen in the prairie pothole country, which harbors marshes that have persisted for some 11,000 years. Let us take a look at how this can happen. As was previously mentioned, the marshy vegetation in potholes often displays a belting pattern that runs from the upland into deep water. Sedge marsh is adjacent to the upland; next is a belt of cattails; then bulrushes; and, finally, water lilies and submerged aquatics. This appearance reflects a highly productive stage in the life of a prairie pothole marsh, but over time this structure can change.

In a prolonged drought, the pothole can dry up completely, although some wetland plants may continue to live on the exposed mud, while their seeds are added to the bottom. When the rains return, the pothole fills; the seeds buried in the mud quickly come to life, and soon the marsh plants are reestablished. Blackbirds, ducks, and Muskrats return. Then, for a reason that is not fully understood, the situation degenerates. The bulrush zone first becomes infested with insects, and the plants begin to die; Muskrat populations increase, and "eat-outs" further decimate the marshy plant cover. Soon much of the marsh vegetation has disappeared; only scattered bulrushes fringe the open water. Heavy algal blooms begin to appear, and even the submerged aquatics may decline. The open pond will persist until the next drought, when it will completely dry up, with its seed bank of aquatics stored in the bottom of the pothole. This time when the rains return, a healthy marsh is restored. In the prairie pothole country, even when marshes seem completely to have disappeared, we can rest assured that they will return, as long as their sites are not drained, filled, or otherwise destroyed.

Man and Marshes

Since marsh plants are so productive, they may be able to play a role in helping to fulfill our energy needs. In the future, Water Hyacinth and other fast-growing aquatics may provide us with burnable methane gas. In Scandinavia, reed grass has been used for fuel, and studies on the possible use of cattails as fuels are under way. Duckweeds and Florida Elodea are two other candidates for fuel production. Recently introduced into Florida, Elodea is an aggressive submerged aquatic that breaks loose from its roots, forming floating masses and clogging waterways, lakes, and ponds. Care must be taken when introducing such aggressive plants, because of the possible effects on other members of the marsh ecosystem.

Wetlands, including marshes—and the often delicately intricate interactions among their natural populations—have much to teach humankind. Paul Errington, who spent his life studying Muskrats in the pothole marshes, wrote, in his classic study *Of Men and Marshes:*

"No species has taught me more about parallels that I think man should be familiar with than has the muskrat. . . . To me, overcrowding is so much the supreme factor underlying stress in the muskrat populations that its lessons may scarcely be overemphasized. It does function as a biological mechanism to reduce, in part, its own evils. . . . The principal moral that the lives of muskrats may have for us may be that the biological foundation of peace is that of moderation."

Although man has destroyed vast amounts of marsh wetlands, one can only hope that a lesson has been learned from the mistakes. It is up to all of us to develop a new ethic in regard to our wetlands—one that will encompass not only humans but all of the creatures that rely on them for their existence.

MARSHES: PLANTS AND ANIMALS

Black-crowned Night-Heron 529
Black Tern 549
Blue-winged Teal 497
California Gull 556
Canada Goose 512
Canvasback 499
Cinnamon Teal 495
Common Goldeneye 506
Common Merganser 507
Common Moorhen 536
Common Snipe 542
Common Yellowthroat 584
Forster's Tern 551
Franklin's Gull 553
Fulvous Whistling-Duck 487
Gadwall 496
Green-backed Heron 534
Great Blue Heron 528
Great Egret 526
Green-winged Teal 490
King Rail 541
Least Bittern 533
Least Sandpiper 545
Limpkin 522
Mallard 492
Marsh Wren 574
"Mexican" Duck 488
Northern Harrier 561
Northern Pintail 498
Northern Shoveler 493
Olivaceous Cormorant 519
Palm Warbler 583
Pied-billed Grebe 483
Purple Gallinule 537
Red-winged Blackbird 580, 588
Redhead 500
Ross Goose 515
Ruddy Duck 510
Sandhill Crane 531
Sedge Wren 575
Semipalmated Sandpiper 543
Sharp-tailed Sparrow 582
Short-eared Owl 565
Snail Kite 558
Snow Goose 513, 514
Snowy Egret 527
Sora 538
Swamp Sparrow 576
Tricolored Blackbird 587
Virginia Rail 540
Western Grebe 482
White-faced Ibis 523
White-fronted Goose 511
Wilson's Phalarope 548
Yellow-headed Blackbird 586
Yellow Rail 539

Mammals

Marsh Rice Rat 596
Masked Shrew 589
Meadow Jumping Mouse 599
Meadow Vole 603
Mink 613
Muskrat 609
Nutria 610
Round-tailed Muskrat 608

THE EVERGLADES

The Seminoles called the Everglades "Pa Hay-Okee," or "grassy waters," words which perfectly depict this river of grass, whose waters move slowly and imperceptibly southward toward the Gulf of Mexico. The drive from Miami to Naples on Alligator Alley or the Tamiami Trail reveals the character of this vast, flat, grassy freshwater plain, which is dotted with low islands of willows or bays. Within the glades, wildlife tends to congregate in the open water sloughs and man-made canals, especially during the drier winter season.

As one approaches the southern lobe of Florida, freshwater saw grass marshes are replaced by brackish marshes and finally by mangrove swamps, which fringe the coastline. In fact the southern half of Everglades National Park is not a saw grass habitat, but is rather a saline mangrove wetland (and is described in *The Audubon Society Nature Guide to the Atlantic and Gulf Coasts).*

Distribution

The Everglades—which originally covered some one and a half million acres—now consists of a belt that is fifty miles wide and one hundred miles long, extending from Lake Okeechobee southward to the southern tip of Florida. It was historically an integral part of the lake's drainage pattern: The summer's overflow moved unobstructed across the glades and into the Gulf. From Lake Okeechobee, which is about twenty feet above sea level, the terrain falls only two or three inches per mile in its southward course, so the movement of the water is scarcely noticeable.

Because of its location—just west of the densely populated coastal cities of Miami and Palm Beach and south of Lake Okeechobee—the Everglades has been drastically modified by man. The area directly south of the lake has been converted to agricultural land by means of drainage canals, and, in the last few decades, an elaborate water-control system has been installed in order to facilitate irrigation and flood control. Large areas along the eastern side have also been drained. Portions of the wetter, central glades still exist, however, and Everglades National Park, which is twice the size of Rhode Island, now preserves a sample of this unique subtropical wetland. To the west of the Everglades is the Big Cypress Swamp, which is discussed in another chapter.

Ecology

As the sea level rose and fell several times during the glacial epoch, the Everglades evolved as a gently sloping plain extending southward from Lake Okeechobee. The soft limestone, called Miami oolite, that was deposited at this time has since been eroded into jagged pinnacles and holes, some of which are many feet across. Where the rock is not exposed, it is covered by a veneer of sand, muck, peat, or marl (a deposit of clay and calcium carbonate); this layer supports the saw grass and its associated communities. In this subtropical climate, the plant and animal life has evolved in response to a cyclical water regime: a rainy season in summer and a dry season in winter, along with periodic droughts.

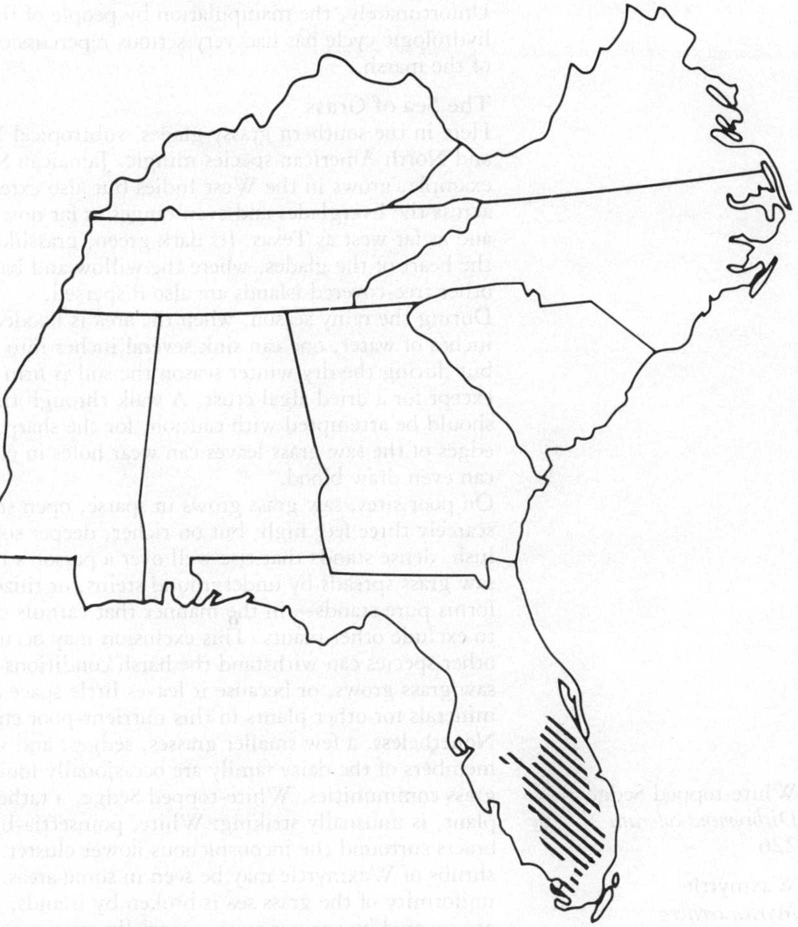

Unfortunately, the manipulation by people of the natural hydrologic cycle has had very serious repercussions on the life of the marsh.

The Sea of Grass

Here in the southern grassy glades, subtropical West Indian and North American species mingle. Jamaican Saw Grass, for example, grows in the West Indies but also extends northward across the Everglades and even ranges as far north as Virginia and as far west as Texas. Its dark green, grasslike leaves cover the heart of the glades, where the willow and bay heads and other tree-covered islands are also dispersed.

During the rainy season, when the area is flooded with several inches of water, one can sink several inches into the wet marl, but during the dry winter season the soil is firm and often bare except for a dried algal crust. A walk through the glades should be attempted with caution, for the sharp, saw-toothed edges of the saw grass leaves can wear holes in clothing and can even draw blood.

White-topped Sedge
Dichromena colorata
226

Waxmyrtle
Myrica cerifera

On poor sites, saw grass grows in sparse, open stands that are scarcely three feet high, but on richer, deeper soil it can form lush, dense stands that rise well over a person's head. Because saw grass spreads by underground stems, or rhizomes, it often forms pure stands—in the manner that cattails do—and tends to exclude other plants. This exclusion may occur because few other species can withstand the harsh conditions under which saw grass grows, or because it leaves little spacc and few minerals for other plants in this nutrient-poor environment. Nonetheless, a few smaller grasses, sedges, and several members of the daisy family are occasionally found within saw grass communities. White-topped Sedge, a rather showy plant, is unusually striking: White, poinsettia-like, leafy bracts surround the inconspicuous flower cluster. Scattered shrubs of Waxmyrtle may be seen in some areas. The uniformity of the grass sea is broken by islands, or heads, that are covered by various trees, especially species of willow and bay. The willow heads usually occur in wet depressions, where the cottony, windborne seeds of the willow establish themselves during a dry period. Willows also border the sloughs (stagnant, backwater areas), such as Taylor Slough, along the Anhinga Trail. With the buildup of organic matter, some of these willow stands may, in time, give way to bay islands. Redbay is an attractive, aromatic evergreen whose lance-shaped leaves are used to flavor soups and meats. Its dark green, glossy leaves are reddish when they first appear and have rust-colored hairs underneath. This feature distinguishes Redbay from hollies, magnolias, and bayberry—evergreens that may also be present on these islands.

Redbay
Persea borbonia
451

American Alligator
Alligator mississippiensis
172

Bay and willow heads often have open water in or around them. These areas harbor Alligators and garfish as well as many other forms of aquatic life. Herons frequently visit and feed around these heads.

Tropical Hammocks

In addition to the willow and bay heads, tropical hammocks—

raised ground supporting tropical trees—are also part of the pattern of the glades.

The hammocks of the Everglades are islands of tropical jungle vegetation. Dominated by West Indian trees, these microcosms grow on elevated ground, which is one to three feet higher than the surrounding glades; this arrangement keeps most of the trees' roots above the saturated soil of the marsh. The acidic humus of the hammock tends to dissolve the surrounding limestone; as a result, moats often encircle the islands. These moats serve as effective barriers against the frequent fires that sweep the glades. Originally the hammocks were covered by magnificent forests of mahogany and other tropical trees, but most hammocks have been cut or otherwise modified by people.

Royal Palm
Roystonea regia

Mahogany
Swietenia mahogoni

Live Oak
Quercus virginiana

Gumbo-limbo
Bursera simarouba

Strangler Fig
Ficus aurea

In Everglades National Park, two hammocks—Royal Palm and Mahogany Hammock—are readily accessible to the visitor and give the flavor of a tropical forest. Large Live Oaks native to the southern United States mingle with subtropical trees, including Gumbo-limbo, bastics, mastics, poisonweeds, and wild coffee. The Gumbo-limbo has unmistakable red-brown, peeling bark that looks like skin. The aerial roots of the Strangler Fig can be seen extending down the trunks of large Live Oaks. As the name implies, this fig literally strangles its host: A seedling starts high on a branch of the oak; as it grows, it puts out a series of octopuslike aerial roots, which become tightly molded to the trunk. When the roots reach the ground, they eventually engulf and kill the oak, leaving the Strangler Fig in its place. Ferns grace the undergrowth, and on tree trunks and branches, air plants and orchids lend a further tropical touch. Finally, the spectacular Royal Palm, for which the hammock is named, towers high, its crown capped with fronds. Frequently cultivated as an ornamental tree in south Florida, this rare native palm is found here as well as in certain parts of the Big Cypress Swamp.

Apple Snail
Pomacea spp.

Snail Kite
Rostrhamus sociabilis
558

Bobcat
Felis rufus
616

Mountain Lion
Felis concolor

These hammocks are also the habitat of the colorful Apple Snail, which has more than fifty color variations. Restricted to Florida and islands in the Caribbean, it has been heavily collected by shell hunters, yet it remains the sole food of the rare Snail Kite. Among the large animals that have been reported in these jungle hardwood habitats are Bobcats and the Florida Panther, an isolated race of the Mountain Lion.

A Slough and Its Wildlife

Within the park there are several major sloughs where open water normally persists during the dry winter season. Let us take a look at Taylor Slough, the site of the famous Anhinga Trail and the Royal Palm Hammock.

As one approaches the slough, its teeming life becomes apparent. Alligators, mostly small ones, are snugged in along the water's edge. A few that are about a foot in length may be active nearby. Garfish—long, slender, primitive creatures, swim slowly about, apparently unaware of the predators nearby.

Purple Gallinule
Porphyrula martinica
537

In a pool covered by water lilies, several Purple Gallinules—

birds with beautiful, iridescent feathers—walk casually about on the lily pads, turning over leaves with their especially well-adapted long toes, searching for aquatic insects and other organisms.

Green Heron
Butorides striatus

Great Blue Heron
Ardea herodias
528

Great Egret
Casmerodius albus

Snowy Egret
Egretta thula
527

Farther along the trail, we pass a willow thicket at the edge of the slough, where a little Green Heron and a stately Great Blue Heron fish in the shallow water. A Great Egret and a Snowy Egret come into view at the next curve of the boardwalk. Turtles sun themselves on rocks or logs. Suddenly a six-foot-long American Alligator comes into view.

Anhinga
Anhinga anhinga
518

Several Anhingas—the birds for which the trail is named—can be seen resting on a willow branch. One holds its wings spread open to dry: Unlike many aquatic birds, Anhingas have oil glands that are poorly developed and cannot keep the birds' feathers dry. Another Anhinga is submerged in an open pool, with only its neck and head above the water; this characteristic swimming posture gives rise to the nickname "Snakebird." The Anhinga spears its fish prey with its long, pointed bill; arriving at a perch, the bird tosses its catch into the air and swallows it headfirst.

In winter, the abundance and variety of wildlife in the slough is striking. During this season, the slough represents the last aquatic lifeline, providing crucial food and shelter for many species. When the rains come in the spring, however, the wildlife disperses.

Drought and Gator Holes

Although the glades are seasonally flooded, occasional droughts are part of the natural cycle to which much of the plant and animal life has become adjusted. During periods of drought, some animals leave, whereas others bury themselves in the muck or marl and aestivate (enter into a more or less torpid state). Crayfish and American Alligators escape the drought in this manner, as does the Greater Siren, a two-legged salamander that balls up in a spherical chamber lined with mucus. Crayfish may burrow as deep as two feet.

Crayfish
Cambarus spp.

Greater Siren
Siren lacertina
106

Alligators may use their feet, snouts, and tails to create pools that stay filled with water during the dry periods, or they may aestivate in a mud-covered den. The gator holes not only provide an aquatic habitat for the Alligator during these dry periods, but they are also critical to many other animals. Large numbers of fish, turtles, snails, and other aquatic creatures move in with the gators, repopulating the surrounding areas when the rains return.

Common Cattail
Typha latifolia
220

Arrowhead
Sagittaria latifolia
247

Marsh Rabbit
Sylvilagus palustris
605

Raccoon
Procyon lotor
614

Gator holes become miniature, marshlike habitats, filled with lily pads, cattails, arrowheads, and other aquatics. On the piles of debris alongside the holes, ferns, wild flowers, and tree and shrub seedlings find new habitats. Birds nest in the new shrubby growth. Turtles may even lay their eggs here, and the Marsh Rabbit, a small-eared, dark-furred rodent, visits these sites in search of vegetation. The Raccoon, an opportunist, may consume turtle eggs or capture the small creatures that have congregated here.

Gator holes are such a vital part of the glades—important in increasing habitat diversity and serving other forms of life during critical periods—that a law has been enacted to protect them within the park.

After the winter's drought, the female Alligator builds a nest of mud and rotting plants, sometimes capped with saw grass. The nest is about eight feet high and two to three feet across. In May or June, from forty to sixty eggs are laid in the nest; after nine weeks of incubation, the young begin to hatch. While still in the egg, they signal the mother with a distinctive call. The mother quickly tears open the nest, and out come the little hatchlings, only eight to ten inches long. Growing at the rate of one foot per year for the first five years, Alligators reach maturity at about ten years of age and can grow as long as twenty feet.

The Alligator is a powerful and potentially dangerous creature, but if unmolested will rarely harm people. In the past, the Alligator was heavily hunted. Skins—to make shoes, purses, and other items—were in great demand; poaching can be a highly profitable business. Some states now have laws forbidding the sale of items made from Alligator skin. This, and the protection now awarded the Alligator as an endangered species, have given this animal a greater chance to survive.

Man and the Everglades

Since the late 1800s, man has attempted to control flooding in southern Florida by building canals. In 1925 and 1928, hurricane-driven water from Lake Okeechobee killed 2500 people. In the mid-1940s, farmland and residential communities flooded, and salt water intruded from the sea—in other words, crucial fresh groundwater was replaced by salt water.

This stimulated the formation of a comprehensive water-control plan that altered the Everglades forever. Extensive levees were built around Lake Okeechobee so that the overflow would no longer naturally spill across the sea of grass to the south. The central feature of the plan involved three major conservation areas south of the lake. The system included an elaborate pattern of levees, canals, and pumping stations, and was designed both to prevent flooding and to provide water for irrigation—since much of the muck-covered glades south of the lake had already been drained for agriculture. The system was also designed to prevent the intrusion of salt water from the ocean, which can be a problem because the land is so flat. It was also intended that the Everglades National Park receive water from this system. However, the expense of moving water to the park proved a deterrent, and vital water was allowed to flow out to sea. Unfortunately, this cost-cutting proved short-sighted and disastrous; in the 1960s, a cycle of very dry weather wreaked havoc in the Everglades. Dead and dying fish were everywhere. Rangers attempted to rescue Alligators stranded in the drying muck; the U.S. Air Force blasted holes in the parched earth to collect water; and an aerator was installed in the slough along the Anhinga Trail as an emergency measure to oxygenate the water.

Following these bad years, legislation was passed requiring a minimum flow of water into Shark and Taylor sloughs and the Park's eastern panhandle. The water is measured according to a monthly schedule that reflects the historical Everglades flow. This influx of fresh water is critical not only to freshwater organisms. Biologists have found that the larval forms of marine shrimp spend a short time in the fresh water of the glades before migrating to the sea, and appear to be dependent upon fresh water for their survival. The annual shrimp fishing profits at Fort Jefferson are estimated to range from $15 million to $20 million, while other commercial fisheries take $1 million of fish and crustaceans from the Park's coastal waters each year. Here, as in the bottomland hardwood swamps, the close connection between fresh and saline aquatic systems becomes apparent, as does the importance of maintaining them in a healthy condition.

But what has this water-modification system done to the overall ecosystem of the Everglades? The draining of thousands of acres of the surrounding glades during this century has lowered the water table and significantly dried out the glades. The water that nourishes the area is now being administered according to law, instead of proceeding as a natural flow from Lake Okeechobee. This radical change has also altered another factor: the frequency and intensity of fires. An eminent ecologist who recognized this problem several decades ago described it in this way: "It is my contention that the herbaceous Everglades and the surrounding pinelands were born in fires; that they can survive only with fires; and that they are dying today because of fires."

At first glance, this statement seems contradictory; yet upon examination, it makes sense. It is presumed that prior to the entry of human beings into the glades, lightning-caused fires burned the glades periodically, even during periods of ample rainfalls. Indeed, saw grass can burn even when its environment is flooded. However, such fires do little damage; in fact they can stimulate the saw grass to greater growth when it resprouts.

As early as the 1950s, personnel in the Park carefully observed lightning-caused fires. Some were extinguished naturally, but others became large conflagrations. Why? The draining of the glades and many years of fire suppression are involved. When fires occur naturally and periodically, dead plant material is regularly eliminated. However, under a program of fire suppression, this material builds up to extraordinary levels. This accumulation provides fuel for hot, highly destructive fires. As a result of the lower water table, fires of recent decades have actually burned the underlying peat and killed the saw grass roots. Once such devastating fires get started, even hammocks or woody islands of vegetation are likely to be consumed.

This situation sharply contrasts with the state of affairs that existed for hundreds of years prior to the entry of human beings onto the scene. During this period, light fires skimmed over the glades when they were wet. It is clear that a change in fire intensity has the capability of destroying the original Everglades pattern.

This new, devastating set of circumstances began with the manipulation of the water, which is critical in maintaining the integrity of these wetlands. Again, the words of my colleague summarize the situation: "Considering the tremendous amount of drainage and artificial lowering of water tables, the entire condition is accentuated to an extreme degree. Then comes a bright day at the end of the dry season. The grass burns. The saw grass roots burn. The peat soil burns. The centuries-old hammocks burn. The world burns. And we blame the fire, not ourselves."

Australian Pine
Casnarina equisetifolia

Cajeput-tree
Melaleuca leucadendron

Brazilian Pepper
Schinus terebinthifolia

Coastal Colubrina
Colubrina arborescens

Grass Carp
Ctenopharyngodon idella
96

Cuban Treefrog
Osteopilus septentrionalis

Fire and a lack of water are not the only problems threatening the Everglades. The introduction of exotic plants and animals poses a further threat to the native flora and fauna. Australian Pine, Cajeput-tree, Brazilian Pepper, and Coastal Colubrina are all fast-growing exotics that readily invade disturbed areas or those with lowered water levels. On my last trip up the eastern side of the Everglades, I was appalled at the rapid takeover by the Cajeput-tree, a flaky, thick-barked Australian species that is quite resistant to fire and to efforts to extirpate it. Although it was introduced many years ago, with the intention of making the Everglades more livable, the Cajeput-tree is now considered to be one of the most serious long-range threats to Everglades National Park. Florida Elodea, or Hydrilla, a submerged aquatic that was introduced in the 1950s as an aquarium plant, now clogs waterways and canals. The oriental Grass Carp, which was introduced in 1963 to control the Elodea, may also become a problem: This fish consumes virtually all aquatic plants, leaving little for other wildlife. A South American toad with a voracious appetite is also at large, as is a Cuban treefrog that preys on native insects.

These are only a few of the many species that have been brought into Florida over the years. The introduction of flora and fauna from other places does not always have adverse effects on the native species, but can often prove disastrous. However—to strike a more optimistic note—one should not forget the positive actions that have come about because of the concern many people have for this unique area. In 1969 the proposed construction of an international jetport on the western edge of the glades brought protests from all over the world. People were worried—not about the economic value of the Everglades, but about the very fact of the continued existence of the area and the animals and plants that make it so interesting. These protesters knew that if the Everglades were to vanish, the world would have lost something unique and very precious. The jetport idea was abandoned, but that does not mean that new threats will not appear in the future. An educated and informed public can be a strong force in protecting this unique part of our natural heritage.

THE EVERGLADES: PLANTS AND ANIMALS

Red Maple
Acer rubrum
479

Black Willow
Salix nigra
453

Silver Maple
Acer saccharinum
478

Northern White-cedar
Thuja occidentalis
428

Atlantic White-cedar
Chamaecyparis thyoides
429

Western Hemlock
Tsuga heterophylla

Red Alder
Alnus rubra
466

Black Spruce
Picea mariana
432

Balsam Fir
Abies balsamea

Larch (Tamarack)
Larix laricina
430

Black Ash
Fraxinus nigra
435

Pin Oak
Quercus palustris
477

Swamp White Oak
Quercus bicolor
476

American Elm
Ulmus americana
465

Sweet Gum
Liquidambar styraciflua

In the northern part of North America, several different types of forested wetlands can be found. Perhaps easiest to recognize are the widely represented Red Maple swamps, which are painted with brilliant splashes of red in the autumn. Conifer swamps, with their evergreen cover, are sometimes mistaken for bogs and thus require a closer look for identification. Some swamps support a mixture of evergreen and deciduous trees. The forested wetlands of the North resemble the surrounding upland forests, but they occur in the lowlands on poorly drained sites; they are frequently associated with streams and have standing water for part of the year.

The northern floodplain forests, like the bottomland hardwood swamps of the South, border the major rivers; they form meandering ribbons of forest and are composed primarily of a variety of hardwoods that find the silty alluvial soil a congenial place to grow. Northern floodplain forests, although blending with those to the south, occur along more rapidly flowing rivers, are frequently flooded for shorter periods of time, and are characterized by different species. Here, Black Willow, cottonwoods, and Silver Maple are among the common trees (in contrast with the Baldcypress, Water Tupelo, and aquatic oaks of the South).

Distribution

These northern wetlands are widely distributed throughout the East, extending as far south as the Appalachians and west to the Great Lakes states. In the Far West, beyond the grasslands, they reappear. Spruce-fir and Northern White-cedar swamps occur northward into the conifer forest region, where bogs are also common. Atlantic White-cedar swamps and bogs extend from Cape Cod southward along the coast. In the Far West, Western Hemlock, Red Alder, and other evergreens predominate in the wetlands. Floodplain forests occur where extensive floodplains have developed along such major rivers as the Connecticut, the Wabash, the Tippecanoe, and the upper Mississippi.

Ecology

Northern boreal swamps are dominated by Black and White spruces, Balsam Fir, Larch (or Tamarack), and Northern White-cedar. On richer sites, cedar may form swamps or bogs, assisted by periodic fires. The slightly more southern hardwood swamp forests are dominated by Red Maple or a variety of other deciduous trees, such as Black and White ashes, Black Gum, Yellow Birch, Pin Oak, Swamp White Oak, and American Elm. Still farther south, Sweet Gum is a significant species.

Like the forests of the surrounding uplands, which they resemble, the northern swamp forests typically have a tree canopy that dominates the community. Often the evergreen swamps are so shady that mosses form a carpet on the forest floor. If there is enough light, though, shrubs can grow beneath the canopy, along with ferns and wild flowers. Some of these forests are layered and thus provide many niches for different forms of animal life.

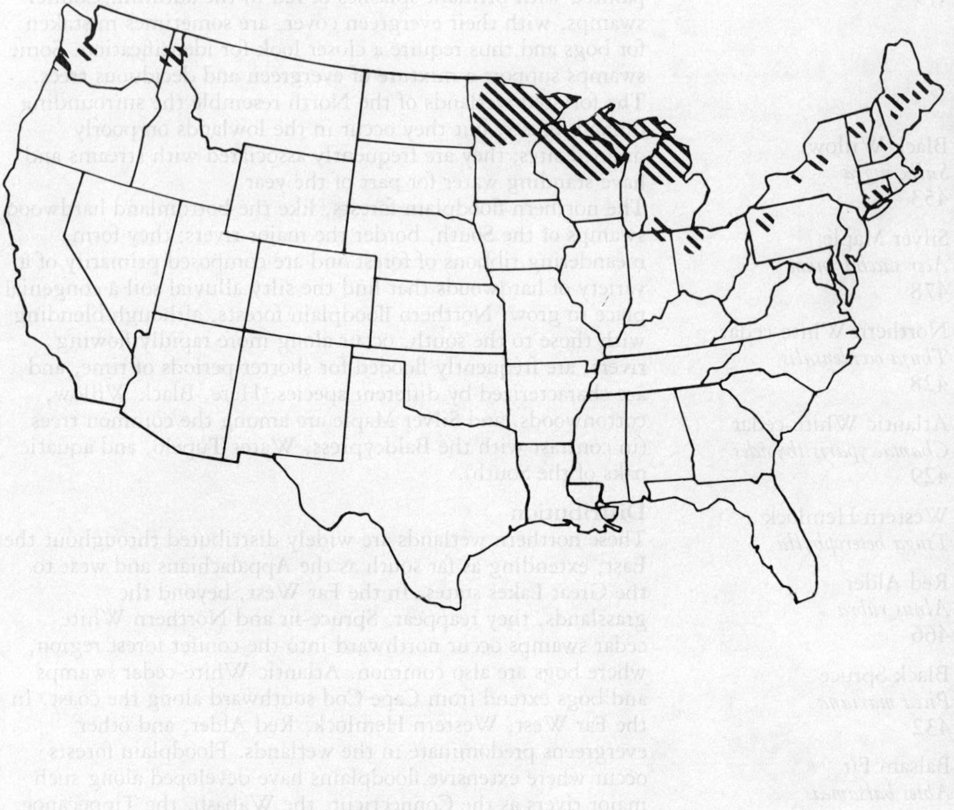

Now let us turn to characterizing one of the more widespread forms of forested wetlands. What follows is an excursion through the seasons in a Red Maple swamp; we will follow the unfolding of life of the typical plants and animals.

The Red Maple Swamp Throughout the Seasons

In winter, when the Red Maple swamp is frozen, one can walk on the snow-covered patches of ice between the hummocks. It is very quiet. Only the tracks in the snow suggest that life is stirring in this cold weather.

Skunk Cabbage
Symplocarpus foetidus
312

As the days begin to lengthen in February, Skunk Cabbage begins to flower. Projecting above the frozen soil are the sharp, tightly-coiled, growing tips and the spathe—a mottled reddish-yellow-green, globe-shaped structure that encloses the flower cluster. The snow has melted from around the flower. Inside the spathe, a ball of flowers—the spadix—is producing pollen.

These flowers, like others in the arum family, often give off a considerable amount of heat. Skunk Cabbage can maintain an internal flower temperature of 68° F for several weeks, even when nighttime temperatures drop below freezing. To produce this heat, Skunk Cabbage has a special internal device that converts much of the stored food in the plant's large underground storage organ to heat energy. The relatively high temperature seems to help spread the foul odor of the flowers and thus aid in attracting pollinating insects.

Heat given off as a result of cellular respiration is ordinarily thought of as a waste product. However, the heat generated in cold weather by the Skunk Cabbage may be critical to its survival. Since it is not growing much at this time, the plant is able to use most of its energy in the form of heat energy rather than as work energy (which is the form needed by rapidly growing plants and active animals). The Skunk Cabbage may be unique among temperate flowering plants in its capacity to generate heat in the winter.

(Jewelweed) Spotted Touch-me-not
Impatiens capensis
279

Yellow Skunk Cabbage
Lysichitum americanum
223

After the Skunk Cabbage has flowered—and with the onset of warm spring weather—large leaves develop, sometimes shading the entire forest floor. (The characteristic skunklike smell is evident when one tears a leaf.) By the middle or end of summer, the leaves have restored the energy that was spent on flowering and fruiting, and have also built up a new supply for next season. Soon the leaves wither and die, leaving ample space for Jewelweed and other swamp wild flowers. On the West Coast, the related Yellow Skunk Cabbage, with its attractive yellow-green spathe, grows in open swamps or wet woods.

One of the first trees to flower is the Red Maple. Even in the winter, a close look will reveal distinctive, globose flower buds on the newest, reddish twigs. Different buds give rise to the new shoots and leaves. After a few warm weeks in early spring, the swampy lowland takes on a reddish tinge as both male and female flowers burst into bloom. The flowers are red; male blossoms may show some yellow on the pollen-bearing stamens. By mid-May the distinctive fruits—the winged samaras that children like to stick on their noses—are rapidly maturing. These seeds are easily dispersed by the wind, which helps to make Red Maple one of our most widespread and common trees.

Wood Frog
Rana sylvatica
14, 149

One of the first spring sounds to come from the pools in the swamp is the ducklike quack of the Wood Frog. Normally forest residents, these frogs concentrate in the wetlands at breeding time. Sometimes the pools boil with activity as they mate. The male firmly clasps the female and remains in the same position until the eggs are laid.

Spicebush
Lindera benzoin
201

Spring Peeper
Hyla crucifer
150

In the shrubby undergrowth, Spicebush blooms at the same time as the cultivated Forsythia, and its tiny, pale yellow flowers lend a diffuse yellow tone to the still-leafless swamp forest. Now, as warmer evenings approach, the inch-long Spring Peeper—one of the smallest American frogs, which is marked by an X on its back—signals the true arrival of spring. It is amazing how much sound these little amphibians can make.

Cinnamon Fern
Osmunda cinnamomea
304

Bead Fern or Sensitive Fern
Onoclea sensibilis

Marsh Marigold
Caltha leptosepala
253

Common Buttercup
Ranunculus acris

Clumps of Cinnamon Ferns become evident as the young fronds uncurl from their distinctive fiddleheads. Nearby are the dried, brown, beadlike spore cases of the Bead, or Sensitive, Fern; its new fronds will appear soon after those of the Cinnamon Fern. Various species of wild flowers spring up, taking advantage of the available light before the dense, leafy canopy closes over. Showy yellow clumps of Marsh Marigold brighten the dark, watery forest floor. Related to the Buttercup, the Marsh Marigold has shiny green leaves, which are sometimes used in cooking.

Spotted Salamander
Ambystoma maculatum
126, 127

Spring also brings forth the strikingly marked Spotted Salamanders, which are six to nine inches long and black with bright yellow spots. Scientists at Connecticut College monitored the species' migrating habits during the breeding season, and found that these animals have a sophisticated homing or piloting instinct that enables them to find their way back to their swamp breeding grounds even after having been deliberately removed and disoriented. The exact nature of the instinct is not clear; however, many experts believe that it may involve the sense of smell.

During the spring, migrating birds return from the South, and some species select the swamp forest for nesting. Studies in Massachusetts revealed that over forty different species of birds breed in Red Maple swamps.

Common Yellowthroat
Geothlypis trichas

Canada Warbler
Wilsonia canadensis

Northern Waterthrush
Seiurus noveboracensis

Ovenbird
Seiurus aurocapillus

Catbird
Dumetella carolinensis

These birds are present in swamp forests because these areas contain niches that fulfill their requirements. Birds choose nesting sites not because specific species of vegetation are present; instead the choice is based on the structure of the plant cover. Some like shrubs, while others prefer saplings or even dead trees. Two brightly colored warblers have slightly different habits: The black-masked Common Yellowthroat, or "Bandit Bird," nests near the ground or in a low shrub; the Canada Warbler constructs a well-hidden nest on or near the ground. The Northern Waterthrush prefers an old stump over water as a nesting site, and the Ovenbird builds a domelike nest on the ground that resembles a Dutch oven. Catbirds tend to select shrubby thickets. Only by choosing different nesting and feeding areas can all of these birds exist together in the swamp forests.

Jack-in-the-pulpit
Arisaema triphyllum
309, 327

The Jack-in-the-pulpit is one of the next marsh plants to bloom. Related to Skunk Cabbage, these plants have a distinctively striped, arching spathe (the "pulpit"), which overshadows an erect spadix ("Jack"). The tiny flowers are located at the base of the spadix; each plant bears both male and female flowers, usually more of one than of the other. Many of the plants seem to start off as male, then produce flowers of both sexes, and eventually may end up with only female flowers. The females yield brilliant clusters of red fruit in the fall.

Why does all this sex transformation occur? Transplant experiments that involve placing different plants in good and poor growing spots have demonstrated that this amazing ability to change from male to female has survival value: It takes more energy to produce fruit than pollen. On poor sites, Jack-in-the-pulpits are mostly male, while, in contrast, on well-lighted, nutrient-rich sites, most of the plants are female.

American Black Duck
Anas rubripes
489

Wood Duck
Aix sponsa
491

Mallard
Anas platyrhynchos
492

Although ducks are usually associated with marshes, there are at least two—the Black Duck and the Wood Duck—that have an affinity for wooded swamps. The Black Duck, which sometimes interbreeds with the familiar Mallard, is by comparison shy and secretive. The Black Duck is really a sooty brown bird with conspicuous white wing linings, drab in comparison with the bright, elegantly plumaged Wood Duck. A favorite game bird, the Black Duck is a hardy species that nests on the ground and likes to keep its brood near the thick swamp cover much of the time.

Swamp Honeysuckle or Clammy Azalea
Rhododendron viscosum
229

Pink Azalea or Pinxter Flower
Rhododendron nudiflorum

The Wood Duck, on the other hand, prefers to nest near the swamp in a hollow tree. The paucity of such niches in most forests—due to cutting or clearing—has necessitated the erection of nest boxes to attract these lovely birds. Within a day or two after a brood of ducklings hatches, the mother may call them to leave the nest. The young ducklings have a special sharp claw that helps them climb up from the bottom of the nesting hole.

Highbush Blueberry
Vaccinium corymbosum
259

Large Purple Fringed Orchid
Habenaria fimbriata
294

Cardinal Flower
Lobelia cardinalis
277

Sweet Pepperbush
Clethra alnifolia
235

By summer the sticky white flowers of the Swamp Honeysuckle, or Clammy Azalea—one of the most fragrant flowers in the swamp shrub layer—are in full bloom. Except in color, they resemble those of the more familiar upland Pink Azalea or Pinxter Flower, also found by the borders of swamps and bogs.

The swamp may dry out by the middle or end of the summer, although some standing water frequently persists. This is the time to look for the Highbush Blueberry shrubs, as they are heavy with fruit that is well worth harvesting—if you can beat the birds to it. Related to cultivated forms, these native berries are equally sweet or sweeter.

In sunny openings, the showy Large Purple Fringed Orchid or the spectacular Cardinal Flower are in full bloom at this time of year. One of the last swamp shrubs to flower is Sweet

Pepperbush. Its fragrant, white, candlelike flower clusters make it easy to recognize.

Spotted Touch-me-not
Impatiens capensis
279

Pale Touch-me-not
Impatiens pallida

Bumblebee
Bombus spp.

By early fall, the shaded bare spots are covered with Spotted Touch-me-not or Pale Touch-me-not, which are both also called Jewelweed. The name Touch-me-not derives from the fruit capsule, which explodes at a light touch to disperse the seeds. Bumble bees enter the spurred flowers in search of nectar and, in the process, pollinate them. However, a closer look reveals that some bees are getting something for nothing. Since their sucking tubes are too short to work the flower from the top, they drill holes in the bottom of the spurs and suck out the sweet liquid, neglecting their pollination duties.

As fall advances, the swamp will turn a brilliant red, as first the Black Gum and then the maples assume their autumn colors. Even as the leaves fall, all of their vital nutrients contribute to the perpetuation of this wetland ecosystem. Some nutrients may flow through the swamp to enter the stream; others remain where they fall, to be added to the rich black muck of the swamp.

Winterberry or Black Alder
Ilex verticillata
244, 328

With the leaves gone, the bright red fruit of the Winterberry, or Black Alder, is more conspicuous. Much sought-after by birds, the newly exposed berries on these native deciduous holly plants can add a bright touch to an otherwise drab landscape.

Snowshoe Hare or "Varying" Hare
Lepus americanus

Raccoon
Procyon lotor
614

With the onset of winter, deer may head for the swampy lowlands, where they will remain throughout the season. This is especially likely to happen in the evergreen cedar swamps. Northern White-cedar swamps also provide excellent wintering grounds—in fact they are so good that the evergreens may be replaced by hardwoods as a result of the deer's selective eating of the young cedars. The Snowshoe or "Varying" Hare—although it is more typical of the northern evergreen or mountain swamps and uplands—also depends on these wetlands for both food and cover year-round. This hare's adaptations to its environment include an ability to change its color from summer brown to winter white, and long, furry feet that act like snowshoes in heavy snow. Raccoons visit the swamp throughout the year in search of the fruiting shrubs that supplement their varied diet.

Blue Jay
Cyanocitta cristata

As snow covers the swamp, the flurry of activity dies down. The breeding birds have gone south, but several permanent residents—among them, the chickadees, the Blue Jay, and various woodpeckers—continue to seek food and cover in these wetlands throughout the winter months.

The seasonal variations in a typical Red Maple swamp are not unlike those in other wooded wetlands. To the north and west, the trees and some of the animals are different, but similar patterns and processes can be observed: for example, the succession of flowering; insects' role in pollination; the return of birds, frogs, and salamanders during the breeding season. New forms replace the old, leaves fall, and in winter, the cycle of life is suspended, but only temporarily, for this is a self-perpetuating system.

Changing Patterns in Swamps

A look at the vegetation dynamics of some of these wetlands can provide interesting insights into their origins and patterns of change.

Swamps tend to develop in poorly drained depressions, because these areas are subject to periodic flooding and have mucky soils that are too wet for the surrounding upland forest species. Some forested swamps have evolved from sedge or cattail marshes that gradually filled in.

A typical sequence of changes might occur as follows: As the water level is lowered, Red Maples and other swamp species become established. As these increase, they shade out the light-demanding marsh plants and create a shady wetland forest. When this happens, the dabbling ducks, Red-winged Blackbirds, and Muskrats—creatures of the marsh—leave, and the newly created swamp attracts a new set of animals.

Red-winged Blackbird
Agelaius phoeniceus
580, 588

Muskrat
Ondatra zibethicus
609

Some of these swamps are affected by agricultural use, as grazing ceases in low, sedgy meadows or marshy areas. Red Maple and its allies usurp the marshy site and return to the status they may once have held before the land was cleared.

Man's impact is evident in many swamps, where multistemmed clumps of trees are present on elevated hummocks. These formations develop following cutting, which causes most deciduous swamp trees to sprout vigorously and to create a new clump of trees around the old stumps.

A forested wetland can also be modified by the permanent raising of the water level. If a road is built across a swamp and the drainage pattern is thus altered so that prolonged flooding occurs, the swamp forest may die. Northern swamp trees are not as flood-tolerant as the Water Tupelo and Baldcypress of the southern bottomlands. Red Maple swamps are usually not flooded for more than a third of the year; continuous flooding kills these trees. Atlantic White-cedar, however, can tolerate a bit more flooding.

In Beaver country, flooding frequently occurs, since Beaver dams along streams that flow through swamps can permanently inundate low-lying swamp forests and the adjacent upland areas. Although a Beaver pond may persist for years, when the food runs out and the Beavers move, the water level will fall; then a marsh or meadow will develop, and eventually a swamp forest may be established on the site of the former pond.

Beaver
Castor canadensis
611

There is good evidence to suggest that fire has historically played an important role in the modification of swamp forests. It is certainly helpful to the development of light-loving species such as the Atlantic White-cedar, which cannot compete successfully with the more shade-tolerant Red Maple. When fire clears away growth in a swamp, an even-aged stand of cedar will soon begin to grow, as long as a seed source is present.

Other natural occurrences also affect swamp systems. Wind storms, for example, blow down large numbers of trees and create openings for species that require a great deal of light.

Swamp forests are not static, but are highly dynamic. Both man and nature have a strong impact on the changing patterns of these wetlands.

Floodplain Forest Dynamics

Although both the southern bottomlands and the northern floodplain forests are exposed to riverine flooding, the two wetland systems differ—not only in the tree species they support, but also in the nature of the flooding they undergo. Along the more rapidly flowing northern rivers, flood waters peak in the spring and then recede, exposing most of the floodplain for the rest of the year. Along sluggish southern rivers, where some of the floodplain is under water most of the time, trees such as Baldcypress and Water Tupelo have adapted to these conditions. Farther north, these trees and the southern aquatic oaks are replaced by willows, cottonwoods, Silver Maple, and their associates.

Let us now take a look at some of the dynamics and interactions that can occur on a typical northern riverine floodplain, such as that along the Connecticut River.

On approaching the floodplain from the upland, we may first encounter an open, sloping meadow that is flooded only by very high waters. Or perhaps there will be an extensive emergent marsh, where Purple Loosestrife, a rather aggressive but lovely introduced aquatic, competes with the native riverine plants. We may pass through the meadow or marsh to reach the floodplain forest, where impressive Silver Maple trees tower eighty feet or more above us. The tree trunks still bear the silt stains from the spring flooding, when the water rose to a level high above our heads. The alluvial silt is wet, and, as we walk toward the river's edge, there are still water-filled stream channels.

Purple Loosestrife
Lythrum salicaria
293

Elsewhere along the river's edge, Black Willow trees form a narrow belt that stabilizes the bank. Although the trees are small, they are suited to their task. If damaged by spring floods or winter ice scouring, the willows rapidly put forth adventitious roots to take the place of those that have been damaged or eroded. Nearer the shore an exposed sandbar, sometimes called a point bar, has also developed and it is being covered by a sandbar willow thicket. The bar may help to build the floodplain or may be washed away by the next major flood.

Beyond the Black Willow belt, the floodplain rises slightly to form a natural levee that is covered by a cottonwood forest. The forest has an open understory except for saplings of Silver Maple. Nearby, a very young cottonwood stand has developed on a levee that was probably formed by a flood in 1955. In an opening along the edge, an unusual vine community of Bur Cucumber has become so dense that it is smothering out some of the little cottonwoods. Such vine communities are a distinctive feature of floodplains; they become established as a result of the constant disturbance—flooding—that enhances their competitive edge.

Bur Cucumber
Sicyos angulatus

Far from the river's edge beyond the cottonwoods, the forest

Sycamore
Platanus occidentalis
480

becomes most impressive. The predominant species is Silver Maple; other trees include Sycamore, American Elm, and White Ash. The open-crowned trees, widely spaced, are two to three feet in diameter. How old are they? We learn from a friend whose house overlooks the floodplain that the river changed its course over 300 years ago. Some of the trees may date back to this major event.

Ostrich Fern
Matteuccia struthiopteris

False Nettle
Boehmeria spp.

Wood Nettle
Laportea canadensis
317

Beautiful fern glades are found in forest openings. Large colonies—some a half acre or more in size—of Sensitive and Ostrich ferns may have been here a long time. There are few, if any, tree seedlings within their dense cover. Although their origin is unknown, some ferns may have been established with the forest, indicating that these glades are probably quite old.

Clearweed
Pilea pumila
318

By late summer, the previously bare soil under the Silver Maples bears a dense cover of False and Wood nettles and Clearweed. This layer of annuals—which tend to establish themselves on bare soil—shows an interesting adaptation to periodic flooding and silting and contrasts with the swamp and upland forest herb layers, which are primarily perennial wildflowers.

Pickerelweed
Pontederia cordata
295

Water Arum
Calla palustris
225

Arrowhead
Sagittaria latifolia
247

Tussock Sedge
Carex stricta

The forest is also interrupted by sloughs, where marshy plants such as Pickerelweed, Water Arum, and Arrowhead thrive. One of the shallow sloughs is on the way to becoming a Tussock Sedge marsh. As the slough fills in and wet soil is periodically exposed, the sedge can become established.

As on the southern bottomland floodplain, we see distinctive belts: the pioneering willows on the rugged river's edge; the cottonwoods on the levee; and the more mature Silver Maple forest on the older, higher, and more stable parts of the floodplain. Will the shorter-lived cottonwoods give way to Silver Maple in the future? Saplings are already established beneath the cottonwoods, but a severe flood like the one in 1955 may damage and uproot them. The cottonwood may persist or it may someday give up its turf. What will be the fate of the older, more mature forest? On other floodplains, especially those in the Midwest, trees may achieve a diameter of six to seven feet, which suggests that the river has not changed its course for a long time.

American Beech
Fagus grandifolia

Tuliptree
Liriodendron tulipifera

A floodplain forest is at the mercy of the river. Older, higher floodplains that are set back from the river's edge may persist and include such typical upland trees as American Beech and Tuliptree. Sometimes these floodplains can put on spectacular floral displays, with vast numbers of wild flowers bursting into bloom. As in the southern bottomland hardwoods, there is a distinctive fauna, which has adjusted to the periodic flooding.

Man also uses these floodplains, for they are among the most productive agricultural lands in the world. The fields are annually enriched by silt from the flooding river, and the farmer has adjusted to this regime. Even though a planting may be lost to floods, the farmer can usually plant again and count on the natural fertility of the land to produce a crop.

NORTHERN SWAMPS AND FLOODPLAIN WETLANDS: PLANTS AND ANIMALS

Red Maple 479
Silver Maple 478
Swamp Cottonwood 470
Swamp White Oak 476
Western Redcedar 427

Birds
Barred Owl 566
Barrow's Goldeneye 505
Black-crowned Night-Heron 529
Black Duck 489
Common Yellowthroat 584
Double-crested Cormorant 520
Little Blue Heron 521, 525
Prothonotary Warbler 585
Red-bellied Woodpecker 570
Red-shouldered Hawk 564
Swamp Sparrow 576
Wild Turkey 567
Wood Duck 491
Yellow-crowned Night-Heron 530

Mammals
Arctic Shrew 594
Black Bear 615
Bobcat 616
Moose 618
Raccoon 614
Smoky Shrew 593
Star-nosed Mole 595
White-tailed Deer 617

SHRUB SWAMPS: PUSSY WILLOW THICKETS, ALDER THICKETS, AND THE POCOSIN

Leatherleaf
Chamaedaphne calyculata
260

Pond Pine
Pinus serotina
431

Pussy Willow
Salix discolor
199, 457

Scrubby, low-growing thickets of evergreen or deciduous shrubs characterize the shrub swamps of North America. Some of the more common types include: northern boggy areas dominated by Leatherleaf (a heath); coastal swamps of the Southeast (called pocosin), which are populated by hollies, bays, and scraggly Pond Pines; and alder and Pussy Willow thickets, which grow in many areas of the continent. Some of the shrub swamps of North America are transitional—on their way to becoming some other kind of wetland; others are relatively stable and may persist for many years or even centuries.

Distribution

Shrub swamps are typical of forested regions and, except for the pocosin, extend throughout the Northeast and westward into the Great Lakes states. They also occur locally in the West. Flooded or poorly drained sites on the edges of lakes, streams, marshes, and forested swamps may host shrub swamps. Alder and the leatherleaf thickets are typically associated with the boreal forest, and old beaver dams provide perfect openings for both alders and Pussy Willows. The pocosin extends from Virginia south to Florida on the sandy coastal plain.

Since many shrub swamps are in flux, our knowledge of them is somewhat limited. However those that are relatively permanent, like the pocosin, are being studied. We shall take a brief look at some of the shrubby wetland communities—at some of their characteristic plants and animals, as well as factors that affect their stability.

Ecology

Shrubby wetlands often flourish in areas once occupied by wet, sedgy meadows. The establishment of these wetlands is related to how the land has been used in the past: Burning, clearing, draining, mowing, and grazing are some of the factors that may favor or suppress these communities. Grazing by animals, for example, suppresses the shrubs, but when grazing ceases, shrubby species proliferate. Where meadows are burned or mowed, shrubs sprout vigorously and form even denser thickets.

Just as shrubs replace the sedge meadow or marsh, they too may be replaced by trees, such as elm, ash, and maple. However, some shrub wetlands persist for fifty years or more, since tree seedlings seem to have difficulty getting through the dense shrubby cover. In other spots where shrub wetlands are long-lived, cold-air drainage and the nature of the soil also seem to have deterred tree growth. European ecologists have used the Scandinavian word *carr,* a term meaning brushwood or copse wood, for these shrubby wetland communities.

Alder Thickets

Collectively, alders can create relatively pure stands that often cover several acres and form miniature forests of trees only ten to twenty-five feet high. Beneath the alder's dense cover, ferns and wild flowers thrive in the wet soil.

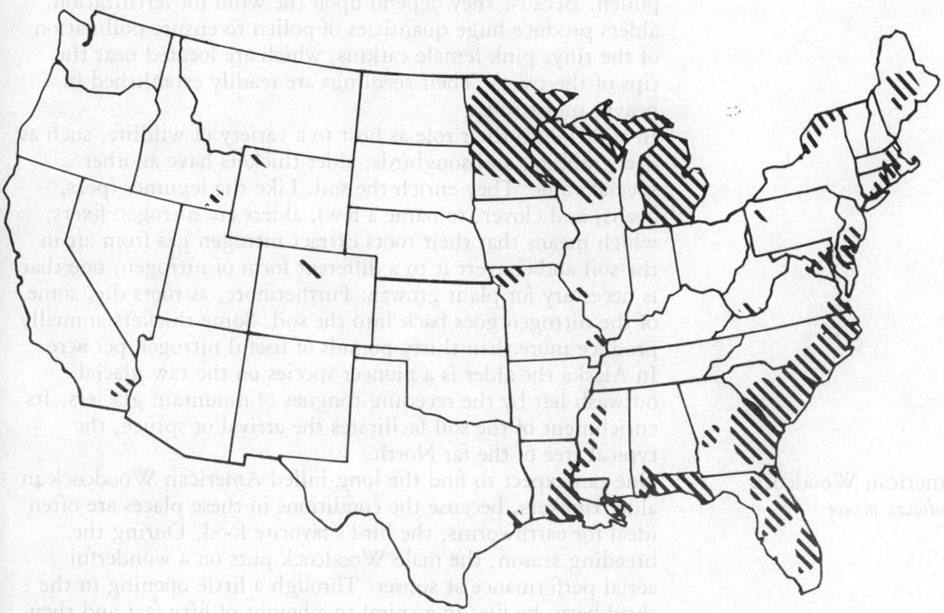

Related to the birches, alders form drooping male catkins or elongated spikes of pollen-laden flowers in the spring. Touching one of the ripe catkins elicits a small cloud of yellow pollen. Because they depend upon the wind for fertilization, alders produce huge quantities of pollen to ensure pollination of the tiny, pink female catkins, which are located near the tips of the twigs. Their seedlings are readily established in heavy, moist soil.

In addition to their role as host to a variety of wildlife, such as deer, rabbits, and songbirds, alder thickets have another special value: They enrich the soil. Like the legumes (peas, beans, and clover, to name a few), alders are nitrogen fixers, which means that their roots extract nitrogen gas from air in the soil and convert it to a different form of nitrogen, one that is necessary for plant growth. Furthermore, as roots die, some of the nitrogen goes back into the soil. Some thickets annually produce more than thirty pounds of useful nitrogen per acre.

In Alaska the alder is a pioneer species on the raw glacial outwash left by the receding tongues of mountain glaciers. Its enrichment of the soil facilitates the arrival of spruce, the typical tree of the far North.

American Woodcock
Scolopax minor

One can expect to find the long-billed American Woodcock in alder thickets, because the conditions in these places are often ideal for earthworms, the bird's favorite food. During the breeding season, the male Woodcock puts on a wonderful aerial performance at sunset. Through a little opening in the shrubbery, he flies in a spiral to a height of fifty feet and then circles to the ground, tweeting all the way. Once on the ground, the bird struts about with wings lowered, uttering a high, nasal *peent* call.

Pussy Willow Thickets

Familiar to many people, Pussy Willows thrive in flooded swamps. This many-stemmed shrub is easily identified by its silky gray catkins, which appear in late winter or early spring from beneath a single bud scale. Pussy Willow thickets occur throughout much of the North; they are especially extensive in the lake-filled boreal forest, where these shrubs may form small forests, and individuals may reach up to nine feet high.

Like the hollies, Pussy Willows produce male and female flowers on separate plants. As the catkins expand and flower, the pollen-laden males turn a showy yellow, while the female catkins remain a duller greenish.

Silky Dogwood
Cornus amomum

Red Osier Dogwood
Cornus stolonifera
325

At times Pussy Willow intermingles with other shrubs, including the red-stemmed, shrubby dogwoods (both Silky and Red-osier dogwoods). Westward, in Wisconsin, the Red Osier becomes dominant, while Pussy Willows occur only occasionally. Tall asters, goldenrods, and sedges grow in the understory, and smaller wild flowers such as bedstraws, bluebells, and marsh ferns grow nearer to the ground.

Leatherleaf and Other Shrub Swamps

Northward in the coniferous forest, Leatherleaf and its evergreen allies, which are tolerant of acidic conditions, often

Buttonbush
Cephalanthus occidentalis
237

American Black Duck
Anas rubripes
489

Water Willow
Justicia americana
263

Swamp Loosestrife
Decodon verticillatus
286

Loblolly-bay
Gordonia lasianthus
460

Redbay
Persea borbonia
451

Sweetbay
Magnolia virginiana
449

Fetterbush
Lyonia lucida

Waxmyrtle
Myrica cerifera

Titi
Cyrilla racemiflora
243

Zenobia
Zenobia pulverulenta

Black Bear
Ursus americanus
615

Cottonmouth
Agkistrodon piscivorus
175, 177, 194

Eastern Diamondback Rattler
Crotalus adamanteus

Pygmy Rattler
Sistrurus miliarius

Copperhead
Agkistrodon contortrix

form low mats of vegetation on poorly drained sites. These mats often are instrumental in the formation of sphagnum bogs.

Some shrub communities, including Buttonbush swamps, are flooded most of the time. Like cattails, the flood-tolerant Buttonbush is an emergent—that is, it grows partially submerged in water. With its white balls of tiny flowers and greenish to reddish-brown fruit balls, this species is quite striking. Buttonbush swamps are favored nesting places for Black Ducks.

Water Willow is an unusual shrub of North American wetlands. It "walks" across the water—its arching branches resprout at the tips where they touch the water. Water Willow forms extensive, low thickets along the edges of lakes and streams, and constantly advances outward. Although it has willowlike leaves, Water Willow (also known as Swamp Loosestrife) is a member of the loosestrife family. It produces attractive pinkish-lavender flowers.

The Pocosin

This Algonquin Indian name means "swamp on a hill"—an allusion to the fact that pocosins form in the elevated spots between streams. These evergreen communities are boggy, underlain by peat, and distinctly shrubby. Found in the Southeast, pocosins developed over the past few thousand years as the Atlantic Ocean receded and freshwater lakes formed along the coast. Gradually, the lakes became filled in with peat, giving rise to these unique evergreen communities. Pond Pine and the various bays—Loblolly-Bay, Redbay, and Sweetbay—as well as numerous shrubs, including Fetterbush, Waxmyrtle, Titi, and Zenobia, are characteristic of these shrubby evergreen wetlands. Where the peat layer is deep, a dense, waist-high, almost impenetrable shrub community develops. On the better sites, the shrubs and trees grow taller, and one can enter the community more easily.

The pocosin is a wildlife haven. In the eastern Carolinas, these communities are the last refuge of the Black Bear. Reptiles, such as Cottonmouth, Eastern Diamondback Rattler, Pygmy Rattler, and Copperhead, also find an undisturbed habitat in the pocosins, especially in the Croatan National Forest of North Carolina, where one can view the different kinds of pocosin communities.

What ecological factors influence or maintain pocosins? Their presence is closely related to fire history, water levels, and peat depths. As it does in the Everglades, fire helps maintain the pocosin as a discrete community.

Fires have influenced the evolution of the surrounding upland pine forest, and during dry periods, these fires have spread to the pocosin. Dry areas obviously burn more readily and thoroughly than wet ones, and in some cases, the peat also burns. Wetter areas burn less intensely, and the species that inhabit these locales respond differently. Sometimes the pocosin shrubs may be killed, but most are quite fire-tolerant and especially capable of resprouting following fire. Of all the species, the Pond Pine is perhaps the most interesting, for it actually seems to require fire. Its cones remain closed for many years until fire sweeps through and causes the scales to separate, thereby releasing the seeds. The fire also prepares a bed, and the winds contribute to the start of a new Pond Pine by carrying the winged seeds to this finely prepared ash bed. This process, which is not unknown to pine species in dry habitats, is certainly an amazing adaptation for a wetland pine.

The pocosin is one of the most interesting shrubby evergreen wetland communities in the world. Not only does it harbor unusual flora and interesting fauna, but it is tied into the surrounding streams, which supply estuaries with fresh, unpolluted water. Pocosins are also important in that they help to stabilize the coastal environment. As pocosins have been destroyed—as a result of either peat removal or drainage for the purpose of converting the land to other uses—rivers have become enriched with excessive nutrient runoff. The over-enrichment of rivers with nutrients and other pollutants can have an adverse effect on the coastal fisheries, for freshwater and coastal systems are closely interrelated.

Unfortunately, the pocosin has decreased markedly throughout its range. In North Carolina it once covered two and a half million acres, but today only one million acres survive. Approximately a third of the land that once supported pocosin has been converted to agricultural use, and about the same amount has been drained for development. There is ample reason to save the remaining part of this environment.

SHRUB SWAMPS: PLANTS AND ANIMALS

Insects and Spiders
American Horsefly 378
Golden-silk Spider 383
Vinegar Fly 381

Butterflies and Moths
Appalachian Brown 400, 408
Broken Dash 424
Creole Pearly Eye 410
Great Gray Copper 403
Harvester 394
Lace-winged Roadside Skipper 411
Palamedes Swallowtail 389
Sedge Skipper 422
Swamp Metalmark 398
White Peacock 404, 406

Trees
Atlantic White-cedar 429
Bebb Willow 458
Black Ash 435
Black Tupelo 443
Buckwheat-tree 446
Dahoon 448
Loblolly-bay 460
Mountain Alder 467
Poison-sumac 441
Pond Pine 431
Possumhaw 469
Possumhaw Viburnum 445
Pussy Willow 199, 457
Red Maple 479
Red Osier Dogwood 444
Redbay 451
Speckled Alder 468
Swamp-privet 456
Sweetbay 449

Birds
American Swallow-tailed Kite 559
Anhinga 518
Barred Owl 566
Black-crowned Night-Heron 529
Double-crested Cormorant 520
Little Blue Heron 521, 525
Prothonotary Warbler 585
Red-bellied Woodpecker 570
Red-shouldered Hawk 564
Swamp Sparrow 576
Wood Duck 491
Yellow-crowned Night Heron 530

Mammals
Arctic Shrew 594
Black Bear 615
Bobcat 616
Cotton Mouse 597
Golden Mouse 598
Moose 618
Raccoon 614
Smoky Shrew 593
Southern Red-backed Vole 601, 602
Star-nosed Mole 595
White-tailed Deer 617

CYPRESS SWAMPS

Spanish Moss
Tillandsia usneoides

Baldcypress
Taxodium distichum
433

Pondcypress
Taxodium distichum var. *nutans*

Cypress swamps are somber, eerie places, associated in most people's minds with the Deep South. The trees themselves are easily recognized by their "knees," which are the aerial roots that protrude out of the dark water, and by their spreading branches, which are draped with trailing gray-green curtains of Spanish Moss. The scene is dominated by the tall, graceful Baldcypress—alone or in conjunction with a smaller variety known as Pondcypress, which occurs on less flooded sites. Where the two occur together, they are sometimes difficult to distinguish. (These trees are not true cypresses of the family Cupressaceae, but are instead classified by most experts with the redwoods, in the family Taxodiaceae. Nonetheless, these wetlands are familiarly known as cypress swamps, a name we will retain for this discussion.) Although they are conifers, Baldcypresses are not evergreen but, like deciduous hardwoods, lose their leaves in the fall—hence the common name.

Distribution

Primarily a southern tree, Baldcypress occurs over a wide area. It reaches its best development in Florida, where it covers over ten percent of the state. The Big Cypress Swamp, a vast area west of the grassy Everglades, includes more than 2000 square miles of cypress scrub, cutover cypress strands (muck-filled depressions), wet prairies, and pinelands. Unfortunately, because of heavy logging and other man-made disturbances, only a few examples of mature Baldcypress remain. One of the best of these is in the Corkscrew Swamp Sanctuary, which is owned by the National Audubon Society. Recently, however, over 500,000 acres of the Big Cypress Swamp were set aside as the Big Cypress National Preserve.

Cypress swamps also occur along the Gulf Coast to eastern Texas (where elements can be found in the Big Thicket Wildlife Refuge), northward into Arkansas (in the White River Refuge) and Tennessee (in the Reelfoot Wildlife Refuge). Baldcypress may also be found in the Mississippi Valley up to southern Illinois and Indiana, and as far north as Delaware along the East Coast. The Okefenokee Swamp in Georgia is dominated by Baldcypress, although it was heavily lumbered in the early part of the century. In the Dismal Swamp of Virginia and North Carolina, Baldcypress mingles with the typical northern swamp hardwoods. Baldcypress is also an important tree discussed in the chapter on "Southern Bottomland Hardwood Swamps."

Ecology

Although Baldcypress grows under a variety of conditions, it does best in a warm, humid climate. Planted trees survive as far north as Massachusetts and Michigan, but the seeds will not mature in cold climates. Driving southward along the coast, one begins to see some of the best Baldcypress stands along the edges of rivers and lakes in the Carolinas. As one crosses the Tamiami Trail from Naples, Florida, and enters the Big Cypress Swamp region, one can see extensive areas of Baldcypress scrub—low, scraggly trees that are struggling to

exist in harsh, rocky conditions. Some of these trees are probably quite old; one that is three inches in diameter may be twenty-five to thirty years of age. Near the road, larger Baldcypresses and the flowering air plants on their trunks occasionally catch one's eye. The reddish, leafy bracts of the flowering stalks are especially showy.

Aside from the stands of Baldcypress scrub in the Big Cypress Swamp, one also encounters cypress domes, or heads, which are elevated areas alongside depressions created by the dissolution of limestone. Some of the domes resemble doughnuts, with trees forming a circle around a "hole" of water in the center. The smaller Pondcypress usually dominates these domes, but Baldcypress may be present in the deeper water near the center. Cypress domes are also scattered within sandy pine forests, where the water is sealed by an underlying clay layer.

The origin of these domes is most likely related to fire and differing soil conditions within the depressions. During severe droughts, bad upland fires probably penetrated their edges, possibly killing all of the trees and even burning up the organic soil. This would have created conditions less favorable for tree growth around the margins of the domes. A very severe fire might kill all the trees and even burn up the soil. Then the depression would fill with water and become a pond.

Some of the best forests in the Big Cypress Swamp develop strands, which cover hundreds or even thousands of acres. Although various explanations have been proposed, the origin of these muck-filled depressions is not clear.

Baldcypress lumber has always been in great demand, because the wood is so durable. It is known in the trade as "wood everlasting."

Raccoon
Procyon lotor
614

Royal Palm
Roystonea regia

Red Maple
Acer rubrum
479

Carolina Ash (Pop Ash)
Fraxinus caroliniana
437

Dahoon Holly
Ilex cassine

Coastal Plain Willow
Salix caroliniana
455

Swamp Bay (Sweetbay)
Magnolia virginiana
449

One of the last mature forests in the Big Cypress to have been cut was the Fakahatchee Strand. Along a fifty-foot-wide swath there is now a memorial drive on the old railroad right-of-way where an extraordinary array of wildlife once could be seen. Herons and egrets constantly flew up from the road. Raccoons, ordinarily nocturnal, fed actively by day in the flooded roadside ditches. Venerable Royal Palms, which fortunately had been left standing, towered above the post-lumbering undergrowth, their cementlike trunks giving way above to bright green leaf sheaths and lovely fronds. Following logging, a dense undergrowth of Red Maple, Carolina or Pop Ash, Dahoon Holly, Coastal Plain Willow, and Swamp Bay developed along the road. In such dense cover, the reestablishment of a cypress forest can be a slow process.

An Emerald Kingdom: Corkscrew Swamp

Although few mature cypresses have survived in Florida, Corkscrew Swamp is an uncut gem that can be visited and enjoyed via a nearly two-mile-long boardwalk, which penetrates the various habitats of this wetland wilderness. The 11,000-acre Corkscrew Swamp Sanctuary is one of the finest cypress swamps in the world. (Corkscrew is a local term for cypress strand.) Originally more than twenty miles long and about three miles wide, the strand that is the Corkscrew Swamp has shrunk to a remnant of its former size: only three miles of the original length remain. One of the best ways of getting acquainted with such a swamp is to be given a guided tour—which will help clarify some of the complex interactions that occur within this wetland ecosystem.

Slash Pine
Pinus elliottii

Saw Palmetto
Paurotis wrightii

As we enter the Corkscrew Swamp from the upland Slash Pine area, which is scattered with Saw Palmettos, the boardwalk crosses an open, grassy meadow, a wet prairie dotted with wetland wild flowers.

At the other side of the wet meadow, we enter a low Pondcypress forest, where most of the trees are relatively small, and their trunks are encrusted with colorful lichens. Several varieties of air plants, including some bromeliads, are also attached to the tree trunks. Their small flowers are encased in colorful bracts on the long, flowering stalks. Members of the pineapple family and related to Spanish Moss, these air plants are not parasites as some people think, but are instead epiphytes, plants that merely "rent" space so that they can have a place in the sun. Because they are not rooted in the soil, air plants must be very frugal and store water and minerals from the rain or dust they collect from the air, in order to carry on photosynthesis. Their silver-gray, overlapping, tightly packed leaves hold water and serve as tiny nurseries where mosquitoes and other aquatic organisms breed.

Wild Pine
Tillandsia fasciculata
283

The most common bromeliad here is Wild Pine, one of a number in the genus found in Florida, and one that favors cypress as a host.

In a sunny spot, a long spray of beautiful yellowish-brown orchids hangs from a Baldcypress. The Cigar, or Cow Horn Orchid, another epiphyte, is easily recognized by its long, cigar-shaped, bulblike structures, which store food and water.

Butterfly Orchid
Encyclia tampensis
265

Clamshell Orchid
Epidendrum cochleatum

Other orchids to look for include the greenish-brown Butterfly Orchid, the most common in Florida, and the yellowish Clamshell Orchid, which is marked by a purple splotch on the lip petal.

Before entering the taller and most impressive part of the swamp, it should be noted that we have already gone through two distinct vegetation belts. This pattern, which is typical of most strands, has resulted from differences in soils, water levels, and fire history. The surrounding pinelands are perpetuated by periodic fires—to which pines are resistant, but which inhibit the growth of other trees. During very dry periods, fires often penetrate the drier edges of the strands, but do not touch the wetter interiors. This process tends to kill the woody growth in the prairie and also creates conditions favorable for the Pondcypress.

Water Lettuce
Pistia stratiotes
308

As we enter the large Baldcypress forest, we find trees of two to four feet in diameter that tower to heights of more than a hundred feet. Ahead, the trail opens out onto Lettuce Lake, a flooded clearing that is surrounded by magnificent cypresses with long trains of Spanish Moss. The water level changes with the seasons, fluctuating between a few inches and more than three feet. Water Lettuce, a floating aquatic, forms a

American Alligator
Alligator mississippiensis
172

Florida Redbelly Turtle
Chrysemys nelsoni
158

Florida Softshell Turtle
Trionyx ferox

"Great White Heron"
Ardea herodias
528

Little Blue Heron
Egretta caerulea
521, 525

Snowy Egret
Egretta thula
527

Louisiana Heron
Egretta tricolor

Great Blue Heron
Ardea herodias
528

White Ibis
Eudocimus albus

Wood Stork
Mycteria americana
524

Pickerelweed
Pontederia cordata
295

Arrowhead
Sagittaria latifolia
247

Limpkin
Aramus guarauna
522

Southern Cricket Frog
Acris gryllus
141, 142

Common Cattail
Typha latifolia
220

Snail Kite
Rostrhamus sociabilis
558

striking, thick green carpet that looks sturdy enough to walk on. Don't try it. Not only is it not strong enough to support anything heavier than a bird, but in addition, if you look closely, you may spot a sizable alligator lurking in the lettuce. Like the sloughs in the Everglades, cypress swamps have their share of these large reptiles. Red-belly Turtles sun themselves on logs emerging from the water, and the Florida Softshell, a swift, aggressive turtle, plies the shallows. A number of White Herons feed on small frogs, tadpoles, and fishes. The smaller, rather drab birds are Little Blue Herons, which, when mature, turn a uniform blue-gray. Also present are Snowy and Great egrets and Louisiana and Great Blue herons. Two large birds fly overhead; the smaller White Ibis has a three-foot wingspan, which is small compared with the five-foot span of the Wood Stork's wings. Whether the Wood Stork will have a successful nesting year here or in other swamps is of great concern to ornithologists and others interested in this magnificent bird. Locally called "Flintheads" because of their naked, gray heads, these storks nest together in enormous numbers; rookeries with up to 10,000 pairs have been recorded. However, in the past few decades, these birds have been on the decline. The primary problem appears to be an inadequate concentration of food fishes in the pools. It is urgent that suitable breeding habitats be preserved if this spectacular bird is to be saved from extinction.

In addition to the lettucelike rosettes of Water Lettuce (a plant that is found in tropical wetlands around the world), the blue spikes of Pickerelweed and belts of Arrowheads with their white, three-petaled flowers add color and diversity to the wetlands. These lush, marshy openings constantly add an organic supplement to the swamp and increase the depth of the rich swamp soil. Eventually the swamp may fill in and become covered with trees and shrubs.

A gray-brown bird the size of a goose feeds on freshwater Apple Snails with its down-curved bill. It is a Limpkin, a relative of the rails and the cranes. Called the "Crying Bird" because of its eerie, wailing call, Limpkins are often seen singly, wading or swimming in shallow water. It gives its *kurr-ee-ow, kra-ow* call often on cloudy days, as well as at dawn or dusk.

Of the ten species of frogs found in Corkscrew, the Southern Cricket Frog, which has a dark triangle between its eyes, is one of the most common; its rapidly repeated cricketlike clicks are a familiar sound in southern wetlands. The largest species, the Pig Frog, is sometimes called the "Bullfrog" in the South; it gets its name from the short, sharp grunt that it utters. The Pig Frog is the source of the edible frogs' legs served in some restaurants. In the wild, this frog floats almost continuously among Cattails and other aquatics.

Masses of the white egg cases of the freshwater Apple Snails can also be seen along the trail. The cases are attached to plant stems, for the eggs must develop above water. These snails are not only an important food source of the Limpkin, but are also the sole food of the Snail Kite, a tropical member of the hawk

Barred Owl
Strix varia
566

American Swallow-tailed Kite
Elanoides forficatus
559

Eastern Kingbird
Tyrannus tyrannus

Green Anole
Anolis carolinensis

Bobcat
Felis rufus
616

White-tailed Deer
Odocoileus virginianus
617

Cougar
Felix concolor

Gray Squirrel
Sciurus carolinensis

Fox Squirrel
Sciurus niger

River Otter
Lutra canadensis
612

Poison Ivy
Rhus radicans

Sweetbay
Magnolia virginiana
449

Redbay
Persea borbonia
451

Titi or Swamp Cyrilla
Cyrilla racemiflora
243

Swamp Lily
Crinum americanum
227

Fire Flag
Thalia geniculata
303

Strangler Fig
Ficus aurea

family that is uncommon in our range. This bird has a thin, sharply curved bill well-suited to extracting the mollusk from its shell. Draining marshes has had a very negative effect on populations of Snail Kites.

One of the largest birds of the Corkscrew Swamp is the Barred Owl. This common species can be heard giving its familiar *who-cooks-for-you?* call from branches; it usually hunts small prey, such as frogs and small mammals.

Throughout the year, a variety of songbirds can be heard throughout the swamp, and during the winter season, northern migrants join them. More than forty species of birds are permanent residents of the sanctuary. Summer residents include the elegant Swallow-tailed Kite—whose dramatically forked tail and back-swept outline are striking identification marks—and the Eastern Kingbird, which is frequently seen hawking insects from a perch in a bush or tree.

A little green lizard, the Green Anole, may be seen skittering across the boardwalk or along the railing. With patience you can get a good look at this handsome reptile—once a principal commodity of the pet trade—which can change color from green to brown in a very short time. During courtship the males display bright pink neck fans.

Animals like Bobcats, Deer, Raccoons, and Cougars also depend upon wetlands much more than one might think. Gray and Fox squirrels are also found in the swamp, along with the River Otter, which is truly dependent on the wetland, and which is sometimes visible from the boardwalk.

The undergrowth is full of a number of interesting plants. Anyone from the north will recognize the wide-ranging Red Maple, a typical tree of northern wetland swamps. Poison Ivy, another familiar plant, is quite tolerant of wet conditions. Its fruits are prized by several birds and other wildlife. The fragrant white flowers of the evergreen Sweetbay, a magnolia, are worth a sniff. They are a small version of the magnificent flowers of the larger magnolias so often cultivated around southern mansions. Redbay, Dahoon Holly, Waxmyrtle, and Titi or Swamp Cyrilla are other plants that provide cover and nesting sites for birds. Pop Ash (a relative of the White Ash, from which baseball bats are made) produces winged fruits that aid in the dispersal of this species.

Ferns are especially common in this rich, moist environment. The most spectacular is the huge, evergreen Leather Fern, which has fronds that grow as long as twelve feet. Clumps of wild Boston or Sword Fern are common. Strap Ferns dangle, strap-fashion, from logs. Up on the branches of some of the trees is the unusual Resurrection Fern. Under dry conditions, its leaves curl and the fern appears dead; when the rains come, it seems magically to come back to life.

In the spaces between the ferns, the beautiful white Swamp Lily—really an amaryllis—may bloom. Clumps of Fire Flags have spoon-shaped leaves and small blue flowers. Strangler Figs find the trees of Corkscrew congenial hosts, eventually engulfing entire trees. In the Lettuce Lake area, one can also see Cabbage Palms and the rare Royal Palm along the trail.

Cabbage Palm
Roystonea oleracea

The latter tree is thought to have been introduced to this area in the early 1960s, when its seed may have been transported from the Fakahatchee by a bird. (Such an event emphasizes the importance of preserving wilderness islands, which provide places for the establishment of rare and unusual species.)

The Marsh

The boardwalk opens out onto a large marsh, which is covered by a rich spectrum of light-loving marsh plants, including Saw Grass, which is common in the Everglades, Pickerelweed, Arrowhead, and a variety of wetland grasses and other sedges. Willow thickets appear here and there, and may increase in number and range until fire halts their advance. Marshes—or prairies, as they are sometimes called—are often part of a cypress-swamp strand. Some have borders of floating sphagnum moss that contain a variety of insectivorous plants, such as Pitcher Plants, Trumpets, and Sundews. In more open water, huge beds of yellow-flowered Horned Bladderwort present a breathtaking sight. This carnivorous plant sucks in tiny aquatic organisms with its many little bladders and digests them to obtain their nutrients.

Trumpet
Sarracenia flava
224

Horned Bladderwort
Utricularia cornuta
218

Cypress swamps are mysterious places. Scattered throughout the South, many can be visited by either boardwalk or boat. In these wetlands, one encounters an amazing diversity of plants and animals. There is considerable evidence that this diversity helps to maintain a stable, healthy ecosystem, although this conclusion is questioned by some experts. Nonetheless, certain species are sensitive to natural phenomena, as is the case with the Wood Stork's reaction to natural water fluctuations. The interaction between different degrees of flooding, soil conditions, and fire has created the mosaic of vegetation types found in the cypress swamp.

What will the fate of these cypress swamps be? Strange as it may seem, these communities depend on fire as well as on water to perpetuate their particular mix of plant and animal life. And the importance of water lies not simply in its presence but also in its annual cycle. Fire plays its part in shaping the domes and maintaining the prairies.

A visit to a cypress swamp is a memorable experience. In early spring, the observation tower in Okefenokee offers a view of the light, bare, spreading branches of the Baldcypress outlined against the still, black swamp water, from which rise the brilliant tips of Golden Club. This is surely a sight worth preserving.

Golden Club
Orontium aquaticum
222

CYPRESS SWAMPS: PLANTS AND ANIMALS

Fishes
Alligator Gar 78
Chain Pickerel 75
Golden Shiner 70
Green Sunfish 54
Least Killifish 101
Pirate Perch 57
Starhead Topminnow 65
Swamp Darter 61
Walking Catfish 83
Warmouth 47

Amphibians
Bullfrog 136, 137
Green Frog 134
Lesser Siren 107
Mud Salamander 111, 116, 118, 119
Red Salamander 120
River Frog 135
Southern Cricket Frog 141, 142
Spring Peeper 150
Striped Chorus Frog 132
Two-lined Salamander 110, 121

Reptiles
American Alligator 172
Black Swamp Snake 181, 183
Brown Water Snake 190
Cottonmouth 175, 177, 194
Florida Red-bellied Turtle 158
Glossy Crayfish Snake 184
Green Water Snake 185
Mud Snake 182
Razorback Musk Turtle 168
Slider 157, 163
Snapping Turtle 151
Southern Water Snake 191, 196
Timber Rattlesnake 193, 197, 198

Wildflowers, Ferns, and Grasses
Arrowhead 247
Buttonbush 237
Butterfly Orchid 265
Cinnamon Fern 304
Crimson Pitcher Plant 280
Delicate Ionopsis 232
Elderberry 242
Golden Club 222
Green Dragon 311
Hibiscus 275
Horned Bladderwort 218
Jack-in-the-pulpit 309, 327
Lizard's Tail 236
Pickerelweed 295
Red Iris 276
Royal Fern 306
Soft Rush 324
Spotted Touch-me-not 279
Swamp Honeysuckle 229
Swamp Rose 273
Sweet Pepperbush 235
Tall Meadow Rue 257
Titi 243
Trumpets 224
Water Hemlock 240
Water Hyacinth 296
Water Lettuce 308
Wild Pine 283
Winterberry 244, 328
Wood Grass 322
Yaupon 329

Mushrooms
Wrinkled Thimble-cap 337

Insects and Spiders
American Horse Fly 378
Golden-silk Spider 383
Vinegar Fly 381

Butterflies and Moths
Appalachian Brown 400, 408
Broken Dash 424
Creole Pearly Eye 410
Harvester 394
Lace-winged Roadside Skipper 411
Palamedes Swallowtail 389

Trees
Baldcypress 433
Black Ash 435
Black Tupelo 443
Carolina Ash 437
Dahoon 448
Loblolly-bay 460
Possumhaw 469
Red Maple 479

Redbay 451
Sweetbay 449
Water-elm 464
Water Tupelo 462

Birds
American Swallow-tailed Kite 559
Anhinga 518
Barred Owl 566
Black-crowned Night-Heron 529
Great Blue Heron 528
Green-backed Heron 534
Limpkin 522
Little Blue Heron 521, 525
Pileated Woodpecker 569
Red-bellied Woodpecker 570
Red-shouldered Hawk 564
Short-tailed Hawk 560
White-faced Ibis 523
Wood Duck 491
Wood Stork 524
Yellow-crowned Night-Heron 530

Mammals
Black Bear 615
Bobcat 616
Cotton Mouse 597
Golden Mouse 598
Raccoon 614
White-tailed Deer 617

SOUTHERN BOTTOMLAND HARDWOOD SWAMPS

Baldcypress
Taxodium distichum
433

Loblolly Pine
Pinus taeda

The southern bottomland hardwoods are river swamps, rarely more than five miles wide, that can stretch half the length of a coastal state. They are made up of forests of different species of gum and oak, and of the graceful Baldcypress—trees that may be either seasonally flooded or covered with water much of the year. Two identifying features of these systems are the fluted or flaring trunks that develop in several species and the presence of knees, or aerial roots, on the Baldcypress. During the winter, the larger trees are virtually without foliage. The bays, hollies, and magnolias, however, lend a touch of evergreen to the undergrowth.

I remember my first visit to the Congaree River hardwoods, a magnificent bottomland forest near Columbia, South Carolina. A colleague and I were undertaking a survey of wetlands to determine which ones should be given National Landmark status. As we penetrated the dark forest of giant gums, oaks, and Loblolly Pine, I knew we had found a gem. We were driven in a water buggy down a flooded woods road to a hunting camp on stilts, which today, along with the surrounding land, forms the Congaree Swamp National Monument. In this mature forest there are forty species of wetland trees, giants that often tower to heights of more than a hundred feet and that measure up to six feet in diameter. These huge specimens are the trees that were spared or overlooked by lumberjacks, and which have, fortunately, been subsequently preserved.

Distribution

When Europeans first arrived in this country, these magnificent bottomland forests covered some thirty million acres; today only about forty percent of this area still supports bottomland hardwood swamps. The remainder has been converted to farmland. Although the crops that are produced are important, such land is often more valuable when left in its natural state.

These river swamps occur on the coastal plain that extends from Virginia south to Florida and westward along the Gulf of Mexico to the Mississippi River drainage basin. They fringe such major southern rivers as the Roanoke, the Pee Dee, the Altamaha, the Alcovy, the Suwannee, the Apalachicola, the Chattahoochee, and the Mississippi—arteries that drain most of the interior of the southeastern and Gulf Coast states.

Anyone who has driven from the Northeast to Florida along one of the coastal routes will recall crossing low bridges for a mile or two just above the dark waters of a flooded swamp forest. Along the Gulf Coast, engineers have constructed elevated highways over these extensive wetland systems.

Ecology

The Mississippi alluvial plain, a major part of the bottomlands region, originally included twenty-four million acres. Today fewer than five million acres—or twenty percent of the region—are left in their original state. Tree cutting and channelization were carried out in the process of draining the land for growing cotton and corn. Now soybeans, a short-

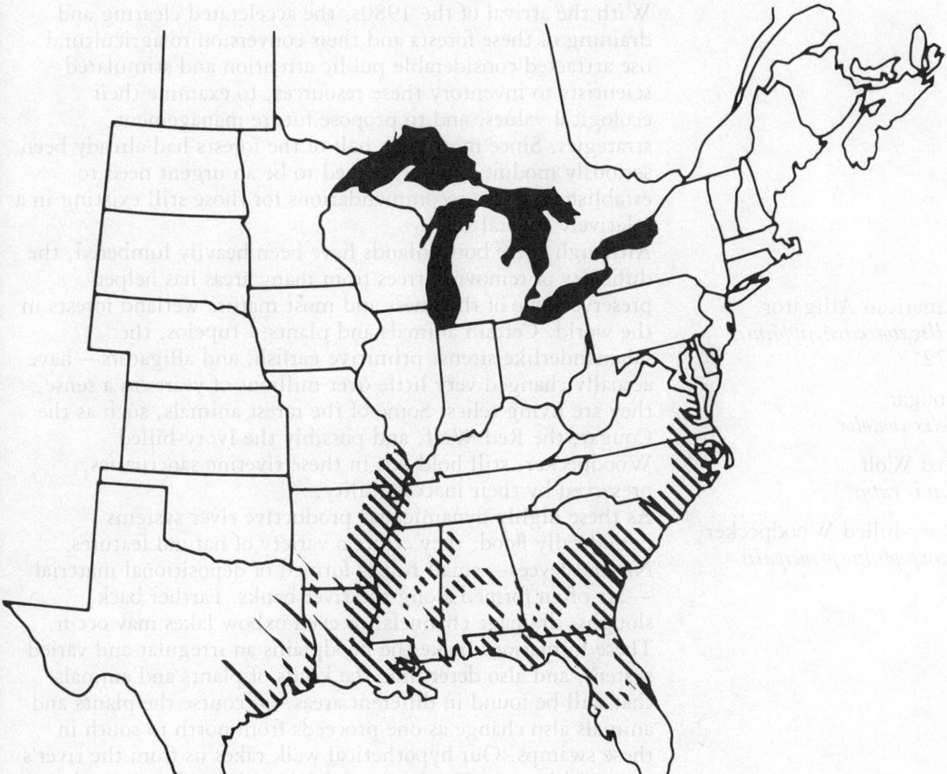

season crop that is well-adapted to the drained bottomland soils—and which is in great demand worldwide—have become a lucrative cash crop in many parts of the South. With the arrival of the 1980s, the accelerated clearing and draining of these forests and their conversion to agricultural use attracted considerable public attention and stimulated scientists to inventory these resources, to examine their ecological values, and to propose future management strategies. Since more than half of the forests had already been seriously modified, there seemed to be an urgent need to establish land-use recommendations for those still existing in a relatively natural state.

American Alligator
Alligator mississippiensis
172

Cougar
Felix concolor

Red Wolf
Canis rufus

Ivory-billed Woodpecker
Campephilus principalis

Although these bottomlands have been heavily lumbered, the difficulty of removing trees from many areas has helped preserve some of the finest and most mature wetland forests in the world. Certain animals and plants—tupelos, the salamanderlike sirens, primitive garfish, and alligators—have actually changed very little over millions of years; in a sense, they are living relics. Some of the rarest animals, such as the Cougar, the Red Wolf, and possibly the Ivory-billed Woodpecker, still hold out in these riverine sanctuaries, preserved by their inaccessibility.

As these highly dynamic and productive river systems periodically flood, they create a variety of natural features. Natural levees—small ridges formed of depositional material—are often formed along the river banks. Farther back, sloughs, drainage channels, or even oxbow lakes may occur. These formations make the floodplains an irregular and varied system, and also determine the kinds of plants and animals that will be found in different areas. Of course the plants and animals also change as one proceeds from north to south in these swamps. Our hypothetical walk takes us from the river's edge and levee across the floodplain, with its sloughs and pools scattered in the higher spots. Thus we see an ever-changing mosaic typical of highly dynamic systems where the river is constantly at work over the floodplain.

The Flooded River's Edge

Water Tupelo
Nyssa aquatica
462

Ogeechee Tupelo
Nyssa ogeche

Water Elm
Ulmus americana

Carolina Ash
Fraxinus caroliniana
437

Pumpkin Ash
Fraxinus profunda

This almost continuously flooded forest along the river's edge is dominated by huge Water Tupelo and Baldcypress, both of which are characterized by swollen or buttressed trunks. Ogeechee Tupelo, which is found in Georgia and northern Florida, is another flood-tolerant gum. A few other trees, such as Water Elm, Carolina Ash, and Pumpkin Ash, may also occur in this belt, which is flooded for eighty to ninety percent of the year.

The trees that can withstand this flooded environment have various ways of aerating their roots. The knees of Baldcypress may be a structural adaptation that helps in this regard, although studies have shown that when the knees are removed, the tree's growth seems unaffected. When flooded, ash trees develop adventitious roots (roots that develop in an unusual spot) to aid air uptake. The tupelos have internal mechanisms for dealing with this problem.

River Otter
Lutra canadensis
612

Bullfrog
Rana catesbeiana
136, 137

Alligator Gar
Lepisosteus spatula
78

Cottonmouth
Agkistrodon piscivorus
175, 177, 194

Banded Water Snake
Nerodia fasciata

Yellow-crowned Night-Heron
Nycticorax violaceus
530

Hooded Merganser
Lophodytes cucullatus
509

Prothonotary Warbler
Protonotaria citrea
585

Along the edge of the sluggish river, water lilies and submerged aquatic plants provide cover for the River Otter, which feeds on Bullfrogs and the large, eel-like salamanders called congo-eels or amphiumas. Nearby, alligators are pursuing gar, a favorite fish, or an occasional Cottonmouth or Banded Water Snake.

In the trees one can spot a chunky bird with a yellowish crown of plumes and a white-checked wing pattern. It is the Yellow-Crowned Night-Heron, a rather solitary and somewhat sinister-looking bird that usually nests in colonies. The Night-Heron's feeding habit is an interesting one: It tosses its catch into the air to swallow it head first. On the water is a small flock of Hooded Mergansers, which are expert divers. The males can be easily distinguished by their fan-shaped, black-bordered white crests. Using both feet and wings to propel themselves, they dive in pursuit of small fish, crayfish, frogs, or aquatic insects. They nest in tree cavities. Songbirds brighten up this dark swamp forest with their songs—especially the golden orange Prothonotary Warbler, a water-loving species that sounds a loud, ascending "sweet-sweet-sweet." Like the Hooded Merganser, the Prothonotary makes its nest in a tree cavity, which is unusual for a warbler.

These heavily flooded forests are not restricted to the water's edge. Sometimes tupelo-cypress stands are formed in sloughs, backwater swamps, or bayous that are almost permanently flooded. When the water briefly recedes from these areas, it is an unforgettable experience to walk among the trees. At Florida's Sutton Lake on the Apalachicola River, where the slough floods to fourteen feet, the massive, steeplelike cypress knees stand twelve feet high, dwarfing the visitor. Some gums may also develop strangely shaped, black aerial knees that resemble stools.

Overcup Oak
Quercus lyrata
475

Water Hickory
Carya aquatica
439

Waterlocust
Gleditsia aquatica

Black Willow
Salix nigra
453

Red Maple
Acer rubrum
479

Silver Maple
Acer saccharinum
478

A dry period is an especially good time to view the flaring trunks of gums and Baldcypress. This unusual shape is a characteristic that may have developed to stabilize trees that are in water so much of the time, and which—since they do not develop a deep, anchoring root system—may thus be more easily blown down. Toppled trees reveal the root system, which spreads horizontally and is massively wider than it is thick. In upright trees, most of the roots are concentrated near the surface, which probably helps these trees get oxygen. The stains on the trees' trunks reflect the high-water mark.

Farther from the River's Edge

As we move from the bank of the river and toward the upland, the vegetation and animals change in response to the degree of flooding. As we enter the area where flooding occurs perhaps only a third of the year, the tupelos and cypresses are replaced by trees such as Overcup Oak, Water Hickory, Waterlocust, Black Willow, Red and Silver maples, magnolias, and bays. These trees, like those closer to the river, can reach three to four feet in diameter and can attain heights of more than one hundred feet. Overcup Oak is quite common and especially easy to recognize: Its acorn is very different from those of most

Sugarberry
Celtis laevigata
463

Diamond Leaf (Laurel) Oak
Quercus laurifolia
447

Water Oak
Quercus nigra
474

Willow Oak
Quercus phellos
452

Swamp Chestnut Oak
Quercus michauxii
473

Raccoon
Procyon lotor
614

White-tailed Deer
Odocoileus virginianus
617

Bobcat
Felis rufus
616

Golden Mouse
Ochrotomys nuttalli
598

Swamp Rabbit
Sylvilagus aquaticus
606

Wood Duck
Aix sponsa
491

Mallard
Anas platyrhynchos
492

Wild Turkey
Meleagris gallopavo
567

Swainson's Warbler
Limnothlypis swainsonii
581

oaks, since the cup, or cap, almost completely covers the fruit. Even nearer the upland, where flooding occurs for yet shorter periods, one can find Sugarberry, Sweetgum, and a number of oaks—Diamond leaf (Laurel), Water, Willow, Swamp Chestnut, Cherrybark—as well as large Lobolly Pine closest to the upland border. These species represent only a sample of the great variety that occurs.

Animals to look for in the floodplain area are the Raccoon—which can also be found at the water's edge—Gray Fox, White-tailed Deer, and Bobcat. Although all of these are typical upland species as well, they can often be highly dependent upon bottomland forests for food and cover. The Golden Mouse and the Swamp Rabbit—the counterpart of the Marsh Rabbit, which occurs farther east—must keep a constant lookout for Fox, Bobcat, and Canebrake Rattler. Swamp Rabbits have slightly splayed feet with strong-nailed toes to facilitate movement over the wet soil. They are also excellent swimmers and can escape from their predators by remaining submerged except for the tip of the nose. One of their favorite foods is cane, a bamboo grass. The Marsh Rabbit has developed a rather amazing adaptation to wetland life: If flooding occurs during the breeding season, a developing embryo may be resorbed into the female's placenta, helping to ensure survival of newborn rabbits.

The Golden Mouse, which is golden cinnamon color above and white beneath, is a great tree climber that can go as high as thirty feet or more. It runs over the branches, using its tail as a balancing pole. High in the trees, it builds a grapefruit-sized nest of Spanish Moss or pine needles. It feeds on acorns and seeds.

Other animals that are closely dependent upon these forests include a number of birds, especially waterfowl and migrating species. The acorn cups from the many kinds of oaks that grow here provide an enormous food supply. For example, it has been estimated that a single, large hundred-year-old Water Oak can produce nearly 30,000 acorns in one year. Collectively, the fruit and seed crops from these bottomland trees provide an invaluable food resource. In the fall, millions of migrating grackles precede the ducks and feed on these acorns. In the Mississippi alluvial floodplain basin, some four million Wood Ducks and two and one-half million Mallards that use the "Mississippi Flyway" appropriate these bottomlands as their winter grounds. The spectacular Wood Duck, considered by many to be the most beautiful North American duck, is highly dependent upon acorns. The Wild Turkeys that breed and nest in the bottomlands are also heavy consumers of the fruit crop. In some years, ten percent or more of the acorn crop is eaten by birds alone.

Among the songbirds are such winter migrants as the beautiful Ruby-crowned Kinglet, White-throated and White-crowned sparrows, American Goldfinch, Pine Siskin, and Purple Finch. One of the permanent residents is the uncommon and generally inconspicuous Swainson's Warbler; this bird, with its distinctive reddish crown, is one of the species that are most admired by bird watchers. It has an affinity for the canebrakes and—oddly—for an entirely different habitat, mountain thickets.

River cane, of which there are large and small species, often forms dense stands. Some of the best canebrakes in the bottomland forest understory are found in central Georgia, along the Ocmulgee River, which drains the heart of the state. The larger species, Giant Cane, grows up to thirty feet in height and forms bamboo poles that reach an inch or more in diameter. An early botanist, William Bartram, recorded canebrakes that were up to forty feet tall with stems reaching three to four inches in diameter—dimensions that approach those of tropical species. In 1765, on the banks of the Altamaha River, Bartram also discovered the Franklinia, a tree that was named in honor of Benjamin Franklin. Twenty-five years after it was discovered, the tree was extinct in the wild, presumably in part as a result of over-collecting. Today this tree, with its beautiful, white, camellialike flower, is found only in cultivation.

Franklinia
Gordonia alatamaha

In addition to the cane, there is a great diversity of ground-inhabiting plants in these areas. As one nears the upland, where the flooding is less prolonged, sedges, ferns, and wildflowers increase in abundance. Old logs and stumps are a particularly good habitat: Twenty-four different kinds of plants have been found in such areas, including the fragrant Spider Lily, which is named for its white, spiderlike petals.

Spider Lily
Hymenocallis liriosme
228

Associated with the canebrakes is a form of the Timber Rattler called the Canebrake Rattler. It and the Copperhead pose a threat to the Swamp Rabbit, which favors the young grass shoots of the cane. The brightly colored Green Treefrog, which has a light stripe along its lower jaw and side, is one of the most conspicuous of the amphibians. When assembled in a large chorus and heard from a distance, these frogs produce a sound reminiscent of cowbells. Heard from nearby, the call becomes a *quank, quank*. This frog's arboreal existence is facilitated by the adhesive discs on its toes. During the day, it sleeps under a leaf or in some other shady spot. Sometimes the Green Treefrog jumps into the air to escape its enemies.

Timber Rattler
Crotalus horridus
193, 197, 198

Copperhead
Agkistrodon contortrix

Green Treefrog
Hyla cinerea

Interactions in the Aquatic Food Chain

Every year the bottomland swamps receive an extraordinary amount of dead plant material that falls from the dense canopy above. Eight to ten tons of leaves per acre may be contributed annually to the detrital food chain. Pure stands of river cane alone can add up to seven tons of material per acre, which is a vast amount of energy-rich grass for the decomposers to consume. In these bottomland forests, as in certain other aquatic environments, two major kinds of food chains operate. The grazer chain involves the direct consumption of leaves, shoots, and fruits; examples might include a rabbit's browsing on young tree shoots and a waterfowl's consumption of acorns. The detrital food chain, which processes decomposed material, is also very important, because so much of the plant material is not consumed directly.

Most of the leaves that fall into the water form a rich organic stew, food for a tremendous number of aquatic organisms. Each season's vast tonnage of leaf fall fuels billions of mostly tiny, shrimplike organisms—the crustaceans. These amphipods and isopods, along with insect larvae and small worms (oligochaetes), work over the dead organic-food supply. These small consumers are extremely numerous; there may be as many as 10,000 of these animals in an area of three square feet.

Most of the creatures that feed on detrital material—including the Crayfish, which is common in these swamps—are shredders: They chew or shred the leaves into small particles and set the stage for another attack by trillions of bacteria and water fungi. When the shredders die, they further enrich the leafy organic matter with their dead bodies, which are protein- or nitrogen-rich. Another important group in this detrital system consists of the scrubbers, such as snails, which scrape the algal and bacterial scum from leaves and other surfaces in the water.

Caddisfly
Rhyacophila fenestra

Stonefly
Perlesta placida

Mayfly
Ephemerella spinifera

Midge
Chironomus attenuatus

As these myriad organisms break down the leaves, they also release feces—which ecologists refer to as fine particulate organic matter, or FPOM. This organic broth feeds the larvae of caddisflies, stoneflies, mayflies, and midges, as well as the clams that strain this food material. As many as 40,000 of these organisms have been recorded in a three-foot-square plot.

In addition to the coarse and fine particulate material, there is dissolved organic matter (DOM), a kind of nutrient juice that leaches out of the leaves after they have fallen into the water; this may account for up to a third of the leaf's weight. Certain organisms quickly ingest these nutrients.

An interesting reversal of the food chain can be seen in the swamps. Bladderworts, fascinating, carnivorous plants closely related to snapdragons, have small, egg-shaped bladders attached to some of their submerged leaves; they use these bladders to capture tiny aquatic organisms, which they digest to obtain protein and nitrogen.

Greater Siren
Siren lacertina
106

Many of these organisms—especially the aquatic insects—are vital links in the important food chains. Many are eaten by fish or other animals, such as the black, eel-like Greater Siren, a common salamander that lacks hind legs. This creature may grow to a length of more than two feet and lay as many as 200 eggs in crayfish burrows. At birth, the Greater Siren is only half an inch long, but it grows quickly. When excited, the Siren gives off a clucking sound, and "yells" when captured. It is preyed on by fish, herons, and alligators.

Six-spotted Fishing Spider
Dolomedes triton
382

Liverwort
Marchantia polymorpha

The Fishing Spider, another creature in the middle range of the food chain, can stay underwater for thirty minutes or more by using the air trapped by its hairy body. Although it feeds on small fish and tadpoles, it can lose its life to larger fish. Frequently this spider hides under Liverwort, a relative of the mosses that forms a green, leafy crust. These tiny plants act as a flood-level indicator by forming dense carpets on the trunks of trees up to the high-water mark.

More than fifty species of fish spawn or feed in this wetland ecosystem. Members of the catfish, sunfish, gar, perch, and sucker families are most common, and their abundance is closely correlated with annual water fluctuations and competition for food, especially for the aquatic organisms dependent upon detritis. Fishermen know how important the floodplain overflow is in controlling both the number and size of Black Bass and Sunfish. Several herring species and the Hickory Shad use sloughs and bayous as their spawning grounds. The Blueback Herring has a remarkable adaptation: It attaches its sticky eggs to submerged twigs or other fixed objects so that they will not be swept downstream. It is estimated that half of the fishes in the lower Mississippi use these swamps during their early stages of development.

Black Bass
Centropistis striata

Sunfish
Lepomis spp.

Hickory Shad
Alosa mediocris

Blueback Herring
Alosa aestivalis

If both the land and water habitats of the swamp environment are considered, it becomes evident that swamps support a tremendous diversity of plant and animal life. Without them there would be no place for many of these organisms.

Human Impact on the Bottomland Forests

Bottomland forests have long served the need for timber. In addition to cypress, many of these areas' hardwoods are valuable timber trees. Commercially used trees of the southern hardwood forests include the Carolina and Pumpkin ashes, American Elm, the tupelos, and nearly twenty species of bottomland oak. If done properly, lumbering need not have an adverse effect on these forests and can be carried on year after year.

American Elm
Ulmus americana
465

As one might expect, fish production is also high in these habitats: Some river swamps annually produce more than 1000 pounds of fish per acre. However, productivity of the swamps is not limited to the bottomlands: The nutrient-rich waters of these areas also have a profound effect on places like Barataria Bay, Louisiana, where a huge number of commercial fish are taken.

Besides fish, these bottomlands provide human beings with waterfowl and fur-bearing animals. The industries and jobs associated with these animals may not be as economically significant as fishing, but to people who live in or near the swamps, hunting or trapping can mean a great deal—either as an income supplement or as a means of providing food. And economics aside, one must also consider the recreational and aesthetic pleasure that such wild places give.

Probably the greatest threat to bottomland swamps has come from efforts to channel or drain them. Such action totally disrupts the ecology of these areas. The pulsing process of the system is lost, and productivity declines drastically. The fish populations alone have been known to drop ninety-eight percent as a result of such measures.

With over half of these wetlands already diverted to other uses, what will be the fate of those that remain? Scientists have helped to give new insight into the wetlands' ecological role, but their future remains to be seen.

SOUTHERN BOTTOMLAND HARDWOOD SWAMPS: PLANTS AND ANIMALS

Fishes
Alligator Gar 78
Chain Pickerel 75
Golden Shiner 70
Green Sunfish 54
Least Killifish 101
Pirate Perch 57
Starhead Topminnow 65
Swamp Darter 61
Warmouth 47

Amphibians
Bird-voiced Treefrog 147
Bullfrog 136, 137
Dwarf Siren 108
Greater Siren 106
Green Frog 134
Lesser Siren 107
Mud Salamander 111, 116, 118, 119
Red Salamander 120
River Frog 135
Southern Cricket Frog 141, 142
Spring Peeper 150
Striped Chorus Frog 132
Two-lined Salamander 110, 121
Two-toed Amphiuma 103

Reptiles
American Alligator 172
Black Swamp Snake 181, 183
Brown Water Snake 190
Cottonmouth 175, 177, 194
Glossy Crayfish Snake 184
Green Water Snake 185
Mud Snake 182
Painted Turtle 159, 161, 162
Razorback Musk Turtle 168
Slider 157, 163
Southern Water Snake 191, 196
Timber Rattlesnake 193, 197, 198

Wildflowers, Ferns and Grasses
Buttonbush 237
Titi 243
Yaupon 329

Mushrooms
Wrinkled Thimble-cap 337

Insects and Spiders
American Horse Fly 378
Golden-silk Spider 383
Vinegar Fly 381

Butterflies and Moths
Appalachian Brown 400, 408
Broken Dash 424
Creole Pearly Eye 410
Harvester 394
Lace-winged Roadside Skipper 411
Palamedes Swallowtail 389

Trees
Atlantic White-cedar 429
Baldcypress 433
Black Ash 435
Black Tupelo 443
Black Willow 453
Buckwheat-tree 446
Carolina Ash 437
Dahoon 448
Honeylocust 434
Loblolly-bay 460
Northern White-cedar 428
Nutmeg Hickory 440
Overcup Oak 475
Poison Sumac 441
Possumhaw 469
Red Maple 479
Redbay 451
Silver Maple 478
Sugarberry 463
Swamp Chestnut Oak 473
Swamp-privet 456
Sweetbay 449
Water-elm 464
Water Hickory 439
Water Oak 474
Water Tupelo 462
Willow Oak 452

Birds
American Swallow-tailed Kite 559
Anhinga 518
Bald Eagle 562
Barred Owl 566
Black-crowned Night-

Heron 529
Common Yellowthroat 584
Double-crested Cormorant 520
Hooded Merganser 509
Little Blue Heron 521, 525
Louisiana Water Thrush 578
Osprey 563
Prothonotary Warbler 585
Red-bellied Woodpecker 570
Red-shouldered Hawk 564
Red-winged Blackbird 580, 588
Swainson's Warbler 581
Swamp Sparrow 576
Wild Turkey 567
Wood Duck 491
Yellow-crowned Night-Heron 530

Mammals
Beaver 611
Black Bear 615
Bobcat 616
Cotton Mouse 597
Golden Mouse 598
Mink 613
Moose 618
Muskrat 609
Raccoon 614
River Otter 612
Smoky Shrew 593
Southern Red-backed Vole 601, 602
Star-nosed Mole 595
Swamp Rabbit 606
White-tailed Deer 617

LAKES AND PONDS

Lakes and ponds are inland bodies of water, which may be either natural or man-made. They can be large or small, deep or shallow, and may vary greatly in their chemical and physical makeup. Whether fed by streams, groundwater, or runoff, lakes and ponds have water as their primary life-support system.

How do lakes and ponds differ? Ponds are usually smaller and shallower, but it is water temperature that principally distinguishes them. The water temperature of ponds is relatively uniform, whereas in lakes—because they are deeper—there is a layering effect: In summer, warmer water lies at the surface, and colder water toward the bottom.

Extensive marshes sometimes develop along the edges of lakes and ponds in water that is only a few feet deep, and there we find such typical marsh plants as cattails, bulrushes, and water lilies. Shallow ponds can become completely engulfed by marshy vegetation, and some may eventually become marshes.

Distribution

In the United States, there are an estimated 100,000 lakes that are over one hundred acres in size, and an uncounted number of smaller lakes and ponds. These bodies of water abound in parts of the country that were once subject to glaciation, including the Northeast and the Great Lakes states. Minnesota, for example, has 17,000 natural lakes; Michigan, 11,000; and Wisconsin, 8700. Thousands of the prairie potholes in the Dakotas and adjacent Canada are also of glacial origin.

In the Southeast, many shallow lakes were formed by the receding ocean, or as a result of the action of river systems or earthquakes, or through the dissolution of limestone rock. Sinkhole lakes are especially common in Florida and Louisiana.

In the mountains of the West, at altitudes of more than 4000 feet, cold-water lakes are of glacial origin, while others, like Oregon's Crater Lake, formed in extinct volcanoes. There are even sand dune lakes, such as Moses Lake in Washington, which occupies a depression formed when sand blew out and the water table rose.

In the Southwest, natural lakes are few; most are playa lakes, which are formed after heavy rains and are temporary in nature. Many kinds of artificial lakes have been created by people: farm ponds; reservoirs; and hydroelectric, irrigation, and flood-control dams. Some, like the Southwest's Lake Mead offer both recreational and electrical resources. Beaver dams are also a force in the creation of lakes.

Ecology

Lakes are of particular importance because they serve as catchment basins for forty percent of the nation's landscape. They supply fresh drinking water, irrigate fields, generate electricity, provide wildlife habitats, and serve as recreational areas where one can fish, boat, and swim. Lakes have always attracted people. Those that partake of the lake's offerings must exercise care to ensure that their activities do not result in pollution problems.

In the energy-flow pattern of lakes or ponds, phytoplankton and other aquatic plants form the base of the food chain, and zooplankton and other aquatic animals serve as primary consumers. They in turn provide food for the secondary consumers, such as fish and snakes. When plants die, their remains contribute to the lake or pond sediments. The detritus food chain, working on these sediments, completes the decomposition process and makes mineral nutrients available once more to the primary producers. The lakes may also receive mineral input from the surrounding land. Groundwater seepage and streams carrying silt and nutrient runoff are further sources of nutrient enrichment.

Lake Trout
Salvelinus namaycush
88

The life in lakes and ponds is controlled by such factors as temperature, light, the amount of nutrients, and the availability of oxygen. For example, Lake Trout require cold-water lakes, whereas sunfishes and bass can tolerate warmer lakes and ponds. Algal blooms occur only in the upper, well-lighted waters of a lake and are limited by the availability of certain nutrients, especially phosphorus. During late summer, when lakes are stratified, oxygen levels can become so low in the bottom waters that large fish kills occur.

Lakes may be categorized as young, middle-aged, or mature. Young or oligotrophic, lakes are usually too deficient in mineral nutrients—particularly phosphorus—to support plant growth. The sediments in these lakes are primarily inorganic. Lacking phytoplankton blooms and rooted plants, the system's productivity is low; the water of such lakes is very clear, like that of Lake Tahoe, which is located between California and Nevada.

Over time, lakes tend to be enriched by introduced nutrients and become middle-aged; the continuation of this process of enrichment eventually leads to maturity. When a lake becomes overly enriched, it is in danger of dying. Such mature lakes are termed eutrophic (literally, "well-fed") and are characterized by an abundance of organic matter in the sediments and much decomposer activity. People have aided in the aging process of lakes by contributing sewage and fertilizer runoff from farmland.

Common Cattail
Typha latifolia
220

Pickerelweed
Pontederia cordata
295

Yellow Pond Lily
Nuphar variegatum
214

Even the shape of lakes can influence their productivity. Those that drop off sharply from the bank are usually oligotrophic, since the development of vegetation is inhibited by the fact that it has no shallow margin to attach to. Bowl-shaped lakes, on the other hand, have a shallow marginal zone, where rooted aquatic plants may easily become established. Small ponds often support a rich cover of emergent plants, such as cattails, Pickerelweeds, and Pond Lilies.

Within a lake, there are three distinct zones, which are known as the littoral, the limnetic, and the profundal. The littoral zone occurs closest to the shore, where the water is relatively shallow; it is here that extensive marshes may develop. Beyond this zone—in the open water away from vegetation, and extending downward from the surface of the lake to the areas where light no longer penetrates—is the limnetic zone, which is the habitat of those organisms that require large amounts of light and oxygen. The third zone—the profundal—includes the remaining area of the lake and the bottom. Here in the darkness are creatures that can tolerate low levels of oxygen and a lack of light. Each zone is productive in its own way and important to the total well-being of the lake ecosystem.

Let us look at some of the aspects of life in lakes and ponds, keeping in mind that although there are differences between these bodies of water, there are also many features that they hold in common. It should be noted that deep marshes with several feet of water support many of the same wetland plants and animals that are found in ponds and the margins of shallow lakes. Therefore, some of the organisms typical of lakes and ponds are covered in detail in the chapter on marshes.

Lake Plants

Besides algae (the microscopic primary producers), rooted, floating, flowering aquatic plants play a major role in ponds and in lakes with shallow margins. In addition, many lakes and ponds have well-developed marshes on their borders. Because these varieties of vegetation are described in the chapter on marshes, only a brief discussion will be included here.

Duckweed
Lemna spp.
313

Water Hyacinth
Eichhornia crassipes
296

Milfoil
Millefolium

In addition to cattails, bulrushes, Pickerelweed, and other typical emergents, water lilies and submerged aquatic plants may be common in well-lighted water. Tiny Duckweed sometimes carpets the water of quiet ponds and lakes, as does Water Hyacinth in the South. Submerged aquatics—either rooted or free-floating—such as Milfoil, bladderworts, Water Celery, and pondweeds are common and become especially abundant in nutrient-rich lakes. Their finely dissected leaves and air-filled stems help buoy them up.

Buttonbush
Cephalanthus occidentalis
237

Water Willow
Justicia americana
263

Two interesting shrubby plants, Buttonbush and Water Willow, are commonly associated with the shallow water of lakes and ponds. The Buttonbush tolerates standing water, just as bulrushes and cattails do. Water Willows form dense growths; wherever they touch the water their arching stems put out new roots and produce new arching shoots.

These plants, along with many others, give lakeshores and ponds a distinctive kind of community. The plants, interesting in themselves, also feed and shelter animal life.

Aquatic Insects and Other Life

Common Water Strider
Gerris remigis
356

In the quiet waters of the littoral zone, the spiderlike Common Water Strider skates on the surface film in search of small organisms that have fallen from above or broken through from below.

Large Whirligig Beetle
Dineutus spp.
348

The Strider's six legs with waxy hairs on their jointed tips keep it afloat. The two front, forward-pointing legs are used primarily for feeding. The Whirligig Beetle, a surface glider, careens about like bumper cars at an amusement park. This frenetic insect seems to be on continuous holiday. With its divided eye half in and half out of the water, it can view two worlds at once. Although a scavenger as an adult, it is a voracious carnivore in its larval form. Adult Whirligigs usually do not appear until midsummer.

The real aerial acrobats of this marshy zone are the dragonflies and damselflies. Often colorful and striking in appearance, these useful predators consume many insects, especially mosquitoes. When at rest, the smaller, delicate damselflies hold the wings upward and backward, while dragonflies park like an airplane, with wings spread horizontally. Immature dragonflies, called nymphs, are ferocious underwater predators, using the highly specialized tongue to catch insect larvae, worms, and even small fish. After a year in the water, a nymph is ready to change its lifestyle; it climbs up onto an emergent plant, sheds its final nymphal skin—which you can sometimes find still clinging to the plant—and zooms off, one of the most skillful fliers in the world. Dragonflies in pursuit of insects have been clocked at twenty miles per hour.

Sometimes you see two dragonflies airborne together, the male clasping the female by the back of the neck just behind the head. This is a part of the mating procedure, during which the eggs are fertilized and the male guards his promiscuous mate from would-be suitors. Dragonfly eggs are fertilized only as they are being deposited; the final mate will be the father of the brood.

Some female dragonflies lay their eggs singly in flight, jabbing the water to deposit each one; it is this behavior that has given them the name "darning needles." Damselflies have their own mating technique. While joined to a female, the male backs down the stem of a Pickerelweed or some other emergent and pushes its mate totally under the water. There the female makes an incision in the plant stem and deposits the eggs. Then the male tows the female out and they fly off together to repeat the process.

(Marbled) Diving Beele
Thermonectes marmoratus
349

Water Boatmen
Corixa spp.
343

Mayfly
Ephemerella spinifera

Giant Water (Scavenger) Beetle
Hydrophilus spp.
347

American Horse Fly
Tabanus americanus
378

There are other fascinating aquatic insects, including the Predaceous Diving Beetles, Water Boatmen, backswimmers, mayflies, giant water beetles, horse flies—and many, many more.

Lakes and ponds abound with more sedentary forms of life as well. Moving slowly but steadily, freshwater snails crawl along underwater in their protective shells, scraping algae from various surfaces with their specially adapted jaws. Some snails are only a quarter of an inch long and are heavily preyed upon by fish. A snail's shell varies in thickness, depending upon the amount of calcium in the water: In nutrient-poor waters, it is transparent, and you can actually see the body inside.

Although they often mate, snails carry both male and female reproductive structures and can reproduce asexually.

Sometimes hydra, which are tiny clublike animals with tentacles, attach themselves to the snail's shell. These opportunistic animals comb the water and strain out microscopic zooplankton as they travel with the snail.

Partially embedded in the sandy bottom, a small freshwater bivalve clam or mussel opens its two shells slightly and feeds by siphoning water through its body by the gills, thus straining out tiny food particles and at the same time absorbing oxygen. The mussel can move along the bottom of the littoral zone on its muscular foot. Its mode of reproduction is most unusual: During the summer, the male sperm enters the female through the siphons and fertilizes the eggs. As the tiny embryos—or glochidia—are expelled, they fall to the bottom with their tiny shells open. It is imperative that an embryo attach itself to a passing fish, or it will die. Once attached, it becomes embedded in the fish's skin, usually either on the gills or fins. Absorbing nourishment from the fish and their own disintegrating bodies, they transform into tiny versions of adult mussels. This relationship illustrates once again organisms' close interdependence, as the mussel is a significant part of the lake food chain. Fish eat those with thinner shells, while Raccoons, Mink, and turtles eat the harder-shelled ones.

Raccoon
Procyon lotor
614

Mink
Mustela vison
613

The Fairy Shrimp is especially common in temporary ponds. These inch-long, bronzy, transparent creatures swim on their backs, appearing irregularly very early in the spring in small, frequently ephemeral, ponds. These beautiful little shrimp are graceful swimmers and well worth searching for at the end of a cold winter. They feed on microscopic floating algae or protozoans. Their eggs appear to require a drying period before hatching and have been known to retain their viability for more than a decade after being dried.

Mud Puppy
Necturus maculosus
104

Hellbender
Cryptobranchus alleganiensis
105

Red-spotted (Eastern) Newt
Notophthalmus viridescens
122, 123

Early spring is also the time when many amphibians—namely salamanders, toads, and frogs—head for lakes and ponds to lay their eggs. Although many live primarily on land and return to water only to lay eggs, a few—like the Mud Puppies and the Hellbenders—have gills and are fully aquatic. Another, the little Red-spotted Newt of eastern North America, spends the early part of its life on land and the rest in the water. During its time on land, the newt is called an eft; you may have seen one crawling over a moist log in the forest. After one to several years as a land dweller, the eft returns to the water, its coat transformed from bright red to a drab, black-dotted olive, with only the row of scarlet spots persisting from the eft stage.

Bullfrog
Rana catesbeiana
136, 137

Green Frog
Rana clamitans
134

Pickerel Frog
Rana palustris
144

Northern Leopard Frog
Rana pipiens
130, 143

(Northern) Cricket Frog
Acris crepitans
133

Many frogs, including the Bullfrog and the Green, Pickerel, Leopard, and Cricket frogs, are associated with lakes and ponds. Although some may at times be found far from water, they all return to lay their eggs. The young develop in the water and leave only when they have completed the change from tadpole to adult.

Snapping Turtle
Chelydra serpentina
151, 152

Turtles of various kinds are also typical of open-water environments. The Snapping Turtle is highly aquatic, preferring warm, shallow ponds with muddy bottoms, where it likes to rest with only its nostrils exposed. The Snapper, which reaches a foot and a half across, has a large head and powerful jaws that enable it to take small ducks, fish, and mammals. Some twenty to fifty eggs are laid in June in a nest near the water; and after several months, with the aid of the summer sun, the young hatch. Prowling skunks and other predators often dig out the leathery eggs, and thus play an important role in regulating turtle populations.

Painted Turtle
Chrysemys picta
159, 161, 162

The beautiful red and black Painted Turtle is one of the earliest to be found basking in the spring sun. In one study, it was calculated that there were approximately forty-two turtles in a three and one-half acre pond, or twelve turtles per acre. By counting the growth rings, or annuli, on the belly, it was estimated that each turtle grew an average of about one and one-half millimeters per year and that some were thirty-five years old. The pond had been created some fifty years earlier. Frogs, tadpoles, fishes, and crayfish are among the prey of the numerous snakes found in or around the shores of lakes and ponds. The common and harmless Northern Water Snake, which reaches a length of three feet, plays an important role in weeding out small fishes. Because the bones of this snake's jaws and head are connected by elastic ligaments, it is capable of swallowing a four- to five-inch fish. After the fish ceases to struggle, the snake begins to swallow it headfirst, using its teeth to move the fish along to its stomach, where powerful enzymes digest it.

Other snakes associated with ponds include the Green Water, the Common Garter, and Rough Green snakes, and the poisonous Pygmy Rattlesnake, which is found in the South. Some snakes lay their leathery eggs along the shore, but the Green Water and Common Garter snakes produce live young.

The populations of larger animals that live along ponds and lakes are quite similar to those found in marshes; they include Muskrats, Nutria, Beavers, and Raccoons. In the northern United States and Canada, the Moose is a common early morning and late evening visitor to ponds filled with Yellow and small White water lilies and other aquatics. From Texas to Illinois and eastward, the Swamp Rabbit can be found feeding on bark and leaves near the edges of ponds. In the Southeast, this species is replaced by the Marsh Rabbit. Small mammals such as the Meadow Vole, the Rice Rat, and the Southern Bog Lemming frequent the wet meadows near lakes and ponds. The Water Shrew is found in the northern United States and ranges southward along the mountains of the East and West. It is an excellent swimmer and diver, and preys on aquatic animals and insects, primarily at night.

Waterfowl and Other Birds

The bird life of lakes and ponds is similar to that of marshes: The surface-feeding dabbling ducks work over the marshy, littoral zone, and the diving ducks feed in deeper water on pondweeds, water lilies, clams, insects, and other aquatic life. Mergansers, Ruddy Ducks, Buffleheads, and Lesser Scaup are often common around fresh water. The marshy areas around lakes and ponds are important not only as breeding and nesting areas, but also as invaluable resting and feeding spots during the birds' long migratory flights; many birds that do not reach their wintering grounds until late in the season rely on these places.

For example, along the Central Flyway (one of the main waterfowl migration routes in North America), more than one million Mallards have been reported on Lake Francis Case in South Dakota during the early winter. Great numbers of ducks

Northern Water Snake
Nerodia sipedon
195

Green Water Snake
Nerodia cyclopion
185

Muskrat
Ondatra zibethicus
609

Nutria or Coypu
Myocastor coypus
610

Beaver
Castor canadensis
611

Moose
Alces alces
618

Swamp Rabbit
Sylvilagus aquaticus
606

Marsh Rabbit
Sylvilagus palustris
605

Meadow Vole
Microtus pennsylvanicus
603

Southern Bog Lemming
Synaptomys cooperi
600

Water Shrew
Sorex palustris
591

Common Merganser
Mergus merganser
507

Ruddy Duck
Oxyura jamaicensis
510

Bufflehead
Bucephala albeola
508

Mallard
Anas platyrhynchos
492

Lesser Scaup
Aythya affinis
503

Snow Goose
Chen caerulescens
513, 514

Canada Goose
Branta canadensis
512

Osprey
Pandion haliaetus
563

Common Loon
Gavia immer
481

Red-throated Loon
Gavia stellata

Belted Kingfisher
Ceryle alcyon
568

use prairie potholes and reservoirs on the Mississippi Flyway. Even the lakelike impoundments of Texas can host enormous concentrations of Lesser Scaup during the migration season. Snow Geese, moving in flocks of as many as 5000, sometimes make the 2000-mile flight from Canada to the Gulf in two days. Their traditional stopping places are Devil's Lake and Sand Lake Refuge in the Dakotas. Playas, artificial lakes, and stock ponds serve a similar role in the Texas Panhandle. In good years, more than 1 million ducks and between 5000 and 10,000 Canada Geese use Buffalo Lake and Muleshoe National Wildlife Refuge as resting places.

In addition to waterfowl, wading birds and other marsh birds are also associated with lakes and ponds. Gallinules, grebes, coots, herons, and bitterns may all be found here. The Osprey and both the Common and Red-throated loons, all fish eaters, are found on lakes and in coastal wetlands. Osprey populations declined drastically in the 1960s because of the use of DDT and other pesticides, which weakened their egg shells and boosted mortality rates. Since the curtailment of use of these insecticides, the Osprey has been recovering. The Common Loon, a strong swimmer and a deep diver, summers on lakes in the northeastern and north-central United States and in Canada; its loud, eerie call evokes the lake country of the North perhaps better than any other sound.

The Belted Kingfisher is a large-headed, big-beaked bird that is well-adapted to diving for fish from its perch on the edge of a pond or lake. It makes tunnels, usually three to six feet long (and occasionally up to fifteen feet long) in the banks of rivers or lakes, where it then makes its nest. The deceptively small, two- to three-inch opening in the bank slopes slightly upward to the nest depression, an excavated area that may be a foot across and half a foot deep. Five to seven eggs are laid. If you look for a Kingfisher nest, you can usually spot one a few feet from the top of the bank; the entrance is marked by two grooves that are created by the bird's feet as it enters and leaves.

The Fish World

Fishes are among the most common and distinctive forms of the animal life found in lakes and ponds. As is the case in rivers and streams, certain fish are associated with warm and cold water. In the cold lakes of Canada and Maine, the common Lake Trout, the largest North American trout, is highly prized by anglers. Once abundant in the Great Lakes, the Lake Trout was heavily preyed on by the Lamprey Eel, which entered the rest of the Great Lakes through Lake Ontario following the construction of the Welland Canal in the late 1800s. By the 1940s, the trout population had declined to less than ten percent of its former size.

The parasitic Lamprey attaches itself to its victims by its suction-cup mouth, sucks the body fluids of the fish (killing the fish in the process), and leaves to find another host. Spawning adults migrate up freshwater streams. The larvae, which are filter feeders, burrow into the stream bed, where they live for four or five years before returning to the lakes as adults. Although the cost has been high, Lampreys are now being controlled, and the Lake Trout is recovering.

Muskellunge
Esox masquinongy
77

Chain Pickerel
Esox niger
75

Largemouth Bass
Micropterus salmoides
34

Northern Pike
Esox lucius
76

There are a number of large northern lake fish—such as members of the pike family—that prefer the littoral zone of a lake. The largest of these, the Muskellunge, can reach six feet in length and weigh one hundred pounds. The common name derives from an Ojibwa Indian word meaning "big, powerful fish." This well-camouflaged fish searches out a submerged tree that offers shade and cover; it will then stubbornly exclude Pickerel and Largemouth Bass from its territory. Once the Muskellunge has sighted its prey its attack is rapid.

The similarly well-camouflaged Northern Pike, a relative of the Muskellunge, prefers heavily vegetated shores. When the two fishes are found together, the Pike is more common, as it is a more efficient competitor. Pike generally range from twelve to twenty-four inches, but occasionally attain a length of four feet. The related Chain Pickerel—at thirty-one inches, the smallest of the genus—is found in the same range, as well as in lakes farther south. Ice-fishing for this Pickerel is a common winter sport in the lake-filled Northeast.

Largemouth Bass often feed in small groups on fish, frogs, and even Meadow Voles. As is true in other species of the sunfish family, it is the male Largemouth Bass that selects and prepares a nest in late spring; using its tail, it fans out a depression several feet in diameter and removes small stones with its mouth. After the female has laid the eggs, the male continues to guard the nest until the young are hatched and ready to leave.

Pumpkinseed
Lepomis gibbosus
53

Bluegill
Lepomis macrochirus
48

Green Sunfish
Lepomis cyanellus
54

Pumpkinseed, Bluegill, and Green Sunfish are smaller sunfishes and typical inhabitants of ponds and lakes. A large Bluegill, which may be a foot long, can lay more than 200,000 eggs in one spawning. Although heavily preyed upon by the larger fish, Bluegills have a tendency to overpopulate small ponds, producing many stunted individuals that are only three to four inches long.

White Sucker
Catostomus commersoni
73

Redhorse
Moxostoma spp.

Lake Chubsucker
Erimyzon sucetta

The bottoms of shallow ponds and lakes, which host a rich array of life, are also attractive to certain bottom-feeding fish. The various bullheads and madtoms, members of the bullhead catfish family, have special chin whiskers, or barbels, that act as sensory organs to help the fish find food as they cruise along the bottom. Several suckers—the White Sucker, the Redhorse, and the Lake Chubsucker—are also bottom feeders, but with a different adaptation: their mouths can be extended vertically to suck up insects, mollusks, and plants. The White Sucker and the Redhorse are found throughout central and eastern North America, whereas the Lake Chubsucker ranges from the Great Lakes to Texas.

When a fish dies, crayfish gather quickly, for these nocturnal carrion feeders have a keen sense of smell. Sometimes hordes will cover a fish, leaving only the skeleton by morning. These scavengers perform an important function in the process of recycling nutrients within a lake or pond.

Microscopic Producers: Phytoplankton

In the open, well-lighted water of the limnetic zone, phytoplankton (tiny plant organisms) are among the lake's important primary producers. When nutrient levels, temperature, and other factors are just right, the phytoplankton population explodes. Frequently, in the spring, there is a sudden flowering of diatoms, which are one-celled algae with highly sculptured silica cell walls that fit together like pillboxes. As the diatoms increase, there is a corresponding increase in the zooplankton—the tiny copepods and water fleas. This burst of life will now provide the common silvery Gizzard Shad with a source of food. This fish has a very small mouth; a plankton feeder like the Baleen Whale, the Gizzard Shad strains microscopic organisms out of the water.

Gizzard Shad
Dorosoma cepedianum
31

When the nutrient level of a lake declines, the algae population declines as well—until late summer, when there may be another nutrient surge favoring a blue-green algal bloom. Although oxygen is still being produced, there are soon so many dead algae falling to the bottom that the decomposers must work overtime. In the process, they deplete the oxygen supply. This often causes serious fish kills, as fish living in the lower levels run out of oxygen.

The blue-green algal blooms are also a constant threat to water supplies, because many of these algae give off toxic products. Before these blooms were brought within chemical control, people died from drinking water heavily contaminated with blue-green algae. Another alga that is especially common in enriched ponds is the threadlike filamentous form, which sometimes floats on the surface as it generates oxygen. This alga is the "scum" that is often visible in many ponds. It should not be mistaken for a blue-green algal bloom, and does not necessarily signal that a pond is unhealthy. Some of these algae will be eaten by ducks, insects, tadpoles, and other creatures, and some will fall to the decomposers.

The Endless Cycle: Decomposers and the Profundal Zone

When plants and animals die, the excess biomass falls to the lower depths and eventually to the bottom. Along the bottoms of ponds and shallow lakes, tiny segmented nematodes sustain themselves by reworking the sediments. The inch-long Segmented Tubifex worm is a reddish bottom dweller that constructs a little tube to live in. Its tail may be seen waving as it feeds with its tiny head burrowed in the mud. Leeches, which are often abundant in warm water, move gracefully, often forming loops with the suckers on each end of their bodies. They rest under stones or logs by day, and at night hunt for dead fish or other organisms. Occasionally they attach themselves to frogs, fish, and even human beings. Lake bottoms are especially rich in life, because it is here that the decomposers assist in recycling materials.

With no light or oxygen, the profundal zone may seem a poor place to live, but certain snails, clams, and insect larvae have evolved ways of coping with life in this harsh environment.

Trillions of anaerobic bacteria—that is, those capable of decomposing this rich organic matter without oxygen—are constantly at work. The little phantom midges, or gnats, resemble mosquitoes but do not feed or bite. The half-inch-long larvae live on the bottoms of deep lakes; those of some species are nearly transparent (hence the common name). The larva travels to the surface at night to prey on shrimplike copepods and to pick up air in its two pairs of air sacs. When the larvae become adults, they form huge swarms that, from a distance, resemble smoke above the lake.

True Midge/Bloodworm
Chironomus spp.

The True Midge, which also resembles a mosquito, has large feathery antennae as an adult; in the larval stage, it is bright red from the hemoglobin it contains and thus is called a Bloodworm. These larvae are important food for many kinds of fishes. They can occur in tremendous numbers and are an important part of the recycling process. Using a special dredge, it is possible to sample the bottom sediments of such lakes and find these small organisms.

Although the decomposers are constantly making nutrients available through the decomposition process, these nutrients appear to be trapped in the bottom sediment. But the lake ecosystem has a unique technique for getting them into the upper waters. The overturning of the lake's waters in both the spring and the fall brings these nutrients up and mixes them with the surface waters, so that they may be used by the photosynthetic organisms.

In spring and fall when lake temperatures are relatively uniform from top to bottom, the wind and currents mix the water so that nutrients at the bottom are circulated to the surface. During the summer the temperature differential of the water column is too great for this to occur, and the lake has warmer water on top and colder water beneath and little or no mixing of the two layers.

The bottom sediments may provide clues about a lake's paleoecology—the structure and relations of plant and animal communities buried in the ancient past. Preserved in the sediments are such remains as the chitinous fossil shells of the tiny, aquatic water flea, Cladoceran, and pollen grains from the plants that once grew around the lake. By bringing up bottom sediments, one can identify these microfossils and reconstruct the history of a lake, as well as the changes in the plant life of the surrounding area. In formerly glaciated areas, such study is limited to a time span of 12,000 to 15,000 years—the time that has elapsed since the last glacier—but farther south, it is possible to reconstruct many more thousands of years of past development. Even early man has left evidence of his presence in the sediments of lakes.

The Fate of Lakes

Probably no single wetland animal is more important than the Beaver in determining the fate of wetlands. These master builders literally create ponds, and once they have chosen their dam sites, almost nothing will discourage these wetland engineers from building on them. Various techniques have been tried (unsuccessfully): dynamiting, keeping lanterns continuously lighted, burning sulfur, and relocating the creatures. Although Beavers may cause flooding on roads and desirable farmlands, their work is invaluable in maintaining an area's water level and in creating habitats for fish, herons, ducks, Muskrats, and Mink. Like Muskrats, Beavers also build lodges, which serve them well during cold winters when the ponds are frozen; at that time, they eat energy-rich bark, which they store on the bottoms of ponds. As woodcutters, Beavers are among the best: They strip the bark with their chisel-like front teeth, which grow continuously. Conical, gnawed stumps near a pond or stream are sure signs that Beavers are, or have been, active. Their favorite foods are poplar or aspen, but other trees are frequently consumed; in an average meal, one Beaver can put away about three pounds of bark.

Beavers must leave an area if their food runs out, and their departure leaves the fate of the pond in question. Without their constant maintenance, the dam that has created the pond will in time begin to leak; the pond may in time look more like a marsh. If the water level continues to fall, the pond may become a beaver meadow, filled with grasses, sedges, and other colorful wetland plants. Eventually, an alder thicket might develop.

There is in fact a tendency for shallow ponds and lakes to become marshy. Many once-deep glacial lakes have filled in and are now covered by boggy vegetation. When the animal plant production is not entirely used by the grazers or decomposers, the surplus organic accumulation contributes to the filling-in process. In many lakes, silt also adds significantly to the filling in. This is true especially of certain lakes with man-made dams, which are rapidly silting in.

In the early 1950s, Arboretum Pond, a shallow body of water at the Connecticut Arboretum, was essentially free of water lilies. But twenty-five years later the pond had been engulfed by these aquatics. In addition, bur reeds and Pickerelweed were advancing toward the center of the pond. Because it was desirable to preserve the open-water setting, something drastic had to be done. Accordingly, one autumn the pond was drained. During the winter, many of the water lily rhizomes (rootlike stems) froze, removing many lilies and the threat of imminent death from the pond.

Bur Reed
Sparganium americanum
315

Other alternative solutions might have included chemical control (which has potential hazards), excavation of the pond, or harvesting the aquatics. The latter technique is used in lakes where submerged aquatics such as Milfoil—a feathery plant like those used in aquariums—have become overabundant. Harvesting has the simple advantage of removing material from a pond rather than adding more of it, as would occur with chemical control techniques. In some areas, aerating devices are being used to restore the health of lakes, since oxygen depletion is often the crux of the problem. The best solutions, of course, are those that remove the cause of the problem.

A classic case of eutrophication reversal is that of Seattle's Lake Washington. The city of Seattle lies between Puget Sound and the west side of the lake, which for many years has borne the brunt of sewage dumping. In the early 1930s, sewage from the city was diverted for a limited time into Puget Sound, and thus lake pollution was reduced. As the city grew, however, more sewage treatment plants began to appear around the lake, until by 1954 there were ten two-stage biological treatment facilities. In the early 1960s, some twenty million gallons of treated sewage effluent were added to the lake each day. By 1955, a blue-green algal bloom had appeared, and it intensified each year. This was a clear indication that the lake was getting sick.

Public concern and demands for a cleanup grew, and in 1963 a project was begun to divert the sewage once again to Puget Sound. By the late 1960s, the lake was looking much better. There was more oxygen in the lower levels and the water was clearer to a greater depth. What is more, the phosphates—the culprits that enhanced the growth of the blue-green algae—were reduced, and along with them the algal bloom.

Thus, cultural eutrophication is reversible: Even badly polluted lakes have an amazing ability to straighten out their systems if given a chance. One strategy, popular in recent years, has been to reduce phosphates in detergents. The presence of phosphates is often the limiting or critical factor in the health of a lake, as was demonstrated here. It is believed that the phosphates will not harm Puget Sound, however, because the dilution is so great. Yet this must be watched closely.

To preserve Lake Tahoe, one of the clearest cold oligotrophic lakes in the world, a special tertiary sewage-treatment facility was constructed, essentially to eliminate nutrient pollution. Elsewhere, other lakes are being rehabilitated.

Other pollutants—for example, pesticides and PCBs (polychlorinated biphenols), as well as chlorinated hydrocarbons—can also threaten life in aquatic systems. Acid rain also threatens many lakes. Sulfur oxides and nitrogen oxides—the result of massive burning of fossil fuels—are constantly falling from the atmosphere along with precipitation. In the mid-1960s—only twenty years ago—the lakes in New York's Adirondack Mountains were noted for their fish populations; but by 1979, half of the lakes above 2000 feet had no fish whatsoever. The lakes had become very acid, with a high concentration of hydrogen (stated as a *p*H of 4.2). The source of the problem—if not all of its ramifications—has been identified by scientists, but the issue is politically sensitive; the solution, which will involve great expense and drastic changes, is currently stymied by the political process.

Although lakes are constantly under stress, it is heartening to know that it is possible for them to recover. Nevertheless, these beautiful ecosystems have a limited carrying capacity and must not be overburdened if their integrity is to be maintained and their pleasures perpetuated.

LAKES AND PONDS: PLANTS AND ANIMALS

Water Hyacinth 296
Water Lettuce 308
Water Smartweed 291
Water Willow 263
Watercress 245
Wild Rice 321
Winterberry 244
Yellow Pond Lily 214
Yellow Water Buttercup 212
Yellow Water Lily 216

Insects and Spiders

American Horsefly 378
Betten's Silverstreak Caddisfly 362
Bluebell 363
Common Backswimmer 345
Common Water Strider 356
Crane Fly 373
Dark Lestes 372
Elisa Skimmer 370
Giant Water Bug 344
Giant Water Scavenger Beetle 347
Green Darner 366
Kirby's Backswimmer 346
Large Whirligig Beetle 348
Marbled Diving Beetle 349
Marsh Fly 380
Purplish-blue Cricket Hunter 377
Red Freshwater Mite 384
Short-stalked Damselfly 367
Six-spotted Fishing Spider 382
Streak-winged Red Skimmer 371
Swift Long-winged Skimmer 368
Twelve-spot Skimmer 369
Vinegar Fly 381
Water Boatman 343
Waterlily Leaf Beetle 355
Western Waterscorpion 357
Widow 364

Butterflies and Moths

Least Skipperling 425
Zebra Swallowtail 390

Birds

American Black Duck 489
American Coot 535
Anhinga 518
Bald Eagle 562
Barrow's Goldeneye 505
Belted Kingfisher 568
Blue Winged Teal 497
Bonaparte's Gull 554
Bufflehead 508
California Gull 556
Canada Goose 512
Caspian Tern 552
Common Loon 481
Common Merganser 507
Common Moorhen 536
Common Tern 550
Double-crested Cormorant 520
Eared Grebe 486
Franklin's Gull 553
Great Blue Heron 528
Greater Scaup 502
Green-backed Heron 534
Green Winged Teal 490
Herring Gull 557
Hooded Merganser 509
Horned Grebe 485
Lesser Scaup 503
Mallard 492
Mute Swan 516
Osprey 563
Pied-billed Grebe 483
Red-necked Grebe 484
Ring-billed Gull 555
Ring-necked Duck 501
Semipalmated Sandpiper 543
Solitary Sandpiper 544
Spotted Sandpiper 546
Western Grebe 482

Mammals

Beaver 611
Moose 618
River Otter 612
Star-nosed Mole 595
Water Vole 604

RIVERS AND STREAMS

The sound of running water is one of the most soothing things in nature. As soon as we hear the splash of a stream, the torrent of a river, or the rush of a falls, we are drawn to the source, where we derive great pleasure from just watching and listening. Streams and rivers—bodies of water on the move—are part of an endless, and endlessly fascinating cycle.
Streams have their origin as springs or seepage, and in turn they feed the rivers as the water makes its way to the sea. As the water evaporates from the sea, it returns to the streams and rivers in the form of precipitation, and the process is repeated.
There is no single characteristic river or stream, for they vary according to the surrounding terrain. Rapidly flowing streams that originate in the mountains eventually enter valleys as large, slower-moving rivers. On the Midwestern plains, the Platte, Missouri, Arkansas, Kansas, and Red rivers extend like giant tentacles into the prairie. Fringed by cottonwoods, elms, and willows, they are sharply defined by their riparian streamside vegetation. In the deserts, the arroyos, which through most of the year support a mere trickle, occasionally carry flash floods after sudden storms.

Distribution

No matter where you are in the United States, you are probably not far from a stream or a river. The nation's river systems are vast, complex patterns that cover the country. Although best developed in the eastern, central, southeastern, and northwestern parts of the country, they are also present in the arid West. Nine major river drainages—constituting all the land drained by a particular river and its branches—are recognized: the St. Lawrence River Basin; the Rio Grande Basin and Gulf Coast; the Mississippi River Basin; the Souris River Basin of Saskatchewan, North Dakota, and Manitoba; the Atlantic and Gulf Coasts; the Colorado River Basin; the Great Basin in the West; the Columbia River Basin; and the Pacific Coast Basin. As one would expect, rivers and streams are best developed where there is ample rainfall and where the volume of precipitation exceeds the rate of evaporation from the land.

Ecology

The life of a river or stream is influenced by many factors, including rapidity of flow, water temperature, amount of oxygen, nutrient levels, and the nature of the bottom. The cold water of rapidly flowing, rocky mountain streams, for example, is rich in oxygen, because it is aerated as it passes over rapids and riffles. However, as this cold, rushing water descends into the valley and slows down, it becomes warmer and less oxygenated.
As major rivers meander across valley floors, they create floodplains, which are areas defined by the spread of the river and created by the deposition of silt as the river advances and retreats. The floodplain is an integral part of the river system: It provides a place where the river can periodically store excess water and lay down a fertile coat of silt.
Although rivers and streams are properly presented as a

Rivers and Drainage Areas

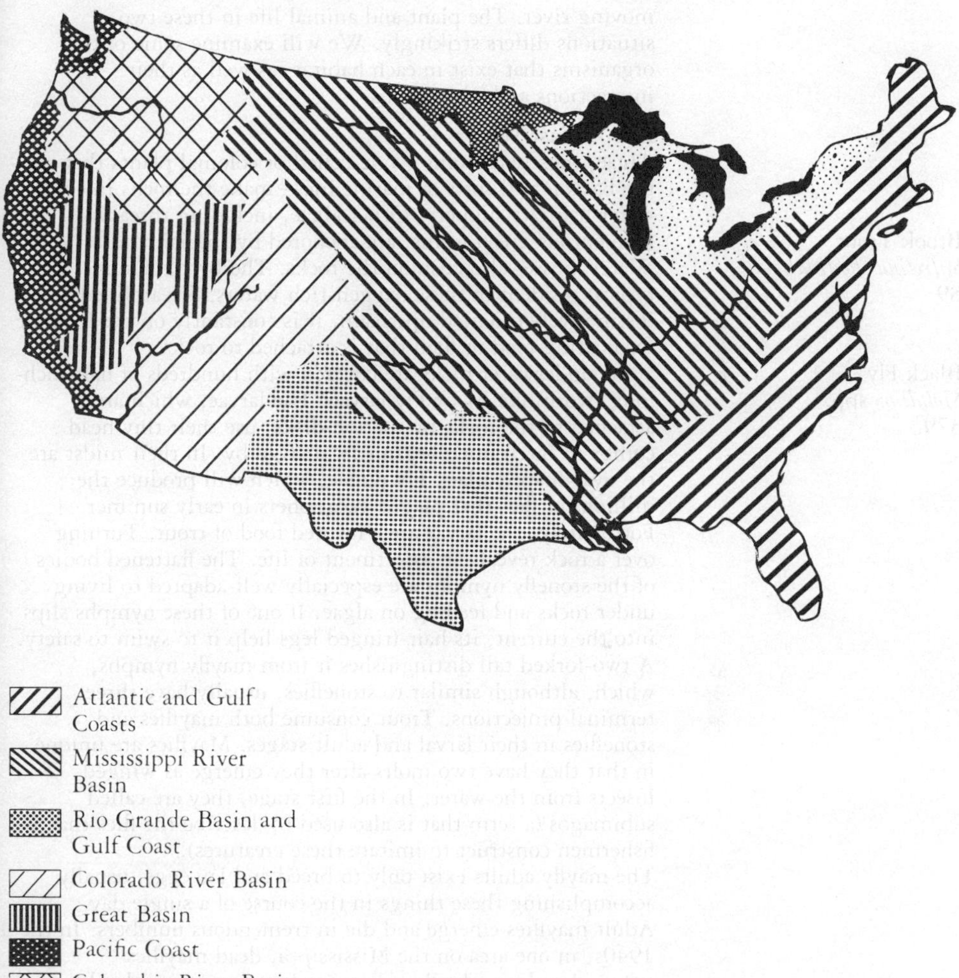

continuum, in which one set of conditions is only gradually replaced by another, two rather distant ecological environments at the extremes of the continuum may be isolated: The cold, fast-moving stream and the warmer, slow-moving river. The plant and animal life in these two situations differs strikingly. We will examine some of the organisms that exist in each habitat, as well as their interactions and adaptations.

Life in Fast Water

Algae, mostly diatoms—one-celled or colonial plants that are the basis for all sorts of marine life—make the rocks in cold-water habitats slippery. Other algae, including threadlike, filamentous green forms, are anchored by special holdfast cells. Water mosses also cushion the rocks. The Brook Trout is a typical resident of these oxygen-rich waters. Streamlined and instinctively oriented upstream, it is constantly on the lookout for floating food or food that is attached to rocks.

Brook Trout
Salvelinus fontinalis
89

Black Fly
Simulium spp.
379

Some underwater rocks are covered with hundreds of half-inch-long, wormlike Black Fly larvae. The larvae, which are attached to the rocks by suction disks, use their tiny head combs to catch microorganisms that go by. In their midst are the oval-shaped Black Fly pupae, which will produce the millions of flies that plague vacationers in early summer. Fortunately, the larvae are a favored food of trout. Turning over a rock reveals an assortment of life. The flattened bodies of the stonefly nymphs are especially well-adapted to living under rocks and feeding on algae. If one of these nymphs slips into the current, its hair-fringed legs help it to swim to safety. A two-forked tail distinguishes it from mayfly nymphs, which, although similar to stoneflies, usually have three terminal projections. Trout consume both mayflies and stoneflies in their larval and adult stages. Mayflies are unique in that they have two molts after they emerge as winged insects from the water. In the first stage, they are called subimagos (a term that is also used to describe the flies that fishermen construct to imitate these creatures).

The mayfly adults exist only to breed and lay eggs, usually accomplishing these things in the course of a single day. Adult mayflies emerge and die in tremendous numbers. In the 1940s, in one area on the Mississippi, dead mayflies accumulated to a depth of three or four feet on one bridge, and a snowplow had to be called out (in July) to clear it.

Sand particles glued together on a rock signal the presence of a caddisworm—the larva of a caddisfly, of which there are many species. In quiet pools, Caddisworms sometimes make their portable homes out of sticks, leaves and pebbles. Perhaps the most unusual kind are the net-building caddisworms, which spin a delicate net to trap tiny food particles. Lying alongside the net, they periodically comb it to check for food.

The coppery, pennylike object that is clamped fiercely to the rock is the water penny, the larva of a land beetle. If this little animal is pried from its spot, we can see the six legs on its underside that help it to hold fast. Among the many other

Eastern Dobsonfly
Corydalus cornutus
359, 360

Crane Fly
Tipula spp.
373

aquatic insects are dobsonfly larvae, also known as hellgrammites and used by fishermen as bait, and crane flies, which as adults resemble giant mosquitoes. These insects are beautifully adapted: They are able to maintain themselves in swift water and to catch fragments of algae and other organic debris; like fish, these creatures have gills that remove oxygen from the water.

Two-lined Salamander
Eurycea bislineata
110, 121

Turning over rocks in streams can be a risky business, especially if the crayfish population is substantial. This lobsterlike creature can pinch one's finger quite hard. From its hiding place under a rock, the crayfish nips out and scavenges food as it passes by.

The Two-lined Salamander is found in association with streams in the Eastern United States. Although most salamanders lay their eggs in quiet pools, the Two-lined Salamander has a special streamside adaptation: It fastens its eggs to rocks in the stream to prevent their being washed away.

Mottled Sculpin
Cottus bairdi
59

Johnny Darter
Etheostoma nigrum
62

Brook Stickleback
Culaea inconstans
63

Rainbow Trout
Salmo gairdneri
91

Brown Trout
Salmo trutta
90

Apache (Arizona) Trout
Salmo apache
93

In addition to trout, many species of sculpins are typical in rapidly flowing cold-water streams. The Mottled Sculpin, found in the Great Lakes region and farther west, feeds on aquatic insects. It was once believed to prey on trout eggs, but this is not the case; in fact, trout may prey on sculpins. Other small fishes, including Johnny Darters, Sticklebacks, and the Blunt-nosed Dace, also enjoy cool, fast-moving water and provide food for game fish. Aside from Brook Trout, one may find Rainbow and Brown trout, as well as Apache, or Arizona, Trout, a threatened species found above 7500 feet in the mountain streams of the Salt and Little Colorado rivers of east-central Arizona.

Sockeye Salmon
Oncorhynchus nerka
95

In the Pacific Northwest, the annual migrations of the anadromous Pacific salmon are a spectacular show. There are four major species: Coho, Sockeye, Chinook, and Chum. After spending two to three years in the ocean, the Coho moves up the Columbia and other rivers in huge numbers, its sole aim to spawn in the stream of its birth. This amazing feat of navigation is apparently accomplished by the fish's sense of smell, for if nose plugs are inserted, the fish go astray. The Coho and Sockeye both have great commercial value. The Chinook, which reaches twenty pounds, is a prized game fish that inhabits the ocean waters from northern California to Alaska; it also enters fresh water to spawn.

American Dipper
Cinclus mexicanus
579

Louisiana Waterthrush
Seiurus motacilla
578

Spotted Sandpiper
Actitis macularia
546

Several streamside birds prefer fast water. In the West, watch for the American Dipper, or "Water Ouzel." A small, drab bird, it searches out aquatic insects in the swiftest of streams and doesn't mind going underwater for them. In the East, the Louisiana Waterthrush teeters and bobs its tail as it feeds along rivers and streams. The Spotted Sandpiper, which is more widespread, has a polka-dotted white breast. It also has a rather comical walk, moving rapidly, almost mechanically, in its search for aquatic life.

River Otter
Lutra canadensis
612

Among the mammals, the River Otter is the acrobat of streams and rivers. One of the most playful of animals, the Otter has a streamlined body that is ideal for frolicking and tobogganing down rapids. Equipped with valved ears and nostrils, it is well adapted to underwater fishing. Sometimes a pair of otters will act together to round up a school of fish, usually consuming their large catch on the stream bank. The Otter's beautiful fur, as well as the suspicion that it depletes populations of fish—especially trout—has unfortunately led to excessive trapping and has greatly reduced its numbers. In fact, the Otter primarily consumes species, such as the crayfish, that are of little interest to fishermen.

Mink
Mustela vison
613

Raccoon
Procyon lotor
614

The Mink, which is discussed more fully in the chapter on marshes, also favors rivers and streams. It is a formidable hunter. Another mammal that frequents swift-moving streams is the Raccoon, an opportunistic eater that uses streams and rivers for the food sources they provide. Other animals whose tracks may often be seen in this environment include deer, foxes, and bears.

Water Arum
Calla palustris
225

Pickerelweed
Pontederia cordata
295

Common Cattail
Typha latifolia
220

Bulrush
Scirpus spp.

Snapping Turtle
Chelydra serpentina
151, 152

Map Turtle
Graptemys geographica
164

Cooter
Chrysemys floridana

Slider
Pseudemys scripta
157, 163

Softshell
Trionyx spp.

Stinkpot
Sternotherus odoratus
155

Razorback Musk Turtle
Sternotherus carinatus
168

Life in Slow Water

In the valley, the river widens, deepens, and slows, and its sediment load is gradually deposited on the silty bottom. As the water warms, its oxygen-holding capacity decreases, and the plants and animals of colder, rushing waters are replaced by forms better able to exploit these different conditions. For example, caddisflies and mayflies may still occur, but new species that are adapted to slower water also are found. The large water strider of the cool stream is replaced by smaller species. Dragonflies fill the air and aquatic insects actively work the rich sediments. The attached algae found in the fast-moving streams are replaced by free-swimming phytoplankton in these slower waters. And in general, there is greater reliance placed on the detrital food chain. Slow-water systems have certain characteristic vegetation. Along the shallow, silty river's edge, for example, Water Arum, Pickerelweed, cattails, bulrushes, and water lilies may signal an emergent marsh. Snapping turtles, which are most often found in ponds and marshes, may be here, but there are other, more typically riverine species. Indeed, virtually every category of freshwater turtle may be found in rivers: Map Turtle, Sawback, Cooter, Slider, Snapping Turtle, and Softshell. The musk turtles, including the Stinkpot and the Razorback, prefer shallow, slow-moving muddy-bottomed rivers. When disturbed, musk turtles gives off a foul-smelling yellow liquid from their musk glands, which are located beneath the carapace. In western Mississippi and Texas, the Razor-backed Musk Turtle, which has prominent ridges on its shell, is abundant in slow-moving rivers and streams. The smooth Softshelled Turtle resembles a leathery pancake; it lacks the typical scales, or scutes, of most turtles. Softshells, which have fully webbed feet, are especially good swimmers. Unlike most turtles, they are swift and aggressive; their long necks reach out to extraordinary lengths as they feed. They are typically found throughout the Mississippi drainage basin in the Midwest.

The fish of slow-water systems are different from their swift-water counterparts. Their flattened bodies are adapted to quiet

Largemouth Bass
Micropterus salmoides
34

Yellow Perch
Perca flavescens
43

water, and they are, in general, less muscular. In the marshy shallows and in deeper water, various sunfishes—including Largemouth Bass—Yellow Perch, Miller's Thumb, Northern Pike, White Sucker, Buffalofish, Gar, eels, and various catfish or bullheads are some of the fishes that make up the rich fauna of these warm rivers, replacing the trout, darters, and sculpins of colder waters.

Northern Pike
Esox lucius
76

White Sucker
Catostomus commersoni
73

Buffalofish
Ictiobus spp.

Often found in open, slow-moving water, the sluggish members of the sucker family have a distinctive sucking mouth that can be extended to the underside of the body in order to feed on insect larvae and other bottom dwellers. One such fish, the Bigmouth Buffalo of the Mississippi and Great Lakes drainage, is especially tolerant of turbidity, a characteristic that gives it an advantage over some of the other river fishes.

Gar
Lepisosteus spp.

Bigmouth Buffalo
Ictiobus Cyprinellus

Channel Catfish
Ictalurus punctatus
87

Also found in this area is the Channel Catfish, which reaches nearly four feet in length and weighs up to fifty pounds. Like other catfish, it has barbels, or whiskers, that act as sensory organs, helping it to find food near the bottom.

Paddlefish
Polyodon spathula
79

With its long snout and nearly scaleless, smooth skin, the Paddlefish is certainly among the most unusual of North American fishes. At one time, individuals reached seven feet in length and weighed up to 150 pounds, but such giants are a rarity today. Paddlefish inhabit the backwaters of the Mississippi River system. Their populations have declined because of pollution and the rerouting of the river, a process that has cut them off from the streams where they once spawned.

Common Carp
Cyprinus carpio
37, 38

Grass Carp
Ctenopharyngodon idella
96

The Common Carp, which was introduced in the late 1800s, and the recently introduced Grass Carp, have proven detrimental to native fish populations; they have crowded other species out and altered the environment. These herbivores eat aquatic plants and can destroy habitats for waterfowl as well as fish. This fact provides one more illustration of the potential hazard of introducing into a new region a species that may lack natural predators and controls, and which therefore may destroy the balance of an ecosystem.

Blue Crab
Callinectes sapidus

Alewives
Alosa pseudoharengus

American Shad
Alosa sapidissima
32

American Eel
Anguilla rostrata
84

Atlantic Salmon
Salmo salar
94

Where the rivers meet the sea, there is a mingling of fresh and salt water, and a new group of species that are tolerant of brackish water—including oysters, Blue Crabs, Alewives, and flounders—replace the freshwater biota. On the East Coast, numerous anadromous species pass through the mouths of rivers on their way to spawn in freshwater streams or at sea. In the spring, American Shad move upstream to spawn, and the female American Eel leaves small cool streams to join her mate in the estuaries and ultimately to spawn in the deep waters off Bermuda. The Atlantic Salmon, which spends its adult life at sea and spawns in cold freshwater streams, has disappeared from much of its former range. On the Connecticut River, however, it is being reestablished with the help of fish ladders constructed around hydroelectric dams on the river.

Riverine Ecosystem Processes

Like all ecosystems, rivers and streams require nutrients as a source of energy, and they have a limited carrying capacity. As linear communities—going from fast to slow water—they illustrate how life can change along an environmental gradient. Finally, rivers and streams are able to cleanse themselves of certain pollutants.

In fast-moving streams and rivers, most of the energy is not produced within the water itself but comes instead from the streamside. One important source is the leaves of trees. In one study in New England, it was found that nearly ninety-nine percent of the energy derived from leaves came from outside the stream; only one percent came from the water mosses; and algae represented an insignificant percentage. This means that decomposing agents are of great importance in breaking down the energy-rich leaves to provide detritus as a source of food for aquatic life. Insects and other animals that decompose in the stream are another energy source. Mineral nutrients come from the weathering of bedrock and soil as the water flows over or through these materials. Rain provides minerals as well. In slower moving streams, detritus and silt may tend to accumulate and provide an especially rich nutrient pool, as in the southern bottomland hardwood forests.

In most stream ecosystems, the detrital food chain plays a more significant role than the grazing food chain, but there are exceptions. Studies at Silver Springs, the famous Florida tourist attraction, demonstrated how submerged Eelgrass, a grasslike arrowhead that is related to marsh species, plays an indirect but important role in the grazing food chain. If one looks carefully, it is possible to see that the blades of the plants are coated with algae, tiny epiphytes that do not harm their host. These diatoms and filamentous green and blue-green algae are in fact the most significant primary producers in the food chain. In scraping off this coating, scientists found that the algae were contributing over a pound of food per square meter.

Eelgrass
Zostera marina

At the base of the food pyramid, the algae begin a process that ultimately reaches the carnivores at the top, such as Gar and Largemouth Bass. However, by the time the top of the pyramid has been reached, little useful energy is left and only one-twentieth of an ounce of fish tissue has been produced. The reason is that in the move from one trophic level to the next most of the useful living material is converted into heat energy, which is not useful to productive organisms. Thus the amount of useful energy available at one level is always greater than that of the next higher level in the food chain.

Another principle that is important to riverine systems involves the way in which ecosystems change along an environmental gradient. For example, if you walk from a cool ravine to a dry, rocky ridge you are well aware of changes in plant and animal life that you will see. Similarly, within just ten to fifteen miles along the course of a cool mountain stream, interesting changes are evident—especially in the fish life. A study conducted in the mountains of Virginia revealed that Brook Trout inhabited the cool, well-oxygenated water in the upper portions of a stream. A little way downstream,

Central Stoneroller
Campostoma anomalum

Common Shiner
Notropis cornutus
67

Longnose Dace
Rhinichtys cataractae

Brook Trout were gradually replaced by Rainbow Trout. Still farther along the stream, the Rainbow was joined by Central Stoneroller, Common Shiner, Longnose Dace, and Common Sucker, all of which are typical of warmer water. The acidity and temperature also changed along the gradient. Slightly more acid along the upper reaches, the water was nearly neutral at the end, and the temperature had increased from 60° to 70° F.

Fishing (or, in technical terms, the removal of part of the stream ecosystem) is an important consideration in the life of many streams; for this reason, another concept—the carrying capacity of an ecosystem—is brought sharply into focus. In this context, the carrying capacity of a stream or river is defined as the maximum number of organisms that the habitat can support without damage to the ecosystem.

How many fish can a trout stream produce, and how much fishing can occur without depleting the breeding stock? Studies in the Sierra Nevada shed some light on this question. Over a ten-year period, a ten-mile trout stream was found to support 15,000 fish, or an average of one hundred and fifty pounds of fish per mile; this figure remained stable even with heavy fishing. It was found that a quarter of the population could be caught without depleting the stock. It is very important in both freshwater and marine fisheries to know what can be removed from these systems without harming them—their sustained yield. It is only by intelligent management of such natural resources that all forms of life, including man, can become integrated in the productivity of rivers and streams.

Another important aspect of flowing ecosystems is their ability to cleanse themselves. When a pollutant such as sewage is introduced into clear water, Tubifex worms, fungi, and bacteria, which are always present in the system, suddenly increase in numbers. Their flurry of activity brings about low oxygen levels, forcing sunfish, bass, aquatic insects, and other animals to move. When the pollutant has been sufficiently diluted, the original inhabitants can return and the stream is healthy once more. However, if too much of any pollutant is added, the organisms are overtaxed and the riverine system can be destroyed.

Many rivers are overburdened beyond their ability to process these organic pollutants. Hazardous waste including toxic, nonorganic pollutants, is another matter. Natural systems have not evolved to cope with these man-made compounds, so it is in our interest to be very careful when disposing of them.

Mankind and the River

Rivers and people have always been linked. In the early days of our country, rivers were used by industry and were major arteries of transportation and trade. Today they still work for us in much the same way. Hydroelectric dams, such as those in the Tennessee Valley, have transformed the lives of people in many regions. On the marshes around the reservoirs, wildlife thrives. Migrating waterfowl rest and feed. Half a

Walleye
Stizostedion vitreum
41

White Crappie
Pomoxis annularis

Black Bass
Centropistis striata

million acres of water provide thousands of people with recreation facilities, and fishermen enjoy catching Walleye, White Crappies, and Black Bass.

In the arid West, the wild Colorado in the Grand Canyon provides exciting recreation, and the fringing cottonwoods and willows give much-needed shade for a trek through the canyon. Although gigantic dams have unfortunately destroyed magnificent scenery and wildlife in places such as Glen Canyon, the new ecosystems that have resulted have created fish and waterfowl habitats and now provide electricity and water for irrigation. But with over a dozen dams on this river, some of these man-made basins are rapidly silting in; in fact, flash floods are frequent in this dry country, and great quantities of soil are carried away.

In northern Minnesota at Lake Itasca, you can step across the Mississippi, here a trickle, as it begins its 2300-mile journey to the Gulf of Mexico. On the way, it drains over a million square miles, or a quarter of the country. The river is heavily used as a water highway for the boats and barges that constantly ply the water from New Orleans northward. Encroachment on the rich floodplains of the Mississippi has necessitated heavy diking to minimize flooding.

It is important to analyze carefully the potential long-range effects of any modification of a naturally functioning ecosystem. In the long run, such planning saves money and the unnecessary destruction of plants and animals.

One further example of the relationship of rivers to the surrounding watershed is the situation at Hubbard Brook in New Hampshire. Here scientists performed a most drastic experiment: They cut all the trees on a small watershed and then killed the roots with herbicides. With no tree cover on the surrounding land, the stream ecology changed dramatically. The water warmed up, and its nutrient content and acidity increased. Although the water looked good enough to drink, the nitrate content was above that permitted by public health standards. With the forest gone, there was little plant life to absorb the minerals in the soil, so they leached into the streams. In contrast to nutrient-tight, forested ecosystems, this system was very leaky. The study also found that the forest can influence the acidity of streams. Although the rain falling on the watershed was highly acid at times, the stream water draining a forested watershed was thirty times less acid than the rain falling on it.

This may be an appropriate place to end our discussion—with the thought that these systems are tied to the surrounding landscape in complex ways that have not yet been fully explored. What we have managed to understand should serve to increase our respect.

RIVERS AND STREAMS: PLANTS AND ANIMALS

Wildflowers, Ferns, and Grasses
American Lotus 215
Arrowleaf Groundsel 205
Cardinal Flower 277
Checkermallow 290
Duckweed 313
Fire Flags 303
Heartleaved Bittercress 246
Monkey flower 298
Mountain Bluebell 300
Mountain Globemallow 289
Red Osier Dogwood 325
Seep Spring Monkeyflowers 217
True Forget-me-not 301
Turtlehead 231
Umbrella Plant 233
Water Buttercup 250
Water Hyacinth 296
Water Willow 263
Watercress 245
Wild Rice 321
Wood Nettle 317
Yellow Pond Lily 214

Insects and Spiders
Betten's Silverstreak Caddisfly 362
Black Fly 379
Brown Darner 365
California Acroneuria 361
Common Backswimmer 345
Common Water Strider 356
Comstock's Net-winged Midge 374
Crane Fly 373
Eastern Dobsonfly 359, 360
Elisa Skimmer 370
Fishfly 358
Giant Water Scavenger Beetle 347
Green Darner 366
Kirby's Backswimmer 346
Large Whirligig Beetle 348
Marsh Fly 380
Purplish-blue Cricket Hunter 377
Red Freshwater Mite 384
Short-stalked Damselfly 367
Six-spotted Fishing Spider 382
Small Mayfly 375
Swamp Milkweed Leaf Beetle 351
Swift Long-winged Skimmer 368
Twelve-spot Skimmer 369
Waterlily Leaf Beetle 355
Willow Borer 352
Willow Leaf Beetle 350

Butterflies and Moths
Cerisy's Sphinx 407
Least Skipperling 425
Milbert's Tortoiseshell 393
Viceroy 392
Western Tiger Swallowtail 388
Zebra Swallowtail 390

Trees
Baldcypress 433
Black Willow 453
Dahoon 448
Possumhaw 469
Red Alder 466
Red Maple 479
Silver Maple 479
Swamp Cottonwood 470
Sycamore 480
Water Tupelo 462

Birds
American Black Duck 489
American Dipper 579
Bald Eagle 562
Bank Swallow 571
Belted Kingfisher 568
Black Crowned Night-Heron 529
Bonaparte's Gull 554
Canada Goose 512
Caspian Tern 552
Common Loon 481
Common Merganser 507
Common Tern 550
Common Yellowthroat 584
Double-crested Cormorant 520
Eastern Phoebe 573
Great Blue Heron 528
Green-backed Heron 534
Harlequin Duck 504
Herring Gull 557
Hooded Merganser 509
Lesser Scaup 503
Louisiana Waterthrush 578
Mute Swan 516
Northern Rough-winged Swallow 572
Osprey 563
Ring-billed Gull 555
Ring-necked Duck 501
Semipalmated Sandpiper 543
Spotted Sandpiper 546
White-Fronted Goose 511

Mammals
Beaver 611
Mountain Beaver 607
Pacific Shrew 590
Pacific Water Shrew 592
River Otter 612
Smoky Shrew 593
Star-nosed Mole 595
Water Shrew 591
Water Vole 604

1 Suwannee River Northern Florida

Rivers and Streams

2 Courtois Creek Huzzah State Forest, Missouri

Rivers and Streams

3 Salmon River Central Idaho

Rivers and Streams

4 **Firehole River** Yellowstone National Park, Wyoming

Rivers and Streams

5 **Colorado River** Southeastern Utah

Rivers and Streams

6 **Beaverhead River** Near Dillon, Montana

Rivers and Streams

7 Bear Lake Rocky Mountain National Park, Colorado

Lakes and Ponds

8 Saint Mary's Lake Glacier National Park, Montana

Lakes and Ponds

9 Lake Superior Northeastern Minnesota

Lakes and Ponds

10 Lake Mead Northern Arizona

Lakes and Ponds

11 Green River Lake Western Wyoming

Lakes and Ponds

12 Channel connecting lakes Boundary Waters Canoe Area, northeastern Minnesota

Lakes and Ponds

13 Beaver meadow bog Victory Bog, north of St. Johnsbury, Vermont

Bogs

14 Spruce bog Northeastern Minnesota

Bogs

15 Black Spruce bog Kylen Lake, Minnesota

Bogs

16 Baldcypress trees

Brunswick County, North Carolina

Cypress Swamps

17 Baldcypress trees

Audubon Sanctuary at Four Holes Swamp, Francis Beidler Forest, near Charleston, South Carolina

Cypress Swamps

18 Baldcypress trees

Okefenokee Swamp, southern Georgia

Cypress Swamps

19 **Wild Rice beds** Vermilion River, Minnesota

Marshes

20 **Marsh with sedges** Crex Meadows, near St. Croix River, Wisconsin

Marshes

21 **Pickerelweed** Potomac River, Virginia

Marshes

22 School Section Marsh

Sandhills region, Nebraska

Marshes

23 Marsh with Common Tule

Gray Lodge Refuge, Butte County, California

Marshes

24 Marsh with Saw Grass

Everglades National Park, Florida

Marshes

25 Beaver pond with lodge Elk Island National Park, Alberta

Lakes and Ponds

26 Red maples on Oaks Pond Central Maine

Lakes and Ponds

27 Ethan Pond White Mountains, New Hampshire

Lakes and Ponds

28 Beaver Pond with water lilies

Acadia National Park, Mount Desert Island, Maine

Lakes and Ponds

29 Pond with Water Lettuce

Southwestern Florida

Lakes and Ponds

30 Pond with Water Hyacinth

Southern Florida

Lakes and Ponds

HOW TO USE THE COLOR PLATES

The color plates on the following pages include nine major groups of animals and plants: fishes; amphibians and reptiles; wildflowers, ferns, and grasses; mushrooms; insects and spiders; butterflies and moths; trees; birds; and mammals.

Table of Contents

For easy reference, a table of contents precedes the color plates. The table is divided into two sections. On the left, we list each major group of animals or plants. On the right, the major groups are usually subdivided into smaller groups, and each small group is illustrated by a symbol. For example, the large group of wildflowers, ferns, and grasses is divided into small groups based on color. Similarly, the large group of amphibians and reptiles is divided into small groups made up of distinctive animals such as turtles or snakes.

Captions for the Color Plates

The black bar above each color plate contains the following information: the plate number, the common and scientific names of the animal or plant, its dimensions, and the page number of the full species description. To the left of each color plate, the habitats where you are likely to encounter the species are always indicated in blue type. Additionally, you will find either a fact helpful in field identification, such as the food that an insect eats (also in blue type), or a range map or drawing.

The chart on the facing page lists the dimensions given and the blue-type information, map, or drawing provided for each major group of animals or plants.

CAPTION INFORMATION

Dimensions	Blue Type/Art
Fishes Maximum length of adult	Range map
Amphibians and Reptiles Maximum length of adult	Range map
Wildflowers, Ferns, and Grasses Plant height and flower length or width, or frond length	Drawing of plant or flower
Mushrooms Approximate size of mature mushroom: height or width of stalked mushroom; width of cup-shaped or unusually shaped mushroom	Specific habitat
Insects and Spiders Length of adult, excluding antennae and appendages	Major food
Butterflies and Moths Wingspan of fully spread adult	Caterpillar's host plants
Trees Leaf, leaflet, or needle length	Winter tree silhouette
Birds Length, usually of adult male, from tip of bill to tail	Range map showing breeding, winter, and/or permanent range
Mammals Length of adult	Range map

Mushrooms

Mushrooms
331–342

Insects and Spiders

Aquatic Bugs and Beetles
343–357
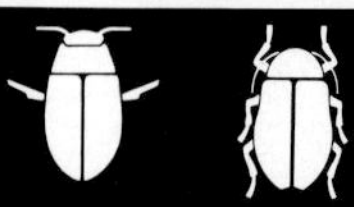

Dobson Flies and Other Long-winged Insects
358–362

Dragonflies and Damselflies
363–372

Flies and Mayfly
373–376, 378–381

Cricket Hunter
377

Spiders and Mite
382–384

Butterflies and Moths

Green
385–387

Swallowtails
388–390

Orange-patterned
391–398

Butterflies and Moths
(*continued*)

Blues and Coppers
399, 403, 405

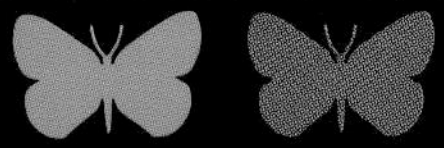

Eyespot Patterns
400–402, 404, 406–410

Skippers
411, 413–414, 416, 419–426

Arctic and Alpine Satyrs
412, 415, 417–418

Trees

Needle-leaf and Scale-leaf Conifers
427–433

Compound Leaves
434–441

Simple Leaves
442–480

Birds

Loon and Grebes
481–486

Ducks, Geese, and Swan
487–516

Pelican and Anhinga
517–518

Birds (*continued*)

31 Gizzard Shad

Dorosoma cepedianum
p. 355
Length: to 16″

Lakes and Ponds; Rivers and Streams

32 American Shad

Alosa sapidissima
p. 355
Length: to 30″

Rivers and Streams

33 Striped Bass

Morone saxatilis
p. 355
Length: to 6′

Rivers and Streams

34 Largemouth Bass *Micropterus salmoides* Length: to 3′2″
p. 356

The Everglades; Lakes and Ponds

35 Quillback *Carpiodes cyprinus* Length: to 24″
p. 356

Lakes and Ponds; Rivers and Streams

36 Smallmouth Buffalo *Ictiobus bubalus* Length: to 3′
p. 357

Lakes and Ponds; Rivers and Streams

37 Common Carp

Cyprinus carpio
p. 357

Length: to 30″

Lakes and Ponds; Rivers and Streams

38 Common Carp

Cyprinus carpio
p. 357

Length: to 30″

Lakes and Ponds; Rivers and Streams

39 White Perch

Morone americana
p. 358

Length: to 19″

Lakes and Ponds; Rivers and Streams

40 White Bass *Morone chrysops* Length: to 18″
p. 358

Lakes and Ponds; Rivers and Streams

41 Walleye *Stizostedion vitreum* Length: to 3′5″
p. 358

Lakes and Ponds; Rivers and Streams

42 Sauger *Stizostedion canadense* Length: to 28″
p. 359

Lakes and Ponds; Rivers and Streams

43 Yellow Perch

Perca flavescens
p. 359

Length: to 15″

Lakes and Ponds; Rivers and Streams

44 Smallmouth Bass

Micropterus dolomieui
p. 360

Length: to 24″

Lakes and Ponds; Rivers and Streams

45 Rock Bass

Ambloplites rupestris
p. 360

Length: to 13″

Lakes and Ponds; Rivers and Streams

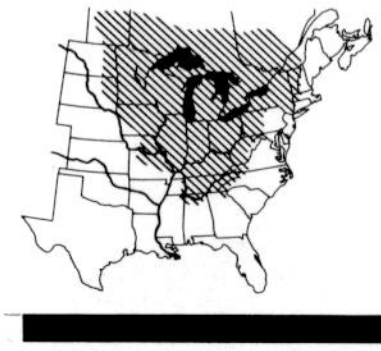

46 Sacramento Perch

Archoplites interruptus
p. 360

Length: to 16″

Swamps and Sloughs

47 Warmouth

Lepomis gulosus
p. 361

Length: to 10″

Swamps; Lakes and Ponds

48 Bluegill

Lepomis macrochirus
p. 361

Length: to 12″

The Everglades; Lakes and Ponds; Rivers and Streams; Sloughs

49 **Spotted Bass** *Micropterus punctulatus* Length: to 24″
p. 361

Lakes and Ponds; Rivers and Streams

50 **Black Crappie** *Pomoxis nigromaculatus* Length: to 16″
p. 362

Lakes and Ponds; Rivers and Streams

51 **Longear Sunfish** *Lepomis megalotis* Length: to 9″
p. 362

Lakes and Ponds; Rivers and Streams

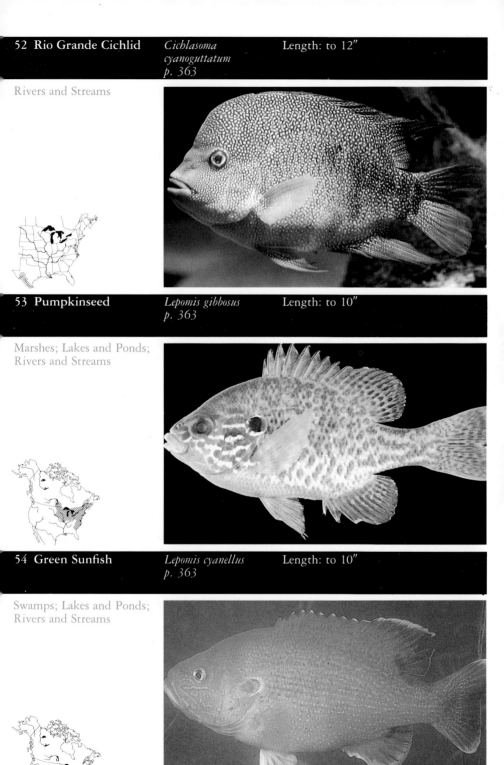

52 Rio Grande Cichlid

Cichlasoma cyanoguttatum
p. 363

Length: to 12″

Rivers and Streams

53 Pumpkinseed

Lepomis gibbosus
p. 363

Length: to 10″

Marshes; Lakes and Ponds; Rivers and Streams

54 Green Sunfish

Lepomis cyanellus
p. 363

Length: to 10″

Swamps; Lakes and Ponds; Rivers and Streams

55 Mozambique Tilapia

Tilapia mossambica
p. 364

Length: to 15″

Lakes and Ponds; Rivers and Streams

56 Sailfin Molly

Poecilia latipinna
p. 364

Length: to 5″

Lakes and Ponds

57 Pirate Perch

Aphredoderus sayanus
p. 365

Length: to 4½″

Bottomland Hardwood Swamps; Lakes and Ponds; Rivers and Streams

58 Stippled Darter *Etheostoma punctulatum* *p. 365* Length: to 3½″

Rivers and Streams

59 Mottled Sculpin *Cottus bairdi* *p. 365* Length: to 4″

Lakes and Ponds; Rivers and Streams

60 Snail Darter *Percina tanasi* *p. 366* Length: to 3″

Rivers and Streams

61 Swamp Darter

Etheostoma fusiforme
p. 366
Length: to 2″

Swamps; Lakes and Ponds; Rivers and Streams

62 Johnny Darter

Etheostoma nigrum
p. 367
Length: to 2½″

Lakes and Ponds; Rivers and Streams

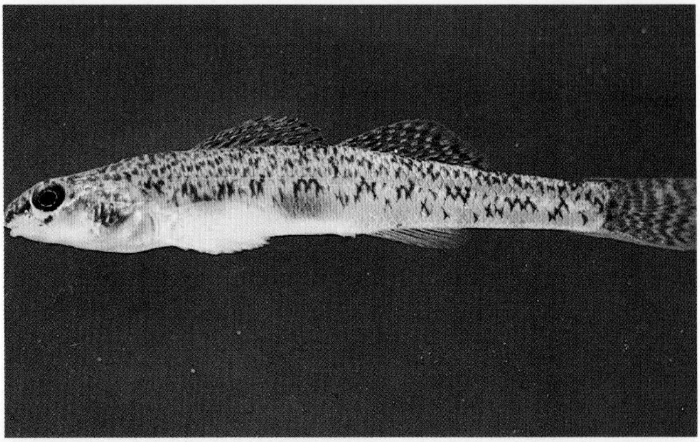

63 Brook Stickleback

Culaea inconstans
p. 367
Length: to 2″

Lakes and Ponds; Rivers and Streams

64 Plains Killifish *Fundulus zebrinus* Length: to 5″
p. 368

Rivers and Streams

65 Starhead Topminnow *Fundulus notti* Length: to 3″
p. 368

Marshes; Swamps; Lakes and Ponds; Rivers and Streams

66 Speckled Chub *Hybopsis aestivalis* Length: to 3″
p. 368

Rivers and Streams

67 Common Shiner *Notropis cornutus* Length: to 6″
p. 369

Rivers and Streams

68 Taillight Shiner *Notropis maculatus* Length: to 3″
p. 369

Lakes and Ponds; Rivers and Streams

69 Brook Silverside *Labidesthes sicculus* Length: to 4″
p. 369

Lakes and Ponds; Rivers and Streams

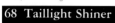

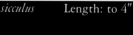

70 Golden Shiner

Notemigonus crysoleucas Length: to 12″
p. 370

Swamps and the Everglades; Lakes and Ponds; Rivers and Streams

71 Pugnose Minnow

Notropis emiliae Length: to 2½″
p. 370

Slow-moving Rivers

72 Pugnose Minnow

Notropis emiliae Length: to 2½″
p. 370

Slow-moving Rivers

73 White Sucker *Catostomus commersoni* Length: to 24″
p. 371

Lakes and Ponds; Rivers and Streams

74 Spotted Sucker *Minytrema melanops* Length: to 20″
p. 371

Rivers and Streams

75 Chain Pickerel *Esox niger* Length: to 31″
p. 372

Swamps; Lakes and Ponds; Rivers and Streams

76 Northern Pike

Esox lucius
p. 372

Length: to 4′4″

Lakes and Ponds; Rivers and Streams

77 Muskellunge

Esox masquinongy
p. 372

Length: to 6′

Lakes and Ponds; Rivers and Streams

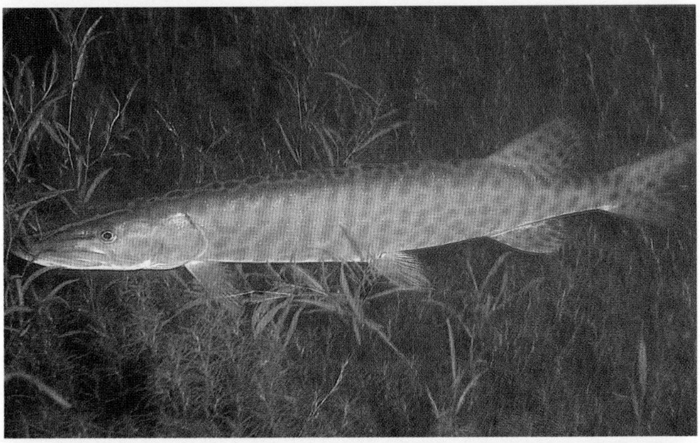

78 Alligator Gar

Lepisosteus spatula
p. 373

Length: to 10′

Swamps; the Everglades; Lakes and Ponds; Rivers and Streams; Bayous

79 Paddlefish *Polyodon spathula* *p. 373* Length: to 7′1″

Lakes and Ponds; Rivers and Streams

80 Shovelnose Sturgeon *Scaphirhynchus platorynchus* *p. 374* Length: to 3′

Rivers and Streams

81 Shovelnose Sturgeon *Scaphirhynchus platorynchus* *p. 374* Length: to 3′

Rivers and Streams

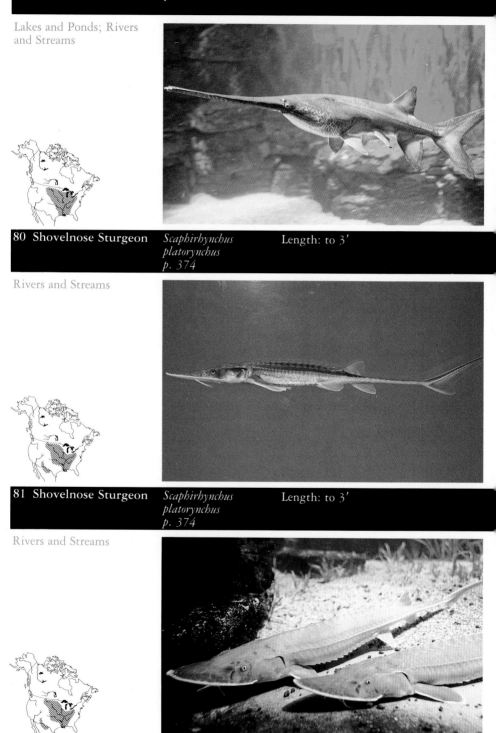

82 Chestnut Lamprey *Ichthyomyzon castaneus* Length: to 15″
p. 374

Rivers and Streams

83 Walking Catfish *Clarias batrachus* Length: to 14″
p. 374

Swamps; the Everglades; Lakes and Ponds

84 American Eel *Anguilla rostrata* Length: to 4′11″
p. 375

Rivers and Streams

85 Tadpole Madtom

Noturus gyrinus
p. 375

Length: to 4½″

Lakes and Ponds; Rivers and Streams

86 Yellow Bullhead

Ictalurus natalis
p. 376

Length: to 18″

Lakes and Ponds; Rivers and Streams

87 Channel Catfish

Ictalurus punctatus
p. 376

Length: to 3′11″

Rivers and Streams

88 Lake Trout *Salvelinus namaycush* Length: to 4′2″
p. 376

Lakes and Ponds; Rivers and Streams

89 Brook Trout *Salvelinus fontinalis* Length: to 21″
p. 377

Lakes and Ponds; Rivers and Streams

90 Brown Trout *Salmo trutta* Length: to 3′4″
p. 377

Lakes and Ponds; Rivers and Streams

91 Rainbow Trout
Salmo gairdneri
p. 378
Length: to 3′9″

Rivers and Streams

92 Cutthroat Trout
Salmo clarki
p. 378
Length: to 30″

Lakes and Ponds; Rivers and Streams

93 Apache Trout
Salmo apache
p. 378
Length: to 18″

Rivers and Streams

94 Atlantic Salmon

Salmo salar
p. 379

Length: to 4′5″

Lakes and Ponds; Rivers and Streams

95 Sockeye Salmon

Oncorhynchus nerka
p. 379

Length: to 33″

Lakes and Ponds; Rivers and Streams

96 Grass Carp

Ctenopharyngodon idella
p. 380

Length: to 3′3″

Rivers and Streams

97 Mosquitofish

Gambusia affinis *p. 380*

Length: to 2½″

The Everglades; Lakes and Ponds; Rivers and Streams

98 Desert Pupfish

Cyprinodon macularius *p. 380*

Length: to 2½″

Rivers and Streams

99 Fathead Minnow

Pimephales promelas *p. 381*

Length: to 4″

Lakes and Ponds; Rivers and Streams

100 Flagfish | *Jordanella floridae* *p. 381* | Length: to 2½″

Lakes and Ponds

101 Least Killifish | *Heterandria formosa* *p. 382* | Length: to 1″

Swamps; the Everglades; Lakes and Ponds

102 Central Mudminnow | *Umbra limi* *p. 382* | Length: to 5″

Bogs; Swamps; Lakes and Ponds

103 Two-toed Amphiuma *Amphiuma means* *p. 384* Length: 18–45¾″

Southern Bottomland Hardwood Swamps and the Everglades

104 Mudpuppy *Necturus maculosus* *p. 384* Length: 8–17″

Lakes and Ponds; Rivers and Streams

105 Hellbender *Cryptobranchus alleganiensis* *p. 384* Length: 12–29⅛″

Rivers and Streams

106 Greater Siren *Siren lacertina* Length: 19¾–38½″
p. 385

Bottomland Hardwood Swamps and the Everglades

107 Lesser Siren *Siren intermedia* Length: 7–27″
p. 386

Swamps and Sloughs

108 Dwarf Siren *Pseudobranchus striatus* Length: 4–9⅞″
p. 386

Bottomland Hardwood Swamps

109 Dwarf Salamander *Eurycea quadridigitata* Length: 2⅛–3½″
p. 387

Lakes and Ponds

110 Two-lined Salamander *Eurycea bislineata* Length: 2½–4¾″
p. 387

Swamps; Rivers and Streams; Floodplains

111 Mud Salamander *Pseudotriton montanus* Length: 2⅞–7⅝″
p. 388

Swamps; Rivers and Streams; Floodplains

112 Dusky Salamander

Desmognathus fuscus Length: 2½–5½″
p. 389

Rivers and Streams; Floodplains

113 Many-lined Salamander

Stereochilus marginatus Length: 2½–4½″
p. 389

Lakes and Ponds; Rivers and Streams

114 Four-toed Salamander

Hemidactylium scutatum Length: 2–4″
p. 390

Bogs and Floodplains

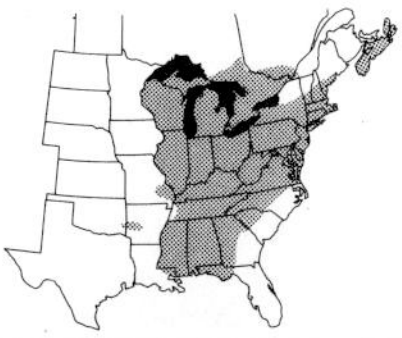

115 California Newt

Taricha torosa
p. 390

Length: 5–7¾″

Lakes and Ponds; Rivers and Streams

116 Mud Salamander

Pseudotriton montanus
p. 388

Length: 2⅞–7⅝″

Swamps; Rivers and Streams; Floodplains

117 Dwarf Salamander

Eurycea quadridigitata
p. 387

Length: 2⅛–3½″

Lakes and Ponds

118 Mud Salamander *Pseudotriton montanus* Length: 2⅞–7⅝″
p. 388

Swamps; Rivers and Streams; Floodplains

119 Mud Salamander *Pseudotriton montanus* Length: 2⅞–7⅝″
p. 388

Swamps; Rivers and Streams; Floodplains

120 Red Salamander *Pseudotriton ruber* Length: 3⅞–7⅛″
p. 391

Swamps; Rivers and Streams

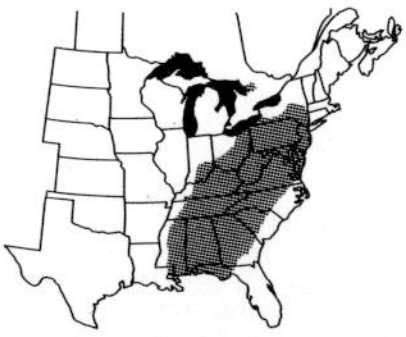

121 Two-lined Salamander | *Eurycea bislineata* *p. 387* | Length: 2½–4¾″

Swamps; Rivers and Streams; Floodplains

122 Eastern Newt | *Notophthalmus viridescens* *p. 391* | Length: 2⅝–5½″

Lakes and Ponds

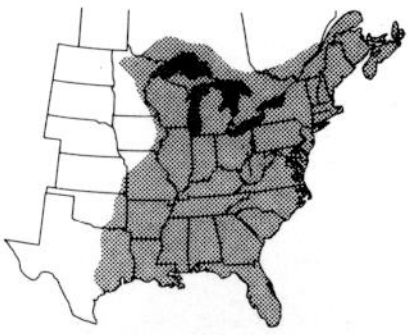

123 Eastern Newt | *Notophthalmus viridescens* *p. 391* | Length: 2⅝–5½″

Lakes and Ponds

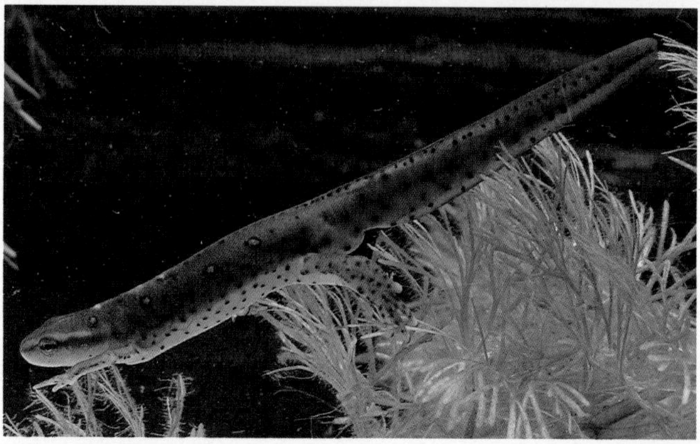

124 Black-spotted Newt

Notophthalmus meridionalis
p. 392

Length: 2⅞–4¼″

Lakes and Ponds; Rivers and Streams

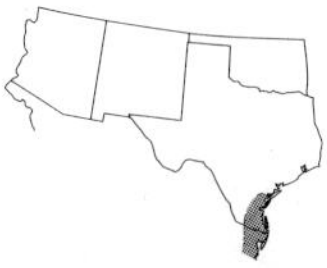

125 Tiger Salamander

Ambystoma tigrinum
p. 392

Length: 6–13⅜″

Lakes and Ponds; Rivers and Streams

126 Spotted Salamander

Ambystoma maculatum
p. 393

Length: 6–9¾″

Swamps

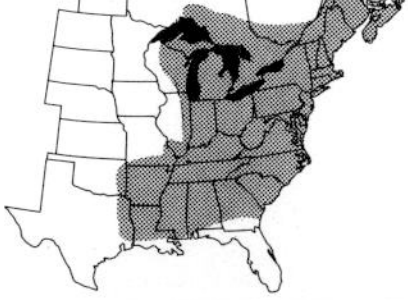

127 Spotted Salamander *Ambystoma maculatum* *p. 393* Length: 6–9¾″

Swamps

128 Pacific Giant Salamander *Dicamptodon ensatus* *p. 394* Length: 7–11¾″

Rivers and Streams

129 Tiger Salamander *Ambystoma tigrinum* *p. 392* Length: 6–13⅜″

Lakes and Ponds; Rivers and Streams

130 Northern Leopard Frog — *Rana pipiens* — Length: 2–5″

p. 394

Marshes; Lakes and Ponds

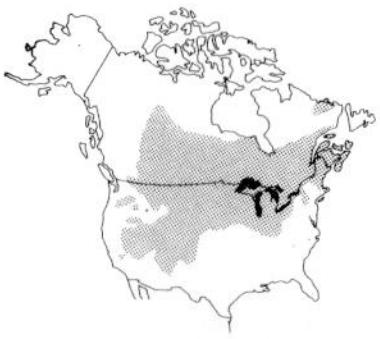

131 Rio Grande Leopard Frog — *Rana berlandieri* — Length: $2\frac{1}{4}$–$4\frac{1}{2}$″

p. 395

Marshes; Lakes and Ponds; Rivers and Streams

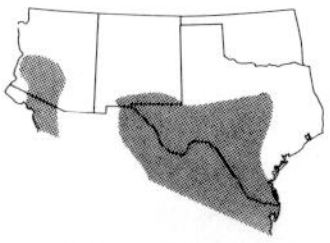

132 Striped Chorus Frog — *Pseudacris triseriata* — Length: $\frac{3}{4}$–$1\frac{1}{2}$″

p. 395

Swamps

133 Northern Cricket Frog *Acris crepitans* p. 396 Length: ⅝–1½″

Lakes and Ponds; Rivers and Streams

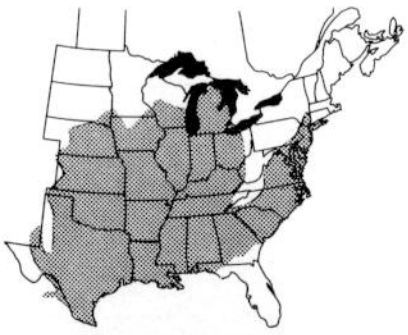

134 Green Frog *Rana clamitans* p. 396 Length: 2⅛–4″

Swamps; Lakes and Ponds

135 River Frog *Rana heckscheri* p. 397 Length: 3¼–5$\frac{5}{16}$″

Swamps; Rivers and Streams

136 Bullfrog *Rana catesbeiana* Length: 3½–8″
p. 397 Female

Lakes and Ponds; Rivers and Streams

137 Bullfrog *Rana catesbeiana* Length: 3½–8″
p. 397

Lakes and Ponds; Rivers and Streams

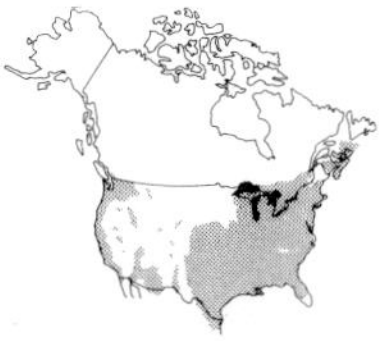

138 Pine Barrens Treefrog *Hyla andersoni* Length: 1⅛–2″
p. 398

Bogs; Swamps; Rivers and Streams

139 Carpenter Frog

Rana virgatipes
p. 398

Length: 1⅝–2⅝″

Bogs; Lakes and Ponds

140 Wood Frog

Rana sylvatica
p. 399

Length: 1⅜–3¼″

Swamps

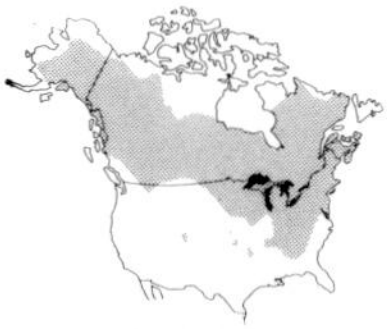

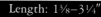

141 Southern Cricket Frog

Acris gryllus
p. 399

Length: ⅝–1¼″

Marshes; Swamps; the Everglades; Lakes and Ponds; Rivers and Streams

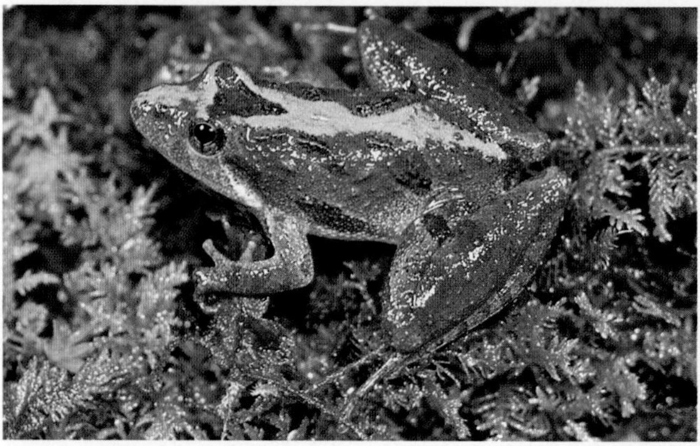

142 Southern Cricket Frog

Acris gryllus
p. 399

Length: ⅝–1¼″

Marshes; Swamps; the Everglades; Lakes and Ponds; Rivers and Streams

143 Northern Leopard Frog

Rana pipiens
p. 394

Length: 2–5″

Marshes; Lakes and Ponds

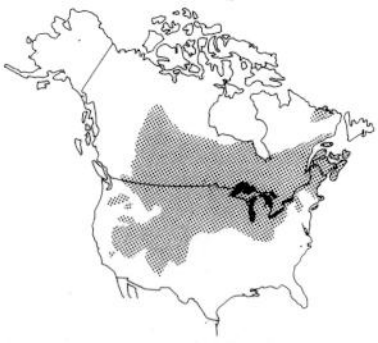

144 Pickerel Frog

Rana palustris
p. 400

Length: 1¾–3 7/16″

Swamps; Rivers and Streams

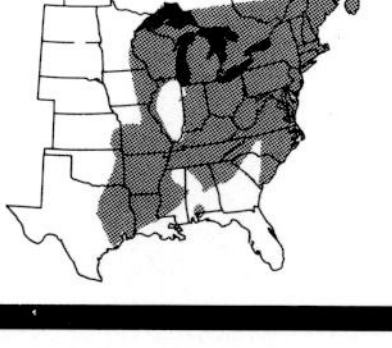

145 Canadian Toad *Bufo hemiophrys* *p. 400* Length: 2–3¼"

Lakes and Ponds

146 Black Toad *Bufo exsul* *p. 401* Length: 1¾–2⅜"

Rivers and Streams

147 Bird-voiced Treefrog *Hyla avivoca* *p. 401* Length: 1⅛–2⅛"

Southern Swamps

148 Brimley's Chorus Frog | *Pseudacris brimleyi* *p. 402* | Length: 1–1¼″

Marshes

149 Wood Frog | *Rana sylvatica* *p. 399* | Length: 1⅜–3¼″ Female

Swamps

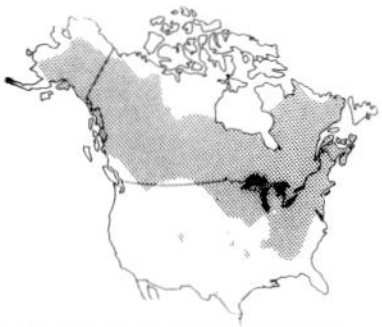

150 Spring Peeper | *Hyla crucifer* *p. 402* | Length: ¾–1⅜″

Swamps

151 Snapping Turtle

Chelydra serpentina
p. 403

Length: 8–18½″

Lakes and Ponds

152 Snapping Turtle

Chelydra serpentina
p. 403

Length: 8–18½″

Lakes and Ponds

153 Mud Turtle

Kinosternon subrubrum
p. 403

Length: 3–4⅞″

The Everglades; Rivers and Streams

154 Mud Turtle

Kinosternon subrubrum
p. 403
Length: 3–4$\frac{7}{8}$″

The Everglades; Rivers and Streams

155 Stinkpot

Sternotherus odoratus
p. 404
Length: 3–5$\frac{3}{8}$″

Lakes and Ponds; Rivers and Streams

156 Spotted Turtle

Clemmys guttata
p. 405
Length: 3$\frac{1}{2}$–5″

Lakes and Ponds; Rivers and Streams

157 Slider *Pseudemys scripta* Length: 5–11⅜″
p. 405

Swamps; Lakes and Ponds; Rivers and Streams

158 Florida Redbelly Turtle *Chrysemys nelsoni* Length: 8–13⅜″
p. 406

The Everglades; Lakes and Ponds; Rivers and Streams

159 Painted Turtle *Chrysemys picta* Length: 4–9⅞″
p. 406

Lakes and Ponds; Rivers and Streams

160 Mud Turtle *Kinosternon subrubrum* Length: 3–4⅞″
p. 403

The Everglades; Rivers and Streams

161 Painted Turtle *Chrysemys picta* Length: 4–9⅞″
p. 406

Lakes and Ponds; Rivers and Streams

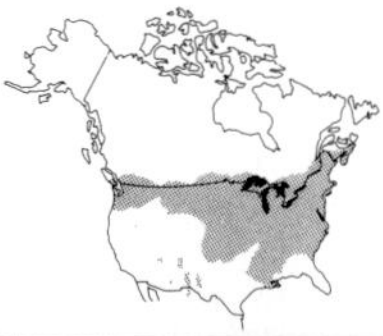

162 Painted Turtle *Chrysemys picta* Length: 4–9⅞″
p. 406

Lakes and Ponds; Rivers and Streams

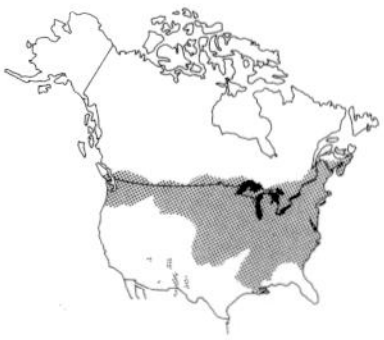

163 Slider *Pseudemys scripta* *p. 405* Length: 5–11⅜"

Swamps; Lakes and Ponds; Rivers and Streams

164 Map Turtle *Graptemys geographica* *p. 407* Length: 4–6¼" (males); 7–10¾" (females)

Lakes and Ponds; Rivers and Streams

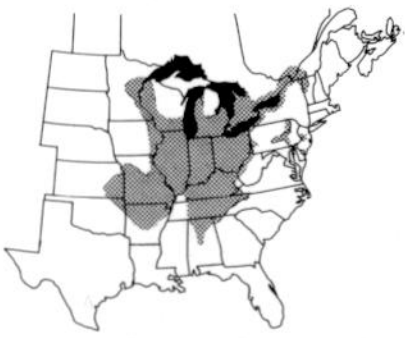

165 Bog Turtle *Clemmys muhlenbergi* *p. 408* Length: 3–4½"

Bogs

166 Wood Turtle | *Clemmys insculpta* | Length: 5–9″
p. 408

Swamps

167 Western Pond Turtle | *Clemmys marmorata* | Length: 3½–7″
p. 409

Marshes; Lakes and Ponds

168 Razorback Musk Turtle | *Sternotherus carinatus* | Length: 4–5⅞″
p. 410

Swamps; Rivers and Streams

169 Flattened Musk Turtle

Sternotherus depressus
p. 410

Length: 3–4½″

Swamps; Rivers and Streams

170 Spiny Softshell

Trionyx spiniferus
p. 410

Length: 5–9¼″ (males); 6½–18″ (females)

Lakes and Ponds; Rivers and Streams

171 Spiny Softshell

Trionyx spiniferus
p. 410

Length: 5–9¼″ (males); 6½–18″ (females)
Female

Lakes and Ponds; Rivers and Streams

172 American Alligator *Alligator mississippiensis* *p. 411* Length: 6′–19′2″

Marshes, Swamps, the Everglades; Lakes and Ponds; Rivers and Streams

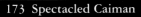

173 Spectacled Caiman *Caiman crocodilus* *p. 411* Length: 4′–8′8″

Marshes and the Everglades; Lakes and Ponds; Rivers and Streams

174 American Crocodile *Crocodylus acutus* *p. 412* Length: 7–15′

The Everglades, Bogs, and Swamps

175 Cottonmouth *Agkistrodon piscivorus* *p. 412* Length: 20–74½" ⊗

Swamps; the Everglades; Lakes and Ponds; Rivers and Streams; Sloughs

176 Smooth Green Snake *Opheodrys vernalis* *p. 413* Length: 14–26"

Marshes

177 Cottonmouth *Agkistrodon piscivorus* *p. 412* Length: 20–74½" ⊗

Swamps; the Everglades; Lakes and Ponds; Rivers and Streams; Sloughs

178 P[redacted] Woods Snake *Rhadinaea flavilata* *p. 414* Length: [redacted]15⅞″

Marshes

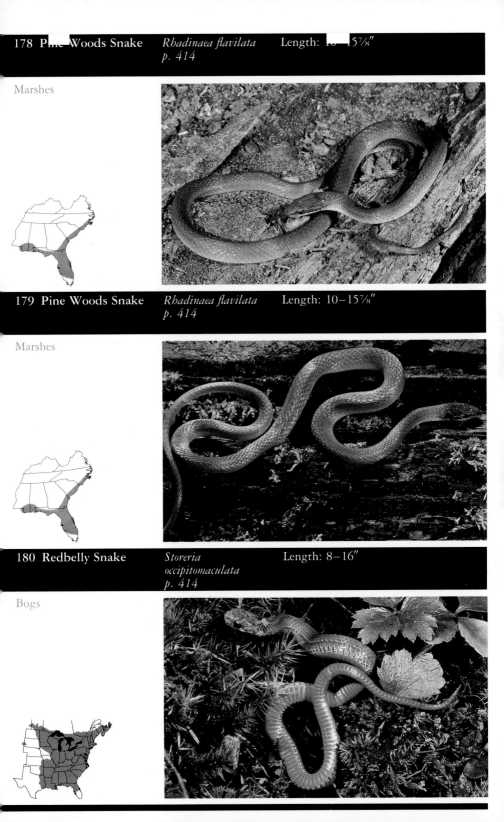

179 Pine Woods Snake *Rhadinaea flavilata* *p. 414* Length: 10–15⅞″

Marshes

180 Redbelly Snake *Storeria occipitomaculata* *p. 414* Length: 8–16″

Bogs

181 Black Swamp Snake *Seminatrix pygaea* Length: 10–18½″
p. 415

Swamps and the Everglades

182 Mud Snake *Farancia abacura* Length: 38–81″
p. 415

Swamps; the Everglades; Floodplains

183 Black Swamp Snake *Seminatrix pygaea* Length: 10–18½″
p. 415

Swamps and the Everglades

184 Glossy Crayfish Snake | *Regina rigida* | Length: 14–31⅜″

p. 416

Swamps; Lakes and Ponds; Rivers and Streams; Floodplains

185 Green Water Snake | *Nerodia cyclopion* | Length: 30–74″

p. 416

Marshes and Swamps

186 Queen Snake | *Regina septemvittata* | Length: 16–36¾″

p. 417

Rivers and Streams

187 Eastern Ribbon Snake

Thamnophis sauritus
p. 417

Length: 18–40″

Bogs and Marshes

188 Striped Crayfish Snake

Regina alleni
p. 418

Length: 13–25¾″

Bogs

189 Brown Snake

Storeria dekayi
p. 418

Length: 10–20¾″

Bogs, Marshes, Swamps, and the Everglades

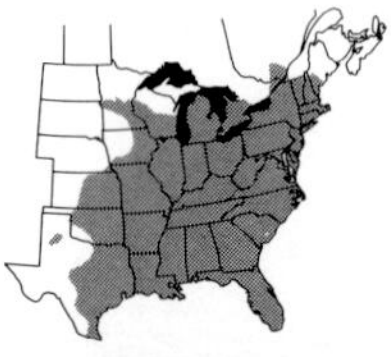

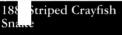

190 Brown Water Snake *Nerodia taxispilota* Length: 28–69″
p. 419

Swamps; Lakes and Ponds; Rivers and Streams

191 Southern Water Snake *Nerodia fasciata* Length: 16–62½″
p. 419

Swamps; Lakes and Ponds

192 Kirtland's Snake *Clonophis kirtlandi* Length: 14–24½″
p. 420

Marshes; Lakes and Ponds

193 Tim[redacted]Rattlesnake

Crotalus horridus
p. 420

Length: 3[redacted]½″

Swamps and the Everglades

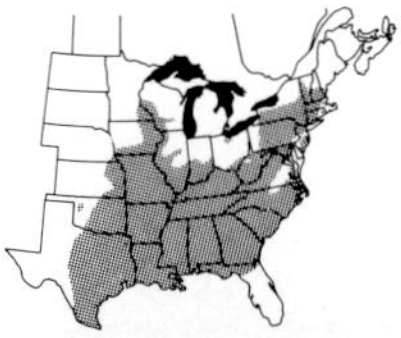

194 Cottonmouth

Agkistrodon piscivorus
p. 412

Length: 20–74½″

Swamps; the Everglades; Lakes and Ponds; Rivers and Streams; Sloughs

195 Northern Water Snake

Nerodia sipedon
p. 421

Length: 22–53″

Marshes; Swamps; Lakes and Ponds; Rivers and Streams

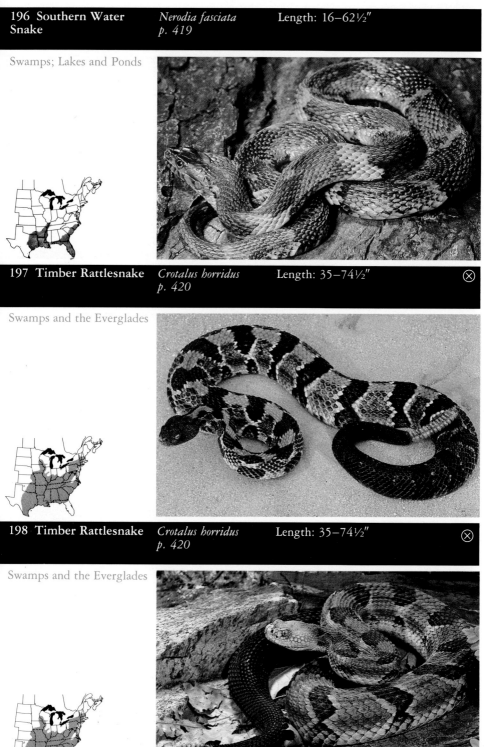

196 Southern Water Snake *Nerodia fasciata* Length: 16–62½″
p. 419

Swamps; Lakes and Ponds

197 Timber Rattlesnake *Crotalus horridus* Length: 35–74½″ ⊗
p. 420

Swamps and the Everglades

198 Timber Rattlesnake *Crotalus horridus* Length: 35–74½″ ⊗
p. 420

Swamps and the Everglades

199 Pussy Willow | *Salix discolor* *p. 423* | Plant height: 2–20′ Flower length: to 2″

Shrub Swamps

200 Tufted Loosestrife | *Lysimachia thyrsiflora* *p. 423* | Plant height: 8–32″ Flower length: about ¼″

Swamps

201 Spicebush | *Lindera benzoin* *p. 423* | Plant height: 6–17′ Flower width: ⅛″

Swamps

202 Hooded Pitcher Plant *Sarracenia minor* *p. 424* Plant height: 6–24″ Flower width: about 2″

Bogs

203 Fringed Loosestrife *Lysimachia ciliata* *p. 424* Plant height: 1–4′ Flower width: ¾″

Marshes

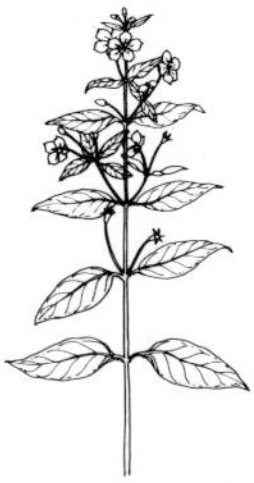

204 Swamp Candles *Lysimachia terrestris* *p. 425* Plant height: 1–3′ Flower width: ½″

Marshes

205 Arrowleaf Groundsel

Senecio triangularis
p. 425

Plant height: 1–5′
Flower width: 1–1½″

Rivers and Streams

206 Nodding Bur Marigold

Bidens cernua
p. 425

Plant height: 1–3′
Flower width: to 2″

Swamps

207 Golden Ragwort

Senecio aureus
p. 426

Plant height: 1–2′
Flower width: ¾″

Swamps

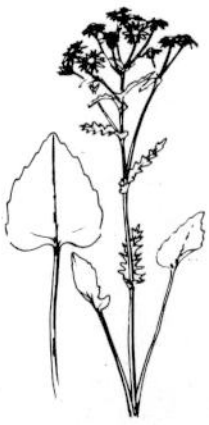

208 Yellow Butterwort *Pinguicula lutea* Plant height: 5–18″
p. 426 Flower width: 1″

Bogs and wet depressions in grassy areas; the Everglades

209 Cowslip *Caltha palustris* Plant height: 1–2′
p. 427 Flower width: 1–1½″

Swamps

210 Yellow-eyed Grass *Xyris iridifolia* Plant height: 2–3′
p. 427 Flower width: about ½″

Wet peat or sand

211 Swamp Buttercup

Ranunculus septentrionalis
p. 427

Plant height: 1–3′
Flower width: 1″

Swamps

212 Yellow Water Buttercup

Ranunculus flabellaris
p. 428

Aquatic
Flower width: ½–1½″

Lakes and Ponds

213 Swollen Bladderwort

Utricularia inflata
p. 428

Aquatic
Flower width: ⅔″

Lakes and Ponds

214 Yellow Pond Lily *Nuphar variegatum* *p. 429* Aquatic Flower width: 1½–2½″

Lakes and Ponds; Rivers and Streams

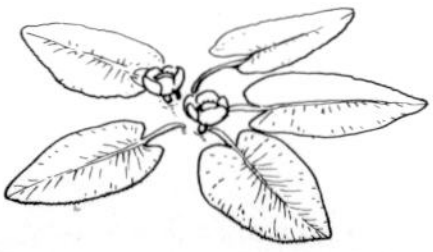

215 American Lotus *Nelumbo lutea* *p. 429* Aquatic Flower width: 6–10″

Lakes and Ponds; Rivers and Streams

216 Yellow Water Lily *Nymphaea mexicana* *p. 430* Aquatic Flower width: 4–5″

Lakes and Ponds

217 Seep-spring Monkeyflower

Mimulus guttatus
p. 430

Plant height: to 3′
Flower length: ½–1½″

Rivers and Streams

218 Horned Bladderwort

Utricularia cornuta
p. 431

Plant height: 2–12″
Flower length: about ¾″

Bogs; Lakes and Ponds

219 Yellow Flag

Iris pseudacorus
p. 431

Plant height: 2–3′
Flower width: 3″

Marshes

220 Common Cattail — *Typha latifolia* — *p. 431*

Plant height: 3–9′
Flower length: on spikes to 6″

Marshes and the Everglades

221 Sweetflag — *Acorous calamus* — *p. 432*

Aquatic
Flower length: clustered on spadix 2–3½″

Marshes

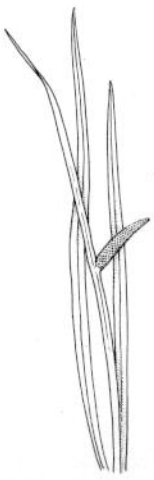

222 Golden Club — *Orontium aquaticum* — *p. 432*

Aquatic
Flower length: clustered on spadix 1–2″

Cypress Swamps; Lakes and Ponds

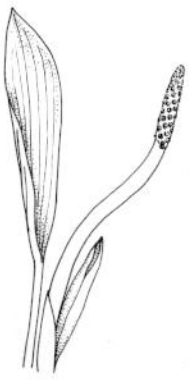

223 Yellow Skunk Cabbage *Lysichitum americanum* p. 433
Plant height: 12–20″
Flower length: bract to 8″

Swamps

224 Trumpets *Sarracenia flava* p. 433
Plant height: 1½–3½′
Flower width: 3–5″

Bogs

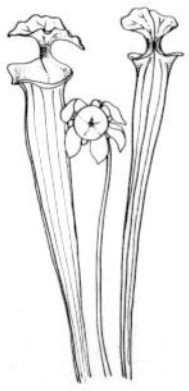

225 Water Arum *Calla palustris* p. 434
Aquatic
Flower length: clustered on spadix 1″

Bogs

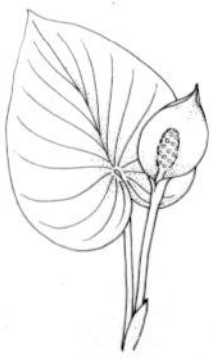

226 White-topped Sedge *Dichromena colorata* *p. 434*
Plant height: 8–24″
Flower length: in spikelet about ¼″

Marshes

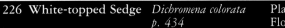

227 Swamp Lily *Crinum americanum* *p. 434*
Plant height: to 3′
Flower width: 4″

Marshes and the Everglades

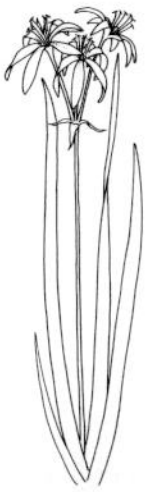

228 Spider Lily *Hymenocallis liriosme* *p. 435*
Plant height: 1½′
Flower width: to 7″

Marshes and the Everglades

229 Swamp Honeysuckle *Rhododendron viscosum* *p. 435* Plant height: 3–9′ Flower width: 1½–2″ ⊗

Swamps

230 Great Laurel *Rhododendron maximum* *p. 436* Plant height: 5–35′ Flower width: 1½–2″ ⊗

Bogs and Swamps

231 Turtlehead *Chelone glabra* *p. 436* Plant height: 1–3′ Flower length: 1–1½″

Rivers and Streams

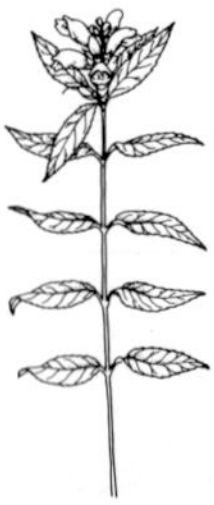

232 Delicate Ionopsis
Ionopsis utricularioides
p. 437
Plant height: 4–15″
Flower width: ¾″

Cypress Swamps and the Everglades

233 Umbrella Plant
Peltiphyllum peltatum
p. 437
Plant height: 2–6′
Flower length: about ¼″

Rivers and Streams

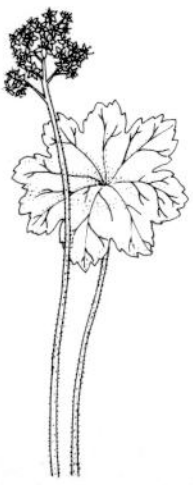

234 Labrador Tea
Ledum groenlandicum
p. 437
Plant height: 1–4′
Flower width: ⅓–½″

Bogs

235 Sweet Pepperbush *Clethra alnifolia* *p. 438* Plant height: 3–10′ Flower width: about ⅓″

Swamps

236 Lizard's Tail *Saururus cernuus* *p. 438* Plant height: 2–5′ Flower length: cluster to 6″

Swamps and the Everglades

237 Buttonbush *Cephalanthus occidentalis* *p. 438* Plant height: 3–10′ Flower length: ⅓″

Swamps; Lakes and Ponds; Rivers and Streams

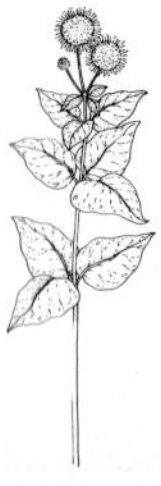

238 Cotton Grass *Eriophorum polystachion*
p. 439
Plant height: 8–40″
Flower width: clusters 2–3″

Bogs

239 Common Pipewort *Eriocaulon septangulare*
p. 439
Plant height: 1½–9″
Flower length: about 1/12″

Marshes; Lakes and Ponds

240 Water Hemlock *Cicuta maculata*
p. 440
Plant height: 3–6′
Flower length: about 1/6″

Marshes and Swamps

241 Water Parsnip *Sium suave* *p. 440*
Plant height: 2–6′
Flower width: clusters 2–3″

Marshes

242 Elderberry *Sambucus canadensis* *p. 441*
Plant height: 3–12′
Flower width: 1/6″

Swamps

243 Titi *Cyrilla racemiflora* *p. 441*
Plant height: to 25′
Flower width: about 1/5″

Swamps

244 Winterberry

Ilex verticillata
p. 441

Plant height: 3–10′
Flower width: clusters 1/4–1/2″

Swamps; Lakes and Ponds

245 Watercress

Nasturtium officinale
p. 442

Creeper
Flower length: about 3/16″

Lakes and Ponds; Rivers and Streams

246 Heartleaved Bittercress

Cardamine cordifolia
p. 442

Plant height: 4–32″
Flower length: 1/2–3/4″

Rivers and Streams

247 Arrowhead | *Sagittaria latifolia* *p. 443* | Plant height: 1–4′ Flower width: ⅔″

Marshes and the Everglades

248 Water Plantain | *Alisma subcordatum* *p. 443* | Plant height: 4–36″ Flower width: ⅙″

Marshes

249 Venus Flytrap | *Dionaea muscipula* *p. 443* | Plant height: 4–12″ Flower width: about 1″

Marshes

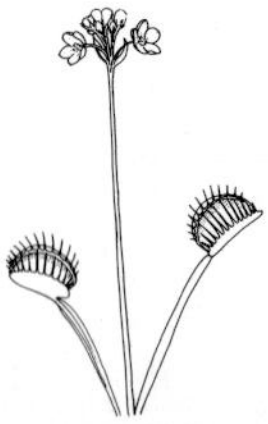

250 Water Buttercup | *Ranunculus aquatilis* *p. 444* | Aquatic
Flower width: ½–¾″

Lakes and Ponds; Rivers and Streams

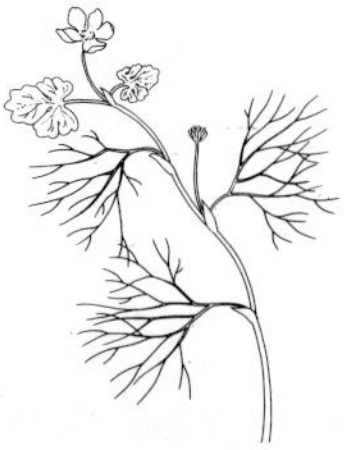

251 Round-leaved Sundew | *Drosera rotundifolia* *p. 444* | Plant height: 4–9″
Flower width: about ¼″

Bogs

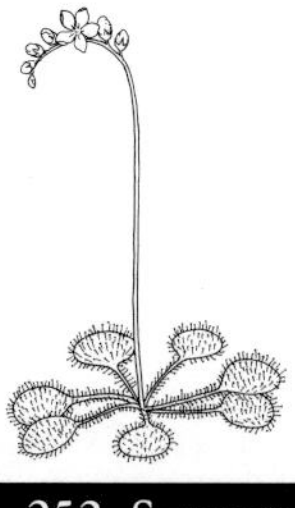

252 Swamp Dewberry | *Rubus hispidus* *p. 445* | Creeper
Flower width: ¾″

Swamps

253 Marsh Marigold *Caltha leptosepala* p. 445 Plant height: 1–8″ Flower width: ½–1½″

Marshes

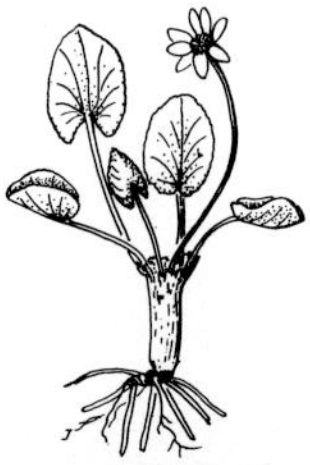

254 Floating Hearts *Nymphoides aquatica* p. 446 Aquatic Flower width: ½–¾″

Lakes and Ponds

255 Fragrant Water Lily *Nymphaea odorata* p. 446 Aquatic Flower width: 3–5″

The Everglades; Lakes and Ponds

256 Goldthread *Coptis groenlandica*
p. 447
Plant height: 3–6″
Flower width: ½″

Bogs

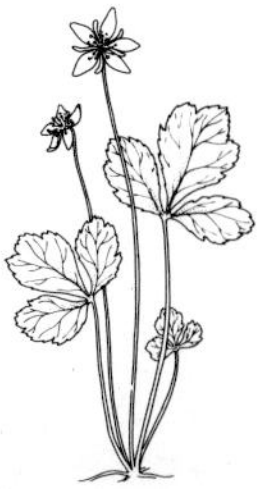

257 Tall Meadow Rue *Thalictrum polygamum*
p. 447
Plant height: 2–8′
Flower width: about ⅓″

Marshes and Swamps

258 Buck Bean *Menyanthes trifoliata*
p. 448
Aquatic
Flower width: ½–¾″

Bogs

259 Highbush Blueberry *Vaccinium corymbosum* *p. 448* Plant height: 5–15′ Flower length: ¼–½″

Swamps

260 Leatherleaf *Chamaedaphne calyculata* *p. 448* Plant height: 1–4′ Flower length: ¼″

Bogs

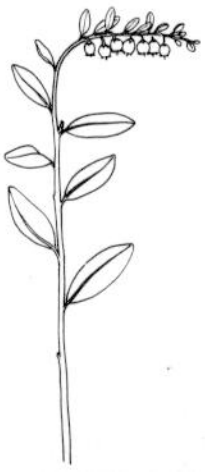

261 Bog Rosemary *Andromeda glaucophylla* *p. 449* Plant height: 10–18″ Flower length: ¼″

Bogs

262 Bog Rein Orchid *Habenaria dilatata* *p. 449*
Plant height: 6–40″
Flower length: about ¼″

Bogs

263 Water Willow *Justicia americana* *p. 450*
Plant height: 1–3′
Flower length: to ½″

Lakes and Ponds; Rivers and Streams

264 Showy Lady's Slipper *Cypripedium reginae* *p. 450*
Plant height: 1–3′
Flower length: 1–2″

Swamps

265 Butterfly Orchid *Encyclia tampensis* *p. 451*
Plant height: 3–12″
Flower width: 1¼–1¾″

Swamps and the Everglades

266 Cranberry *Vaccinium macrocarpon* *p. 451*
Creeper
Flower length: about ½″

Bogs, Swamps, and Lakes and Ponds

267 Swamp Milkweed *Asclepias incarnata* *p. 451*
Plant height: 1–4′
Flower width: ¼″

Marshes

268 Rose Pogonia

Pogonia ophioglossoides
p. 452

Plant height: 3–24″
Flower length: about 1¾″

Bogs and the Everglades

269 Grass Pink

Calopogon pulchellus
p. 452

Plant height: 6–20″
Flower length: 1½″

Bogs and the Everglades

270 Swamp Pink

Arethusa bulbosa
p. 453

Plant height: 5–10″
Flower length: about 2″

Bogs

271 Virginia Meadow Beauty | *Rhexia virginica* *p. 453* | Plant height: 1–2′ Flower width: 1–1½″

Marshes

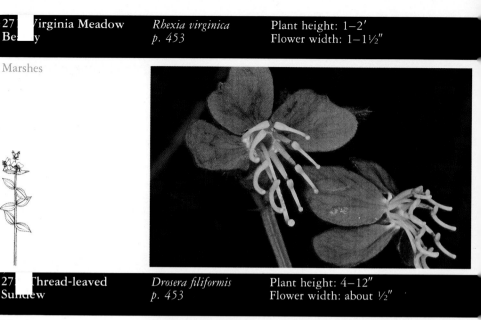

272 Thread-leaved Sundew | *Drosera filiformis* *p. 453* | Plant height: 4–12″ Flower width: about ½″

Marshes

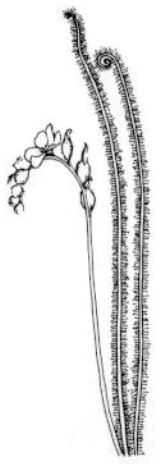

273 Swamp Rose | *Rosa palustris* *p. 454* | Plant height: 2–8′ Flower width: 2–3″

Swamps

274 Swamp Rose Mallow

Hibiscus palustris
p. 454

Plant height: 3–8′
Flower width: 4–7″

Marshes

275 Hibiscus

Hibiscus coccineus
p. 455

Plant height: 3–10′
Flower width: 5–8″

Swamps

276 Red Iris

Iris fulva
p. 455

Plant height: 2–5′
Flower width: about 3″

Swamps

277 Cardinal Flower | *Lobelia cardinalis* *p. 455* | Plant height: 2–4′ Flower length: 1½″

Swamps; Rivers and Streams

278 Turk's-cap Lily | *Lilium superbum* *p. 456* | Plant height: 3–7′ Flower length: 2½″

Marshes and Swamps

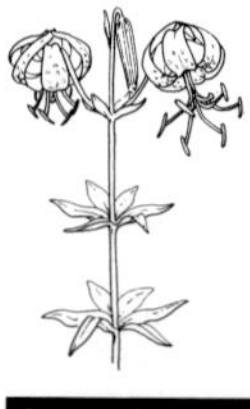

279 Spotted Touch-me-not | *Impatiens capensis* *p. 456* | Plant height: 2–5′ Flower length: 1″

Swamps

280 Crimson Pitcher Plant | *Sarracenia leucophylla* *p. 457* | Plant height: 2–3′ Flower width: 2–3″

Bogs

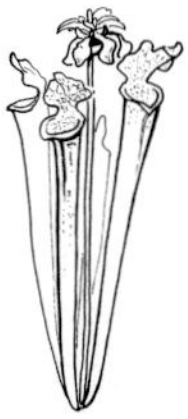

281 Northern Pitcher Plant | *Sarracenia purpurea* *p. 457* | Plant height: 8–24″ Flower width: 2″

Bogs

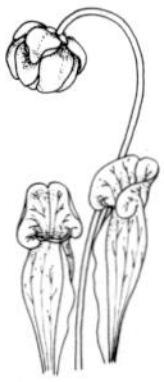

282 California Pitcher Plant | *Darlingtonia californica* *p. 458* | Plant height: to 3′ Flower length: 1½–3½″

Bogs

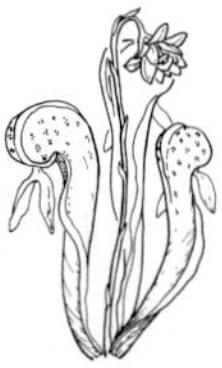

283 Wild Pine

Tillandsia fasciculata
p. 458

Epiphyte
Flower length: 2″

Cypress Swamps and the Everglades

284 Great Hedge Nettle

Stachys cooleyae
p. 459

Plant height: 2–5′
Flower length: 5/8–1″

Swamps

285 Marsh St. Johnswort

Hypericum virginicum
p. 459

Plant height: 8–24″
Flower width: 1/2–3/4″

Marshes

286 Swamp Loosestrife *Decodon verticillatus* *p. 459*
Plant height: to 8′
Flower length: about ½″

Bogs

287 Spotted Joe-Pye Weed *Eupatorium maculatum* *p. 460*
Plant height: 2–6′
Flower length: ⅕″

Swamps

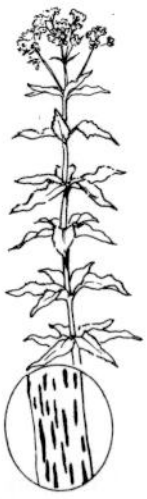

288 Sheep Laurel *Kalmia angustifolia* *p. 460*
Plant height: 1–3′
Flower width: ⅓–½″

Bogs

289 Mountain Globemallow *Iliamna rivularis* *p. 461* Plant height: 3–7′ Flower width: 1–2″

Rivers and Streams

290 Checkermallow *Sidalcea neomexicana* *p. 461* Plant height: 1–3′ Flower width: 1–1½″

Lakes and Ponds; Rivers and Streams

291 Water Smartweed *Polygonum amphibium* *p. 462* Aquatic Flower length: clusters ½–1½″

Lakes and Ponds

292 Marsh Skullcap — *Scutellaria galericulata* *p. 462* — Plant height: 4–32″ Flower length: ½–¾″

Marshes and Swamps

293 Purple Loosestrife — *Lythrum salicaria* *p. 463* — Plant height: 2–4′ Flower width: ½–¾″

Marshes and Floodplains

294 Large Purple Fringed Orchid — *Habenaria fimbriata* *p. 463* — Plant height: 2–4′ Flower length: 1″

Swamps

295 Pickerelweed

Pontederia cordata
p. 463

Aquatic
Flower length: 1/3″

Marshes

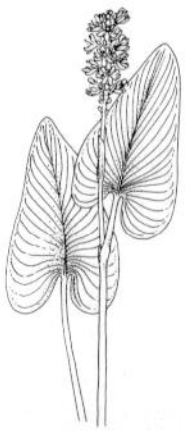

296 Water Hyacinth

Eichhornia crassipes
p. 464

Aquatic
Flower width: 2″

Swamps; the Everglades; Lakes and Ponds; Rivers and Streams

297 Blue Flag

Iris versicolor
p. 464

Plant height: 2–3′
Flower width: 2½–4″

Marshes and Swamps

298 Monkeyflower *Mimulus ringens*
p. 465
Plant height: 1–3′
Flower length: about 1″

Rivers and Streams; wet depressions in grassy areas

299 Virginia Bluebells *Mertensia virginica*
p. 465
Plant height: 8–24″
Flower length: about 1″

Marshes and Floodplains

300 Mountain Bluebell *Mertensia ciliata*
p. 466
Plant height: 6–60″
Flower length: $\frac{1}{2}$–$\frac{3}{4}$″

Rivers and Streams

301 True Forget-me-not *Myosotis scorpioides* *p. 466*

Plant height: 6–24″
Flower width: ¼″

Lakes and Ponds; Rivers and Streams

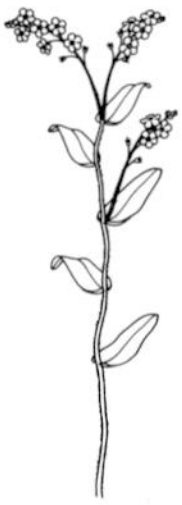

302 Common Butterwort *Pinguicula vulgaris* *p. 467*

Plant height: 2–6″
Flower width: ⅓″

Wet open areas and the Everglades

303 Fire Flags *Thalia geniculata* *p. 467*

Plant height: 3–10′
Flower length: ½–¾″

The Everglades; Lakes and Ponds; Rivers and Streams; Marshy Borders

304 Cinnamon Fern

Osmunda cinnamomea
p. 467

Plant height: 3–5′
Frond length: to 3′

Swamps

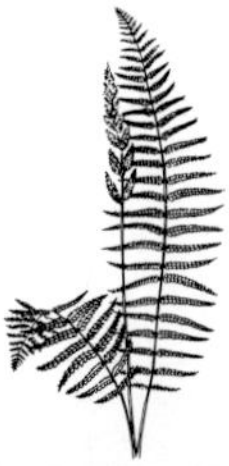

305 Marsh Fern

Thelypteris palustris
p. 468

Plant height: 12–18″
Frond length: 4–28″

Marshes

306 Royal Fern

Osmunda regalis
p. 468

Plant height: 3–6′
Frond length: 3′ or more

Marshes and Swamps

307 Marsh Cinquefoil | *Potentilla palustris* p. 469 | Plant height: 6–20″ Flower width: ¾″

Marshes

308 Water Lettuce | *Pistia stratiotes* p. 469 | Aquatic Flower length: about ½″

Cypress Swamps; the Everglades; Lakes and Ponds

309 Jack-in-the-pulpit | *Arisaema triphyllum* p. 469 | Plant height: 1–3′ Flower length: 2–3″

Swamps

310 Arrow Arum *Peltandra virginica*
p. 470
Plant height: 1–2′
Flower length: 4–7″

Marshes

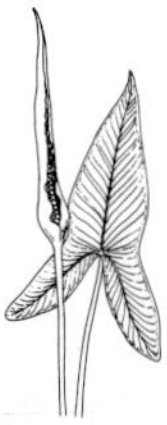

311 Green Dragon *Arisaema dracontium*
p. 470
Plant height: 1–3′
Flower length: 4–8″

Swamps

312 Skunk Cabbage *Symplocarpus foetidus*
p. 471
Plant height: 1–2′
Flower length: 3–6″

Swamps

313 Duckweed *Lemna* spp.
p. 471
Aquatic
Frond length: about 1/16–3/8″

Lakes and Ponds; Rivers and Streams

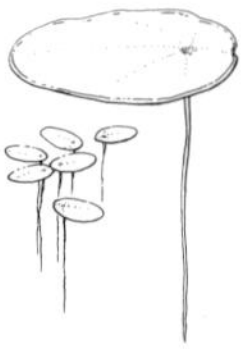

314 Featherfoil *Hottonia inflata*
p. 471
Aquatic
Flower length: 1/3″

Lakes and Ponds

315 Bur Reed *Sparganium americanum*
p. 472
Plant height: 1–3′
Flower width: cluster 1″

Marshes; Lakes and Ponds

316 Water Pennywort *Hydrocotyle americana* *p. 472*
Creeper
Flower width: about 1/16″

Marshes

317 Wood Nettle *Laportea canadensis* *p. 473*
Plant height: 1½–4′
Flower length: about 1/6″

Rivers and Streams

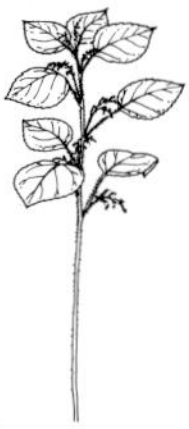

318 Clearweed *Pilea pumila* *p. 473*
Plant height: 4–20″
Flower length: about 1/6″

Marshes and Floodplains

319 Swamp Saxifrage *Saxifraga pensylvanica* *p. 474*
Plant height: 1–3′
Flower width: about 1/6″

Bogs and Swamps

320 False Hellebore *Veratrum viride* *p. 474*
Plant height: 2–7′
Flower width: about 1/2″

Swamps

321 Wild Rice *Zizania aquatica* *p. 474*
Plant height: 3–10′

Brackish Marshes; Lakes and Ponds; Rivers and Streams

322 Wool Grass — *Scirpus cyperinus* *p. 475*
Plant height: 3–5′
Flower length: about ¼″

Marshes and Swamps

323 Giant Reed — *Phragmites australis* *p. 475*
Plant height: 5–15′
Flower length: in scales about ¼″

Marshes

324 Soft Rush — *Juncus effusus* *p. 476*
Plant height: 1½–4′
Flower length: about ⅙″

Marshes and Swamps

325 Red Osier Dogwood

Cornus stolonifera
p. 476

Plant height: 3–10′
Flower width: clusters 1–2″

Shrub Swamps; Rivers and Streams

326 Highbush Blueberry

Vaccinium corymbosum
p. 448

Plant height: 5–15′
Flower length: ¼–½″

Swamps

327 Jack-in-the-pulpit

Arisaema triphyllum
p. 469

Plant height: 1–3′
Flower length: 2–3″

Swamps

328 Winterberry *Ilex verticillata* *p. 441*
Plant height: 3–10′
Flower width: clusters ¼–½″

Swamps; Lakes and Ponds

329 Yaupon *Ilex vomitoria* *p. 477*
Plant height: 5–15′
Flower width: ¼″

Swamps

330 Cranberry *Vaccinium macrocarpon* *p. 451*
Creeper
Flower length: about ½″

Bogs, Swamps, and Lakes and Ponds

331 Yellow Unicorn Entoloma

Entoloma murraii
p. 479

Cap width: ⅜–1¼″

Sphagnum Bogs

Habitat
Damp ground in woods and near swamps

332 Brown Alder Mushroom

Alnicola melinoides
p. 479

Cap width: ⅜–1″

Alder Wetlands

Habitat
Under alder trees in boggy areas

333 Spotted Gomphidius

Gomphidius maculatus
p. 479

Cap width: 1–4″

Larch Bogs

Habitat
Mostly under larch; also under mixed conifers

334 Turpentine Waxy Cap *Hygrophorus pudorinus* Cap width: 2–4″
p. 480

Bogs

Habitat
Under spruce, fir, or hemlock; sometimes in boggy areas

335 Emetic Russula *Russula emetica* Cap width: 1–3″ ⊗
p. 480

Bogs

Habitat
Most frequently in sphagnum moss but also on the ground in mixed woods

336 Chocolate Milky *Lactarius lignyotus* Cap width: ¾–4″
p. 480

Sphagnum Bogs

Habitat
Often in moss in sphagnum bogs and coniferous woods

337 Wrinkled Thimble-cap *Verpa bohemica* Height: 3⅛–4½″
p. 481

Swamps

Habitat
Damp and wet areas in woods

338 Velvety Earth Tongue *Trichoglossum hirsutum* Height: 1⅝–3″
p. 481

Sphagnum Wetlands

Habitat
Various; on rotting wood, on soil, in sphagnum moss

339 Swamp Beacon *Mitrula elegans* Height: ⅞–2¼″
p. 482

Sphagnum Bogs and Swamps

Habitat
Base of stalk usually submerged in shallow pool, growing from decaying leaves or twigs

340 Blue-staining Cup

Caloscypha fulgens
p. 482

Cup width: 3/8–2″

Bogs

Habitat
Boggy areas; also wet places in coniferous woods in mountains

341 Blueberry Cup

Monilinia vaccinii-corymbosi
p. 482

Cup width: 1/4–3/8″

Bogs and Swamps

Habitat
In wet, boggy areas and swamps, on fallen blueberry fruits

342 Silky Parchment

Stereum striatum
p. 483

Cap width: 1/4–3/8″

Swamps

Habitat
Twigs and branches of decaying ironwood

343 Water Boatman | *Corixa* spp. | Length: ¼–½"
p. 485

Lakes and Ponds

Food
Minute algae

344 Giant Water Bug | *Lethocerus americanus* | Length: 1¾–2⅜"
p. 485

Lakes and Ponds

Food
Other insects, tadpoles, small fishes, and salamanders (Caudata)

345 Common Backswimmer | *Notonecta undulata* | Length: ⅜–½"
p. 485

Lakes and Ponds; Rivers and Streams

Food
Insects and other small aquatic animals

346 Kirby's Backswimmer — *Notonecta kirbyi* *p. 486* — Length: 3/8–1/2″

Lakes and Ponds; Rivers and Streams

Food
Insects and other small animals that fall into or live in water, as well as tadpoles, small fishes, and aquatic insects

347 Giant Water Scavenger Beetle — *Hydrophilus* spp. *p. 486* — Length: 1 3/8–1 1/2″

Lakes and Ponds; Rivers and Streams

Food
Decaying remains of aquatic animals or small live animals

348 Large Whirligig Beetle — *Dineutus* spp. *p. 487* — Length: 3/8–5/8″

Lakes and Ponds; Rivers and Streams

Food
Aquatic insects and insects that fall into water; larva eats mites (Hydrachnellae), Snails (Gastropoda), and small aquatic insects

349 Marbled Diving Beetle *Thermonectes marmoratus* *p. 487* Length: 3/8–5/8"

Lakes and Ponds

Food
Smaller insects

350 Willow Leaf Beetle *Chrysomela lapponica* *p. 487* Length: 1/4–3/8"

Rivers and Streams; Floodplains

Food
Foliage of willows (*Salix*)

351 Swamp Milkweed Leaf Beetle *Labidomera clivicollis* *p. 488* Length: 3/8–1/2"

Marshes; Rivers and Streams

Food
Foliage and sometimes flowers of milkweed (*Asclepias*)

352 Willow Borer *Xylotrechus insignis* Length: ½–⅝″
p. 488

Rivers and Streams; Floodplains

Food
Pollen; larva bores into willow (*Salix*)

353 Bombardier Beetle *Brachinus* spp. Length: ¼–⅝″
p. 488

Floodplains

Food
Larva eats pupating insects

354 Green Pubescent Ground Beetle *Chlaenius sericeus* Length: ⅜–⅝″
p. 489

Floodplains

Food
Small insects, slugs and snails (Gastropoda), and other animal matter

355 Waterlily Leaf Beetle

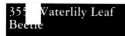

Donacia spp.
p. 489

Length: ¼–½″

The Everglades; Lakes and Ponds; Rivers and Streams

Food
Foliage and pollen of water lily (Nymphaeaceae), skunk cabbage (*Symplocarpus foetidus*), and similar plants; larvae eats submerged parts of plants

356 Common Water Strider

Gerris remigis
p. 490

Length: ½–⅝″

Lakes and Ponds; Rivers and Streams

Food
Aquatic insects

357 Western Waterscorpion

Ranatra brevicollis
p. 490

Length: 1″

Lakes and Ponds

Food
Smaller insects, mites (Hydrachnellae), and aquatic worms

358 **Fishfly** *Chauliodes* spp. Length: ¾–1″
p. 490

Rivers and Streams

Food
Larva eats small aquatic insects

359 **Eastern Dobsonfly** *Corydalus cornutus* Length: 2″
p. 491

Rivers and Streams

Food
Larva eats aquatic insects

360 **Eastern Dobsonfly** *Corydalus cornutus* Length: 2″
p. 491

Rivers and Streams

Food
Larva eats aquatic insects

361 Californian Acroneuria *Acroneuria californica* Length: ⅞" (male); 1¼" (female)
p. 491

Rivers and Streams

Food
Algae

362 Betten's Silverstreak Caddisfly *Grammotaulius bettenii* Length: ¼–⅞"
p. 492

Lakes and Ponds; Rivers and Streams

Food
Larva eats algae and organic debris

363 Bluebell *Nannothemis bella* Length: ¾"
p. 492

Marshes; Lakes and Ponds

Food
Small flying insects, particularly flies (Diptera); nymph eats small aquatic insects and worms

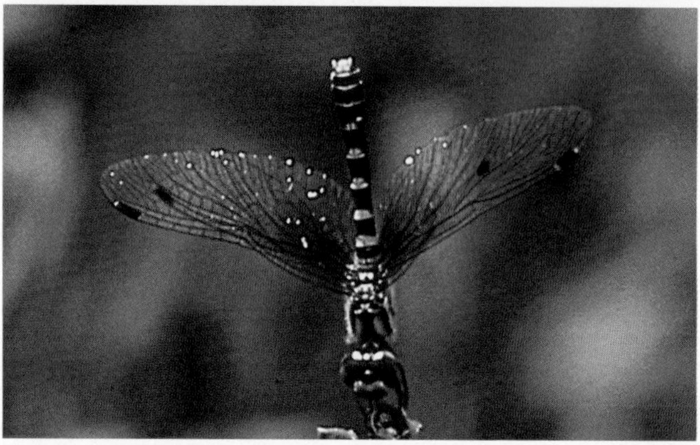

364 Widow *Libellula luctuosa* Length: 1⅝–2″
p. 493

Marshes; Lakes and Ponds

Food
Smaller flying insects; nymph eats small aquatic insects

365 Brown Darner *Boyeria vinosa* Length: 2¾–3⅛″
p. 493

The Everglades; Rivers and Streams

Food
Small insects caught in flight; nymph eats small aquatic invertebrates

366 Green Darner *Anax junius* Length: 2¾–3⅛″
p. 493

The Everglades; Lakes and Ponds; Rivers and Streams

Food
Midges (Chironomidae), mosquitoes (Culicidae), caddisflies (Trichoptera), and other flying insects; nymph eats tadpoles, small fish, and aquatic insects

367 Short-stalked Damselfly | *Argia* spp. *p. 494* | Length: 1⅛–1⅝″ (male); 1⅛–1¾″ (female)

The Everglades; Lakes and Ponds; Rivers and Streams

Food
Smaller insects; nymph eats aquatic insects

368 Swift Long-winged Skimmer | *Pachydiplax longipennis* *p. 494* | Length: 1⅛–1¾″

Lakes and Ponds; Rivers and Streams

Food
Small insects; nymph eats small aquatic insects

369 Twelve-spot Skimmer | *Libellula pulchella* *p. 495* | Length: 1¾–2¼″

Lakes and Ponds; Rivers and Streams

Food
Small insects caught in flight; nymph eats aquatic invertebrates

370 Elisa Skimmer | *Celithemis elisa* *p. 495* | Length: 1⅛–1⅜″

Marshes; the Everglades; Lakes and Ponds; Rivers and Streams

Food
Small flying insects; nymph eats small aquatic insects and worms

371 Streak-winged Red Skimmer | *Sympetrum illotum* *p. 495* | Length: 1⅝–1¾″

Lakes and Ponds

Food
Small flying insects; nymph eats small aquatic insects and worms

372 Dark Lestes | *Lestes congener* *p. 496* | Length: 1⅜–1⅝″ (male); 1¼–1½″ (female)

Lakes and Ponds

Food
Smaller insects such as aphids (Aphididae); nymph eats small aquatic insects

373 Crane Fly

Tipula spp.
p. 496

Length: 3/8–2½″

Lakes and Ponds; Rivers and Streams

Food
Larva eats decaying vegetation, fungi, roots, leaves of emergent and terrestrial plants, and, less often, animal matter

374 Comstock's Net-winged Midge

Agathon comstocki
p. 497

Length: 3/8″

Rivers and Streams

Food
Larva eats algae

375 Small Mayfly

Baetis spp.
p. 497

Length: 1/8–3/8″

Rivers and Streams

Food
Nymph eats microscopic green plants and organic particles in debris

376 House Mosquito *Culex pipiens* Length: ⅛–¼″
p. 497

Swamps; Lakes and Ponds

Food
Male: plant juices; female: blood of birds and mammals, including humans; larva: microscopic algae

377 Purplish-blue Cricket Hunter *Chlorion cyaneum* Length: 1–1⅛″
p. 498

Lakes and Ponds; Rivers and Streams

Food
Crickets (Gryllidae)

378 American Horse Fly *Tabanus americanus* Length: ¾–1⅛″
p. 498

Swamps; Marshes; the Everglades; Lakes and Ponds

Food
Male: pollen and nectar; female: blood of large mammals; larva: aquatic insects and other small animals

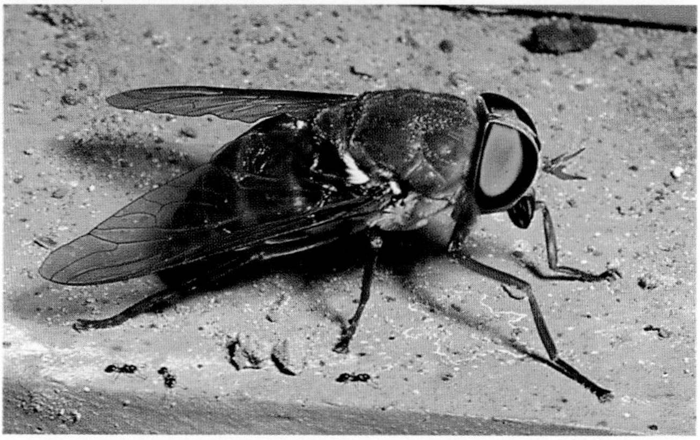

379 Black Fly

Simulium spp.
p. 499

Length: 1/16–1/8″

Rivers and Streams

Food
Male: nectar; female: nectar, blood from birds and mammals; larva: diatoms, bacteria, and other filtered particles

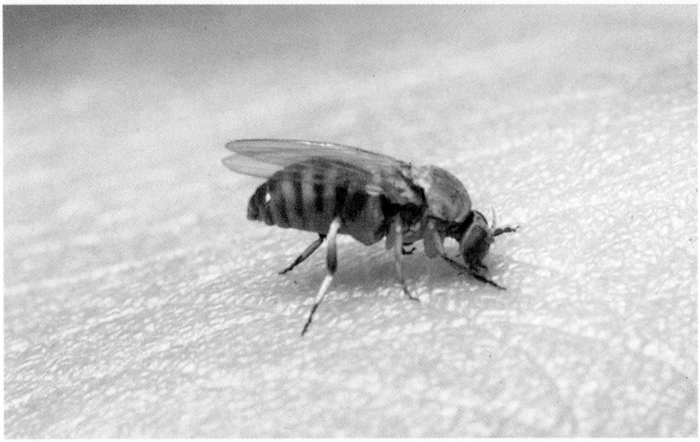

380 Marsh Fly

Tetanocera spp.
p. 499

Length: 1/8–1/4″

Lakes and Ponds; Rivers and Streams

Food
Dew and nectar; larva probably eats freshwater snails (Pulmonata)

381 Vinegar Fly

Drosophila melanogaster
p. 500

Length: 1/16″

Swamps; Marshes; the Everglades; Lakes and Ponds

Food
Nectar and other sugary solutions; larva eats yeasts in fermenting juices

382 Six-spotted Fishing Spider *Dolomedes triton* *p. 500* Length: ⅜–½″ (male); ⅝–¾″ (female)

Lakes and Ponds; Rivers and Streams

Food
Small insects; sometimes tadpoles and small fish

383 Golden-silk Spider *Nephila clavipes* *p. 500* Length: ⅛″ (male); ⅞–1″ (female)

Swamps

Food
Flying insects

384 Red Freshwater Mite *Limnochares americana* *p. 501* Length: ⅛″

Lakes and Ponds; Rivers and Streams

Food
Small insects and mollusks

385 Pink-edged Sulphur *Colias interior* Length: 1⅜–1¾″
p. 503

Bogs and Marshes

Host Plants
Velvet-leaf blueberry (*Vaccinium myrtilloides* or *V. canadense*) and other species of blueberries

386 Scudder's Willow Sulphur *Colias scudderii* Length: 1½–1¾″
p. 503

Willow Bogs

Host Plants
Willows (*Salix*)

387 Hessel's Hairstreak *Mitoura hesseli* Length: ⅞–1″
p. 504

Atlantic White-cedar Bogs

Host Plant
Atlantic white-cedar (*Chamaecyparis thyoides*)

388 Western Tiger Swallowtail | *Pterourus rutulus* *p. 504* | Length: 2¾–3⅞″

Rivers and Streams

Host Plants
Include willows, poplars, and aspens (Salicaceae), several alders (*Alnus*), and sycamores (Platanaceae)

389 Palamedes Swallowtail | *Pterourus palamedes* *p. 505* | Length: 3⅛–5½″

Subtropical Marshes and Swamps

Host Plants
Red bay (*Persea borbonia*), sassafras (*Sassafras albidum*), and sweet bay (*Magnolia virginiana*)

390 Zebra Swallowtail | *Eurytides marcellus* *p. 505* | Length: 2⅜–3½″

Lakes and Ponds; Rivers and Streams

Host Plants
Pawpaw (*Asimina triloba*) in North and other *Asimina* species in South

391 Baltimore — *Euphydryas phaeton* — Length: 1⅝–2½″
p. 506

Bogs

Host Plants
Turtlehead (*Chelone glabra*), false foxglove (*Gerardia grandiflora* and *G. pedicularia*), plantain (*Plantago lanceolata*), and white ash (*Fraxinus americana*)

392 Viceroy — *Basilarchia archippus* — Length: 2⅝–3″
p. 507

Marshes; Rivers and Streams

Host Plants
Willows (*Salix*) preferred

393 Milbert's Tortoiseshell — *Aglais milberti* — Length: 1¾–2″
p. 507

Rivers and Streams

Host Plants
Nettles (*Urtica*)

394 Harvester

Feniseca tarquinius
p. 508

Length: 1⅛–1¼″

Host Plants
Caterpillar carnivorous, feeding exclusively upon wooly aphids of genera *Schizoneura* and *Pemphigus*

395 Arctic Skipper

Carterocephalus palaemon
p. 509

Length: ¾–1¼″

Bogs

Host Plant
In California, purple reedgrass (*Calamagrostis purpurascens*)

396 Bog Fritillary

Proclossiana eunomia
p. 509

Length: 1¼–1½″

Bogs

Host Plants
Alpine bistort (*Polygonum viviparum*), violets (*Viola*), and willows (*Salix*)

397 Frigga's Fritillary
Clossiana frigga
p. 510
Length: 1¼–1⅝″

Bogs

Host Plants
Arctic avens (*Dryas integrifolia*), possibly raspberry (*Rubus*), and willows (*Salix*)

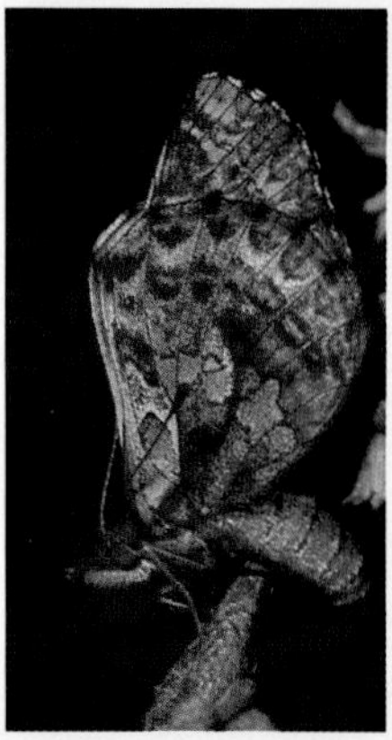

398 Swamp Metalmark
Calephelis muticum
p. 510
Length: ⅞–1⅛″

Bogs and Swamps

Host Plant
Young swamp thistle (*Cirsium muticum*)

399 Bog Copper
Epidemia epixanthe
p. 511
Length: ⅞–1″

Bogs

Host Plant
Wild cranberry (*Vaccinium macrocarpum*)

400 Appalachian Brown *Satyrodes appalachia* Length: 1⅝–2″
p. 511

Bogs and Swamps

Host Plants
Sedges (*Carex*)

401 Mitchell's Marsh Satyr *Neonympha mitchellii* Length: 1½–1¾″
p. 512

Tamarack Bogs

Host Plants
Probably sedges (*Carex*)

402 Eyed Brown *Satyrodes eurydice* Length: 1⅝–2″
p. 512

Marshes

Host Plants
Sedges (*Carex*)

403 Great Gray Copper *Gaeides xanthoides* Length: 1¼–1¾"
p. 513

Marshes and Swamps

Host Plants
Several docks (*Rumex hymenosepalus, R. conglomeratus, R. crispus, R. obtusifolia*)

404 White Peacock *Anartia jatrophae* Length: 2–2⅜"
p. 513

Swamps

Host Plants
Ruellia (*Ruellia occidentalis*) and water hyssop (*Bacopa monniera*)

405 Northern Blue *Lycaeides argyrognomon* Length: ⅞–1¼"
p. 514

Bogs

Host Plants
Lupines (*Lupinus*), crowberry (*Empetrum*), laurel (*Kalmia*), and Hudson Bay tea (*Ledum palustre*)

406 White Peacock

Anartia jatrophae
p. 513

Length: 2–2⅜″

Swamps

Host Plants
Ruellia (*Ruellia occidentalis*) and water hyssop (*Bacopa monniera*)

407 Cerisy's Sphinx

Smerinthus cerisyi
p. 514

Length: 2⅜–3⅜″

Rivers and Streams

Host Plants
Willow foliage (*Salix*)

408 Appalachian Brown

Satyrodes appalachia
p. 511

Length: 1⅝–2″

Bogs and Swamps

Host Plants
Sedges (*Carex*)

409 Eyed Brown

Satyrodes eurydice
p. 512

Length: 1⅝–2″

Marshes

Host Plants
Sedges (*Carex*)

410 Creole Pearly Eye

Enodia creola
p. 515

Length: 2–2¼″

Swamps and Bottomlands

Host Plant
Maiden Cane (*Arundinaria tecta*)

411 Lace-winged Roadside Skipper

Amblyscirtes aesculapius
p. 515

Length: 1–1¼″

Swamps

Host Plants
Unknown

412 Jutta Arctic

Oeneis jutta
p. 516

Length: 1⅞–2⅛″

Bogs

Host Plant
Possibly cotton grass (*Eriophorum spissum*)

413 Window-winged Skipper

Xenophanes trixis
p. 516

Length: 1⅛–1⅜″

Floodplains

Host Plant
Mallows (Malvaceae)

414 Small Checkered Skipper

Pyrgus scriptura
p. 517

Length: ⅝–1″

Marshes

Host Plants
Alkali Mallow (*Sida hederacea*), globemallow (*Sphaeralcea coccinea*), and probably other mallows

415 Bog Elfin *Incisalia lanoraieensis* Length: ⅝–1″
p. 517

Bogs

Host Plants
Needles of black spruce (*Picea mariana*)

416 Lilac-banded Longtail *Urbanus dorantes* Length: 1½–2″
p. 518

Marshes and the Everglades

Host Plants
Include beans (Phaseolus), butterfly-pea (*Clitoria*), and beggar-weed (*Desmodium tortuosum*)

417 Common Alpine *Erebia epipsodea* Length: 1¾–2″
p. 518

Bogs

Host Plants
Grasses (Poaceae)

418 Spruce Bog Alpine *Erebia disa* *p. 519* Length: 1¾–2″

Bogs

Host Plants
Probably grasses (Poaceae)

419 Poweshiek Skipperling *Oarisma poweshiek* *p. 519* Length: 1–1¼″

Marshes

Host Plants
Unknown

420 Saw-grass Skipper *Euphyes pilatka* *p. 520* Length: 1½–1¾″

Marshes and the Everglades

Host Plant
Saw grass (*Mariscus jamaicensis*)

421 Two-spotted Skipper

Euphyes bimacula
p. 520

Length: 1⅛–1¼″

Bogs and Marshes

Host Plants
Sedges (*Carex*)

422 Sedge Skipper

Euphyes dion
p. 521

Length: 1¼–1⅝″

Marshes and Swamps

Host Plants
Lake sedge (*Carex lacustris*) or wool grass (*Scirpus cyperinus*)

423 Mulberry Wing

Poanes massasoit
p. 521

Length: 1–1⅛″

Bogs and Marshes

Host Plants
Grasses (Poaceae) or sedges (Cyperaceae), including tussock sedge (*Carex stricta*)

424 Broken Dash

Wallengrenia otho
p. 522

Length: 1–1¼″

Swamps

Host Plants
Grasses (Poaceae), possibly including St. Augustine grass (*Stenotaphrum secundatum*)

425 Least Skipperling

Ancyloxypha numitor
p. 522

Length: ¾–1″

Marshes; Lakes and Ponds; Rivers and Streams

Host Plants
Include bluegrass (*Poa*) and rice (*Oryza sativa*)

426 Black Dash

Euphyes conspicua
p. 523

Length: 1–1⅜″

Bogs and Marshes

Host Plants
Probably sedges (*Carex*)

427 Western Redcedar *Thuja plicata* p. 525 Leaf length: 1⁄16–1⁄8"; scalelike

Swamps

428[redacted]Northern White-ced[redacted] *Thuja occidentalis* p. 525 Leaf length: 1⁄16–1⁄8"; scalelike

Bogs and Swamps

429[redacted]tlantic White-ced[redacted] *Chamaecyparis thyoides* p. 526 Leaf length: 1⁄16–1⁄8"; scalelike

Bogs and Swamps

430 Tamarack

Larix laricina
p. 526

Needle length: ¾–1″

Bogs

431 Pond Pine

Pinus serotina
p. 527

Needle length: 5–8″

Pocosin

432 Black Spruce

Picea mariana
p. 527

Needle length: ¼–⅝″

Bogs

433 Baldcypress

Taxodium distichum
p. 528

Needle length: 3/8–3/4″

Cypress Swamps and the Everglades

434 Honeylocust

Gleditsia triacanthos
p. 529

Leaflet length: 3/8–1 1/4″

Floodplains

435 Black Ash

Fraxinus nigra
p. 529

Leaflet length: 3–5″

Swamps

436 Green Ash *Fraxinus pennsylvanica* Leaflet length: 2–5″
p. 530

Forested Swamps

437 Carolina Ash *Fraxinus caroliniana* Leaflet length: 2–4½″
p. 530

Forested Swamps and the Everglades

438 Elderberry *Sambucus canadensis* Leaflet length: 1½–4″
p. 531

Swamps

439 Water Hickory

Carya aquatica
p. 532

Leaflet length: 2–5″

Southern Bottomland Hardwood Swamps

440 Nutmeg Hickory

Carya myristiciformis
p. 532

Leaflet length: 2–5″

Southern Bottomland Hardwood Swamps

441 Poison-sumac

Toxicodendron vernix
p. 533

Leaflet length: 2½–3½″

Bogs and Swamps

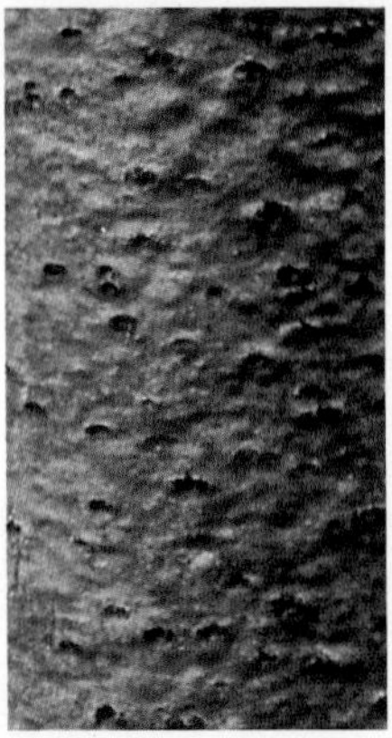

442 Pawpaw *Asimina triloba* *p. 534* Leaf length: 7–10″

Floodplains

443 Black Tupelo *Nyssa sylvatica* *p. 534* Leaf length: 2–5″

Swamps

444 Red Osier Dogwood *Cornus stolonifera* *p. 535* Leaf length: 1½–3½″

Shrub Swamps

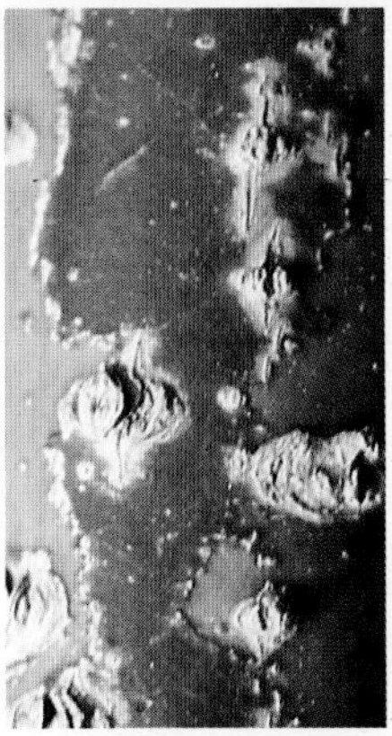

445 Possumhaw Viburnum | *Viburnum nudum* *p. 536* | Leaf length: 2–5″

Swamps; Rivers and Streams

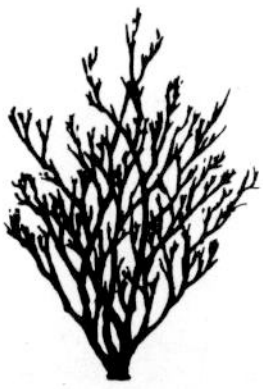

446 Buckwheat-tree | *Cliftonia monophylla* *p. 536* | Leaf length: 1–2″

Swamps

447 Laurel Oak | *Quercus laurifolia* *p. 537* | Leaf length: 2–5½″

Southern Swamps

448 Dahoon

Ilex cassine
p. 537

Leaf length: 1½–3½″

Swamps; the Everglades; Rivers and Streams

449 Sweetbay

Magnolia virginiana
p. 538

Leaf length: 3–6″

Swamps; Floodplains; the Everglades

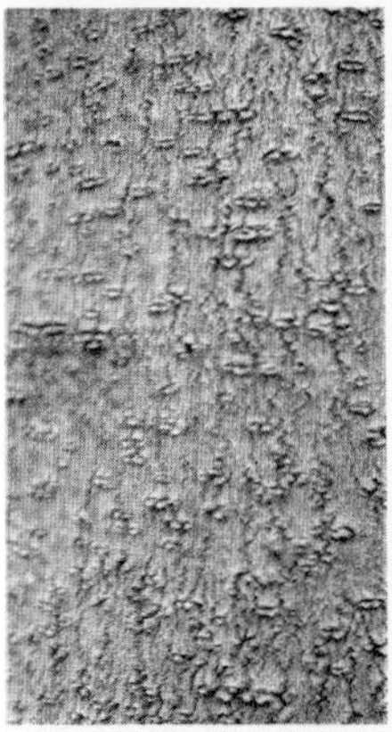

450 Titi

Cyrilla racemiflora
p. 538

Leaf length: 1½–3″

Swamps

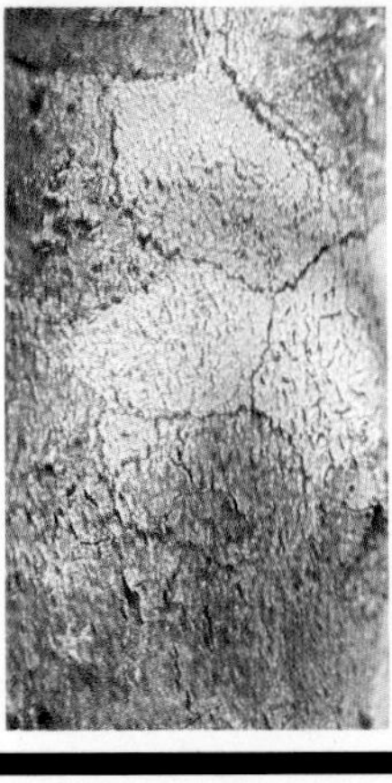

451 **Redbay** *Persea borbonia*
p. 539
Leaf length: 3–6″

Swamps and the Everglades

452 **Willow Oak** *Quercus phellos*
p. 540
Leaf length: 2–4½″

Southern Bottomland Hardwood Swamps

453 **Black Willow** *Salix nigra*
p. 540
Leaf length: 3–5″

Riverine Floodplains

454 Sand[redacted]Willow | *Salix exigua* p. 541 | Leaf length: [redacted]″

Floodplains, Streamsides, and Sandbars

455 Coastal Plain Willow | *Salix caroliniana* p. 541 | Leaf length: 2–4″

Southern Swamps and the Everglades

456 Swamp-privet | *Forestiera acuminata* p. 542 | Leaf length: 1½–4″

Swamps

457 Pussy Willow *Salix discolor* *p. 542* Leaf length: 1½–4¼″

Shrub Swamps and Streamsides

458 Bebb Willow *Salix bebbiana* *p. 543* Leaf length: 1–3½″

Shrub Swamps

459 Balsam Willow *Salix pyrifolia* *p. 544* Leaf length: 2–3½″

Bogs

460 Loblolly-bay *Gordonia lasianthus* *p. 544* Leaf length: 4–6″

Swamps

461 Southern Bayberry *Myrica cerifera* *p. 545* Leaf length: 1½–3½″

Southern Swamps and the Everglades

462 Water Tupelo *Nyssa aquatica* *p. 545* Leaf length: 5–8″

Southern Bottomland Hardwood Swamps

463 Sugarberry *Celtis laevigata* Leaf length: 2½–4″
p. 546

Southern Bottomland Hardwood Swamps

464 Water-elm *Planera aquatica* Leaf length: 2–2½″
p. 546

Swamps

465 American Elm *Ulmus americana* Leaf length: 3–6″
p. 547

Floodplain Forests

466 Red Alder

Alnus rubra
p. 548

Leaf length: 3–5″

Swamps

467 Mountain Alder

Alnus tenuifolia
p. 548

Leaf length: 1½–4″

Swamps

468 Speckled Alder

Alnus rugosa
p. 549

Leaf length: 2–4″

Shrub Swamps and Streamsides

469 Possumhaw *Ilex decidua* *p. 550* Leaf length: 1–3″

Swamps

470 Swamp Cottonwood *Populus heterophylla* *p. 550* Leaf length: 4–7″

Forested Swamps and Floodplains

471 River Birch *Betula nigra* *p. 551* Leaf length: 1½–3″

Riverine Floodplains

472 Eastern Cottonwood *Populus deltoides* *p. 551* Leaf length: 3–7″

Riverine Floodplains

473 Swamp Chestnut Oak *Quercus michauxii* *p. 552* Leaf length: 4–9″

Southern Swamps

474 Water Oak *Quercus nigra* *p. 552* Leaf length: 1½–5″

Southern Bottomland Hardwood Swamps

475 Overcup Oak

Quercus lyrata
p. 553

Leaf length: 5–8″

Southern Bottomland Hardwood Swamps

476 Swamp White Oak

Quercus bicolor
p. 553

Leaf length: 4–7″

Forested Swamps

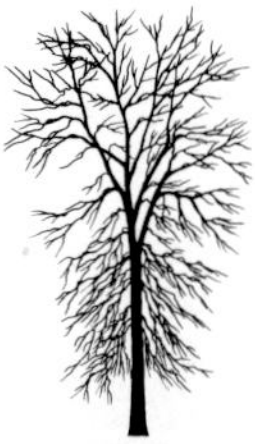
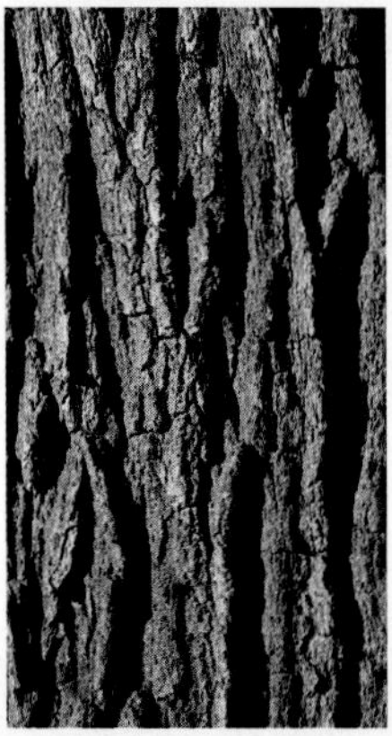

477 Pin Oak

Quercus palustris
p. 554

Leaf length: 3–5″

Forested Swamps

478 Si[redacted]Maple *Acer saccharinum* *p. 555* Leaf [redacted]h: 4–6″

Swamps and Floodplain Forests

479 Red Maple *Acer rubrum* *p. 555* Leaf length: 2½–4″

Swamps

480 Sycamore *Platanus occidentalis* *p. 556* Leaf length: 4–8″

Floodplains

481 Common Loon *Gavia immer* *p. 558* Length: 28–36″

Lakes and Ponds; Rivers and Streams

482 Western Grebe *Aechmophorus occidentalis* *p. 558* Length: 22–29″

Marshes; Lakes and Ponds

483 Pied-billed Grebe *Podilymbus podiceps* *p. 558* Length: 12–15″

Marshes; Lakes and Ponds

484 Red-necked Grebe *Podiceps grisegena* Length: 18–20″
p. 559

Lakes and Ponds

485 Horned Grebe *Podiceps auritus* Length: 12–15¼″
p. 559

The Everglades; Lakes and Ponds

486 Eared Grebe *Podiceps nigricollis* Length: 12–14″
p. 560

Lakes and Ponds; Sloughs

487 Fulvous Whistling-Duck

Dendrocygna bicolor
p. 560

Length: 18–21″

Marshes

488 "Mexican" Duck

Anas platyrhynchos diazi
p. 560

Length: 21–22″

Marshes

489 American Black Duck

Anas rubripes
p. 561

Length: 19–22″

Marshes; Lakes and Ponds; Rivers and Streams

490 Green-winged Teal *Anas crecca* Length: 12–16″
p. 561

Marshes; Lakes and Ponds

491 Wood Duck *Aix sponsa* Length: 17–20″
p. 562

Swamps

492 Mallard *Anas platyrhynchos* Length: 18-27″
p. 562

Marshes; Lakes and Ponds

493 Northern Shoveler *Anas clypeata* Length: 17–20″
p. 562

Marshes and Prairie Potholes

494 American Wigeon *Anas americana* Length: 18–23″
p. 563

Marshes and the Everglades

495 Cinnamon Teal *Anas cyanoptera* Length: 14–17″
p. 563

Marshes

496 Gadwall *Anas strepera* Length: 18–21″
p. 564

Marshes

497 Blue-winged Teal *Anas discors* Length: 14–16″
p. 564

Marshes; the Everglades; Lakes and Ponds

498 Northern Pintail *Anas acuta* Length: 25–30″ (males); 21–23″ (females)
p. 565

Marshes and the Everglades

499 Canvasback *Aythya valisineria* Length: 19–24″
p. 565

Marshes

500 Redhead *Aythya americana* Length: 18–22″
p. 565

Marshes

501 Ring-necked Duck *Aythya collaris* Length: 14–18″
p. 566

The Everglades; Lakes and Ponds; Rivers and Streams

502 Greater Scaup

Aythya marila
p. 566

Length: 15–20″

Lakes and Ponds

503 Lesser Scaup

Aythya affinis
p. 567

Length: 15–18″

Marshes; the Everglades; Lakes and Ponds; Rivers and Streams

504 Harlequin Duck

Histrionicus histrionicus
p. 567

Length: 14½–21″

Rivers and Streams

505 Barrow's Goldeneye *Bucephala islandica* *p. 568* Length: 16½–20″

Forested Lakes and Ponds

506 Common Goldeneye *Bucephala clangula* *p. 568* Length: 16–20″

Bogs; Lakes and Ponds

507 Common Merganser *Mergus merganser* *p. 569* Length: 22–27″

Lakes and Ponds; Rivers and Streams

508 Bufflehead

Bucephala albeola
p. 569

Length: 13–15½″

Bogs; Lakes and Ponds

509 Hooded Merganser

Lophodytes cucullatus
p. 570

Length: 16–19″

Lakes and Ponds; Rivers and Streams

510 Ruddy Duck

Oxyura jamaicensis
p. 570

Length: 14–16″

Marshes

511 Greater White-fronted Goose | *Anser albifrons* | *p. 571* | Length: 26–34″

Marshes; Rivers and Streams

512 Canada Goose | *Branta canadensis* | *p. 571* | Length: 22–26″ (small races); 35–45″ (large races)

Marshes; Lakes and Ponds; Rivers and Streams

513 Snow Goose | *Chen caerulescens* | *p. 572* | Length: 25–31″ "Blue" Goose

Marshes

514 Snow Goose

Chen caerulescens
p. 572

Length: 25–31″

Marshes

515 Ross' Goose

Chen rossii
p. 572

Length: 21–25½″

Marshes

516 Mute Swan

Cygnus olor
p. 572

Length: 58–60″

Lakes and Ponds; Rivers and Streams

517 American White Pelican | *Pelecanus erythrorhynchos* | Length: 55–70″

p. 573

Marshes and the Everglades

518 Anhinga | *Anhinga anhinga* | Length: 34–36″

p. 573

Marshes; Swamps; the Everglades; Lakes and Ponds

519 Olivaceous Cormorant | *Phalacrocorax olivaceus* | Length: 25″

p. 574

Freshwater Marshes

520 Double-crested Cormorant *Phalacrocorax auritus* Length: 30–35″
p. 574

Swamps; Lakes and Ponds; Rivers and Streams

521 Little Blue Heron *Egretta caerulea* Length: 25–30″
p. 574

Swamps and the Everglades

522 Limpkin *Aramus guarauna* Length: 25–28″
p. 575

Marshes and Cypress Swamps

523 White-faced Ibis *Plegadis chihi* p. 575 Length: 19–26″

Marshes

524 Wood Stork *Mycteria americana* p. 576 Length: 40–44″

Cypress Swamps and the Everglades

525 Little Blue Heron *Egretta caerulea* p. 574 Length: 25–30″ Immature

Swamps and the Everglades

526 Great Egret *Casmerodius albus* Length: 35–41″
p. 576

Marshes and the Everglades

527 Snowy Egret *Egretta thula* Length: 20–27″
p. 576

Marshes and the Everglades

528 Great Blue Heron *Ardea herodias* Length: 39–52″
p. 577

Marshes; the Everglades; Lakes and Ponds; Rivers and Streams

529 Black-crowned Night-Heron

Nycticorax nycticorax
p. 577

Length: 23–28″

Marshes; Swamps; the Everglades; Rivers and Streams

530 Yellow-crowned Night-Heron

Nycticorax violaceus
p. 578

Length: 22–27″

Swamps and the Everglades

531 Sandhill Crane

Grus canadensis
p. 578

Length: 34–48″

Marshes

532 American Bittern *Botaurus lentiginosus* Length: 23–34″
p. 578

Marshes and the Everglades

533 Least Bittern *Ixobrychus exilis* Length: 11–14″
p. 579

Marshes

534 Green-backed Heron *Butorides striatus* Length: 15–22″
p. 579

Marshes; the Everglades; Lakes and Ponds; Rivers and Streams

535 American Coot *Fulica americana* Length: 15″
p. 580

Marshes; the Everglades; Lakes and Ponds

536 Common Moorhen *Gallinula chloropus* Length: 13″
p. 580

Marshes; the Everglades; Lakes and Ponds

537 Purple Gallinule *Porphyrula martinica* Length: 11–13″
p. 580

Marshes and the Everglades

538 Sora *Porzana carolina* Length: 8–10″
p. 581

Marshes

539 Yellow Rail *Coturnicops noveboracensis* Length: 6–8″
p. 581

Marshes

540 Virginia Rail *Rallus limicola* Length: 9–11″
p. 582

Marshes

541 King Rail

Rallus elegans
p. 582

Length: 15–19″

Marshes and the Everglades

542 Common Snipe

Gallinago gallinago
p. 582

Length: 10½–11½″

Marshes

543 Semipalmated Sandpiper

Calidris pusilla
p. 583

Length: 6½″

Marshes; the Everglades; Lakes and Ponds; Rivers and Streams

544 Solitary Sandpiper *Tringa solitaria* Length: 7½–9″
p. 583

Lakes and Ponds

545 Least Sandpiper *Calidris minutilla* Length: 5–6½″
p. 584

Marshes

546 Spotted Sandpiper *Actitis macularia* Length: 7½″
p. 584

Lakes and Ponds; Rivers and Streams

547 American Avocet *Recurvirostra americana* *p. 584* Length: 16–20″

Marshes

548 Wilson's Phalarope *Phalaropus tricolor* *p. 585* Length: 9″ Breeding female

Marshes

549 Black Tern *Chlidonias niger* *p. 585* Length: 9–10″

Marshes

550 Common Tern *Sterna hirundo* Length: 13–16″
p. 586

Lakes and Ponds; Rivers and Streams

551 Forster's Tern *Sterna forsteri* Length: 14–16¼″
p. 586

Marshes

552 Caspian Tern *Sterna caspia* Length: 19–23″
p. 586

Lakes and Ponds; Rivers and Streams

553 Franklin's Gull
Larus pipixcan
p. 587
Length: 13½–15½″

Marshes; Lakes and Ponds

554 Bonaparte's Gull
Larus philadelphia
p. 587
Length: 12–14″

Lakes and Ponds; Rivers and Streams

555 Ring-billed Gull
Larus delawarensis
p. 588
Length: 18–20″

Lakes and Ponds; Rivers and Streams

556 California Gull *Larus californicus* Length: 20–23″
p. 588

Marshes; Lakes and Ponds

557 Herring Gull *Larus argentatus* Length: 23–26″
p. 589

Lakes and Ponds; Rivers and Streams

558 Snail Kite *Rostrhamus sociabilis* Length: 16–18″
p. 589

Marshes and the Everglades

559 American Swallow-tailed Kite | *Elanoides forficatus* *p. 589* | Length: 22–24″

Marshes; Swamps; the Everglades

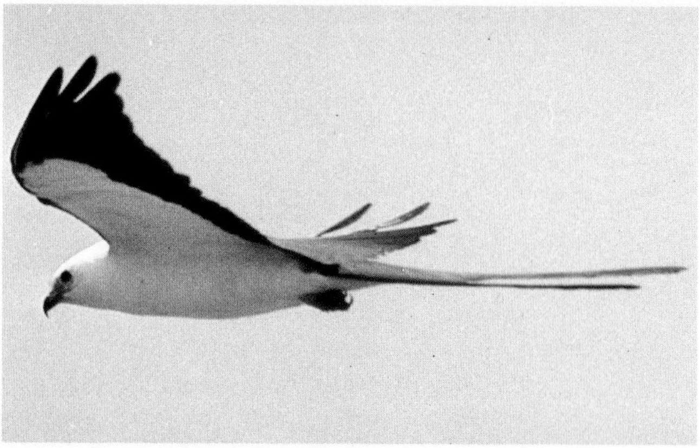

560 Short-tailed Hawk | *Buteo brachyurus* *p. 590* | Length: 13–14″

Cypress Swamps

561 Northern Harrier | *Circus cyaneus* *p. 590* | Length: 16–24″

Marshes and the Everglades

562 Bald Eagle | *Haliaeetus leucocephalus* | Length: 30–31″

p. 590

Marshes; the Everglades; Lakes and Ponds; Rivers and Streams

563 Osprey | *Pandion haliaetus* | Length: 21–24″

p. 591

The Everglades; Lakes and Ponds; Rivers and Streams

564 Red-shouldered Hawk | *Buteo lineatus* | Length: 16–24″

p. 591

Swamps and the Everglades

565 Short-eared Owl *Asio flammeus* *p. 592* Length: 16″

Marshes

566 Barred Owl *Strix varia* *p. 592* Length: 20″

Swamps and the Everglades

567 Wild Turkey *Meleagris gallopavo* *p. 593* Length: 48″ (males); 36″ (females)

Southern Bottomland Hardwood Swamps

568 Belted Kingfisher

Ceryle alcyon Length: 13″

p. 593

Lakes and Ponds; Rivers and Streams

569 Pileated Woodpecker

Dryocopus pileatus Length: 17″

p. 593

Cypress Swamps and the Everglades

570 Red-bellied Woodpecker

Melanerpes carolinus Length: 10″

p. 594

Swamps

571 Bank Swallow

Riparia riparia
p. 594
Length: 4¾–5½″

Rivers and Streams

572 Northern Rough-winged Swallow

Stelgidopteryx serripennis
p. 594
Length: 5–5¾″

Rivers and Streams

573 Eastern Phoebe

Sayornis phoebe
p. 595
Length: 7″

Rivers and Streams

574 Marsh Wren *Cistothorus palustris* Length: 4–5½″
p. 595

Marshes and the Everglades

575 Sedge Wren *Cistothorus platensis* Length: 4–4½″
p. 596

Marshes

576 Swamp Sparrow *Melospiza georgiana* Length: 5″
p. 596

Marshes; Swamps; the Everglades

577 Lincoln's Sparrow *Melospiza lincolnii* *p. 596* Length: 5–6″

Bogs

578 Louisiana Waterthrush *Seiurus motacilla* *p. 597* Length: 6½″

Rivers and Streams

579 American Dipper *Cinclus mexicanus* *p. 597* Length: 7–8½″

Rivers and Streams

580 Red-winged Blackbird | *Agelaius phoeniceus* | p. 597 | Length: 7–9½″ | Female

Marshes

581 Swainson's Warbler | *Limnothlypis swainsonii* | p. 598 | Length: 5″

Bottomland Hardwood Swamps

582 Sharp-tailed Sparrow | *Ammodramus caudacutus* | p. 598 | Length: 5½″

Marshes

583 Palm Warbler

Dendroica palmarum Length: 5½″
p. 599

Bogs and Marshes

584 Common Yellowthroat

Geothlypis trichas Length: 4½–5¾″
p. 599

Marshes; the Everglades; Rivers and Streams

585 Prothonotary Warbler

Protonotaria citrea Length: 5½″
p. 599

Swamps

586 Yellow-headed Blackbird | *Xanthocephalus xanthocephalus* | *p. 600* | Length: 8–11″

Marshes

58[redacted]ricolored Bla[redacted]kbird | *Agelaius tricolor* | *p. 600* | Length: 7½–9″

Marshes

58[redacted]Red-winged Bla[redacted]kbird | *Agelaius phoeniceus* | *p. 597* | Length: 7–9½″ Female

Marshes

589 Masked Shrew

Sorex cinereus
p. 602
Length: 2¾–4⅜″

Bogs and Marshes

590 Pacific Shrew

Sorex pacificus
p. 602
Length: 5⅛–6¼″

Rivers and Streams

591 Water Shrew

Sorex palustris
p. 602
Length: 5⅝–6¼″

Rivers and Streams

592 Pacific Water Shrew *Sorex bendirii* *p. 603* Length: $5\frac{7}{8}$–$6\frac{7}{8}$″

Rivers and Streams

593 Smoky Shrew *Sorex fumeus* *p. 603* Length: $4\frac{1}{4}$–5″

Swamps; Rivers and Streams

594 Arctic Shrew *Sorex arcticus* *p. 603* Length: 4–5″

Bogs and Swamps

595 Star-nosed Mole *Condylura cristata* Length: 5⅞–8¼″
p. 603

Swamps; Lakes and Ponds; Rivers and Streams

596 Marsh Rice Rat *Oryzomys palustris* Length: 7⅜–12″
p. 604

Marshes and the Everglades

597 Cotton Mouse *Peromyscus gossypinus* Length: 6–8⅛″
p. 604

Swamps and the Everglades

598 Golden Mouse *Ochrotomys nuttalli* Length: 5⅞–7½″
p. 605

Swamps

599 Meadow Jumping Mouse *Zapus hudsonius* Length: 7¼–10″
p. 605

Marshes

600 Southern Bog Lemming *Synaptomys cooperi* Length: 4⅝–6⅛″
p. 605

Bogs

601 Southern Red-backed Vole *Clethrionomys gapperi* *p. 606* Length: 4¾–6¼″

Bogs and Swamps

602 Southern Red-Backed Vole *Clethrionomys gapperi* *p. 606* Length: 4¾–6¼″

Bogs and Swamps

603 Meadow Vole *Microtus pennsylvanicus* *p. 606* Length: 5½–7¾″

Marshes

604 Water Vole *Arvicola richardsoni* Length: 7¾–10¼″
p. 606

Lakes and Ponds; Rivers and Streams

605 Marsh Rabbit *Sylvilagus palustris* Length: 14⅛–18″
p. 607

Bottomland Hardwood Swamps and the Everglades

606 Swamp Rabbit *Sylvilagus aquaticus* Length: 20⅞–21¼″
p. 607

Bottomland Hardwood Swamps

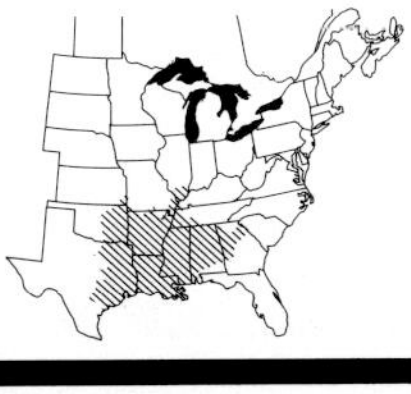

607 Mountain Beaver *Aplodontia rufa* Length: 9⅜–18½″
p. 607

Rivers and Streams

608 Round-tailed Muskrat *Neofiber alleni* Length: 11¼–15″
p. 608

Marshes and the Everglades

609 Muskrat *Ondatra zibethicus* Length: 16⅛–24⅜″
p. 608

Marshes

610 Nutria *Myocastor coypus* Length: 26⅜–55⅛″
p. 609

Marshes

611 Beaver *Castor canadensis* Length: 35½–46″
p. 609

Lakes and Ponds; Rivers and Streams

612 River Otter *Lutra canadensis* Length: 35–51⅝″
p. 610

The Everglades; Lakes and Ponds; Rivers and Streams

613 Mink

Mustela vison
p. 610

Length: 19¼–28¼″

Marshes and the Everglades

614 Raccoon

Procyon lotor
p. 611

Length: 23¾–37⅜″

Swamps and the Everglades

615 Black Bear

Ursus americanus
p. 611

Length: 4½–6¼′

Bogs, Swamps, and the Everglades

616 Bobcat

Felis rufus
p. 612

Length: 28–49$\frac{3}{8}$″

Swamps and the Everglades

617 White-tailed Deer

Odocoileus virginianus
p. 613

Length: 4$\frac{1}{2}$–6$\frac{3}{4}$′

Bogs, Swamps, and the Everglades

618 Moose

Alces alces
p. 614

Length: 6$\frac{3}{4}$–9′

Swamps; Lakes and Ponds

****

Naples Information Resource Center

03/21/2006 5:04 PM 941-513-1122

****

Wetlands /

Niering, William A

00020451

Due: 04/11/2006 11:59 PM

PART III SPECIES DESCRIPTIONS

FISHES

The wetlands of North America harbor a wide variety of fishes. Some are found in fast-moving mountain streams, while others prefer shallow, slow-moving rivers in relatively flat terrain; still others are found in lakes and ponds. The freshwater fishes include the Largemouth Bass—easily the most prized sport fish in the continent—along with other popular species such as salmon, trout, and pickerel. Also included in this group is the Paddlefish, an eerie, primitive-looking creature of sluggish waters. This section describes these and many other important fishes of freshwater habitats.

Gizzard Shad
Dorosoma cepedianum
31

To 16″ (41 cm). Deep, moderately compressed; back dark blue or gray, sides silvery; belly white; 6 or 8 horizontal dusky stripes on upper sides; dusky spot behind gill cover. Head small, mouth small and underneath head; transparent membranous eyelid present. Pelvic fin almost directly under origin of dorsal fin. Last ray of dorsal fin elongate, filamentous. Belly scales platelike, forming distinct keel.

Habitat
Fresh water in large rivers, reservoirs, lakes, and estuaries; also in salt water.

Range
Atlantic Coast and associated rivers from New York to mid-Florida, Gulf of Mexico from mid-Florida to central Mexico; St. Lawrence River, Great Lakes, and Mississippi River system.

Comments
The Gizzard Shad is a very common herbivorous fish associated primarily with freshwater habitats. It has no commercial value, but is a forage fish for larger, carnivorous fishes.

American Shad
Alosa sapidissima
32

To 30″ (76 cm). Elongate, strongly compressed; top and bottom profiles evenly rounded; depth about one-fourth length. Back dark bluish or greenish, sides much paler, belly silvery; dusky spot behind gill cover usually followed by several small, less distinct dusky spots. Head one-fifth or less of length; mouth oblique; eye diameter much less than length of snout. Dorsal fin origin slightly in front of pelvic fin insertion.

Habitat
Bays, estuaries, and fresh water.

Range
From S. Labrador to St. Johns River, Florida; introduced in Pacific from Alaska to Mexico.

Comments
The related Hickory Shad (*A. mediocris*) has a profile that is almost straight at the top and well rounded at the bottom; the lower jaw projects well beyond the upper. This species occurs in a similar habitat from Maine to St. Johns River, Florida. All *Alosa* are schooling species that enter freshwater streams to spawn. None remain long in fresh water, nor do they go far out at sea.

Striped Bass
Morone saxatilis
33

To 6′ (1.8 m). Elongate, moderately compressed; back olive-green to dark blue, sides silvery, belly white, upper sides with 6–9 dark, uninterrupted stripes; dorsal, anal, and caudal fins dusky. Mouth large, lower jaw slightly projecting. Teeth small. Gill cover has 2 flat spines near rear edge. First dorsal fin with 8–10 strong spines, separated from second dorsal by deep notch. Scales extend onto all fin bases except dorsal.

Habitat
Inshore over various bottoms.

Range
Atlantic Ocean and associated rivers from St. Lawrence River to St. Johns River, Florida; Appalachicola River, W. Florida, to Lake Ponchartrain, Louisiana. Most abundant from Hudson River to Chesapeake Bay. Widely introduced into rivers and lakes in much of Mississippi River system, Colorado River, and coastal streams in Washington, Oregon, and California.

Comments
The Striped Bass is a very important sport and commercial fish throughout its range, and large individuals are caught by surf fishing, especially on the Atlantic Coast. It is a delicious food fish. It is anadromous, and spawns prolifically in fresh water.

Largemouth Bass
Micropterus salmoides
34

To 3′2″ (97 cm). Moderately deep, robust; back olive to dark green, mottled; sides greenish yellow with dark midlateral stripe; head greenish gold. Mouth large, extends beyond rear edge of eye. Dorsal, anal, and caudal fins olive; dorsal fins almost separate. Lateral line complete; no scales on bases of soft dorsal and anal fins.

Habitat
Quiet, clear to slightly turbid streams, ponds, lakes, and reservoirs, often with vegetation.

Range
S. Ontario south through Great Lakes, Mississippi River system, and Coastal Plain from N. North Carolina to Texas and northeastern Mexico. Also introduced throughout southern Canada and United States.

Comments
The Largemouth Bass, one of the most highly sought sport fishes in the United States, is caught with live and artificial bait. It is more tolerant of warm water than the Smallmouth Bass, but at higher temperatures it becomes less active.

Quillback
Carpiodes cyprinus
35

To 24″ (61 cm). Deep, compressed, back highly arched; olive to brownish; sides silvery. Head small; snout blunt; mouth on underside, narrow, horizontal; lips with folds, tip of lower lip in front of nostril. Fins plain, dorsal, anal, and caudal fins dusky, paired fins clear; front dorsal fin rays long, longest ray almost as long as fin base; caudal fin forked, with pointed tips. Lateral line complete, straight.

Habitat
Clear to turbid waters of large creeks, rivers, lakes, and reservoirs with firm or soft bottom.

Range
SW. Quebec and S. Ontario west to S. Alberta; Atlantic Coast drainages, NE. Pennsylvania south to South Carolina;

Mississippi River system; Gulf Coast drainages, W. Florida west to Louisiana.

Comments
The Quillback and its related species, including the River Carpsucker (*C. carpio*) and the Highfin Carpsucker (*C. velifer*), are rarely sought, but are occasionally taken by snag fishing.

Smallmouth Buffalo
Ictiobus bubalus
36

To 3′ (91 cm). Deep, moderately compressed, back arched, often with ridge toward front; dark olive to gray, sides grayish to bronze. Head small; snout bluntly rounded; mouth small, horizontal, on underside, below level of eye; lips thick, with folds. Pelvic fins gray-black, other fins dusky; front dorsal fin rays long, less than half length of fin base. Lateral line straight.

Habitat
Clear to slightly turbid rivers with moderate current; also lakes and reservoirs.

Range
Throughout Mississippi River system and Gulf Coast drainages, from Alabama west to Rio Grande.

Comments
Buffalofishes are not popular for sport, but are fished commercially in the Mississippi River and some large lakes. The common name refers to their large size and humped back. The Bigmouth Buffalo (*I. cyprinellus*) and Black Buffalo (*I. niger*), somewhat different in appearance, occur in sluggish rivers, backwaters, and lakes in the Lake Winnipeg drainage, southern Great Lakes drainage, and the Mississippi River system.

Common Carp
Cyprinus carpio
37, 38

To 30″ (76 cm). Robust, moderately compressed; back dark olive, sides lighter, yellowish below; fins dusky-olive. 2 pairs of barbels on upper lip. Dorsal fin long, has 1 stout, serrate spine; anal fin with similar spine. Lateral line complete.

Habitat
Streams, lakes, ponds, sloughs, and reservoirs in turbid or clear water over mud or silt with aquatic vegetation; more common in warm waters.

Range
Introduced in southern Canada, throughout United States, and Mexico.

Comments
Carp were introduced into the United States during the late 1880s by the United States Fish Commission as a food fish. They proved detrimental to native fish populations and have never become as popular for game or food in North America as they are in Europe.

White Perch
Morone americana
39

To 19″ (48 cm). Oblong, moderately compressed, back elevated; back greenish gray or nearly black; sides paler, sometimes with indistinct stripes; belly whitish. Head flattened between eyes; lower jaw slightly projecting; 2 spines on gill cover. Dorsal fins barely connected. Scales extend onto base of dorsal, anal, and caudal fins and head.

Habitat
Brackish water in bays and estuaries; freshwater populations in rivers and lakes, especially in north of range.

Range
From Cape Breton Island, St. Lawrence River, and Lake Ontario to St. Johns River, Florida; most abundant in Hudson River and Chesapeake Bay.

Comments
The White Perch is an important sport and game fish. Its average size is 8″ to 10″ (20 to 25 cm), and the usual weight is 1 lb (500 g) or less. The White Perch probably entered Lake Ontario through the Erie Barge Canal and the Oswego River. It is a recent immigrant to Lake Erie.

White Bass
Morone chrysops
40

To 18″ (46 cm). Deep, compressed; back olive to silvery gray; sides silvery to white, with 6–9 dark, narrow stripes, sometimes interrupted below lateral line; belly yellowish. Mouth extends to middle of eye; lower jaw protrudes; single patch of teeth on back of tongue. First dorsal fin separate from second; second anal spine about half length of third. Scales in lateral line extend onto head.

Habitat
Large streams, lakes, and reservoirs; over firm sand, gravel, or rocks in moderately clear water.

Range
Lake Winnipeg; St. Lawrence River, southern Great Lakes, Mississippi River system, Gulf Coast from Louisiana to Texas and New Mexico. Introduced outside native range.

Comments
The White Bass is found in schools in open water. It feeds primarily on fishes, but also consumes aquatic insects and crustaceans, which it locates by sight rather than scent.

Walleye
Stizostedion vitreum
41

To 3′ 5″ (1 m). Elongate, slightly compressed; olive-brown to brassy greenish yellow above with dusky to black mottlings, belly whitish with yellow-green tinge. Mouth extends to eye. Dorsal fins separate; first dorsal fin dusky with black edge, black blotch on membranes of last 2–3 spines; caudal fin forked, tip of lower lobe white. Lateral line complete.

Habitat
Deep waters of large streams, lakes, and reservoirs over firm sand, gravel, or rocks.

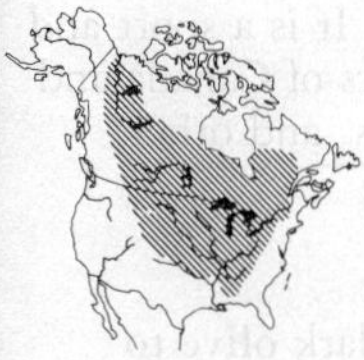

Range
From southern Hudson Bay drainage west to MacKenzie River; south through Great Lakes and Mississippi River system to Arkansas. Eastern Gulf drainage, Alabama and Mississippi. Widely introduced.

Comments
The Walleye is the largest North American species in the perch family and one of the most sought-after sport and food fishes. The largest catch was taken in Old Hickory Lake, Tennessee, in 1960.

Sauger
Stizostedion canadense
42

To 28″ (71 cm). Elongate, almost cylindrical; gray to dull brown, sides brassy to orange with dark markings, often with 3–4 dark saddles extending to middle of sides, belly whitish. Mouth extends past middle of eye. Dorsal fins separate; first dorsal has 2–3 rows of small, black spots and narrow, dusky edge; second dorsal fin has 2 light, narrow bands; caudal fin forked. Lateral line complete.

Habitat
Dingy, turbid waters of large creeks and rivers with moderate to swift current; also lakes and reservoirs.

Range
From Quebec to Alberta; St. Lawrence River and Great Lakes; Mississippi River drainage south to Tennessee, N. Alabama, and Arkansas. Introduced outside native range.

Comments
The Sauger is an important sport and food fish and is harvested commercially in parts of Canada. It eats a variety of small fishes and aquatic invertebrates, which it locates with its eyes.

Yellow Perch
Perca flavescens
43

To 15″ (38 cm). Oblong, moderately compressed; brassy green to golden yellow above with 508 dusky bars across back almost to belly. Mouth extends to middle of eye. Dorsal and caudal fins dusky to olive; pelvic and anal fins light grayish green to reddish orange; dorsal fins separate; 2 anal fin spines. Lateral line complete; cheek and gill cover scaled.

Habitat
Open areas in streams, lakes, ponds, and reservoirs with clear water and aquatic vegetation.

Range
From Nova Scotia to Alberta; Great Slave Lake south to Montana. Atlantic Coast from St. Lawrence River drainage south to South Carolina; Great Lakes drainage; south in Mississippi River drainage to Missouri; Gulf drainages of W. Florida and extreme S. Alabama. Introduced outside native range.

Comments
The Yellow Perch lives in schools in deep water, and moves

into shallower areas to feed at dawn and dusk. It is a sport and food fish and is harvested commercially in parts of Canada and the Great Lakes. Anglers use minnows, worms, and other fishes as live bait.

Smallmouth Bass
Micropterus dolomieui
44

To 24″ (61 cm). Elongate, compressed; back dark olive to brown, sides greenish yellow with bronze reflections, diffuse midlateral bars form dark mottlings. Mouth extends to eye. Dorsal, anal, and caudal fins olive; dorsal fins joined. Lateral line complete. Scales on bases of soft dorsal and anal fins.

Habitat
Cool, clear streams with moderate to swift current over gravel or rocks; lakes and reservoirs.

Range
SW. Quebec and SE. Ontario; New York west to Minnesota, south in Mississippi River system to N. Alabama, N. Arkansas, and E. Oklahoma. Widely introduced.

Comments
One of the most popular sport fishes in eastern North America, this species takes a variety of live bait, minnows, and crayfishes, as well as artificial lures. The Smallmouth Bass spawns earlier than other sunfishes in the same areas.

Rock Bass
Ambloplites rupestris
45

To 13″ (33 cm). Oblong, robust; back olive mottled with dark saddles and bronze blotches, lighter below with rows of dusky spots. Head large; mouth extends to or past middle of large, red eye; cheeks and gill covers scaled. Lateral line complete.

Habitat
Cool, clear, rocky streams and shallow lakes with vegetation and other cover.

Range
Southern Canada, S. Quebec west to Manitoba; from Great Lakes drainage south to N. Alabama and N. Georgia.

Comments
Although small, the Rock Bass is a popular game fish.

Sacramento Perch
Archoplites interruptus
46

To 16″ (41 cm). Moderately elongate, compressed; back olive to black, sides olive-brown, upper sides mottled with 6–8 irregular olive-brown bars, belly whitish. Mouth large, extends to middle of eye. Caudal fin slightly forked. Lateral line complete.

Habitat
Sloughs, sluggish streams, and lakes with vegetation.

Range
Sacramento, San Joaquin, Pajaro, and Salinas rivers and Clear Lake, California. Introduced in Utah, Nevada, Oregon, and California.

Comments
The Sacramento Perch is the only sunfish native to the western United States. In its native range, it declined rapidly as exotic fishes were introduced and its habitat destroyed.

Warmouth
Lepomis gulosus
47

To 10″ (25 cm). Oblong, robust; back and dorsal, anal, and caudal fins dark olive-brown with dusky mottlings, sides lighter with scattered dusky spots, belly yellowish. Head large, wide; gill cover flat not extended; teeth on tongue; mouth extends past middle of reddish eye, which has radiating dusky lines, 4–5 running to edge of gill cover; dark spot on upper part of gill cover. Pectoral fin short, rounded. Lateral line complete.

Habitat
Ponds, swamps, lakes, and sluggish streams with vegetation or debris.

Range
From Maryland, S. Michigan, and S. Wisconsin south to Florida, west to Texas and New Mexico.

Comments
The Warmouth spends much of its time in the cover of dense vegetation. It feeds on small fishes, crayfishes, and aquatic insects. During the late spring and summer, it nests in shallow water.

Bluegill
Lepomis macrochirus
48

To 12″ (30 cm). Deep, compressed, profile rounded under dorsal fin; body and dorsal, anal, and caudal fins dark olive-green; sides lighter, olive with brassy reflections, often with dusky bars; belly whitish. Mouth at tip of snout, not extending past front edge of eye; gill cover flap broad, moderatly long, dusky to black. Pectoral fin long, pointed; second dorsal fin with black blotch near middle of rear rays; anal fin base about half length of dorsal fin base. Lateral line complete.

Habitat
Clear, warm pools of streams, lakes, ponds, sloughs, and reservoirs, usually in shallow water with vegetation.

Range
From S. Ontario, S. Quebec, and Great Lakes drainage south to Florida, west to S. Texas. Introduced throughout United States and northern Mexico.

Comments
The Bluegill is the most common sunfish and probably the most popular freshwater game fish in the United States.

Spotted Bass
Micropterus punctulatus
49

To 24″ (61 cm). Elongate, compressed; back dark olive, sides olive to yellowish with dark, midlateral, diamond-shaped blotches; lower sides have rows of dusky spots forming stripes.

Mouth reaches middle of eye. Dorsal, anal, and caudal fins olive; dorsal fins joined. Lateral line complete; scales on bases of soft dorsal and anal fins.

Habitat
Warm, clear to slightly turbid pools of creeks and rivers; also ponds, lakes, and reservoirs.

Range
From W. West Virginia, SW. Virginia, NW. Georgia, and W. Florida west to E. Texas; S. Ohio to SE. Kansas. Introduced outside native range.

Comments
There are 3 subspecies of Spotted Basses and they are often confused with the Largemouth Bass. The Spotted Bass is a prized game fish and readily takes live or artificial bait.

Black Crappie
Pomoxis nigromaculatus
50

To 16″ (41 cm). Deep, strongly compressed, dorsal profile rounded; back greenish, sides silvery green with dark green to black scattered mottlings not forming bars, belly silvery, dorsal, anal, and caudal fins yellowish green with dusky, wavy lines and white spots. Head long, concave near eye; mouth oblique, extends past middle of eye. Dorsal fins connected without notch. Lateral line complete.

Habitat
Quiet, warm, clear streams, ponds, lakes, and reservoirs.

Range
Quebec, Ontario, and S. Manitoba; eastern and central United States except Atlantic Coast streams from Maine to Virginia. Widely introduced.

Comments
This is a very popular sport and food fish, especially in the southern part of its range. It is generally less abundant than the White Crappie and less tolerant of silty and turbid waters. It feeds day and night, but is most active in the evening.

Longear Sunfish
Lepomis megalotis
51

To 9″ (23 cm). Deep, compressed; back dark olive to blue-green, sides light olive with yellow and blue-green speckles, belly yellow to reddish, cheeks reddish with wavy blue-green stripes. Mouth extends to eye; gill cover flap "ear" long, wider than eye, often edged with white or red. Pectoral fin short, rounded; soft dorsal, anal, and caudal fins reddish orange. Lateral line complete.

Habitat
Pools of streams with moderate current over sand, gravel, or rocks; also reservoirs and lakes.

Range
From SW. Quebec to SE. Manitoba; Mississippi Valley; Gulf Coast drainages, W. Florida west to Rio Grande, Texas, and New Mexico. Introduced outside native range.

Comments
The Longear Sunfish is a popular game fish in most areas. Its food consists of aquatic insects, snails, crustaceans, and fish.

Rio Grande Cichlid
Cichlasoma cyanoguttatum
52

To 12″ (30 cm). Deep, compressed, top profile gently curved; breeding males have hump at nape; dusky to olive above, sides greenish gray with numerous small blue or blue-green to whitish spots and 4–6 dusky bars, dark spots below middle of dorsal fin and near caudal fin base, dusky below. Single nostril each side of snout. Dorsal fins joined, spiny portion much longer. Lateral line interrupted.

Habitat
Warm streams in pools and slack water, usually with aquatic vegetation.

Range
Gulf of Mexico drainages from Rio Grande, Texas, to northern Mexico; introduced in west-central Florida, S. Texas, and other southern states.

Comments
This very attractive fish is easy to keep in an aquarium, but like other cichlids, it digs up the bottom, uproots plants, and is somewhat aggressive if kept with other fishes.

Pumpkinseed
Lepomis gibbosus
53

To 10″ (25 cm). Deep, short, compressed; back dark greenish gold mottled with reddish orange, sides greenish yellow, mottled orange and blue-green, belly yellow-orange. Head small; mouth extends to eye; gill cover flap "ear" stiff, with spot, black toward front, bordered by white above and below, red toward rear; cheeks with wavy bluish lines. Pectoral fin long, pointed; soft dorsal fin spotted, edge yellowish to white. Lateral line complete.

Habitat
Cool, quiet, shallow waters of slow streams, ponds, marshes, and lakes with dense vegetation.

Range
From New Brunswick west to S. Manitoba; south along Atlantic Coast to NE. Georgia; Great Lakes and upper Mississippi River system south to S. Illinois. Widely introduced.

Comments
The Pumpkinseed is not sought by most experienced anglers, but is often caught by beginners. It is aggressive and will take a variety of bait.

Green Sunfish
Lepomis cyanellus
54

To 10″ (25 cm). Robust, moderately elongate, depth less than distance from snout tip to dorsal fin origin; yellowish olive, sides sometimes with dusky bars, belly pale olive, dorsal, anal, and caudal fins olive to dusky, edges whitish to light orange.

Head broad; gill cover flap not extended; mouth extends to middle of eye. Pectoral fin short, rounded; rear base of second dorsal and anal fins often with black blotch. Lateral line complete.

Habitat
Clear to turbid water with little or no current in smaller streams, swamps, and ponds.

Range
Native to southern Great Lakes, Mississippi River basin south to Texas; Alabama west to New Mexico; widely introduced in United States and northern Mexico.

Comments
The Green Sunfish, one of the most common sunfishes, is tolerant of a wide range of environmental conditions.

Mozambique Tilapia
Tilapia mossambica
55

To 15″ (38 cm). Deep, compressed; dark olive to gray above, sides gray-green to yellowish, yellowish below; dorsal and caudal fins have reddish edges; breeding males bluish to black; young silvery with 6–8 bars. Mouth small; lips of breeding males large, blue; single nostril on each side of snout. Dorsal fins jointed; dorsal and anal fins pointed toward rear. Caudal peduncle short, deep; caudal fin rounded. Lateral line interrupted toward rear.

Habitat
Warm, sluggish streams, ponds, and canals with abundant aquatic vegetation; also enters brackish coastal waters.

Range
Widely introduced in southern United States south of North Carolina, Missouri, and central California.

Comments
The Mozambique Tilapia has been introduced for the purpose of weed control and has escaped from ponds where it was cultured for the tropical fish trade. It feeds on aquatic insects and small fishes as well as aquatic weeds, and competes with native game fishes for food and space.

Sailfin Molly
Poecilia latipinna
56

To 5″ (12.5 cm). Oblong, compressed; depth of male about same from dorsal fin toward rear; belly rounded in female and caudal peduncle narrower. Olive with blackish or reddish-orange to yellowish dots on side scales forming stripes. Head small, flattened; mouth small; teeth in several series, outer ones largest. In males, dorsal fin very tall, with blackish spots on membranes between rays forming interrupted narrow bands; caudal fin has dark spots forming bars. Anal fin of males located forward and modified as reproductive organ.

Habitat
Saltwater marshes, ponds, and ditches; also freshwater pools, ponds, and ditches.

Range
Along coast from North Carolina to Yucatán. Inland streams in Florida, Louisiana, and Texas. Introduced in lower Colorado River system.

Comments
These strikingly beautiful fishes feed primarily on plants and organic detritus. A variety with black coloring is bred as a popular aquarium fish. Like many killifishes, they are extemely tolerant of wide ranges in salinity.

Pirate Perch
Aphredoderus sayanus
57

To 4½″ (11.5 cm). Oblong, stout toward front, compressed toward rear; head and body dark olive-grayish with dark spots; underside of head and body yellowish to brownish. Gill cover with sharp spine. Fins dusky, single dorsal fin; no adipose fin; caudal peduncle deep; caudal fin has 1–2 dark bars at base. Lateral line incomplete. Scales on head and body spiny.

Habitat
Backwaters of low-gradient streams, ponds, swamps, and bayous in clear to murky water with abundant plant cover.

Range
Atlantic Coastal Plain, from Long Island south to S. Florida, west to E. Texas; southern Great Lakes drainage from W. New York to SE. Minnesota, and south in Mississippi Valley.

Comments
This fish hides in aquatic vegetation by day, emerging at night to feed. It is more abundant in the southern part of its range.

Stippled Darter
Etheostoma punctulatum
58

To 3½″ (9 cm). Moderately deep, compressed; brownish above with 4 prominent, dark saddles, sides have broad midlateral blue-green band toward rear, males bright red-orange below. Snout longer than eye; fleshy bridge (frenum) connects upper lip to tip of snout; broad black bar under eye; gill membranes narrowly joined, red-orange in males. First dorsal fin has orange edge and black base in males, lighter in females; other fins spotted. Lateral line incomplete.

Habitat
Quiet pools in cool, clear creeks with moderate current.

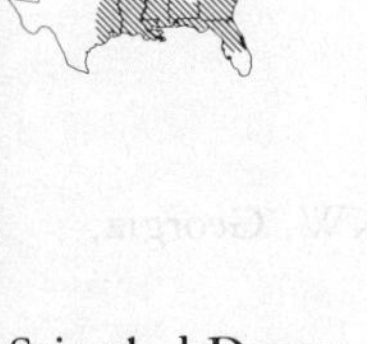

Range
S. Missouri, N. Arkansas, SE. Kansas, and NE. Oklahoma.

Comments
The Stippled Darter spawns during the spring and early summer. Other details of its life history are unknown.

Mottled Sculpin
Cottus bairdi
59

To 4″ (10 cm). Robust, thick toward front, caudal peduncle deep, compressed; back olive to tan, dusky in adult males, sides lighter with dark mottlings, belly whitish; traces of 2 dark saddles sometimes under second dorsal fin, first dorsal fin of males black, edge bright orange, other fins dusky or have faint, narrow, dusky to brown bands. Head broad, flattened; mouth extends to below eye. Pelvic fin has 1 slender spine, 3–4 soft rays. Lateral line incomplete.

Habitat
Clear, cool or cold creeks, rivers, and lakes over rocks.

Range
Quebec, Ontario, central Manitoba south to N. Georgia, west to N. Arkansas; S. Alberta and British Columbia south to W. Colorado, NW. New Mexico, and Utah, west to Oregon.

Comments
The Mottled Sculpin, which feeds on aquatic insects, is frequently cited as a major predator of trout eggs, but this does not appear to be true. Trouts may prey on sculpins.

Snail Darter
Percina tanasi
60

To 3″ (7.5 cm). Robust, thick toward front; back olive-brown with 4 broad, dark saddles extending to lateral line, first under front dorsal fin spines; sides have midlateral blotches; pale green to yellowish below. Head small; snout curved downward; mouth almost horizontal. Fins large; pelvic and anal fins clear; other fins with dark spots forming bars on rays; pectoral fins rounded. Lateral line complete.

Habitat
Clean gravel riffles and shoals in clear streams.

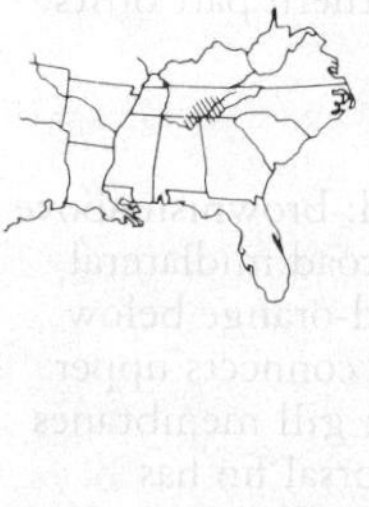

Range
Tennessee River drainage in SE. Tennessee, NW. Georgia, and NE. Alabama.

Comments
The Snail Darter gained notoriety in 1977 when its status as an endangered species delayed construction of a dam in the Tennessee Valley. Congress eventually exempted that dam project from the Endangered Species Act.

Swamp Darter
Etheostoma fusiforme
61

To 2″ (5 cm). Elongate; back dark olive with 8–12 dark blotches; sides tan to greenish, mottled, often with midlateral blotches, belly whitish with dark specks. Snout shorter than eye, curved downward; fleshy bridge (frenum) connects upper lip to tip of snout; spine on gill cover; gill membranes narrowly joined. First dorsal fin with dark bands; caudal fin barred, 3 dark spots at base; caudal peduncle long, slender. Lateral line arched upward, incomplete.

Habitat
Clear or dark, stained, sluggish coastal streams, ponds, and swamps with vegetation over mud, sand, and detritus.

Range
From S. Maine to Florida, west to SE. Oklahoma and E. Texas; W. Tennessee and E. Arkansas south to Louisiana.

Comments
The Swamp Darter is common over most of its range, but little is known of its life history and habits.

Johnny Darter
Etheostoma nigrum
62

To 2½″ (6.5 cm). Slender; yellowish to straw-colored, usually with 5–7 dark saddles and small, dark X-, V-, and W-shaped markings on sides, often merging to form zigzag lines; breeding males blackish. Snout blunt, curved downward; no fleshy bridge (frenum) connecting upper lip to tip of snout; dark lines from snout to eye not joined at midline; gill membranes narrowly joined. Fins have rows of dark spots forming bands; spots dusky in breeding males; pectoral fins vary from clear to barred. Lateral line nearly complete; cheeks usually unscaled.

Habitat
Pools near riffles in clear to slightly turbid creeks and rivers over sand, gravel, or rocks; lake shores.

Range
From S. Quebec and southern Hudson Bay drainage to E. Saskatchewan; Atlantic Coast drainages in S. Virginia and N. North Carolina; upper Mississippi River and Great Lakes drainages west to SE. Wyoming and NE. Colorado and south to SW. Arkansas; Mobile Bay drainage in Alabama and Mississippi.

Comments
This is the most widespread species in the genus *Etheostoma*. It is food for game fishes, but is not an important forage fish. One of the easiest darters to maintain in captivity, it is often used in behavioral studies.

Brook Stickleback
Culaea inconstans
63

To 2″ (5 cm). Compressed; back green to olive, sides lighter with yellowish spots or wavy lines; spawning males dusky-green to black. Dorsal spines short, less than diameter of eye, curved slightly backward. Caudal peduncle slender, without keel; caudal fin rounded. Minute bony plates along lateral line.

Habitat
Small streams, ponds, and lakes with clear, cold water and abundant aquatic vegetation; rarely enters brackish water.

Range
Southeast from southern Hudson Bay drainage, east from E. British Columbia, south from Northwest Territories to New England and Great Lakes; St. Lawrence River, Nova Scotia, and upper Mississippi River system. Introduced in Connecticut, Alabama, and New Mexico.

Comments
Brook Sticklebacks spawn in shallow water, where the male uses vegetation to construct a small, ball-shaped nest with a cavity through its center.

Plains Killifish
Fundulus zebrinus
64

To 5″ (12.5 cm). Elongate, stout toward front; back dark olive; sides silvery yellow to white with 12–28 dark bars, wider, fewer, and darker in males; belly yellowish. Head flat above, scaled; mouth upturned, band of teeth on jaws. Fins large, rounded, yellowish to reddish; dorsal fin origin before anal fin. Caudal peduncle deep; caudal fin margin straight. Scales small.

Habitat
In shallow pools, backwaters, and along edges of streams with slow to moderate current over sand.

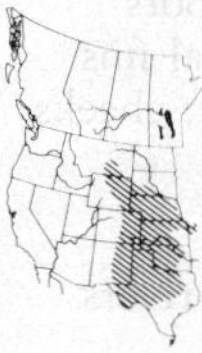

Range
Great Plains east of Rocky Mountains, NW. Missouri and SE. Montana south to Texas; introduced in Colorado and upper Missouri rivers and Rio Grande.

Comments
The Plains Killifish tolerates saline and alkaline waters in which few, if any, other fishes are found.

Starhead Topminnow
Fundulus notti
65

To 3″ (7.5 cm). Short, moderately deep; back dark, sides olive to silvery with dark spots forming stripes; males have faint dusky bars. Silvery spot on top of head; mouth upturned; large, square, black blotch under eye. Fins small; dorsal fin origin behind anal fin origin. Lateral line absent.

Habitat
Lowland marshes, ponds, swamps, and sluggish streams with vegetation.

Range
From southern Lake Michigan drainage south in Mississippi Valley to Louisiana; Gulf Coast streams from north-central Florida west to E. Texas.

Comments
Starhead Topminnows swim at the surface, feeding on aquatic as well as terrestrial insects. Spawning occurs during May and June over dense growths of aquatic plants.

Speckled Chub
Hybopsis aestivalis
66

To 3″ (7.5 cm). Slender; olive to brownish yellow above; sides yellow to silvery, with small, dark, rounded speckles, often with faint, dusky stripe along side; belly silvery. Mouth on underside; barbel long; snout rounded, projects far beyond upper lip; eyes high on head, diameter much less than snout length. Lateral line complete.

Habitat
Channels of large, clear to turbid streams over sand or gravel in moderate current.

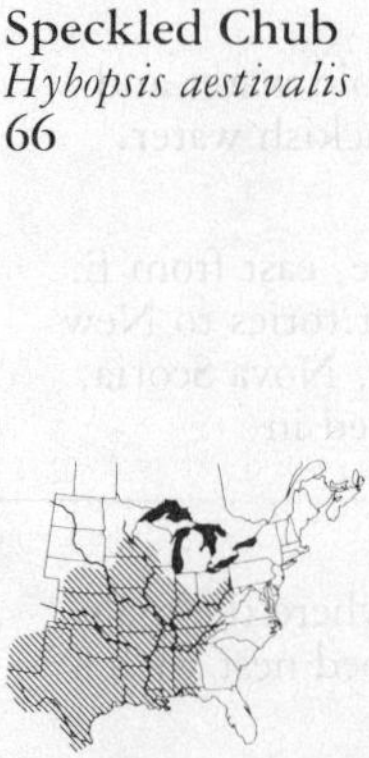

Range
S. Minnesota, Ohio, Nebraska south to Rio Grande drainage in northeastern Mexico, W. Florida, NW. Georgia, Alabama west to Texas.

Comments
The Speckled Chub lives on or near the bottom, and uses taste buds on the head, body, and fins to find the aquatic insects on which it feeds. It spawns in deep, swift water around midday from May through August. Its life span seldom exceeds 1½ years.

Common Shiner
Notropis cornutus
67

To 6″ (15 cm). Deep, compressed; back dusky-olive with dark, wide stripe on back between snout and dorsal fin origin; sides silvery to bluish purple in breeding males. Head moderately large, blunt; mouth large, at tip of snout, oblique; chin without dusky pigment; eye large. Fins clear to rosy, rounded; dorsal fin origin over or in front of pelvic fin insertion. Lateral line complete; lateral scales tall, narrow.

Habitat
Clear, cool creeks and small rivers with moderate current in riffles and pools over firm bottom.

Range
Nova Scotia west to SE. Saskatchewan, south to central Virginia, west to SE. Wyoming, E. Colorado.

Comments
The Common Shiner, as its name implies, is found frequently in much of its range. It is often replaced by the Striped Shiner in streams that have become warm, turbid, and silty. It is often used as bait for basses and other game fishes.

Taillight Shiner
Notropis maculatus
68

To 3″ (7.5 cm). Long, slender; olive to yellowish brown above, scales dark-edged, giving crosshatched appearance; dusky lateral stripe from snout to caudal fin ends in large, black caudal spot; breeding males reddish. Snout rounded; upper jaw projects beyond lower. Dorsal and anal fins crescent-shaped; edges of pelvic, dorsal, and anal fins dusky; leading edge of dorsal fin black. Lateral line incomplete.

Habitat
Clear or dark, stained backwaters and quiet areas of lowland rivers, streams, and lakes with some aquatic vegetation.

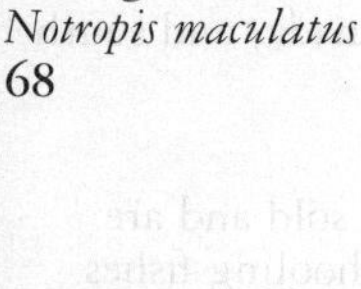

Range
Coastal Plain, S. North Carolina, south to S. Florida, west to E. Texas; in Mississippi River Valley, S. Illinois south to E. Texas.

Comments
The total life span of the Taillight Shiner is 13 to 15 months. It grows rapidly, sometimes reaching sexual maturity and spawning at 6 to 9 months.

Brook Silverside
Labidesthes sicculus
69

To 4″ (10 cm). Elongate, slender, compressed, depth one-seventh length; pale greenish yellow, translucent with silvery lateral band bordered above by dark line; fins transparent; tips of dorsal spines black in males. Head long, flattened above, narrow below; snout longer than eye; jaws pointed, forming beak. Dorsal fins separate, above anal fin; anal fin long; caudal fin forked. Lateral line incomplete.

Habitat
Quiet, clear waters of lakes, ponds, rivers, creeks, and reservoirs.

Range
Great Lakes and St. Lawrence River; Atlantic Coastal Plain from South Carolina to Florida; from Pennsylvania to W. Oklahoma; Mississippi River system from Minnesota to Louisiana.

Comments
Brook Silversides are adapted for living near the surface, where they form large schools during the day and feed on zooplankton and small insects.

Golden Shiner
Notemigonus crysoleucas
70

To 12″ (30 cm). Deep, compressed; back golden to olive, sides light olive with silvery reflections, belly silvery yellow; some fish entirely silvery. Mouth upturned; snout blunt. Belly has pronounced keel between pelvic and anal fins. Dorsal fin slightly crescent-shaped; breeding males have orange on pelvic and anal fins. Lateral line curved downward.

Habitat
Clear, quiet streams, lakes, ponds, and swamps over mud, sand, or rocks, usually near aquatic vegetation.

Range
Native to eastern North America, southern Canada, and south to Texas; widely introduced elsewhere.

Comments
Golden Shiners are the most common bait fish sold and are important forage fish for game fishes. These schooling fishes stay mainly near shore but may venture into open water.

Pugnose Minnow
Notropis emiliae
71, 72

To 2½″ (6.5 cm). Moderately deep, compressed; back yellowish olive, sides silvery with dusky midlateral stripe extending from snout, scales on sides outlined in dark pigment. Snout blunt; mouth small, upturned, almost vertical; barbel occasionally present. Front and rear dorsal fin rays dusky in males; other fins plain. Lateral line complete or interrupted.

Habitat
Clear, sluggish waters with little current and abundant vegetation over organic debris.

Range
Lake St. Clair drainage, Ontario; Coastal Plain, S. South Carolina south to Florida, west to Texas; E. Ohio west to SE. Minnesota, south to S. Texas.

Comments
The upturned mouth of the Pugnose Minnow suggests that this fish feeds in midwater or near the surface. The specific name *emiliae* honors Mrs. Emily Hay, whose husband discovered the species.

White Sucker
Catostomus commersoni
73

To 24″ (61 cm). Elongate, cylindrical, caudal peduncle moderately slender; back dusky-olive, sides greenish yellow with brassy luster; young mottled on sides. Head flattened above; snout blunt; mouth large, on underside; lips thick with many papillae. Fins plain; pelvic axillary scale present. Lateral line complete; front scales crowded.

Habitat
Cool, clear streams and lakes over sand, gravel, or rocks.

Range
Canada and northern United States east of Continental Divide to NW. South Carolina, N. Alabama, N. Arkansas, and N. New Mexico.

Comments
The White Sucker is the most common species of this genus in North America. Anglers do not fish for it, but some are taken during spawning runs in large lift nets and in commercial fisheries.

Spotted Sucker
Minytrema melanops
74

To 20″ (51 cm). Elongate, slightly compressed; back olive usually with dark blotch near base of dorsal fin; sides and belly silvery, scales on sides have black spots forming horizontal stripes; dorsal, anal, and caudal fins light olive. Lips ridged, thin; rear margin of lower lip V-shaped. Dorsal fin short, rear margin concave; caudal fin deeply forked. No lateral line.

Habitat
Lowland streams with deep, clear pools and firm bottoms; overflow ponds, sloughs, lakes, and reservoirs.

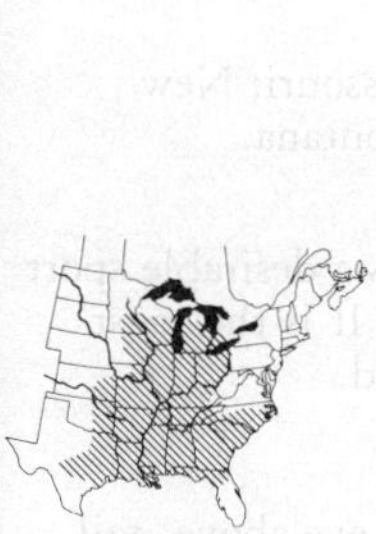

Range
Coastal drainages of North Carolina south to Gulf drainages of N. and W. Florida, west to central Texas; southern Great Lakes drainage; Mississippi River system, Minnesota south to Louisiana.

Comments
Spotted Suckers make spawning runs up rivers and small streams in early spring, and spawn from March to May in swift, shallow riffles. They are intolerant of silty and turbid waters. Redhorses, members of the genus *Moxostoma,* are similar to the Spotted Sucker but have a lateral line and side scales usually without spots. *Moxostoma* species occur in streams, lakes, and rivers in eastern and central North America.

Chain Pickerel
Esox niger
75

To 31″ (79 cm). Elongate, moderately compressed; olive to yellowish brown above, sides with dark, chainlike markings; belly whitish, bold, dark bar under eye. Head long, flat above; snout long, profile concave; lower jaw with 4 large sensory pores on each side; gill cover fully scaled. Caudal fin deeply forked. Lateral line complete.

Habitat
Clean, clear lakes, ponds, swamps, reservoirs, and pools of streams with vegetation.

Range
Nova Scotia, New Brunswick, SW. Quebec; Maine to New York south in Atlantic Coast streams to S. Florida; Mississippi River system, S. Indiana, SE. Missouri south to Louisiana and Georgia.

Comments
In the northeastern United States Chain Pickerels are especially popular sport fishes in the winter, and large numbers are caught through the ice.

Northern Pike
Esox lucius
76

To 4′4″ (1.3 m). Long, head one-fourth total length, tail forked; back dark olive-green to greenish brown, sides lighter, with irregular rows of small, oval, yellow spots and small gold spot on exposed edge of each scale; belly creamy white. Lower jaw protruding, 5 large sensory pores on each side; cheek and upper half of gill cover scaled; dorsal, anal, and caudal fins green to white, occasionally reddish orange, with dark markings; lateral line complete.

Habitat
Lakes, reservoirs, and large streams with little current and abundant aquatic vegetation.

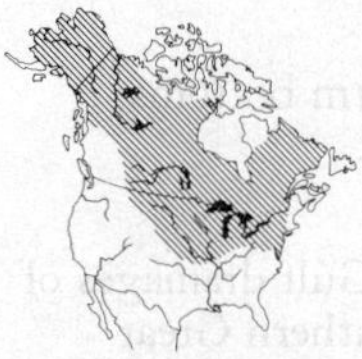

Range
From Alaska south throughout Canada to Missouri; New York, Pennsylvania west to Nebraska and Montana.

Comments
Because of its large size, the Northern Pike is a desirable sport fish and used to be a commercial fish as well. It is the most widely distributed freshwater fish in the world.

Muskellunge
Esox masquinongy
77

To 6′ (1.8 m). Long, head broad, flat to concave above, tail forked; back greenish to light brown; sides greenish gray to silvery usually with dark spots or diagonal bars; belly creamy white; dorsal, anal, and caudal fins greenish to reddish brown with dark markings. Cheeks and gill covers usually scaled only on upper half; lower jaw has 6–9 large sensory pores on each side; lateral line complete.

Habitat
Lakes and reservoirs with thick vegetation; slow, meandering rivers and streams with abundant plant cover.

Range
SE. Manitoba, SW. Ontario east through Great Lakes to St. Lawrence River, south to Pennsylvania, West Virginia, Virginia, N. Georgia, Ohio, Kentucky; upper Mississippi River, Minnesota south to Missouri.

Comments
The largest species in the family, the "Musky" is most sought by anglers. It feeds primarily on fishes, but will eat any animal it can swallow, such as small ducks and amphibians. This species and the Northern Pike have been crossed to produce a more robust fish called the Tiger Muskellunge, commonly stocked in some areas.

Alligator Gar
Lepisosteus spatula
78

To 10′ (3 m). Cylindrical; dark brown above, occasionally spotted, yellowish below. Snout short, broad, length of jaw shorter than remainder of head; teeth large. Dorsal, anal, and caudal fins with few dark spots; young with light stripe along back from tip of snout to upper base of caudal fin, bordered by dark lateral stripes. Caudal fin short, rounded.

Habitat
Large rivers, sluggish lakes, bayous, and reservoirs; in coastal areas frequently enters brackish and marine waters.

Range
Ohio River west from SW. Ohio; Mississippi River south from Illinois; Gulf Coastal plain from W. Florida to Veracruz, Mexico.

Comments
The Alligator Gar is one of the largest freshwater fishes. In some areas it is fished commercially and by anglers. There are unverified reports of attacks on humans.

Paddlefish
Polyodon spathula
79

To 7′1″ (2.2 m). Slightly compressed; snout paddle-shaped; back dark bluish gray, often mottled, lighter on sides, belly white. Mouth very large; eyes small, above front edge of mouth; gill cover flap large, tapering, extending to pelvic fins. Caudal fin deeply forked, lobes about equal. Scales only on caudal peduncle.

Habitat
Backwaters, sluggish pools, bayous, oxbows of large rivers, impoundments, and lakes.

Range
Throughout Mississippi River system; Mobile Bay drainage, Alabama, west to E. Texas; early records from few localities in Lakes Superior, Michigan, Huron, and western Lake Erie.

Comments
Paddlefishes are large, reaching lengths of 7′1″ (2.2 m), weighing 200 pounds (90.7 kg), and living up to 30 years. They are caught by snag fishing during spawning in April and

June, when they congregate below obstructions (dams) and on gravel shoals. Paddlefishes have declined recently due to pollution, channelization, dams, and intensive fishing.

Shovelnose Sturgeon
Scaphirhynchus platorynchus
80, 81

To 3′ (91 cm). Elongate, bony plates sharply keeled; olive to yellowish brown above, sides lighter, white below. Bony head plates with short spines at tip of snout and in front of eye; snout shovel-shaped; bases of 4 barbels in straight line; lower lip with 4 nipplelike lobes; no spiracles. 5 rows of bony plates. Caudal peduncle long, flattened, fully armored; tail heterocercal, upper lobe with long, threadlike filament.

Habitat
Channels of large, turbid rivers with moderate current over firm sand or gravel.

Range
Ohio, Mississippi, Missouri rivers; Mobile Bay drainage, Alabama; Rio Grande in Texas and New Mexico.

Comments
The Shovelnose is the smallest and most common sturgeon in North America, rarely exceeding 3′ (91 cm) in length. It is becoming less common, but is part of the commercial fishery industry along the Mississippi and Missouri rivers.

Chestnut Lamprey
Ichthyomyzon castaneus
82

To 15″ (38 cm). Eel-like; yellowish-olive above; sides, belly, and fins lighter. Eyes small; mouth without jaws, fringed, and when expanded, wider than head; numerous strong, slender teeth. No paired fins; dorsal fin long with shallow notch.

Habitat
Large rivers and reservoirs, ascending small rivers to large creeks to spawn.

Range
Lake Winnipeg, Red River, S. Manitoba; Lake Michigan; Wisconsin, Minnesota, south to E. Tennessee, NW. Georgia west to E. Texas.

Comments
A parasite, the adult Chestnut Lamprey attaches itself to the side of a fish with its sucker mouth, and uses its teeth to rasp a small wound through which it obtains body fluids.

Walking Catfish
Clarias batrachus
83

To 14″ (36 cm). Elongate, broad toward front, compressed toward rear; body dark brown to olive above, lighter below; frequent albino populations white to pinkish. 4 pairs of barbels. Pectoral fins with 1 spine; dorsal and anal fins long, not joined to caudal fin.

Habitat
Lakes, swamps, and canals with little or no current, over mud with debris and aquatic plants.

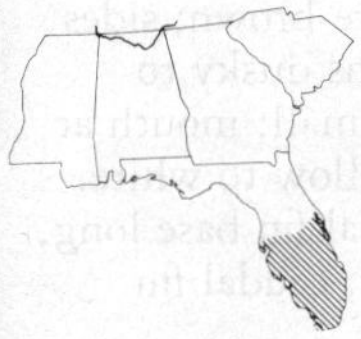

Range
Established in S. Florida; introduced in Georgia, Nevada, and California.

Comments
The Walking Catfish, brought into the United States by the exotic fish business, escaped or was released from fish farms in southern Florida. It has spread rapidly, damaging native fishes in areas where this species has become established.

American Eel
Anguilla rostrata
84

To 4′11″ (1.5 m). Elongate, snakelike, circular in cross section toward front, compressed toward rear. Color variable depending on habitat and age, usually dark brown or greenish above, fading to yellowish white on belly. Head large, about one-eighth of length; mouth at tip of snout, nearly horizontal, lower jaw projects slightly. Pectoral fins well developed; dorsal fin origin far behind pectoral fins; anal fin origin behind dorsal fin origin, both fins continuous with caudal fin. Scales small, elliptical, deeply embedded in skin.

Habitat
Brackish or fresh water, except when migrating and spawning at sea.

Range
Along coast to headwaters of associated rivers from Labrador south to Guyana, including Gulf of Mexico, Antilles, and Caribbean.

Comments
Eels are eaten fresh and smoked, and elvers (young eels) are exported to Europe and Japan for use in aquaculture.

Tadpole Madtom
Noturus gyrinus
85

To 4½″ (11.5 cm). Tadpole-shaped, robust toward front, strongly compressed toward rear; back golden brown to olive-gray; sides gray with narrow, dark midlateral stripe branching out to outline muscle segments; belly yellowish; dorsal, anal, and caudal fins olive. Head deep, rounded eye small; mouth at tip of snout; 4 pairs of barbels. Pectoral fin spine lacks serrations, has poison gland at base. Adipose fin continuous with broad, rounded caudal fin.

Habitat
Low-gradient, quiet, slow streams, sloughs, ponds, and lakes over mud and vegetation.

Range
SW. Quebec west to SE. Manitoba and south to S. Florida and S. Texas; absent from Appalachian highlands.

Comments
The Tadpole Madtom is the most widespread species in the genus. Like most madtoms, it is secretive and frequently hides in empty cans and bottles.

Yellow Bullhead
Ictalurus natalis
86

To 18″ (46 cm). Robust, heavy; back dark olive-brown; sides yellow-brown, not mottled; belly yellowish; fins dusky to olive. Head thick, long, rounded above; eyes small; mouth at tip of snout; 4 pairs of barbels, pair on chin yellow to white. Serrations on rear edge of pectoral fin spine; anal fin base long, about equal to head length; adipose fin present; caudal fin squared off to rounded.

Habitat
Pools and backwaters of sluggish streams, ponds, and lakes; sometimes in slow riffles; usually in areas with heavy vegetation.

Range
SE. Ontario; central eastern United States; widely introduced outside native range.

Comments
The Yellow Bullhead is a good sport and food fish. It is active at night, searching out food along the bottom by relying on its barbels and sense of smell.

Channel Catfish
Ictalurus punctatus
87

To 3′11″ (1.2 m). Slender; back blue-gray; sides light blue to silvery with scattered dark olive to black spots; belly white; fins olive to dusky. Head wide, flat to slightly rounded above; eyes large, above midline of head; upper jaw overhangs lower; 4 pairs of barbels. Adipose fin present; outer edge of anal fin rounded; caudal fin deeply forked.

Habitat
Rivers and large creeks in slow to moderate current over sand, gravel, or rocks; ponds, lakes, reservoirs.

Range
S. Quebec west to S. Alberta; central and east-central United States. Widely introduced.

Comments
The Channel Catfish, weighing more than 50 lbs, is a very popular sport and food fish. It is harvested commercially in some areas and is the principal catfish reared in aquaculture.

Lake Trout
Salvelinus namaycush
88

To 4′2″ (1.3 m). Elongate, slightly compressed; dark olive to gray-green above, blue-gray to greenish bronze below; creamy spots on head, body, adipose fin, and dorsal, anal, and caudal fins; leading edges of pectoral, pelvic, and anal fins reddish orange with narrow whitish margin. Mouth at tip of snout, extends beyond eye. Adipose fin present; caudal peduncle slender; caudal fin deeply forked. Scales small.

Habitat
Deep, cold waters of lakes; rivers in far north.

Range
Alaska; Canada, Great Lakes, Maine south to New York, west to E. Minnesota; introduced outside native range.

Comments
The Lake Trout is the largest trout native to North America. It is highly esteemed as food and is sought by anglers. A large commercial fishery for Lake Trout in the Great Lakes was decimated by pollution and by Sea Lampreys, after the rapid expansion of their population in the 1940s.

Brook Trout
Salvelinus fontinalis
89

To 21″ (53 cm). Elongate, spindle-shaped, depth about one-fifth length. Freshwater coloration: back and sides have red or yellowish tint with lighter wavy lines; sides have red spots within blue halos; belly ordinarily white, reddish in adult males; pectoral, pelvic, and anal fins light orange to red, leading edges white followed by dark, dorsal fin with dark, undulating lines. Marine coloration: back bluish green, becoming silvery on sides, belly white. Fins relatively large; adipose fin present; caudal fin slightly forked.

Habitat
Clear, cool, freshwater streams; tidal streams; rarely in salt water.

Range
Native to eastern Canada and northeastern United States and Great Lakes region south to N. Georgia. Introduced in western United States at higher elevations.

Comments
The Brook Trout, highly esteemed as food and game, is one of the most colorful freshwater fishes. It feeds on a variety of organisms, including other fishes, but primarily on aquatic insects. Spawning occurs in small headwater streams.

Brown Trout
Salmo trutta
90

To 3′4″ (1 m). Elongate, spindle-shaped, moderately compressed; back and sides olive, becoming lighter, belly silvery, numerous red or orange spots, often with halo, scattered on head, body, and dorsal and adipose fins. Pectoral fin inserted well below axis of body; dorsal fin base short, about midway between snout and caudal fin base; adipose fin present; caudal fin squared off.

Habitat
Primarily high gradient freshwater streams; lakes; sea-run populations.

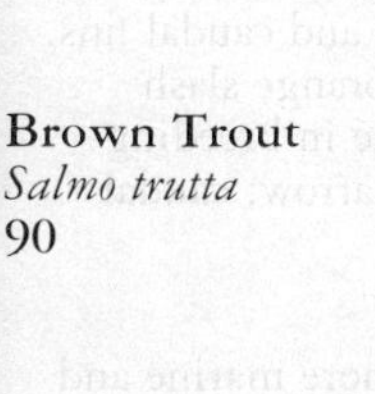

Range
From southern Canada to northeastern United States, south in Appalachians, Mississippi Valley west in Great Lakes; western United States at higher elevations.

Comments
The Brown Trout, native to Europe and western Asia, was introduced into the United States 100 years ago and is now one of the most widespread members of its family. It can tolerate higher temperatures than other salmons and trouts. The young feed on aquatic insects; adults feed on other fishes.

Rainbow Trout
Salmo gairdneri
91

To 3′9″ (1.1 m). Elongate, spindle-shaped. Marine coloration: metallic blue above, silvery white below, with small black spots on back, sides, and dorsal and caudal fins. Freshwater coloration: spots more prominent, distinctive red band on sides. Mouth white; no teeth on back of tongue. Adipose fin present, usually with black edge.

Habitat
Inshore ocean at mid-depths and near surface; spawns in freshwater streams and rivers.

Range
From Bering Sea to S. California. In fresh water, native range confined to lakes and streams of western states bordering Pacific Ocean from Alaska to Baja California; introduced throughout North America in suitable streams and lakes.

Comments
Sea-run Rainbow Trout usually spend 2 to 4 years in their home stream before venturing to sea, where they remain for about 3 years. They return to their home stream in the winter to spawn, and will continue this pattern as long as they survive natural predators. Fish that exist solely in fresh water spawn in the spring. Most males spawn at 1 year, while females may take 6 years to mature. Rainbow Trout are much-sought game fish; they are rarely taken at sea by bait anglers, but do succumb readily to trolled shrimplike flies.

Cutthroat Trout
Salmo clarki
92

To 30″ (76 cm). Elongate, cylindrical or slightly tapering at both ends, moderately compressed; back dark olive; sides variable; silvery, olive, reddish to yellow-orange; belly lighter; dark spots on back, sides, and on dorsal, anal, and caudal fins. Mouth extends beyond eye; bright red to red-orange slash mark on each side of throat, particularly visible in breeding males. Adipose fin present. Caudal peduncle narrow; caudal fin slightly forked. Lateral line complete.

Habitat
Lakes; coastal, inland, and alpine streams; inshore marine and estuarine waters.

Range
From S. Alaska south to N. California; inland from S. British Columbia and Alberta south to New Mexico; E. California east to central Colorado. Introduced in western United States.

Comments
There are more than 10 subspecies of Cutthroat Trouts, locally called "native trout," which vary in coloration and size. The largest specimen, caught in Pyramid Lake, Nevada, in 1925, weighed 41 lbs (18.6 kg), but this strain is now extinct.

Apache Trout
Salmo apache
93

To 18″ (46 cm). Moderately stout, compressed; dark olive to brown above, sides and belly yellow to golden yellow; many dark spots about one-half diameter of pupil on head, back, sides, and fins; large, prominent, dark spot behind eye; lower part of head orange to yellow-orange. Pelvic, dorsal, and anal fins white-tipped; dorsal fin large; adipose fin present. Lateral line complete.

Habitat
Clear mountain streams about 7544′ (2300 m) with riffles and pools.

Range
Headwaters of Salt and Little Colorado rivers, east-central Arizona.

Comments
The Apache Trout, also called the Arizona Trout, was almost totally exterminated by exotic trouts, which hybridize with it and compete for food and habitat. It is a threatened species.

Atlantic Salmon
Salmo salar
94

To 4′5″ (1.3 m). Elongate, moderately compressed; adults brownish above, sides silvery, with numerous small, black spots, sometimes X-shaped, without halos, on head, body, and dorsal fin; males have red patches on sides; young specimens have about 11 dusky bars. Head large, depth about one-fifth length; lower jaw upward-hooked in breeding males. Pectoral fins inserted well below axis of body; dorsal fin short-based, at midpoint of body; adipose fin present; caudal fin slightly forked or notched.

Habitat
Freshwater streams and lakes; coastal waters.

Range
Native in northern Atlantic from Arctic Circle, N. Quebec south to Delaware River; Lake Ontario. Landlocked populations in several New England states.

Comments
This anadromous species spawns in the fall in high gradient streams over gravel. After spawning, the fish are weak and emaciated but do not necessarily die like some other salmonid species. The Atlantic Salmon is a highly valued game fish.

Sockeye Salmon
Oncorhynchus nerka
95

To 33″ (84 cm). Elongate, spindle-shaped, moderately compressed. Freshwater coloration: bright red, head pale green; females may have green and yellow blotches. Marine coloration: bluish green above, silvery below, with fine speckling but no spots. Snout bluntly pointed, mouth at tip of snout. Adipose fin present.

Habitat
Surface waters of open ocean and freshwater streams, rivers, and lakes containing tributary streams for spawning.

Range
From Bering Strait to Sacramento River, California; introduced elsewhere in northern lakes.

Comments
Sockeye Salmon spawn during summer in small tributaries of lakes, where the young spend 1 to 3 years before migrating to the ocean. After living at sea for 2 to 4 years, maturing adults return to their home stream. Sockeye Salmon have the greatest commercial value of all the Pacific salmons.

Grass Carp
Ctenopharyngodon idella
96

To 3′3″ (99 cm). Robust; back olive-brown, sides silvery, belly whitish; upper scales outlined with dusky pigment giving crosshatched appearance. Snout short; head blunt, broad. Dorsal fin origin over pelvic fin insertion; anal fin origin nearer caudal fin base than dorsal fin origin; fins olive to dusky; caudal peduncle short, deep. Lateral line complete.

Habitat
Rivers and large creeks, but adaptable to ponds and reservoirs.

Range
Introduced into more than 35 states.

Comments
This Oriental carp, native to eastern Asia, was introduced into experimental ponds in Alabama and Arkansas in 1963 for aquatic weed control and as a food fish. It feeds primarily on vegetation, grows rapidly, and may eat more than its body weight daily; all are traits that could destroy fish and waterfowl habitats. Stocking of this species is prohibited in some states.

Mosquitofish
Gambusia affinis
97

To 2½″ (6.5 cm). Rather robust, particularly females; compressed. Tan to olive above, pale yellowish below; scales have small, dusky spots near edges; dark bar below eye; many spots present on dorsal and caudal fins; females have conspicuous black spot on belly during reproductive period. Head flattened; mouth small, oblique; lower jaw projects beyond upper. Anal fin of male modified to form reproductive organ.

Habitat
Near surface of fresh or brackish water in ponds, lakes, ditches, backwaters, and sluggish streams.

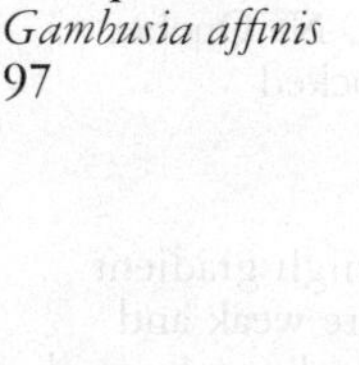

Range
From New Jersey to central Mexico along coast and in associated freshwater streams; Mississippi River basin south from Illinois.

Comments
Because it eats aquatic mosquito larvae, the Mosquitofish has been introduced into many areas to control mosquitoes.

Desert Pupfish
Cyprinodon macularius
98

To 2½″ (6.5 cm). Stout, deep, females deeper-bodied than males; back silvery to olive; sides silvery with 6–9 dusky bars often forming irregular band along side; breeding males iridescent blue. Head short, scaled; mouth at tip of head, upturned. Dorsal and anal fins rounded, dorsal fin often with dusky blotch toward rear; caudal fin edge slightly convex.

Habitat
Marshy backwaters of desert streams and springs.

Range
S. Arizona, S. California, and NW. Mexico.

Comments
The Desert Pupfish grows very rapidly, sometimes reaching lengths of 2″ (5 cm) in a year. Most of the 13 species of *Cyprinodon* in the United States are restricted to springs or streams in the deserts of Texas, New Mexico, Arizona, Nevada, and California. Several species are endangered by development and the introduction of exotic fishes. The best known is the Devils Hole Pupfish (*C. diabolis*), which was the focus of a U.S. Supreme Court water rights case in the 1970s.

Fathead Minnow
Pimephales promelas
99

To 4″ (10 cm). Stout, chubby; back tan to olive; sides silvery to brassy, with dark caudal spot. Breeding males grayish black with pale fleshy pad behind head; pale below dorsal fin. Snout blunt; mouth nearly at tip of snout, oblique. Fins low, rounded; first dorsal fin ray short, splintlike. Lateral line incomplete; scales behind head crowded.

Habitat
Clear pools of creeks, shallow ponds, and lakes over sand, gravel, or mud.

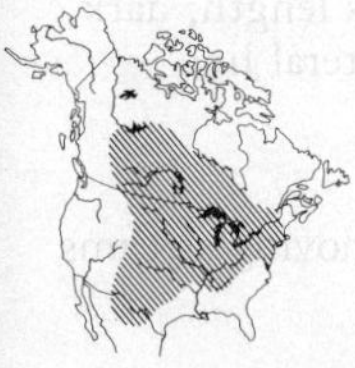

Range
SW. Quebec west to Great Slave Lake, Alberta; northeastern and central United States; northeastern Mexico. Widely introduced.

Comments
The Fathead Minnow, commonly sold as bait, is easily propagated in small ponds, which may yield 400,000 minnows per acre.

Flagfish
Jordanella floridae
100

To 2½″ (6.5 cm). Short, deep, compressed; back olive, sides greenish gold to brassy, males with 7–9 red-orange stripes between scale rows and dark blotch below dorsal fin origin; belly yellowish. Head short, flat above; mouth small, upturned. First dorsal ray short, thick, spinelike.

Habitat
Quiet, shallow waters of ditches, lakes, and ponds with vegetation; commonly enters brackish water.

Range
From north-central Florida south throughout peninsula.

Comments
The Flagfish is primarily a herbivore. It spawns from April

through August over dense mats of vegetation or in small depressions. The male fans the eggs and remains with them until they have hatched.

Least Killifish
Heterandria formosa
101

To 1″ (2.5 cm). Moderately compressed; back golden-brown to olive; sides lighter with 6–9 indistinct bars and dusky midlateral stripe terminating in darker spot. Snout short; mouth at tip of snout; eye large. Dark spot on base of dorsal fin; females have dark spot on base of anal fin; anal fin origin in front of dorsal fin, modified in male to form reproductive organ.

Habitat
Fresh and brackish water in swamps, ditches, ponds, and bayous with abundant aquatic vegetation.

Range
Coastal drainages from S. North Carolina to Louisiana; throughout peninsular Florida.

Comments
Despite its common name, this is a livebearer. It is very hardy and makes an interesting aquarium fish. It is the smallest livebearing vertebrate in the United States.

Central Mudminnow
Umbra limi
102

To 5″ (12 cm). Broad toward front, compressed toward rear; back brownish olive, mottled with black; sides mottled with olive, sometimes barred; belly yellowish. Mouth at tip of snout, extends to middle of eye. Fins dusky; pectoral fins rounded; anal fin under dorsal fin, about half its length; dark bar at base of caudal fin; caudal fin rounded. Lateral line absent.

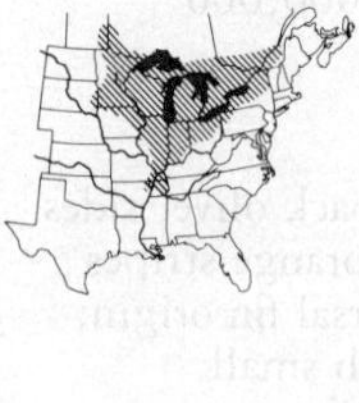

Habitat
Cool ponds, bogs, swamps, and pools of slow-moving streams with abundant vegetation.

Range
S. Manitoba, Great Lakes, and St. Lawrence drainage south to NE. Arkansas and W. Tennessee; W. Pennsylvania west to E. South Dakota.

Comments
The Central Mudminnow is used as bait in some areas.

AMPHIBIANS AND REPTILES

Damp streamside logs, overhanging branches, and mud-covered rocks offer perfect hiding places for many kinds of reptiles and amphibians. Early in the morning, some slow-moving turtles and stealthy snakes may venture out in search of a meal; others, meantime, avoid the heat of the day, never stirring from their homes until nightfall. Frogs and toads noisily announce their presence, while the large American Alligator may lurk nearby, undetected in shadowy shallows. This section describes these and other common amphibians and reptiles of the wetlands.

Two-toed Amphiuma
Amphiuma means
103

18–45¾″ (45.7–116.2 cm). Aquatic eel-like salamander; 4 tiny legs each with 2 toes. Uniformly dark gray to grayish brown above; belly lighter. Average of 58 grooves on sides.

Breeding
Lays eggs June–July in North Carolina and N. Florida, January–February in S. Florida. Female lays about 200 eggs in a damp cavity beneath debris; remains coiled about them during incubation—about 5 months. Hatchlings are about 2⅛″ (54 mm) long.

Habitat
Acid waters of swamps, bayous, drainage ditches.

Range
Coastal plain from SE. Virginia to Florida and E. Louisiana.

Comments
Nocturnal. Amphiumas are ill-tempered and can inflict a nasty bite. Their slippery skins make them difficult to handle. This species prowls shallows for crayfish, frogs, small snakes, and fish. It may leave water temporarily if weather is wet enough. For shelter it digs burrows in muddy bottoms or invades the burrows of other creatures. Long-lived; one is known to have survived 27 years in captivity.

Mudpuppy
Necturus maculosus
104

8–17″ (20.3–43.2 cm). Large aquatic salamander, with feathery maroon gills, 4-toed feet, compressed tail. Gray to rusty brown above, with fuzzy-edged dark blue spots. Belly gray, with dark spots. 15–16 grooves on sides.

Breeding
April–June. Female lays 30–190 eggs, singly attached to underside of stone or log; larvae hatch in 5–9 weeks, at ⅞″ (22 mm). Maturity is reached in 4–6 years.

Habitat
Lakes, rivers, and streams of all descriptions, from muddy, weed-choked shallows to a record depth of 90′ (27.4 m).

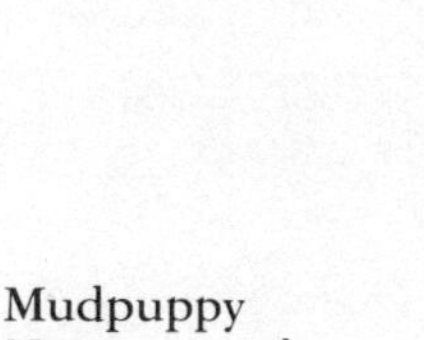

Range
SE. Manitoba to S. Quebec, south to N. Georgia and Louisiana. Introduced into large New England rivers.

Comments
Animals from cold, clear, highly oxygenated water have short gills; those from warm, muddy water, long bushy gills. The various subspecies differ in coloring and pattern. Mudpuppies are nocturnal; they feed on worms, crayfish, and insects.

Hellbender
Cryptobranchus alleganiensis
105

12–29⅛″ (30.5–74 cm). A giant among salamanders; totally aquatic. Body and head flattened; loose flap of skin along lower sides of body. Single pair of circular gill openings on neck. Gray or olive-brown above, with or without dark mottling or spotting. Belly lighter, with few markings. Male smaller than female.

Breeding
Late August–early September in North; September–early November in South. At night males prepare saucer-shaped nest cavity beneath large, flat rocks or submerged logs. Female lays 200–500 yellowish eggs in long strings, forming tangled mass; male positions himself beside or above her and sprays milt. Male guards nest. Larvae hatch in 2–3 months.

Habitat
Clear fast-flowing streams and rivers with rocky bottoms.

Range
SW. New York to N. Alabama and Georgia. Separate populations in Missouri and in Susquehanna River (New York and Pennsylvania).

Subspecies
Two; 1 widespread in wetlands of our range.
Eastern (*C. a. alleganiensis*), spotting variable on body and tail; range as noted except absent in SE. Missouri and NE. Arkansas, where another, more localized subspecies occurs.

Comments
This species is commonly called the Allegheny Alligator or Devil Dog. Fishermen often encounter Hellbenders while searching for insect bait under flat river rocks. Folklore has it that Hellbenders smear fishing lines with slime, drive game fish away, and inflict poisonous bites. In fact, they are harmless; they feed on crayfish, snails, and worms. Captive longevity is 29 years. Long-term survival is threatened by dam construction and pollution.

Greater Siren
Siren lacertina
106

19¾–38½″ (50–97.8 cm). Aquatic; stout, eel-like body; gray or olive above, sometimes with dark spots on head, back, and sides; sides lighter, with many faint greenish-yellow dashes and blotches. External gills, 3 gill slits; 4 front toes on limbs. Tail compressed, with fin; tail tip rounded.

Breeding
Eggs laid February–March. Larvae hatch April–May, are ⅝″ (16 mm) long.

Habitat
Shallow, muddy-bottomed, weed-choked water.

Range
Coastal plain from District of Columbia south through Florida, S. Alabama.

Comments
Nocturnal. Sirens spend the day under debris or rocks, burrowed in mud or thick vegetation. Young are often seen amid water-hyacinth roots. Adults are sometimes caught at night by bait fishermen. When drought dries up their habitat, sirens remain dormant in mud burrows; their skin glands secrete a moisture-sealing cocoon over the body.

Lesser Siren
Siren intermedia
107

7–27″ (17.8–68.6 cm). Aquatic; slender, eel-like body; brown, gray, or blackish above, sometimes with dark spotting. External gills, 3 gill slits; 4 toes on front limbs. Tail compressed, with fin; tail tip pointed. 31–38 grooves on sides. Male larger than female.

Breeding
Nests in winter and early spring. Female lays about 200 eggs in a sheltered cavity. Hatching larvae are ½″ (11 mm) long.

Habitat
Warm, shallow, quiet waters; swamps, sloughs, weedy ponds.

Range
Coastal plain from SE. North Carolina to central Florida, west to parts of Texas and Oklahoma, north to SW. Michigan.

Subspecies
Eastern (*S. i. intermedia*), black or brown with minute black dots, 31–34 grooves on sides; coastal plain, from SE. North Carolina to W. Alabama.
Western (*S. i. nettingi*), brown, olive, or gray with tiny black dots, 34–36 grooves on sides; W. Alabama to E. Texas, north in Mississippi Valley to Michigan.
Rio Grande (*S. i. texana*), largest subspecies, dark gray and unpatterned to light or brownish gray with many dark flecks, 36–38 grooves on sides; lower Rio Grande Valley.

Comments
The Lesser Siren emits a clicking sound when excited, yelps when captured, and squirms vigorously when handled. It eats aquatic invertebrates and plants.

Dwarf Siren
Pseudobranchus striatus
108

4–9⅞″ (10.2–25.1 cm). Smallest siren. Aquatic, gilled throughout life; slender, eel-like. Brown or light gray above, with light stripes on sides. External gills, single gill slit, 3 toes on forefeet; tail finned, tip compressed.

Breeding
In spring. Eggs laid singly on roots of water plants. Larvae hatch about a month later; ⅝″ (14 mm).

Habitat
Shallow ditches, cypress swamps, weed-choked ponds, especially water hyacinth.

Range
Coastal plain of South Carolina and Georgia; Florida, except western panhandle.

Subspecies
Narrow-striped (*P. s. axanthus*), slender, with shortened head, side stripes narrow and pale gray; Okefenokee Swamp, Georgia south to Lake Okeechobee, Florida.
Gulf Hammock (*P. s. lustricolus*), stout and large, head flattened, snout blunt with 3 narrow light stripes within wide dark stripe down back, and 2 side stripes, top one orange-

brown, bottom one silvery white; Gulf Hammock region, Florida.
Everglades (*P. s. belli*), small and slender, head long and narrow, stripes like Gulf Hammock, except side stripes buff; S. Florida.

Comments
Dwarf Sirens are secretive. They dwell among water-hyacinth roots and amid debris at pond bottoms, feeding on tiny invertebrates. During droughts they encase themselves in mud beneath the pond bottom.

Dwarf Salamander
Eurycea quadridigitata
109, 117

2⅛–3½″ (5.4–9 cm). Elongated miniature species, with 4 toes on hind feet. Yellowish to dark brown band runs along back, often with row of dark spots down center and bordered by a darker stripe running from eye to tip of tail.

Breeding
Courts in fall. Lays 1–4 dozen eggs in shallow water, late fall to early winter, singly or in small groups on undersides of leaves and logs. Larvae hatch in 30–40 days, transform April–June at 1½″ (38 mm). Sexually mature by first fall.

Habitat
Margins of pine savannah ponds, swampy areas in low flatwoods.

Range
Coastal plain, North Carolina to Lake Okeechobee, Florida, and west to E. Texas. Isolated populations in Arkansas and Missouri.

Comments
Dwarfs frequent soggy beds of pine needles or damp places under logs. Surface activity is greatest during fall and early winter breeding season.

Two-lined Salamander
Eurycea bislineata
110, 121

2½–4¾″ (6.4–12.1 cm). An abundant brookside species. Broad, basically yellow band above may be tinged with brown, green, or orange-bronze; often darkly speckled. Band bordered by dark brown or black stripe running from each eye well out onto tail. Tail oval, keeled, compressed.

Breeding
A dozen to 100 eggs are laid on undersides of submerged rocks, logs, or aquatic plants; female may guard eggs. Larvae hatch at ½″ (13 mm), transform in 1–3 years at 1¾″ (44 mm).

Habitat
Rock-bottomed brooks, springs, seepages, river swamps, and floodplain bottoms in coastal plain to damp forest floors at high elevations; near sea level to 6000′ (1829 m).

Range
Mouth of St. Lawrence River, Quebec, to N. Florida and west to SE. Ontario, E. Illinois, and Mississippi River.

Subspecies
Northern (*E. b. bislineata*), back stripes tend to break up into dashes or dots on tail, males do not develop downward projections from nostrils; mouth of St. Lawrence River to Virginia and west to Tennessee River.
Southern (*E. b. cirrigera*), back stripes narrow and continue close to tail tip, males with downward projections from nostrils; S. Virginia to N. Florida west to Mississippi River.
Blue Ridge (*E. b. wilderae*), back stripes broad and break up into dots on tail, males with downward projections from nostrils; SW. Virginia to N. Georgia, in southern Blue Ridge Mountains.

Comments
The life history of this species is largely unknown. In some populations larvae retain gills and do not transform. A stocky short-tailed Two-lined Salamander, recognized as *E. aquatica* by some authorities, lives in scattered springs in the South.

Mud Salamander
Pseudotriton montanus
111, 116, 118, 119

2⅞–7⅞″ (7.3–19.5 cm). Stout and strikingly colored, with short legs and tail. Coral-pink, bright red, or brownish-salmon above, generally with well-scattered black spots. Older animals reddish brown to chocolate-brown; spots obscured. Underside reddish or yellowish. Back and belly colors sharply separated. Eyes brown. 16–17 grooves on sides.

Breeding
Late fall to early winter. Female lays 75–190 eggs. Larvae hatch late winter at ¾″ (19 mm), transform in 1½–2½ years when about 3″ (7.6 cm) long.

Habitat
Muddy springs and streams, wooded floodplains, and swampy pools; low elevations.

Range
Chiefly coastal plain and Piedmont areas, S. New Jersey to central Florida; low elevations west of Appalachians from S. Ohio to south-central Tennessee.

Subspecies
Eastern (*P. m. montanus*), scattered spots on back and sides, some belly spotting; S. New Jersey to N. Georgia.
Midland (*P. m. diastictus*), coral-pink to bright red, large spots mostly on back, belly unspotted; west of Appalachians, S. Ohio to S. Tennessee.
Gulf Coast (*P. m. flavissimus*), numerous spots on back and sides, belly unspotted; southern tip of South Carolina west to E. Louisiana.
Rusty (*P. m. floridanus*), back purplish brown without spots, sides streaked, belly spotted; S. Georgia and N. Florida.

Comments
Aquatic larvae live in silt or decaying vegetation; adults in muck, under logs or stones, or in mud burrows along stream banks.

Dusky Salamander
Desmognathus fuscus
112

2½–5½″ (6.4–14.1 cm). The most common dusky. Pale line from eye to angle of jaw. Juveniles have 5–8 pairs of round yellowish or reddish spots on back. Adults tan or dark brown above, plain or mottled; some show alternating pairs of oval to rhombic blotches, often fused to form stripe. Pattern becomes obscured with age by dark pigment. Tail triangular, sharply keeled, compressed. 14 grooves on sides.

Breeding
June–September; lays compact, grapelike cluster of 1–3 dozen eggs near water, beneath rocks, in rotting logs, stream-bank cavities. Larvae hatch in 6–13 weeks at ⅝″ (16 mm); transform in 6–13 months at 1½″ (38 mm).

Habitat
Rock-strewn woodland creeks, seepages, and springs in northern areas; floodplains, sloughs, and mucky sites along upland streams in southern areas. Near sea level to about 5300′ (1615 m).

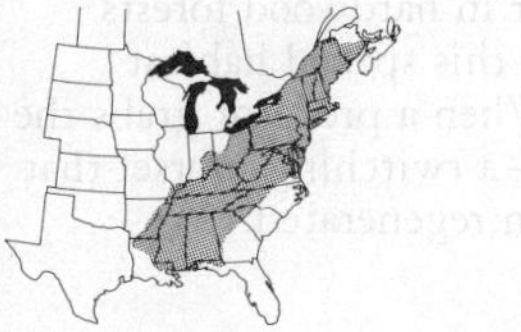

Range
S. New Brunswick and SE. Quebec southwest to Louisiana.

Subspecies
Northern (*D. f. fuscus*), round yellow spots on young that quickly fade as animal ages; S. New Brunswick to E. Kentucky and Carolinas. Another subspecies occurs south to the Gulf of Mexico.

Comments
Where ranges coincide, Dusky Salamanders often share the same stream with other species, but Dusky likes higher stream bank elevations. It is often found with the Red Salamander, and with the Mud Salamander on the coastal plain. It eats insect larvae, sow bugs, and earthworms.

Many-lined Salamander
Stereochilus marginatus
113

2½–4½″ (6.4–11.4 cm). Small brown or dull yellow aquatic species with parallel lines on sides, sometimes indistinct or reduced to a few dark spots. Belly yellow with scattered specks. Head small, narrow, and pointed; short tail; tiny legs.

Breeding
Mates in autumn. In winter female lays 6–100 eggs that adhere singly to aquatic vegetation or in a clump on a log next to water. Larvae hatch in spring at ⅝″ (14 mm), transform in 13–28 months when 2½–2¾″ (54–70 mm) long.

Habitat
Lowland ponds, swamps, drainage ditches, sluggish streams.

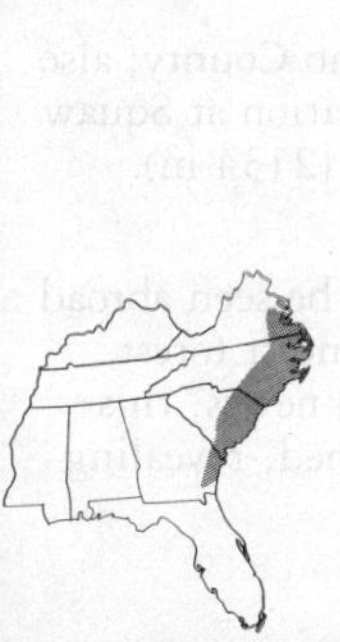

Range
Coastal plain from Virginia to SE. Georgia.

Comments
Occasionally these salamanders are seen under logs or damp sphagnum moss on banks; most are found in water amid bottom debris or the roots of a floating sphagnum mat.

Four-toed Salamander
Hemidactylium scutatum
114

2–4″ (5.1–10.2 cm). A small species distinguished by hind feet with 4 toes and marked constriction at base of tail. Reddish brown above, grayish sides; white belly, with black spots. 13–14 grooves on sides.

Breeding
Late winter to spring. 2–3 dozen eggs, singly attached to sphagnum moss or other plants close to water; female guards eggs until hatching 6–8 weeks later. The aquatic larvae transform in 1½ months at ⅞″ (22 mm). Mature in 2½ years.

Habitat
Bogs, boggy streams, and floodplains; usually associated with sphagnum moss.

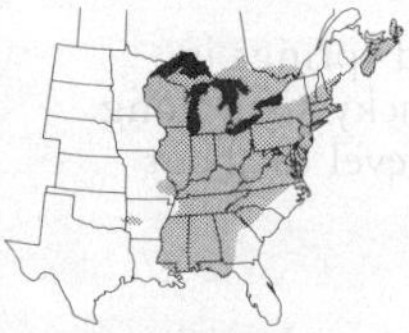

Range
Discontinuous. Chiefly east of Mississippi River; Nova Scotia to Wisconsin south to Gulf; absent from Florida peninsula.

Comments
Adults live under stones and leaf litter in hardwood forests surrounding boggy areas; the need for this special habitat accounts for its spotty distribution. When a predator grabs the Four-toed's tail, it readily breaks off—a twitching morsel that distracts the enemy. A new tail is soon regenerated.

California Newt
Taricha torosa
115

5–7¾″ (12.7–19.7 cm). Rough skin; large eyes and light-colored lower eyelids. Tan to reddish brown above, yellow to orange below. Back and belly colors blend. Breeding male has smooth skin, swollen vent, compressed tail, and toes tipped with black, horny layer.

Breeding
December–May. Female lays 1–2 dozen eggs in spherical masses, on aquatic plants or submerged forest litter. Larvae hatch at about ½″ (11 mm), transform in fall at 2¼″ (5.7 cm) or following spring when larger.

Habitat
Quiet streams, ponds, and lakes and surrounding evergreen and oak forests along coast. Fast-moving streams through digger pine and blue oak communities in Sierra Nevada foothills.

Range
Coastal California from San Diego to Mendocino County; also western slope of Sierra Nevada. Separate population at Squaw Creek, Shasta County. Near sea level to 7000′ (2134 m).

Comments
During the rainy season California Newts may be seen abroad during the day. Dry periods are passed under moist forest litter and in rodent burrows. Like other Pacific newts, this species strikes a warning posture when threatened, revealing its brightly colored underbelly.

Red Salamander
Pseudotriton ruber
120

3⅞–7⅛″ (9.7–18.1 cm). Robust red salamander with short legs and tail. Young coral-red to reddish orange above, adults orange-brown to purple-brown; numerous irregularly shaped black spots. Back and belly colors blend gradually along the sides.

Breeding
Females retreat to nesting sites in early fall, lay 50–100 eggs. Larvae hatch late fall to early winter at ⅞″ (22 mm); transform in 2½ years when 2¾–4¼″ (7–11 cm) long.

Habitat
Springs, their seepages, cool clear brooks and surrounding woodlands, swamps, and meadows; elevations to 5000+′ (1524+ m).

Range
S. New York west to SE. Indiana, southward east of the Mississippi River to the Gulf. Absent from Atlantic coastal plain south of Virginia and from peninsular Florida.

Subspecies
Northern (*P. r. ruber*), edges of back spots diffuse and tending to fuse, small dark spots on belly; S. New York west to N. Indiana, south to Georgia and Alabama.
Southern (*P. r. vioscai*), profusion of minute white flecks, especially on head, black spots usually distinct; S. Georgia to SE. Louisiana, north to W. Tennessee.
Blackchin (*P. r. schencki*), heavy black pigment on jaws; southern Blue Ridge Mountains, south of French Broad River.
Blue Ridge (*P. r. nitidus*), no black spots on latter part of tail, belly unspotted; southern Blue Ridge Mountains, north and east of French Broad River.

Comments
The Red Salamander may be encountered some distance from water, but usually is seen in the leaf litter of spring-fed brooks or under nearby forest debris or rocks.

Eastern Newt
Notophthalmus viridescens
122, 123

2⅝–5½″ (6.5–14 cm). Aquatic and terrestrial forms. Aquatic adult yellowish brown or olive green to dark brown above, yellow below; back and belly both peppered with small black spots. Land-dwelling form is orange-red to reddish brown; varies in size from 1⅜–3⅜″ (3.5–8.6 cm).

Breeding
Late winter to early spring. As season approaches, male develops enlarged hind legs, with black, horny structures on inner surfaces of thighs and toe tips, swollen vent, and broadly keeled tail. Female lays 200–400 eggs singly, on submerged vegetation. Incubation period 3–8 weeks. Hatching larvae average ⅜″ (8 mm). In late summer or early fall they transform to aquatic subadults or land-dwellers.

Habitat
Ponds and lakes with dense submerged vegetation, quiet

stretches or backwaters of streams, swamps, ditches, and neighboring damp woodlands.

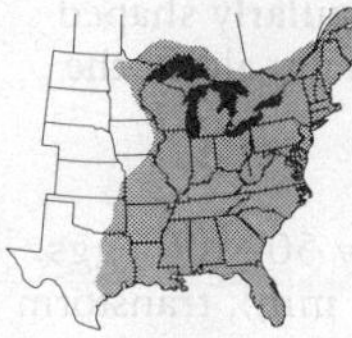

Range
Nova Scotia to Florida and west to SW. Ontario and Texas.

Subspecies
Red-spotted (*N. v. viridescens*), back with series of black-bordered orange-red spots in adult and terrestrial stages; Nova Scotia west to Great Lakes, south to NW. South Carolina, central Georgia, and Alabama.
Broken-striped (*N. v. dorsalis*), broken black-bordered red stripe from head to base of tail on either side of midline, terrestrial form reddish brown with back stripes incompletely bordered by black; coastal plain, NE. North Carolina and SE. South Carolina.

Comments
Adult newts are often seen foraging in shallow water. They prey voraciously on worms, insects, small crustaceans and mollusks, amphibian eggs, and larvae. Newts secrete toxic substances through the skin and so are avoided by fish and other predators. Terrestrial individuals can be found on the forest floor after a shower. Other subspecies, varying in color and pattern, occur within the range.

Black-spotted Newt
Notophthalmus meridionalis
124

2⅞–4¼″ (7.1–11 cm). Aquatic. Covered with black spots. Olive-green above; back edged by narrow, often broken, yellow line. Sides light blue-green, belly yellowish orange to orange.

Breeding
Can occur any time, depending on availability of water.

Habitat
Quiet stretches of streams with submerged vegetation; permanent and temporary ponds, and ditches.

Range
Coastal plain of S. Texas south into Mexico.

Comments
The Black-spotted Newt has no land-dwelling stage. When ponds dry up, both young and adults are forced to find shelter on land; they may be found under rocks and rocky ledges.

Tiger Salamander
Ambystoma tigrinum
125, 129

6–13⅜″ (15.2–40 cm). World's largest land-dwelling salamander. Stoutly built, with broad head and small eyes. Color and pattern extremely variable—large light spots, bars, or blotches on dark background or network of spots on lighter background. Tubercles on soles of feet.

Breeding
Prompted by rain; in North and higher elevations, eggs laid March–June; in South, December–February; in Southwest, July–August. Mates in temporary pools, fishless ponds,

stream backwaters, and lakes soon after ice is out. Egg masses adhere to submerged debris. Hatching larvae are 9/16″ (14 mm) long; transform June–August at about 4″ (90–123 mm).

Habitat
Varied; pine barrens, mountain forests, damp meadows where ground is easily burrowed; arid sagebrush plains; also in mammal burrows; sea level to 11,000′ (3353 m).

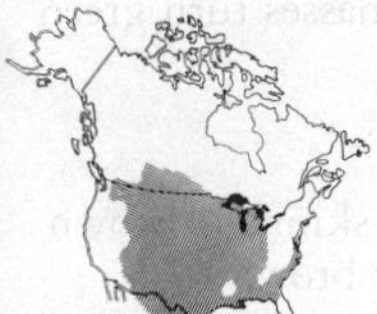

Range
Widespread from central Alberta and Saskatchewan, south to Florida and Mexico, but absent from New England, Appalachian Mountains, Far West.

Subspecies
Eastern (*A. t. tigrinum*), dark with olive spots; East Coast; also central Ohio to NW. Minnesota and south to Gulf of Mexico.
Barred (*A. t. mavortium*), dark with yellow crossbars or blotches; NE. Nebraska to extreme SE. Wyoming, south to south-central Texas and New Mexico, and Mexico.
Arizona (*A. t. nebulosum*), gray with small dark marks; W. Colorado and Utah to south-central New Mexico and central Arizona.
Blotched (*A. t. melanostictum*), dark with yellow to olive blotches or netlike lines; extreme S. British Columbia, E. Washington and central Alberta southeast to S. Wyoming and NW. Nebraska.
Gray (*A. t. diaboli*), light olive to dark brown with small dark spots; S. Saskatchewan and S. Manitoba to Minnesota.
Sonoran (*A. t. stebbinsi*), yellowish spots, belly brown with a few yellow spots; Santa Cruz County, Arizona.

Comments
Tiger Salamanders are often seen at night after heavy rains, especially during breeding season; they live beneath debris near water or in crayfish or mammal burrows. They are voracious consumers of earthworms, large insects, small mice, and amphibians.

Spotted Salamander
Ambystoma maculatum
126, 127

6–9¾″ (15.2–24.8 cm). Stoutly built; black, blue-black, dark gray, or dark brown above, with 2 irregular rows of round, yellow or orange spots beginning on head and extending to tail tip. Belly slate-gray.

Breeding
March–April in North, January–February in the Great Smokies, December–February in South. Heavy rains and warming temperatures prompt migration to breeding ponds. Female lays 1 or more compact, clear or milky egg masses, each containing about 100 eggs, which adhere to submerged branches. Larvae hatch in 1–2 months, are ½″ (13 mm) long; transform in 2–4 months at 2½″ (64 mm).

Habitat
Hardwood forests and hillsides around pools and flooded swampy depressions.

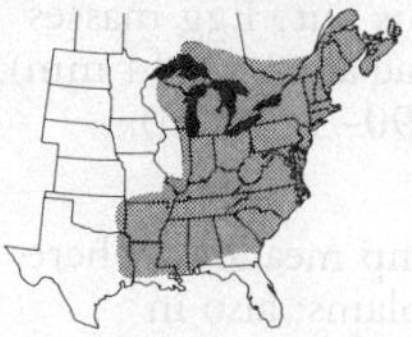

Range
South-central Ontario to Nova Scotia, south to Georgia and E. Texas.

Comments
This species spends most of the time underground, so adults are rarely encountered. Acid rains have so polluted the water in some Northeast ponds that eggs cannot develop and populations have died out. Developing egg masses turn green from a beneficial algae. May live 20 years.

Pacific Giant Salamander
Dicamptodon ensatus
128

7–11¾″ (17.8–30 cm). Robust and smooth-skinned. Brown or purplish, with black mottling. Belly light brown to yellowish white. No foot tubercles; 3 segments on fourth toe of hind foot. 12–13 indistinct grooves on sides.

Breeding
Terrestrial adults breed in spring, in river headwaters. Eggs laid singly, on submerged timber. Hatching larvae, about ⅝″ (16 mm), may transform during or following second year at 3¼–6″ (8.9–15.2 cm).

Habitat
Rivers, their tributaries, and surrounding cool, humid forests.

Range
Extreme SW. British Columbia south along coast to Santa Cruz County, California; Rocky Mountains in Idaho and extreme west-central Montana.

Comments
Most salamanders are voiceless, but the Pacific Giant has been known to emit a low-pitched yelp when captured. Land-dwelling adults live under logs, rocks, and forest litter but are sometimes seen crawling on the surface or even climbing in bushes or trees.

Northern Leopard Frog
Rana pipiens
130, 143

2–5″ (5.1–12.8 cm). Slender brown or green frog with large, light-edged dark spots between light-colored ridges at juncture of back and sides; ridges continuous to groin. Light stripe on upper jaw. Eardrum without light center.

Voice
A low guttural snore lasting about 3 seconds, followed by several clucking notes.

Breeding
March–June. Egg masses are attached to submerged vegetation or laid on bottom.

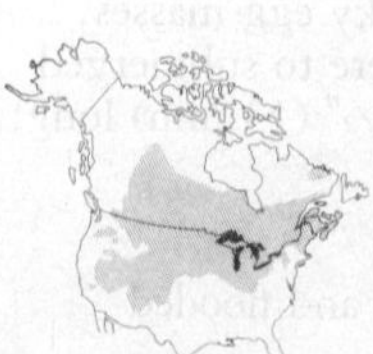

Habitat
From freshwater sites with profuse vegetation to brackish marshes and moist fields; from desert to mountain meadow.

Range
Throughout northern North America, except West Coast.

Comments
Primarily nocturnal. When pursued on land, it flees in zigzag leaps to the security of water.

Rio Grande Leopard Frog
Rana berlandieri
131

2¼–4½″ (6–11.4 cm). Pale green, with large dark spots between russet ridges at juncture of back and sides; ridges broken near hind legs. Light jaw stripe poorly defined.

Voice
A short rapid trill, low in pitch.

Breeding
Year-round. Egg masses are attached to submerged vegetation.

Habitat
Any water or moist conditions, natural or artificial.

Range
SW. Arizona and S. New Mexico to central Texas, south into Mexico.

Comments
Primarily nocturnal. The Rio Grande Leopard Frog can tolerate fairly dry conditions by burrowing under rocks.

Striped Chorus Frog
Pseudacris triseriata
132

¾–1½″ (1.9–3.8 cm). Skin smooth, greenish gray to brown. 3 dark stripes down back; may be broken, reduced, or absent. Dark stripe through eye and white stripe along upper lip. Small round toe tips.

Voice
A rasping, rising trill lasting 1–2 seconds, like the sound of a fingernail running over the teeth of a comb. Males call while sitting upright on floating vegetation.

Breeding
All winter in warmer areas of range, late winter to summer in northern areas.

Habitat
Grassy areas from dry to swampy to agricultural; also suburbs where pollution and pesticides are not a problem; woodlands; and river swamps.

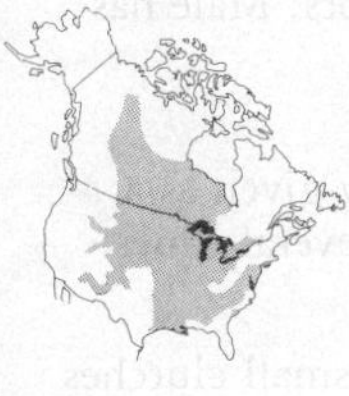

Range
Widespread. Alberta to N. New York (except New England, the northern Appalachians, and the southern coast) south to Georgia, west to Arizona.

Subspecies
Western (*P. t. triseriata*), with dark stripes; Wisconsin to extreme S. Quebec, south through W. New York and north of the Ohio River to central Oklahoma, west to Nebraska and South Dakota, and northeastern Lake Superior; a disjunct population occurs in central Arizona and New Mexico.
Upland (*P. t. feriarum*), with thin dark stripes or rows of small spots; E. Pennsylvania south to the Florida panhandle and

west to E. Texas and Oklahoma, and north to Kentucky. New Jersey (*P. t. kalmi*), larger size, with prominent dark stripes; extreme S. New York along the coastal plain through the Delmarva Peninsula.
Boreal (*P. t. maculata*), with shorter hind legs, and dark stripes or spots; northwestern Canada near Great Bear Lake to N. Ontario, south through N. Michigan to N. New Mexico, west to central Utah, E. Idaho and along the eastern slopes of the Rocky Mountains to British Columbia.

Comments
Nocturnal. Chorus frogs may be heard calling on warm nights in early spring even before all the ice has disappeared from the water. At the slightest threat they slip beneath the surface.

Northern Cricket Frog
Acris crepitans
133

⅝–1½″ (1.6–3.8 cm). Skin rough; greenish brown, yellow, red, or black. Dark triangle between eyes and longitudinal dark stripes on back of thigh. Snout rounded. Legs relatively short. Webbing of hind foot quite extensive, reaching tip of first toe and next-to-last joint of longest toe.

Voice
A shrill, measured clicking.

Breeding
April–August in northern areas; earlier in western areas.

Habitat
Sunny ponds of shallow water with good growth of vegetation in water or on shore; slow-moving streams with sunny banks.

Range
S. New York to Florida panhandle west to Texas and SE. New Mexico, north to South Dakota, Wisconsin, and Michigan.

Comments
Diurnal. These frogs are often abundant but are difficult to catch as they hop among the grass at the water's edge.

Green Frog
Rana clamitans
134

2⅛–4″ (5.4–10.2 cm). Green, bronze, or brown frog; large external eardrum and prominent ridges at juncture of back and sides that do not reach groin. Typically green on upper lip. Belly white with darker pattern of lines or spots. Male has yellow throat and swollen "thumbs."

Voice
Like the twang of a loose banjo string, usually given as a single note, but sometimes repeated rapidly several times.

Breeding
March–August. Eggs are usually laid in 3–4 small clutches attached to submerged vegetation.

Habitat
Lives close to shallow water, springs, swamps, brooks, and edges of ponds and lakes; among rotting debris of fallen trees.

Range
Widespread throughout eastern North America.

Subspecies
Bronze (*R. c. clamitans*), brown or bronze; Carolinas to central Florida and through the Gulf Coast states to E. Texas and S. Arkansas.
Green (*R. c. melanota*), green or greenish brown; S. Ontario east to Newfoundland, south to North Carolina, west to Oklahoma; introduced into Canada, the West, and Hawaii.

Comments
Primarily nocturnal. Green Frogs are not as wary as many other species of frog. They seldom scream in alarm when caught.

River Frog
Rana heckscheri
135

$3\frac{1}{4}$–$5\frac{5}{16}''$ (8–13.5 cm). Large and rough-skinned; dark olive to almost black; light spots along edge of jaws. Belly dark, from gray to almost black, with irregular light spots and lines. Large external eardrum; hind feet webbed to last joint of largest toe. Male has a swollen "thumb" and darker throat than female.

Voice
Sharp grunt or low-pitched snore.

Breeding
April–August. Tadpoles are large, to 5″ (12.7 cm), black with black borders on tail, and transform in about a year.

Habitat
Swamps bordering slow-moving rivers and creeks.

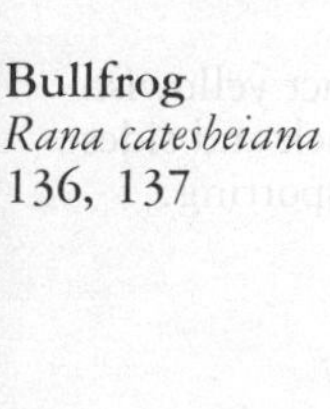

Range
From SE. South Carolina to central Florida.

Comments
Nocturnal. Newly metamorphosed River Frogs apparently have a toxic skin secretion, for water snakes and indigo snakes become violently ill after ingesting them.

Bullfrog
Rana catesbeiana
136, 137

$3\frac{1}{2}$–8″ (9–20.3 cm). The largest frog in North America. Green to yellow above with random mottling of darker gray. Large external eardrum; hind feet fully webbed except for last joint of longest toe. No ridges at juncture of back and sides. Belly cream to white, may be mottled with gray.

Voice
Deep-pitched *jug o'rum* call can be heard for more than a quarter mile on quiet mornings.

Breeding
Northern areas, May–July; southern, February–October. Egg masses are attached to submerged vegetation. Tadpoles are large, 4–$6\frac{3}{4}''$ (10.2–17.1 cm), olive-green, and may take almost 2 years to transform.

Habitat
Aquatic. Prefers ponds, lakes, and slow-moving streams large enough to avoid crowding and with sufficient vegetation.

Range
Eastern and central United States; also New Brunswick and parts of Nova Scotia. Extensively introduced in the western United States.

Comments
Nocturnal. The Bullfrog is usually found on the bank at water's edge. When frightened, it will as soon flee into nearby vegetation as take to the water. Large specimens have been known to catch and swallow small birds and young snakes; its usual diet includes insects, crayfish, other frogs, and minnows. Attempts to commercially harvest frogs' legs have prompted many introductions of the Bullfrog outside its natural range.

Pine Barrens Treefrog
Hyla andersoni
138

1⅛–2″ (2.9–5.1 cm). Bright green with white-edged lavender stripes on side. Hidden surface of thighs orange; toe pads large.

Voice
A nasal honk without much carrying power, repeated about once a second.

Breeding
April–August.

Habitat
Swamps, streams, and acid bog areas.

Range
Population centers are scattered in mid-Atlantic and South.

Comments
Nocturnal. A rare species, the Pine Barrens Treefrog is seldom encountered except at breeding time, when it may be seen at a favorite mating site. Its survival is threatened by habitat destruction, especially the draining of wetlands.

Carpenter Frog
Rana virgatipes
139

1⅝–2⅝″ (4.1–6.7 cm). Small, brown; 4 distinct yellowish stripes down back but no folds at juncture of back and sides. Underside cream to yellow, with random dark spotting. Webbing does not reach tip of longest toe.

Voice
A rhythmic hammering sound.

Breeding
April–August. Eggs laid in clusters are attached to vegetation. Tadpoles transform during the following spring.

Habitat
Sphagnum bogs and sphagnum fringes of lakes and ponds. Also found in tea-colored, slow-moving water with abundant emergent vegetation.

Range
Coastal plain from Pine Barrens of New Jersey to S. Georgia.

Comments
Nocturnal. This frog is often seen wholly out of water but is never far from the edge. When frightened, it leaps into water and hides beneath vegetation, swimming only a short distance before it breaks the surface for a quick look at the pursuer.

Wood Frog
Rana sylvatica
140, 149

1⅜–3¼″ (3.5–8.3 cm). Pink, tan, or dark brown, with prominent dark mask ending abruptly behind eardrum. Light stripe on upper jaw; sometimes light line down middle of back. Ridges at juncture of back and sides prominent. Dark blotch on chest near base of each front leg. Belly white, may have dark mottling. Toes not fully webbed; male has swollen "thumbs."

Voice
A series of short raspy quacks.

Breeding
Early spring, before ice has completely melted from water. Egg masses are attached to submerged vegetation.

Habitat
Moist woodlands in eastern areas; open grasslands in western; tundra in the Far North.

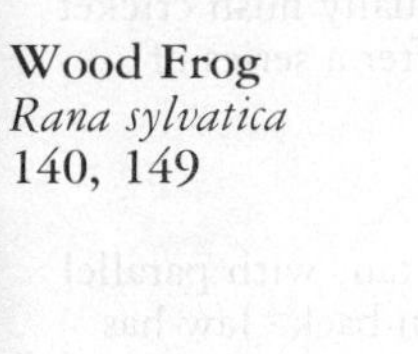

Range
Widespread throughout northern North America.

Comments
This is the only North American frog found north of the Arctic Circle. Primarily diurnal. In the colder parts of its range, the Wood Frog is an explosive breeder. Swarms of pairs lay fertilized eggs within 1 or 2 days, then disappear into the surrounding country. It may venture far from water during summer, and hibernates in forest debris during winter.

Southern Cricket Frog
Acris gryllus
141, 142

⅝–1¼″ (1.6–3.2 cm). Tiny, with rough skin; red, brown, black, or green. Dark triangle between eyes, and longitudinal dark stripes on back of thigh. Snout pointed. Legs relatively long. Webbing of hind foot extensive.

Voice
A rapid cricketlike click of 1 or 2 syllables. Calls while sitting on the ground, usually near edge of water.

Breeding
Throughout the year; infrequent during winter.

Habitat
Margins of swamps, marshes, lakes, streams, and ditches.

Range
The coastal plain from SE. Virginia to Mississippi and E. Louisiana.

Subspecies
Southern (*A. g. gryllus*), SE. Virginia through inland Georgia to Louisiana.
Florida (*A. g. dorsalis*), Georgia coast through Florida peninsula to SE. Alabama.
Coastal (*A. g. paludicola*), NE. Texas coast.

Comments
This species is active throughout the day and a strong jumper. A quick walk along the water's edge will usually flush cricket frogs from cover. Most will stop jumping after a series of erratic leaps.

Pickerel Frog
Rana palustris
144

$1\frac{3}{4}$–$3\frac{7}{16}''$ (4.4–8.7 cm). Smooth-skinned, tan, with parallel rows of dark squarish blotches running down back. Jaw has light stripe. Folds at juncture of back and sides yellow. Belly and undersurfaces of hind legs bright yellow to orange.

Voice
A steady low croak. May call in a rolling snore while under water.

Breeding
March–May. Egg masses attached to submerged vegetation.

Habitat
Slow-moving water and other damp areas, preferably with low, dense vegetation; streams, swamps, and meadows.

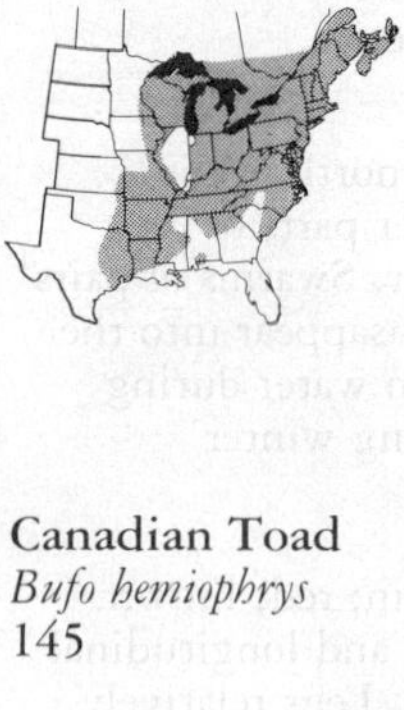

Range
Throughout the eastern states except the extreme Southeast.

Comments
Nocturnal. An irritating skin secretion makes this frog unappetizing to some predators. The secretion will kill other frogs kept in the same collecting container or terrarium. Pickerel Frogs hibernate from October until March or April.

Canadian Toad
Bufo hemiophrys
145

2–$3\frac{1}{4}''$ (5.1–8.3 cm). Large, with bony ridges on head fused into bony hump between eyes. Green to brownish red, with brownish-red warts; light line down middle of back. Parotoid glands oval, somewhat indistinct.

Voice
Short, weak, low-pitched trill, repeated every 15–20 seconds.

Breeding
Through summer, March–September. Eggs are laid in shallow water at edge of ponds and lakes.

Habitat
Margins of ponds, lakes, and potholes.

Range
In Canada from extreme S. Mackenzie and E. Alberta southeast to NE. South Dakota and N. Montana. Separate population in SE. Wyoming.

Subspecies
Canadian (*B. h. hemiophrys*), with wide light line on back; S. District of Mackenzie south and east to Minnesota and NE. South Dakota, west in the south to east-central Alberta.
Wyoming (*B. h. baxteri*), with narrow light line on back; SE. Wyoming.

Comments
Primarily nocturnal. The Canadian Toad readily takes to water to avoid capture. It is also an adept burrower, utilizing 2 tubercles on the hind feet in the same manner as a spadefoot toad.

Black Toad
Bufo exsul
146

1¾–2⅜″ (4.4–6.2 cm). Small; has oval parotoid glands. Heavy dark olive to black mottling separated by light wavy marks. Usually has a light stripe down middle of back. Heavy black blotches on belly.

Voice
A weak chirp.

Breeding
May–July.

Habitat
Quiet streams or springs; sometimes found in grass or open woods.

Range
Deep Springs Valley, Inyo County, California.

Comments
Active at twilight, this aquatic species forages among the grassy tussocks bordering the spring runs at Antelope and Deep Springs. It is now on the California endangered list.

Bird-voiced Treefrog
Hyla avivoca
147

1⅛–2⅛″ (2.9–5.2 cm). Greenish, brownish, or shades of gray, with darker blotches on back; dark-edged light spot beneath eye. Hidden surfaces of thigh green to greenish yellow. Toe pads large.

Voice
The most beautiful frog call in North America: a resonant, birdlike whistle. Males call while perched on shrubs.

Breeding
March–September.

Habitat
Wooded river swamps and bayous. Especially frequent in cypress, tupelo, and other trees that grow in standing water, and creepers that grow among the trees.

Range
Extreme S. Illinois southwest to Florida panhandle and south to Louisiana. Isolated populations in NE. Georgia and on the Georgia–South Carolina border.

Subspecies
Western (*H. a. avivoca*), smaller size, white or pale yellow light spot beneath eye; Illinois to Louisiana and W. Florida. Eastern (*H. a. ogechiensis*), larger size, yellow or green light spot beneath eye; central Georgia and SW. South Carolina.

Comments
Nocturnal. This species is almost never seen except during nighttime choruses; apparently it remains in the treetops during the day. Its skin secretions may cause runny nose and watery eyes in people who handle it.

Brimley's Chorus Frog
Pseudacris brimleyi
148

1–1¼″ (2.5–3.2 cm). Slender, tan with black stripe from snout through eye to groin. Usually 3 longitudinal dark stripes and dark spots on chest. Small round toe tips.

Voice
A rasping trill, of about 1 second, given often.

Breeding
February–April.

Habitat
Marshes and sunny wooded areas where vegetation is not too thick.

Range
The coastal plain from E. Virginia to E. Georgia.

Comments
Brimley's Chorus Frog is primarily nocturnal. It can change color rapidly, depending on temperature and activity.

Spring Peeper
Hyla crucifer
150

¾–1⅜″ (1.9–3.5 cm). Tan to brown to gray, with characteristic dark X on back. Large toe pads.

Voice
A high-pitched ascending whistle, sometimes with a short trill. Chorus sounds like the jingle of bells. Males call from shrubs and trees standing in or overhanging water.

Breeding
In southern areas, November–March; in northern areas, March–June, with the start of warm rains.

Habitat
Wooded areas in or near permanent or temporarily flooded ponds and swamps.

Range
Manitoba to the Maritime Provinces, south through central Florida, west to E. Texas, and north into central Wisconsin.

Comments
Nocturnal. The Spring Peeper is one of the most familiar frogs in the East. Its chorus is among the first signs of spring. Peepers hibernate under logs and loose bark.

Snapping Turtle
Chelydra serpentina
151, 152

8–18½″ (20–47 cm). The familiar "snapper," with massive head and powerful jaws. Carapace tan to dark brown, often masked with algae or mud, bearing 3 rows of weak to prominent keels, and serrated toward the back. Plastron yellow to tan, unpatterned, relatively small, and cross-shaped in outline. Tail as long as carapace; with saw-toothed keels. Tubercles on neck. Wild specimens range to 45 lb. (20.5 kg). Some fattened captives exceed 75 lb. (34 kg).

Breeding
Mates April–November; peak laying season is June. Lays as many as 83 (typically 25–50) spherical eggs in deep, flask-shaped cavity. Each egg is directed into place by alternating movements of hind feet. Incubation, depending on weather, takes 9–18 weeks. In temperate localities, hatchlings overwinter in nest. Females sometimes retain sperm for several years.

Habitat
Fresh water. Likes soft mud bottoms and abundant vegetation. Also enters brackish waters.

Range
S. Alberta to Nova Scotia, south to the Gulf of Mexico.

Subspecies
Four; 2 in our range.
Common (*C. s. serpentina*), blunt tubercles on neck; throughout our range, except Florida.
Florida (*C. s. osceola*), pointed tubercles on neck; throughout the Florida peninsula.

Comments
Highly aquatic, the Snapping Turtle likes to rest in warm shallows, often buried in mud, with only its eyes and nostrils exposed. It emerges in April from a winter retreat beneath an overhanging mud bank, under plant debris, or inside a muskrat lodge. The snapper eats invertebrates, carrion, aquatic plants, fish, birds, and small mammals. It is an excellent swimmer: individuals displaced 2 miles have returned to their capture sites within several hours. Snappers strike viciously when lifted from water or teased and can inflict a serious bite.

Mud Turtle
Kinosternon subrubrum
153, 154, 160

3–4⅞″ (7.6–12.4 cm). Carapace olive to dark brown, patternless, smooth, keelless. Marginal plates not enlarged. Plastron yellow to brown, double-hinged, with 11 plates. Males have well-developed blunt spine at end of tail and rough scale patches on inside of hind legs.

Breeding
Sexually mature at 5–7 years. Breeds mid-March to May; usually nests in June, but October–June nestings have occurred. 1–6 elliptical eggs—hard-shelled, pinkish, or bluish white—are deposited in a cavity dug in plant debris or sandy loam soil. Several clutches laid annually in South.

Habitat
Fresh or brackish water. Prefers shallow, soft-bottomed, slow-moving water with abundant vegetation. Often occupies muskrat lodges.

Range
SW. Connecticut and Long Island south to S. Florida, west to central Texas, and north in the Mississippi Valley to S. Illinois and SW. Indiana; isolated population in NW. Indiana.

Subspecies
Eastern (*K. s. subrubrum*), spotted or mottled head; SW. Connecticut and Long Island to Gulf, northwest to S. Illinois and SW. Indiana, isolated population in NW. Indiana.
Florida (*K. s. steindachneri*), plain or mottled head; peninsular Florida.
Mississippi (*K. s. hippocrepis*), 2 light lines on side of head; SE. Missouri, Arkansas, E. Oklahoma, E. Texas, Louisiana, W. and S. Mississippi, S. Alabama, and extreme W. Florida.

Comments
This species is active April–October. During warmer months it can be seen prowling along the bottom. If the habitat dries up, the turtles may move overland to a permanent body of water or burrow into the mud and remain dormant. Surprisingly terrestrial, they are frequently seen crossing roads; many are killed doing so. Some mud turtles are mild-tempered, while others are feisty and do not hesitate to bite.

Stinkpot
Sternotherus odoratus
155

3–5⅜″ (7.6–13.7 cm). A feisty little turtle with 2 light stripes on head, barbels on chin and throat. Carapace smooth or with 3 keels, unserrated, highly domed, and elongated; olive-brown to dark gray and often obscured by a layer of algae. Juveniles have keeled and patterned carapace with irregular dark streaks or spots. Plastron small, with 11 plates and a single inconspicuous hinge. Male's tail ends in a blunt horny nail; inner surface of hind legs bears 2 small patches of tilted scales. Female's tail very short.

Breeding
Nests February–June, depending on latitude. Mates underwater. Lays 1–9 thick-shelled, elliptical eggs—off-white with stark white band—in shallow nest under rotting stump or in wall of muskrat lodge. Incubation takes 9–12 weeks.

Habitat
Fresh water; prefers quiet or slow-moving, shallow, muddy-bottomed waters.

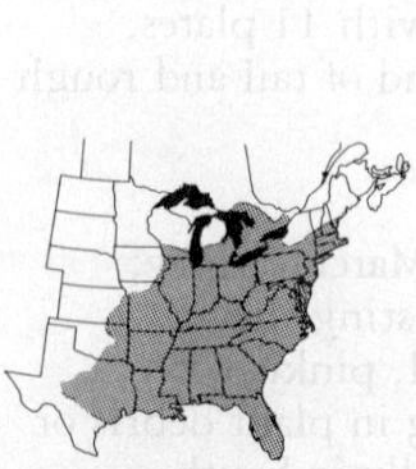

Range
S. Ontario and coastal Maine to Florida, west to central Texas, north to S. Wisconsin.

Comments
This species is also called the Musk Turtle or Stinking Jim. When disturbed, it secretes a foul-smelling, yellowish fluid

from 2 pairs of musk glands under the border of the carapace. Males are aggressive and bite readily. Stinkpot's long neck can bring its jaws as far back as its hind limbs. In early spring it likes to bask in shallows or amid floating vegetation with the center of its carapace exposed to the sun. Stinkpots rarely leave the water, but they occasionally climb trees to bask.

Spotted Turtle
Clemmys guttata
156

3½–5″ (8–12.7 cm). A small, attractive turtle. Carapace black, keelless, unserrated; usually sprinkled with round yellow spots. Spotting on head, neck, and limbs. Plastron creamy yellow with large black blotches along border. Male has brown eyes, tan chin, long thick tail; female has orange eyes and yellow chin.

Breeding
Courts March–May. In June, female digs shallow flask-shaped nest in sun-drenched areas and deposits up to 8 (typically 3–5) flexible-shelled, elliptical eggs. Hatchlings emerge in late August–September or overwinter in nest until spring.

Habitat
Marshy meadows, wet woodlands, boggy areas, beaver ponds, and shallow, muddy-bottomed streams.

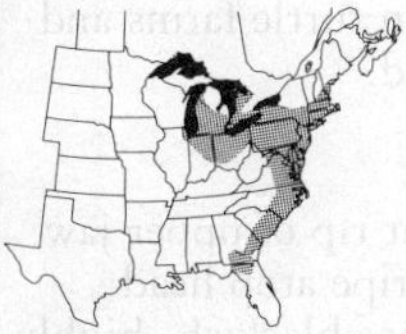

Range
S. Maine south along the Atlantic coastal plain to N. Florida, west through Maryland, Pennsylvania, and S. New York into N. Ohio and Indiana, extreme NE. Illinois and adjacent SE. Wisconsin, S. Michigan, and Ontario.

Comments
Frequently seen basking in the cooler spring months, the Spotted Turtle is difficult to find during the summer, when dense vegetation obscures its movements. It is often found in association with Painted, Wood, and Bog turtles. It winters underwater in soft mud, debris, or muskrat burrows.

Slider
Pseudemys scripta
157, 163

5–11⅜″ (12.7–28.9 cm). The "dime store" turtle. Prominent yellow, orange, or red blotch or stripe behind eyes. Carapace oval, weakly keeled, olive to brown, with pattern ranging from yellow bars and stripes to networks of lines and eyelike spots. Plastron yellow, plain to intricately patterned. Undersurface of chin rounded. V-shaped notch at front of upper jaw. With age, pattern and head blotch may become masked by black pigment, making identification difficult.

Breeding
Mates March–June. Nests June–July. Lays 1–3 clutches of 4–23 oval eggs in nest cavity that may be located some distance from water. Hatchlings emerge in 2–2½ months, but often overwinter in nest. Males mature in 2–5 years.

Habitat
Sluggish rivers, shallow streams, swamps, ponds, and lakes with soft bottoms and dense vegetation.

Range
SE. Virginia to N. Florida west to New Mexico, south to Brazil.

Subspecies
Yellowbelly (*P. s. scripta*), with conspicuous vertical yellow blotch behind eye, vertical yellowish bar on each side plate, and dark round smudges on forward part of plastron; SE. Virginia to N. Florida.
Red-eared (*P. s. elegans*), with wide red stripe behind eye, dark smudge on each plastron plate; Mississippi Valley from N. Illinois to Gulf of Mexico.
Cumberland (*P. s. troosti*), upper portions of Cumberland and Tennessee River valleys from SE. Kentucky and SW. Virginia to NE. Alabama.
Big Bend (*P. s. gaigeae*), with large, black-bordered orange spot on side of head, small orange spot behind eye, carapace with netlike pattern; Big Bend region of Texas and adjacent Mexico, also Rio Grande Valley in south-central New Mexico.

Comments
Fond of basking, Sliders are often seen stacked one upon another on a favorite log. The young eat water insects, crustaceans, mollusks, and tadpoles, then turn to a plant diet as they mature. Millions have been raised on turtle farms and sold as pets. Few have survived to adulthood.

Florida Redbelly Turtle
Chrysemys nelsoni
158

8–13⅜″ (20.3–34 cm). Prominent notch at tip of upper jaw flanked by toothlike cusps; arrow-shaped stripe atop head (shaft between eyes, point at snout). Carapace blackish, highly arched; plates down center convex; red bar on each plate around margin, with dark blotch on underside. Plastron reddish; patternless or with dark semicircles along plate seams that fade with age. Male has elongated, slightly curved claws on front feet.

Breeding
Nests early June–August, but most clutches are laid mid-June to mid-July.

Habitat
Ponds, lakes, sloughs, marshes, mangrove-bordered creeks.

Range
Florida peninsula and Apalachicola area of panhandle.

Comments
Active year-round, the Florida Redbelly is often seen basking on logs or floating mats of vegetation. Because of its thick shell, it can bask for long periods. Adults prefer a diet of aquatic plants.

Painted Turtle
Chrysemys picta
159, 161, 162

4–9⅞″ (10.2–25.1 cm). Carapace olive or black; oval, smooth, flattened, and unkeeled; plate seams bordered with olive, yellow, or red. Red bars or crescents on marginal plates.

Plastron yellow, unpatterned or intricately marked. Yellow and red stripes on neck, legs, and tail. Notched upper jaw.

Breeding
Nests May–July. In north lays 1–2 clutches a year, in south 2–4, of 2–20 elliptical eggs in flask-shaped nest cavity. Hatchlings in north may overwinter in the nest. Incubation averages 10–11 weeks. Males reach maturity in 2–5 years.

Habitat
Slow-moving shallow streams, rivers, and lakes. Likes soft bottoms with vegetation and half-submerged logs.

Range
British Columbia to Nova Scotia, south to Georgia, west to Louisiana, north to Oklahoma, and northwest to Oregon. Isolated populations in the Southwest.

Subspecies
Eastern (*C. p. picta*), seams aligned where plates down center meet those on sides; plastron yellow, not patterned; southeastern Canada through New England and the Atlantic coastal states to N. Georgia and E. Alabama.
Midland (*C. p. marginata*), plates down center not aligned with side plates, plastron yellow with dark blotch in center; S. Quebec and S. Ontario to Tennessee.
Southern (*C. p. dorsalis*), red or yellow stripe down carapace, plastron yellow, not patterned; S. Illinois to Gulf, SE. Oklahoma to central Alabama.
Western (*C. p. belli*), largest subspecies, with light netlike lines on carapace, bars on marginal plates, and intricate branching pattern on plastron; SW. Ontario south to Missouri and west to Oregon and British Columbia; isolated populations in the Southwest. Specimens from areas where ranges of subspecies overlap display an intergradation of characteristics.

Comments
The Painted Turtle is the most widespread turtle in North America. It is fond of basking and often dozens can be observed on a single log. Young turtles are basically carnivorous, but become herbivorous as they mature.

Map Turtle
Graptemys geographica
164

Males 4–6¼″ (10.2–15.9 cm); females 7–10¾″ (17.8–27.3 cm). Carapace greenish to olive-brown, with netlike pattern of thin yellow-orange lines (obscure in adult females); somewhat flattened and with a low keel (with small spines in juveniles). Plastron yellowish; patternless in adults, with black-bordered plate seams in juveniles. Skin greenish with narrow yellow stripes; isolated yellow spot behind eye.

Breeding
Nests May to mid-July. Southern females lay 2 or more clutches a season (northern females, 1) of 12–14 ellipsoidal eggs. Hatchlings emerge mid-August through September or late May or June of following year.

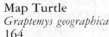

Habitat
Slow-moving rivers and lakes with mud bottoms, abundant aquatic vegetation, and logjams.

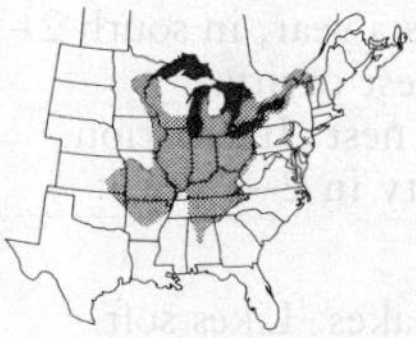

Range
Lake George and Lake Champlain through St. Lawrence and Great Lakes drainage, south to Tennessee and Alabama; also Arkansas and Missouri river drainages. Isolated populations in Delaware River and Susquehanna River drainage.

Comments
Map turtles quickly slide into the water when disturbed. The female's large crushing jaws can break open freshwater clams and large snails. Males and juveniles eat insects, crayfish, and smaller mollusks.

Bog Turtle
Clemmys muhlenbergi
165

3–4½″ (7.6–11.4 cm). A small brown turtle with conspicuous yellow, orange, or reddish blotch on each side of head. Carapace light brown to mahogany (a light brown or orange sunburst pattern may be present on large plates), weakly keeled, and rough or smooth depending on age. Plastron brownish black with yellow along midline; hingeless, with 12 plates. Male has concave plastron and thick tail.

Breeding
Reaches sexual maturity in 5–7 years. Mates during first warm days of spring; nests in June. Lays single clutch of 1–6 (typically 3–4) elliptical, flexible-shelled eggs in nest cavity. Hatchlings emerge August–September after incubation of 6½–9 weeks, or may overwinter in the nest.

Habitat
Sunlit marshy meadows, spring seepages, wet cow pastures, and bogs. Prefers narrow, shallow, slow-moving rivulets.

Range
E. New York and adjacent Massachusetts and Connecticut, south through New Jersey and parts of Pennsylvania, Delaware, and Maryland. Other populations in Finger Lakes region (New York) and parts of Pennsylvania, Virginia, and North Carolina.

Comments
The Bog Turtle, or Muhlenberg's Turtle, is more secretive than rare. Typically active from April to mid-October, the Bog Turtle searches out a wide variety of prey. In spring it often basks atop grassy tussocks. During hot periods it buries itself in mud or vegetative debris, exposing only a small portion of its shell to the sun. Winter is spent buried deep in mud flooded by subterranean waters. It is now protected in most states where it is found.

Wood Turtle
Clemmys insculpta
166

5–9″ (12.7–23 cm). Formed by concentric growth ridges, each large carapace plate looks like an irregular pyramid. Upper shell brown and keeled, appears sculptured and rough.

Plastron yellow, with black blotches usually present along outer margins of plates; hingeless. Skin of neck and forelegs often reddish orange. Male has concave plastron and thick tail.

Breeding
1 clutch of 6–8 (maximum 18) elliptical, flexible-shelled eggs deposited May–June, hatch September–October. In North hatchlings may overwinter in the nest.

Habitat
Cool streams in deciduous woodlands, red-maple swamps, marshy meadows, and farm country.

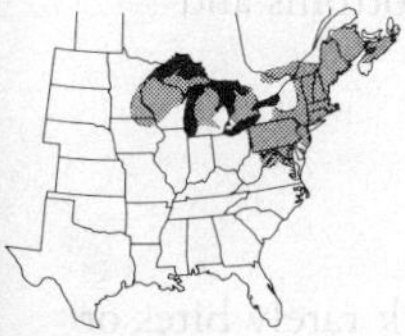

Range
Nova Scotia south to N. Virginia and discontinuously west through S. Quebec and the Great Lakes region to E. Minnesota and NE. Iowa.

Comments
"Ole redlegs" is an excellent climber. After spring rains, it often searches for worms in freshly plowed fields. It also likes slugs, insects, tadpoles, and fruits. The Wood Turtle was once taken for food and now suffers from overcollection and habitat loss. It is currently protected in some states.

Western Pond Turtle
Clemmys marmorata
167

3½–7" (8.9–17.8 cm). Smooth, broad, low carapace olive to dark brown; often marked with network of dark flecks and lines radiating from center of plates. Plastron pale yellow, hingeless; may have dark brown to black blotches along plate margins. Male has concave plastron.

Breeding
Lays 1 clutch of 3–11 oval, hard-shelled eggs, April–August. Hatchlings emerge in about 12 weeks.

Habitat
Ponds and small lakes with abundant vegetation. Also seen in marshes, slow-moving streams, reservoirs, and occasionally in brackish water.

Range
West of Cascade-Sierra Nevada crest from extreme SW. British Columbia south to Baja California. Isolated population in Carson and Truckee rivers in extreme W. Nevada.

Subspecies
Northwestern (*C. m. marmorata*), well-developed triangular plates at groin on part of shell connecting carapace and plastron; British Columbia south to San Francisco Bay, W. Nevada.
Southwestern (*C. m. pallida*), plates at groin small or absent; San Francisco Bay south into NW. Baja California.

Comments
One turtle may challenge another for a favored basking site by extending its neck, opening its mouth, and exposing its yellow-edged jaws and reddish interior.

Razorback Musk Turtle
Sternotherus carinatus
168

4–5⅞″ (10–14.9 cm). Steeply sloped carapace with prominent keel down center. Plates light brown to orangish, accented with small dark spots or radiating streaks and dark borders. Pattern may be lost in older turtles. Plastron yellow; no throat plate; has only 10 plates. Single hinge barely discernible between chest and abdominal plates. Snout somewhat tubular. Barbels on chin only.

Breeding
Cycle poorly known; probably lays 2 clutches a season.

Habitat
Slow-moving streams and rivers with soft bottoms and abundant aquatic vegetation; swamplands.

Range
S. Mississippi west to Texas.

Comments
Unlike other musk turtles the shy Razorback rarely bites or expels musk. It is active from March to November and basks frequently. Good habitats may have 100 turtles an acre.

Flattened Musk Turtle
Sternotherus depressus
169

3–4½″ (7.6–11.4 cm). Carapace extremely flattened. Head and neck greenish, covered with dark, netlike pattern. Barbels on chin only.

Breeding
Little is known.

Habitat
Rock-bottomed streams and their impoundments.

Range
Black Warrior River system in NW. Alabama.

Comments
A shy little turtle, it is most active during early morning.

Spiny Softshell
Trionyx spiniferus
170, 171

Males 5–9¼″ (12.7–23.5 cm); females 6½–18″ (16.5–45.7 cm). Shell covered with soft leathery skin, not horny plates. Carapace olive to tan, with black-bordered "eyespots" or dark blotches and dark line around shell's rim; spiny tubercles on leading edge; 2 dark-bordered light stripes on sides of head.

Breeding
Nests May–August. Digs flask-shaped cavity in bank of sand or gravel exposed to full sunlight and lays 4–32 spherical eggs. Hatchlings emerge late August–October or following spring.

Habitat
Likes small marshy creeks and farm ponds as well as large, fast-flowing rivers and lakes.

Range
Throughout central United States as far west as the

Continental Divide. Separate populations in Montana, S. Quebec, Delaware, and the Gila–Colorado River system of New Mexico and Utah.

Comments
The Spiny Softshell is difficult to approach and fast-moving on land and in water. It is fond of basking on banks, logs, and floating debris. Numerous subspecies occur throughout the range; characteristics may intergrade.

American Alligator
Alligator mississippiensis
172

6′–19′2″ (1.8–5.84 m). Largest reptile in North America. Distinguished from American Crocodile by broad and rounded snout. Generally black with yellowish or cream crossbands that become less apparent with age. Large fourth tooth on bottom jaw fits into a socket in upper jaw, is not visible when mouth is closed. No curved bony ridge in front of eyes.

Voice
During the breeding season adults produce a throaty, bellowing roar heard over considerable distance. Young give a high-pitched call: *y-eonk, y-eonk, y-eonk.*

Breeding
Mates April–May after emerging from hibernation. In June, female builds a mound-shaped nest of mud, leaves, and rotting organic material; deposits about 25–60 hard-shelled eggs in cavity scooped from center of nest. During 9-week incubation period, she remains near nest. The calling of hatching young prompts the female to scratch open the nest to free them. Hatchlings are 9–10″ (22.8–25.4 cm) long and remain with the female for 1–3 years.

Habitat
Fresh and brackish marshes, ponds, lakes, rivers, swamps, bayous, and big spring runs.

Range
Coastal SE. North Carolina to Florida Keys and west along coastal plain to S. Texas; north to extreme SE. Oklahoma and S. Arkansas.

Comments
Alligators are important to the ecology of their habitat. During droughts they dig deep holes, or "dens," which provide water for the wildlife community. They hibernate in dens during the winter. Alligators have been relentlessly hunted for their hides and are much reduced in numbers. Under state and federal protection they are beginning to make a comeback in some areas.

Spectacled Caiman
Caiman crocodilus
173

4′–8′8″ (1.2–2.64 m). Light brown to olive-brown or light yellow, with distinct or indistinct crossbanding on back and tail. Curved bony ridge, or "spectacle," in front of eyes. Enlarged fourth tooth on lower jaw not visible when jaws are closed.

Breeding
August–September. Female builds mound-shaped nest of soil and vegetation, somewhat smaller than alligator's. Clutch averages 28 hard-shelled, elliptical eggs. Hatchlings emerge late October–November; average 8½″ (21.6 cm) long.

Habitat
Ponds, streams, marshes, rivers, and drainage canals.

Range
Introduced from Central and South America; liberated in many areas. A small reproducing population inhabits S. Florida.

Subspecies
Four; 1 in our range, *C. c. crocodilus.*

Comments
In the past 20 years, as a result of protective legislation for alligators, hundreds of thousands of caimans were imported for the pet trade. Most died quickly. Others, which escaped or were released, survived and have been sighted in the wild.

American Crocodile
Crocodylus acutus
174

7–15′ (2.1–4.6 m). Long slender snout distinguishes it from American Alligator. Gray-green, dark olive-green, or gray-brown with dark crossbands on back and tail; crossbands obscure in old adults. Large fourth tooth on bottom jaw visible when mouth is closed. No curved bony ridge in front of eyes, as seen in caimans.

Breeding
Female builds mound-shaped nest of soil, sand, and mangrove peat; lays 35–50 eggs, late April–early May. Hatchlings emerge July–early August, are about 9″ (22.9 cm) long.

Habitat
Florida Bay in Everglades National Park, Biscayne Bay, and Florida Keys; bogs and mangrove swamps.

Range
Extreme coastal S. Florida and the Keys.

Comments
The Florida population, fewer than 500 in number, was declared endangered in 1975. Poaching and construction have reduced their numbers. The adult diet includes crabs, fish, raccoons, and water birds. Drawn to the sounds of hatchlings, the female opens the nest cavity and carefully picks up the young in her mouth and, in a series of trips, carries them to water.

Cottonmouth ⊗
Agkistrodon piscivorus
175, 177, 194

20–74½″ (50.8–189.2 cm). A dark, heavy-bodied water snake; broad-based head is noticeably wider than neck. Olive, brown, or black above; patternless or with serrated-edged dark crossbands. Wide light-bordered, dark brown cheek stripe distinct, obscure, or absent. Head flat-topped; eyes with vertical pupils (not visible from directly above as are eyes of harmless water snakes); heat-sensitive facial pit between eye and nostril, used for locating prey. Young strongly patterned and bear bright yellow-tipped tails. Scales keeled.

Breeding
Live-bearing. Mates spring and fall. August–September, females give birth to 1–15 young, 7–13″ (18–33 cm) long. Females mature in 3 years and give birth every other year.

Habitat
Lowland swamps, lakes, rivers, bayheads, sloughs, irrigation ditches, canals, rice fields, to small, clear, rocky mountain streams; sea level to about 1500′ (450 m).

Range
SE. Virginia south to upper Florida Keys, west to S. Illinois, S. Missouri, south-central Oklahoma, and central Texas. Isolated population in north-central Missouri.

Subspecies
3; broad zones of intergradation.
Eastern (*A. p. piscivorus*), cheek stripe not well defined, snout tip lacks vertical markings; coastal plain, SE. Virginia south through Carolinas, west through central Georgia to Alabama.
Florida (*A. p. conanti*), cheek stripe distinct, 2 vertical dark marks on snout tip; SE. Alabama, S. Georgia, Florida.
Western (*A. p. leucostoma*), head and body markings obscure or absent; SW. Kentucky, W. Tennessee, and W. Alabama, west through S. Missouri to south-central Oklahoma and central Texas.

Comments
Do not disturb or attempt to handle! Its bite can be fatal. When annoyed, the Cottonmouth tends to stand its ground and may gape repeatedly at an intruder, exposing the light "cotton" lining of its mouth. Unlike other water snakes, it swims with head well out of water. Although it may be observed basking during the day, it is more active at night.

Smooth Green Snake
Opheodrys vernalis
176

14–26″ (35.5–66 cm). Small and streamlined; bright grass-green with long tapering tail. Belly white, tinged with pale yellow. Hatchlings bluish gray or dark olive-green. Scales smooth. Scale in front of anus divided.

Breeding
Mates spring and late summer. Lays 3–11 cylindrical-shaped, thin-shelled eggs, late July–August. Young hatch in 4–23 days at 4–6½″ (10–16.5 cm).

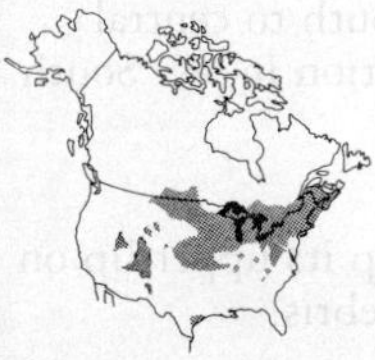

Habitat
Meadows, grassy marshes, moist grassy fields along forest edge; sea level to 9500′ (2900 m).

Range
Nova Scotia west to SE. Saskatchewan, south to North Carolina and NE. Kansas; SE. Idaho and Wyoming south into

NE. and SE. Utah and E. New Mexico; SE. Texas. Numerous scattered populations.

Comments
Active during the day, the Smooth Green Snake is a capable climber, but is largely terrestrial. Its color provides excellent camouflage as it moves through grass and low shrubs in search of insects and spiders.

Pine Woods Snake
Rhadinaea flavilata
178, 179

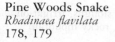

10–15⅞″ (25.4–40.2 cm). Tiny golden-brown or reddish-brown snake with white to yellow belly. Upper lip scales yellowish, some with dark specks. Top of head darker than body; dark stripe runs from snout through eye to corner of mouth. Faint narrow back and side stripes may be present.

Breeding
May–August, female deposits 2–4 eggs. Hatchlings are about 6½″ (16.5 cm) long.

Habitat
Low marshy areas, damp pine flatwoods and hammocks, and coastal islands.

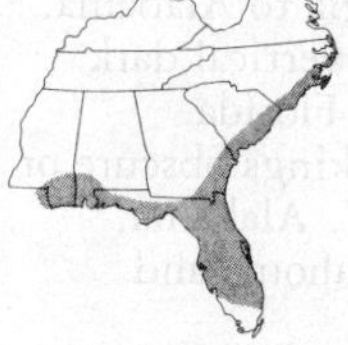

Range
Coastal plain, North Carolina to S. Florida and west to E. Louisiana.

Comments
The secretive "yellow-lipped snake" is most often seen during spring months when the water table is high. It often burrows into the centers of damp rotting pine logs and stumps or under forest litter or loose soil. Although harmless to man, its saliva is mildly toxic to its prey—frogs and lizards.

Redbelly Snake
Storeria occipitomaculata
180

8–16″ (20.3–40.6 cm). A small snake; plain brown, gray, or black, with a single broad light stripe, or 4 faint narrow dark stripes, or all 5, down back. Belly red, orange, or yellow; occasionally jet-black. 3 light spots on nape of neck that sometimes fuse to form collar. Scales keeled.

Breeding
Mates in spring or fall; 1–21 young, 2¾–4″ (7–10 cm) long, are born June–September; mature in 2 years.

Habitat
Mountainous or hilly woodland; sphagnum bogs. Sea level to 5600′ (1700 m).

Range
Extreme SE. Saskatchewan to Nova Scotia, south to central Florida and west to E. Texas. Isolated population in W. South Dakota and E. Wyoming.

Comments
When startled or captured, this snake curls up its upper lip on one or both sides. It hides under lumber or debris.

Black Swamp Snake
Seminatrix pygaea
181, 183

10–18½″ (25.4–47 cm). Glossy black, red-bellied snake. Black back color extends onto ends of belly sides. Scales smooth; last 3–5 rows bear light lines resembling keels.

Breeding
Live-bearing; 2–13 young, 4¼–5½″ (11–14 cm) long, are born August–October.

Habitat
Swamps, cedar and cypress ponds, canals, and drainage ditches, especially areas overgrown with water hyacinth.

Range
Coastal North Carolina to peninsular Florida, west to extreme SE. Alabama. Isolated population in South Carolina.

Subspecies
North Florida (*S. p. pygaea*), 118–124 belly scales; coastal Georgia to central Florida, west to SE. Alabama.
South Florida (*S. p. cyclas*), 117 or fewer belly scales; S. Florida.
Carolina (*S. p. paludis*), 127 or more belly scales; coastal plain of North and South Carolina.

Comments
This species is often found hiding amid mats of aquatic vegetation or seen at night after heavy rains. Eats leeches, small fish, frogs, tadpoles, and Dwarf Sirens. It is timid and does not bite when handled.

Mud Snake
Farancia abacura
182

38–81″ (96.5–205.5 cm). Shiny blue-black snake with pink or red belly bars extending upward on sides. Body cylindrical. Tail short and tipped with a sharp spine. Scales smooth.

Breeding
Mates in spring. July–August, female lays 11–104 eggs in an earthen cavity. She may remain with eggs until hatched in 7–8 weeks, August–September.

Habitat
Swampy, weedy lake margins; slow-moving, mud-bottomed streams; shallow sloughs with rotting logs; floodplains.

Range
SE. Virginia to S. Florida, west to E. Texas, and north in Mississippi Valley to S. Illinois. Isolated population in north-central Alabama.

Subspecies
Eastern (*F. a. abacura*), tops of red bars pointed, 53 or more, SE. Virginia to S. Florida and west to SE. Alabama.
Western (*F. a. reinwardti*), tops of red bars rounded, 52 or fewer; W. Alabama to E. Texas, north in Mississippi Valley to S. Illinois.

Comments
The Mud Snake is especially active on rainy nights and may be seen crossing roads in swampy areas. It does not bite when

picked up, but the captor may be poked with its harmless spine-tipped tail. Eats sirens and amphiumas.

Glossy Crayfish Snake
Regina rigida
184

14–31⅜″ (36–79.7 cm). A stout, small-headed snake; shiny brown or olive-brown with 2 faint dark stripes on back and 2 somewhat more detectable stripes on sides. Belly yellow or cream with 2 rows of crescent-shaped spots. Scales keeled.

Breeding
Poorly known. 7–14 young, about 7″ (18 cm) long, are born in summer.

Habitat
Mucky situations along streams or around edges of ponds, lakes, swamps, freshwater tidal marshes, rice fields, flatwood ponds, floodplains.

Range
Coastal plain, NE. North Carolina to central Florida, west to E. Texas. Isolated population in E. Virginia.

Comments
Though seldom seen, this species is usually observed at night crossing roads or found amid mats of aquatic vegetation. It is sometimes called the "stiff snake" because of its rigid body tone. Subspecies varying in color and pattern occur within range.

Green Water Snake
Nerodia cyclopion
185

30–74″ (76.2–188 cm). Heavy-bodied; olive-green, brownish, or reddish (in south Florida), with indistinct black bars on sides alternating with crossbars on back, more distinct in juveniles. Head seemingly short, series of small scales separating eye from upper lip scales. Belly cream to brown, with or without light spots. Scales keeled.

Breeding
Mates March–April; 4–101 young are born June–August; are 8¾–10¾″ (22–27 cm) long.

Habitat
Marshes, swamps, ditches, canals, bayous, and estuaries. Most frequent in waters with little current and dense vegetation.

Range
Coastal South Carolina through Florida, west to Louisiana and E. Texas, and north through E. Arkansas to extreme S. Illinois.

Subspecies
Green (*N. c. cyclopion*), light spots on dark belly; S. Alabama (Mobile Bay) to Texas and north to S. Illinois.
Florida Green (*N. c. floridana*), unmarked light belly; S. South Carolina through Florida to S. Alabama.

Comments
Though primarily diurnal, this species is often active in the

early evening feeding on minnows and small fishes. The most favorable habitat for the western form is wooded swamp, where many individuals may be seen basking in branches that overhang water. The Florida Green prefers weed-choked marshes, is less inclined to bask, and is somewhat more nocturnal. When captured, Green Water Snakes will bite or smear their captors with musk.

Queen Snake
Regina septemvittata
186

16–36¾″ (40.6–93.3 cm). Tan to olive-brown or chocolate-brown, to almost black, with a yellow stripe on lower side of body. Belly yellow with 4 distinct brown stripes; 2 near midline, 2 along sides. Sometimes 3 faded, indistinct stripes on back. Scales keeled. Scale in front of anus divided.

Breeding
Mates April–May. Live-bearing; 5–23 young, 7½–9″ (19–23 cm) long, are born July–early September.

Habitat
Streams and small rivers with rocky margins and bottoms, and clear sandy-bottomed creeks in coastal plain.

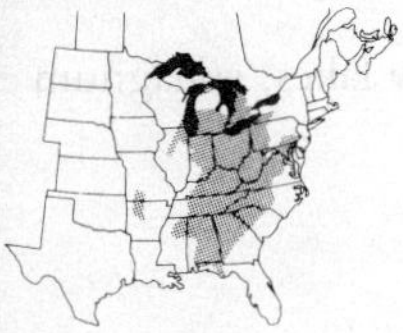

Range
Southern Great Lakes region and SE. Pennsylvania south to Gulf Coast. Isolated populations in N. Michigan and SW. Missouri and NW. Arkansas.

Comments
Active day and night, the Queen Snake is highly aquatic and an excellent swimmer; it drops into water when disturbed. This species feeds almost entirely on crayfish.

Eastern Ribbon Snake
Thamnophis sauritus
187

18–40″ (45.7–101.6 cm). A slender, streamlined garter snake. 3 bright, well-defined stripes usually contrast sharply with dark back and sides. Side stripe involves third and fourth scale rows. A dark, brownish stripe runs along margin of belly scales. Lip scales and belly unmarked. Tail very long, about a third of snake's total length. Scales strongly keeled.

Breeding
Mates in spring. Live-bearing. 3–26 young, 7–9″ (18–23 cm) long, are born July–August, mature in 2–3 years.

Habitat
Wet meadows, marshes, bogs, ponds, weedy lake shoreline, swamps, and shallow, meandering streams.

Range
East of the Mississippi River: Michigan, S. Ontario, and S. Maine, south to the Florida Keys and SE. Louisiana. Isolated colonies inhabit NE. Wisconsin and central Nova Scotia.

Subspecies
Eastern (*T. s. sauritus*), reddish-brown back, yellow side stripes, yellow- or green-tinged orange back stripe; S. Indiana, S. and E. Pennsylvania, SE. New York, and S. New

Hampshire, south to northern side of Lake Pontchartrain, Louisiana, Florida panhandle, and South Carolina.

Comments
This semiaquatic species is almost always encountered in low wet places. It likes to bask in bushes. When startled it takes to water. Unlike water snakes, ribbon snakes glide swiftly across the water's surface. They feed on frogs, salamanders, and small fish. Other subspecies occur within range.

Striped Crayfish Snake
Regina alleni
188

13–25¾″ (33–65.4 cm). Iridescent brown snake with wide yellow or orange stripe on lower side of body. 3 indistinct dark stripes on back; 1 down midline, others running along juncture of back and sides. Belly yellow to orange-brown, plain or marked with scattered dark smudges or with a well-defined row of spots along midline. Scales smooth (keeled on top of tail and in anal region). Scale in front of anus divided.

Breeding
Live-bearing; 6–34 young, 6–7″ (15–18 cm) long, are born June–August.

Habitat
Freshwater marshes, sloughs, canals, shallow lakes, sphagnum bogs, and waters choked by water hyacinth.

Range
S. Georgia and peninsular Florida.

Comments
Highly aquatic, it forages amid hyacinth roots and floating mats of vegetation. The Striped Crayfish Snake is occasionally seen crossing roads or lawns on rainy nights. It feeds on hard-shelled crayfish.

Brown Snake
Storeria dekayi
189

10–20¾″ (25.4–52.7 cm). Small; gray, yellowish brown, brown, or reddish brown, with 2 parallel rows of small dark spots bordering an indistinct wide light back stripe. Belly pale yellow, brown, or pinkish with small black dots along edges. Young have yellowish color. Scales keeled.

Breeding
Live-bearing. Mates spring and fall; 3–31 young, 3¼–4½″ (8–11.4 cm) long, are born June–September.

Habitat
Moist upland woodland to lowland freshwater and saltwater marshes; margins of swamps, bogs, and ponds; vacant lots, gardens, golf courses.

Range
S. Maine, S. Quebec, and S. Minnesota, south to lower Florida Keys, and through Texas and Mexico to Honduras.

Subspecies
Eight; 5 in our range. Intergradation occurs between races.

Comments
The Brown Snake is diurnal, but becomes nocturnal in warm weather. It hides under flat rocks, logs, or trash and is usually found near water or damp places. It feeds on earthworms, slugs, and snails. Large numbers may hibernate together.

Brown Water Snake
Nerodia taxispilota
190

28–69″ (71.1–175.3 cm). Heavy-bodied with large head. Brown to dark brown, with large squarish dark blotches down middle of back, alternating with row of similar blotches on each side. Yellow belly has many prominent dark spots, often arranged in broken rows along sides. Scales keeled.

Breeding
Mates April–May; 14–58 young are born June–October. Newborn are 7–11″ (18–28 cm) long.

Habitat
Lakes, rivers, streams, swamps, marshes, and ponds.

Range
Coastal Virginia through Florida to SW. Alabama.

Comments
This species is primarily active during the day, but is sometimes encountered foraging at night. It feeds on frogs and fishes caught among emergent vegetation along the shore. It is quite arboreal, basking and sleeping on limbs overhanging the water. When frightened it drops from its resting place into the water. It bites readily.

Southern Water Snake
Nerodia fasciata
191, 196

16–62½″ (40.6–158.8 cm). Stout-bodied aquatic snake with dark crossbands over most of body, light stripes on back and at juncture of back and sides, or essentially patternless. Color and pattern highly variable, like Northern Water Snake; where ranges overlap, presence of dark stripe from eye to angle of mouth and large squarish blotches or wormlike markings on belly scales will identify the Southern. Some darken with age.

Breeding
Live-bearing. Mates January–February in extreme southerly parts of range. 2–57 young, 7–10½″ (18–27 cm) long, are born June–August.

Habitat
Fresh- and saltwater situations; permanent lakes, ponds, cypress and mangrove swamps, marshes, and sluggish streams; sea level to about 1000′ (300 m).

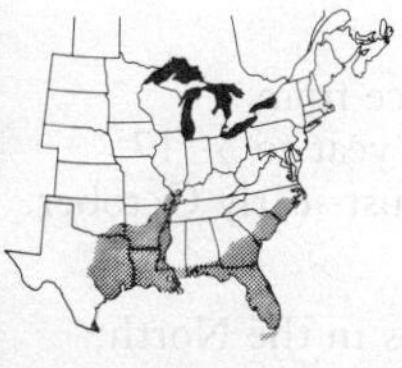

Range
Coastal plain, North Carolina to Florida Keys, west to E. Texas; north in Mississippi River Valley to extreme S. Illinois.

Subspecies
Several; 3 in freshwater wetlands of our range.
Banded (*N. f. fasciata*), red, brown, or black crossbands, most darken with age, squarish spots on belly; coastal plain, North

Carolina to Florida panhandle west to SW. Alabama.
Broad-banded (*N. f. confluens*), 11–17 broad dark crossbands, irregularly shaped yellow interspaces, large squarish blotches on belly; W. Alabama to E. Texas, north in Mississippi River Valley to extreme S. Illinois.
Florida (*N. f. pictiventris*), dark spots on side, wormlike red or black markings on belly; peninsular Florida; intergrades with Banded in panhandle and SE. Alabama; introduced into Brownsville, Texas.

Comments
This species is fond of sunning, but is active mostly at night after heavy rains when frogs are moving about. In cool weather it is often found under plant debris. Commonly mistaken for the venomous Cottonmouth, it defends itself vigorously when disturbed. It feeds on frogs, tadpoles, and fish. Interbreeds extensively with Northern Water Snake in parts of its range.

Kirtland's Snake
Clonophis kirtlandi
192

14–24½″ (35.5–62.2 cm). Slender brown or grayish snake with 2 rows of alternating dark squarish spots (often indistinct) on either side of midline of back and a line of round black spots along each side of red belly. Scales keeled.

Breeding
Early August–late September, female gives birth to 4–15 young, 5–6½″ (13–17 cm) long.

Habitat
Marshy meadows, woodland ponds, open swamplands.

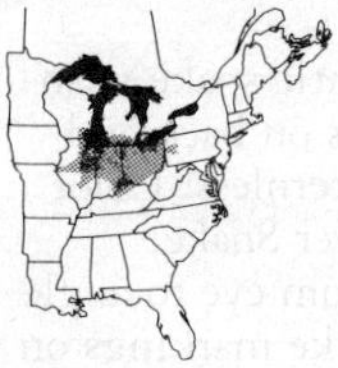

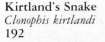

Range
West-central Pennsylvania west through Ohio, S. Michigan, N. Kentucky and Indiana to Illinois.

Comments
Kirtland's Snake dramatically flattens its body when frightened. Although this snake swims well, it is the least aquatic of the water snakes and is rarely encountered in the water. It is usually seen under flat rocks in wet meadows.

Timber Rattlesnake ⊗
Crotalus horridus
193, 197, 198

35–74½″ (88.9–189.2 cm). Northern forms range from yellow through brown or gray to black, with dark back and side blotches on front of body and blotches fused to form crossbands on rear of body. Head unmarked. Southern forms yellowish gray, brownish gray, or pinkish gray, with tan or reddish-brown back stripe dividing chevronlike crossbands; dark stripe behind eye. Both forms have black tail.

Breeding
Mates in autumn and shortly after emergence from hibernation. Female gives birth every other year to 5–17 young, 10–13″ (25–33 cm) long, late August–early October.

Habitat
Remote wooded hillsides with rock outcrops in the North;

unsettled swampy areas, canebrake thickets, and floodplains in the South; sea level to 6600′ (2000 m).

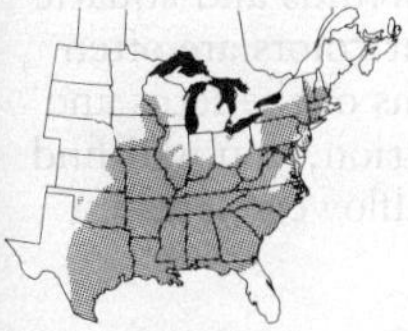

Range
Extreme SW. Maine south to N. Florida, west into SE. Minnesota and central Texas.

Comments
This species is active April to October; in the daytime in spring and fall, and at night during the summer. In northern areas, Timber Rattlesnakes congregate in large numbers about rocky den sites and may overwinter with rat snakes and Copperheads. The Timber Rattlesnake is often encountered coiled up waiting for prey. Until recently, southern populations were recognized as *C. h. atricaudatus,* the Canebrake Rattlesnake.

Northern Water Snake
Nerodia sipedon
195

22–53″ (55.9–134.6 cm). Reddish, brown, or gray to brownish black, with dark crossbands on neck region, and alternating dark blotches on back and sides at midbody. Pattern darkens with age, becoming black. Belly white, yellow, or gray, with reddish-brown or black crescent-shaped spots. No dark line from eye to corner of mouth.

Breeding
Mates April–June; 8–99 (typically 15–30) young are born August–October. Newborn are 6½–12″ (16.5–30 cm) long.

Habitat
Found in most aquatic situations from sea level to about 4800′ (1450 m); lakes, ponds, swamps, marshes, canals, ditches, bogs, streams, rivers; salt marshes of Carolina Outer Banks.

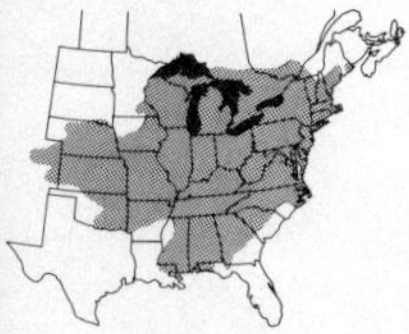

Range
Maine to coast of North Carolina, NW. South Carolina and Georgia to S. Alabama and E. Louisiana, west to E. Colorado and northeast through Minnesota to S. Ontario and Quebec.

Subspecies
Four; 2 widespread in freshwater wetlands of our range. Northern (*N. s. sipedon*), dark back markings wider than spaces between them; S. Maine to North Carolina, west to central Tennessee, N. Indiana, and Illinois, west to E. Colorado, northeast to Minnesota and S. Ontario and Quebec. Midland (*N. s. pleuralis*), dark back markings narrower than spaces between them; N. South Carolina and Georgia through Alabama to E. Louisiana, north to S. Indiana and Illinois, west to E. Oklahoma.

Comments
Active day and night, this snake frequently basks on rocks or stumps. It will flee if given the chance, but flattens its body and strikes repeatedly if cornered. Wounds from its bite bleed profusely because of an anticoagulant in the snake's saliva, but there is no poison. These snakes are often mistaken for venomous "water moccasins" and killed on sight.

WILDFLOWERS, FERNS, AND GRASSES

From early spring to late fall, the wetlands put on a brilliant display of color as thousands of wildflowers burst into bloom. Some are easily recognized; others, such as orchids and aquatic plants, may be less well known. Their bright colors are often especially noticeable against the darker greens of the ferns and grasses that carpet these habitats. In this section, you will find descriptions of some of the most typical wildflowers, grasses, and ferns of the wetlands.

Pussy Willow
Salix discolor
199

A large shrub or small tree with furry flower catkins that appear in the spring before the leaves.
Flowers: catkins with male flowers yellow, up to 2″ (5 cm) long; those with female flowers greenish, approximately 2½″ (6.3 cm) long; both age to yellow-brown; February–May.
Leaves: 2–4″ (5–10 cm) long, oblong to lanceolate, bright green above, whitish below, wavy-toothed above the middle.
Height: 2–20′ (60–600 cm).

Habitat
Damp thickets, swamps, and stream banks.

Range
Across Canada; south through New England to Maryland; west to Kentucky, Missouri, South Dakota.

Comments
For many people the appearance of these flower catkins signals the arrival of spring. The male catkins with their bright yellow stamens are especially showy compared to the more drab female catkins, which appear on separate plants.

Tufted Loosestrife
Lysimachia thyrsiflora
200

Erect stems bear evenly distributed leaves, and yellow flowers in dense, slender racemes in axils of leaves near midstem; entire plant is finely dotted with black or dark purple.
Flowers: corolla with 5 narrow lobes about ¼″ (6 mm) long, with narrow stalks leading to the united base; sepals and petals also dotted with dark purple; May–July.
Leaves: to 6″ (15 cm) long, opposite, lanceolate.
Height: 8–32″ (20–80 cm).

Habitat
Swamps, lakes, and ditches.

Range
N. California to N. Colorado; north throughout much of North America.

Comments
The tight racemes of yellow flowers immediately distinguish this species, the erect stamens giving a fuzzy appearance.

Spicebush
Lindera benzoin
201

A deciduous shrub with dense clusters of tiny, pale yellow flowers that bloom before the leaves from globose buds along the twigs.
Flowers: ⅛″ (3 mm) wide; sepals and petals all alike, 6. Male and female flowers occur on separate plants; March–April.
Leaves: 2–5½″ (5–13.8 cm) long; dark green, oblong, smooth, untoothed, and have an aromatic, spicy fragrance when crushed.
Fruit: ovoid, shiny, red, berrylike drupes.
Height: 6–17′ (1.8–5.1 m).

Habitat
Swamps and wet woods.

Range
Maine south to Florida; west to Texas; north to Missouri, Iowa, and Ontario.

Comments
In the North this plant is thought of as the "forsythia of the wilds" because its early spring flowering gives a subtle yellow tinge to many lowland woods where it is common.

Hooded Pitcher Plant
Sarracenia minor
202

Yellow flowers on a leafless stalk amid clustered, hollow, tubular leaves, patterned near the top with reddish veins and pale spots, expanding at summit into an overarching hood.
Flowers: about 2″ (5 cm) wide; petals 5; sepals 5; stamens numerous; pistil bears an umbrellalike style; spring.
Leaves: 6–24″ (15–60 cm) long, winged along one side.
Height: 6–24″ (15–60 cm), leaves taller than floral stalk.

Habitat
Low pinelands, marshes, bogs.

Range
Coastal plain; North Carolina south to Florida.

Comments
This is the most common of the Florida Pitcher Plants. Because of the hoodlike dome at the tip of the leaf, rain is not collected in this species. Instead, insects and other small organisms are lured up a nectar path on the wing of the leaves and into the hood where there are translucent spots through which the victims try to escape. Unable to do so, they eventually exhaust themselves and drop to the base of the leaf. The plant secretes a liquid that digests the organism and the resulting nutrients are then absorbed by the plant.

Fringed Loosestrife
Lysimachia ciliata
203

The erect stem, simple or branched, bears yellow flowers rising on stalks in the axils of opposite leaves with leafstalks fringed with spreading hairs.
Flowers: ¾″ (2 cm) wide, usually pointing outward or even downward; petals 5, minutely toothed and coming to a sharp point; stamens 10, 5 fertile and separate, 5 rudimentary; June–August.
Leaves: 2½–5″ (6.3–12.5 cm) long, lanceolate to ovate.
Height: 1–4′ (30–120 cm).

Habitat
Damp woods and thickets, floodplains, and marshes.

Range
E. Washington to Arizona; east across most of the United States to Texas, Georgia, Nova Scotia, and Quebec.

Comments
The species name emphasizes the hairy leafstalks of this wetland plant that is sometimes placed in the genus *Steironema*.

Swamp Candles
Lysimachia terrestris
204

The erect stem bears a terminal, spikelike cluster of yellow flowers with 2 red spots at the base of each petal.
Flowers: ½″ (1.3 cm) wide; petals 5 stamens 5; June–August.
Leaves: 1½–4″ (3.8–10 cm) long, lanceolate, opposite, sharp-pointed at both ends. Small, reddish bulblets often present in axils of leaves after flowering.
Height: 1–3′ (30–90 cm).

Habitat
Marshes, moist thickets, low grounds.

Range
Newfoundland, Nova Scotia, and Ontario; south through New England to Georgia; west to Kentucky and Arkansas; north to Iowa, Minnesota, and Manitoba.

Comments
In a wetland garden this showy species will spread rapidly by underground stems. Loomis' Loosestrife (*L. loomisii*), with candlelike clusters of yellow flowers and whorled, very narrow, 1″ (2.5 cm) long leaves, occurs from North Carolina to Georgia. Tufted Loosestrife (*L. thyrsiflora*) looks very different, with flower clusters borne from the axils of the lower leaves. It is found in swamps and bogs in much of Canada, south to New Jersey, west to West Virginia, Missouri, Colorado, and California.

Arrowleaf Groundsel
Senecio triangularis
205

Broadly or narrowly triangular or arrowhead-shaped leaves, with many sharp teeth on edges, grow on several leafy stems that bear yellow flower heads in a branched cluster at top.
Flowers: heads 1–1½″ (2.5–3.8 cm) wide, with about 8 rays ½″ (1.3 cm) long surrounding the small disk, and bracts mostly all the same length, about ½″ (1.3 cm) long, lined up side by side and not overlapping; June–September.
Leaves: 2–8″ (5–20 cm) long.
Fruit: seedlike, with a tuft of slender white hairs at top.
Height: 1–5′ (30–150 cm).

Habitat
Stream banks and other moist places in the mountains.

Range
Alaska and western Canada; south to S. California, Arizona, and New Mexico.

Comments
As indicated by the common and technical names, the triangular leaves are distinctive.

Nodding Bur Marigold
Bidens cernua
206

Numerous yellow flower heads nod as the flowers mature.
Flowers: heads to 2″ (5 cm) wide, usually with 6–8 yellow ray flowers, short in comparison to diameter of darker yellow disk; ray flowers occasionally lacking; August–October.
Leaves: 2–6″ (5–15 cm) long, simple, smooth, opposite, stalkless, narrowly lanceolate to elliptic.

Fruit: seedlike, 4-pronged, toothed.
Height: 1–3′ (30–90 cm).

Habitat

Swamps and wet ground.

Range

Nova Scotia to British Columbia; south to North Carolina and Tennessee; west through Oklahoma, New Mexico, and California.

Comments

The species name is Latin for "nodding." Bur Marigold seeds are sometimes eaten by ducks.

Golden Ragwort
Senecio aureus
207

Smooth plant with yellow daisylike flower heads in flat-topped clusters.
Flowers: ¾″ (2 cm) wide, each head with 8–12 yellow ray flowers and yellow central disk flowers; April–July.
Leaves: basal leaves ½–6″ (1.3–15 cm) long, heart-shaped, with long stalks, rounded teeth; upper stem leaves 1–3½″ (2.5–9 cm) long, pinnately lobed.
Height: 1–2′ (30–60 cm).

Habitat

Wet meadows, swamps, and moist woods.

Range

S. Ontario to Newfoundland; New England south to South Carolina and upland Alabama; west to Missouri; north to North Dakota.

Comments

There are numerous other species in this genus, many of which are typical of uplands.

Yellow Butterwort
Pinguicula lutea
208

A solitary, yellow flower blooms at the end of a leafless, glandular stalk rising from a basal rosette of yellow-green, sticky leaves.
Flowers: 1″ (2.5 cm) wide; tubular, with 5 flattish lobes, the lower lobe tonguelike and spurred; February–May.
Leaves: to 2½″ (6.3 cm) long, lying flat against the ground; ovate to oblong, with rolled edges.
Height: 5–18″ (12.5–45 cm).

Habitat

Moist sandy sites.

Range

Coastal NE. North Carolina south to S. Georgia and Florida; west to SE. Louisiana.

Comments

The sticky leaves of this plant trap insects, which are digested by enzymes secreted by the leaves, and then absorbed as nutrients.

Cowslip
Caltha palustris
209

A succulent plant with glossy, heart- or kidney-shaped leaves and a thick, hollow, branching stem with bright, shiny yellow flowers.
Flowers: 1–1½″ (2.5–3.8 cm) wide; petal-like sepals 5–9; no petals; numerous stamens and pistils; April–June.
Leaves: basal ones 2–7″ (5–17.5 cm) wide, stalked, dark green, shallowly toothed; upper leaves becoming stalkless.
Fruit: in a whorl, each fruit splitting open along one side (follicle).
Height: 1–2′ (30–60 cm).

Habitat
Swamps, marshes, wet meadows, along streams and brooks.

Range
Across Canada; south through New England to North Carolina; west to Tennessee, Iowa, and Nebraska.

Comments
The flowers of this showy spring plant resemble large Buttercups rather than the Marigolds. The leaves are sometimes used as potherbs but require several short boilings with changes of water between. They should not be eaten raw. A smaller species, Floating Marsh Marigold (*C. natans*), found from Alaska southeastward to northern Minnesota, has small white or pinkish flowers and kidney-shaped leaves.

Yellow-eyed Grass
Xyris iridifolia
210

A tufted plant with flat, linear, Irislike leaves and a floral stalk terminated by a reddish-brown, oval head with scalelike bracts enclosing yellow flowers.
Flowers: about ½″ (1.3 cm) wide; petals 3; stamens 6, 3 normal and 3 tufted, sterile; July–September.
Leaves: 16–32″ (40–80 cm) long, about ½″ (1 cm) wide.
Height: 2–3′ (60–90 cm).

Habitat
Wet peat or sand.

Range
North Carolina south to Florida; west to Texas.

Comments
This large southern species is one of more than 15 in the United States. They are grasslike, wetland plants with distinctive conelike heads of overlapping scales in which the flowers are set. The different species are very similar and distinguishing them is difficult without a technical manual. The smaller, widespread Slender Yellow-eyed Grass (*X. torta*) grows to a height of 1′ (30 cm) and has erect, narrow, twisted, needlelike leaves, and tufts of hairs on the flower head.

Swamp Buttercup
Ranunculus septentrionalis
211

Arching or reclining, hollow stems bear bright, glossy, yellow flowers.
Flowers: 1″ (2.5 cm) wide; sepals 5; petals 5, showy; stamens and pistils numerous; April–July.

Leaves: divided into 3-lobed segments, each 1½–4″ (3.8–10 cm) long, on short stalks.
Fruit: dry, seedlike, with winged margins and birdlike beaks, in a globose cluster.
Height: 1–3′ (30–90 cm).

Habitat
Moist woods, thickets, and meadows.

Range
Manitoba to Quebec; south through New England to Maryland; west to Kentucky and Missouri.

Comments
A native, weak-stemmed Buttercup, it is typical of swamps and marshes. Twenty to 30 species of Buttercups are found in a variety of habitats; all are pollinated by flies and bees.

Yellow Water Buttercup
Ranunculus flabellaris
212

An aquatic plant with golden-yellow flowers extending above the water on stout, hollow stems.
Flowers: ½–1½″ (1.3–3.8 cm) wide; sepals 5; petals 5, longer than sepals; stamens and pistils numerous; May–June.
Leaves: submerged ones 1–3″ (2.5–7.5 cm) long, divided into hairlike segments; emerged leaves (when present) ½–2″ (1.3–5 cm) wide, repeatedly divided and lobed.
Fruit: dry, seedlike, in a globose head.
Height: aquatic, with stem to 2′ (60 cm) high.

Habitat
Quiet waters and muddy shores.

Range
Across Canada; south from Maine to North Carolina; west to Louisiana, Kansas, and California.

Comments
Usually found in quiet waters, this plant, with the typical Buttercup flower, occasionally grows on wet shores. In a similar habitat we may find White Water Buttercup (*R. longirostris*), with 5 white petals and submerged leaves.

Swollen Bladderwort
Utricularia inflata
213

A carnivorous, aquatic plant with several yellow flowers on a stem that rises above the water over a wheel-like float of inflated leafstalks.
Flowers: ⅔″ (1.6 cm) wide; 2-lipped; May–November.
Leaves: floating ones to 3″ (8 cm) long; repeatedly divided into threadlike segments; submerged leaves with small, ovoid bladders on some segments.
Height: aquatic, with flower stalks 1½–8″ (3.8–20 cm).

Habitat
Ponds and ditches.

Range
Nova Scotia and New England south to Florida; west to Texas; north to Tennessee; northwest to Indiana.

Comments
When swimming prey, such as minute crustaceans, touch the trigger hairs surrounding the mouth of one of the bladders, a trapdoorlike flap of tissue swings open and the bladder quickly expands, sucking the organisms inside. Enzymes are secreted to dissolve the prey into nutritional elements for the plant.

Yellow Pond Lily
Nuphar variegatum
214

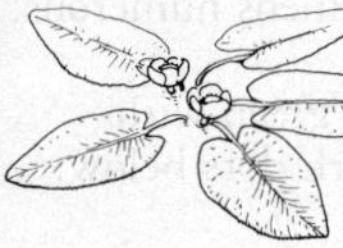

A floating aquatic plant with yellow, cuplike flowers.
Flowers: 1½–2½″ (3.8–6.3 cm) wide; corolla composed of 6 showy, petal-like sepals and numerous small, yellow, stamenlike petals; stamens numerous, in several rows; pistil greenish, disklike, compound, with numerous united parts (carpels) and 7–25 radiating stigmatic surfaces; May–September.
Leaves: 3–15″ (7.5–37.5 cm) long; mostly floating on water, heart-shaped, with V-shaped notch at base.
Height: aquatic.

Habitat
Pond margins and quiet streams.

Range
Across Canada; south to New England, Delaware, and Maryland; west to Ohio, Indiana, Illinois, Iowa, Nebraska, South Dakota, and beyond.

Comments
This is the most familiar yellow Pond Lily in the Northeast. Common Spatterdock (*N. advena*) is very similar, but its leaves are frequently raised above the water. It occurs in the southern United States and as far north as New England, New York, Ohio, Michigan, and Wisconsin. A smaller species, Small Pond Lily (*N. microphyllum*), has leaves only 2–4″ (5–10 cm) long, flowers 1″ (2.5 cm) wide, and a stigmatic disk with 6–10 rays. It occurs in Canada and only as far south as New Jersey. Arrow-leaf Pond Lily (*N. sagittifolium*), found from Virginia to northeast South Carolina, has leaves 3 times as long as they are wide. The leaves and long, stemlike petioles of the Water Lilies and Pond Lilies die back each year and contribute to the organic buildup in lakes and marshes.

American Lotus
Nelumbo lutea
215

An aquatic plant with fragrant, pale yellow flowers and bowl-shaped leaves borne on stalks above the water.
Flowers: 6–10″ (15–25 cm) wide; numerous petals and petal-like sepals intergrade into one another; stamens many. Center of flower has large, convex receptacle, 3–4″ (7.5–10 cm) long, with numerous cavities, each containing a pistil; July–September.
Leaves: 1–2′ (30–60 cm) wide; leafstalk attached in middle.
Height: aquatic, with leaves to 3′ (90 cm) above water.

Habitat
Ponds and quiet streams.

Range
S. Ontario to southern New England and New York; south to Florida; west to Texas; north to Iowa and Minnesota.

Comments
This member of the Water Lily group is recognized by large, umbrellalike leaves and the inverted, conelike structure in the middle of the flowers. It covers extensive areas along the Mississippi River from Iowa to Wisconsin and southward.

Yellow Water Lily
Nymphaea mexicana
216

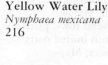

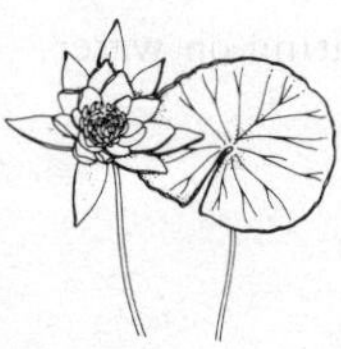

An aquatic plant with bright yellow flowers and floating leaves.
Flowers: 4–5″ (10–12.5 cm) wide, rising about 4″ (10 cm) above the water; sepals 4, green; petals and stamens numerous; spring–summer.
Leaves: 3–5″ (7.5–12.5 cm) wide; ovate, dark green with brown blotches on top, reddish brown with dark dots below.
Height: aquatic.

Habitat
Quiet water, ponds, and ditches.

Range
South Carolina, Florida, and Mexico.

Comments
The lovely flowers are open from midday to late afternoon. When the plants are crowded, the leaves may rise above the water. The plant was first discovered in Mexico, which accounts for the species name. It is also known as the Sun-lotus or Banana Water Lily.

Seep-spring Monkeyflower
Mimulus guttatus
217

An extremely variable, leafy plant ranging from spindly and tiny to large and bushy, with yellow bilaterally symmetrical flowers on slender stalks in upper leaf axils.
Flowers: corolla ½–1½″ (1.3–3.8 cm) long, often with reddish spots near opening, 2 lobes of upper lip bent upward, the 3 lobes of lower lip bent downward; at base of lower lip is a hairy hump that almost closes the opening; March–September.
Leaves: ½–4″ (1.3–10 cm) long, ovate, opposite, edges with sharp teeth.
Height: to 3′ (90 cm).

Habitat
Wet places from sea level to mountains.

Range
Throughout the West; naturalized locally in brooks and meadows of Connecticut and New York.

Comments
In this large genus of several look-alikes with yellow corollas, Seep-spring Monkeyflower is distinguished by the longer upper tooth on the angular calyx.

Horned Bladderwort
Utricularia cornuta
218

The brownish stalk of this carnivorous plant has a few scalelike bracts and 1–5 yellowish, 2-lipped flowers near the summit.
Flowers: about ¾″ (2 cm) long; lower lip large, helmet-shaped, with a pendant spur; June–September.
Leaves: minute, threadlike, underground, seldom seen, occasionally on the surface, bearing minute bladders.
Height: 2–12″ (5–30 cm).

Habitat
Wet, sandy, muddy, or peaty shores; bogs.

Range
Ontario to Nova Scotia; south to Pennsylvania; west to Illinois, Wisconsin, and Minnesota. Also North Carolina south to Florida, and in E. Texas.

Comments
This species differs from many other bladderworts in being terrestrial rather than aquatic, although it may occasionally be submerged. It is able to suck very small organisms in through the bladders and digest them.

Yellow Flag
Iris pseudacorus
219

One to several yellow flowers, on a robust stalk, often overtopped by the long, stiff, swordlike leaves; often found in clumps.
Flowers: 3″ (7.5 cm) wide; sepals 3, backward-curving, nonbearded; petals 3, smaller, narrow, upright; styles 3, arching over sepals, with 3 stamens beneath; June–August.
Leaves: to 3′ (90 cm) tall; arising from a basal cluster and often taller than the stem.
Fruit: 6-angled, oblong capsule, about 2″ (5 cm) long.
Height: 2–3′ (60–90 cm).

Habitat
Marshes, stream margins.

Range
Newfoundland west to Minnesota and southward, widely established.

Comments
This is a showy species. It was introduced from Europe and escaped from cultivation.

Common Cattail
Typha latifolia
220

This tall, stiff plant bears a yellowish, clublike spike of tiny, male flowers extending directly above a brownish cylinder of female flowers.
Flowers: calyx and corolla represented by bristles. Male and female flowers on separate spikes, each to 6″ (15 cm) long. Female flowers with 1 stalked pistil; male flowers usually with 3 stamens. Male flowers fade after pollen is shed, leaving bare stalk; May–July.
Leaves: up to 1″ (2.5 cm) wide and taller than the stem, swordlike, flat, sheathing the stem.
Height: 3–9′ (90–270 cm).

Habitat
Freshwater marshes.

Range
Newfoundland to Alaska; throughout most of United States; also Mexico.

Comments
By its creeping rootstocks, this typical marsh perennial forms dense stands in shallow water and provides a favorable habitat for red-winged blackbirds, as well as other marsh birds, and muskrats. The latter can cause extensive "eat outs," creating areas of open water in the marsh. The rootstock is mostly starch and edible; it was ground into meal by Indians, and the early colonists also used it for food. The young shoots can be eaten like asparagus, the immature flower spikes can be boiled and eaten like corn on the cob, and the sprouts at the tip of the rootstock can be used in salads or boiled and served as greens. The related Narrow-leaved Cattail (*T. angustifolia*) has narrower leaves, up to ½″ (1.3 cm) across, a narrower fruiting head, less than ¾″ (2 cm) wide, and a gap between the male and female flower clusters.

Sweetflag
Acorous calamus
221

This plant emerges from the water with a 2-edged stalk, and an outward-jutting clublike spadix bearing tiny, greenish-yellow flowers.
Flowers: clustered in diamond-shaped patterns on a spadix 2–3½″ (5–9 cm) long; typical spathe lacking; May–August.
Leaves: 1–4′ (30–120 cm) long, stiff, light green, swordlike.
Fruit: small, gelatinous berries that eventually dry.
Height: aquatic, leaves above water 1–4′ (30–120 cm).

Habitat
Swamps, marshes, riverbanks, and small streams.

Range
Nova Scotia; south to North Carolina; west to Texas and Oregon coast.

Comments
This plant, which grows partly in and partly out of the water, reproduces by underground rootstalks that have a sweet odor and flavor and were once used for making candy. All parts of the plant are fragrant when bruised.

Golden Club
Orontium aquaticum
222

An aquatic with long-stalked leaves, and a golden-yellow, clublike spadix.
Flowers: minute, clustered on spadix, 1–2″ (2.5–5 cm) long, with 4–6 sepals, 6 stamens; undeveloped spathe appears as narrow leaf sheath; April–June.
Leaves: blades 5–12″ (13–30 cm) long, elliptical, veined, dark green, extending above or floating upon water.
Fruit: blue-green, bladderlike.
Height: aquatic, 1–2′ (30–60 cm) above waterline.

Habitat
Shallow waters of marshes, swamps, and ponds.

Range
Massachusetts and central New York south to Florida and west to Louisiana, chiefly along coastal plain; inland to Kentucky and West Virginia.

Comments
This emergent perennial is of striking beauty, especially when seen against the backdrop of dark open waters in southern swamps. Its Latin generic name derives from a plant that grows in the Orontes River of Syria.

Yellow Skunk Cabbage
Lysichitum americanum
223

A spike of minute flowers surrounded by a large, conspicuous yellow or cream bract open on one side; grows on a stout stalk in a cluster of giant, erect leaves.
Flowers: bract to 8″ (20 cm) long, often appearing before leaves are fully developed; tiny flowers inconspicuous; April–July, often as the snow melts.
Leaves: 1–5′ (30–150 cm) long, the stalks usually much shorter than the oval blades.
Height: 12–20″ (30–50 cm).

Habitat
Swampy soil.

Range
Alaska to near the coast in central California, east to Montana.

Comments
The common name refers to the skunklike odor of the sap and the fetid odor of the flowers, which draws flies as pollinators. Long ago the peppery sap was used to treat ringworm. The short, fleshy underground stem is eaten by animals. Baked, it supplemented the winter diets of Indians.

Trumpets
Sarracenia flava
224

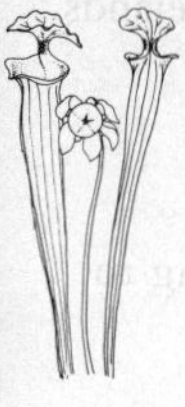

A carnivorous plant with showy, bright yellow, drooping flowers and erect, trumpet-shaped, hollow, inflated leaves; flower has musty odor.
Flowers: 3–5″ (7.5–12.5 cm) wide; sepals 5; petals 5; stamens numerous; style large, disklike; April–May.
Leaves: 1–3′ (30–90 cm) high; hood, purple at constricted neck, arches over opening that collects water.
Height: 1½–3½′ (45–105 cm), flower stalk equal to or taller than leaves.

Habitat
Wet pinelands, bogs.

Range
SE. Virginia south to Florida; west to Alabama.

Comments
A southern plant with hollow leaves that fill with water in which insects and other small organisms drown; their soft

parts are then digested by the plant. A similar species, Trumpet Pitcher Plant (*S. alata*), with fiddle-shaped petals and leaves without the purple constriction at the base of the hood, is found from Alabama to eastern Texas.

Water Arum
Calla palustris
225

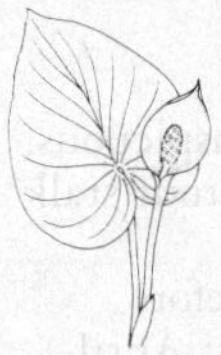

Growing in water among oblong heart-shaped leaves is a broad white spathe around a spadix covered with tiny yellow flowers.
Flowers: clustered on yellow spadix 1″ (2.5 cm) long, inside white, rolled-edge spathe 2″ (5 cm) long; late May–August.
Leaves: usually up to 6″ (15 cm) long, numerous, long-stemmed, glossy dark green.
Fruit: red clustered berries in late summer and autumn.
Height: aquatic, stem above water 6–12″ (15–30 cm).

Habitat
Cool, boggy wetlands and pond edges.

Range
Nova Scotia to Hudson Bay; south to New Jersey and Pennsylvania; west to Minnesota.

Comments
This perennial is a more northerly species than the other arums. It is very showy when in flower, and later when bearing its fruit. The genus name *Calla,* its meaning uncertain, was used by Pliny; the species epithet *palustris* means "of marshes."

White-topped Sedge
Dichromena colorata
226

The spikelets are in a globose cluster enclosed at the base by a set of 5 or 6 long, drooping, white bracts with green tips.
Stem triangular.
Flowers: enclosed in oblong, whitish scales in a spikelet about ¼″ (6 mm) long. Spikelets in a cluster to ⅔″ (1.6 cm) wide. Perianth or petals lacking; stamens 6; style 2-cleft. Bracts under inflorescence widely spreading, unequal, to 3″ (7.5 cm) long; March–November.
Leaves: about 1/12″ (2 mm) wide; grasslike, shorter than the stalk.
Height: 8–24″ (20–60 cm).

Habitat
Brackish or calcareous swamps and marshes, moist pinelands.

Range
Virginia south to Florida; west to Texas.

Comments
The whitish bracts on this sedge are sufficiently striking to make one think it has showy, daisylike flowers.

Swamp Lily
Crinum americanum
227

Small cluster of fragrant, stringy white flowers on a leafless stalk that rises from basal leaves.
Flowers: 4″ (10 cm) wide; 6 narrow, petal-like lobes attached to a long green floral tube; stamens 6, reddish-purple

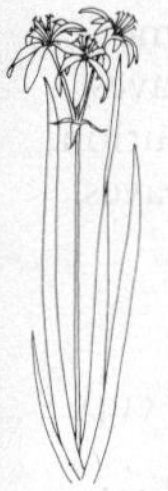

filaments; periodically throughout the year, chiefly spring–fall.
Leaves: to 4′ (1.2 m) long, 1–3″ (2.5–7.5 cm) wide, straplike.
Height: to 3′ (90 cm).

Habitat
Marshes and stream banks.

Range
Along coastal plain, Florida to Texas.

Comments
Despite its common name, this beautiful flower is not a true Lily but a member of the Amaryllis Family. Its floral parts are attached above the ovary rather than below as in Lilies.

Spider Lily
Hymenocallis liriosme
228

Few spidery white flowers borne on 2-edged stalk above basal leaves.
Flowers: to 7″ (17.5 cm) wide, each a long slender tube with 6 radiating lobes (comprising 3 petals and 3 petal-like sepals), inside which is a cup, or crown, of white gauzy tissue from which 6 stamens issue; March–May.
Leaves: to ½″ (1.3 cm) wide, 1′ (30 cm) or more long, straplike, deeply grooved.
Height: 1½′ (45 cm).

Habitat
Marshes and ditches.

Range
Louisiana west to Texas.

Comments
A showy southern member of the Amaryllis Family whose cuplike structure, the "hymen" or membrane, from which the stamens arise, is distinctive, as is the spidery appearance of the long petal-like parts. The species name means "fragrant lily."

Swamp Honeysuckle
Rhododendron viscosum
229

A deciduous shrub with hairy twigs and clusters of fragrant, white, vase-shaped flowers.
Flowers: 1½–2″ (3.8–5 cm) long; corolla 5-lobed, with reddish, sticky hairs; stamens 5, long, curved, projecting beyond corolla; style 1, longer than stamens; June–August.
Leaves: 1–2½″ (2.5–6.3 cm) long; obovate, glossy above, often whitish beneath, with hairs on midrib.
Height: 3–9′ (90–270 cm).

Habitat
Swamps.

Range
Maine south to Georgia; west to Texas.

Comments
This typical wetland shrub is sometimes called the Clammy

Azalea because of its very sticky corolla. The species name means "sticky" in Latin. The flowers appear after the leaves. Another white wetland species of more southern distribution, the Smooth Azalea (*R. arborescens*), has smooth twigs, leaves without hairs, and red stamens.

Great Laurel
Rhododendron maximum
230

A large evergreen shrub with clusters of pinkish-white, cup-shaped flowers on glandular and sticky stalks.
Flowers: 1½–2″ (3.8–5 cm) wide, with 5 blunt corolla lobes; June–July.
Leaves: 4–8″ (10–20 cm) long; leathery, smooth, elliptic-oblong, pointed at base and tip, dark green above, often paler and closely hairy below.
Fruit: smooth brown capsule.
Height: 5–35′ (1.5–10.5 m).

Habitat
Damp woods and forested wetlands.

Range
Maine south to Georgia and Alabama; north to Ohio and S. Pennsylvania; most common from Pennsylvania southward.

Comments
This tall, straggly shrub often forms impenetrable thickets on moist slopes or in swamps. It is frequently used as an ornamental for its showy flowers and handsome foliage. The leaves droop in frost and may curl under lengthwise; the colder the temperature, the tighter the roll. The hard wood may be used for making tools and ornaments.

Turtlehead
Chelone glabra
231

This smooth plant has tight terminal clusters of white (often lavender-tinged), tubular, 2-lipped flowers resembling turtle heads.
Flowers: 1–1½″ (2.5–3.8 cm) long; upper lip arches over hairy lower lip; stamens 4, plus 1 short, sterile stamen; July–September.
Leaves: 3–6″ (8–15 cm) long, opposite, lanceolate, sharply toothed.
Height: 1–3′ (30–90 cm).

Habitat
Wet thickets, stream banks, and low ground.

Range
Ontario to Nova Scotia; south through New England to Georgia; west to Missouri; north to Minnesota.

Comments
The distinctive shape of this flower is reflected in the genus name, derived from the Greek *chelone* ("a tortoise").

Delicate Ionopsis
Ionopsis utricularioides
232

Medium-size, epiphytic orchid producing small bulbs and showy, pinkish-lavender flowers on a loose stalk.
Flowers: ¾″ (2 cm) wide; lavender, spotted and striped with purple; March–April.
Leaves: 1–3, oblong, linear, 4–8″ (10–20 cm) long.
Fruit: capsule, 3-ribbed, ½–1½″ (1.3–3.8 cm) long.
Height: 4–15″ (10–40 cm).

Habitat
Cypress swamps and hammocks.

Range
Florida, West Indies, Mexico, South America.

Comments
This sun-loving orchid is found on exterior branches and often dangles from the tip by long, slender rootlets. Great numbers of flowers can produce the illusion of mist or fog along streams or sloughs.

Umbrella Plant
Peltiphyllum peltatum
233

This plant forms large masses of nearly round, jaggedly toothed leaf blades on rough, hairy stalks; small, pink flowers in large, round, branched clusters grow on stalks slightly taller than leaves.
Flowers: petals 5, pink or white, about ¼″ (6 mm) long; stamens 10; pistil with 2 reddish-purple sections; April–June.
Leaves: to 16″ (40 cm) wide.
Height: 2–6′ (60–180 cm).

Habitat
In and along edges of cold streams.

Range
Central Oregon to central California.

Comments
The luxuriant foliage of this plant sometimes gives a verdant, almost tropical aspect to mountain streams.

Labrador Tea
Ledum groenlandicum
234

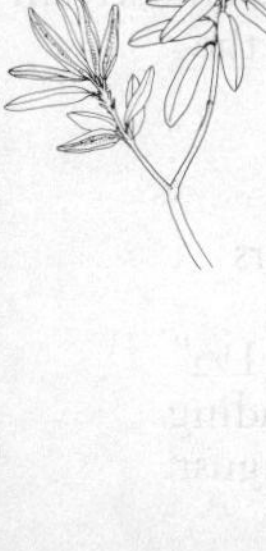

A low, evergreen shrub with densely hairy twigs and rounded terminal clusters of white flowers.
Flowers: ⅓–½″ (8–13 mm) wide; petals 5, spreading; June–August.
Leaves: 1–2″ (2.5–5 cm) long; evergreen, narrow, oblong, rusty-woolly beneath, with rolled margins, slightly fragrant when crushed.
Fruit: 5-valved capsule on a recurved stalk.
Height: 1–4′ (30–120 cm).

Habitat
Peaty soils, especially bogs.

Range
Across Canada to Newfoundland; south to New England and N. New Jersey; west to Ohio; north to Michigan, Wisconsin, and Minnesota.

Comments
This boreal shrub, typical of acidic boggy areas, can easily be recognized by the woolly brown undersurfaces of its leaves. A pleasant tea can be made from them, and they were used for this purpose during the American Revolution.

Sweet Pepperbush
Clethra alnifolia
235

A tall, many-branched, leafy shrub with spikelike, upright clusters of fragrant white flowers.
Flowers: each about ⅓″ (8 mm) wide; stamens 10, style protruding; July–September.
Leaves: up to 3″ (7.5 cm) long; wedge-shaped, sharply toothed above the middle, untoothed at base.
Fruit: small, globular capsules with persistent style.
Height: 3–10′ (90–300 cm).

Habitat
Wetlands, especially swamps, and sandy woods.

Range
Coastal, from S. Maine south to Florida; west to E. Texas.

Comments
This shrub forms sizable patches. Its dry fruiting capsules remain long after flowering and help identify this plant in winter.

Lizard's Tail
Saururus cernuus
236

Many tiny, fragrant, white flowers are on a slender, tapering, stalked spike with a drooping tip.
Flowers: spike to 6″ (15 cm) long; sepals and petals absent; stamens 6–8, showy, about ⅙″ (4 mm) long; pistils 3–4, united; June–September.
Leaves: 3–6″ (7.5–15 cm) long, heart-shaped, indented at base.
Fruit: fleshy, wrinkled.
Height: 2–5′ (60–150 cm).

Habitat
Swamps and shallow water.

Range
Ontario to Rhode Island, Connecticut, and New York; south to Florida; west to Texas, Missouri, and Kansas; north to Illinois and Michigan.

Comments
This is a mostly southern species of shaded marshes and stream margins. The common name refers to the shape of the drooping flower cluster.

Buttonbush
Cephalanthus occidentalis
237

An aquatic shrub with small, white, tubular flowers collectively forming globose "balls."
Flowers: about ⅓″ (8 mm) long, in clusters about 1½″ (3.8 cm) in diameter. Corolla with 4 erect or spreading lobes; stamens 4; style long, protruding; June–August.

Leaves: 3–6″ (7.5–15 cm) long, opposite or whorled, ovate, untoothed, pointed.
Height: 3–10′ (90–300 cm).

Habitat
Swamps, borders of ponds and streams.

Range
S. Ontario to Nova Scotia; south through New England to Florida; west to Texas and beyond; north to Minnesota.

Comments
This species is noted for its ability to withstand flood conditions. The distinctive, ball-like flower and fruit heads account for the common name. The fruits have some appeal to wildlife, especially mallard ducks.

Cotton Grass
Eriophorum polystachion
238

Extensive patches of erect stems with grasslike leaves, topped by 2–8 white, cottony heads in a cluster.
Flowers: cluster of heads 2–3″ (5–7.5 cm) wide; small brownish or blackish scales around base of each individual head in cluster, each scale with a midrib that does not reach tip; July–August.
Leaves: 6–20″ (15–50 cm) long.
Height: 8–40″ (20–100 cm).

Habitat
Cold swamps and bogs.

Range
Throughout the Northern Hemisphere, south to central Oregon, Idaho, NE. Utah, and N. New Mexico.

Comments
The name comes from the Greek for "wool-bearing." The slender bristles of "cotton" are actually modified sepals and petals of minute flowers. There are several similar species.

Common Pipewort
Eriocaulon septangulare
239

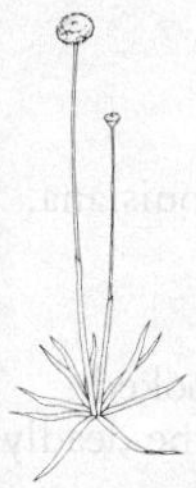

The 7-sided, leafless floral stalk with a grayish-white, knoblike flower head at its summit emerges from the water above a submerged tuft of grasslike basal leaves.
Flowers: about 1⁄12″ (2 mm) long, in a head up to ½″ (1.3 cm) wide; petals 2; flowers interspersed with bracts; bracts also present beneath heads; July–September.
Leaves: 1–4″ (2.5–10 cm) long.
Height: 1½–9″ (3.8–22.5 cm).

Habitat
Still water, edges of ponds and lakes.

Range
Ontario to Nova Scotia; south from New England to Delaware and central Virginia; west to Indiana; north to Minnesota.

Comments
This striking wetland plant with cottony, buttonlike flower

heads is the most common and widespread of several species of Pipeworts. The alternate common name Hatpins is especially appropriate to its overall appearance.

Water Hemlock
Cicuta maculata
240

Smooth, erect, highly branched plant bearing dome-shaped, loose clusters of small white flowers. The sturdy stem is magenta-streaked.
Flowers: florets about ⅙″ (4 mm) long; no bracts beneath flattened umbels, 3″ (7.5 cm) wide; June–September.
Leaves: lower ones to 1′ (30 cm) long, doubly divided, sharp-pointed, toothed, veins ending at notches between the teeth.
Fruit: round, flat, with thick ridges.
Height: 3–6′ (90–180 cm).

Habitat
Wet meadows, thickets, and freshwater swamps.

Range
S. Ontario to Nova Scotia; south through New England to Florida; west to Texas; north through Missouri to Canada.

Comments
Even a very small quantity of this highly poisonous plant can cause death. Its roots have been mistaken for parsnips and other common root crops, with fatal results; cattle, horses, and sheep have died from grazing on it. The plant is not related to true Hemlock (*Tsuga* spp.), but to Poison Hemlock (*Conium maculatum*), the plant used to poison Socrates. In this range it grows as an introduced species, and has a more finely cut compound leaf.

Water Parsnip
Sium suave
241

Fragrant, sometimes aquatic plant with flat clusters of tiny dull white flowers and strongly ridged stems.
Flowers: in clusters (compound umbels) 2–3″ (5–7.5 cm) wide, with narrow, leaflike bracts below umbels; July–September.
Leaves: 4–10″ (10–25 cm) long, pinnately compound; divided into 3–7 pairs of lanceolate, toothed leaflets, with basal ones often submerged and finely cut, 2½–5½″ (6.3–14 cm) long.
Fruit: tiny, ovate, with prominent ribs.
Height: 2–6′ (60–180 cm).

Habitat
Wet meadows and thickets, muddy shores.

Range
Nova Scotia to British Columbia; south to Florida, Louisiana, and California.

Comments
The roots of this plant can be boiled and eaten as a cooked vegetable, but because of the plant's resemblance to the deadly Water Hemlock (*Cicuta maculata*), it is best left alone.

Elderberry
Sambucus canadensis
242

Smooth-stemmed shrub with pinnately compound leaves and flat-topped clusters of tiny, white, fragrant flowers; twigs have large white pith and prominent warty spots (lenticels) on bark.
Flowers: ⅙″ (4 mm) wide, in clusters 2–10″ (5–25 cm) wide; corolla 5-lobed; June–July.
Leaves: opposite, pinnately cut into 5–11 elliptic to lanceolate, toothed leaflets, each 2–6″ (5–15 cm) long.
Fruit: purplish black, berrylike drupes, in clusters.
Height: 3–12′ (90–360 cm).

Habitat
Low ground, wet areas, and borders of fields and copses.

Range
Manitoba to Nova Scotia; south from New England to Florida; west to Louisiana and Oklahoma; north to Minnesota.

Comments
This soft, woody species yields fruit that makes tasty jelly and wine. It is also an important food source for many songbirds and game birds. The genus name comes from Greek *sambuce,* an ancient musical instrument, and refers to the soft pith, easily removed from the twigs and used to make flutes and whistles.

Titi
Cyrilla racemiflora
243

A shrub or small tree with terminal, fingerlike clusters of numerous small white flowers.
Flowers: about ⅕″ (5 mm) wide; clusters 2½–6″ (6.3–15 cm) long; petals 5, pointed; sepals 5, white; June–July.
Leaves: 2–5″ (5–12.5 cm) long; shiny, elliptic, leathery.
Fruit: brownish yellow, berrylike drupe.
Height: to 25′ (7.5 m).

Habitat
Swamps, low pinelands, along watercourses.

Range
Coastal plain, Virginia to Florida; west to Texas.

Comments
This shrub is particularly beautiful in the fall when its foliage turns scarlet or orange. Buckwheat Tree, or Black Titi (*Cliftonia monophylla*), which occurs in southern wetlands, has wider flower clusters and small 4-winged fruits. Also called Leatherwood.

Winterberry
Ilex verticillata
244, 328

A deciduous holly shrub with very small white flowers that grow in the leaf axils.
Flowers: in clusters ¼–½″ (6–13 mm) wide, each flower 4- to 6-parted; June–August.
Leaves: 2″ (5 cm) long, elliptical, toothed but not spiny.
Fruit: berrylike, showy red, less than ¼″ (6 mm) wide, on very short stalks, singly or in small clusters along the branches.
Height: 3–10′ (90–300 cm).

Habitat
Swamps, damp thickets, and pond margins.

Range
Ontario to Nova Scotia; south from New England to Georgia; west to Mississippi; north to Tennessee, Missouri, Michigan, and Minnesota.

Comments
Extremely showy in late fall and early winter when covered with their bright red fruit, these shrubs are either male or female—a trait typical of the Holly Family. Birds are readily attracted to them.

Watercress
Nasturtium officinale
245

The leafy, branched stems of this plant mostly float in water or lie on mud, their tiny white flowers blooming in short racemes on the upturned tips.
Flowers: petals 4, about 3/16″ (5 mm) long; March–October.
Leaves: 1½–5″ (3.8–12.5 cm) long, pinnate, leaflets ovate, terminal leaflet largest.
Fruit: slender pods, each ½–1″ (1.3–2.5 cm) long, gently curved, pointed upward.
Height: creeper, the flower stalks about 4″ (10 cm) high, stems to 24″ (60 cm) long.

Habitat
Quiet streams and freshwater ponds.

Range
Throughout North America.

Comments
Leaves add a mild peppery flavor to salads. *Nasturtium* comes from the Latin *nasi tortium* ("distortion of the nose"), referring to the plant's pungency.

Heartleaved Bittercress
Cardamine cordifolia
246

Several or many leafy stems with white flowers grow from an extensive system of underground runners.
Flowers: petals 4, ½–¾″ (1.3–2 cm) long; June–September.
Leaves: ¾–4″ (2–10 cm) wide, roundish blades with shallowly scalloped margins, indented at base; leaf stalks 2–5 times the length of blades.
Fruit: pods ¾–1½″ (2–3.8 cm) long, slightly flat, slender.
Height: 4–32″ (10–80 cm).

Habitat
Along mountain stream banks, in streams and alpine meadows.

Range
British Columbia; south to N. California; east to New Mexico, Wyoming, and Idaho.

Comments
Some plants in this family were reputed to have medicinal qualities useful in the treatment of heart ailments. Among the

several species in the West, most have pinnately parted or lobed leaves.

Arrowhead
Sagittaria latifolia
247

Aquatic plant with a tall stalk rising from large basal leaves, with white flowers in whorls of 3.
Flowers: ⅔″ (1.6 cm) wide, with 3 white petals, 3 sepals; 7–10 stamens; July–September.
Leaves: 2–16″ (5–40 cm) long, arrow-shaped, vary from broad to narrow, unlobed to lobed (with 2 long backward-projecting lobes).
Height: 1–4′ (30–120 cm).

Habitat
Wet sites or shallow water along lake and stream margins, marshes, and swamps.

Range
Nova Scotia and British Columbia; south to Florida, Mexico, and California.

Comments
This aquatic is closely related to Water Plantain. Several similar species with arrow-shaped leaves are distinguished from one another by number of stamens and petal size. Beneath the muck, rhizomes produce edible starchy tubers, eaten by ducks and muskrats and known as "duck potatoes."

Water Plantain
Alisma subcordatum
248

Tall, spindly, many-branched plant with small white (rarely pink) flowers arranged in whorls.
Flowers: ⅙″ (4 mm) wide, with 3 petals, 3 green sepals; June–October.
Leaves: basal, 2–6″ (5–15 cm) long, olive-green, distinctly veined, elliptical.
Height: 4–36″ (10–90 cm).

Habitat
Shallow water in freshwater marshes, sluggish streams, edges of ponds and lakes.

Range
Quebec; south to New York; west to Wisconsin.

Comments
In this typical emergent aquatic plant, the lower part is often submerged, while the upper part is exposed. If leaves are submerged, they are ribbonlike, not elliptical. The submerged rootlike structure is edible.

Venus Flytrap
Dionaea muscipula
249

An insectivorous plant with a cluster of white flowers at the top of a leafless stalk that rises above a rosette of bristly, folded, basal leaves.
Flowers: about 1″ (2.5 cm) wide; sepals and petals 5; stamens usually 15. All these parts attached at base of ovary; May–June.

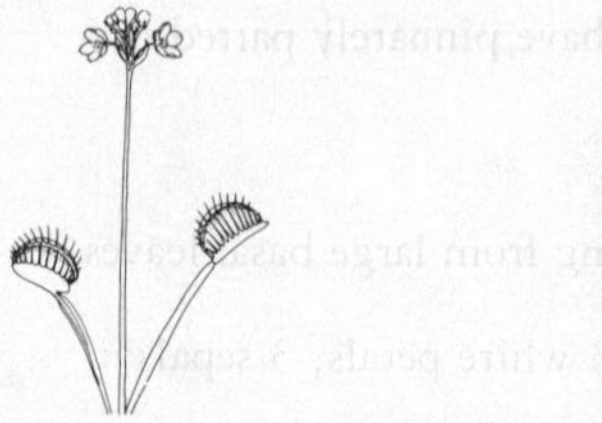

Leaves: 1½–6″ (3.8–15 cm) long; blades folded lengthwise into 2 hinged lobes, green on the outside and often orange on the inside, fringed with long, stout bristles up to ⅓″ (8 mm) long; leafstalks long, winged.
Height: 4–12″ (10–30 cm).

Habitat
Moist sandy areas, pinelands.

Range
Coastal plain of North Carolina and NE. South Carolina.

Comments
When insects or spiders disturb any 2 of the 6 tactile hairs on the upper surface of the folded leaves of this fascinating plant, the hinged halves snap shut, trapping the prey. A chemical secreted by the prey stimulates the plant's secretion of digestive enzymes (this does not take place if the plant is stimulated by an inert object such as a pencil tip). Following digestion of the prey, the nutrients are absorbed and the leaf is reset. This plant is classified as an endangered species in both North and South Carolina and is protected by state law in the former. This is the only species in this family.

Water Buttercup
Ranunculus aquatilis
250

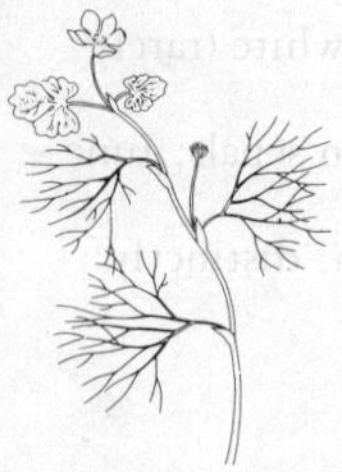

Stems float under and upon the surface of water, generally forming fairly dense beds, the white flowers held by stalks slightly above water.
Flowers: ½–¾″ (1.3–2 cm) wide; petals 5, white, may be yellow at base; May–August.
Leaves: underwater leaves droop when stems are lifted from water, the blades about 1″ (2.5 cm) long on stalks ½–¾″ (1.3–2 cm) long, and finely divided into forked, hairlike segments; leaves that float on surface of water are less divided.
Height: aquatic, with flowers held about 1″ (2.5 cm) above water surface; stems to 3′ (90 cm) long.

Habitat
Ponds and slow streams.

Range
Much of North America.

Comments
The genus name, from the Latin *rana* ("frog"), refers to the wet habitat of some species.

Round-leaved Sundew
Drosera rotundifolia
251

Insectivorous, with white flowers in an elongated cluster on one side of a leafless stalk rising above a rosette of small, reddish, sticky basal leaves.
Flowers: about ¼″ (6 mm) wide; petals 5, often pink-tinged; June–August.
Leaves: blades about ½″ (1.3 cm) long; circular, covered with glandular hairs that exude a sticky substance; leafstalks about 1½″ (3.8 cm) long.
Height: 4–9″ (10–22.5 cm).

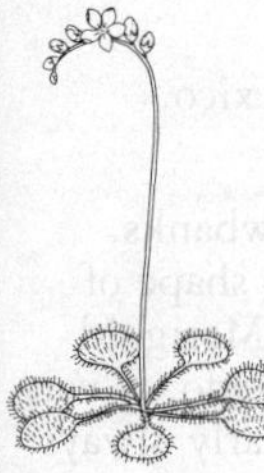

Habitat
Bogs.

Range
Throughout the East and Midwest; also in the West.

Comments
Sundews are able to survive on nutrient-poor soils where other plants are at a disadvantage. A similar species, the Spatulate-leaved Sundew (*D. leucantha*), has oval or spoon-shaped leaves. The very similar northern *D. anglica* has much narrower leaves and grows only as far south as northern Maine, Michigan, and Wisconsin. The Dwarf Sundew (*D. brevifolia*), which has wedge-shaped leaves with shorter stalks in a more compact rosette, is a more southerly species, occurring in damp areas from southern North Carolina to Florida, and west to Tennessee, Arkansas, and Texas.

Swamp Dewberry
Rubus hispidus
252

The trailing, woody stems have weak, backward-directed bristles and erect branches, usually with 3-parted, shiny leaves and loose terminal or axillary clusters of white flowers.
Flowers: ¾″ (2 cm) wide; sepals and petals 5; stamens and pistils many; June–September.
Leaves: leaflets to 2″ (5 cm) long, thick, ovate, toothed, mostly evergreen.
Fruit: red or blackish, blackberrylike.
Height: creeper, with canes 4–12″ (10–30 cm) high.

Habitat
Usually moist thickets, open woods, and clearings.

Range
Ontario, Quebec, and Nova Scotia; south to Maryland and uplands of North Carolina; north to Wisconsin.

Comments
A great many species of dewberries occur, some with bristles and some with stronger prickles. Among the latter is the Prickly Dewberry (*R. flagellaris*), a prostrate plant of drier sites, with stout, curved prickles and usually 5-parted, thin leaves. Southern Dewberry (*R. trivialus*) is widely distributed in the South. These plants and the related Blackberries are among the most important summer foods for songbirds.

Marsh Marigold
Caltha leptosepala
253

There are several leaves at the base of each erect, leafless flowering stem, with usually only 1 white, bowl-shaped flower at tip.
Flowers: ½–1½″ (1.3–3.1 cm) wide; petal-like sepals 5–12; petals absent; stamens many, pistils several; May–August.
Leaves: to 3″ (7.5 cm) long, oblong, with minutely scalloped edges, on stalks either shorter than blade or much longer.
Height: 1–8″ (2.5–20 cm).

Habitat
Wet places high in the mountains.

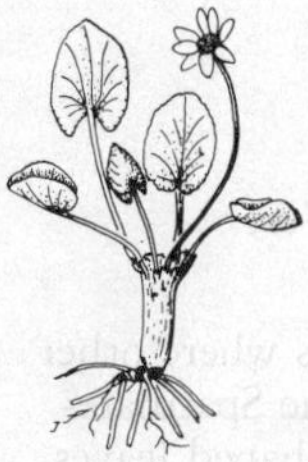

Range
Idaho and Montana to N. Arizona and N. New Mexico.

Comments
Marsh Marigolds bloom very close to receding snowbanks. The alternate common name Elk's Lip refers to the shape of the long leaf of this species. Twin-flowered Marsh Marigold (*C. biflora*), from Alaska to California, east to Colorado, is very similar but has leaves about as wide as long and nearly always 2 flowers on each stem.

Floating Hearts
Nymphoides aquatica
254

A water-lily-like plant with floating, heart-shaped leaves on long stalks, with a flat-topped cluster of small, white flowers rising just below the leaf blade.
Flowers: ½–¾″ (1.3–2 cm) wide; 5 nearly separate petals; July–September.
Leaves: 2–8″ (5–20 cm) long; thick, green above, very veiny beneath.
Height: aquatic.

Habitat
Ponds and slow streams, in the coastal plain.

Range
S. New Jersey to Florida; west to Texas.

Comments
The genus name refers to the plant's resemblance to the Water-lily genus *Nymphaea*. However, its clusters of small, white flowers with only 5 petals make it quite different from the single, many-petaled Water Lilies. Another Floating Hearts (*N. cordata*), with smaller, green leaves mottled with purple above and smooth beneath, occurs from Newfoundland to Florida, west to Louisiana, and north to Ontario.

Fragrant Water Lily
Nymphaea odorata
255

A floating aquatic plant with fragrant white or pink flowers and flat, floating leaves.
Flowers: 3–5″ (7.5–12.5 cm) wide; petals many, narrowing in width toward the center and intergrading with numerous yellow stamens; sepals 4, green; pistil compound, with several united parts (carpels); June–September.
Leaves: 4–12″ (10–30 cm) in diameter; shiny green above, purplish red beneath.
Fruit: fleshy, ripens beneath the water on coiled stalk.
Height: aquatic.

Habitat
Ponds and quiet waters.

Range
Newfoundland to Manitoba; south to Florida; west to Louisiana and Kansas.

Comments
One of the most common white Water Lilies, this plant's

flowers and leaves float on the water. It usually flowers only from early morning until noon. The stomata—tiny openings on the leaf surface through which carbon dioxide and other gases pass into the plant—are on the upper, shiny leaf surface rather than on the lower surface, where they occur on most land plants.

Goldthread
Coptis groenlandica
256

A small plant with solitary white flowers and lustrous, evergreen basal leaves rising from a threadlike, yellow underground stem.
Flowers: ½″ (1.3 cm) wide; sepals 5–7, white, petal-like; petals very small, clublike; stamens numerous; pistils several; May–July.
Leaves: 1–2″ (2.5–5 cm) wide, all basal, palmately divided into 3 leaflets with scalloped, toothed margins.
Fruit: dry pod, splitting open along 1 side.
Height: 3–6″ (7.5–15 cm).

Habitat
Cool woods, swamps, and bogs.

Range
Manitoba to Greenland, Newfoundland, and Nova Scotia; south through New England and New Jersey to the mountains of North Carolina; west to Tennessee, Ohio, Indiana, and Iowa.

Comments
The common name refers to the golden-yellow underground stem that both Indians and colonists chewed to treat mouth sores. (Hence another common name for the plant, Cankerroot.) It was also made into a tea for use as an eyewash.

Tall Meadow Rue
Thalictrum polygamum
257

A tall plant with plumy clusters of white flowers.
Flowers: about ⅓″ (8 mm) wide; sepals greenish white, falling early; petals lacking. Flowers with both male and female flowers on the same plant, or partially unisexual, the female with several pistils and usually some stamens, the male with many erect, threadlike stamens; June–August.
Leaves: compound, bluish to olive-green, divided into roundish, 3-lobed leaflets, each about 1″ (2.5 cm) long.
Fruit: seedlike, in rounded clusters, the lower ones bent backward.
Height: 2–8′ (60–240 cm).

Habitat
Swamps, meadows, and streamsides.

Range
Ontario to Nova Scotia; south through New England to Georgia; west to Tennessee.

Comments
This summer-blooming flower is constantly visited by bees and butterflies. At least 10 other species are found in this range.

Buck Bean
Menyanthes trifoliata
258

Large leaves with long stalks and racemes or narrow clusters of white or purple-tinged, starlike flowers at top of stout stalks, about as high as the leaves.
Flowers: corolla about ½″ (1.3 cm) wide, with a tube ¼–⅜″ (6–9 mm) long (about twice the length of calyx) and 5 or 6 pointed lobes covered with short scales; May–August.
Leaves: 4–12″ (10–30 cm) long; leaflets 1½–5″ (3.8–12.5 cm) long, broadly lanceolate.
Height: aquatic, with leaves and flower stalks 4–12″ (10–30 cm) above water.

Habitat
Bogs and shallow lakes.

Range
From the southern Sierra Nevada and central Colorado north to Canada; eastern United States.

Comments
A species with similar flowers, Deer Cabbage (*Nephrophyllidium crista-galli*), has undivided kidney-shaped leaves, and grows in wet places on the Olympic Peninsula and around the northern Pacific.

Highbush Blueberry
Vaccinium corymbosum
259, 326

A multistemmed shrub with green, or often red, twigs and terminal clusters of small, urn-shaped white flowers.
Flowers: ¼–½″ (6–13 mm) long; corolla 5-toothed; May–June.
Leaves: 1½–3″ (3.8–7.5 cm) long; elliptic, entire, smooth above but usually somewhat hairy beneath.
Fruit: blue berry with whitish bloom; June–August.
Height: 5–15′ (1.5–4.5 m).

Habitat
Swamps or dry upland woods.

Range
Quebec to Nova Scotia; south to Georgia; west to Alabama; north to Wisconsin.

Comments
Our cultivated blueberries have been derived from this tall-growing shrub. It is often found in wet areas, but closely related growths occur in dry sites. These plants are very important to wildlife: their berries are relished by songbirds, game birds, bear, and small mammals; the twigs and foliage are eaten by deer and rabbits.

Leatherleaf
Chamaedaphne calyculata
260

An evergreen shrub with white bell- or urn-shaped flowers, hanging in one-sided racemes.
Flowers: ¼″ (6 mm) long; March–July.
Leaves: ¾–2″ (2–5 cm) long, leathery, elliptical, dull green, and dotted with round, scurfy scales, heaviest on the underside. Older leaves are often brownish-bronze, yellowish beneath.

Fruit: globular capsule.
Height: 1–4′ (30–120 cm).

Habitat
Sphagnum bogs, pond margins.

Range
Across southern Canada to Newfoundland and Nova Scotia; south through New England to Georgia; northwesterly to Iowa and Wisconsin.

Comments
One of many evergreen members of the Heath family, this low, erect, many-branched, circumpolar plant is typical of boggy wetlands and highly acidic sites. It can begin the development of a bog by forming floating mats around the edges of a lake. In Massachusetts the rate of its advance has been recorded at over 1 foot per decade.

Bog Rosemary
Andromeda glaucophylla
261

A low evergreen shrub with pendulous clusters of small, pinkish flowers.
Flowers: ¼″ (6 mm) long, urn-shaped; May–June.
Leaves: 1–2″ (2.5–5 cm) long; alternate, linear, with white bloom beneath and margins enrolled.
Fruit: capsule.
Height: 10–18″ (25–50 cm).

Habitat
Bogs.

Range
Newfoundland and Labrador west to Saskatchewan; south to New Jersey, West Virginia, and west to Indiana and Minnesota.

Comments
Bog Rosemary is one of several heath shrubs often found in boggy areas in association with Leatherleaf (*Chamaedaphne calyculata*), Sheep Laurel (*Kalmia angustifolia*), Bog Laurel (*K. polifolia*), and Labrador Tea (*Ledum groenlandicum*).

Bog Rein Orchid
Habenaria dilatata
262

Erect, leafy stems have many fragrant, white, bilaterally symmetrical flowers in a spike.
Flowers: upper sepal joined to 2 upper petals, forming a hood about ¼″ (6 mm) long; 2 lanceolate sepals 3⁄16–⅜″ (5–9 mm) long, spread horizontally; lip hangs down and is about as long as sepals, the base almost 3 times as wide as slender tip; slender or stout spur extends from back of lip downward and forward beneath flower; June–September.
Leaves: middle ones largest, 2–12″ (5–30 cm) long, narrowly or broadly lanceolate, clasping.
Height: 6–40″ (15–100 cm).

Habitat
Wet or boggy ground.

Range
N. New Mexico to S. California; north through most of the West and northern North America.

Comments
Plants in the Rocky Mountain region often have stouter, shorter spurs. *Habena*, Latin for "reins" or "narrow strap," refers to the narrow lip of some species of *Habenaria*.

Water Willow
Justicia americana
263

An emergent water plant with bicolored flowers borne in dense headlike or spikelike clusters on long, slender flower stalks rising from the leaf axils.
Flowers: to ½″ (1.3 cm) long, 2-lipped; 3-lobed lower lip, white spotted with purple; upper lip pale violet or white, arching over the lower. Only 2 stamens, with purplish-red anthers; June–October.
Leaves: 3–6″ (7.5–15 cm) long, narrow, opposite, willowlike.
Fruit: a brown capsule.
Height: 1–3′ (30–90 cm).

Habitat
Margins of shallow streams, lakes, and ponds; wet shores.

Range
Ontario and Quebec; Vermont and New York south to Georgia; west to Texas; north to Missouri, Kansas, and Wisconsin.

Comments
This plant has underground stems and forms colonies. *J. ovata*, a similar species found from Virginia to Florida, has more loosely flowered spikes.

Showy Lady's Slipper
Cypripedium reginae
264

A stout, hairy, often twisted, leafy stalk bears 1–3 large flowers with a white and pink, pouchlike lip petal.
Flowers: lip 1–2″ (2.5–5 cm) long, white, rose-pink in front, often veined with purple or deep pink, with many shallow, vertical furrows; sepals and side petals waxy white, ovate-lanceolate, spreading; May–August.
Leaves: up to 10″ (25 cm) long, usually 3–7, ribbed, elliptic.
Fruit: elliptic capsule to 1¾″ (4.5 cm) long.
Height: 1–3′ (30–90 cm).

Habitat
Swamps, moist woods, especially limestone sites.

Range
Saskatchewan to Newfoundland; south through New England to the mountains of North Carolina and Tennessee; northwest to North Dakota.

Comments
This flower, the tallest and most beautiful of our northern native Orchids, is especially common in the lake states. It has been overpicked and should be protected from further

exploitation. The glandular hairs of the foliage may cause a rash similar to that caused by Poison Ivy.

Butterfly Orchid
Encyclia tampensis
265

Medium to large epiphyte with 1–3 stiff leaves arising from grayish-green pear-shaped bulbs tinged with purple.
Flowers: 1¼–1¾″ (3.1–4.4 cm) wide; showy, fragrant, greenish yellow striped with magenta; all year.
Leaves: 3–12″ (8–30 cm) long, ½″ (12 mm) wide, linear.
Fruit: capsule, 1–2″ (2.5–5 cm) long.
Height: 3–12″ (8–30 cm).

Habitat
Swamps and hammocks.

Range
North Carolina to Florida.

Comments
This plant is one of the most attractive and widespread orchids; the flowers can vary greatly in color.

Cranberry
Vaccinium macrocarpon
266, 330

The ascending branches of this evergreen, trailing shrub have nodding, pinkish-white flowers in clusters.
Flowers: about ½″ (1.3 cm) long; stamens 8–10, with anthers united into a long, pointed cone; June–August.
Leaves: ⅕–⅔″ (5–16 mm) long; alternate, oval, blunt, shiny above but slightly whitish beneath.
Fruit: dark red, globose berry.
Height: creeper, with branches to 8″ (20 cm) high.

Habitat
Open bogs, swamps, and lake shores.

Range
Newfoundland to Nova Scotia; south to North Carolina; west to Illinois; north to Minnesota.

Comments
Wild cranberries often form low, dense masses in sphagnum-dominated, boggy areas, where they can be picked in fall. They were originally known as Craneberries because their petals and anther "beak" look like a crane's head.

Swamp Milkweed
Asclepias incarnata
267

Deep pink flowers clustered at the top of a tall, branching stem, bearing numerous narrow, lanceolate leaves.
Flowers: ¼″ (6 mm) broad, with 5 recurved petals and elevated central crown divided into 5 parts; June–August.
Leaves: to 4″ (10 cm) long, opposite.
Fruit: an elongated pod, 2–4″ (5–10 cm) long, opening along one side.
Height: 1–4′ (30–120 cm).

Habitat
Swamps, shores, and thickets.

Range
Manitoba, Quebec, and Nova Scotia; from New England south to Georgia; west to Louisiana, and Texas; north to North Dakota.

Comments
The genus was named in honor of Aesculapius, Greek god of medicine, undoubtedly because some species have long been used to treat a variety of ailments.

Rose Pogonia
Pogonia ophioglossoides
268

A slender, greenish stem has a single leaf about midway up and is terminated by a single, rose-pink flower.
Flowers: about 1¾″ (4.5 cm) long; subtended by a leaflike bract up to 1″ (2.5 cm) long. Sepals and petals colored alike; sepals linear-lanceolate, the dorsal one erect; lateral petals ovate, arching over lip petal; lip spatulate, fringed, and bearded in the center with short, yellowish bristles; May–August.
Leaves: to 4¾″ (12 cm) long, solitary, ovate to broadly lanceolate.
Height: 3–24″ (7.5–60 cm).

Habitat
Wet open woods, meadows, swamps, sphagnum bogs.

Range
Ontario to Newfoundland and Nova Scotia; south on coastal plain to Florida; west to Texas; inland to Pennsylvania, Tennessee, Indiana, Illinois, and Minnesota.

Comments
This Orchid is found in places in the eastern United States where soil conditions rather than temperature are the controlling factors.

Grass Pink
Calopogon pulchellus
269

Fragrant, pink flowers in a spikelike cluster of 2–10, open sequentially up the leafless stalk.
Flowers: 1½″ (3.8 cm) long; yellow-bearded lip petal stands erect over 5 similar floral parts (sepals 3 and side petals 2) that spread forward and laterally; column incurved, somewhat petal-like; March–August; throughout year in Florida.
Leaves: to 12″ (30 cm) long, single, basal, grasslike.
Height: 6–20″ (15–50 cm).

Habitat
Bogs and bog meadows; acid, sandy or gravelly sites.

Range
Ontario to Nova Scotia and Newfoundland; south through New England and the Atlantic states to Florida; west to Texas; through Central and Lake states to Minnesota, Iowa, Missouri, Arkansas, and Oklahoma.

Comments
This delicate, sweet-smelling Orchid often springs from

sphagnum moss and is easily recognized by the bearded, uppermost lip petal and single, grasslike leaf.

Swamp Pink
Arethusa bulbosa
270

The smooth stalk, with 1–3 ensheathing, scalelike bracts, has a single, bright pink, scented flower at its summit.
Flowers: about 2″ (5 cm) long; showy lip petal spotted with darker pink and crested with 3 rows of yellow or whitish hairs; side petals 2, arch over lip; sepals 3, erect; May (south)–August (north).
Leaves: absent when plant is in flower, grow to 9″ (22.5 cm) as fruit matures.
Fruit: 6-ribbed, elliptical capsule, about 1″ (2.5 cm) long.
Height: 5–10″ (12.5–25 cm).

Habitat
Bogs, swamps, and wet meadows.

Range
Ontario and Newfoundland to Quebec; south through New England to the mountains of North Carolina; northwest through the Central and Lake states to Minnesota.

Comments
Named for the fountain nymph Arethusa, the flower suggests an animal's open mouth. Its unusual lip petal serves as a platform for insects, especially bumble bees, which enter the flower for nectar and pick up the powdery pollen masses as they leave.

Virginia Meadow Beauty
Rhexia virginica
271

Several pink flowers are in broad, terminal clusters on a sturdy 4-sided, slightly winged stem.
Flowers: 1–1½″ (2.5–3.8 cm) wide; petals 4; 8 prominent stamens, anthers opening by pores; July–September.
Leaves: ¾–2½″ (2–6.3 cm) long; paired, ovate to elliptic, toothed, rounded at base; 3–5 prominent veins.
Fruit: urn-shaped capsule with 4 points.
Height: 1–2′ (30–60 cm).

Habitat
Wet sands and peats.

Range
Nova Scotia to Ontario; south to Florida; west to Mississippi, Tennessee, and Missouri.

Comments
Members of this genus have a distinctive urn-shaped fruit that Thoreau once compared to a little cream pitcher. Although the family is mostly tropical, we have at least 10 native species.

Thread-leaved Sundew
Drosera filiformis
272

Insectivorous plant with lavender-rose flowers in an elongated cluster on one side of a leafless floral stalk, curved at the tip, which rises in the midst of erect, threadlike, sticky basal leaves.

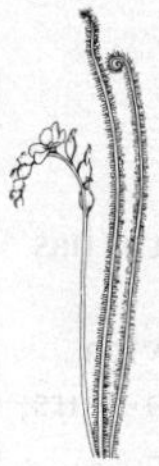

Flowers: about ½″ (1.3 cm) wide; petals 5; June–September.
Leaves: to 12″ (30 cm) long; covered with stalked glands.
Height: 4–12″ (10–30 cm).

Habitat
Wet sandy areas near coast.

Range
Massachusetts to S. New Jersey and from South Carolina to N. Florida; west to Louisiana.

Comments
This striking member of the Sundew family is distinctive, with its stringy leaves covered with glistening droplets of sticky exudate. Insects trapped in the sticky hairs are digested by plant enzymes. Researchers have fed these plants fruit flies labeled with the radioactive isotope nitrogen-15 and have found that substantial quantities of protein from the insects end up in the storage roots.

Swamp Rose
Rosa palustris
273

Pale crimson-pink flowers on branches sparsely armed with stout, hooked spines.
Flowers: 2–3″ (50–80 cm) wide, petals 5; June–August.
Leaves: 4–5″ (10–12.5 cm) long; pinnately compound, with narrow stipules.
Fruit: fleshy hip, red with bristly calyx.
Height: 2–8′ (60–240 cm).

Habitat
Swamps and wet thickets.

Range
Florida west to Arkansas, north to Minnesota, east to Wisconsin, Michigan, and Ontario east to Nova Scotia.

Comments
A showy, bushy rose with conspicuous fruits. Its flowers are pollinated primarily by bees.

Swamp Rose Mallow
Hibiscus palustris
274

This tall, coarse plant has large, pink, 5-lobed, musky-smelling flowers, usually single on short stalks from leaf axils.
Flowers: 4–7″ (10–17.5 cm) wide; stamens numerous, forming column around style, with anthers outside; 5 style branches and stigmas protrude from end of column. Narrow, green, leaflike bracts present beneath calyx; July–September.
Leaves: 4″ (10 cm) long; yellow-green, ovate, toothed, pointed; white down beneath.
Fruit: 5-parted capsule.
Height: 3–8′ (90–240 cm).

Habitat
Tidal marshes and inland freshwater marshes.

Range
Coastal; from Massachusetts to Florida; Great Lakes region from New York to Indiana, Illinois, and Michigan.

Comments
This strikingly showy species is often found along edges of salt marshes but is more common in upper-valley wetlands.

Hibiscus
Hibiscus coccineus
275

Large perennial herb with conspicuous 5-pointed leaves and large, solitary, deep red flowers.
Flowers: 5–8″ (12–20 cm) wide, petals 5; stamens forming tube around style; summer.
Leaves: palmately divided into narrow, toothed segments, 2–10″ (5–25 cm) long.
Fruit: capsule.
Height: 3–10′ (90–300 cm).

Habitat
Southern swamps.

Range
Georgia and Florida.

Comments
This showy mallow thrives in warm southern climates but is not hardy much north of Philadelphia. It dies back each year and seed pods frequently persist.

Red Iris
Iris fulva
276

Showy, reddish-brown flowers with 6 widely spreading petal-like parts are on a slender stalk taller than the swordlike leaves.
Flowers: about 3″ (7.5 cm) wide; sepals 3, recurved, non-bearded, petal-like; petals 3, narrower, recurved; stamens 3, hidden under 3 petal-like, arching styles; May–June.
Leaves: to 3′ (90 cm) long, about ½″ (1.3 cm) wide; form a basal cluster.
Fruit: 6-sided capsule about 2″ (5 cm) long.
Height: 2–5′ (60–150 cm).

Habitat
Wet grasslands or swamp margins.

Range
SW. Illinois south to Alabama and Louisiana; north to Missouri.

Comments
This beautiful southern Iris of wet sloughs and swampy woods is distinctively flat-topped compared to other Irises.

Cardinal Flower
Lobelia cardinalis
277

Many brilliant red, tubular flowers in an elongated cluster on an erect stalk.
Flowers: 1½″ (3.8 cm) long, 5-petaled with 2 lips; upper with 2 lobes, lower with 3; united stamens form a tube around style and extend beyond corolla; narrow leaflike bracts beneath flowers; July–September.
Leaves: to 6″ (15 cm) long, alternate, lanceolate, toothed.
Height: 2–4′ (60–120 cm).

Habitat
Damp sites, especially along streams.

Range
S. Ontario and Quebec to New Brunswick; south to Florida; west to S. Texas; north to Minnesota.

Comments
One of our handsomest deep red wildflowers, Cardinal Flower is pollinated chiefly by hummingbirds, since most insects find it difficult to navigate the long tubular flowers. Although relatively common, overpicking has resulted in its scarcity in some areas.

Turk's-cap Lily
Lilium superbum
278

The tall, flowering stem bears several somewhat drooping, orange flowers, spotted reddish brown, with strongly recurved petals and petal-like sepals; a green streak at the base of each flower segment forms a green "star."
Flowers: 2½″ (6.3 cm) long, with stamens exposed, bearing dangling brown anthers; July–September.
Leaves: 2–6″ (5–15 cm) long; lanceolate, alternate or whorled.
Fruit: a capsule.
Height: 3–7′ (90–210 cm).

Habitat
Wet meadows, swamps, and woods.

Range
S. New Hampshire, Massachusetts, and New York; south to Georgia and Alabama.

Comments
The largest and most spectacular of the native Lilies; up to 40 flowers have been recorded on a single plant. The recurved sepals and petals, which presumably resemble a type of cap worn by early Turks, and the showy extruded stamens, are distinctive features. Indians used the bulbs for soup.

Spotted Touch-me-not
Impatiens capensis
279

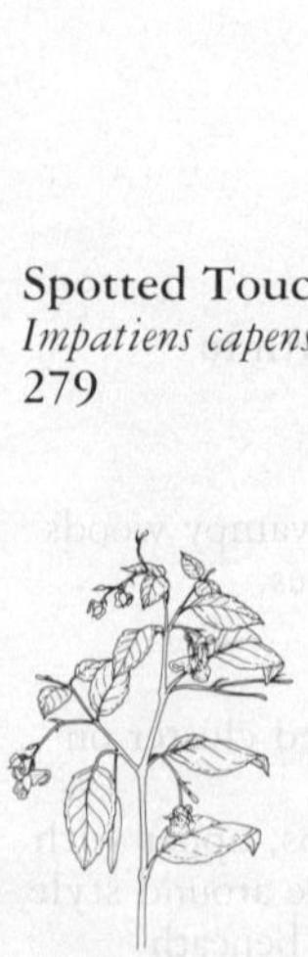

Tall, leafy plant with succulent translucent stems and pendent golden-orange flowers splotched with reddish brown.
Flowers: 1″ (2.5 cm) long; 1 calyx lobe colored as petals, with a sharply spurred sac ¼″ (6 mm) long; other 2 sepals green; 3 petals, 2 of them 2-lobed, open out at mouth; July–October.
Leaves: 1½–3½″ (3.8–8.8 cm) long, thin, ovate, pale and glaucous underneath.
Fruit: swollen capsule that explodes at maturity when touched, expelling seeds.
Height: 2–5′ (60–150 cm).

Habitat
Shaded wetlands.

Range
Saskatchewan to Newfoundland; south to Florida and Texas; west to Oklahoma; north to Missouri.

Comments
An annual that often occurs in dense stands, it is especially adapted to hummingbird visitation, but bees and butterflies are also important pollinators. If the leaves are submerged, they have a silvery look. The stem juice is said to relieve itching from Poison Ivy and has also been used to treat athlete's foot. Scientific data confirm the fungicidal qualities.

Crimson Pitcher Plant
Sarracenia leucophylla
280

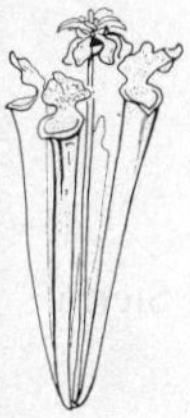

A carnivorous plant with nodding, brownish-red flowers and clusters of erect, hollow, pitcherlike leaves, colored at the top with reddish-purple veins on a white background, and topped by an erect, roundish hood with wavy margin.
Flowers: 2–3″ (5–7.5 cm) wide; petals 5, fiddle-shaped; stigma distinctive, forming a large, reddish-green, umbrellalike structure in center of flower; March–April.
Leaves: 2–3′ (60–90 cm) tall.
Height: 2–3′ (60–90 cm), flower stalk as tall as leaves.

Habitat
Sandy bogs.

Range
Coastal plain; Georgia to N. Florida; west to Mississippi.

Comments
Insects and other small organisms are attracted to the plant by the colorful leaf opening and by nectar secreted inside. They fall into the collected water and are unable to escape. They are then digested by plant enzymes or by bacterial action, thereby providing essential nutrients.

Northern Pitcher Plant
Sarracenia purpurea
281

A carnivorous plant with a large, solitary, purplish-red flower on a leafless stalk rising above a rosette of bronzy, reddish-green, hollow, inflated, curved leaves.
Flowers: 2″ (5 cm) wide; petals 5; stamens numerous; style expanded into an umbrella-shaped structure; May–August.
Leaves: 4–12″ (10–30 cm) long, with a broad flaring terminal lip covered with stiff, downward-pointing hairs.
Fruit: capsule.
Height: 8–24″ (20–60 cm).

Habitat
Sphagnum bogs.

Range
Saskatchewan to Labrador and Nova Scotia; south through New England to Florida; west to Texas; north to Indiana, Illinois, and Minnesota.

Comments
A striking plant with lipped, pitcherlike leaves that collect water; organisms attracted to the colored lip have difficulty crawling upward because of the recurved hairs and eventually fall into the water and drown. Enzymes secreted by the plant aid in the digestion of the insect but much of the breakdown

is passive, a result of bacterial activity. The plant absorbs the nutrients, especially nitrogenous compounds. A southern species, Parrot Pitcher Plant (*S. psittacina*), has many prostrate "pitchers" with hooked lips like a parrot's bill.

California Pitcher Plant
Darlingtonia californica
282

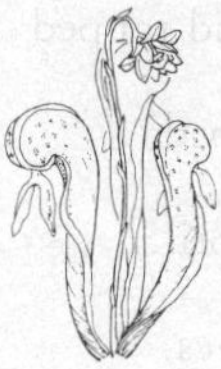

Several tubular leaves with hoodlike tops grow in a cluster; 1 yellow-green and maroon flower hangs at the tip of a leafless stalk.
Flowers: sepals 5, yellow-green, petal-like, 1½–3½″ (3.8–8.8 cm) long; petals 5, maroon, shorter than sepals; green, bell-shaped ovary; April–August.
Leaves: 4–20″ (10–50 cm) long; 2 long, flat appendages beneath hood.
Height: to 3′ (90 cm).

Habitat
Coastal bogs and mountain streams and seeps.

Range
Most of W. Oregon to NW. California and the central Sierra Nevada.

Comments
Insects or other small organisms, attracted to the nectar secreted by the hood and appendages, enter the hole beneath the hood. Once inside, numerous down-pointing hairs discourage escape, and they are decomposed by various microorganisms in the fluid in the tubular base. Nutrients thus released are absorbed by the Pitcher Plant.

Wild Pine
Tillandsia fasciculata
283

An air plant with inconspicuous flowers in the axils of showy bracts, which are usually red.
Flowers: 2″ (5 cm) long, with violet petals and protruding stamens and style; arranged in numerous spikes up to 6″ (15 cm) long on stalks about as long as the leaves; bracts about 1½″ (3.8 cm) long, ranging in color from yellow to red or green; January–August.
Leaves: 12–20″ (30–50 cm) long, in rosettes, grayish green with brown bases, lanceolate to linear, stiff.
Height: epiphyte.

Habitat
Cypress swamps; in hammocks, usually on cypress trees.

Range
Florida.

Comments
This is the most common of the Wild Pines that occur as epiphytes, especially on Bald Cypress. Although they grow on the trees, they get their nourishment from the air, rain, and minerals leached from the host tree. There are 15 other species of *Tillandsia* in Florida.

Great Hedge Nettle
Stachys cooleyae
284

Stout, 4-sided, leafy stems grow in patches and have deep reddish-lavender bilaterally symmetrical flowers in whorls at intervals in a spike at top.
Flowers: corolla ⅝–1″ (1.5–2.5 cm) long, upper lip projecting like a short hood, lower lip 3-lobed, much longer, bent downward; June–August.
Leaves: 2½–6″ (6.3–15 cm) long, opposite, all with stalks, broadly lanceolate, bearing blunt teeth on margins.
Height: 2–5′ (60–150 cm).

Habitat
Swamps and moist low ground from sea level to moderate elevations.

Range
S. British Columbia to S. Oregon, from the eastern slope of the Cascade Mountains to the Pacific Coast.

Comments
The moist habitat is typical for Hedge Nettles. Other western species may have smaller, paler flowers and middle and upper leaves without stalks.

Marsh St. Johnswort
Hypericum virginicum
285

A marsh herb with pink flowers clustered at the top of the leafy stem and in the axils of the paired leaves.
Flowers: ½–¾″ (1.3–2 cm) wide; sepals 5, often purple-red; petals 5; 3 groups of 3 stamens, alternate, with 3 large, orange glands; July–August.
Leaves: 1–2½″ (2.5–6.3 cm) long; opposite, ovate, light green, stalkless, heart-shaped at base, dotted with translucent glands.
Height: 8–24″ (20–60 cm).

Habitat
Wet sandy areas, swamps, and bogs.

Range
Coastal, from Nova Scotia to southern New England and New York; south to Florida; local in Ohio, Indiana, and Illinois, along Great Lakes.

Comments
This wetland perennial differs in flower color from most of the St. Johnsworts, which are yellow. It and other St. Johnsworts with similar stamen arrangements are placed by some in the genus *Triadenum.* The related Marsh St. Johnswort species *H. tubulosum,* found only as far north as southeast Virginia, southern Indiana, and Missouri, has the base of the leaves rounded or tapered, not heart-shaped.

Swamp Loosestrife
Decodon verticillatus
286

Arching stems have showy, deep pink flowers in tufts in the axils of the upper, opposite or whorled, willowlike leaves.
Flowers: about ½″ (1.3 cm) long; bell-shaped; petals 5, wedge-shaped; stamens 10, 5 long and protruding, 5 short; July–August.

Leaves: 2–6″ (5–15 cm) long; lanceolate.
Fruit: round capsule.
Height: stem arching, to 8′ (2.4 m) long.

Habitat
Swamps, bogs, edges of shallow water, wet soils.

Range
Ontario, central Maine, and S. New Hampshire; south to Florida; west to Louisiana; north to S. Illinois.

Comments
The many intertwining, arching stems of this herb- to shrub-like plant may form sizable patches at the edges of lakes and sluggish streams or on floating bog mats. Wherever a stem touches the water, air-filled, spongy tissue may develop. This tissue buoys the stem so that it may root and form a new arching stem.

Spotted Joe-Pye Weed
Eupatorium maculatum
287

Atop a sturdy purple or purple-spotted stem, hairy above, is a large pinkish-purplish, flat-topped cluster of fuzzy flower heads.
Flowers: heads ⅕″ (5 mm) wide, in clusters 4–5½″ (10–14 cm) wide, of all disk flowers; July–September.
Leaves: 2½–8″ (6.3–20 cm) long, in whorls of 3–5, thick, lanceolate, coarsely toothed.
Height: 2–6′ (60–180 cm).

Habitat
Damp meadows, thickets, and shores.

Range
Across southern Canada and northern United States; south to Maryland, Ohio, Illinois, New Mexico, and Arizona.

Comments
This is one of several similar species. Sweet Joe-Pye Weed (*E. purpureum*) has a greenish stem, a dome-shaped cluster of dull pink flower heads, and foliage that smells like vanilla when crushed. Hollow Joe-Pye Weed (*E. fistulosum*) has a hollow stem, and *E. dubium* is a smaller species with ovate leaves. Folklore tells that an Indian, "Joe Pye," used this plant to cure fevers and that the early American colonists used it to treat an outbreak of typhus.

Sheep Laurel
Kalmia angustifolia
288

An evergreen shrub with small, deep pink, saucer-shaped flowers in dense clusters around the stem, mostly below the leaves.
Flowers: ⅓–½″ (8–13 mm) wide; petals 5. The 10 stamens, with anthers tucked into pockets of the corolla, pop out when touched; May–August.
Leaves: 1½–2″ (3.8–5 cm) long; in whorls of 3, oblong, dark green above, pale beneath when mature.
Fruit: globular capsule, persisting through winter.
Height: 1–3′ (30–90 cm).

Habitat
Dry or wet sandy or sterile soil, old fields, and bogs.

Range
Manitoba to Newfoundland and Nova Scotia; south to Virginia and the mountains of Georgia; northwest to Michigan.

Comments
Sometimes called Lambkill, this small shrub is poisonous to livestock. Because of its clonal habit it can form sizable stands. The flowers are miniatures of the larger Mountain Laurel (*K. latifolia*). Pale or Bog Laurel (*K. polifolia*) has pink flowers in terminal clusters, two-edged twigs, and opposite leaves with rolled margins, very white beneath. It is a northern bog plant and occurs only as far south as northern New Jersey and Pennsylvania. Two other species are found in the South.

Mountain Globemallow
Iliamna rivularis
289

A stout plant with large, maplelike leaves and showy pink or pinkish-lavender flowers in long, loose racemes at top of stem, and in shorter racemes in upper leaf axils.
Flowers: 1–2″ (2.5–5 cm) wide; petals 5; many stamens joined at base, forming a tube around branched style, each branch ending in a tiny knob; June–August.
Leaves: 2–8″ (5–20 cm) wide, nearly round, 5 or 7 triangular lobes.
Fruit: many segments in a ring, each containing 3 or 4 seeds.
Height: 3–7′ (90–210 cm).

Habitat
Springs and along mountain streams.

Range
British Columbia through E. Washington to E. Oregon; east to Montana; south to Utah and Colorado.

Comments
The several western Globemallow species are commonly found in wet places, recognizable by their maplelike leaves and pink or rose petals.

Checkermallow
Sidalcea neomexicana
290

Many deep pink flowers crowded in narrow, leaning sprays top the leafy stems.
Flowers: 1–1½″ (2.5–3.8 cm) wide; petals 5; stamens many, joined at base, forming a tube around style, whose slender branches have no knobs at tip; June–September.
Leaves: lowest to 4″ (10 cm) wide, nearly round, 5–7 shallow lobes with coarse teeth; upper are smaller, palmately divided into usually 7 lobes.
Height: 1–3′ (30–90 cm).

Habitat
Moist, often heavy soil, in mountain valleys and along streams and ponds at lower elevations.

Range
E. Oregon to S. California; east to New Mexico, Colorado, and Wyoming; also northern Mexico.

Comments
The many Checkermallows with pink flowers, from coastal marshes to moderate elevations in the mountains, are difficult to distinguish and differentiated only by technical details.

Water Smartweed
Polygonum amphibium
291

Long, prostrate stems grow across mud or in water, and end with erect, dense, narrowly egg-shaped pink flower clusters.
Flowers: clusters ½–1½″ (1.3–3.8 cm) long; each flower with 5 petal-like segments less than ¼″ (6 mm) long; June–September.
Leaves: to 6″ (15 cm) long, narrowly elliptic.
Height: aquatic, with floral stalks 3–6″ (7.5–15 cm) high, and stems up to 7′ (2.1 m) long.

Habitat
In mud or floating on still fresh water.

Range
Newfoundland to Minnesota; Saskatchewan, Montana, and Washington; south to Connecticut, Pennsylvania, and California.

Comments
The pink flower masses are very attractive, but since the plants grow quickly, they can become an unwelcome weed in decorative ponds. Their seeds provide food for waterfowl. The similar species *P. coccineum,* also called Water Smartweed and very common, has narrower, longer clusters of flowers on stalks covered with glandular hairs.

Marsh Skullcap
Scutellaria galericulata
292

Grows in patches, with blue, bilaterally symmetrical flowers, 1 blooming in each axil of the upper leaves.
Flowers: ½–¾″ (1.3–2 cm) long, with upper lobe of corolla helmet-shaped, lower lobe bent downward; upper and lower lips of calyx without teeth, and across top of upper lip is a raised crest; June–September.
Leaves: ¾–2″ (2–5 cm) long, opposite, lanceolate, faintly scalloped on edges.
Height: 4–32″ (10–80 cm).

Habitat
Wet meadows, swamps, and along streams at moderate elevations.

Range
Throughout the West, extending south to central California, N. Arizona, and N. New Mexico.

Comments
In the West, where many species prefer dry sites, this is one that prefers a moist habitat.

Purple Loosestrife
Lythrum salicaria
293

An erect stem has a spike of purple-pink flowers above opposite or whorled, unstalked leaves.
Flowers: ½–¾″ (1.3–2 cm) wide; petals 4–6, wrinkled; stamens as many or twice as many as petals; flowers of 3 types, each with different stamen and pistil lengths; June–September.
Leaves: 1½–4″ (3.8–10 cm) long; lanceolate to linear, the lower ones downy, clasping the stem.
Height: 2–4′ (60–120 cm).

Habitat
Wet meadows, floodplains, and roadside ditches.

Range
Newfoundland, Quebec, Nova Scotia, and New England; south to North Carolina; west through West Virginia, Ohio, Indiana, Missouri, and Minnesota to W. Washington.

Comments
This showy, magenta-flowered perennial, a European introduction, covers acres of wetlands, providing a truly spectacular sight. It is an aggressive species and tends to crowd out native aquatics valuable to wildlife.

Large Purple Fringed Orchid
Habenaria fimbriata
294

The deeply fringed, fragrant, lavender flowers are in a many-flowered, elongated cluster on a leafy stem.
Flowers: 1″ (2.5 cm) long; upper sepal and 2 lateral petals, erect; lateral sepals ovate, spreading; lower "lip" petal with 3 fan-shaped, fringed lobes and backward-pointing spur; sepal and petals similarly colored; June–August.
Leaves: lower ones to 8″ (20 cm) long, ovate to lanceolate, sheathing the stem; upper ones small, lanceolate.
Height: 2–4′ (60–120 cm).

Habitat
Cool moist woods, wet meadows, and swamp margins.

Range
Newfoundland to New England; south to Maryland and West Virginia; in the mountains to North Carolina and Tennessee; northwest to Wisconsin and Ontario.

Comments
A close-up of the individual flowers reveals the striking beauty of these Fringed Orchids. The method of pollination by moths is interesting. The pollen masses (pollinia) bear a sticky disk that protrudes below the anther. As the moth extends its tongue into the spur of the lip petal and then out again, it pulls the pollen mass from the anther and carries it to another flower, where cross-pollination occurs.

Pickerelweed
Pontederia cordata
295

An aquatic herb with a creeping rhizome beneath the water and violet-blue flower spikes extending above water.
Flowers: ⅓″ (8 mm) long; funnel-shaped, with 3-lobed upper lip, the middle one marked with 2 yellow spots; 3 lower

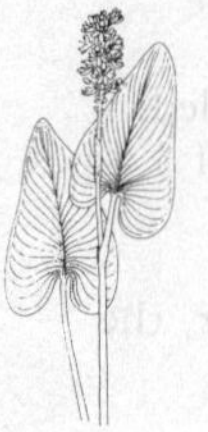

flower parts separate; stamens 6, 3 long and 3 short, often undeveloped; 2 bracts present beneath flower spike, the lower one resembling the basal leaves, the upper one a sheath; June–November.
Leaves: 4–10″ (10–25 cm) long, basal, heart-shaped, indented at bases and tapering to a point, extend above water.
Fruit: seedlike.
Height: aquatic, with flower stalk 1–2′ (30–60 cm) above water.

Habitat
Freshwater marshes, edges of ponds, lakes, and streams.

Range
Ontario to Nova Scotia and New England; south to N. Florida; west to Missouri and Oklahoma; north to Minnesota.

Comments
This emergent aquatic, with its leaves and flowers above water and portions of the stem under water, is found typically in shallow, quiet water. The seeds can be eaten like nuts and the young leafstalks cooked as greens. Deer also feed on these plants. The common name suggests that this plant, as well as the fish known as pickerel, occupy the same habitat.

Water Hyacinth
Eichhornia crassipes
296

A floating aquatic plant with a spike of showy, bluish-purple or lavender, funnel-shaped flowers.
Flowers: about 2″ (5 cm) wide and long; 6-lobed, the upper lobe larger with a conspicuous yellow spot; sepals similar to the petals; stamens 6; all year.
Leaves: 1–5″ (2.5–12.5 cm) broad, roundish or kidney-shaped, bright green, shiny; leafstalks with inflated "bulbs," filled with spongy, air-filled tissue, that act as floats.
Height: aquatic, with flower stalk to 16″ (40 cm) above water.

Habitat
Swamps, freshwater marshes, streams, lakes, and ditches.

Range
Virginia south to Florida; west to Texas and Missouri.

Comments
An introduced tropical plant, it spreads rapidly, clogging waterways in the southern states. It may have some potential for removing excessive nutrients from overly enriched aquatic systems. If the plants are harvested periodically, the nutrient load in the water can be reduced. This plant can screen heavy metals and other toxins from polluted water.

Blue Flag
Iris versicolor
297

Several violet-blue flowers with attractively veined and yellow-based sepals are on a sturdy stalk among tall swordlike leaves that rise from a basal cluster.
Flowers: 2½–4″ (6.3–10 cm) wide; sepals 3, nonbearded; petals 3, narrower, erect; styles 3, 2-lobed, arching over sepals; stamens 3, hidden under styles; May–August.

Leaves: 8–32″ (20–80 cm) long, ½–1″ (1.3–2.5 cm) wide; pale green to grayish.
Fruit: bluntly 3-lobed, erect capsule.
Height: 2–3′ (60–90 cm).

Habitat
Swamps, marshes, and wet shores.

Range
Manitoba to Nova Scotia; south through New England to Virginia; west to W. Pennsylvania, Ohio, Michigan, Wisconsin, and Minnesota.

Comments
This is a showy native Iris of northeastern wetlands. Insects attracted to the sepals must crawl under the tip of a style and brush past a stigma and stamen, thus facilitating pollination. The rhizome is extremely poisonous, but it was dried and used in small amounts as a cathartic and diuretic by Indians and colonists. A similar southern wetland species, occurring from Virginia to Florida and Texas, is Southern Blue Flag (*I. virginica*). It is a smaller plant, to 2′ (60 cm) tall, with bright green leaves that often lie on the ground or water. A coastal, brackish-water species called Slender Blue Flag (*I. prismatica*) has extremely narrow, grasslike leaves that are less than ¼″ (6 mm) wide; it occurs from Maine to Georgia and Tennessee. The name "Flag" is from the Middle English *flagge,* "rush" or "reed."

Monkeyflower
Mimulus ringens
298

Asymmetrical, 2-lipped, blue-purple flowers rise from the axils of opposite leaves that clasp the square stem.
Flowers: about 1″ (2.5 cm) long; upper lip 2-lobed, erect; lower lip 3-lobed, with 2 yellow spots on inside; stamens 4; white throat of corolla nearly closed; June–September.
Leaves: 2–4″ (5–10 cm) long; unstalked, oblong to lanceolate.
Height: 1–3′ (30–90 cm).

Habitat
Wet meadows and stream banks.

Range
Saskatchewan to Nova Scotia; south to Georgia; west to Alabama, Louisiana, and NE. Texas.

Comments
The flower looks something like a monkey's face, hence the common and genus names, the latter from the Latin *mimus* ("a buffoon"). The lavender-flowering Sharp-winged Monkeyflower (*M. alatus*) has stalked leaves and a winged stem. It is more common southward and westward in wet sites.

Virginia Bluebells
Mertensia virginica
299

Erect plant with smooth gray-green foliage and nodding clusters of pink buds that open into light blue trumpet-shaped flowers.

Flowers: about 1″ (2.5 cm) long; corolla 5-lobed; March–June.
Leaves: basal leaves 2–8″ (5–20 cm) long; stem leaves smaller, alternate, oval, untoothed.
Height: 8–24″ (20–60 cm).

Habitat
Moist woods; rarely, meadows; especially on floodplains.

Range
S. Ontario; W. New York south to N. North Carolina and Alabama; west to Arkansas and E. Kansas; north to Minnesota.

Comments
When it grows in masses, this species makes a spectacular show, especially in the Midwest. A smaller, trailing, rosy-pink-flowered species, Sea Lungwort (*M. maritima*), occurs on beaches from Newfoundland to Massachusetts.

Mountain Bluebell
Mertensia ciliata
300

A plant with clumps of leafy stems and loose clusters of narrowly bell-shaped, blue flowers turning pink with age.
Flowers: corolla 5-lobed, ½–¾″ (1.3–2 cm) long, tubular part same length as the bell-like end; May–August.
Leaves: 1¼–6″ (3.1–15 cm) long, tapered at base, the lower ones on long petioles.
Fruit: divided into 4 small, wrinkled segments.
Height: 6–60″ (15–150 cm).

Habitat
Stream banks, seeps, and wet meadows.

Range
Central Idaho to central Oregon and the Sierra Nevada; east to W. Montana, W. Colorado, and N. New Mexico.

Comments
Mertensias are also called Lungworts after a European species with spotted leaves that was believed to be a remedy for lung disease. Similar species differ in the proportions of the corolla.

True Forget-me-not
Myosotis scorpioides
301

Sprawling plant with several tiny, light blue tubular flowers with golden eyes, growing on small, curving, divergent branches that uncoil as the flowers bloom.
Flowers: ¼″ (6 mm) wide, corolla 5-lobed; May–October.
Leaves: 1–2″ (2.5–5 cm) long, oblong, blunt, hairy, mostly stalkless.
Height: 6–24″ (15–30 cm).

Habitat
Stream borders and wet places.

Range
Newfoundland south to Florida and Louisiana; west to Wisconsin; Pacific Coast.

Comments
This European introduction, which was once extensively cultivated, has now been naturalized around lakes, ponds, and streams. In bud, the tightly coiled flower cluster resembles a scorpion; hence the species name. The Tufted Forget-me-not (*M. sylvatica*) is now commonly cultivated and is becoming established in drier habitats of the northeastern United States. The Smaller Forget-me-not (*M. laxa*), with much smaller flowers, is native to North America, particularly in wet places.

Common Butterwort
Pinguicula vulgaris
302

A solitary violet flower tops a leafless stalk that rises from a basal rosette of sticky leaves.
Flowers: ⅓″ (8 mm) wide; corolla tubular, with 5 flattish lobes, the lower lobe spurred; June–August.
Leaves: to 2″ (5 cm) long, lying flat against the ground; yellow-green, with uprolled edges, straplike, shiny, sticky.
Height: 2–6″ (5–15 cm).

Habitat
Wet rocks, open soils in limestone areas.

Range
Alaska to NW. California, across Canada to N. Vermont, central New York, Michigan, and Minnesota.

Comments
This carnivorous plant has greasy leaves on whose surface insects are caught and digested by enzymes.

Fire Flags
Thalia geniculata
303

Tall perennial herb with long basal leaves and pairs of small flowers in open panicles.
Flowers: ½–¾″ (1.3–2 cm) long; petals 3, bluish purple subtended by bracts, sepals 3, minute; most of year.
Leaves: large, broad, lanceolate, arising from underground rhizomes; each blade to 20″ (50 cm) long.
Fruit: indehiscent.
Height: 3–10′ (90–300 cm).

Habitat
Borders of lakes and swamps.

Range
S. Florida, West Indies.

Comments
The light green foliage on their stalks gives these conspicuous plants the name "flags." They are related to the banana and the canna.

Cinnamon Fern
Osmunda cinnamomea
304

Tall, vigorous fern growing as separate plants in arching circular clusters.
Leaves: pinnately compound; fronds to 3′ (90 cm) long and covered by tufts of cinnamon-brown wool in spring.
Reproduction: brownish spore-producing fronds appear in

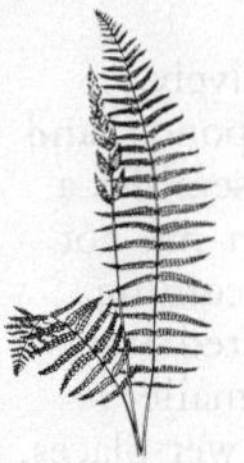

spring as separate stalks and then wither, while green vegetative fronds persist.
Height: 3–5′ (90–150 cm).

Habitat
Swamps.

Range
Newfoundland west to Minnesota; south to Florida, Texas, New Mexico.

Comments
Widely found in wet areas, Cinnamon Ferns often occur in association with the somewhat similar and related Interrupted Fern (*O. claytoniana*); fertile leaflets (pinnae) interrupt the vegetative fronds.

Marsh Fern
Thelypteris palustris
305

Delicate yellow-green fern forming sizable patches in open, sunny, wet areas.
Leaves: fronds 4–28″ (10–70 cm) long, lance-shaped, with pointed tips; widest near base.
Reproduction: fertile fronds are erect on long stalks; numerous brownish sporangia clusters (sori) on underside of frond.
Height: 12–18″ (30–45 cm).

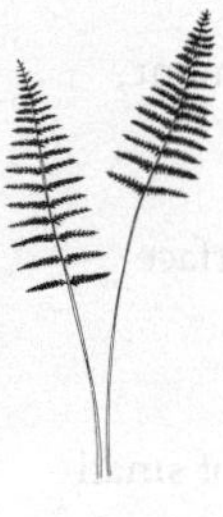

Habitat
Marshes, margins of lakes, ponds and bogs.

Range
S. Newfoundland west to SE. Manitoba; south to New England, Georgia, Tennessee, west to Oklahoma.

Comments
This species is one of the most common wetland ferns.

Royal Fern
Osmunda regalis
306

A robust, erect fern with fronds terminated by light brown, spore-bearing leaflets.
Leaves: fronds large, 3′ (1 m) long or more; twice cut, pinnately compound; resemble leaves of the locust tree; leaflets 1–2″ (2.5–5 cm) long.
Reproduction: fertile leaflets terminal, densely clustered, producing sporangia.
Height: 3–6′ (90–180 cm).

Habitat
Along streams and lakes; bogs and marshes.

Range
Newfoundland west to Saskatchewan; south to Florida, Texas, and tropical America.

Comments
The Royal Fern is one of several ferns that produce their spores on modified leaflets, not on the underside of the fronds.

Marsh Cinquefoil
Potentilla palustris
307

Reddish trailing stems rooting in mud or water and bearing purple flowers.
Flowers: ¾″ (18 mm) wide; magenta-purple within and greenish without, due to long green sepals; June–August.
Leaves: long-stalked, pinnately compound, 2–4″ (5–10 cm) long; 5–7 oblong leaflets, sharply toothed, each 1–2″ (2.5–5 cm) long.
Fruit: small, smooth, seedlike achene.
Height: 6–20″ (15–50 cm).

Habitat
Swamps, bogs, stream banks.

Range
Circumboreal, south to New Jersey, Ohio, and California.

Comments
This is the only cinquefoil with purple flowers.

Water Lettuce
Pistia stratiotes
308

Small floating aquatic plant with inconspicuous white flowers on a spadix embedded in a rosette of green leaves.
Flowers: male florets at apex of spadix; female at base. Spathe small, greenish white, about ½″ (1.3 cm) long; April.
Leaves: 2–10″ (5–25 cm) long, velvety, parallel-ribbed; rosette about 6″ (15 cm) wide.
Height: aquatic, to 10″ (25 cm) above water.

Habitat
Still waters of ponds, ditches, and swamps; slow-moving streams.

Range
Florida west to Texas.

Comments
This aggressive plant rapidly covers vast expanses of open water in southern wetlands, especially cypress swamps. Its growth is so dense and compact that it looks like solid ground.

Jack-in-the-pulpit
Arisaema triphyllum
309, 327

Distinctive "Jack-in-the-pulpit" formation grows beneath large leaves.
Flowers: curving ridged hood (the spathe or "pulpit"), green or purplish brown, often streaked or mottled, envelops an erect club (the spadix or "Jack") 2–3″ (5–7.5 cm) long. Spadix bears tiny separate male and female flowers at the base; April–June.
Leaves: 1 or 2, long-stemmed, 3-parted, veined, dull green.
Fruit: cluster of shiny red berries on spadix, late summer–fall.
Height: 1–3′ (30–90 cm).

Habitat
Damp woods and swamps.

Range
S. Quebec and New Brunswick; south through Appalachians and coastal plain to Florida; west to Lousiana and E. Texas.

Comments
Some authorities recognize 1 species, and others 3, based on minor differences in leaves, spathe, and size. Because of needlelike calcium oxalate crystals in the underground tuber, it is peppery to the taste and causes a strong burning reaction if eaten raw. This unpleasant property can be eliminated by cooking, and American Indians gathered the fleshy taproots (corms) as a vegetable.

Arrow Arum
Peltandra virginica
310

Aquatic plant with large, long-stalked fleshy leaves and a green, wavy-margined, tapering, leaflike spathe curled around a rodlike spadix.
Flowers: spathe 4–7″ (10–17.5 cm) long; female flowers at base of clublike spadix, male above; May–July.
Leaves: 1–2′ (30–60 cm) long, arrowhead shape, with prominent veining.
Fruit: black or blackish-green berries in clusters.
Height: 1–2′ (30–60 cm).

Habitat
Shallow waters of ponds and slow-moving rivers, swamps, and marshes.

Range
S. Ontario and Quebec; S. Maine south to Florida; west to Texas; north to Michigan.

Comments
This aquatic is especially common in and along shallow waterways, where it may occur in large colonies.

Green Dragon
Arisaema dracontium
311

Solitary greenish inflorescence similar to Jack-in-the-pulpit, but with a less dominant hood (spathe) and a curious long-tipped spadix (the "dragon's tongue") protruding several inches beyond the narrow spathe.
Flowers: tiny greenish-yellow male and female flowers at base of spadix 4–8″ (10–20 cm) long; May–June.
Leaves: single, compound, long-stalked, with 5–15 pointed, dull green leaflets, central ones to 8″ (20 cm) long.
Fruit: orange-red and green berries.
Height: 1–3′ (30–90 cm).

Habitat
Wet woodlands, low rich ground, stream banks, in neutral or basic soils.

Range
S. Ontario and Quebec; Vermont south to Florida; west to Texas; north to Wisconsin and Minnesota.

Comments
As with Jack-in-the-pulpit, the tuberous taproot of this plant can burn the mouth severely if ingested uncooked. Far less common than Jack-in-the-pulpit, Green Dragon is considered comparatively rare.

Skunk Cabbage
Symplocarpus foetidus
312

Emerging from moist earth in early spring, a large brownish-purple and green, mottled, shell-like spathe enclosing a knob-like spadix covered with tiny flowers. By late spring a tight roll of fresh green leaves beside the spathe unfolds to form huge, dark green, cabbagy leaves that may carpet an area.
Flowers: floral leaf (spathe) 3–6″ (7.5–15 cm) long; February–May.
Leaves: 1–2′ (30–60 cm) long, to 1′ (30 cm) wide, veined, on stalks rising directly from ground.
Height: 1–2′ (30–60 cm).

Habitat
Open swamps and marshes, along streams, wet woodlands.

Range
Nova Scotia and Quebec to Ontario and Minnesota; south to Georgia and Tennessee.

Comments
This distinctive plant of marshy woods sprouts so early in spring that the heat of cellular respiration resulting from its rapid growth actually melts snow or ice around it. Its strong fetid odor, especially when the plant is bruised, resembles decaying flesh and lures insects that pollinate it.

Duckweed
Lemna spp.
313

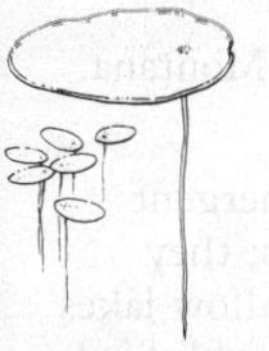

Tiny floating plants often forming a carpetlike cover on the water's surface.
Flowers: inconspicuous, highly reduced with a single anther or 1 or 2 flask-shaped ovaries.
Leaves: no true leaves, but small rounded thalli or fronds, about 1/16–3/8″ (1.5–10 mm) long, with 1 or more roots, depending on species.
Fruit: small, thin-walled, 1-seeded and inflated.
Height: aquatic.

Habitat
Ponds, quiet water.

Range
Throughout North America.

Comments
These are the simplest and among the smallest flowering plants. They reproduce by making new plants from old ones. Duckweeds are especially relished by waterfowl.

Featherfoil
Hottonia inflata
314

An aquatic plant with several thick, hollow, inflated, upright stalks emerging from the water and bearing tiny, greenish-white flowers in terminal clusters and in circles at the joints.
Flowers: 1/3″ (8 mm) long; petals 5, white, inconspicuous compared to the 5 larger, linear, green sepals; April–June.
Leaves: 3/4–2 1/2″ (2–6.3 cm) long, crowded at base of plant, alternate, opposite, or whorled, pinnately compound, divided into narrow segments.
Height: aquatic, with stem 3–8″ (7.5–20 cm) above water.

Habitat
Pools, ditches, and stagnant ponds, usually in more than 1′ (30 cm) of water.

Range
New England and New York; south to Florida, west to Texas; north to Missouri, Illinois, Indiana, and Ohio.

Comments
The unusual appearance of this floating aquatic plant is due to the ½″ (1.3 cm) thick, inflated, floral stalks, constricted at the joints and essentially leafless. Plants are abundant for a season, then vanish for 7 or 8 years before appearing again.

Bur Reed
Sparganium americanum
315

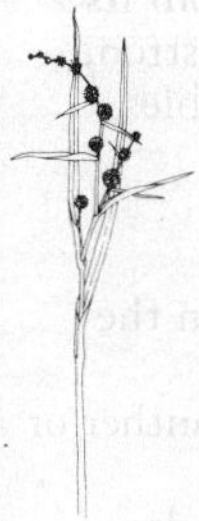

An erect, grasslike, aquatic plant with zigzag stalks bearing ball-like heads of tiny green flowers.
Flowers: sepals and petals represented by chaffy scales. Female flowers with 1 stigma; male flowers with 5 stamens. Female flowers in heads 1″ (2.5 cm) wide, on stem below 5–9 smaller heads of male flowers. Male flowers wither and die after pollen is shed. Pistil of female flower has 1 stigma; May–August.
Leaves: to 3′ (90 cm) long, 2–4½″ (5–11.3 cm) wide; keeled beneath, flat, soft-textured, partly submerged.
Fruit: Female heads form burlike green masses of beaked, seedlike fruits.
Height: 1–3′ (30–90 cm).

Habitat
Shallow water and muddy shores.

Range
Newfoundland to Minnesota; south to Florida and Montana.

Comments
The Bur Reeds represent an important group of emergent plants that are partly in and partly out of the water; they frequently form dense stands along the edges of shallow lakes and ponds. The seeds are eaten by waterfowl and marsh birds, and muskrats feed on the entire plant. The Great Bur Reed (*S. eurycarpum*) reaches a height of 7′ (2.1 m), has 2 stigmas, not 1 as in the rest of the group; it is widely distributed. Floating Bur Reed (*S. fluctuans*) has a floating stem, and floating ribbonlike leaves; it is found in cold ponds and lakes across Canada and New England west to Minnesota.

Water Pennywort
Hydrocotyle americana
316

Creeping or weakly erect marsh plant with clusters of tiny greenish-white flowers arising from the leaf axils.
Flowers: about ¹⁄₁₆″ (1.5 mm) wide, 5-parted, in clusters of 1–5; June–September.
Leaves: ½–1¾″ (1.3–4.4 cm) wide, roundish, doubly scalloped, deep basal notch.
Height: creeper, with runners arising from leaf axils.

Habitat
Damp woods, meadows.

Range
Newfoundland and Nova Scotia; south through New England to Maryland and upland North Carolina; west to Tennessee; northwesterly to Minnesota.

Comments
There are numerous species of Pennyworts with distinctive, rounded, pennylike leaves on stems that creep or float.

Wood Nettle
Laportea canadensis
317

Clusters of small, greenish flowers are in the leaf axils on a stout stem with stinging hairs; female flowers are in loose, elongated clusters in upper axils; male flowers in shorter clusters in lower axils.
Flowers: about ⅙″ (4 mm) long; female with 4 sepals, 1 pistil; male with 5 sepals, 5 stamens; petals absent; July–September.
Leaves: 2½–8″ (6.3–20 cm) long, alternate, thin, ovate, long-stalked, coarsely toothed.
Fruit: dry, seedlike, crescent-shaped.
Height: 1½–4′ (45–120 cm).

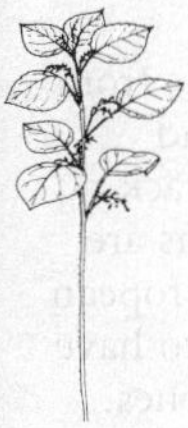

Habitat
Low woods, stream banks.

Range
Manitoba to Quebec and Nova Scotia, south to Florida; west to Mississippi, Oklahoma, and Missouri.

Comments
The flowers of the similar Stinging Nettle (*Urtica dioica*) are in tighter, slender axillary clusters and the leaves are opposite and have heart-shaped bases.

Clearweed
Pilea pumila
318

A small, translucent-stemmed annual with short, curved clusters of inconspicuous, greenish-white flowers in the leaf axils. Plant lacks stinging hairs.
Flowers: about ⅙″ (4 mm) long; female flowers with 3-parted calyx, 1 pistil; male flowers with 4-parted calyx, 4 stamens; July–October.
Leaves: 1–5″ (2.5–12.5 cm) long; opposite, ovate, conspicuously veined, coarsely toothed.
Fruit: dry, seedlike, green (often marked with black).
Height: 4–20″ (10–50 cm).

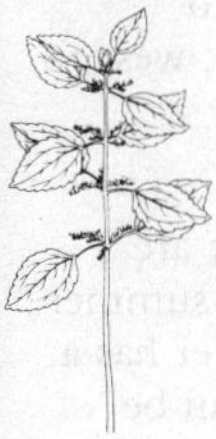

Habitat
Moist, shaded places.

Range
Throughout eastern Canada and New England; south to Florida and Texas; west to Iowa and Kansas.

Comments
The distinctive clear stem, soft and with a watery look, is responsible for the common name. It is restricted to shady areas, where it may form a continuous cover over moist soil.

Swamp Saxifrage
Saxifraga pensylvanica
319

A stout, hairy, sticky flower stalk has branched clusters (at first compact but later elongated and loose) of small flowers, usually yellowish green.
Flowers: about ⅙″ (4 mm) wide; petals 5; stamens 10, pistils 2, united; April–June.
Leaves: 4–8″ (10–20 cm) long; basal, ovate to lanceolate, nearly toothless.
Height: 1–3′ (30–90 cm).

Habitat
Wet meadows and prairies, swamps, bogs, and banks.

Range
Maine south to North Carolina; west to West Virginia, Missouri, and Illinois.

Comments
This is a large Saxifrage of wet areas; the genus name is from the Latin *saxum* ("a stone") and *frangere* ("to break") and alludes either to the supposed ability of the plant to crack rocks (in the crevices where some members of the genus are found) or to the stonelike bulblets on the roots of a European species. In earlier times, the Saxifrages were assumed to have medicinal value in dissolving kidney or gallbladder stones.

False Hellebore
Veratrum viride
320

A stout plant with large leaves clasping a stem that bears a branching cluster of greenish, star-shaped, hairy flowers.
Flowers: about ½″ (1.3 cm) wide; sepals 3, petal-like; petals 3; stamens 6, curved; May–July.
Leaves: 6–12″ (15–30 cm) long, 3–6″ (8–15 cm) wide; large, parallel along veins.
Fruit: 3-lobed capsule.
Height: 2–7′ (60–210 cm).

Habitat
Swamps, wet woods, and meadows.

Range
New Brunswick, Quebec, and New England; south to Maryland and, in uplands, to Georgia and Tennessee; west to Minnesota.

Comments
The ribbed, yellow-green leaves of this wetland plant are conspicuous in spring; the plant withers away before summer. The rootstock is poisonous, as is the foliage. The latter has a burning taste and is usually avoided by animals; it can be lethal.

Wild Rice
Zizania aquatica
321

A robust annual grass usually growing in flooded sites and producing large flowering panicle bearing conspicuous male flowers below the female flowers, producing rice above.
Flowers: borne in panicle with scales that enclose stamens and pistil in separate spikelets; females about ½–¾″ (1.3–2 cm) long; June–August.

Leaves: 20–40″ (50–100 cm) long.
Fruit: dark-colored, elongated grain, ½–¾″ (1.3–2 cm) long.
Height: 3–10′ (90–300 cm).

Habitat
Marshes, ponds, lakes, borders of sluggish rivers.

Range
Nova Scotia east to Manitoba, southwest to Minnesota, south to Nebraska and Texas.

Comments
American Indians harvest the rice in Minnesota. It is also grown commercially there and in California.

Wool Grass
Scirpus cyperinus
322

A compound umbel, made up of many spikelets on branching rays, is at the top of a triangular or nearly round stem and is surrounded by spreading green, leaflike bracts; spikelets woolly in fruit.
Flowers: spikelets about ¼″ (6 mm) long, ovoid to cylindric, their reddish to brownish scales ovate to lanceolate, with 6 protruding bristles representing the sepals and petals; stamens 3; style 3-cleft. Bracts under inflorescence unequal, drooping at the tips; August–October.
Leaves: up to 2′ (60 cm) long and ½″ (1.3 cm) wide; rough-margined.
Height: 3–5′ (90–150 cm).

Habitat
Swamps and wet meadows.

Range
Newfoundland and Nova Scotia; south from New England to Florida; west to Oklahoma and E. Texas; north to Minnesota.

Comments
This is one of several species of important wetland plants, many of them emergents, that provide food and cover for waterfowl and other wildlife. Nearly 30 species occur in the East.

Giant Reed
Phragmites australis
323

A tall, thick-stemmed grass producing large, initially reddish, then silver, plumelike terminal clusters and smooth, flat, sharp, blue-green leaves; floral masses become increasingly downy and purplish gray as they mature.
Flowers: tiny, lacking petals; stamens 3; styles 2. Flowers enclosed in scales about ¼″ (6 mm) long; scales grouped into spikelets subtended by a tuft of silky hairs. Cluster of spikelets to 1′ (30 cm) long; August–September.
Leaves: blades up to 20″ (50 cm) long and 2″ (5 cm) wide, with rough margins; sheathe stem at base.
Height: 5–15′ (1.5–4.5 m).

Habitat
Fresh and brackish marshes, ditches.

Range
Throughout the continent, but more abundant along the coasts.

Comments
This tall and striking plant rarely produces seed but spreads vigorously by underground stems (rhizomes), often running over the surface of the ground for 17–34′ (5.1–10.2 m). It can form dense stands that exclude all other wetland species. It is the dominant vegetation of the still extant Hackensack Meadows of New Jersey, where it filters pollutants from the greater New York-New Jersey metropolitan area, thus serving a vital role. In New England, tidal gates across estuaries have restricted tidal flow and created heavily brackish conditions on tidal marshes, with the result that Giant Reed has replaced extensive areas of tidal marsh grasses. It is native both to the American and European continents.

Soft Rush
Juncus effusus
324

The soft, grasslike stems of this strictly wetland plant are in clumps and each bears clusters of very small, greenish-brown, scaly flowers, the clusters diverging from one point on the side of the stalk near the top.
Flowers: about ⅙″ (4 mm) long; sepals 3; petals 3; and stamens 3; July–September.
Leaves: lacking or represented only by spearlike basal sheaths up to 6″ (15 cm) long.
Height: 1½–4′ (45–120 cm).

Habitat
Swamps, marshes, and damp open ground.

Range
Throughout southern Canada and northern United States.

Comments
This common marsh plant is one of many rushes, most of which are found in wet soil or water. Muskrats feed on the rootstalks, and various wetland wading birds find shelter among the stems.

Red Osier Dogwood
Cornus stolonifera
325

This shrub has flat-topped clusters of small, creamy-white flowers and deep red, smooth twigs with white pith.
Flowers: clusters 1–2″ (2.5–5 cm) wide; petals 4; May–August.
Leaves: 2–4″ (5–10 cm) long; opposite, ovate, pale beneath, with veins curving.
Fruit: cluster of white, berrylike drupes.
Height: 3–10′ (90–300 cm).

Habitat
Shores and thickets.

Range
Alaska to Newfoundland; south to West Virginia; west to California.

Comments
This is the most showy of the red-twigged dogwoods. The genus name comes from the Latin *cornu* ("horn") and alludes to the hardness of the wood. A European species has long been used for making butchers' skewers; hence the common name Dogwood, derived from the Old English word *dagge* ("dagger"). A closely related species, Silky Dogwood (*C. amomum*), has slightly hairy red twigs with tan pith and blue fruits.

Yaupon
Ilex vomitoria
329

A southern shrub or small tree with evergreen leaves and numerous tiny greenish-white flowers.
Flowers: male and female flowers on separate plants, male in stalked clusters of 3–9, female in unstalked clusters of 1–3. Calyx lobes, petals, and stamens 4; March–May.
Leaves: ¾–1½″ (2–3.8 cm) long, leathery, lanceolate to ovate, smooth, finely toothed, dark green and shiny above, pale green below.
Fruit: berrylike, bright red, about ⅕″ (5 mm) in diameter, translucent.
Height: 5–15′ (1.5–4.5 m), occasionally to 26′ (8 m).

Habitat
Swamps, wet woods, rarely in sand hills.

Range
Virginia south to Florida; west to Texas and Arkansas.

Comments
This distinctive native shrub bears decorative red berries seldom eaten by birds. The species name alludes to the fact that an infusion made from the leaves was used by Indians as a laxative and emetic in purification rites. The common name derives from a Catawba Indian word for "small tree."

MUSHROOMS

The damp ground of bogs, marshes, swamps, and streambanks offers the perfect habitat for many different kinds of mushrooms. Some grow on the ground, while others spring to life on fallen tree trunks and branches. Some species are quite inconspicuous; others lend a touch of unexpected color—bright reds and oranges—to somber areas. This section provides descriptions of some of the most familiar and conspicuous mushrooms that grow in North America's wetlands.

Yellow Unicorn Entoloma
Entoloma murraii
331

Cap ⅜–1¼″ (1–3 cm) wide; stalk 2–4″ (5–10 cm) tall. Cap yellow to yellow-orange, conical at maturity, silky and shiny, with short spike jutting from tip. Young mushrooms have yellow gills that turn pinkish as spores mature; somewhat distant, attached to stalk. Stalk dry and yellow.

Season
June–October.

Habitat
Damp ground in woods and near swamps.

Range
Generally throughout the eastern United States.

Comments
Although this beautiful little mushroom is not common, it is occasionally abundant when conditions are extremely favorable.

Brown Alder Mushroom
Alnicola melinoides
332

Cap ⅜–1″ (1–2.5 cm) wide; stalk 1–1⅝″ (2.5–4 cm) tall. Cap honey-colored, darker on low-knobbed center, lighter at radially lined and wavy margin, with very slightly roughened surface. Gills somewhat distant, yellow to rusty brown, attached to stalk. Stalk narrow and brittle, yellowish to brownish.

Season
July–November.

Habitat
Under alder trees in boggy areas.

Range
Primarily in Pacific Northwest, but widely distributed.

Comments
This mushroom is in a vaguely defined group popularly called LBMs (little brown mushrooms), which includes a large number of similar species. The habitat in this case is a clue to identification.

Spotted Gomphidius
Gomphidius maculatus
333

Cap 1–4″ (2.5–10 cm) wide; stalk 1–3″ (2.5–7.5 cm) tall. Cap light cinnamon to reddish brown, slimy, smooth, and blackening when handled. Gills white at first, then gray; distant; attached to stalk and running down it a bit. Stalk whitish with yellow at base, with many purple-black fibers on lower half.

Season
August–November.

Habitat
Mostly under larch, especially in northern larch bogs.

Range
Widely distributed across northern North America.

Comments
This edible species may appear wherever larch thrives, but is most common in Idaho. The similar Slimy Gomphidius (*G. glutinosus*) has a brown cap and is often found with spruce.

Turpentine Waxy Cap
Hygrophorus pudorinus
334

Cap 2–4″ (5–10 cm) wide; stalk 2–4″ (5–10 cm) tall. Cap buff-pink or pale tan, smooth and sticky, with inrolled margin when young. Gills white to slightly pink, waxy, somewhat distant; slightly running down stalk. Stalk white to pink, dry, with white tufts above and sometimes tapered at base.

Season
August–October; to January in California.

Habitat
Under spruce, fir, or hemlock; sometimes in boggy areas.

Range
Northern North America, extending south to Arizona and California in the West.

Comments
Despite this mushroom's unpleasant flavor (note the common name), some people do eat it. This species occurs in a few varieties differing in minor details.

Emetic Russula ⊗
Russula emetica
335

Cap 1–3″ (2.5–7.5 cm) wide; stalk 2–4″ (5–10 cm) tall. Cap bright red varying to deep pink. The cap is sticky with a striate margin. Gills are off-white, close, and attached to the stalk. The white to off-white stalk may widen at the base. There is no ring.

Season
August–September.

Habitat
Most frequently in sphagnum moss but also on the ground in mixed woods.

Range
Widely distributed throughout North America.

Comments
Usually regarded as poisonous, the Emetic Russula is nevertheless eaten by some. The extremely acrid taste will discourage most people. In any event, it cannot be recommended for the table since it closely resembles other species whose toxic properties are unknown.

Chocolate Milky
Lactarius lignyotus
336

Cap ¾–4″ (2–10 cm) wide; stalk 2–4¾″ (5–12 cm) tall. Cap chocolate-brown to blackish brown, with small knob; dry, velvety. Gills attached to stalk; variably spaced, from close to somewhat distant; white when young, becoming pale ochre as spores mature. Stalk same color as cap, usually a bit furrowed; dry, powdery-velvety.

Season
August–October.

Habitat
Often in moss in sphagnum bogs and coniferous woods.

Range
Eastern North America west to Wisconsin.

Comments
This mushroom, like many of its close relatives, exudes a white milky juice called latex. If you slice the mushroom, the latex will stain the sliced surface pinkish. The Chocolate Milky is not edible.

Wrinkled Thimble-cap
Verpa bohemica
337

Cap ⅜–1″ (1–2.5 cm) wide; ¾–1¼″ (2–3 cm) high; stalk 2⅜–3¼″ (6–8 cm) tall. Cap yellow-brown, distinctly wrinkled and skirtlike, attached only at top of stalk. Stalk smooth, cylindrical, white, occasionally with faint furrows.

Season
Late March–early May.

Habitat
Damp and wet areas in woods.

Range
Widely distributed throughout North America.

Comments
Although this mushroom is eaten by many people, it cannot be recommended here because some people react adversely to it. As the common name suggests, it looks like a thimble atop a finger.

Velvety Earth Tongue
Trichoglossum hirsutum
338

Head ¼″ (5 mm) wide near top, ¹⁄₁₆–⅛″ (1.5–3 mm) wide near base; ⅜–⅝″ (1–1.5 cm) high; stalk 1¼–2⅜″ (3–6 cm) tall. Head (not clearly distinct from stalk) black or brownish black, more or less narrowly elliptical, compressed laterally and sometimes with a distinct fold; with dark, bristly hairs. Stalk slender, velvety, colored like head, also with bristly hairs.

Season
July–October.

Habitat
Various: on rotting wood, on soil, in sphagnum moss.

Range
Eastern United States generally; also Idaho and West Coast states.

Comments
This species (and several look-alikes) is unquestionably frequently overlooked because of its small size and somber coloration. Its range is probably wider than is now known.

Swamp Beacon
Mitrula elegans
339

Head ⅛–⅜″ (0.3–1 cm) wide, ¼–⅝″ (0.5–1.5 cm) high; stalk ⅝–1⅝″ (1.5–4 cm) tall. Head yellow or pale orange, irregularly elliptical, smooth. Stalk varies from white to pinkish; translucent, smooth.

Season
May–July.

Habitat
Base of stalk usually submerged in shallow pool, growing from decaying leaves or twigs. Also grows on decaying vegetation in wet soil.

Range
Most of northern North America; south on East Coast to Tennessee.

Comments
This mushroom was formerly mistaken for a very similar European species, *Mitrula paludosa.* Similar species exist in the United States.

Blue-staining Cup
Caloscypha fulgens
340

Cup ⅜–2″ (1–5 cm) wide; no stalk. Cup with irregular shape, sometimes split on one side. Exterior green to bluish green, fading to orange-yellow except for margin. Interior bright orange-yellow, sometimes with blue-green stains. Mushroom brittle.

Season
May–July.

Habitat
Boggy areas; also wet places in coniferous woods in mountains.

Range
Eastern North America west to Montana; also in Rocky Mountains and California.

Comments
A few similar mushrooms grow in different locales, usually at different times during the year.

Blueberry Cup
Monilinia vaccinii-corymbosi
341

Cup ¼–⅜″ (0.5–1 cm) wide, ¼–⅜″ (0.5–1 cm) high; stalk ⅜–1¼″ (1–3 cm) tall. Cup almost closed when young, opening wide revealing fawn-colored inner surface. Outer surface brownish with a satiny sheen. Stalk brownish gray or darker, and smooth.

Season
March–May.

Habitat
In wet, boggy areas and swamps, on fallen blueberry fruits; occasionally on blueberry twigs.

Range
Massachusetts to North Carolina.

Comments
The Blueberry Cup is one of a few interesting species that grow in early spring on fallen overwintered fruits such as cherries and peaches.

Silky Parchment
Stereum striatum
342

Cap ¼–⅜″ (0.5–1 cm) wide; no stalk. Caps silvery gray, thin, rounded, silky and shiny, sometimes attached to one another, growing from a central point. Fertile undersurface light buff to brown, smooth.

Season
All year.

Habitat
Twigs and branches of decaying ironwood (*Carpinus*), often in swampy woods.

Range
Northeastern and midwestern United States.

Comments
One of many mushrooms that grow in tiers on trees, this small species can be easily seen with a magnifier. It can be found where ironwood (sometimes called hornbeam) grows.

INSECTS AND SPIDERS

Among the most numerous animals on earth, insects and spiders are also fascinating. Some have carved out a niche for themselves as tiny predators in an immense landscape; others have developed complex social systems of communal life. Wetlands are tremendously important as breeding grounds and for many species whose larvae live in the water; other insects, such as dragonflies, spend most of their adult lives near water as well. Included here are descriptions of the most common and typical insects, spiders, and related creatures of the wetlands.

Water Boatmen
Corixa spp.
343

¼–½″ (5–13 mm). Elongate oval. Gray to brown, upper surface usually with fine crossbands. Head concave, concealing forward portion of thorax and making fore wings appear to arise immediately behind head. Triangular shield where elytra meet thorax usually concealed. Fore legs short, outermost segments of legs scooplike. Middle and hind legs are flattened, paddlelike. Hind pair fringed with hair.

Habitat
Ponds, puddles, and birdbaths.

Range
Worldwide.

Life Cycle
Oval eggs are cemented to underwater supports, sometimes forming a dense crust. They hatch in 7–15 days.

Comments
Unless a birdbath is scrubbed almost daily, Water Boatmen will come to feed on algae. Some species are attracted to artificial light at night.

Giant Water Bug
Lethocerus americanus
344

1¾–2⅜″ (45–60 mm) long, ¾–1″ (20–25 mm) broad. Wingspan: to 4⅜″ (110 mm). Large, flat. Brown. Beak short and stout. Front femora heavy, with groove to accommodate folded tibiae. Hind legs flat, fringed. Fore wings leathery.

Habitat
Shallow freshwater ponds and pools, among bottom vegetation.

Range
Throughout the United States and Canada.

Life Cycle
In late spring or early summer, eggs are attached in rows of 100 or more on plants or other supports above water. Nymphs emerge in about 2 weeks. Adult female alternates between feeding and mating and lays 150 or more eggs in lifetime, but few nymphs survive because of cannibalism and predators.

Comments
Both the large nymph and the adult feign death if picked up, but they can stab suddenly with their beaks, injecting the anesthetic saliva used to subdue prey.

Common Backswimmer
Notonecta undulata
345

⅜–½″ (10–13 mm). Black underneath; white to dark green on back. Fore wings ivory-white with red markings and dark overlapping tips. Compound eyes large, black. Legs brown; fore and middle legs used for grasping, much longer hind legs flattened, fringed with hair, used for rowing.

Habitat
Ponds and slow-flowing shallow streams.

Range
Throughout North America.

Life Cycle
Elongated white eggs are attached to plant stems underwater, where they hatch in a few weeks. Nymphs are active predators. Adults of first generation appear in July and overwinter. 1–2 generations a year.

Comments
Occasionally, a backswimmer will attack a person's bare hand or leg in the water, earning its reputation as a water bee.

Kirby's Backswimmer
Notonecta kirbyi
346

⅜–½″ (10–13 mm). Black beneath, white to green or black on back. Fore wings yellowish white with dark tips. Compound eyes large, black. Legs brown and long, particularly hind legs, which are flattened and bear a fringe of hair on tibiae and outermost leg segments.

Habitat
Ponds and slow-flowing shallows of streams.

Range
Middle Atlantic states.

Life Cycle
Elongated white eggs are cemented to underwater plant stems, hatching in a few weeks. Nymphs often feed on their own species. Adults of first generation appear in July. 2 generations a year.

Comments
Master predators, backswimmers catch their victims by quietly swimming underneath them. If disturbed, backswimmers dive to the bottom and at intervals rise to the surface to get air.

Giant Water Scavenger Beetles
Hydrophilus spp.
347

1⅜–1½″ (34–38 mm). Elongate oval, strongly convex above, almost flat below. Brown, gray, or shiny black; legs reddish black. Short antennae clubbed, inconspicuous. Long slender lip palps held forward, easily mistaken for antennae.

Habitat
Ponds and slow streams.

Range
Throughout North America.

Life Cycle
Female deposits 120–140 yellow eggs in silken cocoonlike egg case with a hornlike "mast." The case is left to float or attached to some underwater object. Larvae feed underwater. In late summer fully grown larvae leave water to prepare pupal cells in moist earth. Adults emerge in less than 2 weeks and return to water. 1–2 generations a year.

Comments
Some adults creep under litter on land to overwinter; others are active under ice all winter and live more than 1 year. On summer nights these insects often leave water and fly about.

Large Whirligig Beetles
Dineutus spp.
348

3/8–5/8" (9–15 mm). Broadly oval, flattened. Black, often with a bronzy sheen. Elytra have 9 impressed lines.

Habitat
Surface film of ponds and slow streams.

Range
Throughout North America.

Life Cycle
Eggs are deposited in rows or masses on submerged plants. Aquatic larvae hunt prey, including mites, snails, and small aquatic insects, crawl out of water when fully grown, and construct pupal cases of sand and debris. Adults overwinter on plants or in mud. 1 generation a year.

Comments
Adults gather in restless swarms a few feet across. If threatened, a few may dive while the rest swim erratically away at the surface.

Marbled Diving Beetle
Thermonectes marmoratus
349

3/8–5/8" (10–15 mm). Broadly oval, flattened, with smooth contours. Black. Thorax and elytra have gold markings. Abdomen has yellowish spots.

Habitat
Ponds.

Range
Texas, Arizona, California, and Mexico.

Life Cycle
Eggs are attached to underwater plants. Larvae emerge to pupate in mud near pond. Adults return to pond. Larvae and adults survive dry periods by burrowing into mud.

Comments
Large swarms of these beetles sometimes fly to artificial lights at night. Other members of this genus are widespread in northern states and Canada.

Willow Leaf Beetle
Chrysomela lapponica
350

1/4–3/8" (7–9 mm). Oval, flattened. Elytra either reddish above with black spots resembling those of ladybug beetles or unspotted dark metallic purple. Both forms black below.

Habitat
River edges and floodplains.

Range
United States and southern Canada.

Life Cycle
Eggs are laid in spring on willow leaves, where larvae feed. Full-grown larvae pupate while hanging head downward from a leaf or twig.

Comments
The Unspotted Poplar Leaf Beetle (*Lina tremulae*), 3/8–5/8"

(9–15 mm), is bronze-black with red elytra. It was introduced accidentally from Europe and is now common in both eastern and western states and provinces.

Swamp Milkweed Leaf Beetle
Labidomera clivicollis
351

⅜–½″ (8–12 mm). Oval, strongly convex. Bluish or greenish black; elytra orange to yellow with 2 black marks in an X across midline. Male has 1 large projecting tooth on outside of each front femur and 1 on inside.

Habitat
Marsh and stream edges where swamp milkweed grows.

Range
Most of North America.

Life Cycle
Long yellow eggs cemented to milkweed leaves. Larvae drop to the ground and pupate there. Adults emerge by late summer.

Comments
These beetles often overwinter as adults in mullein plants and creep deep among the woolly leaves, which shrivel but do not fall off until the dead plant collapses in spring.

Willow Borer
Xylotrechus insignis
352

½–⅝″ (14–15 mm). Almost cylindrical, narrowed between front portion of thorax and elytra. Male velvety reddish brown with yellow lines on face and front portion of thorax and with 3 marks across elytra. Female is black with reddish antennae and legs and with variable yellow crossbands on front portion of thorax and elytra. Antennae longer than head and front portion of thorax. Elytra do not reach tip of abdomen.

Habitat
Rivers and floodplains.

Range
California, Oregon, and Arizona.

Life Cycle
Eggs are laid on bark of trees. Larvae tunnel into willow, later pupate close to bark surface. 1 generation a year.

Comments
These beetles are often seen on flower clusters, where they nibble pollen; they run with an antlike gait. Other species of this genus are dark brown with yellow markings. All have a Y-shaped ridge on the front of the head.

Bombardier Beetles
Brachinus spp.
353

¼–⅝″ (5–15 mm). Head, front portion of thorax, antennae, and legs brownish yellow. Elytra grooved lengthwise, squarish at rear end; powder-blue to darker blue, slightly metallic.

Habitat
Moist floodplains of rivers and near lakes, where temporary ponds form after storms.

Range
Throughout the United States and southern Canada.

Life Cycle
Eggs are laid singly in mud cells on stones and plants. Larvae feed as external parasites until they kill the host, then scavenge on its remains. They pupate and overwinter in chamber of host. Adults emerge in spring after seasonal floods.

Comments
These beetles are named for their unusual defense mechanism —they emit from their anal glands toxic liquid that instantly vaporizes into puffs, making a protective screen that can stain people's skin.

Green Pubescent Ground Beetle
Chlaenius sericeus
354

⅜–⅝″ (10–16 mm). Elongate oval. Bright green above, black below. Antennae and legs pale brownish yellow. Elytra bluish or green with fine lengthwise grooves and short hair.

Habitat
Floodplains, along edges of lakes and streams.

Range
Throughout North America.

Life Cycle
Eggs are deposited singly in purse-shaped cells made of mud, twigs, and leaves. Larvae pupate in fall and adults emerge in spring. 1 generation a year.

Comments
This beetle emits a leatherlike odor when disturbed, then runs to a new hiding place. Most species in this genus are covered with silky hair. They are distinguishable only by inconspicuous details.

Waterlily Leaf Beetles
Donacia spp.
355

¼–½″ (6–12 mm). Elongate, slender, flattened. Bronze, with green or yellow gloss. Antennae about half as long as body; legs long; outermost leg segments broad. Elytra are pitted in lengthwise rows and conceal tip of abdomen.

Habitat
Water lilies, pickerel weed, and other floating plants on ponds, slow streams, and protected shores of large lakes.

Range
Throughout North America.

Life Cycle
Female cuts holes through water lily pads, then with tip of abdomen cements eggs to the underwater surface of leaves. Larvae spin silken pupal shelters below leaves. Adults emerge in 10 months. Adults fly June–September.

Comments
Active by day, these beetles are fast fliers. Only a specialist can distinguish the 36 different species in this genus.

Common Water Strider
Gerris remigis
356

½–⅝″ (12–16 mm). Flattened, elongate. Dark brown to black. Short fore legs. Long slender middle and hind legs. Mostly wingless.

Habitat
Surfaces of ponds, slow streams, and other quiet waters.

Range
Throughout North America.

Life Cycle
Courtship and mating involve communication by ripples in the water's surface film. Female lays parallel rows of cylindrical eggs on an object at water's edge. Nymphs mature in about 5 weeks. Adults live many months, and in northern parts of their range they overwinter under fallen leaves.

Comments
These insects are called "Skaters" in Canada and "Jesus Bugs" in Texas because they "walk" on the water.

Western Waterscorpion
Ranatra brevicollis
357

1″ (25 mm) with 1″ (25 mm) paired tail-like breathing tubes. Very elongate, sticklike. All brown. Upper part of thorax narrow and necklike, no wider than head at compound eyes. Slender middle and hind legs, each about as long as body.

Habitat
Bottoms of shallow ponds, among debris and vegetation.

Range
California.

Life Cycle
Eggs are thrust into soft tissues of underwater plants or bottom debris. Nymphs are full grown in a few months and may overwinter before or after final molt to adulthood.

Comments
Swaying gently with the wind, this insect resembles a walkingstick. Both sexes produce scratchy sounds underwater by rasping together rough areas on the enlarged front leg bases (coxae) and the grooves into which the coxae fit.

Fishflies
Chauliodes spp.
358

¾–1″ (20–25 mm). Body and wings ash-gray. Jaws small, compound eyes dark and prominent, legs weak. Antennae, ⅜″ (9 mm) or more, have soft comblike projections along 1 side.

Habitat
Vegetation along streams.

Range
Throughout North America; individual species more restricted.

Life Cycle
Eggs are laid in masses near water, into which larvae crawl. They cling to vegetation with strong legs and seize prey in

powerful jaws. Larvae pupate in cells prepared in mud along the shore. Adults are active at night May–August.

Comments
These large insects are easy to capture because they fly so slowly and are so poorly coordinated. They rest on foliage by day and fly to lights at night.

Eastern Dobsonfly
Corydalus cornutus
359, 360

2″ (50 mm). Wingspan: to 4⅞″ (125 mm). Head almost circular, front portion of thorax squarish, slightly narrower. Wings translucent, grayish with dark veins. Jaws of male half as long as body, curved and tapering to tips, held crossing one another; female's jaws are shorter and capable of biting forcefully.

Habitat
Close to fast-flowing water, on alders, willows, and other woody vegetation.

Range
East of the Rocky Mountains.

Life Cycle
Rounded masses containing 100–1000 or more eggs are laid on rocks, branches, and objects close to water. Each mass is coated with a whitish secretion. Larvae drop into the water or crawl to reach feeding grounds. After 2 or 3 growing seasons, they crawl out of the water and prepare pupal cells under stones or logs, where they overwinter. Adults emerge in early summer.

Comments
Fishermen use dobsonfly larvae, called hellgrammites, as bait, since trout seem to be attracted to them as a natural food.

Californian Acroneuria
Acroneuria californica
361

Male ⅞″ (23 mm). Wingspan: ⅞–1⅛″ (23–30 mm). Female 1¼″ (31 mm). Wingspan: 1⅝–2⅛″ (40–54 mm). Upper part of thorax flat, wider at front than rear. Front portion of thorax narrower than head, broader than long. Brown, mottled with yellow. Abdomen yellowish at tip, darker near rear. Projections from tail yellowish brown. First antennal segment brown, pale toward tip. Legs brown with a dark band near tip of femora, outermost leg segments blackish. Wings have dark veins.

Habitat
Near rapid streams.

Range
California, Oregon, and Washington.

Life Cycle
Masses of eggs are deposited in water. Nymphs take 1 year or more to become adults, depending on the water temperature. Full-grown, they climb onto stones near water's edge, complete final molt, and fly away.

Comments
This common stonefly, one of 400 species in North America, is found near mountain streams in late spring and summer. Nymphs can survive in near-freezing water. Like most stoneflies, it is a poor flier and rarely strays from the water's edge.

Betten's Silverstreak Caddisfly
Grammotaulius bettenii
362

¼–⅞″ (7–23 mm). Wingspan: 1⅜–1⅝″ (35–41 mm). Body and wings dark yellowish brown. Head and upper part of thorax raised into yellowish warts with white hair. Antennae yellowish except for first antennal segment, which is greenish white and as long as head. Legs pale yellowish; fore femora bear 2 black spines at tip; fore tibiae have about 20 yellow or black spines; outermost segments of fore legs spiny below. Wings have short silvery streaks.

Habitat
Near freshwater ponds and slow broad streams, on foliage, twigs, and tree bark.

Range
Oregon to British Columbia.

Life Cycle
Eggs are deposited singly through surface film at edge of water. Larvae gather fragments of dead leaves and twigs, cement them with salivary silk until their bodies are encased in cylindrical tubes, which they drag everywhere while feeding from the front opening. They molt several times inside tubes and, when fully grown, close tube ends and pupate inside. Adults break through tubes, rise to water surface, and fly off.

Comments
This species was named in honor of Dr. Cornelius Betten of Cornell University, whose book on the Trichoptera of New York State appeared in 1934.

Bluebell
Nannothemis bella
363

¾″ (18–20 mm). Wingspan: 1–1⅜″ (25–35 mm). Very small. Body black and yellow, becoming powder-blue with age. Wings clear or amber-tinged near base.

Habitat
Stagnant pools in marshy places.

Range
Maine to Florida, west to Louisiana, north to Ontario.

Life Cycle
Female washes off eggs in water, where nymphs develop slowly. Adults may be found April–September.

Comments
This is the smallest North American dragonfly. Naiads inhabit narrow water-filled holes. Adults perch on grass stems in the sunshine, making brief flights to catch midges and other prey.

Widow
Libellula luctuosa
364

1⅝–2″ (42–50 mm). Wingspan: 1⅛–3½″ (30–90 mm). Body dark brown, sometimes with yellow stripes on sides; thorax somewhat hairy. Fore and hind wings blackish brown up to halfway toward tip; wing tips clear or smoky-brown.

Habitat
Near ponds, small lakes, and marshes.

Range
Ontario and Atlantic Coast to Georgia and Gulf Coast, west to Texas and northern Mexico, north to South Dakota.

Life Cycle
Female, often unattended by male, drops eggs into pond water. Nymphs crawl a few feet or more from water, cling to vegetation, and emerge as adults in April in the South, in late summer in the North.

Comments
These slow-flying dragonflies are easy to catch with a net. Their wings are disproportionately large, making these insects look bigger than they are.

Brown Darner
Boyeria vinosa
365

2¾–3⅛″ (70–80 mm). Wingspan: 3⅛–3⅞″ (80–98 mm). Body brown with 2 large pale yellow spots on each side of thorax. Wings have brown spot at base and yellowish spot on front margin.

Habitat
Shadowy edges of free-flowing streams.

Range
Nova Scotia to Florida, west to Texas, north to Illinois.

Life Cycle
Mated pair rests on a lily pad while the female lowers abdomen into water to free eggs. Nymphs crawl about 1′ out of water to transform to adults in May in New England and in October in Alabama.

Comments
These good fliers are seldom seen very far from home streams. Naiads live under stones and trash near woodland streams.

Green Darner
Anax junius
366

2¾–3⅛″ (70–80 mm). Wingspan: to 4⅜″ (110 mm). Thorax green, abdomen blue to purplish gray. Wings with pale yellowish area toward tips, darkening as insect ages. Targetlike mark on face. Compound eyes brown.

Habitat
Near ponds and slow streams.

Range
Throughout North America, less common in the West.

Life Cycle
Female inserts eggs singly into slit cut in stem of a submerged

plant. Fully grown naiads crawl out of the water in early spring or late summer to transform into adults.

Comments
The Green Darner is one of the fastest and biggest of the common dragonflies.

Short-stalked Damselflies
Argia spp.
367

Male 1⅛–1⅝″ (28–42 mm); female 1⅛–1¾″ (29–43 mm). Body blue and purple with few black markings, or brown to yellow with many black markings. Tibiae bear 2 rows of stiff bristles. Clear wings stalked only to level of first crossvein.

Habitat
Near gently flowing streams and lakes.

Range
Atlantic and Gulf coasts to Mexico, north to British Columbia; individual species more restricted.

Life Cycle
Female, unattended or held by male, lays eggs in wet wood. Sometimes both female and male enter water and remain submerged half an hour or more. Naiads are usually found in gentle water.

Comments
Adults alight on bare sunny places or on boulders projecting from the water. They are alert, seldom resting long in one place—hence their nickname, "Dancers."

Swift Long-winged Skimmer
Pachydiplax longipennis
368

1⅛–1¾″ (27–45 mm). Wingspan: to 3½″ (88 mm). Stout. Mostly blue; thorax with pale yellowish-green sides and 3 brown stripes. Abdomen blue-violet. Face white; top of head metallic blue a few days after emergence. Wings clear to slightly smoky, often with a brownish cloud beyond middle.

Habitat
Large ponds and broad streams.

Range
Throughout North America.

Life Cycle
Female generally flies parallel to water surface, flicking the tip of abdomen downward to wash off eggs. Nymphs clamber over submerged objects, generally transforming into adults close to water's edge. Adults fly late April–late September in North.

Comments
This swift-flying skimmer is hard to capture. When two males meet, they face each other and dart upward together, often out of sight. Females generally rest on trees away from the shore unless they are laying eggs.

Twelve-spot Skimmer
Libellula pulchella
369

1¾–2¼″ (45–58 mm). Wingspan: to 3⅛″ (80 mm). Head and thorax chocolate to light brown. Abdomen gray-brown to whitish. Each wing has 3 brown spots; male develops milky cast on wing between spots, female clear in these areas. Sometimes abdomen shows whitish bloom with age.

Habitat
Near ponds or broad, slow regions of rivers.

Range
Most of the United States.

Life Cycle
Female drops eggs singly into water or settles on plants to attach eggs to stems close to water surface. Adults fly late May–September near the Canadian–United States border.

Comments
This skimmer often rests on lily pads or plants overhanging the water.

Elisa Skimmer
Celithemis elisa
370

1⅛–1⅜″ (29–35 mm). Wingspan: 2¼–2⅜″ (56–60 mm). Patterned in red and black. Front portion of thorax is fringed with long brown hair; thorax has black stripe along middle of back, widest at front. Abdomen black with reddish triangular spots on each segment. Tail-like appendages orange. Wings dark reddish at base, brownish or black at tip; a small, vague, brown or black spot in membrane.

Habitat
Marshes, shallow bays, slow streams, and ponds.

Range
Nova Scotia to Florida, west to Texas, north to Minnesota.

Life Cycle
Female dips tip of abdomen through water surface to wash off eggs. Nymphs probably overwinter. Adults begin to emerge in early spring and fly April–October.

Comments
This dragonfly perches on tall plants rising above the marsh. Medium-sized compared to other members of the genus, this species is the most widely distributed in northern states and Canada, but seldom becomes abundant.

Streak-winged Red Skimmer
Sympetrum illotum
371

1⅝–1¾″ (42–45 mm). Wingspan: 2⅛–2½″ (55–65 mm). Head and thorax reddish brown and hairy; thorax with 2 white spots on each side. Abdomen red with row of pale spots on each side. Wings clear with reddish or brown veins.

Habitat
Near reedy pond edges.

Range
NW. Wyoming to Texas, west to California, north to British Columbia, especially Vancouver Island.

Life Cycle
Mated pair flies in tandem above water, while female washes off as many as 30 eggs individually. Then pair goes separately to rest on nearby twigs. Nymphs overwinter in water. Adults are active mid-June–late July.

Comments
As it flies low near pond margins, this skimmer's bright scarlet body is clearly visible against the green reeds.

Dark Lestes
Lestes congener
372

Male 1⅜–1⅝″ (35–42 mm); female 1¼–1½″ (32–38 mm); larger in the West. Male bronzy-black above with yellowish markings; last 2 abdominal segments grayish. Female paler, abdomen reddish brown. Wings clear.

Habitat
Ponds and flooded stream edges.

Range
S. Ontario to New Jersey, west to California, north to British Columbia.

Life Cycle
Eggs are deposited on plants high above the water or rather indiscriminately on live or dead dry foliage in fall. When vegetation collapses in winter, eggs are submerged underwater, where nymphs hatch. Adults emerge late in July.

Comments
This dark-colored, late-flying damselfly produces eggs that can survive frost as well as dry air.

Crane Flies
Tipula spp.
373

⅜–2½″ (8–65 mm). Wingspan: to 3″ (75 mm). Slender; abdomen longer than thorax and head combined. Grayish brown to golden, depending on species. Antennae with many segments, threadlike or narrowly feathery in males. Thorax has deep V-shaped crease above and acute or round point between wing bases. Females of some species wingless. Legs very slender, usually twice as long as body. Females have sharp egg-laying organ.

Habitat
Humid areas and wet ground, often near streams or lakes in mud or wet moss.

Range
Throughout North America.

Life Cycle
Slender eggs are usually laid in or on moist soil. Fully grown larvae pupate in soil or mud, where pupae usually overwinter. Adults emerge in spring. 1 or more generations a year.

Comments
Mating swarms of males "dance" above a bush or treetop waiting to seize females. Then each pair settles on foliage to

mate. The larvae are often eaten by skunks and moles; adults are devoured by birds and bats.

Comstock's Net-winged Midge
Agathon comstocki
374

⅜″ (10 mm). Spindlelike; thorax domed. Dull yellowish gray with dark gray pattern. Eyes large, black, not quite meeting. Antennae slender with short hair. Legs long, especially hind pair. Wings broad, clear; knoblike specialized hind wings long with flat, black triangular tips pointing toward body.

Habitat
Near fast-flowing streams.

Range
California to British Columbia.

Life Cycle
Eggs are laid on wet rocks beside fast streams. Larvae creep into the water, using special ventral suckers to move and cling to rocks. After pupal stage is completed, pupae float to the surface, burst open, and adults fly off.

Comments
Midges are most often seen resting on evergreen needles. This species was formerly included in the genus *Bibiocephala*.

Small Mayflies
Baetis spp.
375

⅛–⅜″ (3–11 mm) excluding 2 tail filaments. Dark brown to reddish brown. Male's abdominal segments 2–6 pale or transparent. Fore wings clear; hind wings much reduced, often difficult to see.

Habitat
Near shallow flowing water.

Range
Throughout North America; most species in central and eastern Canada.

Life Cycle
Eggs hatch in 2–5 weeks. Nymphs swim upstream by wagging the abdomen side to side. In warm streams adults emerge any month, with 2 or more generations a year. In colder water 1 generation matures in summer.

Comments
These mayflies are usually found near the water's edge among vegetation and are relatively easy to catch with a net. Adults of the first generation are larger and darker than those of a second.

House Mosquito
Culex pipiens
376

⅛–¼″ (4–5 mm). Thorax light brown to brownish gray. Abdomen banded white and brown above. Proboscis brown. Wings brown. Male's antennae more feathery than female's.

Habitat
Near swamps, ponds, and other bodies of stagnant water.

Range
Throughout North America; subspecies more limited in distribution.

Life Cycle
Eggs are deposited in raftlike masses of 100–300 on water surface film. They hatch in 1–5 days. Larvae feed head down in water. They pupate after 1–2 weeks. Adults emerge after a few days. Many generations are possible, the last overwintering as adults.

Comments
The Northern House Mosquito (*C. p. pipiens*), found in the northern United States and Canada, is the most common night-flying mosquito. The Southern House Mosquito (*C. p. quinquefasciatus*) is common in the Southeast, ranging west to California.

Purplish-blue Cricket Hunter
Chlorion cyaneum
377

1–1⅛" (25–29 mm). Large. 1-segmented "waist" between thorax and abdomen. Blue-black or metallic green. Front outermost leg segments bear 1 tooth. Wings blackish.

Habitat
Wet meadows and shores of streams or ponds.

Range
Texas, New Mexico, Arizona, and northern Mexico.

Life Cycle
Female hunts cricket, using stinger to anesthetize victim, which is then dragged or carried to nest site. Female prepares a deep tunnel in muddy soil, pushes the cricket inside, and deposits 1 egg. The wasp larva chews into cricket's body, eats internal organs, and eventually pupates in cell beside remains of cricket.

Comments
This wasp is uncommon within its fair-sized range.

American Horse Fly
Tabanus americanus
378

¾–1⅛" (20–28 mm). Large, broad. Head tan to ash-gray between large green eyes and on rear surface. Antennae reddish brown. Thorax brownish to blackish with gray hair. Abdomen is blackish red-brown with short gray hair across rear margin. Hind tibiae do not have spurs. Wings smoky; brown to black near base.

Habitat
Near swamps, marshes, and ponds.

Range
Newfoundland to Florida, west to Texas and northern Mexico, north to Canadian Northwest Territories.

Life Cycle
Egg masses are attached to plants overhanging fresh water, into which larvae drop. Larvae overwinter in muddy bottom 2

winters, then pupate in spring. Males are short-lived, but females may survive until fall.

Comments
When the female bites, the wound inflicted often continues to bleed for several minutes because the fly's saliva contains an anticoagulant that prevents clotting. A single animal may suffer a debilitating loss of blood if many of these insects attack it.

Black Flies
Simulium spp.
379

1/16–1/8″ (2–4 mm). Humpbacked, head pointing downward. Grayish brown to shiny black. Antennae thick, often with many segments. Wings smoky to clear; veins near front margin heavy, others delicate.

Habitat
Near running water in forests, mountains, and tundra.

Range
Labrador south to Georgia, west to California and Mexico, north to Alaska.

Life Cycle
Eggs are laid on stones or leaves at the edge of rapidly flowing streams, or on the water surface itself. Larvae tumble into water. Fully grown larvae pupate in cocoons that coat rocks in water, resembling moss. Adults burst out, rise on a bubble of trapped air, and fly away in late spring and early summer.

Comments
Biting adults are the bane of the North Country and mountain resorts, particularly early in the season. Some species transmit waterfowl malaria, which accounts for up to half of the deaths of ducks, geese, swans, and turkeys.

Marsh Flies
Tetanocera spp.
380

1/8–1/4″ (4–6 mm). Body and legs brownish yellow. Eyes red. Antennae project forward prominently. Femora bristly. Wings yellow to amber, usually with brownish spot near middle of front margin and with other markings.

Habitat
Near ponds, streams, and wet meadows.

Range
Throughout North America, more common in the North than the South.

Life Cycle
Incompletely known.

Comments
This small fly runs about on marsh plants along the banks of woodland streams and ponds.

Vinegar Fly
Drosophila melanogaster
381

1/16" (2 mm). Body short in proportion to oval wings. Brownish yellow with dark crossbands on last 3 abdominal segments in male. Eyes bright red. Legs brownish yellow; front outermost leg segments of male have black "sex combs," important in courtship. Male's abdomen rounded, female's pointed. Feathery bristle at tip of antennae.

Habitat
Ponds, marshes, and swamps on wet decaying plant matter; on rotting fruit; also in homes.

Range
Worldwide.

Life Cycle
Female lays up to 200 slender grayish-white eggs, each with 2 short respiratory tubes projecting above surface of moist food. Eggs hatch in 2 days. Larvae creep to drier sites and transform to adults in 4–5 days. Adults are ready to mate in 2 days and live 2 weeks. Surviving male may mate with its own daughters, but female seldom produces fertile eggs with sons.

Comments
These flies are so named because of their attraction to the sour odor of fermentation and bacterial waste. They are alternately known as Pomace Flies because the sour odor comes from pomace—the liquid squeezed from crushed fruit or seeds.

Six-spotted Fishing Spider
Dolomedes triton
382

Male 3/8–1/2" (9–13 mm); female 5/8–3/4" (15–20 mm) with legspan to 2½" (64 mm). Greenish brown with silvery-white lengthwise stripes along each side of cephalothorax and abdomen. Abdomen has 12 white spots. Undersurface paler, except for 6 black spots between leg bases.

Habitat
Slow-flowing streams or ponds.

Range
East of the Rocky Mountains in the United States and southern Canada; rare in Rocky Mountains and Great Plains.

Life Cycle
Female sometimes carries egg sac across open water and holds or stays close to sac until most spiderlings have dispersed. Egg sacs are produced June–September, occasionally in April.

Comments
Sometimes these spiders are eaten by fish. They are often seen scampering over waterside plants.

Golden-silk Spider
Nephila clavipes
383

Male 1/8" (4 mm); female 7/8–1" (22–25 mm). Female's cephalothorax pale gray with 3 black spots on each side; legs dark with brownish bands and conspicuous tufts of black hair on first and last pairs of legs. Female's abdomen brownish green, spotted with white in irregular pattern. Male's body color drabber; legs also have tufts of black hair.

Habitat
Shaded woodlands and swamps.

Range
Southeastern United States.

Web
Strong, slightly inclined orb with notchlike support lines. Web may measure 2–3′ (1 m) across.

Life Cycle
Female attaches elongated egg mass to undersurface of leaf and then rests nearby. Spiderlings disperse, each to make web elsewhere. At first, they build only two-thirds of a web, leaving the top somewhat irregular across from principal support line.

Comments
During the day the spider hangs head downward from the underside of the web near the meshlike center or hub. The spider repairs the webbing each day, replacing half but never the whole web at one time.

Red Freshwater Mite
Limnochares americana
384

1/8″ (3 mm). Red. Smooth, globular, somewhat elongated. Legs hairy.

Habitat
Ponds and slow-flowing streams.

Range
Throughout North America.

Life Cycle
Eggs are dropped in water at random and settle to the bottom. Larvae creep or swim to aquatic invertebrate animals, mostly insects, on which they attach themselves as external parasites. Nymphs and adults are active predators.

Comments
Fish appear to avoid freshwater mites, although many must be eaten accidentally along with water insects.

BUTTERFLIES AND MOTHS

Wetlands vegetation provides ample shelter, moisture, and nectar for a large variety of butterflies. These delicate creatures are often abundant after a rainfall, and in very wet years the numbers of some species are large indeed. Some are found in open spaces near ponds and streams that support abundant legumes and grasses. A few species are migratory, turning up at various times during the year. This section describes many of the most common butterflies and moths of the wetlands.

Pink-edged Sulphur
Colias interior
385

$1\frac{3}{8}$–$1\frac{3}{4}''$ (35–44 mm). Rounded wings with bright pink fringes and body hair. Above, male yellow with black borders; female yellow or white with vestiges of borders on fore wing. Both sexes have yellow to orange hind-wing cell spot above and silver, pink-rimmed cell spot on hind wing beneath. Below, fore wing dull yellow, hind wing slightly olive.

Life Cycle
Pale, pitcher-shaped egg laid singly. Caterpillar bright yellow-green with lighter back stripes and red-edged side stripes surrounded by bluish; overwinters.

Flight
1 brood; early June–August.

Habitat
Marshes and bogs. Also transitional open spaces such as burns, clearings, meadow edges, woodland roadsides.

Range
British Columbia to Newfoundland, south in mountains and cool woodlands to Oregon, Lake States, New York, Pennsylvania, and Virginia.

Comments
Some other *Colias* have pink fringes, but other marks usually distinguish them; none is edged with such a rich rose when fresh. Like other sulphurs, the males of the slow-flying Pink-edged Sulphur gather at mud puddles and take nectar often; bristly sarsaparilla is visited in Maine, various asters in Washington.

Scudder's Willow Sulphur
Colias scudderii
386

$1\frac{1}{2}$–$1\frac{3}{4}''$ (38–44 mm). Male clear yellow above, slightly greenish below; female usually white, sometimes pale yellowish. Wing margin above black on male, virtually absent on female. Cell spot black on fore wing above and below, yellow on hind wing above, silver on hind wing below. Pink fringe.

Life Cycle
Unreported.

Flight
1 brood; late June at southern edge of range into late August at high altitudes.

Habitat
Willow bogs and willow-fringed meadows from Douglas-fir zone up to timberline.

Range
NE. Utah and SW. Wyoming through Colorado into N. New Mexico in higher mountain ranges.

Comments
Generally, Scudder's Willow Sulphur remains in wet or dry meadows near its host plants, even though it is a stronger flier than most sulphurs.

Hessel's Hairstreak
Mitoura hesseli
387

⅞–1″ (22–25 mm). Above, male dark brown; female somewhat reddish. Below, deep green to bluish green; fore wing has 1 white band just inside margin; 2 white hind-wing bands, bordered by brown; white dash nearest tail concave outwardly; brown patches outside band just behind middle of hind wing. Fore-wing cell below has 1 or 2 white dots.

Life Cycle
Egg green; becomes yellow-white. Caterpillar, to ⅝″ (16 mm), bluish green with white marks. Chrysalis, to ⅜″ (10 mm), dark brown.

Flight
2 broods; May and July.

Habitat
Bogs and swamps close to white-cedar.

Range
Mostly along Atlantic from New Hampshire and Massachusetts south to North Carolina, along Gulf from Florida to Mississippi.

Comments
The rather rare Hessel's Hairstreak and the more common Olive Hairstreak represent a classic example of sibling species; 2 species that are nearly indistinguishable. While the Olive Hairstreak is a widespread colonizer feeding only on redcedars, Hessel's Hairstreak confines itself to inaccessible Atlantic white-cedar (*Chamaecyparis thyoides*) swamps.

Western Tiger Swallowtail
Pterourus rutulus
388

2¾–3⅞″ (70–98 mm). Above and below, lemon-yellow with black tiger-stripes across wings and black yellow-spotted margins. 1 or 2 orange spots and several blue spots near black tail on hind wing; blue continuous all around outer margin of hind wing below. Yellow spots along outer black margin of fore wing below run together into band; uppermost spot on border of hind wing above and below is yellow.

Life Cycle
Egg deep green, shiny, spherical. Caterpillar, to 2″ (51 mm), deep to light green, swollen in front, accentuating large yellow eyespots with black and blue pupils. Dark brown, woodlike chrysalis overwinters slung from a twig or trunk.

Flight
February in S. California, May in Washington, normally June–July in mountain areas. Up to 3 broods in low altitudes and latitudes, 1 in cooler places with shorter seasons.

Habitat
Widespread, but normally near moisture—canyons, watersides, trails, roadsides, parks and gardens; sagelands and mesas with creeks.

Range
British Columbia south to Baja California, east through

Rockies to Black Hills, and High Plains of Colorado and New Mexico. Rare east of Rockies.

Comments
The Western Tiger may be the most conspicuous butterfly in the West. The eastern and western species essentially replace each other along a diagonal line, northwest to southeast, although there may be some slight hybridizing along the dividing line. Such east-west species-pairs are not unusual among butterflies. In Western canyons, males of several species of swallowtails gather in spectacular numbers around mud puddles or beside streams, with the Western Tiger usually predominating.

Palamedes Swallowtail
Pterourus palamedes
389

3⅛–5½″ (79–140 mm). Very large with rounded wings. Blackish brown above, rimmed by yellow spots and crossed midwing by yellow band which is broken on fore wing but is entire on hind wing, where it ends in bright blue spot. Below, fore wing has 2 rows of yellow border-spots; hind wing has orange spots enclosing row of blue and gold to olive clouds and long, straight yellow bar parallel to abdomen down inner third of hind wing below.

Life Cycle
Yellowish-green egg. Grass-green caterpillar, to 2″ (51 mm), has double set of rimmed, orange, false eyespots with black pupils. Possibly overwinters as a caterpillar as well as a chrysalis, unusual for group. Chrysalis, to 1⅝″ (41 mm), slightly mottled, greenish.

Flight
April–August in mid-range; February–December in up to 3 broods in Florida.

Habitat
Subtropical wetlands, coastal swamps, and humid woods with standing water.

Range
Resident from S. Maryland to S. Florida, throughout Southwest, around Gulf to S. Texas and northern Mexico. North in Mississippi Valley to Missouri.

Comments
This butterfly is the signature swallowtail of the great swamps—the Everglades, the Great Dismal, Okefenokee, Okeechobee, and Big Cypress. In common with a number of swamp skippers, the adults love to take nectar from pickerelweed.

Zebra Swallowtail
Eurytides marcellus
390

2⅜–3½″ (60–89 mm). Long triangular wings with swordlike tail. Above, chalk-white to hint of blue-green with black stripes and bands; hind wing above has 2 deep blue spots at base and bright scarlet spot closer to body. Below, black-bordered scarlet stripe runs through middle of hind wing.

Width of black stripes and length of tails vary with season and brood: spring zebras are paler, smaller, shorter tailed; summer individuals are larger and darker with very long white-edged tails, exceeding 1″ (25 mm). Antennae rust-colored.

Life Cycle
Green egg. Caterpillar, to 2⅛″ (54 mm), banded with black and yellow, band on hump broader than others. Overwintering chrysalis, to 1″ (25 mm), is green or brown, stockier and more compact than that of other swallowtails found in the United States.

Flight
March–December in 4 broods on Gulf, April–October in 2 broods in Midwest; first brood most numerous.

Habitat
Waterside woodland passageways, shrubby borders, meadows, riversides, lakeshores and marshes; absent from mountains.

Range
Lake States and Ontario, east to southern New England, south along Atlantic to central Florida and Gulf, and west to eastern Great Plains.

Comments
The aptly named Zebra is the most abundant regular North American representative of the kite swallowtails, named for their triangular wings and long sharp tails. Despite a large range, the Zebra occurs only near pawpaw or its relatives—it usually fails to adapt to suburban development.

Baltimore
Euphydryas phaeton
391

1⅝–2½″ (41–64 mm). Above, black with numerous cream-colored dots, several red-orange spots near base of wings, and border of red-orange half moons. Similar below with more cream-color and orange. New England individuals smallest, with wide red border; Ozark region individuals largest, with narrower red border.

Life Cycle
Eggs laid in clusters. Young caterpillar feeds in silk nests and overwinters half grown. Mature caterpillar, to 1″ (25 mm), black with orange side stripes and many black branching spines. Chrysalis, to ¾″ (19 mm), white, black, and orange; adult emerges after only 10 days.

Flight
1 brood; May–July.

Habitat
Wet meadows in woodlands in the Northeast; sphagnum bogs in Lake States; hillsides and drier ridges in open mixed hardwoods in Ozarks.

Range
SE. Manitoba to Nova Scotia south to Nebraska, Arkansas, and Georgia.

Comments
While often seen in damp turtlehead stands in the Northeast, the Baltimore has been found to have many other host plants and habitats. The caterpillars of Connecticut colonies, for example, feed on false foxglove among rocky oak woods.

Viceroy
Basilarchia archippus
392

2⅝–3″ (67–76 mm). Above and below, rich, russet-orange with black veins, a black line usually curving across hind wing, white-spotted black borders, and white spots surrounded by black in diagonal band across fore-wing tip. Color ranges from pale tawny in Great Basin to deep, mahogany-brown in Florida.

Life Cycle
Egg compressed oval. Caterpillar, 1–1¼″ (25–32 mm), mottled brown or olive with saddle-shaped patch on back; fore parts humped; 2 bristles behind head. Chrysalis, to ⅞″ (22 mm), also brown and cream-colored with brown, rounded disk projecting from back.

Flight
2, 3, or more broods depending upon latitude; April–September in middle latitudes, later in South. Sometimes a distinct gap between broods, with no adults for some weeks in mid- to late summer.

Habitat
Canals, riversides, marshes, meadows, wood edges, roadsides, lakeshores, and deltas.

Range
North America south of Hudson Bay, from Great Basin eastward, and west to eastern parts of Pacific States.

Comments
In each life stage, the Viceroy seeks protection through a different ruse. The egg blends with the numerous galls that afflict the willow leaves upon which it is laid. Hibernating caterpillars hide themselves in bits of leaves they have attached to a twig. The mature caterpillar looks mildly fearsome with its hunched and horned foreparts. Even most birds pass over the chrysalis, thinking it is a bird dropping. The adult, famed as a paramount mimic, resembles the distasteful Monarch.

Milbert's Tortoiseshell
Aglais milberti
393

1¾–2″ (44–51 mm). Above and below 2-toned; inner dark and outer light, separated by a sharp border. Above, inner dark area chocolate-brown with 2 red-orange patches along leading edge of fore wing, outer part has yellow band blending into bright orange band. Below, inner area purplish brown; outer band tan. Dark margin above and below punctuated by faint blue bars, has irregular outline.

Life Cycle
Egg pale green; deposited in clusters, often several hundred together. Caterpillars at first live in colonies in silken nests,

later become solitary, folding up a leaf to live in. Mature caterpillar black with narrow yellow band above and green side stripes, white speckled with 7 rows of short spines. Chrysalis grayish or greenish tan, thorny. Adults overwinter.

Flight
2 or 3 broods where season permits; spring, summer, and fall.

Habitat
Dry stream beds and canals, riversides, beaches, meadows, alpine rockslides, roads, and trails.

Range
Far North except Alaska, south to S. California, Oklahoma east to West Virginia.

Comments
This unmistakable butterfly prefers northern latitudes and higher altitudes, although it occupies lowlands if they are cool enough. Extremely versatile, it inhabits every kind of place within its range, from cold desert to rain forest and city lot to alpine summit. Milbert's Tortoiseshell may sometimes be seen even in midwinter on a warmish day in many temperate areas.

Harvester
Feniseca tarquinius
394

1⅛–1¼″ (28–32 mm). Above, orange-brown to orange-yellow (sometimes nearly white) with blackish-brown borders and splotches; fore-wing outer margin bulges outwards. Below, fore wing mostly brownish with yellowish and darker spots; hind wing has dots and fine grayish circular markings.

Life Cycle
Caterpillar carnivorous, feeds exclusively upon woolly aphids. When mature, greenish-brown caterpillar, about ½″ (13 mm), buries itself among dead prey; becomes covered with whitish aphid secretions and debris caught on long body hair. Back of chrysalis has a "monkey's face" design.

Flight
Multiple broods in far South, 3 broods north to New York, 1–2 broods farther north; April–May and July–September.

Habitat
Damp areas, such as swampy glades, wooded riverbanks, and forest trails; often around alders, but host aphids also occur on witch hazel, wild currant, hawthorn, beech, ash, and others.

Range
Nova Scotia and the Maritime Provinces south to Florida, west to Ontario and central Texas.

Comments
The Harvester is the sole American representative of an Old World tropical group of carnivorous gossamer wings. The adults are rather sluggish and fly slowly, never moving far from their host aphids. They usually do not visit flowers, but do alight on twigs and leaves to take aphid honeydew.

Arctic Skipper
Carterocephalus palaemon
395

¾–1¼″ (19–32 mm). Above, fore wing and hind wing dark brown with crisply outlined, clear orange orbs in bands just inside margin and across cell parallel to margin. Below, fore wing yellow-orange with open black checks; hind wing brandy-tan or russet with several silver or pale yellow, black-rimmed orbs.

Life Cycle
Egg greenish white. Caterpillar dusky-green or ivory with dark stripe above and yellow stripe on sides above rows of dark spots; overwinters. Chrysalis resembles a bit of faded grass.

Flight
1 brood; late May–early August.

Habitat
Streambanks, bogs, mixed upland forests, sedge lowlands, woodland trails, and subarctic meadows.

Range
Alaska, Canada, and northern United States south to Pennsylvania, Minnesota, Wyoming, and central California.

Comments
Despite its name, this species is more sub-Arctic than Arctic and it is well known in many lands. In England, where it is known as the Chequered Skipper, it is an endangered species. But this species is still fairly common in northern North America.

Bog Fritillary
Proclossiana eunomia
396

1¼–1½″ (32–38 mm). Small. Rust-orange above with fine black lines and dots, and darker at base. Below, crisply marked; fore wing like upper side; hind wing rich chestnut alternating with cream-white or silver-white bands across wing, and along margin, row of black-rimmed pearly spots just inside margin (yellowish in southern Rocky Mountains).

Life Cycle
Egg small, cream-colored, with vertical ribs. Reddish-brown caterpillar has branched spines; overwinters half grown.

Flight
1 brood; briefly during June in Northwest, June–August in Rockies.

Habitat
Bogs in spruce and other conifer forests, and arctic-alpine tussock bogs.

Range
Alaska east to Labrador, south to Wisconsin and Maine, and in Rocky Mountains to central Colorado.

Comments
Eastern populations were once thought to appear for only 4–5 days, but are now known to fly during several weeks. In cool, cloudy weather, Bog Fritillaries hide among mosses and heaths to await the warming sun.

Frigga's Fritillary
Clossiana frigga
397

1¼–1⅝″ (32–41 mm). Orange above with black bars and spots; dark scales at base. Below, fore wing like upper side but paler; hind wing dark brown at base with golden-brown band and outer half soft violet-gray; white rectangle containing dark dot lies near base on leading edge.

Life Cycle
Chrysalis overwinters.

Flight
1 brood; June–July.

Habitat
Willow bogs in coniferous forests; alpine bogs or tundra areas in Arctic.

Range
Alaska southeast to N. Quebec and Ontario, and south to British Columbia, Colorado, and Michigan.

Comments
Frigga's Fritillary slows its activity in cloudy weather. It prefers to fly or to bask, with wings spread, on flowers or grass on sunny days. On Baffin and Victoria islands the butterfly flies over the tundra when the brief summer and intermittent sunshine permit. The species is named for the wife of the chief Norse god, Odin.

Swamp Metalmark
Calephelis muticum
398

⅞–1⅛″ (22–28 mm). Wings angular. Above, uniform deep mahogany with fine, blacker scalloping; silver-green metallic markings form continuous band. Below, yellow to orange-brown with black to lead-gray flecks.

Life Cycle
Sculptured egg. Caterpillar pale green with plumelike hair, few or no black spots along back; overwinters partially grown. Chrysalis has silken girdle, surrounds itself with fuzzy hair of caterpillar woven into loose mat.

Flight
1 brood; July–August.

Habitat
Wet meadows, swamps, and bogs.

Range
W. Pennsylvania across north-central Great Lakes States to SE. Minnesota; recorded once in New England.

Comments
Swamp and Northern metalmarks are best distinguished by habitat and geography. The Swamp Metalmark is found in more northern and wetter areas. Although basically they do not overlap, together the ranges of the Swamp, Northern, and Little metalmarks cover most of the United States east of the Mississippi. This pattern suggests that these 3 metalmarks may have developed relatively recently from a common ancestor.

Bog Copper
Epidemia epixanthe
399

⅞–1″ (22–25 mm). Small. Above, male dark brown with purple gloss and some dark spots; female duller and somewhat grayish, often with bright orange margins. Below, both sexes yellow to white, with some black spots (heavier on fore wing); red marks form row just inside margin of hind wing.

Life Cycle
Largely unknown. Egg overwinters.

Flight
1 brood; late June–late July or August.

Habitat
Closely restricted to acid bogs and boggy marshes where wild cranberry grows.

Range
Newfoundland west to the Riding Mountains of Manitoba (and possibly E. Saskatchewan), south to Minnesota, Michigan, Wisconsin, N. Ohio, NW. Indiana, Pennsylvania, and New Jersey.

Comments
The Bog Copper is found in relatively small numbers. Some colonies in New York are known to have only 50–100 individuals year after year. This species is more common in the East and more local and scarce farther west. Observers can find Bog Coppers perching on cranberries and other bog shrubs, or flying feebly among plants.

Appalachian Brown
Satyrodes appalachia
400, 408

1⅝–2″ (41–51 mm). Wings rounded. Above, olive-brown, paler toward tip of fore wing. Below, gray-tan or violet-brown. Black eyespots just inside margin above and below, those below ringed with white and yellow and with white pupils. Darker brown lines cross underside; line nearest eyespots is mildly wavy, not radically zigzagged.

Life Cycle
Caterpillar slender, green and yellow-striped; has 2 horns with red tips in front and rear. Chrysalis green, streamlined.

Flight
1 brood in northern part of range, more farther south; June–August in Maine and June–October in N. Florida.

Habitat
Wooded areas near standing or slow-moving water: swamps, streamsides, bogs, and springs; also edges and roadsides along woods.

Range
E. South Dakota, Quebec, and Maine, south in Appalachians to Mississippi and west-central Florida.

Comments
The Appalachian Brown and the Eyed Brown are excellent examples of sibling species—close relatives, similar in appearance, that may occur in many of the same areas, and yet

have quite different characteristics. The Appalachian Brown dwells in dispersed, damp, brushy marshes and is never plentiful, but the Eyed Brown is abundant in wet, open meadows. Both are vulnerable to development of wetlands.

Mitchell's Marsh Satyr
Neonympha mitchellii
401

1½–1¾″ (38–44 mm). Wings rounded. Above, mahogany-brown, sometimes with eyespots from below vaguely showing through. Below, dull brown crossed by dark orange-brown lines; 4 eyespots just inside margin on fore wing and 5–6 eyespots on hind wing have yellow rims and bluish-silver centers; eyespots are round or slightly oval (but not narrow and elongated); largest hind-wing eyespots usually third and fourth. Beyond eyespot row is reddish line, followed by gray line near margin.

Life Cycle
Egg pale green, globe-shaped. Caterpillar lime-green with contrasting stripes, fine, white, raised stippling all over, and 2 fleshy horns extending at rear. Chrysalis green, rounded over back with large bump on back of head, small horns at front of head.

Flight
1 brood during 2-week period; normally first 2 weeks of July, may be advanced or delayed depending upon weather.

Habitat
Tamarack bogs with poison sumac, adjacent wet meadows, and slightly drier meadows.

Range
S. Michigan, N. Indiana, N. Ohio, and N. New Jersey.

Comments
Discovered in Michigan in the 1880's, this little brown butterfly has one of the most restricted ranges in North America. The special kinds of bogs it requires have largely been eliminated by agriculture and urban development. Although there are populations in both New Jersey and Ohio, the species has never been found in intervening Pennsylvania.

Eyed Brown
Satyrodes eurydice
402, 409

1⅝–2″ (41–51 mm). Wings rounded. Above, warm tan to olive-brown, often but not always with light patch on outer third of fore wing. Variable dark eyespots near margins of both wings above and below; eyespots have small white pupils below. Below, light brown crossed by darker, deeply zigzagged lines near yellow-rimmed eyespots.

Life Cycle
Caterpillar slender, light green, with lengthwise yellow and dark green stripes and red-tipped horns extending from head and tail. Chrysalis green, with small, blunt hook on head.

Flight
1 staggered brood; June–September.

Habitat
Open, damp meadows, sedge marshes, and wetter parts of prairies.

Range
South-central Northwest Territories, south through Dakotas to NE. Colorado, east across Canada and northeastern United States south to N. Illinois and Delaware.

Comments
This locally abundant species occupies a very broad range and is familiar throughout much of the Northeast; its colonies are small, separate, and local. Some lepidopterists consider a dark, large race that is indigenous to the prairie states to be a separate species, called the Smoky Eyed Brown (*S. fumosus*). It has disappeared from much of its former territory as the moist grasslands have been drained, plowed, or inundated by reservoirs. For many years, the Eyed and Appalachian browns were thought to be a single species.

Great Gray Copper
Gaeides xanthoides
403

1¼–1¾″ (32–44 mm). Large. Male above uniform gray-brown, with orange scaling and small black dots along hind-wing margin. Female above has few black spots and often light orange scaling, especially on fore wing; orange margins on hind wing more extensive than male. Both sexes below very light gray with small black spots and either prominent orange hind-wing margins (East) or thin orange hind-wing marginal band (West).

Life Cycle
Egg white. Mature caterpillar green, yellow-green, or magenta with dark orange stripes. Chrysalis pink-buff; found in loosely constructed cocoon of silk and soil in debris.

Flight
1 brood; late May–early August.

Habitat
In West, dry slopes, sandy flats, and dry riverbeds. In East, prairie swamps, marshes, and meadows.

Range
Oregon south to Baja California, east through Rockies and across to Great Plains from Manitoba to Oklahoma.

Comments
The Great Gray Copper is the largest American copper and one of the largest gossamer wings. Its rapid and jerky flight makes this butterfly difficult to watch, except when it stops to take nectar from milkweed.

White Peacock
Anartia jatrophae
404, 406

2–2⅜″ (51–60 mm). Fore-wing tip extends slightly, rounded; hind wing bluntly tailed. Above and below, white, blending to buff and orange in margins, overlaid with pattern of brown and orange scrawls and small black eyespots.

Life Cycle
Egg pale yellow. Caterpillar black and spiny with silver spots. Chrysalis green, darkening with age; smooth.

Flight
Year-round except in cold weather.

Habitat
Swampy places, watersides, shorelines, and disturbed ground.

Range
S. Florida and S. Texas, straying occasionally as far north as Kansas and Massachusetts; also much of the American Tropics.

Comments
Much more limited to the Tropics than its relative the Buckeye, the White Peacock also invades the North. However, it is neither as strong a flier nor as hardy as the Buckeye, and remains a rarity outside its southern range.

Northern Blue
Lycaeides argyrognomon
405

⅞–1¼″ (22–32 mm). Above, male bright silvery purple-blue with narrow dark border; female gray-brown with rows of orange spots around margins above. Dirty white to light fawn below; black line along extreme outer margins thin, becoming inflated at veins forming distinct triangular spots; row of silvery blue-green, orange, and black spots just inside margin below somewhat pale and reduced, especially in West.

Life Cycle
Pale gray-green egg laid singly.

Flight
1 brood; June–August, later at higher elevations.

Habitat
Open areas, heaths, and bogs in northern coniferous and mixed forests; cool zones in western mountains.

Range
Alaska and Yukon east to Minnesota and Maritimes; British Columbia south to central California in mountains and coastal bogs; Pacific Northwest to S. Colorado in Rockies.

Comments
The Northern Blue is the butterfly hikers often stir from muddy spots along the Cascade Crest Trail. Vladimir Nabokov, an accomplished lepidopterist, devoted many years of meticulous study to Northern Blues and their allies.

Cerisy's Sphinx
Smerinthus cerisyi
407

Wingspan: 2⅜–3⅜″ (60–85 mm). Fore wings variable, marked with contrasting light and dark gray or tawny brown. Hind wings rosy pink with tawny outer margin and black and blue eyespot. Caterpillar is bluish green and has a few diagonal yellow streaks and a green and yellow horn at rear.

Flight
May and June.

Habitat
River margins and low ground, where willows grow.

Range
Coast to coast in the northern United States and Canada, south along the Rocky Mountains to Arizona, and along the Sierra Mountains to California.

Comments
The Cerisy's sphinx caterpillar feeds on willow foliage.

Creole Pearly Eye
Enodia creola
410

2–2¼″ (54–57 mm). Wings slightly scalloped. Above, olive-brown; below, lavender to bluish gray. Wings above and below have rows of prominent dark eyespots just inside margin (without pupils above) and darker brown irregular lines. Underside highlighted by pearly reflections. Male has conspicuous patches of dark, raised scent scales between veins of fore wing above. Female normally has 5 full fore-wing eyespots; portion of brown line nearest eyespots irregularly convex.

Life Cycle
Unrecorded.

Flight
2 broods; April–October.

Habitat
Shaded hardwoods, especially among swampy canebrakes and near marshy streams.

Range
S. Illinios and SE. Virginia south to E. Texas and Georgia.

Comments
The noticeable dark patches on the wings of Creole males are composed of raised sex scales, which produce sex attractants called pheromones. The Pearly Eye (*Enodia portlandia*), a similar species, lacks these patches and mates at dusk, while the Creole Pearly Eye mates during the daytime. Nonetheless, the Creole Pearly Eye flies well into dusk and perhaps sometimes at night. While these 2 shade-tolerant satyrs sometimes share habitats, they use different niches.

Lace-winged Roadside Skipper
Amblyscirtes aesculapius
411

1–1¼″ (25–32 mm). Dark gray-brown above and below, with distinctive network of whitish spot bands and connecting white veins on hind wing below, showing through to hind wing above. Fore-wing spots buff above, whiter below, in full curved band.

Life Cycle
Unknown.

Flight
Successive broods in South, 1 brood in North; January–September.

Habitat
Swamps, canebrakes, wooded areas, edges of woods, and forest paths.

Range
Connecticut south to Florida and west to Missouri and New Mexico.

Comments
This skipper flies in the Great Dismal Swamp, on the edges of the vast wetland.

Jutta Arctic
Oeneis jutta
412

1⅞–2⅛″ (48–54 mm). Variable between populations and sexes. Above, basically dense grayish or olive-brown with more or less yellow to ocher between veins near margins, forming patches or even bands; within the yellow are prominent black eyespots with or without white pupils; male has dark patch of scent scales in fore-wing cell. Below, fore wing similar to upper side; hind wing striated with barklike tones of gray and brown, with darker gray, highly irregular median band (not obvious in all populations); eyespots on hind wing, if present, are small.

Life Cycle
Egg yellowish white. Caterpillar buff- and olive-striped. Chrysalis yellow-green with greener wing cases and brown dots on abdomen.

Flight
1 brood; June–July.

Habitat
Black spruce and tamarack sphagnum bogs and northern taiga in East; lodgepole pine forest glades in Rocky Mountains; cotton grass tundra.

Range
Circumpolar: Alaska and most of subarctic Canada east to Maritimes; south down Rockies to Utah and Colorado; N. Minnesota, Wisconsin, Michigan, and Maine.

Comments
The range of the Jutta Arctic takes in much of the boggy boreal forest belt of the Northern Hemisphere. It finds younger, damper sphagnum bogs with cotton grass more favorable than older, drier muskeg with denser trees. This species is more accessible in the cold, high lodgepole pine forests of the Rocky Mountains, where it flies frequently with the Meadow Fritillary. In Alaska, the Jutta Arctic tends to be smaller and duller, while it reaches its largest size and brightest markings in Nova Scotia.

Window-winged Skipper
Xenophanes trixis
413

1⅛–1⅜″ (28–35 mm). Slightly sickle-shaped, pointed fore wing. Above, buff-brown with numerous white glassy spots in centers of both fore wing and hind wing, which give bright pearly reflections. Below, fore-wing spot in band and that of hind wing expand to fill entire wing out to brown margin.

Life Cycle
Caterpillar dotted, brown-headed. Chrysalis tan and speckled, white-powdered, and hairy.

Flight
July in United States, longer in tropics.

Habitat
Floodplains and clearings.

Range
Extreme S. Texas to Argentina.

Comments
This singular butterfly merely grazes our region; it may be a stray, a periodic colonist, or a species whose range is slowly advancing northward.

Small Checkered Skipper
Pyrgus scriptura
414

⅝–1″ (16–25 mm). Tiny. Shiny dark gray to dark brown above, with small and separate white checks. No basal spot on hind wing above. Long white fringes with little dark checkering. Below, fore wing gray-olive; hind wing crossed by alternating rows of clean white and olive-tan, without black outlines.

Flight
Successive broods; most of year in California and Southwest, April–August further north.

Habitat
Marshes in California; open grasslands, prairies, high plains, abandoned fields, and canal sides.

Range
SE. Alberta and North Dakota south to Mexico and west to Arizona, S. Nevada, California, and Baja California.

Comments
This species is one of the few butterflies to emerge just after the snow melts in foothill canyons. It also flies in parched weedy patches in late summer.

Bog Elfin
Incisalia lanoraieensis
415

⅝–1″ (16–25 mm). Smallest elfin. Dull gray-brown above, darker below. Hind wing below scalloped with dark, smudged, zigzag bands. Margins checkered black and white.

Flight
1 brood; May–June.

Habitat
Spruce-tamarack bogs and muskegs.

Range
SE. Quebec, New Brunswick, and Maine; old records for New Hampshire.

Comments
Bog Elfins dwell with Jutta Arctics and Bog Fritillaries—northern butterflies that push south in the cold acid bogs of the East. Along with Bog Coppers, Bog Elfins occur only in these northeastern mires, but the copper is far more widespread than the elfin.

Lilac-banded Longtail
Urbanus dorantes
416

1½–2″ (38–51 mm). Long-winged and long-tailed. Grayish brown above with a loose series of glassy white spots on fore-wing disk and near fore-wing tip. Below, fore wing similar but paler, purplish near tip; hind wing purplish frosty-gray, with dark brown spots at base, 2 dark bands across disk, and 1 band on margin. Checkered buff fringe.

Life Cycle
Egg shiny green. Caterpillar rose-orange to chartreuse, reddish toward ends, with light spots, short hair, and black head. Chrysalis light brown.

Flight
3 or more broods; June–October.

Habitat
Saw grass marshes, hardwood hammocks, and edges of woodlands.

Range
S. Arizona, S. New Mexico, S. Texas, and S. Florida south to Argentina and Antilles. Also S. California (rarely).

Comments
Well-established in Florida, the Lilac-banded Longtail prefers shade to open sunshine, and darts back and forth across paths and clearings until landing beneath a leaf. It takes nectar from lantana, Spanish needles, and ironweed.

Common Alpine
Erebia epipsodea
417

1¾–2″ (44–51 mm). Wings rounded. Above, dark brown, crossed by reddish-orange patches or bands usually containing eyespots with white pupils. 2 eyespots uppermost on fore wing are larger than others. Below, fore wing similar to upper side but paler, or sometimes reddish orange; hind wing usually frosted with gray over outer third, and sometimes also at base; darker brown median band usually not very outstanding. Hind-wing eyespots often ringed with yellow or pale orange.

Life Cycle
Egg pale yellowish white, nearly spherical; laid singly or in small groups. Caterpillar striped green; overwinters when young and resumes feeding in spring, pupating in loose shelter of silk and grass blades.

Flight
1 brood; early June–late August for about 3 weeks, earlier in lowlands and southern part of range and later at higher elevations and latitudes.

Habitat
Mountain meadows, bogs, clearings, and lower arctic-alpine tundra; sage flats; northern prairie parklands; often in association with aspens.

Range
Central Alaska south in Coast Ranges and Rockies to eastern and central Oregon and New Mexico, and east to central Montana and W. Manitoba.

Comments
Strictly a North American species, the Common Alpine occurs farther south than any other New World alpine. While the other Rocky Mountain alpines are confined to the high country, this species flies down almost to the foothills, where moisture permits. Its adaptability and broad taste in habitat have allowed it to spread more widely than most satyrs.

Spruce Bog Alpine
Erebia disa
418

1¾–2″ (44–51 mm). Above, blackish brown, normally fore wing has 4 eyespots, orange-rimmed and often with minute white pupils; orange rings may be broad and nearly contiguous or become a diffuse, orange patch. Below, fore wing chestnut-brown with 4 eyespots repeated; hind wing frosted hoary brown usually with broad, darker band across middle and 2 white spots—1 along leading edge, 1 at end of cell; spots sometimes join, becoming white patch bordering dark band. Fringes checkered tan and gray.

Life Cycle
Unreported.

Flight
1 brood; June–July.

Habitat
Spruce bogs, taiga forests, and damp arctic slopes.

Range
Alaskan North Slope east to Hudson Bay, south to S. British Columbia and N. Minnesota.

Comments
As its name implies, the Spruce Bog Alpine is particularly fond of moist locations. Unlike most alpines, it even takes moisture at mud puddles. When it settles in its characteristic posture with its wings closed, the white spots are clearly evident.

Poweshiek Skipperling
Oarisma poweshiek
419

1–1¼″ (25–32 mm). Wings sharply pointed at tip. Above, fore wing dark brown with bright orange leading edge above cell; hind wing dark brown, with some gold near base. Below, fore wing dark at base with some orange on leading edge and at tip; hind wing dark brown on inner marginal third without orange ray, rest of hind wing below has silvery veins; light brown near abdomen.

Life Cycle
Unrecorded.

Flight
1 brood; June–July.

Habitat
Marshy lakeshores and wetlands.

Range
Dakotas eastward probably to Lake States, Iowa, Illinois, and Nebraska.

Comments
Local and known from rather few sites, this species can be numerous in the right places. Drainage of the prairie pothole wetlands may be one important factor in this butterfly's overall scarcity.

Saw-grass Skipper
Euphyes pilatka
420

1½–1¾″ (38–44 mm). Wings triangular. Male bright orange-tan, with dark borders and small black patch of scent scales. Female pale tawny-orange above with distinct, broad, dark brown borders; dark patch in light area extends near leading edge. Below, hind wing dark tan; fore wing tawny with black base, tan margin, and tip.

Life Cycle
Caterpillar yellow-green with black dots and brown head.

Flight
2 broods in Virginia; spring and fall. Several broods in Florida; most of year.

Habitat
Wetlands with saw-grass stands.

Range
Virginia to Florida and Mississippi.

Comments
The Saw-grass Skipper's caterpillars draw blades of saw grass together, constructing tubes in which they conceal themselves. Adults fly to pickerelweed for nectar.

Two-spotted Skipper
Euphyes bimacula
421

1⅛–1¼″ (28–32 mm). Pointed wings. Dark above; male tawny-orange on broad patch around scent scales; female usually has 2 tiny yellowish fore-wing spots above. Below, both sexes have tawny-orange fore wing with 2 bright yellow spots on disk, on male patch of scent scales occasionally shows through; hind wing dull yellow-tan with bright yellow veins. Wing fringes and palpi white; head and collar orange.

Life Cycle
Egg pale green. Otherwise unrecorded.

Flight
1 brood; late June–July.

Habitat
Bogs, marshes, pond edges and nearby fields, and sedgy meadows in acid areas.

Range
Ontario to Nebraska; E. Colorado to Maine, south along coast to Carolinas.

Comments
Although it enters the South, the Two-spotted Skipper is mainly a northern resident. Members of the genus survive in a wide array of wetlands, but this species prefers cool climates.

Sedge Skipper
Euphyes dion
422

1¼–1⅝″ (32–41 mm). Relatively rounded wings. Male fore wing above tawny-orange with broad brown margin, black patch of scent scales; female fore wing above brown with row of tawny-orange spots. Both sexes have hind wing above brown with bright orange ray from cell toward margin. Below, fore wing orange on upper half and tip of leading edge, black lower edge with lighter spots; hind wing reddish tan with 1 or 2 pale streaks.

Life Cycle
Egg pale green. Caterpillar yellow-green with black head.

Flight
1 brood; July–August in New Jersey.

Habitat
Swamps, marshes, wet meadows, and bogs with dense stands of sedges and tall grasses; also woodland shorelines.

Range
Wisconsin and Ontario, south to Texas and N. Florida.

Comments
The Sedge Skipper occupies a wide range, but colonies occur very locally and it rarely seems common in one area. Although this agile butterfly is capable of powerful flight, it seldom wanders far from beds of the host plants. A particularly dark population inhabits the southeastern states.

Mulberry Wing
Poanes massasoit
423

1–1⅛″ (25–28 mm). Wings stubby. Dark black-brown above with or without minute spotting, orange on males, white on females. Below, fore wing similar to upper side; hind wing brown to maroon with band of bright yellow, angular spots, 1 elongated into crossbar.

Life Cycle
Egg chalk-white. Caterpillar olive with long yellow hairs.

Flight
1 brood; midsummer.

Habitat
Bogs or marshes with sedges or tussocks, and extensive tallgrass meadows.

Range
Minnesota, Ontario, New Hampshire south to Maryland and west to South Dakota, Nebraska, and Illinois.

Comments
Although widespread and sometimes numerous, the Mulberry Wing favors vulnerable, specialized wetland habitats, making it very local.

Broken Dash
Wallengrenia otho
424

1–1¼″ (25–32 mm). Brown above with tawny-orange patches on male fore wing and smaller, tawny-orange spots on female fore wing. Male has conspicuous patch of scent scales broken into 2 segments, interrupted by square, copper-brown patch. Below, reddish tan; hind wing has band of vague, pale spots.

Life Cycle
Caterpillar pale green with dark mottling; cuts circular pieces of grass blades to construct case and overwinters in it.

Flight
1 or 2 broods in North; summer. 3 broods in South; April–October.

Habitat
Swamps, woods, pastures, hayfields.

Range
Chiefly East and Gulf coasts; Maryland to Texas south to Costa Rica.

Comments
The Broken Dash thrives in an array of habitats throughout its extensive Atlantic range, so its choice of grasses must be extremely wide.

Least Skipperling
Ancyloxpha numitor
425

¾–1″ (19–25 mm). Small; wings rounded. Above, orange and black; fore wing variable, entirely black or with heavy orange-gold at base, along leading edge, and near cell; hind wing above gold with broad black border. Below, fore wing black with gold tip, leading edge, and border; hind wing clear orange-gold.

Life Cycle
Egg glossy yellow. Caterpillar light green with brown head. Chrysalis brown and white with blunt head.

Flight
2 broods in Colorado; late June to mid-July and August–September. 3 broods in New England; May–October. 4 broods in Texas; April–November.

Habitat
Reservoirs, ditches, ponds, and streams; moist pastures, meadows, and marshes.

Range
Saskatchewan east to Nova Scotia, south to Florida, and west

to Texas, barely reaching western edge of Great Plains in Colorado.

Comments
Very common in much of the East, the Least Skipperling flies feebly among tall grasses, and is easy to spot because of its distinctive, 2-toned wings.

Black Dash
Euphyes conspicua
426

1–1⅜″ (25–35 mm). Male tawny on fore wing above with broad brown borders and conspicuous patch of scent scales. Female almost black on fore wing above with curved band of glassy yellow spots. Hind wing above of both sexes has distinctive patch of light spots (tawny-orange on male, yellowish on female) crossed by dark veins on otherwise dark hind wing. Below, fore wing and hind wing rich rust-colored with light spots.

Life Cycle
Unknown.

Flight
1 brood; July–August, sometimes earlier farther south.

Habitat
Marshes, marshy meadows, mildly acid woodland bogs, wet tallgrass prairies.

Range
Ontario south through Minnesota to Nebraska, and east through Massachusetts, Ohio, and Virginia.

Comments
The unwary Black Dash perches on tall grasses and takes nectar from the blossoms of buttonbush and swamp milkweed. In June, this butterfly flies together with the Mulberry Wing in the Great Dismal Swamp of Virginia.

TREES

A variety of distinctive trees grow in the wetlands, including many common and widespread conifers and hardwoods. Stately larches and spruces are found in bogs and wet areas of the north, while other species, such as the Baldcypress and Water Tupelo, are found in very wet, swampy areas farther south. The fruit of many species is an important source of food for a wide range of animals, and trees also offer shelter and nesting material for many mammals and birds. Included in this group are descriptions of some of the most common and typical trees of the wetlands.

Western Redcedar
Thuja plicata
427

Large to very large tree with tapering trunk, buttressed at base, and a narrow, conical crown of short, spreading branches drooping at ends; foliage is resinous and aromatic.
Height: 100–175′ (30–53 m) or more. Diameter: 2–8′ (0.6–2.4 m) or more.
Leaves: evergreen; opposite in 4 rows; 1/16–1/8″ (1.5–3 mm) long. Scalelike, short-pointed; side pair keeled, flat pair usually without gland-dot; shiny dark green, usually with whitish marks beneath.
Bark: reddish brown, thin, fibrous, and shreddy.
Twigs: much branched in horizontal plane, slightly flattened in fanlike sprays, jointed.
Cones: 1/2″ (12 mm) long; clustered and upright from short, curved stalk; elliptical, brown; with 10–12 paired, thin, leathery, sharp-pointed cone-scales; 6 usually bearing 2–3 seeds with 2 wings.

Habitat
Swamps, moist, slightly acid upland soils; forming widespread forests with Western Hemlock, also with other conifers.

Range
SE. Alaska southeast along coast to NW. California; also SE. British Columbia south in Rocky Mountains to W. Montana; to 3000′ (914 m) in north; to 7000′ (2134 m) in south.

Comments
Indians of the Northwest Coast carved their famous totem poles, hollowed out war canoes, and split lumber for their lodges from this durable softwood. Indians also used the wood for boxes, batons, and helmets and the fibrous inner bark for rope, roof thatching, blankets, and cloaks.

Northern White-cedar
Thuja occidentalis
428

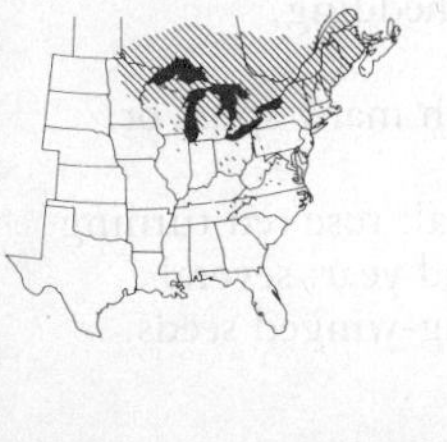

Resinous and aromatic evergreen tree with an angled, buttressed, often branched trunk and a narrow, conical crown of short, spreading branches.
Height: 40–70′ (12–21 m). Diameter: 1–3′ (0.3–0.9 m).
Leaves: evergreen; opposite in 4 rows; 1/16–1/8″ (1.5–3 mm) long. Scalelike; short-pointed; side pair keeled, flat pair with gland-dot. Dull yellow-green above, paler blue-green beneath.
Bark: light red-brown; thin, fibrous, shreddy, and fissured.
Twigs: branching in horizontal plane; much flattened; jointed.
Cones: 3/8″ (10 mm) long; elliptical; light brown; upright from short curved stalk; with 8–10 paired, leathery, blunt-pointed cone-scales, 4 usually with 2 tiny narrow-winged seeds each.

Habitat
Adapted to swamps and to neutral or alkaline soils on limestone uplands; often in pure stands.

Range
SE. Manitoba east to Nova Scotia and Maine, south to New York, and west to Illinois; south locally to North Carolina; to 3000′ (914 m) in south.

Comments
Also known as the Eastern Arborvitae. Probably the first North American tree introduced into Europe, it was discovered by French explorers and grown in Paris about 1536. The year before, tea prepared from the foliage and bark, now known to be high in vitamin C, saved the crew of Jacques Cartier from scurvy. It was named *arborvitae,* Latin for "tree-of-life," in 1558. The trees grow slowly and reach an age of 400 years or more.

Atlantic White-cedar
Chamaecyparis thyoides
429

Evergreen, aromatic tree with narrow, pointed, spirelike crown and slender, horizontal branches.
Height: 50–90′ (15–27 m). Diameter: 1½–2′ (0.5–0.6 m).
Leaves: evergreen; opposite; 1/16–1/8″ (1.5–3 mm) long. Scalelike; dull blue-green, with gland-dot.
Bark: reddish brown; thin, fibrous, with narrow connecting or forking ridges, becoming scaly and loose.
Twigs: very slender, slightly flattened or partly 4-angled, irregularly branched.
Cones: tiny, ¼″ (6 mm) in diameter; bluish purple with a bloom, becoming dark red-brown; with 6 cone-scales ending in short point; maturing in 1 season; 1–2 gray-brown seeds under cone-scale.

Habitat
Wet, peaty, acid soils; forming pure stands in swamp or bog forests.

Range
Central Maine south to N. Florida and west to Mississippi in narrow coastal belt; to 100′ (30 m).

Comments
Also known as the Southern White-cedar. Ancient logs buried in swamps have been mined and found to be well preserved and suitable for lumber. Pioneers prized the durable wood for log cabins, including floors and shingles. During the Revolutionary War, the wood produced charcoal for gunpowder.

Tamarack
Larix laricina
430

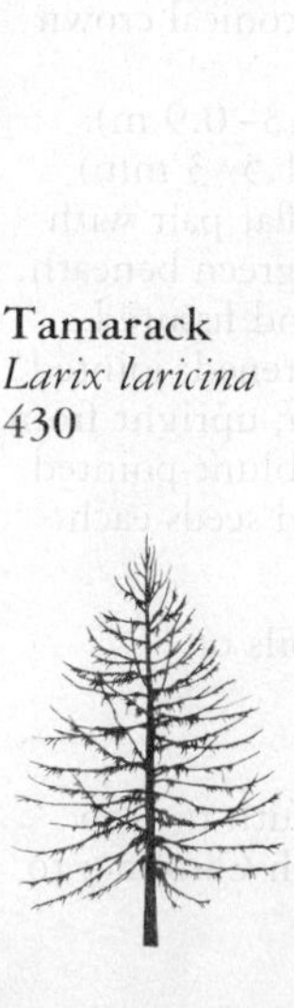

Deciduous tree with straight, tapering trunk and thin, open, conical crown of horizontal branches; a shrub at timberline.
Height: 40–80′ (12–24 m). Diameter: 1–2′ (0.3–0.6 m).
Needles: deciduous; ¾–1″ (2–2.5 cm) long, 1/32″ (1 mm) wide. Soft, very slender, 3-angled; crowded in cluster on spur twigs, also scattered and alternate on leader twigs. Light blue-green, turning yellow in autumn before shedding.
Bark: reddish brown; scaly, thin.
Twigs: orange-brown; stout, hairless, with many spurs or short side twigs.
Cones: ½–¾″ (12–19 mm) long; elliptical; rose red turning brown; upright, stalkless; falling in second year; several overlapping cone-scales; paired brown long-winged seeds.

Habitat
Wet peaty soils of bogs and swamps; also in drier upland loamy soils; often in pure stands.

Range
Across northern North America near northern limit of trees from Alaska east to Labrador, south to N. New Jersey, and west to Minnesota; local in N. West Virginia and W. Maryland; from near sea level to 1700–4000′ (518–1219 m) southward.

Comments
Also known as the Hackmatack or the Eastern Larch. One of the northernmost trees, the hardy Tamarack is useful as an ornamental in very cold climates. Indians used the slender roots to sew together strips of birch bark for their canoes. Roots bent at right angles served the colonists as "knees" in small ships, joining the ribs to deck timbers.

Pond Pine
Pinus serotina
431

Medium-sized tree with open, rounded or irregular crown of stout, often crooked branches.
Height: 40–70′ (12–21 m). Diameter: 1–2′ (0.3–0.6 m).
Needles: evergreen; 5–8″ (13–20 cm) long; 3 in bundle; slender, stiff; yellow-green.
Bark: blackish gray or reddish brown; furrowed into scaly plates.
Cones: 2–2½″ (5–6 cm) long; nearly round or egg-shaped; shiny yellow; almost stalkless; remaining closed on tree many years; cone-scales slightly raised and keeled, with weak prickle usually shed.

Habitat
Swamps, shallow bays, and ponds; often in nearly pure stands.

Range
S. New Jersey and Delaware south to central and NW. Florida, near sea level.

Comments
Also known as the Marsh Pine or the Pocosin Pine. "Pocosin" is an Indian name for pond or bog, alluding to this species' habitat. The Latin name *serotina,* meaning "late," refers to the cones, which remain closed for years before opening, often following a fire. After fires or other damage, seedlings and trees will produce sprouts from roots.

Black Spruce
Picea mariana
432

Tree with open, irregular, conical crown of short, horizontal or slightly drooping branches; a prostrate shrub at timberline.
Height: 20–60′ (6–18 m). Diameter: 4–12″ (0.1–0.3 m).
Needles: evergreen; ¼–⅝″ (6–15 mm) long. Stiff, 4-angled, sharp-pointed; spreading on all sides of twig from very short leafstalks. Ashy blue-green with whitish lines.
Bark: gray or blackish, thin, scaly; brown beneath; cut surface of inner bark yellowish.

Twigs: brown; slender, hairy, rough, with peglike bases.
Cones: ⅝–1¼″ (1.5–3 cm) long; egg-shaped or rounded; dull gray; curved downward on short stalk and remaining attached, often clustered near top of crown; cone-scales stiff and brittle, rounded and finely toothed; paired brown long-winged seeds.

Habitat

Wet soils and bogs including peats, clays, and loams; in coniferous forests; often in pure stands.

Range

Across northern North America near northern limit of trees from Alaska and British Columbia east to Labrador, south to N. New Jersey, and west to Minnesota; at 2000–5000′ (610–1524 m).

Comments

Black Spruce is one of the most widely distributed conifers in North America. The lowest branches take root by layering when deep snows bend them to the ground, forming a ring of small trees around a large one.

Baldcypress
Taxodium distichum
433

Large, needle-leaf, aquatic, deciduous tree often with cone-shaped "knees" projecting from submerged roots, with trunks enlarged at base and spreading into ridges or buttresses, and with a crown of widely spreading branches, flattened at top.
Height: 100–120′ (30–37 m) or more. Diameter: 3–5′ (0.9–1.5 m), rarely 10′ (3 m) or more.

Needles: deciduous; ⅜–¾″ (10–19 mm) long. Borne singly in 2 rows on slender green twigs, crowded and featherlike; flat, soft, and flexible. Dull light green above, whitish beneath; turning brown and shedding with twig in fall.
Bark: brown or gray; with long fibrous or scaly ridges, peeling off in strips.
Cones: ¾–1″ (2–2.5 cm) in diameter; round; gray; 1–2 at end of twig; several flattened, 4-angled, hard cone-scales shed at maturity in autumn; 2 brown, 3-angled seeds nearly ¼″ (6 mm) long, under cone-scale. Tiny pollen cones in narrow drooping cluster 4″ (10 cm) long.

Habitat

Very wet, swampy soils of riverbanks and floodplain lakes that are sometimes submerged; often in pure stands.

Range

S. Delaware to S. Florida, west to S. Texas and north to SE. Oklahoma and SW. Indiana. Below 500′ (152 m); locally in Texas to 1700′ (518 m).

Comments

Also known as the Cypress or the Swamp-cypress. Called the "wood eternal" because of the heartwood's resistance to decay, Baldcypress is used for heavy construction, including docks, warehouses, boats, and bridges. Planted as an ornamental northward in colder climates and in drier soils. Easily seen in Big Cypress National Preserve near Naples, Florida.

Honeylocust
Gleditsia triacanthos
434

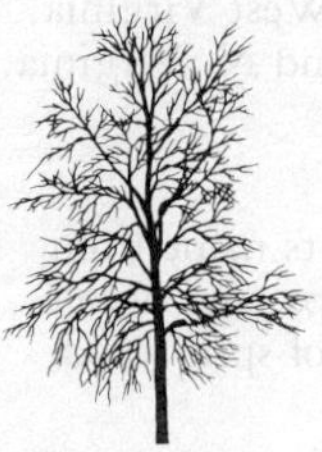

Large spiny tree with open, flattened crown of spreading branches.
Height: 80′ (24 m). Diameter: 2½′ (0.8 m).
Leaves: alternate; pinnately and bipinnately compound; 4–8″ (10–20 cm) long; the axis often with 3–6 pairs of side axes or forks; in late spring. Many oblong leaflets ⅜–1¼″ (1–3 cm) long; paired and stalkless, with finely wavy edges. Shiny dark green above, dull yellow-green and nearly hairless beneath; turning yellow in autumn.
Bark: gray-brown or black, fissured in long, narrow, scaly ridges; with stout brown spines, usually branched, sometimes 8″ (20 cm) long, with 3 to many points.
Twigs: shiny brown, stout, zigzag, with long spines.
Flowers: ⅜″ (10 mm) wide; bell-shaped, with 5 petals, greenish yellow, covered with fine hairs; in short narrow clusters at leaf bases in late spring; usually male and female on separate twigs or trees.
Fruit: 6–16″ (15–41 cm) long, 1¼″ (3 cm) wide; a flat pod, dark brown, hairy, slightly curved and twisted, thick-walled; shedding unopened in late autumn; many beanlike, flattened, dark brown seeds in sweetish, edible pulp.

Habitat
Moist soils of river floodplains in mixed forests; sometimes on dry, upland limestone hills; also in waste places.

Range
Extreme S. Ontario to central Pennsylvania, south to NW. Florida, west to SE. Texas, and north to SE. South Dakota; naturalized eastward; to 2000′ (610 m). Planted in western states.

Comments
Also known as the Sweet-Locust or the Thorny-locust. Livestock and wildlife consume the honeylike, sweet pulp of the pods. Honeylocust is easily recognized by the large, branched spines on the trunk; thornless forms, however, are common in cultivation and are sometimes found wild.

Black Ash
Fraxinus nigra
435

Tree with narrow, rounded crown of upright branches.
Height: 30–50′ (9–15 m). Diameter: 1′ (0.3 m).
Leaves: opposite; pinnately compound; 12–16″ (30–41 cm) long. 7–11 leaflets 3–5″ (7.5–13 cm) long, 1–1½″ (2.5–4 cm) wide; paired (except at end); broadly lance-shaped; finely saw-toothed; stalkless. Dark green above, paler beneath with tufts of rust-colored hairs along midvein; brown in autumn.
Bark: gray; corky, in soft scaly plates that rub off easily.
Twigs: gray, stout, becoming hairless.
Flowers: ⅛″ (3 mm) long; purplish, without calyx or corolla; in small clusters of many flowers each; before leaves in early spring. Male and female flowers on separate trees.
Fruit: 1–1½″ (2.5–4 cm) long; key with broad oblong wing extending to base of flat body; hanging in clusters; maturing in late summer.

Habitat
Wet soils of swamps, peat bogs, and streams, especially cold swamps where drainage is poor; in forests.

Range
SE. Manitoba east to Newfoundland, south to West Virginia, and west to Iowa; local in NE. North Dakota and N. Virginia; to 3500′ (1067 m).

Comments
The northernmost native ash, Black Ash takes its name from the dark brown heartwood. Baskets, barrel hoops, and woven chair bottoms are made from thin tough strips of split wood.

Green Ash
Fraxinus pennsylvanica
436

Tree with dense crown of shiny green foliage.
Height: 60′ (18 m). Diameter: 1½′ (0.5 m).
Leaves: opposite; pinnately compound; 6–10″ (15–25 cm) long; 5–9 (usually 7) leaflets 2–5″ (5–13 cm) long, 1–1½″ (2.5–4 cm) wide; paired (except at end); lance-shaped or ovate; coarsely saw-toothed or almost without teeth; mostly hairless. Shiny green above, green or paler and slightly hairy beneath; turning yellow in autumn.
Bark: gray, in scaly ridges, with reddish inner layer.
Twigs: green, becoming gray and hairless; slender.
Flowers: ⅛″ (3 mm) long; greenish; without corolla; in small clusters of many flowers each; before leaves in early spring. Male and female flowers on separate trees.
Fruit: 1¼–2¼″ (3–6 cm) long; yellowish key with narrow wing extending nearly to base of narrow body; hanging in clusters; maturing in late summer and autumn.

Habitat
Moist alluvial soils along streams in floodplain forests.

Range
SE. Alberta east to Cape Breton Island; south to N. Florida, west to Texas; to 3000′ (914 m) in southern Appalachians.

Comments
The most widespread native ash, this species extends westward into the plains and nearly to the Rocky Mountains. A northeastern variation with twigs, leafstalks, and underleaf surfaces all densely covered with hairs has been called Red Ash.

Carolina Ash
Fraxinus caroliniana
437

Tree with 1, or sometimes more than 1, trunk, often enlarged at base and leaning, and a rounded or narrow crown.
Height: 30–50′ (9–15 m). Diameter: 1′ (0.3 m).
Leaves: opposite; pinnately compound; 6–12″ (15–30 cm) long; 5 or 7 (sometimes 9) leaflets 2–4½″ (5–11 cm) long, 1–2″ (2.5–5 cm) wide; paired (except at end); elliptical or ovate; long-pointed; coarsely saw-toothed; slightly thickened; slender-stalked. Green above, paler or whitish and often slightly hairy beneath.

Bark: light gray; thin and scaly, becoming rough and furrowed.
Twigs: light green to brown, usually hairless, slender.
Flowers: ⅛″ (3 mm) long; without corolla; in small clusters of many flowers each; before leaves in early spring. Male flowers yellowish, female flowers greenish, on separate trees.
Fruit: 1¼–2″ (3–5 cm) long; yellow-brown key with broad elliptical wing extending to base of flat body, sometimes 3-winged; hanging in clusters, maturing in summer and autumn.

Habitat
Wet soils of swamps and riverbanks flooded part of year; in swamp forests.

Range
NE. Virginia to S. Florida and west to SE. Texas; to 500′ (152 m).

Comments
Carolina Ash is the ash that ranges farthest to the southeast. Its large, broadly winged, flat keys are distinctive.

Elderberry
Sambucus canadensis
438

Large shrub or small tree with irregular crown of few, stout, spreading branches, clusters of white flowers, and many small black or purple berries.
Height: 16′ (5 m). Diameter: 6″ (15 cm).
Leaves: opposite; pinnately compound; 5–9″ (13–23 cm) long; with yellow-green axis. 3–7 leaflets 1½–4″ (4–10 cm) long, ¾–2″ (2–5 cm) wide; paired (except at end); elliptical; sharply saw-toothed; stalkless or nearly so. Shiny green above, dull light green and hairy along midvein beneath. Leaves sometimes partly bipinnate, with up to 13 leaflets.

Bark: light gray or brown with raised dots; smooth or becoming fissured and rough.
Twigs: light green, stout, angled, with ringed nodes and thick white pith.
Flowers: ¼″ (6 mm) wide; with white corolla of 5 or 4 lobes; fragrant; many in upright flat-topped, much-branched clusters, 4–8″ (10–20 cm) wide; in late spring and early summer, shedding early.
Fruit: ¼″ (6 mm) in diameter; black or purplish-black berry; juicy and slightly sweet; 5 or fewer 1-seeded nutlets; maturing in late summer and autumn.

Habitat
Wet soils, especially in open areas near water at forest edges.

Range
SE. Manitoba east to Nova Scotia, south to S. Florida, and west to S. Texas; to 5000′ (1524 m).

Comments
Also known as Elder. This common, widespread shrub sprouts from roots. Elderberries are used for making jelly, preserves, pies, and wine. Birds and mammals of many species

also feed on the berries. The bark, leaves, and flowers have served in home remedies. Whistles, popguns, and other toys can be made by removing the thick pith from the stems.

Water Hickory
Carya aquatica
439

Large tree with tall straight trunk, slender upright branches, narrow crown, and bitter inedible nuts.
Height: 70–100′ (21–30 m). Diameter: 1½–2½′ (0.5–0.8 m).
Leaves: alternate; pinnately compound; 9–15″ (23–38 cm) long, with dark red, hairy axis. Usually 9–13 leaflets 2–5″ (5–13 cm) long; lance-shaped; long-pointed at tip; slightly curved; finely saw-toothed; mainly stalkless. Dark green and hairless above, often hairy beneath.
Bark: light brown; thin, fissured into long platelike red-tinged scales.
Twigs: brown; slender, becoming hairless.
Flowers: tiny; greenish; in early spring before leaves. Male, with 6–7 stamens, many in slender drooping catkins, 3 hanging from 1 stalk. Female, 2–10 flowers at tip of same twig.
Fruit: 1–1½″ (2.5–4 cm) long; broadly elliptical; much flattened; 4-winged; becoming dark brown; with thin husk splitting to middle; 4 or fewer in cluster. Nut flattened, 4-angled, thin-shelled, with bitter seed.

Habitat
Low wet flatlands, especially clay and flats, often submerged, in floodplains and swamps; bottomland hardwood forests.

Range
SE. Virginia south to central Florida, west to E. Texas, and north to S. Illinois; to 400′ (122 m).

Comments
Both the common and scientific names describe this hickory occupying wettest soils. The bitter nuts are consumed by ducks and other wildlife. Water Hickory is the tallest of all hickories; the national champion measures 150′ (45.7 m).

Nutmeg Hickory
Carya myristiciformis
440

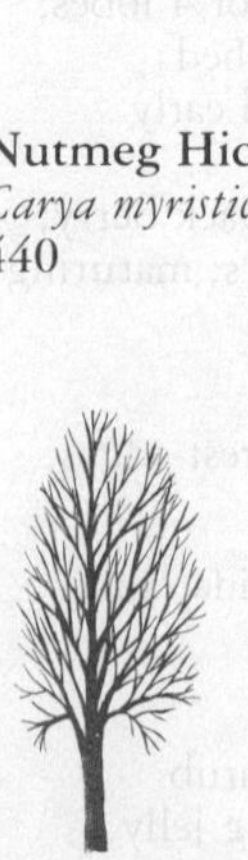

Tree with tall straight trunk, stout branches, narrow open crown of handsome bronze foliage, and edible nuts.
Height: 80′ (24 m). Diameter: 2′ (0.6 m).
Leaves: pinnately compound; 7–14″ (18–36 cm) long, with slender scurfy hairy axis. 5–9 leaflets, 2–5″ (5–13 cm) long; broadly lance-shaped; finely saw-toothed; short-stalked. Dark green and hairy above, shiny whitish beneath; becoming bright golden bronze in autumn.
Bark: gray or brown; fissured, with long thin scales.
Twigs: brown, with tiny yellow or brown scales; slender.
Flowers: tiny; greenish; in early spring before leaves. Male, with 6–7 stamens, many in slender drooping catkins, 3 hanging from 1 stalk. Female, 2–10 flowers at tip of twig.
Fruit: 1¼–1½″ (3–4 cm) long; elliptical; short-pointed;

becoming yellow-brown; covered with scurfy hairs; with thin husk splitting along 4 ridges nearly to base. Hickory nut thick-shelled, with edible seed.

Habitat
Moist soil of valleys and lower uplands in hardwood forests.

Range
Scattered from South Carolina west to E. Texas and SE. Oklahoma; also northeastern Mexico; to 500′ (152 m).

Comments
The common and scientific names of this patchily distributed hickory refer to the nutmeglike shape of the nut. Nutmeg Hickory is easily recognized by the brownish hue produced by numerous tiny scales on various parts. The wood is marketed as Pecan and has similar uses.

Poison-sumac
Toxicodendron vernix
441

Poisonous yet attractive narrow-crowned shrub or small tree with waxy whitish berries and dramatic fall foliage.
Height: 25′ (7.6 m). Diameter: 6″ (15 cm).
Leaves: alternate; pinnately compound; 7–12″ (18–30 cm) long; with reddish axis. 5–13 leaflets 2½–3½″ (6–9 cm) long; paired except at end; ovate or elliptical; without teeth; short-stalked. Shiny dark green above, paler and slightly hairy beneath; turning scarlet or orange in early autumn.

Bark: gray or blackish; thin; smooth or slightly fissured.
Twigs: reddish when young, turning gray with many orange dots; hairless.
Flowers: ⅛″ (3 mm) long; with 5 greenish petals; many, in long, open, branching clusters to 8″ (20 cm) long; male and female on same or separate plants; in early summer.
Fruit: ¼″ (6 mm) in diameter; rounded and slightly flat; whitish, 1-seeded, shiny and hairless; numerous, in drooping branched clusters; maturing in early autumn and often remaining attached until spring.

Habitat
Wet soil of swamps, bogs, seepage slopes, and frequently flooded areas; in shady hardwood forests.

Range
Extreme S. Quebec and Maine south to central Florida, west to E. Texas, and north to SE. Minnesota; mostly confined to Atlantic and Gulf coastal plains and Great Lakes region; to 1000′ (305 m).

Comments
One of the most dangerous North American plants. The clear, very toxic sap turns black on exposure and, for many people, causes a rash upon contact. A black varnish can be made from the sap, as in a related Japanese species. The fruit of Poison-sumac is not toxic to birds or animals and is consumed by many kinds of wildlife, such as bobwhites, pheasants, grouse, and rabbits, especially in winter, when other food is scarce.

Pawpaw
Asimina triloba
442

Shrub or small tree that forms colonies from root sprouts, with straight trunk, spreading branches, and large leaves.
Height: 30′ (9 m). Diameter: 8″ (20 cm).
Leaves: 7–10″ (18–25 cm) long, 3–5″ (7.5–13 cm) wide. Alternate; spreading in 2 rows on long twigs; reverse ovate, broadest beyond middle, short-pointed at tip, tapering to base and short leafstalk; covered with rust-colored hairs when young. Green above, paler beneath; turning yellow in autumn. Bruised foliage has disagreeable odor.
Bark: dark brown, warty, thin.
Twigs: brown; often with rust-colored hairs; ending in small hairy buds.
Flowers: 1½″ (4 cm) wide; 3 triangular green to brown or purple outer petals, hairy with prominent veins; nodding singly on slender stalks; in early spring.
Fruit: 3–5″ (7.5–13 cm) long, 1–1½″ (2.5–4 cm) in diameter; berrylike; brownish; cylindrical; slightly curved, suggesting a small banana; edible soft yellowish pulp has flavor of custard. Several shiny brown oblong seeds.

Habitat
Moist soils, especially floodplains; in understory of hardwood forests.

Range
S. Ontario and W. New York, south to NW. Florida, west to E. Texas, and north to SE. Nebraska; to 2600′ (792 m) in southern Appalachians.

Comments
Pawpaw is the northernmost New World representative of a chiefly tropical family, which includes the popular tropical fruits Annona, Custard-apple, Sugar-apple, and Soursop. The wild fruit was once harvested, but the supply has now decreased greatly due to the clearing of forests. The small crop is generally consumed only by wildlife, such as opossums, squirrels, raccoons, and birds.

Black Tupelo
Nyssa sylvatica
443

Tree with a dense, conical or sometimes flat-topped crown, many slender, nearly horizontal branches, and glossy foliage turning scarlet in autumn.
Height: 50–100′ (15–30 m). Diameter: 2–3′ (0.6–0.9 m).
Leaves: alternate; 2–5″ (5–13 cm) long, 1–3″ (2.5–7.5 cm) wide. Elliptical or oblong; not toothed (rarely with a few teeth); slightly thickened; often crowded on short twigs. Shiny green above, pale and often hairy beneath; turning bright red in early autumn.
Bark: gray or dark brown; thick, rough, deeply furrowed into rectangular or irregular ridges.
Twigs: light brown; slender, often hairy, with short spurs.
Flowers: greenish; at end of long stalks at base of new leaves in early spring; many tiny male flowers in heads ½″ (12 mm) wide; 2–6 female flowers 3/16″ (5 mm) long; male and female usually on separate trees.

Fruit: 3/8–1/2″ (10–12 mm) long; berrylike, elliptical, blue-black; with thin bitter or sour pulp; stone slightly 10- to 12-ridged; maturing in autumn.

Habitat
Moist valleys and uplands in hardwood and pine forests.

Range
Extreme S. Ontario east to SW. Maine, south to S. Florida, west to E. Texas, and north to central Michigan; local in Mexico; to 4000′ (1219 m), sometimes higher in southern Appalachians.

Comments
Also known as the Blackgum or the Pepperidge. A handsome ornamental and shade tree, Black Tupelo is also a honey plant. The juicy fruit is consumed by many birds and mammals. Swamp Tupelo (var. *biflora*), a variety with narrower oblong leaves, occurs in swamps in the Coastal Plain from Delaware to eastern Texas.

Red Osier Dogwood
Cornus stolonifera
444

Large, spreading, thicket-forming shrub with several stems, clusters of small white flowers, and small whitish fruit; rarely a small tree.
Height: commonly 3–10′ (1–3 m), rarely to 15′ (4.6 m).
Diameter: 3″ (7.5 cm).
Leaves: opposite; 1 1/2–3 1/2″ (4–9 cm) long, 5/8–2″ (1.5–5 cm) wide. Elliptical or ovate; short- or long-pointed; without teeth; 5–7 long curved sunken veins on each side of midvein. Dull green above, whitish green and covered with fine hairs beneath; turning reddish in autumn.
Bark: gray or brown; smooth or slightly furrowed into plates.
Twigs: purplish red, slender, hairy when young, with rings at nodes.
Flowers: 1/4″ (6 mm) wide; with 4 spreading white petals; many, crowded in upright flattish clusters, 1 1/4–2″ (3–5 cm) wide; in late spring and early summer.
Fruit: 1/4–3/8″ (6–10 mm) in diameter; whitish, juicy; stone with 2 seeds; maturing in late summer.

Habitat
Moist soils, especially along streams; forming thickets and in understory of forests.

Range
Central Alaska east to Labrador and Newfoundland, south to N. Virginia, and west to California; also northern Mexico; to 5000′ (1524 m); to 9000′ (2743 m) in the Southwest.

Comments
Red-osier Dogwood is useful for erosion control on stream banks. The common name recalls the resemblance of the reddish twigs to those of some willows called osiers, used in basketry. The Latin species name, meaning "bearing stolons," refers to the rooting of branch tips touching the ground and forming new shoots.

Possumhaw Viburnum
Viburnum nudum
445

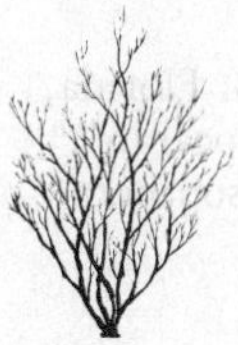

Shrub or small tree with spreading, open crown of irregular branches, many small, white or yellowish flowers, and small blue fruit.
Height: 16′ (5 m). Diameter: 4″ (10 cm).
Leaves: opposite, 2–5″ (5–13 cm) long, 1–2½″ (2.5–6 cm) wide. Elliptical to narrowly elliptical; edges turned under and without teeth or slightly wavy; slightly thick; with prominent curved side veins raised beneath. Shiny green and becoming hairless above; paler, rusty scurfy (especially when young), and with tiny dots beneath; turning red in autumn. Short leafstalk covered with rust-colored hairs.
Bark: gray to brown; smooth.
Twigs: brown; slender; rusty scurfy when young; ending in long-pointed bud covered with rust-colored hairs.
Flowers: ½″ (12 mm) wide; with 5 rounded creamy-white or yellowish corolla lobes, in upright short-stalked flat clusters, 2½–5″ (6–13 cm) wide; in spring.
Fruit: 5/16″ (8 mm) in diameter; nearly round; turning from pink to deep blue or blue-black with a bloom; bitter pulp; slightly flat stone; on slender stalks; maturing in autumn.

Habitat
Moist soil near streams and swamps and less frequently in upland slopes; in open forests, pinelands, and thickets as well.

Range
SW. Connecticut to central Florida, west to E. Texas, and north to central Arkansas and W. Kentucky; to 3000′ (914 m).

Comments
As the common name suggests, opossums consume the small, blue fruit; deer also browse the foliage. This shrub is sometimes also referred to as Swamphaw, alluding to one of its favored habitats. The scientific species name *nudum,* meaning "naked," refers to the stalked, leafless flower clusters.

Buckwheat-tree
Cliftonia monophylla
446

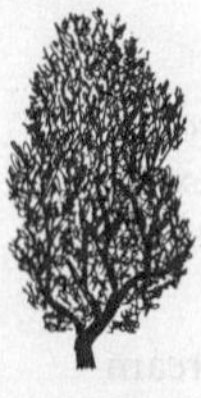

Evergreen, thicket-forming shrub or small tree with short, often crooked trunk, many branches, and a narrow crown.
Height: 20′ (6 m). Diameter: 6″ (15 cm).
Leaves: evergreen; alternate; 1–2″ (2.5–5 cm) long, 3/8–3/4″ (10–19 mm) wide; narrowly elliptical; thick and leathery; with vein along straight border and tiny gland-dots; almost stalkless. Shiny dark green above, paler and often whitish beneath.
Bark: dark red-brown or gray; scaly, becoming furrowed, thick, and spongy.
Twigs: numerous; reddish brown, slender, stiff.
Flowers: 1/4″ (6 mm) wide; with 5–8 white petals, sometimes pinkish-tinged; fragrant; in narrow clusters 1–2½″ (2.5–6 cm) long, with narrow reddish brown bracts; in early spring.
Fruit: 1/4″ (6 mm) long; elliptical, shiny yellow, 2–4 winged; in showy clusters; maturing in late summer, turning brown, remaining closed and often attached until spring.

Habitat
Wet, sandy, acid soils of bays and swamps.

Range
SE. Georgia and N. Florida west to SE. Louisiana; to 200′ (61 m).

Comments
Also known as the Titi or the Black Titi. The persistent winged fruit, similar to the fruit of Buckwheat, makes identification easy. Grown as an ornamental for the fragrant early flowers, shiny evergreen foliage, and showy fruit, it is also a honey-producing plant.

Laurel Oak
Quercus laurifolia
447

Large, nearly evergreen tree with dense, broad, rounded crown.
Height: 60–80′ (18–24 m). Diameter: 1–2½′ (0.3–0.8 m).
Leaves: alternate; 2–5½″ (5–14 cm) long, ⅜–1½″ (1–4 cm) wide. Narrowly oblong; diamond- or lance-shaped, often broadest near middle; bristle-tipped; edges straight (rarely, with few lobes or teeth); thin or slightly thickened; usually hairless. Shiny green or dark green above, light green and slightly shiny beneath; shedding in early spring and nearly evergreen.
Bark: brown to gray, smooth; becoming blackish, furrowed.
Acorns: ½″ (12 mm) long; nearly round, a quarter or less enclosed by shallow cup of blunt hairy scales; short-stalked or nearly stalkless; becoming brown; maturing second year.

Habitat
Moist to wet well-drained sandy soil along rivers and swamps; sometimes in pure stands.

Range
SE. Virginia to S. Florida, west to SE. Texas, and north locally to S. Arkansas; to 500′ (152 m).

Comments
Common and Latin species names refer to the resemblance of the foliage to Grecian Laurel (*Laurus nobilis*), of the Mediterranean region. A handsome shade tree, widely planted in the Southeast.

Dahoon
Ilex cassine
448

Evergreen shrub or small tree with rounded, dense crown and abundant, bright red berries.
Height: 30′ (9 m). Diameter: 1′ (0.3 m).
Leaves: evergreen; alternate; 1½–3½″ (4–9 cm) long, ¼–1¼″ (0.6–3.2 cm) wide. Oblong or obovate; slightly thick and leathery; usually without teeth or spines; edges often turned under. Shiny dark green and becoming hairless above, light green (and densely hairy when young) beneath.
Bark: dark gray; thin, smooth to rough and warty.
Twigs: slender, covered with silky hairs, becoming brown.
Flowers: 3⁄16″ (5 mm) wide; with 4 rounded white petals; on

short stalks mostly at base of new leaves in spring; male and female on separate plants.
Fruit: ¼″ (6 mm) in diameter; berrylike, round, shiny red (sometimes yellow or orange), short-stalked; mealy bitter pulp; 4 narrow, grooved, brown nutlets; maturing in autumn, remaining attached in winter.

Habitat
Wet soils along streams and swamps, sometimes sandy banks or brackish soils.

Range
SE. North Carolina south to S. Florida, and west to S. Louisiana; to 200′ (61 m); also Bahamas, Cuba, Puerto Rico and 1 variety in Mexico.

Comments
Planted as an ornamental for the evergreen foliage and profuse red fruit used in Christmas decorations. The common name apparently is of American Indian origin.

Sweetbay
Magnolia virginiana
449

Tree with narrow, rounded crown that sheds its leaves in winter or is almost evergreen southward, and with aromatic spicy foliage and twigs.
Height: 20–60′ (6–18 m). Diameter: 1½′ (0.5 m).
Leaves: alternate; 3–6″ (7.5–15 cm) long, 1¼–2½″ (3–6 cm) wide. Oblong, blunt at tip, without teeth, slightly thickened; short-stalked, becoming shiny green above, whitish and finely hairy beneath.

Bark: gray; smooth, thin, aromatic.
Twigs: with ring scars at nodes; ending in buds covered with whitish hairs.
Flowers: 2–2½″ (5–6 cm) wide; cup-shaped, with 9–12 white petals; fragrant; in late spring and early summer.
Fruit: 1½–2″ (4–5 cm) long; conelike; elliptical; dark red; composed of many separate pointed fruits, each with 2 red seeds; maturing in early autumn.

Habitat
Wet soils of coastal swamps and borders of streams and ponds.

Range
Long Island south to S. Florida and west to SE. Texas; local in NE. Massachusetts; to 500′ (152 m).

Comments
This attractive, native ornamental is popular for its fragrant flowers borne over a long period, showy conelike fruit, handsome foliage of contrasting colors, and smooth bark. Introduced into European gardens as early as 1688.

Titi
Cyrilla racemiflora
450

Small tree with short, stout, crooked trunk and spreading crown or a much-branched shrub, with glossy foliage, profuse, tiny, whitish flowers, and clusters of tiny fruit.
Height: 30′ (9 m). Diameter: 8″ (20 cm).

Leaves; alternate; clustered near end of twig; 1½–3″ (4–7.5 cm) long, ⅜–1″ (1–2.5 cm) wide. Narrowly oblong, usually widest beyond middle, blunt or slightly notched at tip; without teeth; slightly thickened; hairless. Shiny green above, paler beneath; turning orange and red in autumn. Deciduous or evergreen in the South in subtropical and tropical climates.
Bark: gray and smooth, becoming reddish brown, thin, and scaly; whitish pink and spongy at base.
Twigs: brown, slender, hairless.
Flowers: ⅛″ (3mm) wide; with 5 pointed white petals, sometimes pinkish-tinged; fragrant; short-stalked; crowded in upright narrow clusters 4–6″ (10–15 cm) long; in early summer.
Fruit: ⅛″ (3 mm) long; beadlike or egg-shaped, pointed or rounded, brown or yellow, spongy; in clusters; 2-celled, with 4 or fewer tiny seeds; maturing in late summer, not opening.

Habitat
Moist soils of river floodplains and riverbanks, flatwoods, and borders of sandy swamps and ponds.

Range
SE. Virginia south to central Florida and west to SE. Texas; to 500′ (152 m).

Comments
Also known as Swamp Cyrilla. This tree also is native in the West Indies and from Central America to Brazil. In the upper mountain forests of Puerto Rico, Titi is a large tree known as *palo colorado* ("red tree") because of its reddish-brown bark and wood.

Redbay
Persea borbonia
451

Handsome, aromatic, evergreen tree, with dense crown.
Height: 60′ (18 m). Diameter: 2′ (0.6 m).
Leaves: evergreen; alternate; 3–6″ (7.5–15 cm) long, ¾–1½″ (2–4 cm) wide. Elliptical or lance-shaped; short-stalked; thick and leathery, with edges slightly rolled under. Shiny green above, pale with whitish or rust-colored hairs beneath.
Bark: dark or reddish brown; furrowed into broad scaly ridges.
Flowers: ³⁄₁₆″ (5 mm) long; light yellow; several in long-stalked cluster at leaf base; in spring.
Fruit: ½–⅝″ (12–15 mm) long; nearly round; shiny dark blue-black; with 6-lobed cup at base, thin pulp, and rounded seed; maturing in autumn.

Habitat
Wet soils of valleys and swamps, also sandy uplands and dunes, in mixed forests.

Range
S. Delaware south to S. Florida and west to S. Texas; to 400′ (122 m).

Comments
The wood, which takes a beautiful polish, is used for fine cabinetwork and also for lumber. The spicy leaves can be used

to flavor soups and meats. Birds eat the bitter fruit. Swampbay (var. *pubescens*) is a variety found in coastal swamps; its twigs and lower leaf surfaces are covered with rust-colored hairs.

Willow Oak
Quercus phellos
452

Tree with conical or rounded crown of many slender branches ending in very slender, pinlike twigs with willowlike foliage.
Height: 50–80′ (15–24 m). Diameter: 1–2½′ (0.3–0.8 m).
Leaves: alternate; 2–4½″ (5–11 cm) long, ⅜–¾″ (10–19 mm) wide. Narrowly oblong or lance-shaped, with tiny bristle-tip; edges straight or slightly wavy. Light green and slightly shiny above, dull light green and sometimes with fine gray hairs beneath; turning pale yellow in fall.
Bark: dark gray, smooth, and hard; becoming blackish, rough, and fissured into irregular narrow ridges and plates.
Acorns: ⅜–½″ (10–12 mm) long and broad; nearly round, with shallow cup; becoming brown; maturing second year.

Habitat
Moist alluvial soils of lowlands, chiefly floodplains or bottomlands of streams; sometimes in pure stands.

Range
New Jersey south to NW. Florida, west to E. Texas, and north to S. Illinois; to 1000′ (305 m).

Comments
A popular street and shade tree with fine-textured foliage, widely planted in Washington, D.C., and southward. Its disadvantage, however, is that it becomes too large to be grown around houses. City squirrels as well as wildlife consume and spread the acorns.

Black Willow
Salix nigra
453

Large tree with 1 or more straight and usually leaning trunks, upright branches, and narrow or irregular crown.
Height: 60–100′ (18–30 m). Diameter: 1½–2½′ (0.5–0.8 m).
Leaves: alternate; 3–5″ (7.5–13 cm) long, ⅜–¾″ (10–19 mm) wide. Narrowly lance-shaped; often slightly curved to one side; long-pointed; finely saw-toothed; hairless or nearly so. Shiny green above, paler beneath.
Bark: dark brown or blackish; deeply furrowed into scaly, forking ridges.
Twigs: brownish; very slender, easily detached at base.
Flowers: catkins 1–3″ (2.5–7.5 cm) long; with yellow hairy scales; at end of leafy twigs in spring.
Fruit: 3/16″ (5 mm) long; reddish-brown capsules; hairless; maturing in late spring.

Habitat
Wet soils of banks of streams and lakes, especially floodplains; often in pure stands and with cottonwoods.

Range
S. New Brunswick and Maine south to NW. Florida, west to

S. Texas, and north to SE. Minnesota; also from W. Texas west to N. California; local in northern Mexico; to 5000′ (1524 m).

Comments
The largest and most important New World willow with one of the most extensive ranges across the country. In the lower Mississippi Valley it attains commercial timber size, reaching 100–140′ (30–42 m) in height and 4′ (1.2 m) in diameter. The numerous uses of the wood include millwork, furniture, doors, boxes, barrels, toys, and pulpwood. In pioneer times the wood was a source of charcoal for gunpowder.

Sandbar Willow
Salix exigua
454

Thicket-forming shrub with clustered stems or, rarely, a tree, with very narrow leaves.
Height: 3–10′ (1–3 m), sometimes to 20′ (6 m). Diameter: 5″ (13 cm).
Leaves: alternate; 1½–4″ (4–10 cm) long, ¼″ (6mm) wide. Linear; very long-pointed at ends; few tiny, scattered teeth or none; varying from hairless to densely hairy with pressed, silky hairs; almost stalkless. Yellow-green to gray-green on both surfaces.

Bark: gray; smooth or becoming fissured.
Twigs: reddish brown or yellowish brown; slender, upright; hairless or with gray hairs.
Flowers: catkins 1–2½″ (2.5–6 cm) long; with hairy yellow scales; at end of leafy twigs in spring.
Fruit: ¼″ (6 mm) long; light brown capsules; usually hairy; maturing in early summer.

Habitat
Wet soils, especially riverbanks, sandbars, and silt flats.

Range
Central Alaska east to Ontario and New York, southwest to Mississippi, and west to S. California; also local east to Quebec and Virginia, and in northern Mexico; to 8000′ (2438 m).

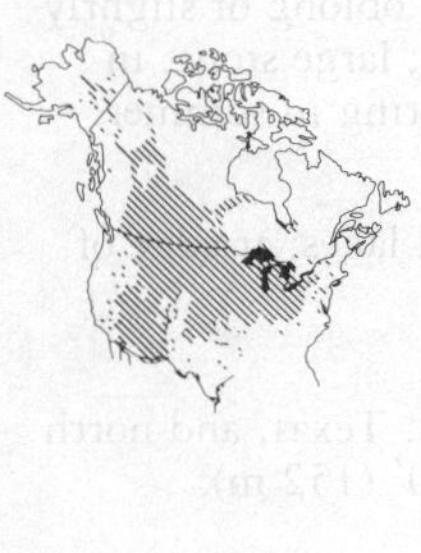

Comments
This hardy species has perhaps the greatest range of all tree willows: from the Yukon River in central Alaska to the Mississippi River in southern Louisiana. A common and characteristic shrub along streams throughout the interior, especially the Great Plains and Southwest, it is drought-resistant and suitable for planting on stream bottoms to prevent surface erosion.

Coastal Plain Willow
Salix caroliniana
455

Shrub or small tree with spreading or drooping branches.
Height: 30′ (9 m). Diameter: 1′ (0.3 m).
Leaves: alternate; 2–4″ (5–10 cm) long, ½–¾″ (12–19 mm) wide. Lance-shaped; finely saw-toothed; densely hairy when young. Green above; whitish and nearly hairless beneath. Leafstalks hairy.

Bark: gray to blackish; fairly smooth, furrowed into broad scaly ridges.
Twigs: brown; slender, limber; hairy when young.
Flowers: catkins 3–4″ (7.5–10 cm) long; greenish or yellowish; at ends of leafy twigs in spring.
Fruit: ¼″ (6 mm) long; long-pointed capsules; light reddish brown; maturing in late spring or early summer.

Habitat
Wet soils of stream banks and swamps.

Range
S. Pennsylvania south to S. Florida, west to central Texas, and north to SE. Nebraska; to 2000′ (610 m).

Comments
This is the common small tree willow found at low altitudes in the southeastern United States.

Swamp-privet
Forestiera acuminata
456

Shrub or small tree with slender, often leaning trunks, forming thickets at water edges, and with paired, diamond-shaped leaves.
Height: 25′ (7.6 cm). Diameter: 4″ (10 cm).
Leaves: opposite; 1½–4″ (4–10 cm) long, ½–1″ (1.2–2.5 cm) wide. Diamond-shaped or ovate, long-pointed at both ends; with small teeth beyond middle; almost hairless; long-stalked. Yellow-green above, paler beneath.
Bark: dark brown; thin, smooth.
Twigs: light brown, slender.
Flowers: tiny, greenish yellow, without petals; in small clusters along twig in early spring before leaves. Male and female flowers on separate plants.
Fruit: ⅜–⅝″ (10–15 mm) long; narrowly oblong or slightly curved, dark purple or blackish; thin pulp; large stone; in short clusters of several flowers each; maturing in summer.

Habitat
Wet soils bordering streams, swamps, and lakes; at edge of swamp forests.

Range
S. South Carolina to N. Florida, west to E. Texas, and north to central Illinois and SW. Indiana; to 500′ (152 m).

Comments
This relative of privet (*Ligustrum*) grows in swamps. The scientific name describes the long-pointed leaves.

Pussy Willow
Salix discolor
457

Many-stemmed shrub or small tree with open rounded crown; silky, furry catkins appear in late winter and early spring.
Height: 20′ (6 m). Diameter: 8″ (20 cm).
Leaves: alternate; 1½–4¼″ (4–11 cm) long, ⅜–1¼″ (1–3 cm) wide. Lance-shaped or narrowly elliptical; irregularly wavy-toothed; stiff; hairy when young; slender-stalked. Shiny green above, whitish beneath.

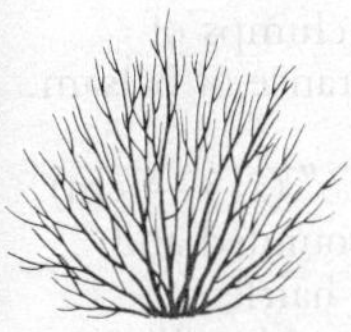

Bark: gray; fissured, scaly.
Twigs: brown; stout; hairy when young.
Flowers: catkins 1–2½″ (2.5–6 cm) long; cylindrical; thick with blackish scales; covered with silky whitish hairs; in late winter and early spring long before leaves.
Fruit: 5/16–½″ (8–12 mm) long; narrow capsules; light brown; finely hairy, in early spring before leaves.

Habitat
Wet meadow soils and borders of streams and lakes; usually in coniferous forests.

Range
N. British Columbia to Labrador, south to Delaware, west to NE. Missouri, and north to N. Wyoming and North Dakota; to 4000′ (1219 m).

Comments
The large flower buds burst and expose their soft silky hair, or "pussy fur," early in the year. In winter, cut Pussy Willow twigs can be put in water and the flowers forced at warm temperatures. Some twigs will produce beautiful golden stamens, while others will bear slender greenish pistils. The Latin species name refers to the contrasting colors of the leaf surfaces, which aid in recognition.

Bebb Willow
Salix bebbiana
458

Much-branched shrub or small tree with broad, rounded crown.
Height: 10–25′ (3–7.6 cm). Diameter: 6″ (15 cm).
Leaves: alternate; 1–3½″ (2.5–9 cm) long, 3/8–1″ (1–2.5 cm) wide. Elliptical; often broadest beyond middle; short-pointed at ends; slightly saw-toothed or wavy; firm; slightly hairy. Dull green above, gray or whitish and net-veined beneath.

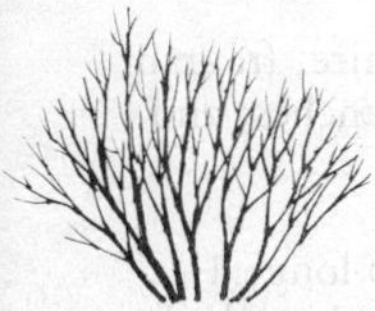

Bark: gray; smooth, becoming rough and furrowed.
Twigs: reddish purple; slender, widely forking; with pressed hairs when young.
Flowers: catkins ¾–1½″ (2–4 cm) long; with yellow or brown scales; on short, leafy stalks; before or with leaves.
Fruit: 3/8″ (10 mm) long; very slender capsules, hairy, brown, ending in point; long-stalked; maturing in early summer.

Habitat
Moist open uplands and borders of streams, lakes, and swamps.

Range
Central and SW. Alaska south to British Columbia and east to Newfoundland, south to Maryland, west to Iowa, and south in Rocky Mountains to S. New Mexico; to 11,000′ (3353 m) southward.

Comments
Bebb Willow is the most important "diamond willow," a term applied to several species that sometimes have diamond-shaped patterns on their trunks. These are caused by fungi, usually in shade or poor sites.

Balsam Willow
Salix pyrifolia
459

Usually a shrub, sometimes a small tree, with clumps of slender stems branched near the top and a fragrance of balsam.
Height: 20′ (6 m). Diameter: 4″ (10 cm).
Leaves: alternate; 2–3½″ (5–9 cm) long, 1–1½″ (2.5–4 cm) wide. Ovate or elliptical, short-pointed, base rounded and usually notched; finely saw-toothed, becoming hairless, aromatic. Dark green above, paler and whitish with yellow midvein and conspicuous network of small veins beneath.
Bark: gray, smooth, thin.
Twigs: shiny reddish brown, slightly stout, hairless, with shiny, bright red winter buds.
Flowers: catkins 1–1½″ (2.5–4 cm) long; yellowish; on short, leafy twigs; in late spring.
Fruit: ¼″ (6 mm) long; dark orange, hairless capsules; maturing in early summer.

Habitat
Cold, wet bogs.

Range
Yukon, south to E. British Columbia and across Canada to Labrador, south to Maine, and west to Minnesota; to 2000′ (610 m).

Comments
Also known as the Bog Willow. The common name refers to the aromatic, gland-toothed young leaves, while the Latin species name means "pear leaf." In winter Balsam Willow is easily recognized by the shiny reddish-brown twigs and the bright red buds.

Loblolly-bay
Gordonia lasianthus
460

Evergreen tree or shrub with showy, large, white, fragrant flowers; narrow, compact crown of upright branches; and shiny, leathery foliage.
Height: 60′ (18 m). Diameter: 1½′ (0.5 m).
Leaves: evergreen; alternate; 4–6″ (10–15 cm) long, 1–2″ (2.5–5 cm) wide. Narrowly elliptical or lance-shaped; short-pointed; finely saw-toothed; thick and leathery; short-stalked. Shiny dark green, turning red before falling irregularly throughout the year.
Bark: dark red-brown or gray; thick, deeply furrowed into narrow flat ridges.
Twigs: dark brown, stout, hairless.
Flowers: 2½″ (6 cm) wide; cup-shaped; with 5 large rounded white petals, waxy and silky on outer surface, and with many yellow stamens; fragrant; borne singly on long reddish stalks at leaf bases; in summer.
Fruit: ½″ (12 mm) in diameter; an egg-shaped capsule, pointed, gray, hairy, hard; 5-celled, and splitting along 5 lines to below middle; several long-winged brown seeds; maturing in autumn.

Habitat
Wet soil of bays and edges of swamps; also in sandhills; with various hardwoods and conifers.

Range
E. North Carolina south to central Florida and west to S. Mississippi; to 500′ (152 m).

Comments
The bark was once used locally for tanning leather. The Latin species name means "hairy-flowered." This genus includes about 30 species; all the others are in southeastern Asia and Indomalaysia.

Southern Bayberry
Myrica cerifera
461

Evergreen, aromatic, resinous shrub or small tree with narrow rounded crown.
Height: 30′ (9 m). Diameter: 6″ (15 cm).
Leaves: alternate; 1½–3½″ (4–9 cm) long, ¼–¾″ (6–19 mm) wide; those toward end of twigs often smaller. Reverse lance-shaped; coarsely saw-toothed beyond middle; slightly thickened and stiff; aromatic when crushed; short-stalked. Shiny yellow-green with tiny dark brown gland-dots above, paler with tiny orange gland-dots and often hairy beneath.
Bark: light gray; smooth, thin.
Flowers: tiny; yellow-green; in narrowly cylindrical clusters ¼–¾″ (6–19 mm) long; at base of leaf. Male and female on separate trees; in early spring.
Fruit: ⅛″ (3 mm) in diameter; 1-seeded drupes; warty; light green, covered with bluish-white wax; several crowded in a cluster; maturing in autumn; remaining attached in winter.

Habitat
Moist, sandy soil, in fresh or slightly brackish banks, swamps, hammocks, flatwoods, pinelands, and upland hardwood forests.

Range
S. New Jersey south to S. Florida, west to S. Texas, and north to extreme SE. Oklahoma; to about 500′ (152 cm).

Comments
Also known as the Candle-berry or the Southern Waxmyrtle. One of the very few Puerto Rican trees native also in the United States north of Florida, this popular evergreen ornamental is used for screens, hedges, landscaping, and as a source of honey. Colonists separated the fruit's waxy covering in boiling water to make fragrant-burning candles, a custom still followed in some countries.

Water Tupelo
Nyssa aquatica
462

Large aquatic tree with swollen base, long, straight trunk, narrow, open crown of spreading branches, and large leaves.
Height: 100′ (30 m). Diameter: 3′ (0.9 m).
Leaves: alternate; 5–8″ (13–20 cm) long, 2–4″ (5–10 cm) wide, sometimes larger. Ovate; often with a few large teeth; slightly thickened; with long hairy leafstalks. Shiny dark green above, paler and hairy beneath.
Bark: dark brown or gray; furrowed into scaly ridges.
Twigs: reddish brown; stout, hairy when young.

Flowers: greenish; on long stalks back of new leaves in early spring; many male flowers ¼″ (6 mm) long in heads ⅝″ (15 mm) wide; solitary female flowers ⅜″ (10 mm) long; male and female usually on separate trees.
Fruit: 1″ (2.5 cm) long; oblong, berrylike, dark purple; with thin sour pulp; stone with 10 winglike ridges; maturing in early autumn.

Habitat
Swamps and floodplains of streams, close to the water, where submerged a few months each winter and spring; often in pure stands.

Range
SE. Virginia south to N. Florida, west to SE. Texas, and north to S. Illinois; to 500′ (152 m).

Comments
Also known as the Tupelo-gum. This aquatic tree was named *Nyssa* after one of the ancient Greek water nymphs or goddesses of lakes and rivers. The name Tupelo is from Creek Indian words meaning "swamp tree."

Sugarberry
Celtis laevigata
463

Tree with broad, rounded, open crown of spreading or slightly drooping branches.
Height: 80′ (24 m). Diameter: 1½′ (0.5 m).
Leaves: alternate in 2 rows, 2½–4″ (6–10 cm) long, ¾–1¼″ (2–3 cm) wide. Broadly lance-shaped, long-pointed, often curved; 2 sides unequal; without teeth, sometimes with a few; 3 main veins from base; thin. Dark green and usually smooth above, paler and usually hairless beneath.

Bark: light gray; thin, smooth, with prominent corky warts.
Twigs: greenish, slender, mostly hairless.
Flowers: ⅛″ (3 mm) wide; greenish; male and female at base of young leaves in early spring.
Fruit: ¼″ (6 mm) in diameter; orange-red or purple 1-seeded drupes; dry and sweet; slender-stalked at leaf bases.

Habitat
Moist soils, especially clay, on river floodplains; sometimes in pure stands but usually with other hardwoods.

Range
SE. Virginia south to S. Florida, west to central and SW. Texas, and north to central Illinois; also northeastern Mexico; to 2000′ (610 m).

Comments
Also known as the Sugar Hackberry. Robins, mockingbirds, and other songbirds eat the sweetish fruits. Principal uses of the wood are for furniture, athletic goods, and plywood.

Water-elm
Planera aquatica
464

Elmlike tree with broad crown of spreading branches.
Height: 40′ (12 m). Diameter: 1′ (0.3 m).
Leaves: alternate; in 2 rows; 2–2½″ (5–6 cm) long, ¾–1″

(2–2.5 cm) wide. Ovate, short-pointed, base rounded with unequal sides; wavy-toothed with blunt gland-tipped teeth; many straight side veins; slightly thickened. Dull dark green and rough above, paler beneath.
Bark: light brown or gray; thin, shedding in large scales and exposing red-brown inner layers.
Flowers: ⅛″ (3 mm) wide; greenish; in early spring. 1–3 male flowers from bud; 1–3 female or bisexual flowers at leaf base of same twig.
Fruit: ⅜″ (10 mm) long; an elliptical drupe; warty or tubercled, dry, light brown, 1-seeded, short-stalked; maturing in early spring and not opening.

Habitat
Wet soil of riverbanks and swamps, especially where flooded annually.

Range
SE. North Carolina to N. Florida, west to E. Texas, north to extreme S. Illinois; to 500′ (152 m).

Comments
This distinctive and uncommon small tree is the only species of its genus; however, fossil relatives have been found in Eurasia.

American Elm
Ulmus americana
465

Large, handsome, graceful tree, often with enlarged buttresses at base, usually forked into many spreading branches, drooping at ends, forming a very broad, rounded, flat-topped or vaselike crown, often wider than high.
Height: 100′ (30 m). Diameter: 4′ (1.2 m), sometimes much larger.

Leaves: alternate in 2 rows; 3–6″ (7.5–15 cm) long, 1–3″ (2.5–7.5 cm) wide.
Elliptical, abruptly long-pointed, base rounded with sides unequal; doubly saw-toothed; with many straight parallel side veins; thin. Dark green and usually hairless or slightly rough above, paler and usually with soft hairs beneath; turning bright yellow in autumn.
Bark: light gray; deeply furrowed into broad, scaly ridges.
Twigs: brownish, slender, hairless.
Flowers: ⅛″ (3 mm) wide; greenish; clustered along twigs in early spring.
Fruit: ⅜–½″ (10–12 mm) long; elliptical flat 1-seeded keys (samaras), with wing hairy on edges, deeply notched with points curved inward; long-stalked; maturing in early spring.

Habitat
Moist soils; valleys and floodplains; mixed hardwood forests.

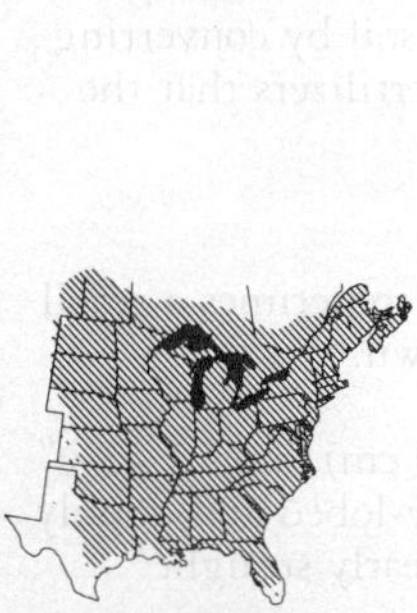

Range
SE. Saskatchewan east to Cape Breton Island, south to central Florida, and west to central Texas; to 2500′ (762 m).

Comments
This well-known, once abundant species, familiar on lawns

and city streets, has been ravaged by the Dutch Elm disease, caused by a fungus introduced accidentally about 1930 and spread by European and native elm bark beetles.

Red Alder
Alnus rubra
466

Graceful tree with straight trunk, pointed or rounded crown, and mottled, light gray to whitish, smooth bark.
Height: 40–100′ (12–30 m). Diameter: 2½′ (0.8 m), sometimes larger.
Leaves: alternate; in 3 rows; 3–5″ (7.5–13 cm) long, 1¾–3″ (4.5–7.5 cm) wide. Ovate to elliptical, short-pointed at both ends, slightly thickened, wavy-lobed and doubly saw-toothed, edges slightly turned under, with 10–15 nearly straight parallel veins on each side. Dark green and usually hairless above, gray-green with rust-colored hairs beneath.
Bark: mottled light gray to whitish, smooth or becoming slightly scaly, thin; inner bark reddish brown.
Twigs: slender, light green, covered with gray hairs when young, with 3-angled pith.
Flowers: tiny; in spring before leaves. Male yellowish, in drooping, narrowly cylindrical catkins 4–6″ (10–15 cm) long, ¼″ (6 mm) wide. Female reddish, in narrow cones ⅜–½″ (10–12 mm) long.
Cones: ½–1″ (1.2–2.5 cm) long; 4–8 on short stalks, elliptical, with many hard black scales; remaining attached; tiny, rounded, flat nutlets with 2 narrow wings; maturing in late summer.

Habitat
Moist soils including loam, gravel, sand, and clay, along streams and lower slopes; often in nearly pure stands.

Range
SE. Alaska southeast to central California; also local in N. Idaho; to 2500′ (762 m).

Comments
The leading hardwood in the Pacific Northwest, Red Alder is used for pulpwood, furniture, cabinetwork, and tool handles. It is planted as an ornamental in wet soils and is a pioneer on landslides, roadsides, and moist sites after logging or fire. Red Alder thickets are short-lived and serve as a cover for seedlings of the next coniferous forest. Alder roots, like those of legumes, often have swellings or root nodules containing nitrogen-fixing bacteria, which enrich the soil by converting nitrogen from the air into chemicals like fertilizers that the plants can use.

Mountain Alder
Alnus tenuifolia
467

Shrub with spreading, slender branches or sometimes a small tree with several trunks and a rounded crown.
Height: 30′ (9 m). Diameter: 6″ (15 cm).
Leaves: alternate; in 3 rows; 1½–4″ (4–10 cm) long, 1–2½″ (2.5–6 cm) wide. Ovate or elliptical, wavy-lobed and doubly saw-toothed, rounded at base, with 6–9 nearly straight

parallel veins on each side. Dull dark green above, light yellow-green and sometimes finely hairy beneath.
Bark: gray, thin, smooth, becoming reddish gray and scaly.
Twigs: slender, reddish and hairy when young, becoming gray, with 3-angled pith.
Flowers: tiny; in early spring before leaves. Male yellowish, in catkins 1–2¾″ (2.5–7 cm) long. Female brownish, in narrow cones ¼″ (6 mm) long.
Cones: ⅜–⅝″ (10–15 mm) long; 3–9 clustered on short stalks; elliptical, with many hard black scales; maturing in late summer and remaining attached. Tiny, elliptical, flat nutlets.

Habitat
Banks of streams, swamps, and canyons in moist soils.

Range
Central Alaska, Yukon, and Mackenzie southeast mostly in mountains to New Mexico and central California; near sea level in north; to 9000′ (2743 m) in south.

Comments
This is the common alder throughout the Rockies. The Navajo Indians made a red dye from the powdered bark.

Speckled Alder
Alnus rugosa
468

A low and clump-forming shrub; sometimes a small tree.
Height: 20′ (6 m). Diameter: 4″ (10 cm).
Leaves: alternate; in 3 rows; 2–4″ (5–10 cm) long, 1¼–3″ (3–7.5 cm) wide. Elliptical or ovate, broadest near or below middle; doubly and irregularly saw-toothed and wavy-lobed; with 9–12 nearly straight parallel veins on each side; short, hairy stalks. Dull dark green with network of sunken veins above; whitish green and often with soft hairs, and with prominent veins and veinlets arranged in rows.

Bark: gray, smooth.
Twigs: gray-brown, slender, slightly hairy when young; with 3-angled pith.
Flowers: tiny; in early spring before leaves. Male in drooping catkins 1½–3″ (4–7.5 cm) long. Female in cones ¼″ (6 mm) long.
Cones: ½–⅝″ (12–15 mm) long; elliptical, blackish, hard, short-stalked; maturing in autumn; with tiny rounded flat nutlets.

Habitat
Wet soil along streams and lakes, and in swamps.

Range
Widespread across Canada from Yukon and British Columbia to Newfoundland, south to West Virginia, west to NE. Iowa, and north to NE. North Dakota; almost to northern limit of trees; in south to 2600′ (792 m).

Comments
The Latin species name, meaning "rugose" or "wrinkled," refers to the network of sunken veins prominent on the lower

leaf surfaces. Planted as an ornamental at water edges. Alder thickets provide cover for wildlife, browse for deer and moose, and seeds for birds.

Possumhaw
Ilex decidua
469

Deciduous shrub or small tree with spreading crown and bright red berries.
Height: 20′ (6 m). Diameter: 6″ (15 cm).
Leaves: deciduous; mostly clustered on short spur twigs; alternate on vigorous twigs; 1–3″ (2.5–7.5 cm) long, ⅜–1¼″ (1–3 cm) wide. Spoon-shaped or narrowly obovate; finely wavy-toothed. Dull green above, paler and hairy on veins beneath.
Bark: light brown to gray; thin; smooth or warty.
Twigs: light gray, slender, hairless.
Flowers: ¼″ (6 mm) wide; with 4 rounded white petals; on slender stalks at end of spur twigs; in spring; male and female on separate plants.
Fruit: ¼″ (6 mm) in diameter; berrylike; red; bitter pulp; 4 narrow grooved nutlets; short-stalked; in clusters; maturing in autumn, remaining attached in winter.

Habitat
Moist soils along streams and in swamps.

Range
Maryland south to central Florida, west to Texas, and north to SE. Kansas; to about 1200′ (366 m).

Comments
Possumhaw is conspicuous in winter, with its many, small, red berries along leafless, slender, gray twigs. Opossums, raccoons, other mammals, songbirds, and gamebirds eat the fruit of this and related species.

Swamp Cottonwood
Populus heterophylla
470

Tree with narrow, rounded crown and stout branches, found in wet soils.
Height: 80′ (24 m). Diameter: 2′ (0.6 m).
Leaves: alternate; 4–7″ (10–18 cm) long, 3–6″ (7.5–15 cm) wide. Broadly ovate; blunt or rounded tip; heart-shaped or rounded at base; fine, curved teeth. Densely covered with white hairs when unfolding; becoming hairless and dark green above, remaining woolly and pale beneath. Leafstalks slender, rounded, hairless.
Bark: brown; furrowed into scaly ridges.
Twigs: stout; covered with white hairs when young.
Flowers: catkins (1–2½″ (2.5–6 cm) long; brownish; male and female on separate trees; in early spring.
Fruit: ½″ (12 mm) long; egg-shaped capsules; brown; long-stalked; maturing in spring and splitting into 2–3 parts; tiny cottony seeds.

Habitat
Wet sites, often submerged in floodplains and edges of swamps, with willows, Baldcypress, and Water Tupelo.

Range
Connecticut south to E. Georgia and from NW. Florida west to E. Louisiana, north to S. Michigan; to 800′ (244 m).

Comments
Because of its rapid growth, Swamp Cottonwood is sometimes planted as a shade tree.

River Birch
Betula nigra
471

Often leaning and forked tree; irregular, spreading crown.
Height: 40–80′ (12–24 m). Diameter: 1–2′ (0.3–0.6 m).
Leaves: alternate; 1½–3″ (4–7.5 cm) long, 1–2¼″ (2.5–6 cm) wide. Ovate or nearly 4-sided; coarsely doubly saw-toothed or slightly lobed; usually with 7–9 veins on each side. Shiny dark green above, whitish and usually hairy beneath; turning dull yellow in autumn.
Bark: shiny pinkish brown or silvery gray; separating into papery scales; becoming thick, fissured, and shaggy.
Twigs: reddish brown, slender, hairy.
Flowers: tiny; in early spring. Male yellowish, with 2 stamens, many in long drooping catkins near tip of twigs. Female greenish, in short upright catkins back of tip of same twig.
Cones: 1–1½″ (2.5–4 cm) long; cylindrical, brownish, upright, short-stalked; with many hairy scales and hairy 2-winged nutlets; maturing in late spring or early summer.

Habitat
Wet soil of stream banks, lakes, swamps, and flood plains; with other hardwoods.

Range
SW. Connecticut south to N. Florida, west to E. Texas, and north to SE. Minnesota; local in Massachusetts and S. New Hampshire; to 1000′ (305 m); to 2500′ (762 m) in southern Appalachians.

Comments
This is the southernmost New World birch and the only birch that occurs at low altitudes in the Southeast. Its ability to thrive on moist sites makes it useful for erosion control.

Eastern Cottonwood
Populus deltoides
472

Large tree with a massive trunk often forked into stout branches, and broad, open crown of spreading and slightly drooping branches.
Height: 100′ (30 m). Diameter: 3–4′ (0.9–1.2 m), often larger.
Leaves: alternate; 3–7″(7.5–18 cm) long, 3–5″ (7.5–13 cm) wide. Triangular; long-pointed; usually straight at base; curved, coarse teeth; slightly thickened; shiny green, turning yellow in autumn. Leafstalks long, slender, flattened.
Bark: yellowish green and smooth; becoming light gray, thick, rough, and deeply furrowed.
Twigs: brownish; stout, with large resinous or sticky buds.
Flowers: catkins 2–3½″ (5–9 cm) long; brownish; male and female on separate trees; in early spring.

Fruit: ⅜″ (10 mm) long; elliptical capsules, light brown; maturing in spring and splitting into 3–4 parts; many on slender stalks in catkin to 8″ (20 cm) long; many cottony seeds.

Habitat
Bordering streams and in wet soils in valleys; in pure stands or often with willows. Pioneers on new sandbars and bare floodplains.

Range
Widespread. S. Alberta east to extreme S. Quebec and New Hampshire, south to NW. Florida, west to W. Texas, and north to central Montana; to 1000′ (305 m) in east, to 5000′ (1524 m) in west.

Comments
The common name refers to the abundant cottony seeds; another name, Necklace Poplar, alludes to the resemblance of the long, narrow line of seed capsules to a string of beads. Although short-lived, it is one of the fastest-growing native trees.

Swamp Chestnut Oak
Quercus michauxii
473

Large tree with compact, rounded crown and chestnutlike foliage.
Height: 60–80′ (18–24 m). Diameter: 2–3′ (0.6–0.9 m).
Leaves: alternate; 4–9″ (10–23 cm) long, 2–5½″ (5–14 cm) wide. Obovate, broadest beyond middle; edges wavy with 10–14 rounded teeth on each side; abruptly pointed at tip; gradually narrowed to base. Shiny dark green above, gray-green and with soft hairs beneath; turning brown or dark red in fall.
Bark: light gray; fissured into scaly plates.
Acorns: 1–1¼″ (2.5–3 cm) long; egg-shaped, a third or more enclosed by deep thick cup with broad base, composed of many overlapping hairy brown scales; stalkless or short-stalked; maturing first year.

Habitat
Moist sites including well-drained, sandy loam and silty clay floodplains along streams; sometimes in pure stands.

Range
New Jersey south to N. Florida, west to E. Texas, and north to S. Illinois; to 1000′ (305 m).

Comments
It is also called Basket Oak because baskets were woven from fibers and splints obtained by splitting the wood. These strong containers were used to carry cotton from the fields.

Water Oak
Quercus nigra
474

Tree with conical or rounded crown of slender branches, and fine textured foliage of small leaves.
Height: 50–100′ (15–30 m). Diameter: 1–2½′ (0.3–0.8 m).
Leaves: alternate; 1½–5″ (4–13 cm) long and ¾–2″ (2–5 cm) wide. Obovate or wedge-shaped; broadest near rounded and

slightly 3-lobed tip; bristle-tipped; gradually narrowed to long-pointed base; sometimes with small lobes on each side. Dull blue-green above, paler with tufts of hairs along vein angles beneath; turning yellow in late fall, shedding in winter.
Bark: dark gray, smooth; becoming blackish and furrowed into narrow scaly ridges.
Acorns: ⅜–⅝″ (10–15 mm) long and broad; nearly round, with shallow, saucer-shaped cup; becoming brown; maturing second year.

Habitat
Moist or wet soils of lowlands, including floodplains or bottomlands of streams and borders of swamps; also moist uplands; often with Sweetgum.

Range
S. New Jersey south to central Florida, west to E. Texas, and north to SE. Missouri; to about 1000′ (305 m).

Comments
A handsome, rapidly growing shade tree for moist soils in the Southeast; however, Water Oak is short-lived.

Overcup Oak
Quercus lyrata
475

Tree with rounded crown of small, often drooping branches, with acorns almost covered by the cup, and narrow deeply lobed leaves.

Height: 60–80′ (18–24 m). Diameter: 2–3′ (0.6–0.9 m).
Leaves: alternate; 5–8″ (13–20 cm) long, 1½–4″ (4–10 cm) wide. Narrowly oblong; deeply divided into 7–11 rounded or short-pointed lobes, the longest near short-pointed tip; pointed base. Dark green and slightly shiny above, gray-green and with soft hairs or nearly hairless beneath; turning yellow, brown, or red in fall.
Bark: light gray; furrowed into scaly or slightly shaggy ridges or plates.
Acorns: ½–1″ (1.2–2.5 cm) long; nearly round, almost enclosed by large rounded cup of warty gray scales, the upper scales long-pointed; usually stalkless; maturing first year.

Habitat
Wet clay and silty clay soils, mostly on poorly drained floodplains and swamp borders; sometimes in pure stands.

Range
Delaware to NW. Florida, west to E. Texas, and north to S. Illinois; to 500′ (152 m), sometimes slightly higher.

Comments
The Latin species name, meaning "lyre-shaped," refers to the leaves.

Swamp White Oak
Quercus bicolor
476

Large tree with a narrow, rounded, open crown of often-drooping branches.
Height: 60–70′ (18–21 m). Diameter: 2–3′ (0.6–0.9 m).
Leaves: alternate; 4–7″ (10–18 cm) long, 2–4½″ (5–11 cm)

wide. Obovate, rounded or blunt at tip, broadest beyond middle, gradually narrowed to pointed base; edges wavy with 5–10 shallow rounded lobes on each side. Green and slightly shiny above, soft whitish hairs beneath; turning brown to red in fall.
Bark: light gray; with large thin scales, becoming furrowed into plates.
Acorns: ¾–1¼″ (2–3 cm) long; egg-shaped; a third or more enclosed by deep cup of many distinct scales, becoming light brown; usually 2 on long slender stalk, maturing first year.

Habitat
Wet soils of lowlands, including stream borders, floodplains, and swamps subject to flooding; in mixed forests.

Range
Extreme S. Ontario east to extreme S. Quebec and Maine, south to Virginia, west to Missouri, and north to SE. Minnesota; local to SW. Maine, North Carolina, and NE. Kansas; to 1000′ (305 m), locally to 2000′ (610 m).

Comments
The Latin species name, meaning "two-colored," refers to the leaves, which are green above and whitish beneath.

Pin Oak
Quercus palustris
477

Straight-trunked tree with spreading to horizontal branches (lowermost branches tend to droop), very slender pinlike twigs, and a broadly conical crown.
Height: 50–90′ (15–27 m). Diameter: 1–2½′ (0.3–0.8 m).
Leaves: alternate; 3–5″ (7.5–13 cm) long, 2–4″ (5–10 cm) wide. Elliptical; 5–7 deep lobes nearly to midvein with few bristle-tipped teeth and wide rounded sinuses; base short-pointed. Shiny dark green above, light green and slightly shiny with tufts of hairs in vein angles along midvein beneath; turning red or brown in fall.

Bark: dark gray; hard; smooth, becoming fissured into short, broad, scaly ridges.
Acorns: ½″ (12 mm) long and broad; nearly round; becoming brown; a quarter to a third enclosed by thin saucer-shaped cup tapering to base; maturing second year.

Habitat
In nearly pure stands on poorly drained, wet sites, including clay soils on level uplands; less common on deep, well-drained bottomland soils.

Range
Extreme S. Ontario to Vermont, south to central North Carolina, west to NE. Oklahoma, and north to S. Iowa; to 1000′ (305 m).

Comments
Named for the many short side twigs or pinlike spurs. A popular, graceful lawn tree with regular compact form and fine-textured foliage, Pin Oak is hardy and easily transplanted because the shallow fibrous root system lacks tap roots.

Silver Maple
Acer saccharinum
478

Large tree with short, stout trunk, few large forks, spreading, open, irregular crown of long, curving branches, and graceful leaves deeply cut toward the midvein.
Height: 50–80′ (15–24 m). Diameter: 3′ (0.9 m).
Leaves: opposite; 4–6″ (10–15 cm) long and nearly as wide. Broadly ovate, deeply 5-lobed and long-pointed (middle lobe often 3-lobed); doubly saw-toothed, with 5 main veins from base; becoming hairless; slender drooping reddish leafstalk. Dull green above, silvery white beneath; turning pale yellow in autumn.
Bark: gray; becoming furrowed into long scaly shaggy ridges.
Twigs: light green to brown; long, spreading and often slightly drooping, hairless; with unpleasant odor when crushed.
Flowers: ¼″ (6 mm) long; reddish buds turning greenish yellow; crowded in nearly stalkless clusters; male and female in separate clusters; in late winter or very early spring before leaves.
Fruit: 1½–2½″ (4–6 cm) long including long broad wing; paired, widely forking keys; light brown, 1-seeded; maturing in spring.

Habitat
Wet soils of stream banks, floodplains, and swamps; with other hardwoods.

Range
S. Ontario east to New Brunswick, south to NW. Florida, west to E. Oklahoma, north to N. Minnesota; to 2000′ (610 m), higher in mountains.

Comments
Its rapid growth makes Silver Maple a popular shade tree; however, its form is not generally pleasing, its brittle branches are easily broken in windstorms, and the abundant fruit produces litter.

Red Maple
Acer rubrum
479

Large tree with narrow or rounded, compact crown and red flowers, fruit, leafstalks, and autumn foliage.
Height: 60–90′ (18–27 m). Diameter: 2½′ (0.8 m).
Leaves: opposite; 2½–4″ (6–10 cm) long and nearly as wide. Broadly ovate, with 3 shallow short-pointed lobes (sometimes with 2 smaller lobes near base); irregularly and wavy saw-toothed, with 5 main veins from base; long red or green leafstalk. Dull green above, whitish and hairy beneath; turning red, orange, and yellow in autumn.
Bark: gray; thin, smooth, becoming fissured into long, thin, scaly ridges.
Twigs: reddish, slender, hairless.
Flowers: ⅛″ (3 mm) long; reddish; crowded in nearly stalkless clusters along twigs; male and female in separate clusters; in late winter or very early spring before leaves.
Fruit: ¾–1″ (2–2.5 cm) long including long wing; paired forking keys; red turning reddish brown; 1-seeded; maturing in spring.

Habitat
Wet or moist soils of stream banks, valleys, swamps, and uplands and sometimes on dry ridges; in mixed hardwood forests.

Range
Extreme SE. Manitoba east to E. Newfoundland, south to S. Florida, west to E. Texas; to 6000′ (1829 m).

Comments
Red Maple is a handsome shade tree, displaying red in different seasons. Pioneers made ink and cinnamon-brown and black dyes from a bark extract. It has the greatest north-south distribution of all tree species along the East Coast.

Sycamore
Platanus occidentalis
480

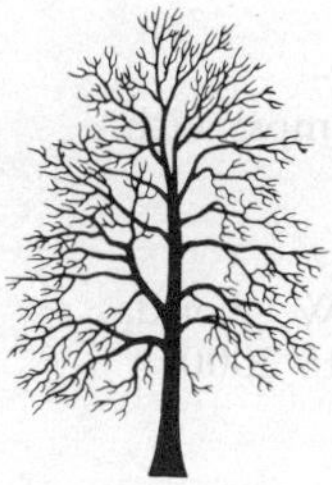

One of the largest eastern hardwoods, with an enlarged base, massive, straight trunk, and large, spreading, often crooked branches forming a broad open crown.
Height: 60–100′ (18–30 m). Diameter: 2–4′ (0.6–1.2 m), sometimes much larger.
Leaves: alternate; 4–8″ (10–20 cm) long and wide (larger on shoots). Broadly ovate, with 3 or 5 shallow broad short-pointed lobes; wavy edges with scattered large teeth; 5 or 3 main veins from notched base. Bright green above, paler beneath and becoming hairless except on veins; turning brown in autumn. Leafstalk long, stout, covering side bud at enlarged base.
Bark: smooth, whitish and mottled; peeling off in large thin flakes, exposing patches of brown, green, and gray; base of large trunks dark brown, furrowed into broad scaly ridges.
Twigs: greenish, slender, zigzag, with ring scars at nodes.
Flowers: tiny; greenish; in 1–2 ball-like drooping clusters; male and female clusters on separate twigs; in spring.
Fruit: 1″ (2.5 cm) in diameter; usually 1 brown ball hanging on long stalk, composed of many narrow nutlets with hair tufts; maturing in autumn, separating in winter.

Habitat
Wet soils of stream banks, floodplains, and edges of lakes and swamps.

Range
SW. Maine, south to NW. Florida, west to S. central Texas, north to E. Nebraska; also northeastern Mexico; to 3200′ (975 m).

Comments
Sycamore survives on exposed upland sites such as old fields and strip mines. A shade tree, it grows to a larger trunk diameter than any other native hardwood. The present champion's trunk is about 11′ (3.4 m) in diameter; an earlier giant's was nearly 15′ (4.6 m). The hollow trunks of old, giant trees were homes for chimney swifts in earlier times.

BIRDS

A tremendous number of birds—large and small, silent and noisy—find a congenial home in North American wetlands. Fish-loving species, such as herons, find perfect hunting in this wet country, while other birds look for insects and small amphibians under logs and along the margins of ponds. The bright shoulders of the Red-winged Blackbird add a touch of color to somber-looking marsh vegetation, while the inconspicuous American Woodcock is perfectly concealed by fallen leaves on damp ground. And millions of waterfowl—ducks, geese, and swans—use wetlands year-round as nesting or wintering grounds, or as stopping-off places in their yearly migrations. This section describes these and many other typical birds of the wetlands.

Common Loon
Gavia immer
481

28–36″ (71–91 cm). Goose-sized. Heavy, long-bodied water bird with thick pointed bill held horizontally. In summer, head and neck black with white collar; back black with white spots. In winter, crown, hind neck, and upperparts grayish; throat and underparts white. Rides low in the water.

Voice
Wild maniacal laugh, also a mournful yodeled *oo-AH-ho* with middle note higher, and a loud ringing *kee-a-ree, kee-a-ree* with middle note lower. Often calls at night.

Habitat
Forested lakes and rivers; oceans and bays in winter.

Range
Breeds from Aleutian Islands, Alaska, and Northern Canada south to New Hampshire, Montana, and California. Winters south to the Gulf Coast.

Comments
It is known for its call, a far-carrying wail heard on its northern breeding grounds and occasionally during migration. Loons are expert divers and have been caught in nets as much as 200 feet below the surface. Their principal food is fish.

Western Grebe
Aechmophorus occidentalis
482

22–29″ (56–74 cm) Largest North American grebe. Long neck. Head, neck, and body slate-blackish above, white below; long, yellow bill. Long white wing stripe shows in flight. Sexes look alike year round.

Voice
A rolling *kr-r-rick!,* given most often on its breeding grounds, but frequently heard from wintering birds as well.

Habitat
Large lakes with marshy regions for breeding; in winter, mainly an inshore seabird.

Range
Breeds on prairie lakes and other big lakes of the West from British Columbia south to S. California and sparsely to Mexico, east to Lake Winnipeg. Winters from the central British Columbia coast south to central Mexico, on some inland waters.

Comments
The mating display of these grebes is spectacular. Hundreds of paired birds display together, both sexes dancing and posturing like mirror images as they race across the water.

Pied-billed Grebe
Podilymbus podiceps
483

12–15″ (30–38 cm). Small, drab brown grebe with thick, short, chickenlike bill, no crest. White beneath tail; black bill ring and throat in summer, white throat and bill in winter.

Voice
A low, hollow, yelping *eeow-eeow-eeow-keeowm-kowm-kowm.*

Habitat
Marshes, ponds, and ditches with shallow water and dense marsh vegetation; open water in winter or on migration.

Range
Breeds throughout the Americas, except the subarctic and subantarctic regions. Winters in central British Columbia and all western and southern states with open water. Also on seacoasts.

Comments
The Pied-billed Grebe may mix with other waterfowl, but it is usually solitary; breeding pairs are secretive and sometimes only one pair is found on a pond.

Red-necked Grebe
Podiceps grisegena
484

18–20″ (46–51 cm). Largest grebe in eastern North America. A slender water bird with long rufous neck; whitish cheeks; dark cap; long, pointed yellow bill. Grayish body. Similar in winter, but neck gray. The long yellow bill separates it from all other North American grebes. In flight it can be distinguished from loons by its smaller size and white wing patches.

Voice
Nasal honk. Also a loonlike wail.

Habitat
Ponds and lakes in summer; bays and estuaries in winter.

Range
Northern Canada and Alaska southeast to S. Minnesota; more rarely to Quebec and New Hampshire. Winters south to Long Island, rarely to Florida.

Comments
Highly aquatic, grebes can swim with only their head above water, concealing themselves in low pond vegetation. The young, striped in black and white, are often seen riding on the parent's back. Like loons, grebes are expert divers.

Horned Grebe
Podiceps auritus
485

12–15¼″ (30–39 cm). Breeding birds of both sexes have rufous lower parts and neck, black head, and 2 buffy tufts on head. In winter gray above, white below; short, thin neck and much white on face, ear area, and neck, contrasting with blackish cap. Straight bill.

Voice
A high squeal and a sharp *ka-raa* heard on the nesting grounds. Otherwise generally silent.

Habitat
Small lakes and ponds. Coastal bays, oceans in winter.

Range
From the Yukon Delta east to Hudson Bay, and east-central Ontario, and North Dakota west to Idaho, Washington, and British Columbia. Winters on both coasts.

Comments
In contrast to the Eared Grebe, this bird primarily eats fish and tadpoles rather than insects. Horned Grebes are solitary or form loose aggregations, wintering mainly on the coasts.

Eared Grebe
Podiceps nigricollis
486

12–14″ (30–36 cm). Teal-sized bird, a bit smaller than the Horned Grebe. Breeding birds rufous below with black head and neck, golden ear tufts (neck of Horned Grebe is rufous). In winter plumage, dark neck and dark ear region contrasting with whitish face distinguish it from the Horned Grebe; bodies of both dusky above, white below. Bill upturned; that of Horned Grebe is straight. Both have red eyes.

Voice
On the breeding grounds, a loud *ker-yeep!*

Habitat
Large lakes and sloughs where part of the water is overgrown with emergent vegetation.

Range
Southwestern Canada through the western United States south to the desert belts. Also in the Old World. Winters south to Mexico.

Comments
Adult and young alike feed on insects. These birds migrate at night, and large congregations may be seen at lakes or seaside coves, where they dive for tiny crustaceans.

Fulvous Whistling-Duck
Dendrocygna bicolor
487

18–21″ (46–53 cm). A long-legged, long-necked, gooselike duck. Body mainly tawny, with a white stripe on the side; rump and underside of the base of the tail are white.

Voice
Clear double whistle. Called "Squealer" by hunters.

Habitat
Rice fields, freshwater marshes, and wet meadows.

Range
Resident in S. California, Texas, and S. Florida, and locally southward to Brazil.

Comments
Although Fulvous Whistling-Ducks in North America breed only in southern Texas and southern California, they occasionally wander; small flocks have turned up as far away as Utah and Nova Scotia.

"Mexican" Duck
Anas platyrhynchos diazi
488

21–22″ (53–56 cm). Plumage of both sexes in all seasons resembles that of female Mallard: dark, streaked buff overall with blue patch on inner flight feathers bordered in front and back with white. Bill of male is yellow-green; female's, dusky orange. No white in tail.

Voice
Resembles that of the Mallard: the male utters a *kwek-kwek-kwek-kwek;* the female, a loud quack.

Habitat
Marshes.

Range
Northeastern Mexico and adjacent parts of Arizona, New Mexico, and W. Texas.

Comments
This small, dark subspecies of the Mallard is a nonmigratory form. Until recently it was considered to be a separate species. A 1966 census counted fewer than 300 "Mexican" Ducks in the United States.

American Black Duck
Anas rubripes
489

19–22″ (48–56 cm). Sooty brown with conspicuous white wing linings, olive or greenish bill. Sexes alike. The female Mallard is paler, sandier, has bill mottled with orange.

Voice
Typical duck quack.

Habitat
Marshes, lakes, streams, coastal mud flats, and estuaries.

Range
Eastern and central North America, from Manitoba and Labrador to Texas and Florida.

Comments
It is believed that widespread interbreeding between American Black Ducks and Mallards has resulted in recent years in a decrease of "pure" Blacks. Actually the name is a misnomer, for the bird appears black only at a distance; it was formerly more aptly known as the "Dusky Duck."

Green-winged Teal
Anas crecca
490

12–16″ (30–40 cm). A small, dark duck. Male has chestnut head, green ear patch, flashing green patch on inner flight feathers, pale gray sides, and pinkish breast with a vertical white stripe down the side. Female is dark brown.

Voice
Clear repeated whistle. Females quack.

Habitat
Marshes, ponds, and marshy lakes.

Range
Aleutians, N. Alaska, Manitoba, and Quebec south to New York, Nebraska, and California. Winters south to Central America and the West Indies.

Comments
Green-winged Teal are among the fastest flying ducks and are therefore popular game birds. They wheel in compact flocks

like shorebirds. They are hardy, being among the last ducks to reach their winter habitat in fall, the first to depart in spring.

Wood Duck
Aix sponsa
491

17–20″ (43–51 cm). A beautiful, crested, multicolored small duck. Male patterned in iridescent greens, purples, and blues with a distinctive white chin patch; red, rather long bill; long tail. Female grayish with broad white eye-ring.

Voice
Loud *wooo-eeek.* Also softer *peet* and *cheep* notes.

Habitat
Wooded rivers and ponds; wooded swamps. Visits freshwater marshes in late summer and fall.

Range
British Columbia, Nova Scotia, and Minnesota south to Florida and Texas. Winters north to Washington in the West and New Jersey in the East, rarely farther north.

Comments
The Wood Duck's habit of nesting in cavities enables it to breed in areas lacking suitable ground cover. The young leave the nest soon after hatching, jumping from the nesting cavity to the ground. Once in the water, they travel through wooded ponds with their mother.

Mallard
Anas platyrhynchos
492

18–27″ (46–68 cm). Male has a green head, white neck-ring, chestnut breast, and grayish body. Inner feathers of wing (speculum) are metallic purplish blue, bordered in front and back with white. Female mottled brown with white tail and purplish-blue speculum, bill mottled orange and brown.

Voice
Males utter soft, reedy notes; females, a loud quack.

Habitat
Ponds, lakes, and marshes. Semidomesticated birds may be found on almost any body of water.

Range
Breeds from Alaska and Greenland south to Virginia, Texas, and northern Mexico. Winters south to Central America and the West Indies.

Comments
Ancestor of the common white domestic duck, wild Mallards frequently interbreed with domestic stock, producing a bewildering variety of patterns and colors. These ducks also hybridize with wild species such as the closely related American Black Duck.

Northern Shoveler
Anas clypeata
493

17–20″ (43–51 cm). Large "shovel" bill. Male has green head, white body, and chestnut flanks. Female streaked brown with pale blue wing patches; similar to female Blue-winged

Teal but larger, with the distinctive bill. Both sexes have pale blue shoulder patches.

Voice
Low croak, cluck, or quack.

Habitat
Marshes and prairie potholes; also on salt or brackish marshes.

Range
Alaska, N. Mackenzie and Manitoba, south to Nebraska, Colorado and S. California; occasionally farther east and south. Winters north to British Columbia and Georgia, and in smaller numbers to New England.

Comments
Like the closely related Blue-winged Teal, the Northern Shoveler is among the first ducks to arrive in the fall and the last to leave in the spring. It feeds on minute aquatic animals by straining water through comblike teeth along the sides of its long, expanded bill. It also eats aquatic plants.

American Wigeon
Anas americana
494

18–23″ (46–58 cm). Male is brownish with white crown, green ear patch, and bold white shoulder patches easily visible in flight. Female is mottled brown with grayish head and whitish shoulder patch. Pale blue bill and feet in both sexes.

Voice
Distinctive whistled *whew-whew-whew.* Also quacks.

Habitat
Marshes, ponds, and shallow lakes.

Range
Alaska, Mackenzie, and Minnesota south to Nebraska and N. California, rarely farther east. Winters south to Central America and the West Indies.

Comments
The American Wigeon, or "Baldpate," is a wary species, often seen on marshy ponds in the company of diving birds such as coots, Redheads, and Canvasbacks. They wait at the surface while the other birds dive, then snatch the food away when the birds reappear. They also visit grain fields and meadows to graze, like geese, on tender shoots.

Cinnamon Teal
Anas cyanoptera
495

14–17″ (35–43 cm). Male bright rufous, with a pale blue patch along the leading edge of each wing. Female mottled sandy brown and dusky, with pale blue wing patches; not distinguishable in the field from female Blue-winged Teal.

Voice
A soft *quack;* various chattering and clucking notes.

Habitat
Prairie marshes, ponds, and slow-moving streams bordered with reeds.

Range
Western North America from Aleutian Islands, regularly east to Saskatchewan, Nebraska, and W. Texas, and occasionally east to New York and the Carolinas. Also in South America.

Comments
This western relative of the Blue-winged Teal often associates with that species in areas where both occur. Like the Blue-wing, these birds migrate south in late summer and early fall, a month or two ahead of the other dabbling ducks.

Gadwall
Anas strepera
496

18–21″ (46–53 cm). A medium-sized duck with a white patch on hind edge of wing. Male mottled gray with a black rump and sandy brown head. Female similar but brown.

Voice
Ducklike quack. Also utters *kack-kack*s and whistles.

Habitat
Freshwater marshes, ponds, and rivers; locally in salt marshes.

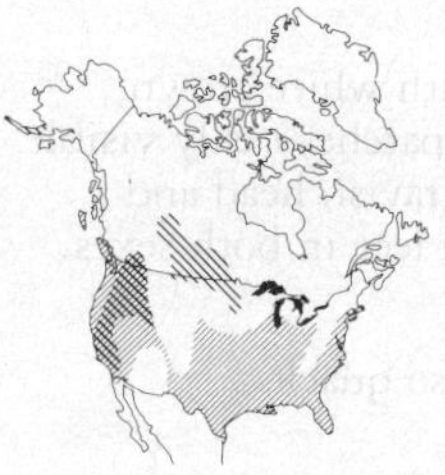

Range
Alaska and New England south to North Carolina and California. Winters north to southern New England.

Comments
This relative of the Mallard has the widest range of any duck, breeding almost throughout the North Temperate Zone. Known to hunters as the "Gray Duck," it is a popular game bird and is abundant in winter in southern marshes.

Blue-winged Teal
Anas discors
497

14–16″ (35–40 cm). A small brownish duck with pale blue shoulder patches. Male has a gray head and white crescent in front of eye. Female mottled brown, similar to female Green-winged Teal but grayer, with pale blue shoulder patches like the male.

Voice
Soft lisping or peeping note. Female utters a soft quack.

Habitat
Marshes, shallow ponds, and lakes.

Range
British Columbia, Quebec, and Newfoundland to North Carolina, the Gulf Coast, and S. California. Winters south to northern South America.

Comments
On low marshy prairies in the central part of the continent, where this duck is most numerous, virtually every pond and pothole has a breeding pair. The male commonly "stands guard" on the pond while the female is incubating. Unlike other dabbling ducks that form pairs in the fall, this teal begins courting in the spring and often does not acquire the familiar breeding plumage until December or January.

Northern Pintail
Anas acuta
498

Males 25–30″ (63–76 cm), females 21–23″ (53–58 cm). Slim, graceful duck with a slender neck. Male has brown head and white neck with white line extending up the side of the head. Central tail feathers long, black, and pointed. Female streaked brown, similar to female Mallard but paler, grayer, and slenderer, with brown patch on inner flight feathers that is bordered with white at the rear edge only; tail is more pointed than in female Mallard.

Voice
Distinctive 2-toned whistle. Females quack.

Habitat
Marshes, prairie ponds, and tundra; sometimes salt marshes in winter.

Range
Breeds from Alaska and Greenland south to W. Pennsylvania, Nebraska, and California. Locally and occasionally farther east. Winters south to Central America and the West Indies.

Comments
The Northern Pintail, widely distributed and common, is a strong flier and long-distance migrant like the Mallard. Seeds of aquatic plants are its main food, but in winter small aquatic animals are also taken; when freshwater habitats freeze over, it resorts to tidal flats, where it feeds on snails and small crabs.

Canvasback
Aythya valisineria
499

19–24″ (48–61 cm). Male has a whitish body, black chest, and reddish head with low forehead. The long bill gives the head a distinctive sloping profile. Female gray-brown, with similar profile. At a distance males can be distinguished from Redheads by their white bodies, the male Redhead's body being largely gray.

Voice
Males grunt or croak. Females quack.

Habitat
Nests on marshes; winters on lakes, bays, and estuaries.

Range
Alaska, Mackenzie, and Manitoba south to Minnesota, Nebraska, and California. Winters from British Columbia and Massachusetts south to the Gulf Coast and to Central America.

Comments
Although they breed mainly in the West, each fall large numbers migrate eastward to winter on the Great Lakes and along the Atlantic Coast. In recent years their numbers have declined drastically, chiefly because of the draining of the large marshes they require to breed.

Redhead
Aythya americana
500

18–22″ (46–56 cm). Male gray, with brick-red head and black breast. Female duller and browner, with a light area around base of bill; more round-headed than female

Ring-necked Duck. Both sexes have a pale gray wing stripe and a pale blue-gray bill. Similar Canvasback has a whitish body and sloping forehead and bill.

Voice
Like the meow of a cat; also quacks.

Habitat
Nests in marshes, but at other times is found on lakes and bays; often on salt water in winter.

Range
Breeds from British Columbia, Mackenzie, and Manitoba south to New Mexico, and rarely in eastern states. Winters from California, the Great Lakes, and southern New England south to Guatemala and the West Indies.

Comments
Redheads do most of their feeding at night, spending the daylight hours resting on water. This beautiful duck has suffered greatly from hunting and the destruction of its habitat; it has declined in numbers until it is one of the least common North American ducks.

Ring-necked Duck
Aythya collaris
501

14–18″ (35–46 cm). Male has black back and breast; purple-glossed, black-appearing head; pale gray flanks; vertical white mark on side of breast. Female brownish, paler around the base of the bill, and has a narrow white eye-ring. Bill pale gray with a white ring. The shape of the head—high and angular—distinguishes this bird from the scaups.

Voice
Soft purring notes, but usually silent.

Habitat
Wooded lakes, ponds, and rivers; seldom on salt water.

Range
Alaska, Manitoba, and Newfoundland south to Maine, Colorado, and California. Winters south to Mexico and the West Indies.

Comments
This species might better be called the Ring-billed Duck, for its chestnut neck-ring is usually seen only at close range, while the white ring on the bill is a prominent field mark.

Greater Scaup
Aythya marila
502

15–20″ (38–51 cm). Male has very light gray body; blackish chest; and black-appearing, green-glossed head. Female is a uniform dark brown with white patch at base of bill. Often seen in large flocks on open water.

Voice
Usually silent; croaking calls on the breeding grounds.

Habitat
Lakes, bays, and ponds; in winter, often on salt water.

Range
Alaska and northern Canada east to Hudson Bay and in Maritime Provinces. Winters mainly along Pacific, Gulf, and Atlantic coasts.

Comments
It is most commonly seen in large rafts, often composed of thousands of birds, on big inland lakes. When these lakes freeze over, the birds move to salt water. Although the two scaups can be difficult to tell apart, any very large flock of scaups on the northeast coast in winter may be assumed to be the Greater.

Lesser Scaup
Aythya affinis
503

15–18″ (38–46 cm). Similar to the Greater Scaup but crown is higher, giving the head a more angular appearance. Male has its head glossed with purple, not green. Females are dark brown with a small white face patch, not easily distinguishable from the female Greater Scaup. In flight, the white stripe is shorter, whereas in the Greater Scaup the stripe extends three-fourths of the wing's length.

Voice
Seldom heard. Sharp whistles and guttural scolding notes.

Habitat
Ponds and marshes; in migration and winter it occurs on lakes, rivers, and ponds, in southern states on salt water.

Range
Breeds from interior Alaska and northern Canada south to British Columbia, Montana, and Iowa, and occasionally farther east. Winters regularly from British Columbia and Massachusetts south to the Gulf of Mexico and South America.

Comments
In the northern states, where the Greater Scaup is more common in winter, the Lesser is often found in small parties on fresh water, while in the South it is seen in large flocks on lakes and salt water.

Harlequin Duck
Histrionicus histrionicus
504

14½–21″ (37–53 cm). Rather small. Breeding male is slate-blue with bright chestnut flanks and bold white markings outlined in black—as on a clown or harlequin—most conspicuous on head and wings. Female and nonbreeding male dark with 2 or 3 small white patches on head; male also shows some white on wing.

Voice
Mostly silent. Male utters high, squealing notes; female, a harsh croak.

Habitat
Near rushing water around boulders; in mountain streams during the nesting season and, in winter, around partly submerged ledges of rocky seashores.

Range
Baffin Island; Greenland, Iceland, mountainous Pacific North America; Alaska to California and Wyoming. In the West, it winters along the Pacific Coast.

Comments
In the Georgia Strait–Puget Sound area of Washington and British Columbia these ducks may be seen all year. The earliest breeders leave for coastal streams on the nearby mainland in April. The males return at the end of June or later, when other males are still courting their females at sea, and wait for their Rocky Mountain home streams to thaw, at which time they can nest.

Barrow's Goldeneye
Bucephala islandica
505

16½–20″ (42–51 cm). Male differs from the Common Goldeneye in having white crescent in front of eye. Flattened, blocky profile with low, abrupt forehead; black head glossed with purple with more of a crest than in Common Goldeneye, and sides extensively black. In flight, both sexes show less white on inner wing than Common Goldeneye. Female has brown head, white collar, grayish body; bill usually orange-yellow during mating season, whereas Common Goldeneye female shows this color only on tip of bill.

Voice
Generally silent except for a whining sound produced by its wings in flight. Clicking, grunting, and whistling notes are uttered during courtship or brood care.

Habitat
Breeds near forested lakes. Winters on bays and along the coast.

Range
SW. Alaska, British Columbia, southward in mountains to N. Wyoming; also in far northeastern Canada, Greenland, and Iceland. Winters with Common Goldeneyes or other diving ducks along the northwestern Pacific Coast and, sparingly, on open waters of the Rocky Mountain states.

Comments
This duck's family life is identical to that of the Common Goldeneye. Mating displays occur all winter. The male dips his bill in the water, then raises his head straight up and arcs it over his back while uttering a peculiar whistle.

Common Goldeneye
Bucephala clangula
506

16–20″ (41–51 cm). Medium-sized diving duck closely resembling Barrow's Goldeneye. In spring, male has black back and tail; white neck, sides, and underparts; head shiny green-black with large, round white spot in front of eye. Plumage of summer male, female, and juvenile is gray with darker gray wings and tail; large head is brown with white collar separating it from gray neck. Solid-white wing patch visible in flight.

Voice
Courting male a shrill *jeee-ep;* female may utter a low quack.

Habitat
Lakes and bogs in coniferous forests.

Range
From Alaska through forested Canada and northern United States, but mainly east of the Rockies. Winters on coasts or on rivers and deep lakes from SE. Alaska to Gulf Coast and California.

Comments
Goldeneyes fly swiftly, usually in small flocks. The males' wingbeat produces a whistle (hence the ducks' colloquial name, "Whistler"). The area where the male meets the incubating female is her territory, as is the vicinity of the nest hole, often far from the lake territory.

Common Merganser
Mergus merganser
507

22–27″ (56–68 cm). Male has flashing white sides, green head, white breast, and long, thin red bill. Female has gray body and sides; brownish crested head sharply set off from white throat. Red-breasted Merganser is similar, but has gray sides, white neck-ring, and rust-colored breast.

Voice
Low rasping croak.

Habitat
Wooded rivers and ponds; in winter, also on salt bays.

Range
SE. Alaska, Manitoba, and Newfoundland south to northern New England, Michigan, and California. Winters south to northern Mexico and the Gulf Coast (rare).

Comments
Although preferring to feed on lakes, they are often driven to rivers by cold weather; there they are found in flocks of 10 to 20 birds, all facing upstream and diving in pursuit of fish.

Bufflehead
Bucephala albeola
508

13–15½″ (33–39 cm). Smallest North American duck. Breeding male white with shiny black back and with large white patch on head conspicuous against green- and purple-glossed black forehead and nape. Female dark overall with pale breast, blackish head with white oval below and behind eye. Both sexes show white patch on inner wing in flight.

Voice
Male gives a squeaky whistle; female a low quack.

Habitat
Northern coniferous forest with small ponds and bogs surrounded by open water and trees.

Range
Alaska to N. Ontario and south through British Columbia to

N. California. In winter, in most of America where waters remain open and on Pacific and Atlantic coasts.

Comments
These sprightly, beautiful ducks fly fast and usually close to the water. They are quite tame; when flushed, they often circle back and settle in their original places.

Hooded Merganser
Lophodytes cucullatus
509

16–19″ (40–48 cm). A small duck with a slender, pointed bill. Male has white, fan-shaped, black-bordered crest; dark blackish body; dull rusty flanks; white breast with 2 black stripes down the side. Female is dull gray-brown with head and crest warmer brown. Both sexes show a white wing patch in flight.

Voice
Hoarse grunts and chatters.

Habitat
Wooded ponds, lakes, and rivers; sometimes in tidal channels in winter.

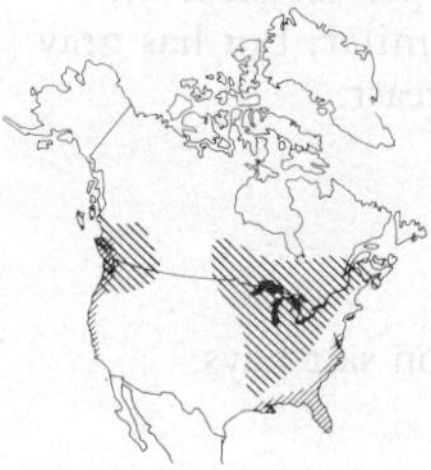

Range
Alaska, Manitoba, and Nova Scotia south to Tennessee, Nebraska, and Oregon; occasionally in southeastern states. Winters from British Columbia, Nebraska, and New England south to Mexico and the Gulf Coast.

Comments
The smallest of our mergansers, they are most often seen along rivers and in estuaries during the fall and winter. They are usually found in flocks of up to a dozen, and when startled are among the fastest flying of our ducks.

Ruddy Duck
Oxyura jamaicensis
510

14–16″ (35–40 cm). A small, chunky duck with a long tail that is often held straight up. Male in breeding plumage has a chestnut body, black crown, and white cheeks. Female and winter male are dusky brown with whitish cheeks—crossed by a brown stripe in the female. Bill of male is blue in breeding season, black at other times.

Voice
Mostly silent. Courting male makes a series of clucking notes.

Habitat
Freshwater marshes, marshy lakes and ponds; sometimes shallow salt bays and rivers in winter.

Range
Breeds from British Columbia, Mackenzie, and Quebec south to the Gulf Coast and through Central America to northern South America. Winters north to British Columbia and Massachusetts.

Comments
This duck is one of the most aquatic members of the family,

and like a grebe can sink slowly out of sight. They seldom fly, escaping from danger by diving or concealing themselves in marsh vegetation.

Greater White-fronted Goose
Anser albifrons
511

26–34″ (66–86 cm). Smaller than a domestic goose. Gray-brown with white patch on face at base of pink bill; feet orange. Irregular black spots or black areas on the gray belly prompted hunters' names: "Specklebelly" or "Speck." Immatures gray without face patch or speckled belly.

Voice
A cackling quite different from the high-pitched barking of the Snow Goose or the deep honking of Canadas. A ringing *gli-gli* or *gla-gla-gla* call.

Habitat
Tundra during breeding season. Migrates through marshy areas and river estuaries to winter on freshwater marshes from early October to May.

Range
The commonest Arctic goose from northern Russia across the Siberian tundra, and from Alaska to the western Canadian Arctic and Greenland. Winters regularly in the western United States, particularly in the Central Valley of California.

Comments
These geese migrate and winter in large flocks; each flock contains many smaller family units consisting of two speckled adults and up to five unspeckled young.

Canada Goose
Branta canadensis
512

Small races 22–26″ (56–66 cm); large races 35–45″ (89–114 cm). Brownish body with black head and long black neck; conspicuous white cheek patch.

Voice
Rich, musical honking.

Habitat
Lakes, bays, rivers, and marshes. Often feeds in open grassland and stubble fields.

Range
Alaska and Baffin Island south to Massachusetts, North Carolina, and California. Winters south to northern Mexico and the Gulf Coast. Widespread as a semidomesticated bird in city parks and reservoirs.

Comments
When people speak of "wild geese," it is generally this species they have in mind. Familiar in every state and province, a common sight is their V-shaped flocks in migration. There is much geographical variation in size. Tolerant of man, some even nest in city parks and suburbs and are especially noticeable in late summer and early fall, when they gather on golf courses and large lawns to molt.

Snow Goose
Chen caerulescens
513, 514

25–31″ (64–79 cm). Smaller than the domestic goose. Those that nest in Siberia and in the Arctic tundra of western North America are pure white with black wing tips, pink feet, and stout pink bill with black margin. Juveniles mottled with brownish gray and have dark bill. In the eastern Arctic most individuals are white, but a blue phase occurs (formerly considered a separate species, the "Blue Goose"): upperparts bluish gray, underparts brownish gray, head and upper neck white. Blue phase birds have spread westward in recent decades and are now found among the thousands of white Snow Geese wintering in California.

Voice
A rather high, nasal *how-wow*.

Habitat
Tundra and marsh.

Range
Arctic areas of Asia and North America.

Comments
In the Far North, fresh plant shoots are scarce in early spring, but the geese arrive fattened, with good reserves, from "staging areas"—thawed prairie marshes where they may spend up to several weeks at a time as they make their leisurely way northward. Snow Geese graze the fields and marshes of Pacific coastal areas and the Southwest all winter.

Ross' Goose
Chen rossii
515

21–25½″ (53–65 cm). Like Snow Goose but Mallard-sized. White with black wing tips; stubby bill pink with a dark base, lacks dark margin found in Snow Goose.

Voice
A weak cackling note.

Habitat
Tundra in summer; freshwater marsh in winter.

Range
The small population of this species (totaling about 32,000) nests in a limited area of the central Canadian Arctic. Winters mainly in California's Sacramento Valley.

Comments
This relatively rare bird is carefully monitored by both Canadian and United States game biologists, but some hunting is allowed on its winter grounds.

Mute Swan
Cygnus olor
516

58–60″ (147–152 cm). Wingspan: 95″ (2.3 m). All white; bill of adults is orange with black knob at the base. Young birds are similar, but dingy.

Voice
Unlike other swans, it is usually silent except for some hissing and grunting notes. Loud trumpeting call rarely heard.

Habitat
Ponds, rivers, coastal lagoons, and bays.

Range
Introduced from Europe into the northeastern United States; most frequent in southern New England, SE. New York, New Jersey, and Maryland; also established locally in Michigan.

Comments
With its wings arched over its back and its neck in a graceful S-curve, the male is extremely handsome on the water. A breeding pair will defend the nest and young against all comers, including humans, using their wings and bills.

American White Pelican
Pelecanus erythrorhynchos
517

55–70″ (140–179 cm). Wingspan: 96″ (2.8 m). Huge white bird with a massive yellow bill and black wing tips.

Voice
Low grunts or croaks on the nesting ground; usually silent.

Habitat
Marshy lakes and along the Pacific and Texas coasts. Winters chiefly in coastal lagoons.

Range
Breeds from British Columbia and Mackenzie south to W. Ontario and California; also on the Texas coast. Winters from Florida and S. California south to Panama.

Comments
A flock of migrating American White Pelicans is a majestic sight—a long line of ponderous birds, flapping and sailing in unison. These birds ride rising air currents to great heights, where they soar gracefully in circles. They often capture fish cooperatively, forming a long line, beating their wings and driving the prey into shallow water, where they seize the fish in their large, pouched bills.

Anhinga
Anhinga anhinga
518

34–36″ (86–91 cm). A blackish bird of southern swamps with a very long, slender neck and long tail. Male's plumage has greenish iridescence; upper surface of wings silvery gray. Female has tawny brown neck and breast, black belly.

Voice
Low grunt similar to that of the cormorant.

Habitat
Freshwater ponds and swamps with thick vegetation, especially cypress.

Range
Atlantic and Gulf coasts from North Carolina to Texas and in the Mississippi Valley north to Arkansas and Tennessee. South to southern South America.

Comments
It is also known as the Snakebird because its body is

submerged when swimming so that only its head and long, slender neck are visible above the water. Its long, dagger-shaped, serrated bill is ideally suited for catching fish.

Olivaceous Cormorant
Phalacrocorax olivaceus
519

25″ (63 cm). Duck-sized. Black with olive sheen; orange throat pouch. Double-crested larger, has yellow throat patch.

Voice
Piglike grunts.

Habitat
Brackish and fresh water, breeding in trees and low bushes.

Range
Coasts of Louisiana and Texas to southern South America.

Comments
Like other cormorants, it perches on dead branches or posts in the water, where it spreads its wings to dry. These birds sometimes join in communal fishing, lining up across a stream and moving forward with flailing wings to drive the fish into shallow water.

Double-crested Cormorant
Phalacrocorax auritus
520

30–35″ (76–89 cm). Goose-sized. Slender-bodied, dark bird with a long neck and a slender, hooked bill that is usually tilted upward when swimming. Orange throat pouch. Stands upright when perched. Larger than the Olivaceous Cormorant of the Gulf Coast, and lacks its white-bordered throat pouch. Tufts on the crown are rarely visible.

Voice
Deep guttural grunt.

Habitat
Lakes, rivers, swamps, and coasts.

Range
Breeds from Alaska and Newfoundland south to Mexico and the Bahamas. Winters north to Long Island and S. Alaska.

Comments
The Double-crested is the most familiar cormorant in the East. Except in the Northeast during the winter, and along the Gulf Coast, it is the only cormorant. Cormorants migrate in large, V-shaped flocks like migrating geese but are silent in flight.

Little Blue Heron
Egretta caerulea
521, 525

25–30″ (63–76 cm). Wingspan: 41″ (1 m). Adult slate-blue with maroon neck; immature is white, usually with dark tips to primaries. Grayish bill with black tip; greenish legs. Young birds acquiring adult plumage have a spotted or patched appearance.

Voice
Usually silent. Squawks when alarmed. Croaks, grunts, and screams at the nest site.

Habitat
Freshwater swamps and lagoons in the South; coastal thickets on islands in the North.

Range
East coast from New York to Texas and inland to Oklahoma. Winters north to South Carolina. Also in South America.

Comments
This is one of the most numerous herons in the South and may be observed in large mixed groups of herons and egrets.

Limpkin
Aramus guarauna
522

25–28″ (64–71 cm). Goose-sized. Grayish brown with white spots and streaks. Long, slender, downcurved bill. Flight is jerky, with a rapid upstroke and a slower downstroke.

Voice
Loud, wailing *krrr-ow*.

Habitat
Wooded swamps and marshes.

Range
Local in S. Georgia and Florida, ranging from the Okefenokee Swamp to the Everglades. South to southern South America.

Comments
This bird is chiefly nocturnal. Its loud, strident, eerie call, a familiar night sound in the Florida marshes, sounds like a human in distress, so the Limpkin is known locally as the crying bird.

White-faced Ibis
Plegadis chihi
523

19–26″ (48–66 cm). Long legs, long neck, and long curved bill. Chestnut-brown, with a green and violet sheen on upperparts. In breeding plumage both sexes have a conspicuous white marking around chin and eye. Juveniles lighter below and lack sheen.

Voice
A low quacking call given in flight.

Habitat
Large marshes, with nesting colony hidden in inaccessible reedbed or willow-covered area.

Range
Breeding range has contracted. Still breeds in the West, from California across to S. Idaho, Nevada, Utah, Colorado, and the Texas coast. Also in South America. Winters in southernmost California and in Mexico.

Comments
Feeding ibises are versatile, wading and probing in mud for crayfish but also walking through wet meadows to take grasshoppers and frogs. In flight to and from the roost they present an unforgettable view as long, wavering lines of large, dark, curlew-like birds speed toward the horizon.

Wood Stork
Mycteria americana
524

40–44″ (102–112 cm). Wingspan: 66″ (1.5 m). White with black flight feathers and tail. Head and neck bare, dark gray. Bill long, stout, and slightly curved, black in adults and yellow in immatures. Flies with its neck extended.

Voice
Dull croak. Usually silent except around nest. Young clatter endlessly.

Habitat
On or near the coast, breeding chiefly in cypress swamps; also in mangroves.

Range
Breeds in Florida; wanders to South Carolina and Texas, occasionally farther. Also in South America.

Comments
These birds perch motionless on a bare branch or slowly stalk through marshes in search of food. They are sometimes seen circling high in the air on rising thermal air currents. They nest in enormous colonies numbering up to 10,000 pairs, but in recent years their numbers have declined drastically.

Great Egret
Casmerodius albus
526

35–41″ (89–104 cm). Wingspan: 55″ (1.4 m). A large, all-white heron with a yellow bill and black legs. In Florida the white form of the Great Blue Heron, known as the "Great White Heron," is larger, with greenish-yellow legs.

Voice
Deep guttural croak. Also loud squawks in nesting colony.

Habitat
Freshwater and salt marshes, marshy ponds, and tidal flats.

Range
Oregon, Wisconsin, and Massachusetts to southern South America. Winters regularly north to South Carolina and the Gulf Coast.

Comments
One of the most magnificent of our herons, it has fortunately recovered from long persecution by plume hunters. Like the Great Blue Heron, it feeds alone, stalking fish, frogs, snakes, and crayfish in shallow water.

Snowy Egret
Egretta thula
527

20–27″ (51–68 cm). Wingspan: 38″ (1 m). A small white heron with a slender black bill, black legs, and yellow feet. In the breeding season it has long lacy plumes on its back. Similar to young of the Little Blue Heron, but that species has a stouter, bluish-gray bill and greenish-yellow legs and feet.

Voice
Harsh squawk.

Habitat
Salt marshes, ponds, rice fields, and shallow coastal bays.

Range
N. California, Oklahoma, and Maine to southern South America. Winters north to California and South Carolina.

Comments
During the 19th and early 20th centuries, Snowy Egrets were slaughtered almost to extinction for their fine plumes, used to decorate hats. Fortunately, complete protection has enabled them to increase their numbers again.

Great Blue Heron
Ardea herodias
528

39–52″ (99–132 cm). Wingspan: 70″ (1.8 m). A common, large, grayish heron with a yellowish bill. Flies with neck folded; the Sandhill Crane flies with the neck extended.

Voice
Hoarse, guttural squawk.

Habitat
Lakes, ponds, rivers, and marshes.

Range
Alaska, Quebec, and Nova Scotia south to Mexico and the West Indies. Winters as far north as New England and southern Alaska. Also breeds in the Galapagos Islands.

Comments
This large heron is frequently found standing at the edge of a pond or marshy pool, watching for fish or frogs, which are its principal food. It also feeds on small mammals, reptiles, and occasionally birds.

Black-crowned Night-Heron
Nycticorax nycticorax
529

23–28″ (58–71 cm). Wingspan: 44″ (1.1 m). A medium-sized, stocky, rather short-necked heron with black crown and back, gray wings, and white underparts; short, black bill; pinkish or yellowish legs. In breeding season it has 2 or more long white plumes on back of head. Young birds are dull gray-brown lightly spotted with white.

Voice
Harsh, barking *quawk!*, most often heard at night or at dusk. A bewildering variety of croaking, barking, and screaming calls are uttered in the nesting colony.

Habitat
Marshes; swamps, and wooded streams.

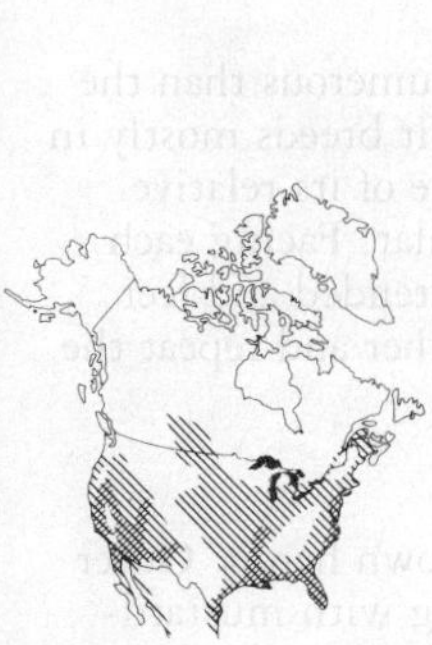

Range
Washington, Saskatchewan, Minnesota, and New Brunswick, to southern South America. Winters in southern half of the United States.

Comments
As its name implies this species is largely nocturnal, spending daylight hours roosting in trees or reedbeds. It is best known for its loud calls.

Yellow-crowned Night-Heron
Nycticorax violaceus
530

22–27″ (56–68 cm). Wingspan: 44″ (1.1 m). Medium-sized heron. Adult is slate-gray with black head, white cheeks, yellowish crown and plumes, black bill, and orange legs. In flight the feet extend beyond the tail. Immature birds are grayish, finely speckled with white above, like young Black-crowned Night-Herons but with a thicker bill and longer legs.

Voice
Quawk like that of Black-crowned Night-Heron but higher in pitch.

Habitat
Wooded swamps and coastal thickets.

Range
Massachusetts to Florida and west to Texas; mainly near the coast, but north along the Mississippi River and its larger tributaries, rarely to the central states. Also warmer portions of Middle and South America and West Indies.

Comments
Contrary to popular opinion, herons do not stab a fish (it would then be difficult to release) but grasp it in their bill, toss it in the air, and swallow it head-first.

Sandhill Crane
Grus canadensis
531

34–48″ (86–122 cm). Wingspan: 80″ (2 m). Very tall, with long neck and long legs. Largely gray with red forehead. Plumage often appears rusty because of iron stains from the water of tundra ponds. Unlike herons, cranes fly with the neck outstretched and with the upstroke faster than the downstroke.

Voice
Loud, rattling *kar-r-r-o-o-o*.

Habitat
Large freshwater marshes, prairie ponds, and marshy tundra; also on prairies and grainfields during migration and in winter.

Range
Alaska and Arctic Islands south to Michigan, Minnesota, and California; also in Gulf states from Florida to Texas. Winters in Arizona, Texas, Mexico, and California. Also in Cuba.

Comments
Apparently this species was always more numerous than the larger Whooping Crane, and the fact that it breeds mostly in the remote Arctic has saved it from the fate of its relative. The mating dance of the cranes is spectacular. Facing each other, they leap into the air with wings extended and feet thrown forward. Then they bow to each other and repeat the performance, uttering loud croaking calls.

American Bittern
Botaurus lentiginosus
532

23–34″ (58–86 cm). A medium-sized, brown heron. Outer wing appears blackish in flight, contrasting with mustard-brown of inner wing and body. At close range the bird shows a black streak on each side of the throat.

Voice
Peculiar pumping sound, *oong-KA-chunk!*, repeated a few times and often audible for half a mile.

Habitat
Freshwater and brackish marshes and marshy lake shores.

Range
British Columbia, Manitoba, and Newfoundland to Maryland, Kansas, and S. California; also in Texas, Louisiana, and Florida. Winters north to British Columbia, Ohio, and Delaware, occasionally farther north.

Comments
This species is secretive, preferring to freeze and trust its concealing coloration when approached rather than flush like other herons. When an observer is nearby it will often raise its head, point its bill skyward, and sway slowly from side to side, as if imitating waving reeds. If the observer gets close the bittern will fly off, uttering a low barking call.

Least Bittern
Ixobrychus exilis
533

11–14″ (28–35 cm). A tiny heron with blackish back and conspicuous buff wing patches and underparts. Female and young are similar but duller.

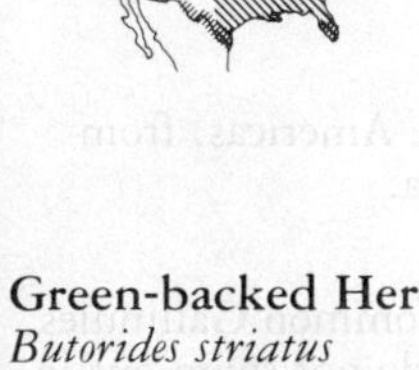

Voice
Soft *coo-coo-coo,* easily unnoticed.

Habitat
Freshwater marshes where cattails and reeds predominate.

Range
Southern Canada and northern United States to S. Texas and the West Indies. Winters from the Gulf Coast south. Also breeds in South America.

Comments
Although locally common, this heron is very secretive. It is reluctant to fly, depending on its cryptic color pattern to escape detection. The best way to see it is to wait at the edge of a cattail marsh—eventually one may rise, fly over the cattails, and drop out of sight again.

Green-backed Heron
Butorides striatus
534

15–22″ (38–56 cm). Crow-sized. A small dark heron with bright orange or yellowish legs. Head and neck chestnut, crown black with a small crest, back and wings green-gray.

Voice
Explosive, rasping *skyow!* Also croaks, cackles, and clucks.

Habitat
Lake margins, streams, ponds, and marshes.

Range
British Columbia, Minnesota, and New Brunswick south to southern South America. Winters north to South Carolina, the Gulf Coast, and California.

Comments
The most common heron in much of its range, all it requires is a pond or stream with thick bushes or trees nearby for nesting and soft, muddy borders in which to search for its prey. A retiring bird, it is often first noticed when it flushes unexpectedly from the edge of water and flies off uttering its sharp call note.

American Coot
Fulica americana
535

15″ (38 cm). Slate-gray with a conspicuous white bill; greenish legs and lobed feet.

Voice
Fowl-like clucking, cackles, grunts, and other harsh notes.

Habitat
Open ponds and marshes; in winter, also in saltwater bays.

Range
Southern Canada to northern South America.

Comments
Coots are the most aquatic members of their family, moving on open water like ducks and often feeding with them. They are excellent swimmers and divers, and they eat various aquatic plants.

Common Moorhen
Gallinula chloropus
536

13″ (33 cm). A ducklike swimming bird that constantly bobs its head while moving. Slaty gray with a prominent red bill with yellow tip and red frontal shield (adults); white under its tail, which it cocks up.

Voice
Squawking notes similar to those of coots. Other calls sound like frogs and are rather harsh in tone.

Habitat
Freshwater marshes and ponds with cattails and other aquatic vegetation.

Range
Nearly cosmopolitan in distribution. In the Americas, from southern Canada to southern South America.

Comments
Common Moorhens—formerly known as Common Gallinules—are closely related to coots and rails but do not swim out in the open water as much as coots and hide in reeds much less than rails.

Purple Gallinule
Porphyrula martinica
537

11–13″ (28–33 cm). Chicken-sized. Rich purplish blue with green upperparts, white underside of base of tail, yellowish-green legs, red-and-yellow bill, and light blue frontal shield.

Voice
Squawking and cackling. Also guttural grunts.

Habitat
Freshwater marshes with lily pads, pickerelweed, and other aquatic vegetation.

Range
The Carolinas and Tennessee to Florida and Texas; wanders to the northern states. South to southern South America.

Comments
This beautiful bird is often observed walking on lily pads, using its very long toes, and may even sometimes be seen climbing up into low bushes. When walking or swimming it constantly jerks its head and tail.

Sora
Porzana carolina
538

8–10″ (20–25 cm). Quail-sized. Gray-breasted with a black face and stubby yellow bill. Upperparts mottled brown; lower abdomen banded with black and white. Young birds lack the black face and have buff breasts.

Voice
Most familiar call is a musical series of piping notes rapidly descending the scale. When an intruder approaches a nest the adults come boldly into view, uttering an explosive *keek!*

Habitat
Chiefly freshwater marshes and marshy ponds; rice fields and salt marshes in winter.

Range
British Columbia, Mackenzie, and Newfoundland south to Pennsylvania, Oklahoma, and Baja California; winters north to California and to the Carolinas.

Comments
These birds are especially numerous in fall and winter in southern marshes and rice fields, where they are primarily seed-eaters. The greatest threat to them is the destruction of the freshwater marshes where they breed: they have consequently become scarce in heavily populated areas.

Yellow Rail
Coturnicops noveboracensis
539

6–8″ (15–20 cm). Sparrow-sized. Brownish-buff with a short yellow bill and yellow feet. Shows a white wing patch in flight.

Voice
Series of clicks in groups of 2 or 3: *click-click, click-click-click.*

Habitat
Grassy marshes and wet meadows.

Range
Central Canada south to North Dakota, and in New Brunswick, Quebec, and Maine. Winters from the Carolinas, Florida, and the Gulf Coast.

Comments
All rails are secretive, but none more than this tiny bird. It is

also rare, and many veteran bird-watchers have never seen one. The best way to see one is to follow a mowing machine in a damp meadow in the Deep South during September or October. When the uncut grass is reduced to a small patch, one or more birds may flush into view.

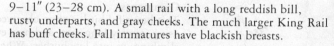

Virginia Rail
Rallus limicola
540

9–11″ (23–28 cm). A small rail with a long reddish bill, rusty underparts, and gray cheeks. The much larger King Rail has buff cheeks. Fall immatures have blackish breasts.

Voice
Series of descending grunts and a far-carrying *ticket-ticket-ticket-ticket.*

Habitat
Freshwater and brackish marshes; salt marshes in winter.

Range
Breeds from British Columbia, Minnesota, and Newfoundland south to Guatemala. Winters regularly north to Virginia, occasionally farther north.

Comments
This common but elusive marsh bird is most often detected by its call. It seldom flies, preferring to escape intruders by running through protecting marsh vegetation. When it does take wing, it often flies only a few yards before dropping out of sight into the marsh.

King Rail
Rallus elegans
541

15–19″ (38–48 cm). A secretive, chicken-sized marsh bird with a long, slightly curved bill. Head, neck, and underparts rusty; back mottled brown. Similar to Virginia Rail but larger and without gray face patch. Clapper Rail is grayer.

Voice
Series of deep resonant notes, *beep-beep-beep-beep,* etc., usually more rapid at the end.

Habitat
Freshwater marshes and roadside ditches; wanders to salt marshes in fall and winter.

Range
Minnesota and Massachusetts south to Florida, Texas, and northern Mexico. Winters regularly from the Gulf Coast southward. Also breeds in Cuba.

Comments
This large rail is common in the larger freshwater marshes of the interior. Although difficult to see, its loud call, consisting of deep grunting and clucking notes, often reveals its presence.

Common Snipe
Gallinago gallinago
542

10½–11½″ (26–29 cm). A long-billed, brownish shorebird with striped back, usually seen when flushed from the edge of a marsh or a pond. Fast, erratic flight.

Voice
Sharp, rasping *scaip!* when flushed.

Habitat
Freshwater marshes, ponds, flooded meadows, and fields; more rarely in salt marshes.

Range
Alaska, Hudson Bay, and Labrador south to Massachusetts, Indiana, and California; more rarely farther south. Winters regularly north to British Columbia and Virginia.

Comments
Although snipes commonly migrate in flocks at night, during the day they scatter and usually feed alone. They seek food early in the morning and in late afternoon, and seem to be more active on cloudy days.

Semipalmated Sandpiper
Calidris pusilla
543

6½″ (16 cm). Brownish gray above, white below; short, straight bill; black legs.

Voice
A soft *krip.* Also a conversational chatter while feeding.

Habitat
Coastal beaches, lake and river shores, flats, and pools in salt marshes.

Range
N. Alaska and Canada south to Hudson Bay. Winters from the southeastern United States and Mexico to South America.

Comments
These small sandpipers are perhaps the most numerous shorebirds in North America, sometimes occurring by the thousands on migration. The name "Semipalmated," referring to the birds' toes, means "partially webbed." Actually the toes are only slightly lobed at their bases, but they do enable the birds to walk on mud without sinking.

Solitary Sandpiper
Tringa solitaria
544

7½–9″ (19–23 cm). Slightly smaller than a Robin. Dark gray back with light spotting; lighter on head with white eye-ring; white below with greenish legs. In flight, shows dark wings and flashy tail, dark in center, cross-barred white on sides. Bill straight and rather long.

Voice
High, clear *pee-weet* or *hueet* calls as it flushes.

Habitat
Breeds in swampy bogs and lakes in the northern forest; during nonbreeding season, along muddy shores of pools.

Range
In coniferous forests north to Alaska and from treeline in Alaska to central Canada. Transient across the West in migration. Winters in Central and South America.

Comments
Well named, this species does not migrate in flocks. It feeds along the edges of irrigation canals and small ponds, especially where cattle are watered.

Least Sandpiper
Calidris minutilla
545

5–6½″ (13–17 cm). Smaller than Western Sandpiper. Short thin dark bill, yellowish legs, light brown breast, and striped brown underparts. Least Sandpipers appear warm brown; in winter they look drab or gray; but leg color does not change.

Voice
A high *preep* or *pree-rreeep*.

Habitat
Nests in tundra marshes, bogs; tidal mud flats, grassy pools, and flooded fields in winter.

Range
Low Arctic tundra from Alaska to Labrador, even bogs in the Maritime Provinces. Visits the Pacific and other coastal states in great numbers in winter, though some flocks proceed south to Central and South America.

Comments
A very common sandpiper of mud flats and wet grassy areas. It is tame in the presence of man. As a tightly bunched flock twists and turns in unison, the birds alternately flash white bellies and dark backs.

Spotted Sandpiper
Actitis macularia
546

7½″ (19 cm). Robin-sized. In breeding plumage olive-brown above, black spots below; lacks spotting in fall and winter.

Voice
Clear *peet-weet;* also a soft trill.

Habitat
Almost anyplace with water nearby.

Range
N. Alaska and Canada to southern United States. Winters from southern United States to South America.

Comments
This is one of the best-known of American shorebirds. Its habit of endlessly bobbing the rear part of its body up and down has earned it the vernacular name "teeter-tail." When flushed from the margin of a pond or stream, it is easily identified by its distinctive flight—short bursts of rapidly vibrating wingbeats alternating with brief glides low over the water.

American Avocet
Recurvirostra americana
547

16–20″ (40–51 cm). Pigeon-sized. Slender and long-legged. Upperparts and wings patterned in black and white; underparts white. Head and neck rust-colored in summer, white in winter. Bill very thin and strongly upturned.

Voice
Loud repeated *wheep*.

Habitat
Freshwater marshes and shallow marshy lakes; breeds locally in salt or brackish marshes. Many move to the coast in winter.

Range
Washington and Manitoba south to Texas and California. Winters from S. Texas and California to Guatemala. Uncommon but regular on Atlantic coast in fall.

Comments
Avocets feed much like Spoonbills, sweeping their bills from side to side along the surface of the water to pick up crustaceans, aquatic insects, and floating seeds.

Wilson's Phalarope
Phalaropus tricolor
548

9″ (23 cm). A strikingly patterned shorebird with pearl gray head and back, white underparts, a black stripe through eye and down the neck, and chestnut markings on breast and back. In fall plumage pale gray above, white below.

Voice
Soft *quoit-quoit-quoit*.

Habitat
Prairie pools and marshes, lake and river shores, marshy pools along the coast.

Range
From southwestern and south-central Canada to central and western United States. Winters in southern South America.

Comments
This species does not have fully lobed toes and so rarely swims, spending no time at sea. It is limited to the Western Hemisphere and breeds much farther south than the others.

Black Tern
Chlidonias niger
549

9–10″ (23–25 cm). A medium-sized tern with solid black head and underparts; gray wings and moderately forked gray tail; in fall and winter the head and underparts are white, with dusky smudging around the eyes and back of the neck.

Voice
Sharp *kick;* when disturbed, a shrill *kreek*.

Habitat
Freshwater marshes and marshy lakes in summer; sandy coasts in migration and in winter.

Range
Breeds from Quebec, Alaska, Mackenzie, and south to Pennsylvania, Missouri, and California. Winters in South America.

Comments
This tern usually nests in small groups and in shallow water.

The nests are sometimes conspicuous; perhaps this is why the young often leave the nest at the first sign of an intruder.

Common Tern
Sterna hirundo
550

13–16″ (33–40 cm). Pigeon-sized. White with black cap and pale gray back and wings. Red bill with black tip. Deeply forked tail.

Voice
Kip-kip-kip. Also *TEEaar*.

Habitat
Lakes, ponds, rivers, coastal beaches, and islands.

Range
Labrador south to the Caribbean and west to Wisconsin and Alberta. Winters from Florida to southern South America.

Comments
A grasp of the field marks of other terns is best gained by comparison with these most common of "sea swallows." They are a familiar sight on almost all large bodies of water where protected nesting sites exist. Sensitive to disturbance during the breeding season, whole colonies often fail to breed successfully because of disruption by humans and, as a result, their numbers are slowly declining.

Forster's Tern
Sterna forsteri
551

14–16¼″ (36–41 cm). Medium-sized tern. White with light silvery-gray mantle, primaries silvery; tail light gray. In summer black cap, bright orange-red bill with black tip. In winter black cap molts to white but black patch remains around eye; bill black.

Voice
A low, nasal *ky-yarr* and a harsh, nasal buzzy *zraa*.

Habitat
Marshes near open shallow water.

Range
From the Canadian prairies south to south-central California (and San Diego) and across to Colorado; on the southeastern Atlantic north to New Jersey; also Gulf Coast. Winters to Central and South America.

Comments
Terns have forked tails and longer, more slender wings than gulls. They feed almost entirely by plunge-diving on fish; gulls usually feed from the surface of the water.

Caspian Tern
Sterna caspia
552

19–23″ (48–58 cm). Gull-sized. Largely white, with black cap and pale gray back and wings; heavy bright red bill and dusky underwing.

Voice
Low, hoarse *kraa*. Also a shorter *kow*.

Habitat
Sandy or pebbly shores of lakes and large rivers, and along seacoasts.

Range
Mackenzie, the Great Lakes, and Newfoundland south to the Gulf Coast and Baja California. Winters north to California and North Carolina.

Comments
Much less gregarious than other terns, Caspians usually feed singly. Pairs breed by themselves, in small colonies, or may attach themselves to colonies of other birds such as the Ring-billed Gull.

Franklin's Gull
Larus pipixcan
553

13½–15½″ (34–39 cm). Small gull. Breeding adults have gray back, white underparts, and black head; in flight show gray wings with black-and-white wing tips, a distinct white bar separating the black areas from the gray; red bill and feet. From September to April or May head is white, washed with slate-gray on nape and ear regions. Immatures have brownish gray above and white below, with a black tail band, and acquire at least a partial hood by spring.

Voice
Kuk-kuk-kuk. Also a nasal *karrr.*

Habitat
Open country around prairie lakes.

Range
Throughout the prairies. Colonies have been found from Alberta to Manitoba in the North and from Montana and Oregon to Iowa in the South. Migrate south for winter. Some winter on Gulf Coast; most in South America.

Comments
These gulls are considered beneficial, since they feed mainly on insects, including those that damage crops. In late fall they feed on grasshoppers and dragonflies.

Bonaparte's Gull
Larus philadelphia
554

12–14″ (30–35 cm). A small, delicate gull, silvery-gray above with conspicuous white patches on the leading edge of the outer wing. Black on head of breeding adults is lacking in winter. Young birds have dark markings on the upper surface of the wing and a black tail band.

Voice
Rasping *tea-ar;* a soft, nasal snarling note.

Habitat
Forested lakes and rivers; winters along the coast, in estuaries, and at the mouth of large rivers.

Range
Breeds in interior of northwestern Canada and in Alaska.

Winters along both coasts, on the Atlantic from southern New England southward.

Comments
Breeding in the Far North, these beautiful gulls are most often seen on lakes and rivers during migration or along the coast in winter. They keep to themselves, seldom joining the larger gulls at dumps. They feed in tidal inlets and at sewage outlets, picking scraps of food from the water.

Ring-billed Gull
Larus delawarensis
555

18–20″ (45–50 cm). Adult silvery gray on back, white on head, tail, and underparts. Similar to Herring Gull but smaller, with yellow feet and with narrow black ring around bill. Young birds are mottled brown, paler than a young Herring Gull, with blackish tail band and flesh-colored legs.

Voice
Loud, raucous mewing cry, like the Herring Gull but higher-pitched.

Habitat
Lakes and rivers; many move to salt water in the winter.

Range
Alaska and Labrador south to the Great Lakes and California. Winters from southern New England south to Cuba.

Comments
In most of the northern part of the United States the Ring-billed Gull is known as a winter visitor, less common than the Herring Gull. But in some inland areas and in the Deep South it is the more numerous of the two species.

California Gull
Larus californicus
556

20–23″ (51–58 cm). Similar to Herring Gull, but smaller, with darker gray back and upper surface of wing, dark eye, reddish eye-ring, and greenish legs; bill of breeding birds has red spot overlapped by black. Winter and immature birds have black bar near tip of bill and lack red eye-ring of adults.

Voice
A shuddering, repetitive *kee-yah.*

Habitat
In breeding season, on interior lakes and marshes; in winter, mostly on seacoast.

Range
Northern prairie provinces east to North Dakota, south to NW. Wyoming and Utah, west to NE. California. Winters mainly on the Oregon, California, and Baja California coasts; in lesser numbers inland.

Comments
The California Gull attained fame when great numbers arrived at the Mormon colony near the Great Salt Lake and devoured a locust swarm that threatened the settlers' first crop.

Herring Gull
Larus argentatus
557

23–26″ (58–66 cm). Adult white with light gray back and wings; black wing tip with white spots. Feet pink or flesh-colored. First-year birds brownish.

Voice
Loud rollicking call, *kuk-kuk-kuk, yucca-yucca-yucca,* and other raucous cries.

Habitat
Lakes, rivers, estuaries, and beaches.

Range
Breeds from Alaska and Greenland south to the Carolinas, and is spreading.

Comments
This is the common "sea gull" inland and along the coast. In recent years it has become abundant, probably due to the amount of food available at garbage dumps, and has extended its range southward along the Atlantic Coast, often to the detriment of colonial birds such as terns and Laughing Gulls.

Snail Kite
Rostrhamus sociabilis
558

16–18″ (40–46 cm). Wingspan: 44″ (1 m). Crow-sized. Male dark slate color; its white tail has a dark broad band; female is brown, heavily streaked below with banded tail like male's. Red (male) or orange (female and young) legs.

Voice
Low cackle, chatter, or neigh, but seldom heard.

Habitat
Freshwater marshes and lakes.

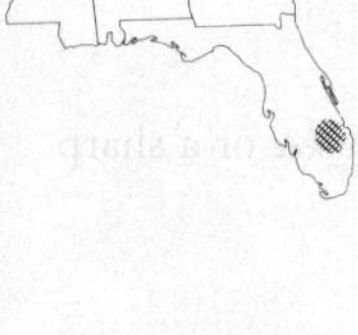

Range
Mainly Lake Okeechobee and Loxahatchee in S. Florida. Widespread in Central and South America.

Comments
The Snail Kite feeds exclusively on snails of the genus *Pomacea,* found in shallow ponds and swampy places. The kite's slender, sharply hooked bill easily extracts the living animal from the unbroken shell.

American Swallow-tailed Kite
Elanoides forficatus
559

22–24″ (56–61 cm). Wingspan: 50″ (1.3 m). A graceful bird of prey, with long, pointed wings and deeply forked tail. Head and underparts white, back wings and tail black.

Voice
Shrill squeals or whistles. Also a soft twittering.

Habitat
Swamps, marshes, river bottoms, and glades in open forests.

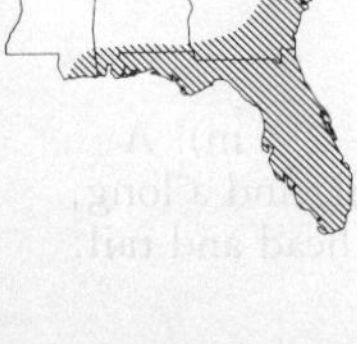

Range
Breeds mainly on or near the coast from South Carolina to Florida, formerly to Texas; local farther inland in the Gulf states, rare farther north. South to southern South America.

Comments
The Swallow-tail's flight as it rides air currents or swoops rapidly after its prey is graceful, buoyant, and effortless. It spends much of the daylight hours on the wing.

Short-tailed Hawk
Buteo brachyurus
560

13–14″ (33–35 cm). Wingspan: 35″ (1 m). Crow-sized. A small, chunky hawk with 2 phases: the light phase is dark above and white below; the dark phase is black above and below except for some light mottling on the belly, chin, and wing linings. Both phases have banded black-and-white tail. Immature is tawny-buff below with dark streaks.

Voice
Cackles and warning screams, but is seldom heard except at nest.

Habitat
Chiefly cypress and mangrove swamps.

Range
Local in S. Florida. Throughout tropical America.

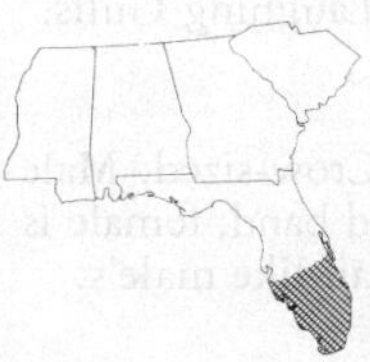

Comments
This rare bird is easily identified in either color phase, being the only hawk in the area that is pure black or pure white below. It often perches low on poles or trees near swampy areas, and darts out after birds.

Northern Harrier
Circus cyaneus
561

16–24″ (40–61 cm). Wingspan: 42″ (1.1 m). Long-winged, long-tailed hawk with a white rump, usually seen soaring unsteadily over marshes with its wings held in a shallow V. Female and young are brown above, streaked below, young birds with a rusty tone. Male, seen less than young birds and females, has gray back, head, and breast.

Voice
Usually silent. At the nest it utters a *kee-kee-kee-kee* or a sharp whistle.

Habitat
Marshes and open grasslands.

Range
Eastern Aleutians, Alaska, Mackenzie, and Newfoundland to Virginia and northern Mexico. Winters north to British Columbia, Wisconsin, and New Brunswick.

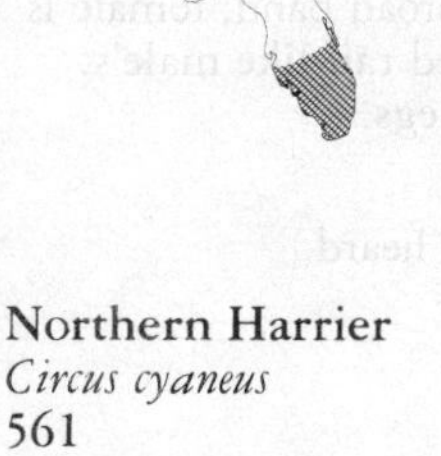

Comments
This is the only North American member of a group of hawks known as harriers. All hunt by flying close to the ground, taking small animals by surprise.

Bald Eagle
Haliaeetus leucocephalus
562

30–31″ (76–79 cm). Wingspan: 72–90″ (1.8–2.3 m). A large blackish eagle with white head, white tail, and a long, heavy yellow bill. Young birds lack the white head and tail.

Voice
Squeaky cackling.

Habitat
Lakes, rivers, marshes, and seacoasts.

Range

Formerly bred throughout most of North America, but now restricted as a breeding bird to Aleutians, Alaska, parts of northern and eastern Canada, northern United States, and Florida. In winter, along almost any body of water.

Comments
Eating dead fish stranded on beaches and riverbanks has caused many Bald Eagles to absorb large amounts of pesticides, which interfere with the birds' calcium metabolism and result in thin-shelled and often infertile eggs. Once a familiar sight along rivers and coasts, our national bird is today known mainly as an occasional migrant. Current studies indicate that numbers are increasing with the phasing out of harmful pesticides.

Osprey
Pandion haliaetus
563

21–24″ (53–61 cm). Wingspan: 54–72″ (1.4–1.8 m). A large, long-winged "fish hawk." Brown above and white below; white head with dark brown line through eye and on side of face. Wing shows distinct bend at the "wrist."

Voice
Loud, musical chirping.

Habitat
Lakes, rivers, and seacoasts.

Range

Breeds from Alaska and Newfoundland south to Florida and the Gulf Coast. Winters regularly from the Gulf Coast and California south to Argentina.

Comments
This hawk is well adapted for capturing fish, which comprise its entire diet. The soles of Ospreys' feet are equipped with sharp, spiny projections that give the bird a firm grip on its slippery prey. It hovers until a fish nears the surface, then suddenly plunges feet-first into the water, grasping the fish in its talons.

Red-shouldered Hawk
Buteo lineatus
564

16–24″ (40–61 cm). Wingspan: 40″ (1 m). Large, long-winged hawk with rust-barred underparts, reddish shoulders, a narrowly banded tail, and a translucent area near the tip of the wing, visible from below. Young birds are streaked below and are best distinguished from young Red-tailed Hawks by their somewhat smaller size, narrower tail, and longer, narrower wings.

Voice
Shrill scream, *kee-yeeer,* with a downward inflection.

Habitat
Deciduous woodlands, especially where there is standing water.

Range
Minnesota and New Brunswick south to the Gulf Coast, and on the Pacific Coast from N. California to Baja California. Winters north to southern New England and the Ohio Valley.

Comments
This hawk generally avoids the upland forests inhabited by the Red-tailed Hawk, and is more often found in lowlands, especially swampy woods and bogs.

Short-eared Owl
Asio flammeus
565

16″ (40 cm). Crow-sized. A long-winged, tawny-brown owl of open country, rather heavily streaked, and with a blackish patch around each eye. The short ear tufts are rarely visible.

Voice
Usually silent; on the nesting ground gives a variety of barks, hisses, and squeals.

Habitat
Freshwater and salt marshes; open grassland, prairies, dunes; open country generally during migration.

Range
Breeds locally from Alaska and northern Canada south to New Jersey and California; winters in the southern part of the breeding range south to Guatemala. Also in South America.

Comments
This owl is most commonly seen late in the afternoon, as it begins to move about in preparation for a night of hunting. It can often be identified at a great distance by its habit of hovering; its flight is erratic and bounding.

Barred Owl
Strix varia
566

20″ (51 cm). Wingspan: 44″ (1.1 m). A large, stocky owl, gray-brown with cross-barring on the neck and breast and streaks on the belly; no ear-tufts.

Voice
A loud, barking *hoo, hoo, hoo, hoo, hoo, hoo-hooo-aw!;* a variety of other barking calls and screams.

Habitat
Low, wet woods and swamp forest.

Range
East of the Rockies from central Canada to the Gulf of Mexico and in mountains as far south as Honduras.

Comments
This owl is seen only by those who seek it out in its dark retreat, usually a thick grove of trees in lowland forest. There it rests quietly during the day, coming out at night to feed on rodents, birds, frogs, and crayfish.

Wild Turkey
Meleagris gallopavo
567

Males 48″ (122 cm); females 36″ (91 cm). Similar to the domestic turkey but more slender; tail tipped with chestnut-brown or rust color.

Voice
Familiar *gobble* of the domestic bird. Also clucks and yelps.

Habitat
Southern bottomland hardwood forests, open woodlands and forests with scattered natural or man-made clearings.

Range
Locally common from Wyoming, Illinois, and New York to Mexico and the Gulf Coast. Formerly more widespread.

Comments
No bird is more distinctively American than the "Wild Turkey." Although well known to the American Indians and widely used by them as food, certain tribes considered these birds stupid and cowardly and did not eat them for fear of acquiring these characteristics.

Belted Kingfisher
Ceryle alcyon
568

13″ (33 cm). Pigeon-sized. Bushy crest; daggerlike bill; blue-gray above, white below. Male has a blue-gray breast band; female similar but with a chestnut belly band.

Voice
Loud, penetrating rattle, given on the wing and when perched.

Habitat
Rivers, lakes, and saltwater estuaries.

Range
Breeds from Alaska and Canada and throughout United States. Winters south to Panama and the West Indies.

Comments
Kingfishers often hover like a tern over water where a fish is visible and dive vertically for the prey. They may also take crabs, crayfish, salamanders, lizards, mice, and insects.

Pileated Woodpecker
Dryocopus pileatus
569

17″ (43 cm). Crow-sized. Black with white neck stripes, conspicuous white wing linings, and a prominent red crest.

Voice
Call flickerlike, but louder, deeper, and more *cuk-cuk-cuk-cuk-cuk,* rising and then falling in pitch.

Habitat
Dense forest and borders.

Range
Breeds from southern Canada to the Gulf states and the mountains of the western United States.

Comments
Despite its size, this elegant woodpecker is adept at keeping

out of sight. Obtaining a close view of one usually requires careful stalking.

Red-bellied Woodpecker
Melanerpes carolinus
570

10″ (25 cm). Robin-sized. Barred black and white above; pale buff below; sexes similar except that male has red crown and nape, female has red nape only. A red patch on the lower abdomen is seldom visible in the field.

Voice
Chuck-chuck-chuck, descending in pitch. Also a loud, oft repeated *churrrr.*

Habitat
Open and swamp woodland; comes into parks during migration and to feeders in winter.

Range
Chiefly southeastern United States west to Texas, ranging north to Minnesota, Michigan, and Connecticut.

Comments
The common woodpecker over much of the South, it is scarcer farther north but has expanded its breeding range in recent years to New York and southern New England.

Bank Swallow
Riparia riparia
571

4¾–5½″ (12–14 cm). Sparrow-sized—our smallest swallow. Brown above, dull white below; breast crossed by a distinct brown band; tail notched. Rough-winged Swallow is warmer brown, with dusky throat and breast without distinct brown band.

Voice
Series of buzzy notes, *bzt-bzt-bzt;* also a twitter.

Habitat
Rivers and streams, especially near sandbanks; more widespread during migration.

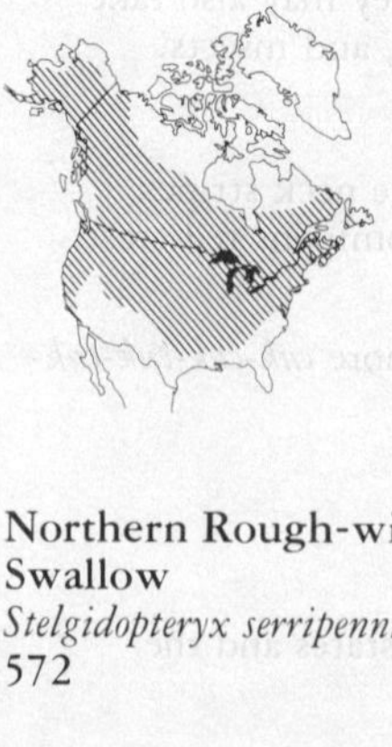

Range
Breeds from Alaska and Labrador south to Virginia, Texas, and California. Winters in South America.

Comments
Bank Swallows originally nested only in steep, sandy riverbanks, but like other swallows they have adapted to man and now nest in the sides of man-made excavations. They breed in colonies of from two or three pairs to a few thousand.

Northern Rough-winged Swallow
Stelgidopteryx serripennis
572

5–5¾″ (13–14 cm). Sparrow-sized. Brown back with dusky throat and upper breast. The similar Bank Swallow has pure white underparts with the breast crossed by a brown band.

Voice
Buzzy notes much like Bank Swallow's, but deeper and more rasping.

Habitat
Streams and rivers, especially in the vicinity of steep banks and man-made structures providing nest sites.

Range
British Columbia, Michigan, and New Brunswick south to northern Argentina. Winters from Gulf Coast southward.

Comments
The name "Rough-winged" comes from tiny hooks on the outer primary, which give the feather a rough feel. The function of these hooks, found also in a group of unrelated African swallows, is unknown.

Eastern Phoebe
Sayornis phoebe
573

7″ (17 cm). Dull olive-green without an eye-ring or wing bars. Wags its tail.

Voice
Clear *phoe-be,* repeated many times; the second syllable is alternately higher or lower than the first. Distinctive *chip.*

Habitat
Open woodland near streams; cliffs, bridges, and buildings with ledges.

Range
Breeds in Canada and the United States east of the Rockies, south to the northern limits of the Gulf states. Winters from Virginia and the Gulf Coast south to Mexico.

Comments
The Phoebe arrives early in spring and departs late in fall, sometimes even staying through the winter in the northern states. In the absence of insects its winter food is berries.

Marsh Wren
Cistothorus palustris
574

4–5½″ (10–14 cm). Smaller than a sparrow. Brown above, pale buff below, with a bold white eyebrow and white streaks on the back.

Voice
Liquid gurgling song ending in a mechanical chatter.

Habitat
Fresh and brackish marshes with cattails, reeds, bulrushes, or sedges.

Range
British Columbia, Manitoba, and New Brunswick south to Florida, the Gulf Coast, and northern Mexico. Winters north to New Jersey, along the Gulf Coast, and on the Pacific Coast north to Washington.

Comments
The male has a number of mates, each of which builds a nest of her own. In addition, the male may also build up to half a dozen "dummy" nests, often incomplete, one of which may be used as a roost.

Sedge Wren
Cistothorus platensis
575

4–4½″ (10–11 cm). A tiny, secretive wren of grassy marshes. Buff-colored, with finely streaked crown and back. Best distinguished by voice and habitat.

Voice
A series of harsh notes, sounding like tapping 2 pebbles together; often heard at night.

Habitat
Grassy freshwater marshes and sedges, also brackish marshes and wet meadows in winter.

Range
Saskatchewan, Manitoba, and New Brunswick south to Delaware, Missouri, and Kansas; Central America south to Tierra del Fuego and the Falkland Islands. Winters north to New Jersey and Tennessee. Very local.

Comments
It is most often seen as it is flushed from grass and flies off only to drop from view a few feet away. Its flight is distinctive, the wings vibrating stiffly as the bird seems to float over the ground. Like other wrens it builds "dummy" nests, often hidden in dense marsh grass.

Swamp Sparrow
Melospiza georgiana
576

5″ (13 cm). A chunky, dark sparrow with unstreaked underparts, bright rufous cap, and rusty wings; back and tail dark brown; face and breast gray; throat white.

Voice
Sweet, musical trill, all on 1 note.

Habitat
Freshwater marshes and open wooded swamps; in migration with other sparrows in weedy fields, parks, and brush piles.

Range
From east-central Canada south to east-central United States; winters south to the Gulf of Mexico.

Comments
A bird of the wetlands during the breeding season, the Swamp Sparrow appears in a variety of other habitats during migration and winter. It is rather shy, but responds readily to any squeaking noise, and can usually be lured into view.

Lincoln's Sparrow
Melospiza lincolnii
577

5–6″ (13–15 cm). Small, brownish bird with gray cheek, pale buffy mustache stripe, and buffy breast streaked with brown.

Voice
Song a low gurgling stanza that ends after some rising phrases. Calls are *tik* and a buzzy *tzee*.

Habitat
Moist and brush-covered bogs, meadows; also mountain meadows with willow thickets or other dense clumps of vegetation.

Range
Breeds in the boreal forest from coast to coast, and along western mountain chains to S. California and New Mexico. Winters from the southwestern states to Central America.

Comments
When not singing, it is wary and secretive. In winter, a lone Lincoln's Sparrow is often seen among other sparrows wintering on the Pacific Coast and in bushy areas inland.

Louisiana Waterthrush
Seiurus motacilla
578

6½″ (16 cm). Sparrow-sized. Dark olive brown above, white and streaked below. Frequently bobs tail.

Voice
Song is 3 clear notes followed by a descending jumble.

Habitat
Prefers swift-moving brooks on hillsides and, where the Northern Waterthrush is absent, occurs in river swamps and along sluggish streams.

Range
Minnesota, Ontario and central New England, south to Georgia and Texas. Winters from Mexico and the West Indies to northern South America.

Comments
This bird is very similar to the Northern Waterthrush. The Northern Waterthrush has a narrower eyebrow stripe that is buff or yellow.

American Dipper
Cinclus mexicanus
579

7–8½″ (18–22 cm). Uniformly slate-gray, wren-shaped bird with stubby tail; feet yellowish.

Voice
Vigorous singers, their loud bubbling song carries over the noise of rapids. Call is a sharp *zeet.*

Habitat
Near clear fast streams with rapids.

Range
From Alaska to mountains of Central America, and from Pacific Coast to eastern slope of the Rockies.

Comments
The "Water Ouzel"—its British name—feeds on insect life of streams. Where water is shallow and runs over gravel, the American Dipper appears to "water-ski" on the surface.

Red-winged Blackbird
Agelaius phoeniceus
580, 588

7–9½″ (17–24 cm). Smaller than a Robin. Male is black with bright red shoulder patches. Female and young are heavily streaked with dusky brown.

Voice
Rich, musical *O-ka-LEEEE!*

Habitat
Marshes, swamps, and wet and dry meadows; pastures.

Range
Breeds from Alaska and Newfoundland south to Florida, the Gulf Coast, and central Mexico. Winters regularly north to Pennsylvania and British Columbia.

Comments
Although primarily a marsh bird, the Red-wing will nest near virtually any body of water and occasionally breeds in upland pastures. Each pair raises two or three broods a season, building a new nest for each clutch. After the breeding season, the birds gather with other blackbirds in flocks.

Swainson's Warbler
Limnothlypis swainsonii
581

5″ (13 cm). A plain warbler, olive-brown above and whitish beneath, with a rufous cap and a whitish line over each eye.

Voice
3 or 4 clear notes followed by several rapid descending notes, described as *whee-whee-whee-whip-poor-will*.

Habitat
Wooded swamps and southern canebrakes; also rhododendron thickets in the mountains.

Range
Southern portions of Illinois, Indiana, Ohio, and Maryland south to southeastern United States. Winters in Cuba, Jamaica, and Yucatán south to Honduras.

Comments
This dull-colored warbler is shy and retiring, dwelling in remote, often impenetrable swamps and cane thickets. If not for its song—like that of a Hooded Warbler or a water thrush—it would frequently be overlooked.

Sharp-tailed Sparrow
Ammodramus caudacutus
582

5½″ (14 cm). The combination of a dark cap, gray ear patch, and a bright orange-buff triangular area on the face distinguishes this species.

Voice
A dry, insect-like *kip-kip-zeeeee*.

Habitat
Inland grassy, freshwater marshes and in drier parts of salt marshes.

Range
Locally from central Canada to the middle Atlantic states; winters chiefly on the south Atlantic and Gulf coasts.

Comments
These birds spend most of their lives in dense, coarse marsh grass, and by the end of the breeding season their plumage is so badly worn that little of the distinctive pattern remains visible.

Palm Warbler
Dendroica palmarum
583

5½″ (14 cm). An olive-drab, streaked, ground-feeding warbler with bright olive rump, bright yellow undertail coverts, and a distinctive habit of wagging its tail. The underparts vary from yellow to dull whitish; adults in spring have a rufous cap.

Voice
Weak, dry, buzzy trill.

Habitat
In summer, bogs in the North; during migration, open places, especially weedy fields and borders of marshes.

Range
Central Canada to the extreme northern portions of the United States. Winters from southern United States to the West Indies and Honduras.

Comments
The Palm Warbler is one of the first warblers to arrive in the spring, and at this season is commonly found feeding quietly on the ground, sometimes with flocks of sparrows.

Common Yellowthroat
Geothlypis trichas
584

4½–5¾″ (11–15 cm). Adult male has black mark edged toward crown with white. Olive green above, bright yellow below, fading into dull white on belly. Female lacks mask, is brownish-olive above, buffy below with some yellow, especially on throat. Immature male dull-colored, often some black on face.

Voice
Song is repeated *whichity-whichity-whichity*, sometimes with an additional *which*. Call is a low *djip*.

Habitat
Meadows, fields, edges of thickets, streams, marshes, and other places with open, low vegetation.

Range
Widespread from coast to coast and from the treeline to southern Mexico.

Comments
This meadow bird, formerly called "Yellowthroat," is common throughout North America, but we get a glimpse of it only when the male climbs the tallest stalk and utters his abrupt song.

Prothonotary Warbler
Protonotaria citrea
585

5½″ (14 cm). Male golden-orange with blue-gray wings; no wing bars; large white spots in tail. Female similar but duller.

Voice
Song is a ringing *sweet-sweet-sweet-sweet-sweet-sweet-sweet*. Also a canarylike flight song. Call is a loud, metallic *chip*.

Habitat
Wooded swamps, flooded bottomland forest, and streams with dead trees.

Range
Mainly in the southeastern states north to Minnesota, Michigan, and New York. Winters from southern Mexico to northern South America.

Comments
This is one of the characteristic birds of the southern swamplands, where its bright plumage is conspicuous in the gloomy, cypress-lined bayous. It is unusual among warblers in that it nests in holes in trees.

Yellow-headed Blackbird
Xanthocephalus xanthocephalus
586

8–11″ (20–28 cm). Robin-sized. Male much larger than the female; head, neck and upper breast bright yellow, blackish elsewhere; and conspicuous white markings on the wings. Female duller and lighter; yellow on the chest, throat, and face; no white wing marks.

Voice
Harsh, incessant *oka-wee-wee* and *kruck* call, coming from many individuals in a colony, blends into a loud, wavering chorus.

Habitat
Freshwater marshes.

Range
A western bird, extending into the prairie states and provinces.

Comments
Visiting a blackbird colony in a marsh or slough in spring is an exciting experience. Some males are always in display flight, with head stooped, feet and tail drooped, wings beating in a slow, accentuated way. Some quarrel with neighbors over boundaries while others fly out to feed.

Tricolored Blackbird
Agelaius tricolor
587

7½–9″ (19–23 cm). Similar to Red-winged Blackbird. Male is black but with dark red epaulets, very broadly margined with white. Female more slate-colored than the brownish-dusky Red-wing and lacks streaks on the rump and belly.

Voice
Calls rather similar to those of the Red-wing but song is more nasal, less musical.

Habitat
Cattail marshes, marshy meadows, and rangeland.

Range
A California bird, it is restricted to the Klamath marshes at the Oregon border, California west of the Sierra, and the coast to northern Baja California. Not seasonally migratory, but moves its nesting colonies to wherever more food is available.

Comments
More colonial than the Red-winged Blackbird, its territories are crowded, with nests often less than 5 or 6 feet apart. Colonies in the Central Valley contain thousands of birds.

MAMMALS

The North American wetlands provide a variety of habitats for many different kinds of mammals, large and small. Moose and other large animals graze year-round on willows and other wetlands species; Beavers make their elaborate homes in ponds and streams; and ferocious Minks and other carnivores prowl swamps and marshes for prey. This section describes these and other common mammals of the wetlands.

Masked Shrew
Sorex cinereus
589

2¾–4⅜″ (7.1–11.1 cm) long. Very small. Brownish above; belly silvery or grayish. Long tail brown above, buff below.

Habitat
Various; moist fields, bogs, marshes, moist or dry woods.

Range
Throughout northern North America south to Washington, Idaho, south-central Utah, north-central New Mexico, Nebraska, Iowa, Indiana, extreme N. Kentucky, Maryland, and south throughout the Appalachians.

Comments
This small secretive shrew is primarily nocturnal and rarely seen. Although all shrews are noted for their voracious appetites, the Masked Shrew's is particularly large; its daily consumption often equals or exceeds its own weight.

Pacific Shrew
Sorex pacificus
590

5⅛–6¼″ (12.9–16 cm) long. In summer dark reddish brown to dark brown. In winter cinnamon above; slightly lighter below. Long tail usually tan or brown above and below, but sometimes indistinctly bicolored.

Habitat
Spruce and redwood forests; stands of alder-skunk cabbage along stream edges.

Range
Pacific Coast from N. California to S. Oregon.

Comments
Unlike most North American shrews, the Pacific Shrew is nocturnal. It feeds on slugs and snails, centipedes, amphibians, insect larvae, and other invertebrates.

Water Shrew
Sorex palustris
591

5⅝–6¼″ (14.4–15.8 cm) long. Very dark or black above; belly grayish white. Long tail. Hind feet have fringe of hairs.

Habitat
Among boulders along mountain streams or in sphagnum moss along mountain lakes.

Range
Most of Canada south throughout NE. California, through Utah, with an isolated population in the White Mountains of E. Arizona; the central states to NE. South Dakota, N. Minnesota, Wisconsin, and Michigan; and New England south through the Applachians to North Carolina.

Comments
At home in and around water, this shrew can dive to the bottom, but when it stops swimming, air entrapped in the fur pops it back to the surface like a cork. Owing to the fringe of hairs on the hind foot, which increases the foot's surface area and traps air bubbles, the shrew can actually run on the water surface.

Pacific Water Shrew
Sorex bendirii
592

5⅞–6⅞″ (14.7–17.4 cm) long. Large. Dark brown above and below. Long tail. Hind toes slightly fringed.

Habitat
Marshes, along streams, sometimes in moist forests.

Range
Coastal N. California north to extreme SE. British Columbia.

Comments
This shrew is the largest member of its genus in North America. It can run on top of the water for several seconds, gaining buoyancy from the air trapped in its partially fringed toes; it can also dive to the bottom.

Smoky Shrew
Sorex fumeus
593

4¼–5″ (11–12.7 cm) long. Brownish in summer; grayish in winter. Long tail dark brown above and lighter, sometimes yellowish, below.

Habitat
Various types of moist wooded areas, but also in deep woods, swamps, and along streams where woods and fields meet.

Range
Northeastern United States south through the mountains to E. Tennessee, N. Georgia, and N. South Carolina, and north to S. Ontario, Quebec, New Brunswick, and Nova Scotia.

Comments
Active in even the coldest weather, the Smoky Shrew commonly lives in extensive burrows in the leaf mold of the forest floor. It makes a leaf nest in a hollow log or stump, or under rocks.

Arctic Shrew
Sorex arcticus
594

4–5″ (10.1–12.6 cm) long. Tricolored fur: dark brown back, light brown sides, and grayish belly tinged with buff; pattern more distinct in winter. Long tail.

Habitat
Swamps, bogs, marshes, and grass-sedge meadows.

Range
Across much of Canada and Alaska south to North Dakota, extreme NE. South Dakota, Minnesota, Wisconsin, and Michigan's Upper Peninsula.

Comments
Unlike other shrews, these are quite docile, can be handled, and seldom attempt to bite. They have a low rapid chatter.

Star-nosed Mole
Condylura cristata
595

5⅞–8¼″ (15.2–21.1 cm) long. Black. Long hairy tail. Large digging forelegs. 22 pink fleshy projections on nose.

Habitat
Wet woods, fields, or swamps; sometimes relatively dry areas, lawns.

Range
The Northeast from SE. Labrador south through much of Minnesota, NE. Indiana, N. Ohio, south through the Appalachians, and along coastal Virginia. Isolated populations along Georgia coast.

Comments
This mole's tentacle-like nose projections are mobile and very sensitive, apparently helping it to find its way about the burrow and locate food. When the Star-nosed Mole forages, its tentacles are constantly in motion; however, when it eats, they are clamped together out of the way.

Marsh Rice Rat
Oryzomys palustris
596

7⅜–12″ (18.7–30.5 cm) long. Grayish brown above; pale buff below. Long sparsely furred tail, showing scales that are brown above, paler below. Feet whitish.

Tracks
In soft mud or dust, hindprint ⅜″ long, with 5 toes printing; foreprint slightly smaller, with 4 toes printing. Walking stride, 2″, with hindprint directly behind foreprint, or slightly overlapping.

Habitat
Mostly marshes; also drier areas among grasses or sedges.

Range
Mainly southeastern United States: E. Texas (with isolated populations in extreme S. Texas) north to SE. Kansas, SE. Missouri, S. Illinois, S. Kentucky, E. North Carolina, and north to SE. Pennsylvania and S. New Jersey.

Comments
The Marsh Rice Rat swims underwater with ease, foraging on the tender parts of aquatic plants. Also included in its diet are crabs, fruits, insects, snails, and the fungus *Endogone*.

Cotton Mouse
Peromyscus gossypinus
597

6–8⅛″ (15.2–20.5 cm) long. Reddish brown above; white below. Tail short-haired, usually bicolored, slightly less than half total length.

Habitat
Woodlands; swamps; brushlands; rocky areas; beaches.

Range
Southeastern United States: from E. Texas and SE. Oklahoma east to SE. Virginia, E. North Carolina, E. South Carolina, Georgia, and Florida.

Comments
Skillful climbers, Cotton Mice run up trees and are fairly strong swimmers, both useful adaptations for the southern swamps where they are most abundant. These nocturnal rodents nest on sandy ridges along the bayous, often in or under logs or palmetto scrub, and have been known to invade buildings.

Golden Mouse
Ochrotomys nuttalli
598

5⅞–7½″ (15–19 cm) long. Golden cinnamon above; white below, often tinged with yellowish brown. Tail long.

Habitat
Greenbrier thickets; boulder-strewn hemlock slopes; brushy hedgerows; swamps.

Range
Extreme E. Texas and Oklahoma; S. Missouri and S. Illinois to East Coast; S. Virginia south to midpeninsular Florida.

Comments
This highly arboreal, gregarious mouse often climbs trees to 30′ or more. It runs about the high branches with ease, using its long prehensile tail for balance and support.

Meadow Jumping Mouse
Zapus hudsonius
599

7¼–10″ (18.7–25.5 cm) long. Yellowish sides; brownish back; white belly. Long tail with tip usually not white.

Habitat
Mainly moist fields; but also brush, brushy field, marsh, stands of touch-me-not (*Impatiens*), woods with thick vegetation.

Range
S. Alaska and most of southern tier of Canadian provinces; northeastern United States west to E. Wyoming, and south to NE. Oklahoma and NE. Georgia.

Comments
When startled from a hiding place, this species may take a few long jumps of 3–4′, then shorter ones, but generally soon stops and remains motionless, which is its best means of eluding predators. In spring, animal foods are particularly important, with caterpillars, beetles, and other insects constituting about half of its diet. It feeds on the seeds of grasses and many other green plants as they ripen. In summer and fall, the subterranean fungus *Endogone* forms part of its diet.

Southern Bog Lemming
Synaptomys cooperi
600

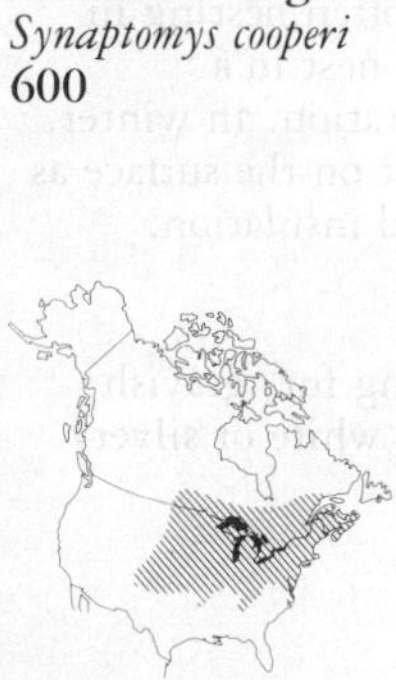

4⅝–6⅛″ (11.8–15.4 cm) long. Brown above; silvery below. Very short tail brownish above, lighter below.

Habitat
Grassy meadows; sometimes burrows in northeastern forests; rarely bogs.

Range
SE. Manitoba east to Newfoundland, south to Kansas, NE. Arkansas, W. North Carolina, NE. Virginia.

Comments
This lemming lives in a system of subsurface runways and burrows about 6″ below the ground; it also commonly uses the runways of other small mammals. Its globular grass nest, up to 7″ in diameter with 2 to 4 entrances, may be in an underground chamber or above ground among vegetation.

Southern Red-backed Vole
Clethrionomys gapperi
601, 602

4¾–6¼″ (12–15.8 cm) long. Rust-reddish above; sides buff or grayish; gray to buff-white below. Tail short, slender, slightly bicolored. Gray phase may occur in the Northeast.

Habitat
Cool, damp forests; bogs, swamps.

Range
Southern tier of Canadian provinces south into Oregon; entire Rocky Mountain system to Arizona and New Mexico; Allegheny Mountain system to North Carolina, North and South Dakota, Minnesota, Wisconsin, upper half of southern peninsular Michigan, and New England south to Maryland.

Comments
These voles use natural runways along rocks and logs and burrows of other animals when available; they do not make elaborate burrow systems.

Meadow Vole
Microtus pennsylvanicus
603

5½–7¾″ (14–19.5 cm) long. Color variable: from yellowish brown or reddish brown peppered with black, to blackish brown above; usually gray with silver-tipped hair below. Tail long, dark above, lighter below. Feet dark.

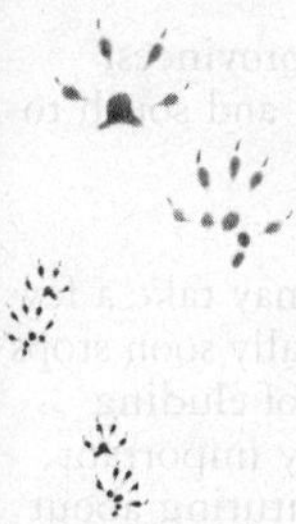

Tracks
In light snow, hindprint ⅝″ long, with 5 toes printing; foreprint ½″ long, with 4 toes printing; hindprints ahead of foreprints, with distance between individual walking prints ½–⅞″; straddle, approximately 1½″.

Habitat
Marshes, swamps, woodland glades, mountaintops, fields.

Range
Canada and Alaska (except for northern portions) south and east to N. Washington, Idaho, Utah, New Mexico, Wyoming, Nebraska, N. Missouri, N. Illinois, Kentucky, NE. Georgia, and South Carolina.

Comments
Also called the Field Mouse. This vole lives in a system of surface runways and underground burrows, often nesting in the burrows during the summer; it may also nest in a depression on the surface under matted vegetation. In winter, the Meadow Vole usually places its grass nest on the surface as long as there is snow cover for protection and insulation.

Water Vole
Arvicola richardsoni
604

7¾–10¼″ (19.8–26.1 cm) long. Large. Long fur, grayish brown to reddish brown above; grayish with white or silvery wash below. Long bicolored tail.

Habitat
Along upland streams and lakes.

Range
SE. and SW. British Columbia and SW. Alberta south

through central and E. Washington to central and E. Oregon, N. Idaho, north-central Utah, and W. Wyoming.

Comments
This large, semiaquatic vole is an excellent swimmer and often enters water to avoid predators. It lives in colonies along waterways, constructing its burrows among sedges or below alders or willows. In winter, it moves farther from water.

Marsh Rabbit
Sylvilagus palustris
605

14⅛–18″ (35.2–45 cm) long. Dark brown above with nape dark cinnamon; belly white. Very small tail, gray mixed with brown below. Short, broad ears; feet small, red-brown above.

Habitat
Bottomlands, swamps, lake borders, and coastal waterways.

Range
SE. Virginia southwest to Florida.

Comments
When threatened, a Marsh Rabbit takes to water; it may then float with only eyes and nose exposed. To elude a pursuer if cut off from water, it will run a zigzag trail.

Swamp Rabbit
Sylvilagus aquaticus
606

20⅞–21¼″ (53–54 cm) long. Largest cottontail. Short, coarse fur; brownish gray mottled with black above; whitish below. Thin tail white below. Feet rust-colored. Ears 2½–2⅝″ (63–67 mm) long.

Habitat
Bottomlands, swamps, and canebrakes.

Range
E. Texas and E. Oklahoma east to S. Illinois and N. Georgia.

Comments
Also known as the Cane-cutter Rabbit. This excellent swimmer not only takes to water when pursued, as will other rabbits, but will swim simply to get about. To elude predators it may remain submerged except for its nose. It rests under thick brush and will hide in hollow logs or the burrows of other animals.

Mountain Beaver
Aplodontia rufa
607

9⅜–18½″ (23.8–47 cm) long. Woodchucklike but smaller, with a short, heavy body. Dark brown above; lighter brown below. Blunt head; short legs; small ears and eyes; tiny tail. 5 toes on all feet, with first toe on front foot a flattened nail, other front toes with very long strong claws.

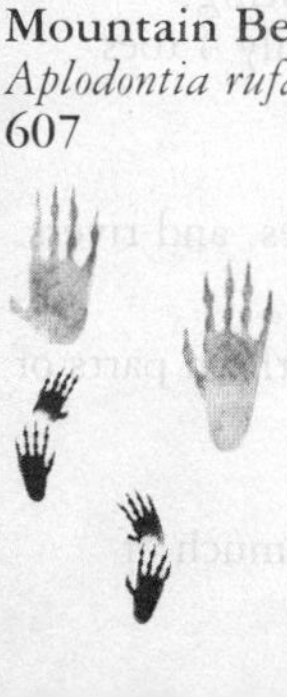

Tracks
Narrow, under 2″ long; hindprints larger than foreprints and may overlap them.

Habitat
Moist forests, especially near streams.

Range
Extreme SW. British Columbia, W. Washington, W. Oregon, N. California, extreme west-central Nevada.

Comments
The common name Mountain Beaver is misleading, as this rodent is neither a beaver nor does it prefer a mountainous habitat; the name may have derived from its beaverlike habit of diverting streams into its tunnels or from its occasional gnawing of bark and cutting of limbs. Active throughout the year, this mostly nocturnal animal occasionally browses during the day, especially in autumn. Its labyrinthine burrow system is usually shallow, near cover, and used by other animals.

Round-tailed Muskrat
Neofiber alleni
608

11¼–15″ (28.5–38.1 cm) long. Large aquatic rodent. Dense fur, dark brown above and below, with silky sheen when dry. Tail long and round. Ears and eyes small. Hind feet webbed.

Tracks
In mud, hindprint approximately 1½″ long; foreprint to 1″ long, printing slightly ahead of overlapping hindprint.

Habitat
Marshes.

Range
SE. Georgia and peninsular Florida.

Comments
Although primarily nocturnal, this squeaky-voiced rodent is sometimes active by day and tends to be gregarious. Its house of tightly woven grasses or sedges usually rests on a base of decayed vegetation with two entrances just below the surface of the water.

Muskrat
Ondatra zibethicus
609

16⅛–24⅜″ (40.9–62 cm) long. Large rodent. Dense glossy fur, dark brown above, lighter on sides; finer, softer, and paler below to nearly white on throat. Small dark patch occasionally on chin. Long tail scaly, nearly naked, vertically flattened and tapering to a point. Eyes and ears small. Hind feet partially webbed and larger than forefeet.

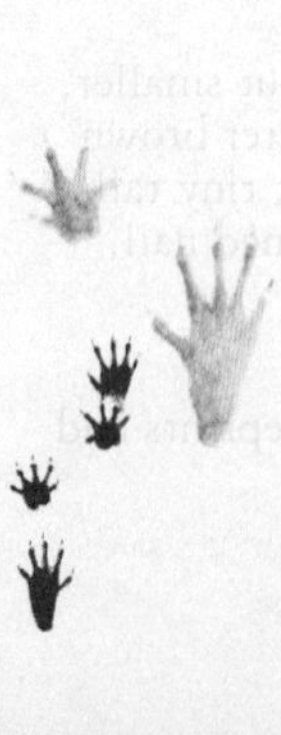

Tracks
Hindprint in mud 2–3″ long, with all 5 toes printing; foreprint half as long, narrower, generally with only 4 toes printing (fifth toe is vestigial).

Habitat
Fresh, brackish, or saltwater marshes, ponds, lakes, and rivers.

Range
Most of United States and Canada, except for southern parts of United States and arctic regions of Canada.

Comments
Excellent swimmers, these aquatic rodents spend much of

their time in water. Propelled along by their slightly webbed hind feet and using their rudderlike tail for guidance, they can swim backward or forward with ease; they dislike strong currents and avoid rocky areas. Their large houses commonly contain one nesting chamber with one or more underwater entrances.

Nutria
Myocastor coypus
610

26⅜–55⅛″ (67–140 cm) long. Large aquatic rodent. Brown above; somewhat lighter below. Long, scaly, sparsely haired round tail. Muzzle and chin whitish. Ears and eyes small. Incisors dark orange, protruding beyond lips. Hind feet longer than forefeet, with inner 4 toes webbed. Males larger than females.

Tracks
Similar to those of Muskrat but larger, with hind feet showing webbing between inner 4 toes.

Habitat
Marshes; ponds; streams.

Range
Widely introduced, especially in the Southeast, but also in Maryland, S. New Jersey, scattered locations in the Great Plains, N. Oregon, and Washington.

Comments
Also known as the Coypu. Although it often feeds on land, when disturbed the Nutria returns to the water, often with a loud splash. It can remain submerged for several minutes and often floats just under the surface with only eyes and nose exposed. Its nest of plant materials is made either in a burrow dug in a riverbank with entrance above water, above ground or in shallow water, or in the burrows of other animals or the lodges of Beavers or Muskrats.

Beaver
Castor canadensis
611

35½–46″ (90–117 cm) long. Very large rodent. Dark brown. Large black scaly tail, horizontally flattened, paddle-shaped. Large hind feet, black, webbed, with inner 2 nails cleft.

Tracks
Usually only 3 or 4 of the 5 toes print, leaving wide, splay-toed track 3″ long. Webbed hind feet leave fan-shaped track often more than 5″ wide at widest part, at least twice as long as forefeet; webbing usually shows in soft mud.

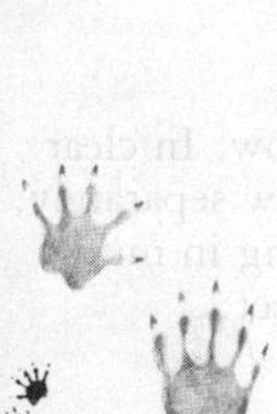

Habitat
Rivers, streams, marshes, lakes, and ponds.

Range
Most of Canada and United States, except for most of Florida, much of Nevada, and S. California.

Comments
Beavers living along a river make burrows with an underwater entrance in the riverbank; those in streams, lakes, and ponds

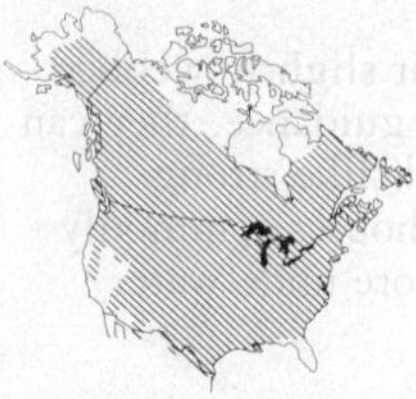

usually build dams that generally incorporate a lodge, which has one or more underwater entrances and living quarters in a hollow near the top; wood chips on the floor absorb excess moisture and a vent admits fresh air. The chief construction materials in the northern parts of its range—poplar, aspen, willow, birch, and maple—are also the preferred foods.

River Otter
Lutra canadensis
612

35–51⅝″ (88.9–131.3 cm) long. Elongated body. Dark brown (looks black when wet) with paler belly; throat often silver-gray; prominent whitish whiskers. Long tail thick at base and gradually tapering to a point; feet webbed. Males larger than females.

Tracks
3¼″ wide or more; often show only heel pad and claws; toes fan out widely, but webbing rarely prints, except in mud. Running stride 1–2′.

Habitat
Primarily along rivers, ponds, and lakes in wooded areas, but will roam far from water.

Range
Alaska and most of Canada south to N. California and N. Utah; in the East, from Newfoundland south to Florida; extirpated from most areas of Midwest.

Comments
The River Otter is active by day if not disturbed by human activity. Well adapted to its aquatic life, it has a streamlined body, rudderlike tail, and ears and nostrils valved to keep out water. It swims rapidly both underwater and on the surface. To observe its surroundings, it raises its head high and treads water. It can remain submerged for several minutes. Also at ease on land, the River Otter runs fairly well. Its permanent den is often dug into banks, with underwater and exposed entrances, and contains a nest.

Mink
Mustela vison
613

19¼–28¼″ (49.1–72 cm) long. Sleek-bodied with lustrous fur, uniformly chocolate-brown to black with white spotting on chin and throat. Tail long, somewhat bushy. Males larger than females.

Tracks
Fairly round, 1¼–1¾″ wide, more than 2″ in snow. In clear print, heel pad and all 5 slightly webbed toes show separately; semiretractile claws may show. Hind feet 2¼″ long in mud, 3½″ in snow, and placed nearly in prints of forefeet.

Habitat
Along rivers, creeks, lakes, ponds, and marshes.

Range
Most of United States and Canada except Arizona, S. California, S. Utah, S. New Mexico, and W. Texas.

Comments
Minks of both sexes are hostile to intruders, and males fight viciously in or out of breeding season. They maintain hunting territories by marking with a fetid discharge from the anal glands, which is at least as malodorous as a skunk's, although it does not carry as far. They swim very well, often hunting in ponds and streams, and can climb trees but do so rarely. Like weasels, Minks kill by biting their victims in the neck. Muskrats are preferred prey, but many rabbits, mice, chipmunks, fish, snakes, frogs, young snapping turtles, and marsh-dwelling birds are taken; Minks occasionally raid poultry houses. They eat on the spot or carry prey by the neck to their dens, where any surplus is cached. They den in protected places near water, often in a Muskrat burrow, an abandoned Beaver den, or hollow log, or they may dig their own den in a streambank; all dens are temporary.

Raccoon
Procyon lotor
614

23¾–37⅜″ (60.3–95 cm) long. Reddish brown above, with much black; grayish below. Distinguished by a bushy tail with 4–6 alternating black and brown or brownish-gray rings and a black mask outlined in white. Ears relatively small.

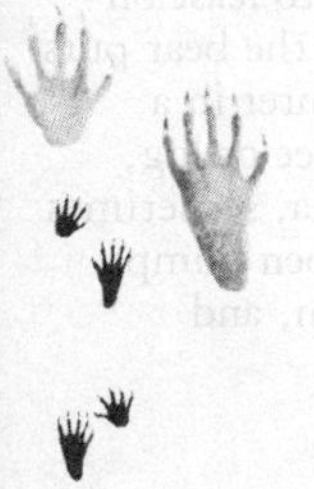

Tracks
Hindprint 3¼–4¼″ long, much longer than wide. Foreprint much shorter, 3″, almost as wide as long; claws show on all 5 toes. Stride 6–20″, averaging 14″.

Habitat
Various, but most common along wooded streams.

Range
Southern edge of southern provinces of Canada; most of United States except for portions of the Rocky Mountain states, central Nevada, and Utah.

Comments
Native only to the Americas, the Raccoon is nocturnal and solitary except when breeding or caring for its young. Although territories overlap, when 2 meet, they growl, lower their heads, bare their teeth, and flatten their ears; the fur on the backs of their necks and shoulders stands on end, generally with the result that both back off.

Black Bear
Ursus americanus
615

4½–6¼′ (137–188 cm) long. In the East, nearly black; in the West, black to cinnamon with white blaze on chest. A "blue" phase occurs near Yukatat Bay, Alaska, and individuals are nearly white on Gribble Island, Alaska. Snout tan or grizzled; in profile straight or slightly convex. Males much larger than females.

Tracks
Broad footprints 4″ long, 5″ wide turning in slightly at the front and showing 5 toes on fore and hind feet. Hindprints 7–9″ long, 5″ wide.

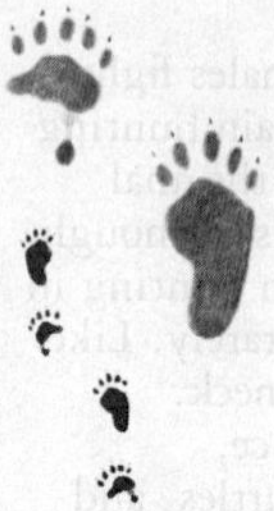

Habitat
In the East, primarily forests and swamps; in the West, forests and wooded mountains seldom higher than 7000′ (2100 m).

Range
Most of Canada, Alaska, south on West Coast through N. California, in Rocky Mountain states to Mexico, N. Minnesota, Wisconsin, and Michigan; in New England, New York, and Pennsylvania south through Appalachians; in Southeast, most of Florida, and S. Louisiana.

Comments
This uniquely American bear, although primarily nocturnal, may be seen at any time. It is solitary except briefly during mating season and when congregating to feed at dumps. Its walk is clumsy, but in its bounding trot it attains surprising speed, with bursts up to 30 mph. A powerful swimmer, it also climbs trees, either for protection or food. Though classed as a carnivore, most of its diet consists of vegetation. In spring, the bear peels off tree bark to get at the inner, or cambium, layer; it tears apart rotting logs for grubs, beetles, crickets, and ants. A good fisherman, the Black Bear often wades in streams or lakes, snagging fish with its jaws or pinning them with a paw. It rips open bee trees to feast on honey, honeycomb, bees, and larvae. In the fall, the bear puts on a good supply of fat, then holes up for the winter in a sheltered place, such as a cave, crevice, hollow tree or log, roots of a fallen tree, and, in the Hudson Bay area, sometimes a snowbank. Bears are often a problem around open dumps, becoming dangerous as they lose their fear of man, and occasionally people have been killed by them.

Bobcat
Felis rufus
616

28–49⅜″ (71–125 cm) long. Tawny (grayer in winter), with indistinct black spotting. Short, stubby tail with 2 or 3 black bars and black tip above; pale or white below. Upper legs have dark or black horizontal bars. Face has thin, often broken black lines radiating onto broad cheek ruff. Ears slightly tufted. Males larger than females.

Tracks
Fore and hind prints about same size, 2″ long, slightly longer than wide, with 4 toes, no claw marks. Trail very narrow, sometimes as if made by a 2-legged animal, because hind feet are set on, close to, or overlapping foreprints; 9–13″ between prints.

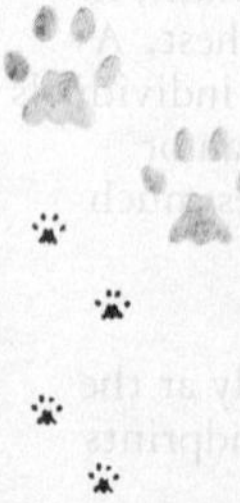

Habitat
Primarily scrubby country and broken forests.

Range
Spottily distributed from coast to coast, southern Canada into Mexico. Probably most plentiful in Far West, from Idaho, Utah, and Nevada to Pacific and from Washington to Baja California. Scarce or absent in most of central and lower Midwest.

Comments
Found only in North America, where it is the most common wildcat, the Bobcat gets its common name from its stubby, or "bobbed," tail. The Bobcat is an expert climber. Sometimes it rests on a boulder or a low tree branch, waiting to pounce on small game that passes; its mottled fur provides excellent camouflage. If hard pressed, it will swim. It uses the same hunting pathways repeatedly to prey mostly on the Snowshoe Hare and cottontail rabbit but also eats mice, squirrels, Porcupines, and cave bats. Unless prey is very scarce, it will not eat carrion. Small prey is consumed immediately; larger kills are cached and revisited. The Bobcat occasionally preys upon livestock, especially poultry. Its variety of calls sound much like those of the domestic cat, although its scream is piercing and when threatened, it utters a short and resonant "cough-bark."

White-tailed Deer
Odocoileus virginianus
617

4½–6¾′ (134–206 cm) long. Tan or reddish brown above in summer; grayish brown in winter. Belly, throat, nose band, eye ring, and inside of ears white. Tail brown, edged with white above, often with dark stripe down center, white below. Black spots on sides of chin. Bucks' antlers with main beam forward and several unbranched tines behind; a small brow tine. Antler spread to 3′ (90 cm). Does normally lack antlers.

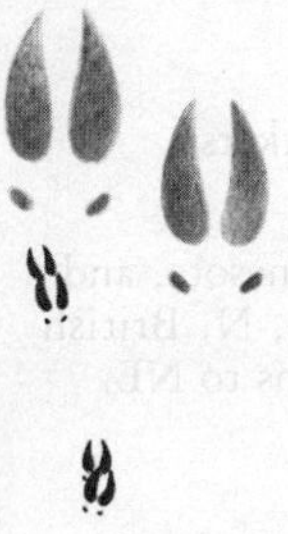

Tracks
Like narrow split hearts, pointed end forward, about 2–3″ long; dewclaws may print twin dots behind main prints in snow or soft mud. In shallow snow (1″ deep), buck may drag its feet, leaving drag marks ahead of prints; in deeper snow, both bucks and does drag feet. Straddle 5–6″ wide. Stride, when walking, 1′; when running, 6′ or more, and hindprints sometimes register ahead of foreprints; when leaping, 20′.

Habitat
Farmlands, brushy areas, woods, and swamps.

Range
Southern half of southern tier of Canadian provinces; most of United States except most of California, Nevada, Utah, N. Arizona, SW. Colorado, and NW. New Mexico.

Comments
Although primarily nocturnal, deer may be active at any time, grazing on green plants, including aquatic ones in the summer; eating acorns, beechnuts, and other nuts and corn in the fall; and in winter, browsing on woody vegetation, including the twigs and buds of viburnum, birch, maple, and many conifers. Although primarily an upland animal, they frequent marshes as grazers and especially cedar swamps in winter where the evergreen foliage serves as an important winter food. If alarmed, the Whitetail raises, or "flags," its tail, exhibiting a large, bright flash of white; this "hightailing" communicates danger to other deer or helps a

fawn follow its mother in flight. Deer usually bed down near dawn, seeking concealing cover. They are good swimmers and graceful runners, with top speeds to 35 mph, though in flight they do not run great distances but flee to the nearest cover. When nervous, Whitetails snort through their noses and stamp their hooves, a telegraphic signal that alerts other deer nearby to danger. Bucks and does herd separately most of the year, but in winter gather together, or "yard up."

Moose
Alces alces
618

6¾–9′ (206–279 cm) long. Largest deer in the world. Horse-size. Long, dark brown hair. High, humped shoulders; long, pale legs; stubby tail. Huge pendulous muzzle; large dewlap under chin; large ears. Males much larger than females, with massive palmate antlers, broadly flattened. Antler spread usually 4–5′ (120–150 cm); record of 81″ (206 cm).

Tracks
Cloven prints; usually more than 5″ long; 6″ long and 4½″ wide in large bull. Lobes somewhat splayed in snow, mud, or when running. Dewclaws often print behind main prints in snow, mud, or when running, lengthening print to 10″. Stride 3½–5½′ when walking, more than 8′ when trotting or running.

Habitat
Spruce forest, swamps, and aspen and willow thickets.

Range
Most of Canada; in the East south to Maine, Minnesota, and Isle Royale in Lake Superior; in the West, Alaska, N. British Columbia and southeast through Rocky Mountains to NE. Utah and NW. Colorado.

Comments
Moose are solitary in summer, but several may gather near streams and lakes to feed on willows and aquatic vegetation, including the leaves of water lilies. When black flies and mosquitoes torment them, Moose may nearly submerge themselves or roll in a wallow to acquire a protective coating of mud. Good swimmers, they can move at speeds of 6 mph for up to 2 hours at a time. Migrating up and down mountain slopes seasonally, they may herd in winter, packing down snow, which facilitates movement; then they browse on woody plants, including the twigs, buds, and bark of willow, balsam, aspen, dogwood, birch, cherry, maple, and viburnum. During mating season, mid-September–late October, bulls do not gather a harem but stay with one cow for about a week and then with another. Bulls thrash brush with antlers, probably to mark territory. Occasionally they battle, but generally threat displays prompt one to withdraw; if horns interlock, both may perish. After a gestation of 8 months, 1–2 calves are born, light colored but not spotted. Within a couple of weeks they can swim; at about 6 months they are weaned; and just before the birth of new calves they are driven off. Life span is up to 20 years.

PART IV APPENDICES

GLOSSARY

Abdomen In insects, the hindmost of the three subdivisions of the body; in spiders, the hindmost of the two subdivisions of the body.

Alternate Arising singly along the stem, not in pairs or whorls.

Anal fin The median fin behind the anus.

Annual Having a life cycle completed in one year or season.

Anther The saclike part of a stamen, containing pollen.

Axil The angle formed by the upper side of a leaf and the stem from which it grows.

Barbel In fishes, a fleshy projection of the skin, often threadlike, usually found near the mouth, chin, or nostrils.

Bipinnate With leaflets arranged on side branches off a main axis; twice-pinnate; bipinnately compound.

Bract A modified and often scalelike leaf, usually located at the base of a flower, a fruit, or a cluster of flowers or fruits.

Brood A generation of butterflies hatched from the eggs laid by females of a single generation.

Calyx A collective term for the sepals of a flower, usually green.

Catkin A compact and often drooping cluster of reduced, stalkless, and usually unisexual flowers.

Caudal fin In fishes, the fin on the hindmost part of the body.

Caudal peduncle The part of the body of a fish between the posterior end of the anal fin base and the caudal fin base.

Cell The area of a butterfly's wing that is entirely enclosed by veins; also called discal cell.

Cephalothorax The first subdivision of a spider's body, combining the head and the thorax.

Compound eye One of the paired visual organs consisting of several or many light-sensitive units, or ommatidia, usually clustered in a radiating array.

Corolla Collective term for the petals of a flower.

Disk The central portion of a butterfly's wing, tangential to the upper and lower margins (*adj.* discal).

Diurnal Active during the daytime hours.

Dorsal fin The fin along the midline of the back, supported by rays; often notched or divided into separate fins.

Elytron The thickened forewing of beetles, serving as protective covers for the hind wings (*pl.* elytra).

Entire Smooth-edged, not lobed or toothed.

Epiphyte A plant growing on another plant but deriving little or no nutrition from it; also called an air plant.

Eutrophic Rich in nutrients but seasonally deficient in oxygen; said of a lake or pond.

Eyespots Spots resembling eyes on winged insects.

Femur The third segment of an insect's leg.

Flight feathers In birds, the long, well-developed feathers of the wings and tail, used during flight.

Head A crowded cluster of flowers on very short stalks, or without stalks as in the sunflower family.

Herb A plant with soft, not woody, stems that dies to the ground in winter.

Host plant The food plant of a caterpillar.

Inflorescence A flower cluster on a plant; especially the arrangement of flowers on a plant.

Insertion The point at which each paired fin is joined to the body.

Introduced Intentionally or accidentally established in an area by man, and not native; exotic or foreign.

Involucre A whorl or circle of bracts beneath a flower or flower cluster.

Lacustrine Of or having to do with lakes.

Lanceolate Shaped like a lance, several times longer than wide, pointed at the tip and broadest near the base.

Larva A post-hatching immature stage that differs in appearance from the adult and must metamorphose before assuming adult characters (e.g., a tadpole).

Lateral line A series of tubes or pored scales associated with the sensory system; usually extending from just behind the opercle to the base of the caudal fin.

Leaflet One of the leaflike parts of a compound leaf.

Limnetic zone The middle zone of a lake, extending from the zone of open-water vegetation to the point at which light no longer penetrates.

Lobed Indented on the margins, with the indentations not reaching to the center or base.

Margin The edge of the wing.

Maxilla The rear and usually larger of two bones forming the upper jaw.

Molt The periodic loss and replacement of feathers; most species have regular patterns and schedules of molt.

Node The place on the stem where leaves or branches are attached.

Oblanceolate Reverse lanceolate; shaped like a lance, several times longer than wide, broadest near the tip and pointed at the base.

Obovate Reverse ovate; oval, with the broader end at the tip.

Oligotrophic Poor in nutrients; said of a lake or pond.

Opposite leaves Leaves occurring in pairs at a node, with one leaf on each side of the stem.

Ovary The swollen base of a pistil, within which seeds develop.

Paired fins In fishes, the fins that occur in pairs—the pectorals and the pelvics.

Palmate Having three or more divisions or lobes, looking like the outspread fingers of a hand.

Palp A sensory structure associated with an insect's mouthparts.

Palustrine Of or having to do with a marsh, bog, or swamp.

Papilla A small, nipplelike projection, often occurring in groups (*pl.* papillae).

Parotoid gland A large glandular structure on each side of the neck or behind the eyes of toads and some salamanders.

Peat Partially decomposed plant matter (especially sphagnum) found in bogs and swamps.

Pectoral fins In fishes, the paired fins attached to the shoulder girdle.

Pedicel The stalk of an individual flower.

Peduncle The main flower stalk or stem holding an inflorescence.

Pelvic fins In fishes, the paired fins on the lower part of the body, usually just below or behind the pectoral fins.

Perennial Living more than two years; also, any plant that uses the same root system to produce new growth.

Petal Of a flower, the basic unit of the corolla; flat, usually broad, and brightly colored.

Petiole The stalklike part of a leaf, attaching it to the stem.

Pinnate leaf A compound leaf with leaflets along the sides of a common central stalk, much like a feather.

Pistil The female organ of a flower, consisting of an ovary, style, and stigma.

Plastron The lower part of a turtle's shell.

Pocosin A flat, swampy evergreen community of the coastal southeastern U.S. that forms on elevated areas between streams.

Pollen Spores formed in the anthers that produce male cells.

Prehensile Adapted for grasping or wrapping around; said of the toes, claws, and tails of certain animals.

Primaries The outermost and longest flight feathers on a bird's wing.

Proboscis A prolonged set of mouthparts adapted for reaching into or piercing a food source.

Profundal zone The deep portion of a lake or pond, where light does not penetrate.

Pupa The inactive stage of insects during which the larva transforms into the adult, completing its metamorphosis.

Raceme A long flower cluster on which individual flowers each bloom on a small stalk all along a common, larger, central stalk.

Ray In fishes, one of the supporting structures in the fin membranes, either flexible (soft ray) or stiff (spine).

Ray flower The bilaterally symmetrical flowers around the edge of the head in many members of the sunflower family; each ray flower resembles a single petal.

Regular flower A flower with petals and/or sepals arranged around the center, like the spokes of a wheel; always radially symmetrical.

Rhizome A horizontal underground stem, distinguished from roots by the presence of nodes, often enlarged by food storage.

Riverine Of, resembling, produced by, or relating to a river; situated on or near a riverbank.

Rosette A crowded cluster of leaves; usually basal, circular, and appearing to grow directly out of the ground.

Saprophyte A plant lacking chlorophyll and living on dead organic matter.

Scent scales Specialized scales that produce and disperse sex attractants.

Sepal A basic unit of the calyx, usually green, but sometimes colored and resembling a petal.

Sessile leaf A leaf that lacks a petiole, the blade being attached directly to the stem.

Sheath A more or less tubular structure surrounding a part, as the lower portion of a leaf surrounding the stem.

Shrub A woody plant, smaller than a tree, with several stems or trunks arising from a single base; a bush.

Simple eye A light-sensitive organ consisting of a convex lens bulging from the surface of the head, concentrating and guiding light rays to a cup-shaped cluster of photoreceptor cells. Also called an ocellus.

Simple leaf A leaf with a single blade.

Slough A sluggish creek in a tidal flat, a marsh or a bottomland.

Spadix A dense spike of tiny flowers, usually enclosed in a spathe, as in members of the arum family.

Spathe A bract or pair of bracts, often large, enclosing the flowers.

Spawn To release eggs and sperm into the water.

Spike An elongated flower cluster, each flower of which is without a stalk.

Stamen One of the male structures of a flower, consisting of a threadlike filament and a pollen-bearing anther.

Stigma The tip of a pistil, usually enlarged, that receives the pollen.

Stipules Small appendages, often leaflike, on either side of some petioles at the base.

Stolon A stem growing along or under the ground; a runner.

Style The narrow part of the pistil, connecting ovary and stigma.

Sucking disc In fishes, an adhesive structure; a disc formed by a jawless mouth, the union of paired fins, or a modification of the dorsal spines.

Taproot Main root, growing vertically downward, from which smaller, lateral roots extend.

Tarsus The foot section of the butterfly leg, which has hooks at the end for clinging.

Thorax The subdivision of the body between head and abdomen, consisting of three segments (the prothorax, mesothorax, and metathorax) and bearing whatever legs and wings are present.

Tubercle A raised, wartlike knob, often with spines.

Tussock A thick tuft of sedge or other vegetation forming a small hummock of solid ground in a marsh or bog.

Umbel A flower cluster in which the individual flower stalks grow from the same point, like the ribs of an umbrella.

Venation The pattern of veins on a wing.

Vent The anus; the opening of the cloaca to the outside of the body.

Whorl A circle of three or more leaves, branches, or pedicels at a node.

Wing bar A conspicuous crosswise wing mark.

Wing stripe A conspicuous mark running along the opened wing.

BIBLIOGRAPHY

Amos, William H.
The Life of the Pond. (Our Living World of Nature).
New York: McGraw-Hill Book Co., 1967.

Carr, Archie.
The Everglades. (The American Wilderness).
New York: Time-Life Books, 1973.

Errington, Paul L.
Of Men and Marshes.
New York: The Macmillan Co., 1957.

Glob, P. V.
The Bog People: Iron-Age Man Preserved.
Ithaca, New York: Cornell University Press, 1969.

Horwitz, Elinor L.
Our Nation's Lakes.
Washington, D.C.: U.S. Environmental Protection Agency, 1980.
Our Nation's Wetlands: An Interagency Task Force Report.
Washington, D.C.: U.S. Government Printing Office, 1978.

Kirk, Paul W., Jr.
The Great Dismal Swamp.
Charlottesville: University Press of Virginia, 1979.

Kusler, Jon A.
Our National Wetland Heritage: A Protection Guidebook.
Washington, D.C.: The Environmental Law Institute, 1983.

Magee, Dennis W.
Freshwater Wetlands: A Guide to Common Indicator Plants of the Northeast.
Amherst: University of Massachusetts Press, 1981.

Meanley, Brooke.
Swamps, River Bottoms and Canebrakes.
Barre, Massachusetts: Barre Publishers, 1972.

Niering, William A.
The Life of the Marsh: The North American Wetlands. (Our Living World of Nature).
New York: McGraw-Hill Book Co., 1966.

Russell, Franklin.
The Okefenokee Swamp. (The American Wilderness).
New York: Time-Life Books, 1973.

Thomas, Bill.
The Swamp.
New York: W. W. Norton & Co., Inc., 1976.

Usinger, Robert L.
The Life of Rivers and Streams. (Our Living World of Nature).
New York: McGraw-Hill Book Co., 1967.

Weller, Milton W.
Freshwater Marshes: Ecology and Wildlife Management.
Minneapolis: University of Minnesota Press, 1981.

CREDITS

Photo Credits

The numbers in parentheses are plate numbers. Some photographers have pictures under agency names as well as their own.

David H. Ahrenholz (391 left and right, 405 left and right, 409, 412, 418, 425 left and right)
Peter Alden (560)
Ruth Allen (270, 272)
Ronn Altig (265, 592)
Dennis Anderson (233)

Animals Animals
Tom Brakefield (131) Breck P. Kent (106, 166) Zig Leszczynski (127, 128, 150, 178, 180, 187, 198) Raymond A. Mendez (382) Lynn M. Stone (132, 174)

Ray E. Ashton, Jr. (135)
Ron Austing (309, 574)
Karölis Bagdonas (396 left)
Frank S. Balthis (4)
Roger W. Barbour (51, 60, 72, 162, 167, 196, 591, 593, 597, 600)
Thomas M. Baugh (65)
John Behler (172)
Michael Beug (332)
Les Blacklock (209, 289)
W. Frank Blair (145)
Tom Bledsoe (547)
J. Harry Boulet, Jr. (281 left)
Mabel Boulet (220, 277)
Edmund Brodie (103, 124)
Edward B. Brothers (32)
Richard T. Bryant (53, 57, 61, 66, 79, 81, 85, 99, 100, 101)
Jean T. Buermeyer (213)
Sonja Bullaty and Angelo Lomeo (427 right, 428 left and right, 429 left and right, 430 left and right, 431 right, 432 left and right, 433 left and right, 436 left and right, 437 left and right, 438 left and right, 439 left and right, 440 left and right, 442 left and right, 443 left and right, 444 left and right, 445 left and right, 448 left and right, 449 left and right, 450 left and right, 451 left and right, 452 left and right, 453 left and right, 457 left and right, 459 right, 460 left and right, 461 left and right, 462 left and right, 463 left and right, 465 left and right, 468 left and right, 469 left and right, 470 left and right, 471 right, 472 left and right, 473 left and right, 474 left and right, 475 left and right, 476 left and right, 477 left and right, 478 left and right, 479 left and right, 480 right)
James H. Carmichael, Jr. (605)
Ken Carmichael (490)
Robert P. Carr (199 left, 401)
Patricia Caulfield (Cover)
David Cavagnaro (427 left, 466 left and right, 467 left)
Patrice Ceisel (31, 40, 43)

Scooter Cheatham (441 left and right, 446 right, 456 left and right)
Herbert Clarke (514, 519, 540, 548, 577, 586)

Click/Chicago
Tom Dietrich (7) Phil and Judy Sublett (15, 19, 20)

Bruce Coleman Inc.
Fred J. Alsop (566) Jen and Des Bartlett (393 right) S. C. Bisserot (217) Robert P. Carr (264 left, 424 left) E. R. Degginger (45) Jack Dermid (3rd frontispiece) John Ebeling (300) M. P. L. Fogden (308) J. Markham (604) Leonard Lee Rue III (37) Joy Spurr (282 right)

Joseph T. Collins (47, 87, 177)
Stephen Collins (221, 222, 256, 266, 267, 285, 298, 314, 316, 324–326)
Ed Cooper (223, 282 left)

Cornell Laboratory of Ornithology
Caulion Singletary (538) Frederick K. Truslow (585) Y. R. Tymbtra (572)

Charles V. Covell, Jr. (422 right)
Helen Cruickshank (556)
James A. Cunningham (204, 240, 257 right, 271)
Thase Daniel (208, 276, 280 left and right)
Kent and Donna Dannen (246)
Harry Darrow (387, 390, 399 left, 408, 416, 420, 423 right, 426 left and right, 530, 546, 561)
Thomas W. Davies (371, 417)
Frances V. Davis (336)
Edward R. Degginger (8, 90, 91, 122, 154, 163, 234, 260, 278, 296, 358, 377)
David M. Dennis (109, 120, 121, 125)
Jack Dermid (16, 17, 21, 28, 107, 112–114, 123, 133, 157, 160, 176, 179, 183, 189, 191, 197, 255, 431 left, 447 left, 524, 526, 528, 533, 569)
Larry Ditto (510)
Neil H. Douglas (38)

DRK Photo
Stephen J. Krasemann (238, 580) Wayne Lankinen (545)

Wilbur H. Duncan (321, 455 right, 464 right)
Robert L. Eikum (227, 447 right)
Harry Ellis (134, 320, 327)
Harry Engels (214, 505, 523, 563, 618)
Chuck Farber (386)
Jon Farrar (22)
Jacob Faust (581)
William E. Ferguson (346, 351, 352, 354, 357, 359, 360, 407)
Kenneth W. Fink (488, 489, 495–497, 504, 511, 515, 525, 537)
Jeff Foott (4th frontispiece, 5th frontispiece, 30, 531, 562, 579, 583)

Joseph Giunta (295)
Daniel W. Gotshall (34, 54)
Don Gray (13)
William D. Griffin (529, 532)
Annie Griffiths (12, 14)
Pamela J. Harper (273, 464 left, 471 left)
John L. Harris (68, 71, 102)
Frank Hedges (413)

Grant Heilman Photography
Runk/Schoenberger (315)

Walter H. Hodge (434 left, 480 left)
Warren Jacobi (487)
Isidor Jeklin (509)
Charles C. Johnson (206, 207, 215, 216, 218, 219, 228, 232, 245, 249, 254, 284, 286, 287, 290, 302, 311)
Bill Jordan (458 left and right)
J. Eric Juterbock (108, 111, 142)
R. Y. Kaufman/Yogi, Inc. (512)
Steven Kaufman (521)
G. C. Kelley (483)
John Kohout (435 left and right)
Dwight R. Kuhn (199 right)
Carl Kurtz (319)
Wayne Lankinen (9, 481, 485, 516, 517, 543, 544)
Tom and Pat Leeson (494)
Jack Levy (388, 403 left)
Ken Lewis (248 right, 317)
William B. Love (168, 173, 175)
Kenneth E. Lucas (33, 76, 89)
Chalmers and Dean Luckhart (307, 454 right, 467 right) John A. Lynch (201 right, 248 left, 257 left, 261, 305)
John R. MacGregor (149, 153, 237, 263, 268, 279, 310, 602, 603)
Thomas W. Martin (588)
Virginia Mayfield (570)
Joe McDonald (559)
John Menge (341)
Anthony Mercieca (491, 493, 502, 536, 555, 616)
Paul Miliotis (363, 370)
Lorus J. and Margery Milne (365, 366)
Robert W. Mitchell (313, 343, 349, 356, 381)
C. Allan Morgan (55, 347, 362, 375, 535)
David Muench (1, 5, 6, 10, 11, 26)
Tom Myers (56, 88, 95, 97)

National Audubon Society Collection/Photo Researchers, Inc.
N. E. Beck, Jr. (350) Charles R. Belinky (151, 328)
A. Cosmos Blank (344) John Bova (550) Ken Brate (335, 345, 415) Henry Bunker IV (158) Patricia Caulfield (202, 224)
Joseph T. Collins (117, 129, 156, 159, 164, 177, 188) Helen Cruickshank (553) Kelly Dean (236) R. W. Dimond (283)
Phil Dotson (614) Robert J. Erwin (59, 105, 193, 549)
H. F. Flanders (329) Michael P. Gadomski (144, 230) Farrell

Grehan (288) Samuel Grimes (558) James Hancock (557) Russ Kinne (84) Michael Phillip Manheim (330) Karl H. Maslowski (578, 599, 606, 613) Karl and Stephen Maslowski (595) Tom McHugh (96, 607) Tom McHugh/Dallas Aquarium (52) Tom McHugh/Steinhart Aquarium (83, 98) Sturgis McKeever (116, 141, 147, 148, 210, 596) Irvin L. Oakes (312) Charlie Ott (601) Richard Parker (241, 322) George Porter (139) Lawrence Pringle (225) Noble Proctor (201 left, 203, 239, 252, 259, 292) William Ray (564) James H. Robinson (348, 384) Leonard Lee Rue III (137, 161, 242, 243, 589, 612) J. R. Simon (571) Alvin E. Staffan (136, 170, 195) Mary M. Thacher (244) Lovett Williams (608) Myron Wood (253)

Nebraska Game and Parks Commission (39, 41, 42, 46, 62, 73)
Peter Nice (415, 395 left)
Phillip Nordin (414)
Boyd Norton (3)
J. Oldenettel (518)
Paul A. Opler (421 left and right)
Robert T. Orr (1st frontispiece, 339)
Robert and Margaret Orr (262 left and right)
Arthur Panzer (507, 573)
Robert Perron (27)
William Pflieger (35, 64, 67, 80, 82, 86)
Jan Erik Pierson (520)
John Pitcher (484)
Rod Planck (513)
Betty Randall and Robert Potts (434 right, 459 left)
P.C.N. Pritchard (152)
James Rathert (582)
John T. Ratti (482, 541)
G. Gable Ray (542)
Susan Rayfield (231, 318, 323)
Hans Reinhard (492)
Dorothy M. Richards (211)
John N. Rinne/U.S. Forestry Service, Rocky Mountain Station (92, 93)
Sam Ristich (342)

Root Resources
Ben Goldstein (522)

Edward S. Ross (353, 361, 364, 369, 372, 378, 379, 392 right)
William Roston (49, 50, 58, 69)
Leonard Lee Rue III (304, 609, 610, 617)
Kit Scates (334, 340)
John Shaw (355, 376, 383 left and right, 393 left, 402, 404, 406)

John G. Shedd Aquarium
Patrice Ceisel (36, 63, 78)

Ervio Sian (498, 508, 554, 565)

Robert S. Simmons (119, 126, 130, 138, 140, 165, 181, 182, 184–186, 190, 194)
Richard Singer (394 right, 403 right)
Caulion Singletary (2nd frontispiece, 226)
Arnold Small (24, 486, 499, 500, 503, 506, 527, 587)
Robert Burr Smith (590)
Richard Spellenberg (454 left)
Joy Spurr (205, 250, 258, 291, 337)

Tom Stack and Associates (2)
Michael P. Gadomski (294)

Alvin E. Staffan (104, 110, 115, 118, 192, 229, 235, 274, 297, 539, 576, 584, 598, 611)
Douglas Stamm (48, 74, 75, 77)
David M. Stone (293)
Lynn M. Stone (29, 212, 251, 264 right)
Gayle Strickland (410, 411, 424 right)
Walter Sturgeon (331)
Rick Sullivan and Diana Rogers (446 left, 455 left)
K. H. Switak (146)
Ian C. Tait (568)
George Taylor (392 left)
Bill Thomas (18)
Frank S. Todd (501, 567)
Edmund Tylutki (333, 338)
Tom J. Ulrich (615)
U.S. Fish & Wildlife Service (44)
R. Van Nostrand (534)
Gilbert Van Ryckevorsel (94)
Richard C. Vogt (169, 171)
Richard K. Wallace (70)
Wardene Weisser (552)
Larry West (143, 269, 281 right, 299, 380, 385, 395 right, 398, 400, 422 left, 423 left)
Jack W. Wilburn (23, 25, 275, 306, 575)
D. Dee Wilder (373, 374)
John Wilkie (396 right, 397 left and right, 419 left and right)
Anthony M. Wilkinson (594)
Curtis E. Williams (367, 368)
Marilyn Wolff (303)
E. N. Woodbury (389, 394 left)
David Wright (399 right)
Robert Zappalorti (155)
C. Fred Zeillemaker (551)
Dale and Marian Zimmerman (247)
Jack Zucker (200, 301)

Illustrations

The drawings of plants and fishes and the tree silhouettes were executed primarily by Dolores R. Santoliquido. The following artists also contributed to this guide: Daniel Allen, Bobbi Angell, Robin Jess, Steven Phillips, and Wendy A. Zomlefer. Dot Barlowe contributed the drawings of mammal tracks.

INDEX

Numbers in boldface type refer to plate numbers. Numbers in italic refer to page numbers.

ACKNOWLEDGMENTS

I am especially grateful to J. Henry Sather for his excellent suggestions regarding the organization and presentation of this text. His continuous help throughout the project has been most appreciated. I would also like to acknowledge the many persons who freely supplied wetland materials for possible inclusion: Robert Askins, Ellen Baldocchino David E. Brown, Edward Carlson, Helen B. Correll, Antoni W. H. Damman, Frank E. Egler, Katherine C. Ewel, Kathleen Feeney, Frank C. Golet, Eville Gorham, James Habeck, James L. Hainline, Marjorie M. Holland, Gary W. Kramer, Aimlee D. Laderman, Joseph S. Larson, Jack Major, Kenneth J. Metzler, Gordon H. Orians, Frank W. Reinchenbacker, C. J. Richardson, William S. Robertson, Jr., Ronald Rozsa, Richard Spellenberg, Paul F. Springer, V. Daniel Stiles, William Walker, Milton W. Weller, William O. Wilen, and Joy Zedler.

Special thanks go to Mrs. Rose Fishman for her continuous secretarial assistance. I also owe much to my wife, Cathy, for typing my various drafts and providing constant encouragement. It has been a tremendous pleasure working with the entire staff at Chanticleer Press. The dedication of Mary Beth Brewer is especially acknowledged. I also wish to thank Susan Costello for her constant concern and assistance as well as the many others who contributed, particularly Ann Whitman, who edited the habitat essays, and Marian Appellof, who coordinated the species accounts.

William A. Niering

CHANTICLEER STAFF

Prepared and produced by Chanticleer Press, Inc.
Founding Publisher: Paul Steiner
Publisher: Andrew Stewart

Staff for this book:

Editor-in-Chief: Gudrun Buettner
Executive Editor: Susan Costello
Managing Editor: Jane Opper
Series Editor: Mary Beth Brewer
Text Editor: Ann Whitman
Associate Editor: Marian Appellof
Assistant Editor: David Allen
Editorial Assistant: Karel Birnbaum
Production: Helga Lose, Amy Roche
Art Director: Carol Nehring
Art Associate: Ayn Svoboda
Picture Library: Edward Douglas, Dana Pomfret
Maps and Symbols: Paul Singer
Natural History Consultant: John Farrand, Jr.

Design: Massimo Vignelli

All editorial inquiries should be addressed to:
Chanticleer Press
568 Broadway, Suite #1005A
New York, NY 10012

To purchase this book, or other National Audubon Society illustrated nature books, please contact:
Alfred A. Knopf, Inc.
201 East 50th Street
New York, NY 10022
(800) 733-3000